The Origins of an International Legal Orde

Legal History Library

VOLUME 86

Studies in the History of International Law

VOLUME 33

The titles published in this series are listed at *brill.com/shil*

The Origins of an International Legal Order of Peace and Justice

Peace through Law

By

Matthias Philipp Packeiser

BRILL | NIJHOFF

ISSN 1874-1793
ISBN 978-90-04-43980-1
ISBN 978-90-04-75412-6 (PDF)
DOI https://doi.org/10.1163/9789004754126

Library of Congress Cataloging-in-Publication Data
A CIP catalog record for this book has been applied for at the Library of Congress.

Brill Nijhoff and Koninklijke Brill BV are part of De Gruyter Brill.
www.degruyterbrill.com

Questions about General Product Safety Regulation: productsafety@degruyterbrill.com

Cover illustration: Peace Palace under construction. Photograph by C.J. de Gilde, 1910. Reproduced by kind permission of the Carnegie Foundation – Peace Palace.

Für Anja und Levin

Contents

Acknowledgments

When I began my doctoral studies, on which this book is based, I was motivated by academic curiosity and a desire to explore a period dating back just over 100 years. As might be expected, states, politicians, and scholars were dealing with very similar questions in the decades before the outbreak of World War I as their counterparts do today. In other cases, however, the results of those efforts can now be seen; some of the norms and ideas created back then have evolved into fundamental and indispensable elements of contemporary public international law.

Tracing the historical and philosophical roots of some aspects of today's international legal order was a great experience. However, the project also presented me with an unexpected opportunity. It enabled me to expand my research beyond a purely European perspective, familiarize myself with alternative approaches to international law, and significantly broaden my personal and professional horizons. I benefited enormously from this intellectual journey and would therefore like to thank those who made it possible. When writing a list of people who have contributed to a project, there is always a risk of forgetting someone. If this happens, I humbly apologize.

Nevertheless, I would like to make an attempt:

Firstly, I would like to thank the institutions and their representatives who enabled me to undertake this project. These are Tilburg University and the University of Hamburg, in particular the Albrecht Mendelssohn Bartholdy Graduate School of Law. I have found wonderful companions, supporters, and friends at these institutions, and I am grateful to them for sharing with me the experience of writing a doctoral thesis. I cannot overstate the value of their help and input. First and foremost, I would like to express my deepest gratitude to my supervisors: Prof. Dr. Stefan Oeter and Prof. Dr. Markus Kotzur at the University of Hamburg, and Prof. Dr. Randall Lesaffer at Tilburg University. Without their encouragement, invaluable academic guidance, and above all, patience, it would have been impossible to carry out the project and achieve the same results. I would also like to thank the other institutions that supported my research, including the DAAD for funding my attendance at several conferences, Indiana University for welcoming me as a visiting scholar, and the German Federal Foreign Office for opening their library to me.

I would also like to thank my friends and family for their active support during this time. Above all, I would like to express my deepest gratitude to my two grandparents, who I miss very much; my parents; and, of course, my beloved wife. Without you, none of this would have been possible.

Matthias P. Packeiser

CHAPTER 1

Introduction

> Mankind must put an end to war before war puts an end to mankind.[1]
>
> John. F. Kennedy before the UN General Assembly, September 25, 1961

1 Introductory Remarks

John F. Kennedy (1917–1963), then acting president of the United States, uttered the aforementioned words before the UN General Assembly on September 25, 1961, right in the midst of the *Cold War*. Only around a year later, 384 days to be precise, the world came to face the imminent danger of falling into a nuclear abyss during the *Cuba Crisis* (October 14–28, 1962). The prospect of the outbreak of an nuclear war between the United States and the Soviet Union terrified the entire world. Their confrontation over the deployment of Soviet ballistic missiles in Cuba bore the tangible risk of resulting in a devastating global war; a possible *Third World War*. This conflict is a perfect example for how close peace, on the one hand, and millions of deaths and unimaginable destruction, on the other hand, can lie together in certain situations. In 1962, a war was only avoided because the leaders of the two superpowers demonstrated sufficient caution and serenity in the decisive moments of the crisis. Why – many of us might wonder today – did they allow this situation to escalate in the first place and why did it happen in a way that led the entire world close to death, chaos, and devastation?

At second thought, however, we must ask ourselves if this development should actually surprise us. War has been a constant phenomenon in human history,[2] and it is still pervasive today in almost the entire world. Despite their

1 Address by President John F. Kennedy to the UN General Assembly, September 25, 1961.

2 Compare, e.g.: Deon Visser, 'A Brief Perspective on Military Preparedness in History' in Thean Potgieter and Ian Liebenberg (eds.), *Reflections on War: Preparedness and Consequences* (SUN Press 2012) 33.

 | DOI:10.1163/9789004754126_002

brutal and devastating nature, wars have always been – and still are – waged on a highly frequent base.[3] With the Russian annexation of the Crimea in February 2014 and the Russian launch of a full-scale invasion of Ukraine in February 2022, the continuing omnipresence of wars was shown again in the most brutal and fatal way. In fact, wars must even be considered as a decisive factor for the development of the culture in Europe, as they used to substantially affect the growth of the population, the economy, and basically every other aspect of peoples' lives.

After 1945, the frequency of wars declined in European affairs (but, of course, without disappearing entirely). *World War II* – this unprecedented and deeply inhuman war – had cost an estimated 60 million lives and marked a bloody turning point in history. As a consequence, the United Nations were established through the *Charter of San Francisco* in 1945; and Europe was stepwise pacified through the European integration process, which resulted in peace among its members and stability on most of the continent. But despite such regional developments and achievements, still today, there are just very few states that are not involved in any kind of armed conflict. In fact, according to an article published by the British newspaper *The Independent* in 2014, only 11 states worldwide abstained from using military means for the settlement of conflicts at the time of the publication.[4] Therefore, it cannot be ignored that war continues to play a crucial role in international relations, and that states keep invoking it on a regular base.

War can bear a multitude of different names – e.g., wars of conquest, crusades, and humanitarian interventions[5] – and it can be waged for many different reasons. Therefore, it is difficult to speak of uniformity regarding its reasons or its form.[6] In addition to that, the face of warfare has changed dramatically over the centuries. Industrialization (including the introduction of mass production), technical innovations, and military modernizations (especially since the late 18th century) resulted in the industrialization and modern-

---

3 Bernd Hüppauf, *Was ist Krieg? Zur Grundlegung einer Kulturgeschichte des Kriegs* (Transcript 2013) 9.

4 Adam Withnall, 'World peace? These are the only 11 countries in the world that are actually free from conflict' (*The Independent,* August 14, 2014) <https://www.independent.co.uk/news/world/politics/world-peace-these-are-only-11-countries-world-are-actually-free-conflict-9669623.html> accessed October 22, 2018.

5 Angelika Nußberger, *Das Völkerrecht: Geschichte, Institutionen, Perspektiven* (C.H. Beck 2009) 57.

6 Stephen Neff, *War and the Law of Nations: A General History* (Cambridge University Press 2005) 1.

ization of warfare.[7] Modern wars no longer have much in common with hand-to-hand combat from the *Middle Ages* or earlier times. Instead, warfare has become highly technologized and industrialized, which, in turn, has brought about an entirely new level of destructiveness. The *U.S.-American Civil War* (1861–1865) was probably the first industrial war and the *Russo-Japanese War* (1904–1905) demonstrated the inhumanity and brutality of modern warfare. They both clearly showed the murderous effects of the new military technologies and of the concept of total war (at least on a regional level).[8] *World War I* then demonstrated the same again – but at the global scale.[9] It was fought with new weapons such as flame-throwers, gas, tanks, heavy artillery, and many other military features, introduced at the beginning of the 20th century, allowing for highly efficient killing on the battlefields. In subsequent years, nuclear bombs, drones, cruise missiles, and other deadly advances were made. These technologies increased the inhumanity and brutality of war once more. However, the devastating nature of war is a fact that has remained constant throughout history. Wars have always been murderous clashes between two or more (somehow organized) groups of people, often resulting from the purely (power) political interests of rulers, and fought at the expense of the population(s).

Today, war is governed internationally by legal constraints and limitations. Article 2.4 was written into the *UN Charter* at the end of *World War II* and is one (or maybe even: *the*) central element of the current international legal order. It sets out the following:

> All members shall refrain in their international relations from the threat or use of force against the territorial integrity or political independence of any state, or in any other manner inconsistent with the Purposes of the United Nations.[10]

Its introduction constituted the final stage of the development toward the introduction of legal restrictions of the use of force in international relations and – as its final consequence – toward an abolition of war by law that had

7 Hew Strachan, 'Military Modernization 1789–1918' in C.W. Blanning (ed.), *The Oxford History of Modern Europe* (Oxford University Press 2000) 76–77.

8 Tohmatsu Haruto, 'Approaching Total War: Ivan Bloch's Disturbing Vision' in John Steinberg, et al. (eds.), *The Russo-Japanese War in Global Perspective: World War Zero*, vol. 2 (Brill 2007) 199 et seq.

9 Compare: John Hinshaw and Peter N. Stearns, *Industrialization in the Modern World: From the Industrial Revolution to the Internet*, vol. 1 (ABC Clio 2013) 505–506.

10 Article 2.4 UN Charter.

begun long before. Regarding the more recent history, Randall Lesaffer (*'Too Much History'* from 2015) emphasized that (in this regard) a new "[…] evolution started at the turn of the 20th century with the two *Hague Peace Conferences* (1899/1907)."[11] Later, during the 1920s and 1930s, agreements were concluded that explicitly prohibited the use of force; such as the *Briand-Kellogg-Pact* in Europe (1928) or the *Saavedra Lamas Treaty* in America (1933). The former, for example, outlined, in Article 2, that adhering states agreed "[…] that the settlement or solution of all disputes or conflicts of whatever nature or of whatever origin they may be, which may arise among them, shall never be sought except by pacific means".

This development later resulted in the complete substitution of the *ius ad bellum* by the *ius contra bellum*; namely in the form of (the above-cited) Article 2.4 UN Charter in 1945.[12] To speak today of a world free of conflicts, or to claim that international law effectively expelled war from international relations is, nevertheless, illusionary. But although war remains a common phenomenon of today's international relations, the sole fact that it is prohibited under international law, and that the *Crime of Aggression* is persecuted from July 17, 2018, onwards by the *International Criminal Court*,[13] already constitutes enormous progress in comparison to earlier times.

The process of outlawing war is a long and stony path, or, in other words, a development that has a long history with an uncountable number of twists and turns. While certain authors praised and idealized war, others held diametrically dissenting opinions and detested it. Heraclitus (ca. 520–460 BC) serves as a good example for a philosopher who regarded the use of force as natural and inevitable.[14] He glorified war as "[…] the father of all things".[15] Another example for this approach would be Pierre-Joseph Proudhon (*'La Guerre et la Paix'*, 3rd edition from 1861) who stated that "[…] la guerre s'affirme dans l'humanité comme justicière, héroique et divine".[16] Desiderius Erasmus (ca.

11 Randall Lesaffer, 'Too much History: From War as Sanction to the Sanctioning of War' in Marc Weler (ed.), *The Oxford Handbook of the Use of Force in International Law* (Oxford University Press 2015) 35. See also: Oona A. Hathaway and Scott J. Shapiro, *The Internationalists: And their Plan to Outlaw War* (Simon & Schuster 2018) 109.

12 Compare: Randall Lesaffer, 'Too much History' (n 11 in Chapter 1) 35 et seq.

13 *Historic Activation of the Crime of Aggression* <http://www.coalitionfortheicc.org/explore/icc-crimes/crime-aggression> accessed October 29, 2018.

14 Duane L. Cady, *From Warism to Pacifism: A Moral Continuum* (Temple University Press, U.S. 2010) 2.

15 Quoted in English, e.g., in John F. Donahue, *Food and Drink in Antiquity: Readings from the Graeco-Roman World* (Bloomsbury Academic 2015) 207.

16 Pierre-Joseph Proudhon, *La Guerre et la Paix* (3rd ed., A. Lacroix, Verboeckhoven & Co 1861) 109. Analogously translated by the author of the present book: "[…] war serves in

1466–1536), on the other hand, was probably (one of) the sharpest critic(s) of war during the *Renaissance*.[17] Other examples for publicly expressed opposition against war can be found in the works of Maximilien de Béthune, duc de Sully (1560–1641), William Penn (1644–1718), and Immanuel Kant (1724–1804).[18] Although these three authors did not oppose the use of force in all circumstances, their – and many other authors' – contributions paved the way for the emergence of the peace movement in the 19th century. They were henceforth responsible for the spreading of such concepts, and for the further development of ideas for the establishment (and preservation) of perpetual peace. Another notable example for an influential opponent of war was Ivan de Bloch (1836–1902), a Warsaw banker and financier. He published a six-volume treatise in 1898 called *'Is War Now Impossible?'*,[19] in which he described the horrors of modern warfare and analyzed its problems and irrationality.[20] According to Jost Dülffer (*'Regeln gegen den Krieg?'* from 1981), Czar Nicholas II was influenced by Bloch's conclusions,[21] when he launched his initiative for disarmament, which led to the convening of the *First Hague Peace Conference* in 1899.

This conference, the *First Hague Peace Conference* from 1899, is doubtlessly a key event in the development of international law. With the decision to constitute the *Permanent Court of Arbitration* (hereinafter: PCA) as a first international institution for peaceful settlement of state-to-state conflicts, the conference delegates took a major step toward the juridification and pacification of international relations. But again, just as in the case of the above-mentioned *Cuban Crisis*, war and peace kept lying very closely together. For example, Great Britain, one of the leading advocates of the PCA, started its campaign for the forceful occupation of the Boer Republics in Southern Africa (in the *Second Boer War* 1899–1902) only a few months after the conclusion of the conference in The Hague (1899), and, in 1914, the world was plunged into chaos with the outbreak of *World War I*.

World War I did even more than causing uncountable numbers of deaths and devastating entire regions, as it also constituted the (preliminary) end of a

---

human society as a judge, heroic and divine". See also: Klaus von Beyme, *Politische Theorien im Zeitalter der Ideologien 1789–1945* (VS Verlag für Sozialwissenschaften 2002) 672.

17 Compare: Desiderius Erasmus, *Querela Pacis* (originally published in 1517).

18 Duane L. Cady, *From Warism to Pacifism* (n 14 in Chapter 1) 9.

19 Ivan S. Bloch, *Is War Now Impossible? Being an Abridgment of "The War of the Future in its Technical, Economic and Political Relations"* (Richards 1898/99).

20 Jost Dülffer, *Regeln gegen den Krieg? Die Haager Friedenskonferenzen von 1899 und 1907 in der internationalen Politik* (Ullstein 1981) 31.

21 Ibid 32.

period in which the concept of preserving peace through legal means achieved so far unprecedented popularity under the eyes of the entire world. Especially since the late 19th century, numerous high-ranked politicians, state leaders, international lawyers, etc. had started to share (and to promote) the conviction that peace had to be established on the international sphere for preventing the outbreak of wars. One of their most crucial claims was to replace war as an instrument for conflict settlement at the international level through peaceful means such as compulsory negotiations, arbitral measures, or even through legal procedures. Even certain state leaders began supporting (some of) these ideas and promoted them on the international level. This development demonstrates the increased popularity and influence of pacific concepts; and it shows that they managed between the late 19th century and the eve of *World War I* to leave the sphere of the peace movement (where they had remained throughout most of the 19th century) and to become seriously discussed topics among growing parts of the populations, in the media, and even on international conferences.

One of the most prominent pacific approaches of that time is often summarized under the term *peace through law*; the idea to bind the use of force by law.[22] Supporters of this approach aimed to restrict the *ius ad bellum* – the states' right to wage war[23] – by the introduction of an international system, which functioned on the base of (the rule of) law, followed legal procedures, and handled state-to-state conflicts in sole accordance with law (or arbitration), instead of by force. For the 18th and 19th centuries, those ideas remained widely utopian. But by the beginning of the 20th century, many authors, peace activists, politicians, and international lawyers put a lot of hope into the concept. They propagated it openly, gathered a quickly growing number of supporters, and developed these ideas and concepts further. Their initiatives – even though incapable of preventing the outbreak of *World War I* in the end – shaped international law and the process of abolishing war in international relations in a lasting and substantial manner which – ultimately – paved the way for outlawing war after *World War II*.

22 Lothar Brock, 'Frieden durch Recht: Anmerkungen zum Thema in historischem Kontext' in Peter Becker, Reiner Braun & Dieter Deiseroth (eds.), *Frieden durch Recht?* (Berliner Wissenschafts-Verlag 2010) 16.

23 Mary Ellen O'Connell, 'Historical Development and Legal Basis' in Dieter Fleck (ed.), *The Handbook of International Humanitarian Law* (3rd ed., Oxford University Press 2013) 1. According to her, *ius ad bellum* is defined as the "[…] body of rules which determines when resort to armed force is permissible".

2 Scope

The book deals with the concept of *ius ad bellum* and the endeavors made during the pre-*World War I* period (with a special focus on the years between 1899 and 1914) to limit the right to wage war. Attempts were made at that time to realize such limitations through the implementation of direct constraints of this right or by the introduction of (obligatory) mechanisms for the peaceful settlement of conflicts (such as arbitration, adjudication, commissions of inquiry, etc.), which ruled out the recourse to force in certain situations. The evolution of the *ius contra bellum* was certainly one of the most important and decisive changes of the transition from *classic international law* in the 19th century to *modern international law* of the 20th century.[24] Therefore, these endeavors, ideas, and concepts did not only provide the basis for the abolition of the use of force by law, and for the implementation of supremacy of law over force after *World War II*. But they were also essential in shaping the current international legal order.

Focusing on this very period allows extending the prevailing understanding of the process of abolishing war under international law in a decisive way. Randall Lesaffer (*'Peace Through Law: The Hague Conferences and the Rise of the Ius Contra Bellum'* from 2017'), for example, claimed that the two Hague Conferences were often (and sometimes they still are) regarded as only "[…] two first, modest steps in the incremental process leading to the prohibition of the use of force between states through the Covenant of the League of Nations (1919), the Pact of Paris (1928), and the Charter of the United Nations (1945)."[25] In great shares of the existing literature on this topic, the contribution of these conferences, as well as other advances in this regard during this period, to the development from an almost absolute and judicially widely unrestricted *ius ad bellum*[26] to the creation of the UN system under which the use of force was prohibited, is often described as even small or entirely insignificant.[27] This

24 Compare: Randall Lesaffer, 'Too much History' (n 11 in Chapter 1) 35–36.

25 Randall Lesaffer, 'Peace through law: the Hague Peace Conferences and the rise of the *ius contra bellum*' in Maartje Abbenhuis et al. (eds.), *War, Peace and International Order? The Legacies of the Hague Conferences of 1899 and 1907* (Routledge 2017) 32.

26 Ibid.

27 Compare, e.g., some of the following studies: Anthony Clark Arend and Robert J. Beck, *International Law and the Use of Force: Beyond the UN Charter Paradigm* (Routledge 1993) 15–25; Ian Brownlie, *International Law and the Use of Force by States* (Oxford University Press 1963) 23–25, 51–129; Ruth Henig, *The League of Nations* (Haus Publishing 2010) 1–24; Niels Blokker, 'The Security Council and the Use of Force on Recent Practice' in Niels Blokker and Nico Schrijver (eds.), *The Security Council and the Use of Force: Theory and Reality – A Need for Change?* (Brill 2005) 4.

approach to the history of international law and to the intellectual and legal foundations of today's international order, however, appears to fall short with regard to the actual influence and importance of this era (in particular concerning the process of abolishing war by law). By closely examining the period between the late 19th century and the beginning of *World War I*, it will be demonstrated in the following that considerably more crucial, influential, and remarkable results took place during that time than set out in many studies on the topic. In fact, both the international legal order and international legal thinking underwent substantial changes during these years[28] and (the conception of) international law was shaped in such a decisive way that (the roots of) later developments – such as the establishment of the *Permanent Court of International Justice* (in 1922) – can be traced back to initiatives from before *World War I*. By following this approach, the present book will offer a new perspective on the process of outlawing war by extending the scope of research on this topic in the pre-*World War I* period.

In addition to that, the book also strikes a new path by not exclusively focusing on (what is referred to in the context of the present book as) the *'North-Atlantic World'*. The latter term comprises Europe as well as the United States; the two most powerful regions in the world at the turn from the 19th to the 20th century. Great Britain, Germany, France, Austria-Hungary, Russia, and – with some limitations – also Italy[29] were considered great powers at the time. These nations had extensive colonial empires, and were economically, militarily, and financially (among) the strongest in the world. Outside of Europe, there were only two more great powers; the United States, which

28 This view is also held, e.g., by the authors of the following studies: Arthur Eyffinger, *The 1899 Hague Peace Conference: The Parliament of Man, the Federation of the World* (Kluwer Academic Publishers 1999); Maartje Abbenhuis et al. (eds.), War, Peace and International Order? (n 25 in Chapter 1); Marcus M. Payk, *Frieden Durch Recht? Der Aufstieg des modernen Völkerrechts und der Friedensschluss nach dem ersten Weltkrieg* (De Gruyter Oldenbourg 2018); Miloš Vec, 'From the Congress of Vienna to the Paris Peace Treaties of 1919' in Bardo Fassbender and Anne Peters (eds.), *The Oxford Handbook of the History of International Law* (Oxford University Press 2012) 654–678; Francis Anthony Boyle, *Foundations of World Order: The Legalist Approach to International Relations 1898–1922* (Duke University Press 1999); Jost Dülffer, Regeln gegen den Krieg? (n 20 in Chapter 1); Calvin DeArmond Davis, *The United States and the Second Hague Peace Conference: American Diplomacy and International Organization 1899–1914* (Duke University Press 1975); Maartje Abbenhuis, *The Hague Conferences and International Politics, 1898–1915 (Bloomsbury Academic 2018)*.

29 John Lowe, *The Great Powers, Imperialism, and the German Problem, 1865–1925* (Routledge 1994) 18.

achieved this status around the turn of the 20th century,[30] and Japan, which rose to a great power as a result of the *Russo-Japanese War*.[31] Moreover, the then-prevailing international order stemmed (to a great extent) from European tradition and the European conception of international law ('*European public law*').[32] Therefore, the North-Atlantic states played highly influential roles in most global developments at the time and had a crucial impact on the conception of international law. Consequently, it is impossible to ignore them when it comes to an in-depth study of public international law in this period. However, concentrating on these two world regions alone (Europe and North America) does not suffice. The family of independent states consisted of more nations than the great powers, but also comprised smaller states from Europe as well as from other parts of the world. A global approach to the topic of international law therefore must consider other perspectives and regional developments as well since international law was already a topic of global importance. At the *Second Hague Peace Conference* from 1907, 44 nations (and thus almost all the states recognized as independent at the time) came together for discussing reforms of the international order. For being able to draw a complete and comprehensive picture, it, therefore, is indispensable to consider developments, ideas, and advances from other world regions too. But because of the comparable small number of independent countries in Africa and Asia at that time (or better: of African and Asian countries recognized as independent by the great powers), linguistic challenges, and the fact that Japan was the only Asian nation being in a position that allowed it to substantially influence the developments under review, it seems more promising to concentrate primarily on Latin America – as the other major focal point within this project.[33]

30 John Oldfield, 'Remembering the Maine: the United States, 1898 and Sectional Reconciliation' in Angel Smith and Emma Dávila-Cox (eds.), *The Crisis of 1898: Colonial Redistribution and Nationalist Mobilization* (Palgrave Macmillan 1999) 59. See also: Martti Koskenniemi, 'The Ideology of International Adjudication and the 1907 Hague Conference' in Yves Daudet (ed.), *Topicality of the 1907 Hague Conference, the Second Peace Conference* (Brill 2008) 135 et seq.

31 Compare: Gbingba T. Gbosoe, *Modernization of Japan* (iUniverse 2006) 59 et seq.

32 Alexander Orakhelashvili, 'The Idea of European International Law' (2006) 17 The European Journal of International Law 316–347.

33 Africa is also spared from the considerations in the present thesis because it was (almost) entirely colonized by European powers at that time. Even the two independent Boer Republics which existed in the late 19th century were annexed by Great Britain between 1899 and 1902 (*Second Boer War*). Compare: Chris Ash, *Kruger, Kommandos & Kak: Debunking the Myths of the Boer War* (30 Degree South Publ. 2014).

The decision to extend the scope of the present book beyond the North Atlantic world and to include also (as a key source for outer-European approaches to international law) Latin America, appears necessary for drawing a broader and more comprehensive picture of the then-prevailing state (and conception) of international law. Numerous highly important developments took place in the context of the mutual relationships of (Latin) American countries with regard to limiting and outlawing war. In addition to that, a surprisingly progressive approach was pursued by Latin American countries toward the use of obligatory arbitration during the 19th century. Those two aspects encourage the decision to take this world region into close consideration when it comes to dealing with the development of international law and international legal thinking between the late 19th century and 1914. Thus, by incorporating and reviewing the particular Latin American notion of international law, and the state practice from this world region, a new perspective will be offered with regard to *global* changes of the conception of international law at the time.

Ius ad bellum, and the prevailing understanding of it between the *First Hague Peace Conference* (1899) and 1914, are at the heart of this book. In the course of the subsequent analysis, it will be demonstrated that the introduction of methods for the peaceful settlement of international conflicts, attempts made in the same direction, and the conclusion of provisions directly affecting *ius ad bellum* imposed (first) actual limitations on the states' right to use force during the period under review and – which might be even more important – that these developments also led to a substantial change of the dominant understanding within the international community concerning the conception of *ius ad bellum*.

For that purpose, a multitude of different developments in the 19th and early 20th centuries will be taken into consideration and will be analyzed. In particular, this involves the emergence of the idea to introduce (obligatory) mechanisms for the peaceful settlement of conflicts and the striving for the institutionalization of such mechanisms in the form of international courts (arbitral or judicial ones). Consequently, actual achievements made in the fields of arbitration and adjudication are reviewed in order to analyze their impact on the *ius ad bellum*. Moreover, other attempts made in the same direction are considered as well. By analyzing which and what kind of initiatives were launched for realizing *peace through law* during the period under review, conclusions will be drawn concerning the then existing set of opinions and views regarding the (limitation of the) *ius ad bellum*. Thereby, it will be possible to determine whether a number, or even a majority, of states were already willing to adapt the international order in accordance with principles stemming from the *peace through law* approach and whether the dominant notion from these days regarding the *ius ad bellum* was already influenced by this concept. Finally, also direct limitations of the *ius ad bellum* in form of explicit prohibitions of the use of force in certain areas of international relations will be considered (for example, in the form of projects that aimed for banning the use of force entirely in certain contexts or which involved the introduction of compulsory *cooling periods*, obligating the parties of a conflict to wait for a certain time before taking recourse to arms).

By dealing with these objects, the overall picture of the situation of the *ius ad bellum* before the eve of *World War I* will be completed, and a telling insight will be provided regarding the question whether (the majority of) states were already willing to accept a limitation of their right to wage war. By following this approach, the book covers a highly influential era within the development of general international law and, in particular, within the process of replacing the *ius ad bellum* with an *ius contra bellum*.

3 Structure and Methodology

The present book is structured into seven chapters. Following the introduction in Chapter 1, Chapter 2 offers an insight into the theoretical background of the concepts under review. It introduces the concept of *ius ad bellum*, and its history before the turn of the 20th century. The same is also done with regard to arbitration, adjudication, and the conceptual differentiation between these two instruments. Chapter 3 concentrates on arbitration and adjudication in the North Atlantic context during the 19th century. The chapter deals with the state practice regarding isolated and obligatory arbitration during that time, and with the emergence of ideas concerning the change of the prevailing international system. The peace movement and international lawyers played particularly decisive roles in this regard; therefore, the chapter also gives a great deal of attention to them, their ideas concerning (obligatory) arbitration, and their proposal to introduce adjudication to international law, which was first articulated around the middle of the century. In Chapter 4, the corresponding situation in Latin America will be analyzed, while paying special attention to the dedication of Spanish American countries to obligatory arbitration and to the idea of creating defensive unions (against outer-Spanish American threats). Chapter 5 then concentrates on the period from 1899 to 1905. During these years, the *First Hague Peace Conference* (*1899*) and the *Second Pan-American Conference* (*1901/02*) took place. Furthermore, the *Permanent Court of Arbitration* was established (as a result of the *First Hague*

Peace Conference) and a quickly growing number of states started to conclude bi-lateral obligatory arbitration treaties. While Chapter 5 mainly concentrates on arbitration, Chapter 6 (which deals with the period between 1906 and 1914) focuses more on adjudication and on attempts to create international courts of law. In this regard, the *Third Pan-American Conference* (*1906*), the *Second Hague Peace Conference* (*1907*), the *Washington Conference* (*1907*), and a series of other meetings in which a varying number of great(er) powers participated in the aftermath of the *Second Hague Peace Conference* are the most important events. Together, these (last) two chapters provide an insight into the situation under international law regarding the understanding of the *ius ad bellum* and the states' willingness to limit their right to wage war between the *First Hague Peace Conference* (1899) and the eve of *World War I*. Finally, Chapter 7 summarizes again the results and conclusion of this book.

The present book takes into consideration general historical events and developments, just as much as those that concern the then prevailing state practice, international legal scholarship, the agenda of the peace movement, and several other aspects. Following this approach (*'law in context'*) allows to compare the then prevailing state practice and the states' opinions regarding (obligatory) arbitration and adjudication with ideas and concepts discussed in legal scholarship and among peace activists during the 19th and early 20th centuries. Such ideas were often of a highly progressive nature and aimed at changing the international legal order. Consequently, concepts developed by peace activists and legal scholars are contrasted in this book with actually realized (as well as attempted) changes and developments within the international legal system; in particular, with regard to the introduction of (obligatory) arbitration and adjudication.

This approach offers the opportunity to determine the influence of the work of peace activists and progressive legal scholars on international law as well as on the states' view on their proposals. The late 19th century experienced an enormous growth with regard to the importance that was attached to international law, public opinion, scholarly work, and the ideas of the peace movement. Therefore, their initiatives and concepts bore the potential of having a considerable impact on the thinking and acting of politicians and state leaders. Moreover, although it is also important to draw conclusions from the (types of) treaties that were concluded at that time, from the actions that were taken by states, and from proposals that were made by the government officials at international gatherings, it is equally indispensable to widen the scope beyond sole state practice. In order to fully understand the period under consideration and the developments that took place at that time, it is equally necessary to focus on discussions among peace activists and international lawyers on the further development of international law, their highly favorable approach to (obligatory) arbitration, and the emergence of the idea to implement adjudication in international law. Therefore, the book will not only review developments made by states and those that states attempted to realize, but it will also set those developments in relation with concepts and ideas for replacing war by law (*peace through law*). Applying this approach allows to determine what influence these concepts had on state practice and the shape of international law. Thereby, their ideological and conceptual background will be identified and the prevailing understanding (as well as minority views) on the *ius ad bellum* will be determined. Furthermore, it will be possible to conclude why certain actions were taken and some concepts were realized, while others failed or why they were ignored by states.

Apart from ideological developments, the present book also focuses on state practice with regard to (the conclusion of) obligatory arbitration treaties and the use of isolated arbitration. The frequency of the use of these instruments will be analyzed in order to get an impression of the states' acceptance of peaceful measures for the settlement of international conflicts and of their willingness to abstain from invoking force for this purpose. By analyzing the states' openness for subjecting themselves in their mutual bi- and multi-lateral relations to obligatory arbitration commitments, conclusions can be drawn concerning their general approach toward limiting their right to wage war through bi- and multi-lateral agreements. Therefore, the frequency of the use of arbitration is used in order to determine whether a majority of states was already willing to subject their mutual conflicts on an obligatory base to arbitral settlements, to accept, thereby, limitations of their right to wage war, and, consequently, to turn away from the understanding of the *ius ad bellum* that had prevailed during most of the 19th century.

Moreover, the book also pays particular attention to multi-lateral conferences. These events were held to discuss and introduce substantial changes to the international legal order. Subjects such as the conclusion of bi-lateral obligatory arbitration treaties or the increased use of isolated arbitration in bilateral relations were – beyond any doubt – important developments. However, they did not affect the international system in a global and encompassing way. For realizing changes that went further than bi-lateral relations or that even had worldwide dimensions, it required the support of the (majority of the) community of states. Consequently, it was only possible to introduce multi-lateral obligatory arbitration agreements, international courts of arbitration, or even truly judicial tribunals to the international order if a sufficiently great number of states supported these initiatives. The book concentrates on the aforementioned topics because by concluding such obligations and creating those institutions, the states agreed on the introduction of (compulsory) means of conflict settlement that involved all signatory states. Thereby, they introduced limitations of their right to wage war (as they could not freely invoke this right any longer without violating the afore-concluded multi-lateral treaties and obligations) and, consequently, changed the prevailing understanding of the *ius ad bellum*.

In order to determine why and whether states were actually willing to subject at least parts of their international relations to obligatory conflict settlement by arbitration or adjudicative measures and to create institutions of voluntary (or even compulsory) courts, the present book focuses particularly on multi-lateral conferences. In the framework of these events, the most progressive proposals were made and discussed by the participating states. Moreover, this approach allows identifying the positions and opinions held by the participating states concerning potential changes of the international legal order and the introduction of new institutions. Whereas states could usually easily avoid giving their opinions on certain ideas or could even simply ignore them, the special circumstances at multi-lateral conferences forced them to openly declare their opinion on certain topics. Therefore, the protocols of the conferences offer an opportunity to determine which countries supported certain proposals – and which countries objected them. By setting their behavior from the conferences in relation to general political events and their foreign political approaches, conclusions will be drawn regarding the overall mood within the community of states regarding reforms and changes of international law as well as regarding the particular positions of certain countries with regard to the topics addressed in this book. By also identifying the sources and origins of the concepts that were proposed at these multi-lateral gatherings and by reviewing further going ideas discussed within the peace movement and among legal scholars, the book provides explanations for the emergence of certain ideas and the adoption of new policies. Additionally, it also examines failed attempts to achieve further going results, opinions and statements issued by governments, legal scholarship, and ideas propagated by the peace movement in order to provide a picture as broad and comprehensive as possible of the relevant developments in the period under review.

Reviewing all these aspects, alongside the actual changes, is of essential importance for the book because a number of initiatives for the adoption of certain far-reaching and advanced agreements failed during this period only because of the opposition of (influential) minorities. This aspect is worth examining, as the fact that a majority of states supported the adoption of more advanced concepts shows that the dominant notion within the community of states was probably more progressive than it was indicated by the results that were actually achieved. Therefore, an in-depth analysis of events such as the *First* and *Second Hague Peace Conference*, the *Pan-American Conferences*, and many other developments in these years – also with regard to proposals that failed – provides substantial insights regarding the readiness of (the majority of) states to strive for further reaching reforms and changes of the international legal order prior to *World War I*. By analyzing the opinions expressed at these events, the concluded acts, and also the presented proposals, conclusions will be drawn regarding the dominant view concerning international law among states and their willingness to agree to the introduction of limitations of their *ius ad bellum*.

All in all, the approach in this book is two-fold. On the one hand, it takes into consideration actual changes and developments under international law (in other words: the state practice), while on the other hand, it also carries out a study of the history of the ideas underlying these changes. It looks at the attempts that were made to realize these concepts and draws conclusions from developments concerning the prevailing understanding of states, legal scholars, peace activists, and the general public regarding the *state of the art* of international law between the late 19th and the early 20th centuries.

CHAPTER 2

The Theoretical Background

> Drei Phasen sind es, die jede geistige Bewegung durchzumachen hat: In der ersten wird sie verlacht, in der zweiten bekämpft und in der dritten wirft man ihr vor, dass sie offene Türen einrennt.[1]
>
> BERTHA VON SUTTNER

1 *Ius ad Bellum*

The term *ius ad bellum* comprises the branch of international law that determines the legality of the use of force by states.[2] It needs to be distinguished from *ius in bello*, which is the set of international legal rules coming into effect after the outbreak of a war. *Ius in bello* governs the states' conduct in wars (it regulates how wars are fought), but does not deal with the question whether waging war is a legitimate decision in the respective situation.[3] Accordingly, the two concepts can be summarized as follows, *ius ad bellum* determines when and under which conditions wars can legally be waged while *ius in bello* governs the states' conduct during armed conflicts.[4]

1.1 *The* Just War Doctrine

Before the 19th century, the *Just War Doctrine* was the dominant concept determining the legitimacy of the use of force by states. To gain a first impres-

---

1 The quote is derived from the cover page of: Alfred H. Fried, *Handbuch der Friedensbewegung* (Outlook Verlag 2011). Transl.: Every intellectual movement has to pass three stages: In the first one the movement is laughed at, in the second one it is deeply rejected, and in the third one it is accused of preaching to the converted.

2 Christopher Greenwood, 'The Relationship between ius ad bellum and ius in bello' (1983) 9 Review of International Studies 221. Also: Keiichiro Okimoto, *The Distinction and Relationship between* Jus ad Bellum *and* Jus in Bello (Hart Publishing 2011) 1.

3 Christopher Greenwood, 'The Relationship between ius ad bellum and ius in bello' (n 2 in Chapter 2) 221.

4 Keiichiro Okimoto, *The Distinction and Relationship between* Jus ad Bellum *and* Jus in Bello (n 2 in Chapter 2) 1.

 | DOI:10.1163/9789004754126_003

sion of this doctrine, and of its history, reference should be made to Lynn H. Miller (*'The Contemporary Significance of the Doctrine of Just War'* from 1964). According to her,

> [t]he *bellum justum* doctrine first took shape in Christian moral theology at a time when the church was attempting to become the universal religion of a universal political order. As such, it was forced to take a stand on war as an instrument of policy. Saint Augustine's basic distinction between the just and the unjust war [...] formed the basis for meeting an urgent political need of the time, i.e., defense against the invasion of the barbarians. He held that if a war results from a just cause, it may be waged in the knowledge that it is permitted by God, whereas, if such a condition is lacking, the war is the product of evil men who seek aggrandizement for themselves in defiance of God's will. The purpose of war is not victory, but the restoration of an ordered society.[5]

Evidently, the origin of the *Just War Doctrine* can be traced back to the 5th century AD (or even to earlier years).[6] It was a moral–philosophical approach to war that did not outright oppose war; however, the use to force was intended to be the last resort. Furthermore, the doctrine demanded that certain requirements were fulfilled in order to achieve legitimization and justification for waging wars.[7] Meaning, resorting to force required a just cause.[8] Employing war under the *Just War Doctrine* was an instrument of law meant to be employed for the promotion of good.[9] Consequently, only one of the parties of an armed conflict could fight a just war. The other party would not be justified to invoke force, and, thus, would be fighting an unjust war.[10]

---

5 Lynn H. Miller, 'The Contemporary Significance of the Doctrine of Just War' (1964) 16 World Politics 254–255.

6 Keiichiro Okimoto, *The Distinction and Relationship between* Jus ad Bellum *and* Jus in Bello (n 2 in Chapter 2) 1.

7 Philipp von dem Knesebeck, *Soldaten, Guerilleros, Terroristen: Die Lehre des gerechten Krieges im Zeitalter asymmetrischer Konflikte* (Springer 2014) 50 et seq.

8 Mary Ellen O'Connell, 'The Prohibition of the Use of Force' in Nigel D. White and Christian Henderson (eds.), *Research Handbook on the International Conflict and Security Law* (Edward Elgar Pub 2013) 90.

9 Stephen Neff, *War and the Law of Nations* (n 6 in Chapter 1) 29.

10 Compare in this regard: Randall Lesaffer, 'Too much History' (n 11 in Chapter 1) 38. According to him, the consequence of this arrangement was the following: "Only one side had a right to be in the war and could thus benefit from the so-called jura belli, the rights of war such as the right to use violence, to take loot, to hold enemy persons to

This approach already represented a vast improvement when compared with earlier times. Until the emergence of the *Just War Doctrine*, it had been the prevailing view that war was a regular phenomenon of (international) politics.[11] In Ancient Greece, peace was even understood as just a temporary state. War, on the other hand, was considered as a normal element of politics.[12] This concept still prevailed during the early Roman Empire. It was only given up when stoic philosophers brought forth the idea of natural law in the third century BC.[13] According to this concept, there was only one single justice that binds together all peoples,[14] and which constitutes one common system under which all people lived. Disorder, arbitrariness, and chaos were to be extinguished. Peace, on the other hand, was regarded as the natural and lawful state of international affairs, whereas war was an exception to it. Accordingly, the use of force constituted a breach of the natural legal order, which could only be justified if it had been launched for a greater common good (such as the rule of law).[15] When the Roman Empire abandoned the persecution of Christians in 325 AD, and when it raised Christianity to its state religion around 380 AD, this approach merged with Christian beliefs.[16] Beforehand, Christians had upheld absolute pacifism. But due to this development, their pacifist worldview was confronted with the need to protect the Empire against

---

random, or to make conquests. The soldiers on the unjust side only retained their natural right of self-defense in the case of personal attack."

11 Stephen Neff, *War and the Law of Nations* (n 6 in Chapter 1) 30.

12 Joan-Antoine Mallet, 'War and Peace in Plato's Political Thought' (2017) 1 The Philosophical Journal of Conflict and Violence 88. Also: Stephen Neff, *Justice Among Nations* (Harvard University Press 2014) 7. There, Neff mentioned the following regarding the understanding of war in Ancient Greece: "There was a general, if somewhat vague, belief that wars should be undertaken only if there is a just cause for them. And in certain contexts at least, there were sometimes rules – or at least expectations – that certain restraints on violence would be observed." However, on the other hand, Neff also stressed the following with regards to the general conception of international law at that time (ibid): "The international law in question […] was an assemblage of practices and not an expression of any set of deep-seated general principles."

13 Michael Bertram Crowe, *The Changing of the Profile of the Natural Law* (Springer 1977) 28 et seq. See also: Thomas Weatherall, *Ius Cogens – International Law and Social Contract* (Cambridge University Press 2015) xv.

14 Stephen Neff, *War and the Law of Nations* (n 6 in Chapter 1) 33.

15 Ibid 34. Neff makes an important remark in this context by stating the following: "There can be no doubt that may, if not all, of these formal causes were merely 'cover stories' given for public consumption or for formal purpose, with the true cause of the conflict lying elsewhere, in such considerations as political rivalry, greed for power, and the like."

16 Randall Lesaffer, *European Legal History: A Cultural and Political Perspective* (Cambridge University Press 2012) 268.

inner and outer enemies.[17] Therefore, Christians began to accept war as a *realpolitik* necessity and even brought it into accordance with Christian principles by constituting the *Just War Doctrine.*[18]

Saint Augustine (354–430 AD), an early Christian theologian, is often credited for having been the first to conceptualize the doctrine[19] (although Marcus Tullius Cicero had already held a similar approach in *'De Officiis'* from 44 BC).[20] Over the following centuries, the concept was further developed; e.g., in the *'Decretum Gratiani'* (1140 AD), a fundamental medieval canon law text,[21] and by Thomas de Aquinas (1225–1274).[22] According to Randall Lesaffer (*'Too Much History'* from 2015), Aquinas distinguished

> […] three conditions for a war to be just: *auctoritas, causa justa,* and *recta intention. Auctoritas* meant that a war could only be waged by or under the authority of a sovereign. Most late-medieval writers did not list possible just causes but confined themselves to a broad definition. In general, it boiled down to the view that a just war was a reaction against a prior or threatening injury by the enemy – 'ulcisi iniuriam' in the words of Augustine. It was a form of law enforcement (*executio juris*), of forcible self-help in the absence of a superior authority to which to turn.[23]

---

17 Joachim Von Elbe, 'The Evolution of the Concept of the Just War in International Law' (1939) 33 The American Journal of International Law 665–688.

18 Mary Ellen O'Connell, 'The Prohibition of the Use of Force' (n 8 in Chapter 2) 92.

19 Joachim Von Elbe, 'The Evolution of the Concept of the Just War in International Law' (n 17 in Chapter 2) 665–688.

20 Cicero, *De Officiis* (44 BC) Book 1, No. 34 (re-published, e.g., in Walter Miller, *Cicero de Officiis: With an English Translation by Walter Miller* (Heinemann 1928) 36 et seq.). See also: Gerhard Luf, 'Der "gerechte Krieg" – rechtsphilosophische Überlegungen zur Renaissance eines überwunden geglaubten Konzepts', in Daniela Demko, Kurt Seelmann, and Gerd Brudermüller (eds.), *Kriegs-Recht* (Königshausen u. Neumann 2013) 43; G.A. Harrer, 'Cicero on Peace and War' (1918) 13 The Classical Journal 26 et seq.

21 Gratianus (de Clusio), *Decretum magistri Gratiani* (1140), re-published, e.g., by Aemilius Friedberg in 1879. See also: Randall Lesaffer, 'Too much History' (n 11 in Chapter 1) 37.

22 Thomas de Aquinas, *Summa Theologica, Secunda Secundae* (1265–1273) Quaestio 40, Art. 1–4 (republished, e.g., in Benzinger Brothers, *The "Summa Theologica" of St. Thomas Aquinas, Part II* (Benziger Bros. 1917) 500 et seq.

23 Randall Lesaffer, 'Too much History' (n 11 in Chapter 1) 37. See also: Laurens Winkel, 'Francisco de Vitoria on Just War on Both Sides and on the Legal Position of Burgundy' (2007) 57 The Legal History Review 356.

The *Just War Doctrine* remained the dominant approach towards *ius ad bellum*[24] during the Middle Ages, wherefore the right to wage war was closely linked with Christian ideals and concepts.

The understanding of *ius ad bellum* only changed during the first half of the 16th century. The *Reformation* undermined and, in the end, caused the collapse of the religious unity in Western and Central Europe by challenging the dominance of the Catholic Church. Due to the omission of Catholicism as the dominant religion in Europe and because of the division of the European community of states into Catholic and Protestant nations, the *Just War Doctrine* lost its primary source of legitimacy; i.e., the universally applicable canon law and ecclesiastical jurisdiction.[25] Furthermore, substantial changes to the European order – especially the emergence of great dynastic powers (such as, e.g., England, France, Spain, and Habsburg),[26] the discoveries made in the New World, and reforms carried out in the military sector (e.g., the massification of armies, navies, and warfare) – required a modification of *ius ad bellum* to adapt it to the new situation and needs.[27] Consequently, from the 16th century onwards, war became more than a mere instrument for the enforcement of law and the redress of wrongs. The theory behind war had to be adjusted for keeping pace with the developments.

1.2 *The Concept of* Legal War

The general concept of the *Just War Doctrine* did not disappear during the 16th, 17th, and 18th centuries since numerous scholars and theologians continued to uphold its principles. However, others began to detach their understanding of *ius ad bellum* from the idea that only one side of a war could be justified in employing force. Francisco de Vitoria (1483–1546), Balthasar de Ayala (1548–1584), and Alberico Gentili (1522–1608) were among the most influential authors who did the latter. Vitoria upheld the *Just War Doctrine* and was convinced that wars could only be just on one side. He did, however, recognize that both parties could be excused from sin and divine punishment if they believed in good faith (and because of an invincible error) to have

24 Compare: Stephen Neff, *War and the Law of Nations* (n 6 in Chapter 1) 49–82.

25 Randall Lesaffer, 'Too much History' (n 11 in Chapter 1) 39.

26 Antonio Cassese, 'States: Rise and Decline of the Primary Subjects of the International Community' in Bardo Fassbender and Anne Peters (eds.), *The Oxford Handbook of the History of International Law* (n 28 in Chapter 1) 49.

27 Randall Lesaffer, 'Too much History' (n 11 in Chapter 1) 39.

fought a just war.[28] By applying this modified approach, he lowered the strict interpretation of the *Just War Doctrine* by adding a subjective element to it (the so-called *bellum iustum ex utraque parte*[29]). Ayala and Gentili, on the other hand, went considerably further. They entirely abandoned the religious aspects of the *Just War Doctrine* and based their approaches to *ius ad bellum* on Roman law and earthly considerations. They held the view that wars only need to be waged and to be formally declared by a sovereign in order to be legal.[30] Accordingly, the element of *auctoritas* became the most important factor for them in this regard. According to them, both sides of state-to-state conflicts had to be regarded as being equally entitled to wage war, and to equally enjoy the benefits of the laws of war. This resulted in a substantial conceptual shift of the function that was assigned to war. War used to be an instrument of law enforcement of just demands under the *Just War Doctrine*. In the 16th century, however, its conception began to change. War came to be conceived as fulfilling the function of a legal trial (respectively: a method of dispute settlement). In other words, the outcome of a war was now considered to determine the attribution of property and other claims.[31] War had become a substitute of legal proceedings between conflicting nations,[32] wherefore states were regarded to be entitled, under the positive law of nations, to take recourse to force whenever it pleased them. Consequently, the legality of wars was no longer dependent on just causes.[33]

Notwithstanding the aforementioned changes, the deviations from the traditional *Just War Doctrine*, and the developments towards a concept of *Legal War*, the requirement to present a just cause was not completely removed. The question (stemming from natural law), whether a war was just and legitimated in the eyes of God, remained an important aspect that concerned the afterlife and eternal salvation. At that time, religion was still an indispensable element of people's lives and, thus, this issue deeply concerned them and affected both their thoughts and actions. When examining the thinking and scholarship of international law at the time, for example, the writings of Hugo

28 Ibid 40. Also: Wilhelm Grewe, *The Epochs of International Law* (De Gruyter 2000) 204. Also: Laurens Winkel, 'Francisco de Vitoria on Just War on Both Sides and on the Legal Position of Burgundy' (n 23 in Chapter 2) 357 et seq.

29 An English translation of Francisco de Vitoria's *De Iure Belli* (1532) is available in Ernest Nys (ed.), *De Indis et De Iure Relections: Being Parts of Relections Theologicae XII* (Oceana Publications Inc. 1917). For Victoria's remark on '*bellum iustum ex utraque parte*', see page 177 (§32).

30 Randall Lesaffer, 'Too much History' (n 11 in Chapter 1) 40.

31 Walter Rech, *Enemies of Mankind: Vattel's Theory of Collective Security* (2013) 108.

32 Randall Lesaffer, 'Too much History' (n 11 in Chapter 1) 40.

33 Walter Rech, Enemies of Mankind (n 31 in Chapter 2) 108.

Grotius' (1583–1645), it becomes apparent that the requirement to present a just cause, and considerations concerning natural law, continued to play an important role. For his groundbreaking work, '*De Iure Belli Ac 'Pacis"* (from 1625),[34] Grotius was praised by many authors as the "Father of International Law".[35] Regarding his role in and his contribution to the process of shaping international law, Randall Lesaffer (*'Aggression before Versailles'* from 2018) concluded the following:

> The *jus ad bellum* of the 17th and 18th centuries operated two different, but inter-connected, conceptions of war: just war and legal war. The doctrine of just war had reached its classical articulation in the writings of canonists and theologians from the 12th and 13th centuries. The concept of legal war was a product of the civilian jurisprudence of the 12th – 15th centuries. In his *De Jure Belli ac Pacis*, Hugo Grotius (1583–1645) recycled both concepts and gave them a place within his dualist systematization of the law of nations. Whereas just war pertained to the natural law of nations, which applied in conscience (in foro interno), legal war, or bellum solemne as he labelled it, pertained to the positive law of nations, which applied to the external relations between states (in foro externo). After Grotius, this dualism of operating two different sets of norms with relation to war – one at the level of natural justice and one at the level of its effect under the positive law of nations – became mainstream and remained so until the 19th century.[36]

The positive law of nations was a secular approach to international law that concentrated entirely on states as both its authors and its only subjects.[37] Accordingly, rights and duties applied only to them, and states alone were entitled to make law. Furthermore, the positive law of nations was detached from natural law and its religious aspects. It was considered to originate from the consent of states[38] and, therefore, comprised only human-made law (such

---

34 See, e.g., the following edition of his work: Hugo Grotius, *De Iure Belli Ad Pacis* (1631) <https://archive.org/details/bub_gb_VIRnoA4gKxwC> accessed August 10, 2018.

35 Amos S. Hershey, 'History of International Law Since the Peace of Westphalia' (1912) 6 The American Journal of International Law 31. For a dissenting and more critical view on Grotius, see also: Oona A. Hathaway and Scott J. Shapiro, *The Internationalists* (n 11 in Chapter 1) 94 et seq.

36 Randall Lesaffer, 'Aggression before Versailles' (2018) 29 The European Journal of International Law 777.

37 Stephen Neff, *War and the Law of Nations* (n 6 in Chapter 1) 49–82, 85.

38 Peter Haggenmacher, 'People in Portrait: Hugo Grotius' in Bardo Fassbender and Anne Peters (eds.), *The Oxford Handbook of the History of International Law* (n 28 in Chapter 1) 1098.

as statuary law and customary law). Other aspects, such as moral or religious considerations – which were dominant factors in natural law – no longer played a role in the positive law of nations.[39] From the 16th to the middle of the 18th century, these two concepts – natural law and the positive law of nations – existed side by side.[40] It was only when religion suffered an even greater and rapidly increasing loss of importance during the second half of the 18th century, due to the *Enlightenment*, that the positive law of nations pushed aside natural law and became the dominant approach in international law (and international legal thinking). Despite this development, the underlying ideas of the *Just War Doctrine* were never completely washed away either, as the concept was deeply rooted in European legal thinking.[41] Therefore, just cause and the *Just War Doctrine* remained key factors in state practice. Governments continued to put a lot of effort in issuing formal declarations of war in order to present reasonable and just causes and to rationalize their decision to go to war to other states, to their populations, and to God.[42]

Despite the duality of the two concepts between the 16th and the middle of the 18th century, the role of war changed remarkably during this period. Under the *Just War Doctrine*, the use of force had been limited to the redress of wrongs and was therefore regarded as an instrument of law enforcement.[43] The concept of *Legal War*, however, did not provide for similar limitations. Wars became fights between two sovereigns in their entireties; in which all subjects and objects were viable targets.

1.3 *The Situation in the 19th Century*

The early modern understanding of *ius ad bellum* changed when the dualism of the two legal regimes – natural law and the positive law of nations – came to an end in the 19th century. This century was generally a time of immense social, political, as well as technological changes.[44] The trend during these

39 Stephen Neff, *War and the Law of Nations* (n 6 in Chapter 1) 85. See also: Mary Ellen O'Connell, 'The Prohibition of the Use of Force' (n 8 in Chapter 2) 94. Joseph Chitty, *The Law of Nations or Principles of the Law of Nature Applied to the Conduct and Affairs of Nations and Sovereigns from the French Monsieur de Vattel* (T. & J.W. Johnson 1852).

40 Rüdiger Wolfrum, 'International Law', *The Max Planck Encyclopedia of Public International Law* (Oxford University Press 2012) 820–836, §30.

41 Mary Ellen O'Connell, 'The Prohibition of the Use of Force' (n 8 in Chapter 2) 95.

42 Compare: Randall Lesaffer, 'Too much History' (n 11 in Chapter 1) 43.

43 Ibid 42. See also: Stephen Neff, *War and the Law of Nations* (n 6 in Chapter 1) 100–102.

44 Miloš Vec, 'From the Congress of Vienna to the Paris Peace Treaties of 1919' (n 28 in Chapter 1) 655. According to him, the quote stems from: Jürgen Osterhammel, *Die Verwandlung der Welt. Eine Geschichte des 19. Jahrhunderts* (C. H. Beck 2009).

years towards global transformations and globalization was not without consequences for the concepts of international law and *ius ad bellum* either. Both underwent deep changes when they were adapted to new worldviews and newly arising legal theoretical considerations. The change of the so-far prevailing international system was caused by the ongoing secularization of international law and the emergence of legal positivism in the 19th century; consequently, natural law and the *Just War Doctrine* lost importance and influence in international legal scholarship.[45] Legal positivism not only became the dominant theory in the field of law (in general), but also in international law. Therefore, natural law was pushed aside and reduced to a mere code of morality.[46] Furthermore, other developments also contributed to the changes of the prevailing international system: in particular, the *Napoleonic Wars* (1803–1815), which threw Europe into chaos and brought the former international system to an end, and the subsequent *Congress of Vienna* (1814/1815) at which the international order was re-modelled. To guarantee peace and stability under the new system in Europe, public law was re-established at this occasion, and a new balance of power was introduced through territorial and political shifts and adjustments.[47] In addition to that, the four victorious European great powers (Great Britain, Russia, Austria-Hungary, and Prussia) created the *Concert of Europe* for preserving this equilibrium. France joined the group in 1818 and, for the next decades, the *Concert* provided a forum for the great powers, in the context of which they could co-ordinate their actions and take joint decisions for the preservation of order and stability in Europe.

The period between 1815 and 1853 is known today as the *European Restoration.* Diplomacy and conferences were the great powers' instruments of choice during that time for the achievement of their goals and formed the cornerstones of the new system. No conflict or territorial change in Europe could arise without attracting the attention of the *Concert.* Its members regarded every European dispute as a potential threat to peace and for the carefully protected balance of power. Therefore, they would meet for conferences whenever a conflict arose, in order to coordinate joint actions for the re-establishment of peace, stability, and order. Apart from the *Concert,* a second framework for cooperation was created at the *Congress of Vienna*, in the form

45 Ian Brownlie, *International Law and the Use of Force by States* (n 27 in Chapter 1) 14.

46 Randall Lesaffer, 'Too much History' (n 11 in Chapter 1) 45.

47 Gordon A. Craig, *Geschichte Europas 1815–1980: Vom Wiener Kongreß bis zur Gegenwart* (C.H. Beck 1983) 23–30. Also: Ian Brownlie, *International Law and the Use of Force by States* (n 27 in Chapter 1) 19.

of the *Holy Alliance*.[48] It was a coalition of the conservative powers Austria-Hungary, Prussia, and Russia, and differed from the *Concert* in the decisive point that its members feared revolutions and potential overthrows so much that they regarded all trends towards democracy, liberalism, and secularism as major threats to peace, stability, and their own privileged positions. Therefore, they attempted to suppress any such trends as soon as they arose anywhere in Europe, whereby forcing the continent into a period of political standstill.

The *Holy Alliance* and the *Concert* were the great powers' instruments for the fulfilment of their claim to leadership in Europe between 1815 and 1853.[49] They dominated the continent and left smaller states scant room for political maneuvers. Whenever smaller states were involved in a conflict, the great powers (but not the smaller states themselves, even if they were directly affected by the conflict) met for conferences and brought the conflicts to an end by finding compromises suitable to the great powers.

In this regard, the interests of the great powers constituted the crucial factors in state practice, along whose lines the decisions were made about for the settlement of conflicts. The interests of the smaller states, on the other hand, were vastly ignored. The conferences in *Troppau* (1820), *Laibach* (1821), or *Verona* (1822), or the meetings in 1830 on the future of Belgium and Greece,[50] constituted telling examples of this practice. The great powers followed the aforementioned approach and forced the (directly affected) smaller states to comply with their wishes. They did so by applying political pressure and demonstrating joint military strength. This arrangement resulted in the emergence of a system based on legalized hegemony of the five European great powers over smaller nations;[51] a system that embraced the inequality of states in Europe, and those worldwide.[52] Neither before nor thereafter did a group of states ever dominate the world so exclusively and absolutely.[53] The system created in Vienna was equally recognized by smaller states (which acknowledged the right of the *Concert* to settle all kinds of disputes and which sometimes even

48 Compare for example: ibid 29–30. Also: Christoph Nonn, *Das 19. und 20. Jahrhundert* (UTB 2014) 118–119; Wolfgang von Hippel and Bernhard Stier, *Europa zwischen Reform und Revolution 1800–1850* (UTB 2012) 66–70.

49 Wilhelm G. Grewe, *Die Epochen der Völkerrechtsgeschichte* (Nomos 1984) 502.

50 For these conferences, please compare ibid 505 et seq.

51 Miloš Vec, 'From the Congress of Vienna to the Paris Peace Treaties of 1919' (n 28 in Chapter 1) 659. Also: Gerry Simpson, *Great Powers and Outlaw States: Unequal Sovereigns in the International Legal Order* (Cambridge University Press 2004) 91 et seq.

52 Theresa Reinold, *Sovereignty and the Responsibility to Protect: The Power of Norms and the Norms of the Powerful* (Routledge 2013) 30. See also: Wilhelm G. Grewe, *Die Epochen der Völkerrechtsgeschichte* (n 49 in Chapter 2) 501–535.

53 Wilhelm G. Grewe, *Die Epochen der Völkerrechtsgeschichte* (n 49 in Chapter 2) 505.

explicitly asked the great powers to do so) and by international lawyers.[54] Thereby, the decisions of the *Concert* were (indirectly at least) attributed the status of sources of international law.[55]

Even though this arrangement resulted into the institutionalization of inequality between states, and caused a period of political standstill in Europe, the years between 1815 and 1853 were also an era of peace in Europe, without almost any major wars.[56] When compared to earlier times, this constituted a novum, as war had always played a decisive role in international politics and had occurred regularly before 1815 in inter-European relations.[57] Therefore, it should be considered a remarkable change of their attitudes that the great powers refrained from taking recourse to force in their mutual relations for 38 years. In fact, the use of force between states became an exceptional and unusual event under the *Congress*-system.[58] International law, however, played a rather secondary role in state practice at that time. Conference diplomacy and the great powers' hegemony over the continent dominated international relations instead.[59] Furthermore, not only did the frequency of wars decrease significantly during the first half of the 19th century, but states were also *de facto* limited by the *Vienna Settlement* to invoke force. Neither the great powers nor smaller states seem to have been free to wage war at that time. This was not due to international norms preventing recourse to arms but resulted from the nature of the *Concert*-system and the policy pursued by the (conservative) great powers, which was to preserve the *status quo* at all costs. They suppressed any attempt made by smaller states to change the territorial distribution of the *Vienna Settlement* and the current system. Thereby, the great powers effectively prevented wars from being waged by smaller states. That

---

54 Matthias Schulz, 'Paradoxes of a Great Power Peace: The Case of the Concert of Europe', in Thomas Hippler and Miloš Vec (eds.), *Paradoxes of Peace in Nineteenth Century Europe* (Oxford University Press 2015) 136.

55 Ibid.

56 John Mueller, 'Changing Attitudes towards War: The Impact of the First World War' (1991) 21 British Journal of Political Science 13. See in Miller's article also *Table 1* (page 14). It provides an overview of the number of soldiers killed or wounded in battle between 1630 and 1919. These figures make clear that hardly any wars were fought in the days between 1815 and 1854 in Europe whereas war had been an absolutely common phenomenon prior to 1815. See also: Martti Koskenniemi, *The Gentle Civilizer of Nations: The Rise and Fall of International Law 1870–1960* (Cambridge University Press 2002) 11.

57 John Mueller, 'Changing Attitudes towards War' (n 56 in Chapter 2) 13.

58 Miloš Vec, 'From the Congress of Vienna to the Paris Peace Treaties of 1919' (n 28 in Chapter 1) 660.

59 Bob Reinalda, *Routledge History of International Organizations – From 1815 to the Present Day* (Routledge 2009) 26–27.

being said, the great powers could not invoke their right to the use of force either. Those that tried to wage war for the enforcement of their will would have had to face the joint opposition of the other four members of the *Concert*, all of whom were keen not to concede gains of power, influence, or territory to any of the others. Thereby, the great powers also successfully deterred one another from taking individual actions in this regard.

The only real advancements of international law during the first half of the 19th century were the fight against slavery, the introduction of the principle of free navigation on rivers, and certain adaptations of diplomatic law.[60] Apart from progresses made in these thematically very limited fields, international law did not exercise much influence on state practice at the time. In certain areas of international relations, governments even seem to not have cared at all about complying with international law,[61] while in other areas, referring to international law and to certain legal principles remained an essential element of international policy.

Recourse to legal arguments was taken, in particular, in the context of topics such as sovereignty, the reasoning of interventions by the *Concert*, and with regards to *ius ad bellum*. But the emergence of legal positivism also played a decisive role in shaping international law. International lawyers began to embrace this approach in the first half of the century and turned it into the leading doctrine in international legal scholarship in the second half.[62] According to this doctrine, international legal norms and regulations had to be consensually accepted by the states in order to bind them.[63] In its purest and strictest interpretation, legal positivism provided that only those rules and obligations were legally binding which were based on treaties or customary law that had been explicitly accepted in advance by the respective states. With regards to *ius ad bellum*, its understanding by leading scholars of international law also changed by the later parts of the 19th, a development that was also deeply influenced by legal positivist considerations.[64] These scholars not

60 Miloš Vec, 'From the Congress of Vienna to the Paris Peace Treaties of 1919' (n 28 in Chapter 1) 659.

61 Ibid 660. In this context, Vec referred, e.g., to international debt regulations.

62 Wilhelm G. Grewe, *Die Epochen der Völkerrechtsgeschichte* (n 49 in Chapter 2) 591.

63 Ibid 592. Also: Amnon Lev, 'The Transformation of International Law in the Nineteenth Century' in Alexander Orakhelashvili (ed.), *Research Handbook on the Theory and History of International Law* (Edward Elgar Pub 2011) 111.

64 Randall Lesaffer, 'Too much History (n 11 in Chapter 1) 46. Also: Agatha Verdebout, 'The Contemporary Discourse on the Use of Force in the Nineteenth Century: A Diachronic and Critical Analysis' (2014) 1 Journal on the Use of Force and International Law 223–245. On page 234, she comes to the following conclusion regarding the situation in the 19th century: "[...] the use of force (war and intervention) was generally considered as pro-

only argued in favor of an unrestricted *ius ad bellum* so long as no provisions existed that were consensually concluded by the respective states, and which explicitly banned war from their mutual relations, but they also aimed for the complete detachment of *ius ad bellum* from any other legal considerations, as they considered it to fall outside the scope of positive law.[65] For them, ethical considerations stemming from the *Just War Doctrine* did not play a role under legal positivism. Carl von Clausewitz's famous remark pointed in the same direction. According to him, war was "[…] not merely an act of policy but a true political instrument, a continuation of political intercourse, carried on with other means."[66] Therefore, scholars advocating such approaches held the view that that the use of force was to be considered as generally governed by reason and controlled by the dictates of policy.[67] As a consequence, a realization of this concept would have resulted in an essentially unlimited right to wage war.[68] For example, Paul Heilborn (*'Handbuch des Völkerrechts'* from 1912) even claimed that it was the dominant view in legal scholarship that there did not exist any limitations of the right to wage war and that, consequently, resorting to force was allowed at any time.[69] However, it should also be borne in mind what authors such as Agatha Verdebout (*'The Contemporary Discourse on the Use of Force in the Nineteenth Century'* from 2014)[70] and Randall Lesaffer (*'Aggression before Versailles'* from 2018) argued regarding the dominant understanding of *ius ad bellum* during the 19th century. According to them, the *ius ad bellum* (and the traditional doctrine of it) kept considerably more restrictive normative power and survived to a larger extent than commonly accepted.[71] Consequently, a differentiated view must be applied in this regard. It appears as if only some international scholars considered *ius ad bel-*

hibited as a logical consequence of the principle of the equal sovereignty of states, according to which each had the right to the respect of their mutual independence. As such, one can only be struck when reading in contemporary literature that classical international law 'scholars agreed that every sovereign state could have recourse to war whenever seemed advisable'."

65 Joachim Von Elbe, 'The Evolution of the Concept of the Just War in International Law' (n 17 in Chapter 2) 682.

66 Carl von Clausewitz, *On War* (trans. and edited by Michael Howard and Peter Paret, University Press Group 1993) 98–99.

67 Ibid 101. See also: Thomas Waldman, 'Politics and War: Clausewitz's Paradoxical Equation' (2010) 40 Parameters 48–60.

68 Wilhelm G. Grewe, *Die Epochen der Völkerrechtsgeschichte* (n 49 in Chapter 2) 624.

69 Paul Heilborn, *Handbuch des Völkerrechts*, vol. 1 (W. Kohlhammer 1912) 23.

70 Agatha Verdebout, 'The Contemporary Discourse on the Use of Force in the Nineteenth Century' (n 64 in Chapter 2) 223, 227.

71 Randall Lesaffer, 'Aggression before Versailles' (n 36 in Chapter 2) 789–790.

lum as entirely unrestricted during the 19th century, while many other authors held a decisively different approach.[72] The latter seem to have maintained the view that waging wars and using force could constitute, at least in principle, violations of international law.[73] Additionally, it should also be noted that the afore-mentioned approaches were, first and foremost, academic and theoretical views on *ius ad bellum*. They did not fully reflect the state practice at that time. Finally, legalist ideals spread slowly among states during the late 19th century and the states proved to be particularly unresponsive to legal positivist consideration in the context of *ius ad bellum*. Contrary to the claim for an unrestricted right to wage war in legal scholarship, states continued to uphold the practice of providing justifications and reasoning for their decisions to go to war.[74]

Governments continued to provide justification for going to war due to the ever-growing importance of public opinion, and in order to seek backing by allied states. Had they not convinced the population, and allied states, of the need to take recourse to force in a particular situation, governments would have run the risk of lacking the necessary support for waging wars. Therefore, public justification of wars continued to play a key role in state practice. Although the reasons for war that were invoked changed over the years; it remained common practice to claim that wars were defensive and in response to earlier wrongs. Governments regularly justified wars by invoking reasons such as the need to defend the own territorial integrity, the security of the nation, vital interests, their nation's honor, or other legitimate rights.[75] Hence, despite the claim for an unrestricted *ius ad bellum* in (parts of) legal scholarship, states continued to provide reasons for their decision to wage war in order to demonstrate that they were fighting defensive (and therefore, justified) wars.[76] This practice had many similarities with the *Just War Doctrine*: States persisted in claiming that their rights had been infringed and that, therefore, the use of force was necessary as a reaction to these wrongdoings. Consequently, they claimed to be simply defending themselves and their rights, and

---

72 Ibid 790 et seq. In this regard, Lesaffer listed, *inter alia*, the following authors as examples: Johann Caspar Bluntschli, *Das moderne Völkerrecht der civilisirten Staaten: Als Rechtsbuch dargestellt* (C. H. Beck 1868) 289; William E. Hall, *International Law* (Clarendon Press 1880) 51; Georg Friedrich von Martens, *Précis du droit des gens moderne de l'Europe fondé sur les traités et les usages: Pour servir d'introduction à un cours politique et diplomatique* (3rd ed., J.C. Dieterich 1821) 432.

73 Randall Lesaffer, 'Aggression before Versailles' (n 36 in Chapter 2) 791.

74 Randall Lesaffer, 'Too much History' (n 11 in Chapter 1) 46. See also: Ian Brownlie, *International Law and the Use of Force by States* (n 27 in Chapter 1) 40–44.

75 Randall Lesaffer, 'Too much History' (n 11 in Chapter 1) 46.

76 Ibid.

not to have initiated or caused the conflict. But these justifications were often nothing more than shallow pretenses that were issued to wage wars, without having to admit to being the actual aggressor.[77]

The system established at the *Congress of Vienna* had guaranteed peace and stability for almost 40 years. However, the prevailing repressive approach at that time towards liberalism, nationalism, and democratic ideas in numerous European countries resulted in growing dissatisfaction among major parts of the populations, which bore the potential for enormous explosive force. When severe economic problems arose during the 1840s, this situation escalated in revolutions across several European countries in 1848.[78] Although the ruling classes were able to re-constitute their power, and stop revolutions in the end, the situation between the great powers had already worsened and had become dominated by mistrust due to these events.[79] Furthermore, nationalist tendencies and pure power considerations replaced the aim of a stable equilibrium among the great powers, following the events of 1848.

The most important and fatal clash of national interests, and of the powers' attempts to extend their spheres of influence during these years, was the *Crimean War* (1853–1856) between Russia on the one hand, and France and Great Britain on the other. The five European great powers came together for a meeting in Paris in 1856 to negotiate peace in the context of this conflict and to re-establish stability in Europe. However, this was the last gasp of the *Concert of Europe*. In the years between 1856 and 1871, open struggles for power, and even wars, once again became common phenomena in Europe. For example, France entered a colonial rivalry for outer-European territories with Great Britain, the Italian states hurled themselves into a revolutionary war between 1861 and 1871, which resulted in the formation of the united Italian Kingdom, and Prussia strove for unifying Germany.[80] Prussia's actions alone caused three wars – between Prussia and Denmark in 1864, Prussia and Austria in 1866, and Germany and France in 1870/71. None of the other great powers sought to prevent these conflicts,[81] even though the balance of power and territorial order that had been established by the *Vienna Settlement*, was considerably shaken, if not

77 Lassa Oppenheim, *International Law – A Treatise*, vol. 2 (Longmans 1906) 71.

78 Compare: Stacie E. Goddard, 'When Right Makes Might: How Prussia Overturned the European Balance of Power' (2008/09) 33 International Security 111. See also: William J. Orr, Jr., 'British Diplomacy and the German Problem, 1848–1850' (1978) 10 Albion: A Quarterly Journal Concerned with British Studies 213 et seq.; Paul W. Schroeder, 'The 19th-Century International System: Changes in the Structure' (1986) 39 World Politics 4.

79 Gordon A. Craig, *Geschichte Europas 1815–1980* (n 47 in Chapter 2) 126.

80 Wilhelm G. Grewe, *Die Epochen der Völkerrechtsgeschichte* (n 49 in Chapter 2) 510.

81 Stacie E. Goddard, 'When Right Makes Might: How Prussia Overturned the European Balance of Power' (n 78 in Chapter 2) 111, 115 et seq.

entirely shattered, by these events. Thus, the great powers had turned away from the *Concert*-system. Instead, they pursued pure power policy (*realpolitik*) after 1848,[82] which also becomes apparent when taking into account the reasons invoked to justify the wars in this period (1848–1871). The arguments given in their favor were often shallow and mere pretexts. Instead of responding to earlier wrongdoings and infringements, they were oft times driven by pure nationalist considerations.[83]

Nationalism had arisen in the 18th century and provided – to give an admittedly cursory definition – that all those individuals belonged to a nation who shared the same language, history, and ethnical background, and who lived in the same country or on the same territory.[84] This ideology coincided with France's, Germany's, and Italy's desire for change. Both Germany and Italy strove for unifications, whereas France wanted to regain their former hegemonic position in Europe, which they had lost as a result of the *Vienna Settlement*.[85] All three countries hoped for territorial gains, more influence, and might – and they all held these goals to be appropriate and reasonable because of the conviction that they, as nations, were entitled to them. In addition to that, nationalism coincided with the pure-power policy after 1848, an approach that regarded every option or action as viable as long as it was capable of resulting in advantages for the own nation.[86] This approach complied to a great extent with Clausewitz's above-mentioned notion that war was not a legal but a purely political instrument. His followers developed this view into the understanding that the decision to go to war belonged to the exclusive sphere of politics, and that states were entitled to wage wars for their purposes whenever they saw fit.[87] Consequently, great powers fought several wars at that time because of purely nationalist and *realpolitik* interests.

During the following period, the years between 1871 and the turn of the 20th century, peace returned to Europe. Italy and Germany had achieved their unifications, whereas France had suffered a heavy defeat in the *German-Franco*

---

82 Frank Möller, 'Vom revolutionären Idealismus zur Realpolitik. Generationswechsel nach 1848?' (2003) 36 Historische Zeitschrift. Beihefte, New Series 77–78. See also: Gordon A. Craig, *Geschichte Europas 1815–1980* (n 47 in Chapter 2) 126.

83 Paul W. Schroeder, 'The 19th-Century International System' (n 78 in Chapter 2) 7.

84 Christoph Nonn, *Das 19. Und 20. Jahrhundert* (n 48 in Chapter 2) 196–197. See also: Jörg Fisch, *Europa zwischen Wachstum und Gleichheit 1850–1914* (UTB 2002) 297–301.

85 Jörg Fisch, *Europa zwischen Wachstum und Gleichheit 1850–1914* (n 84 in Chapter 2) 72–73.

86 Paul W. Schroeder, 'The Nineteenth Century System: Balance of Power or Political Equilibrium?' (1989) 15 Review of International Studies 138.

87 Nicholas Renger and Caroline Kennedy-Pipe, 'The State of War' (2008) 84 International Affairs 894.

War, which deteriorated their position for the following years.[88] Consequently, many European states once again strove for stability after 1871, at least in the European context. The international order and power structure until the turn of the century were characterized by bi- and multi-lateral alliances between the great powers. By concluding them, the great powers aimed for stability, obtaining guarantees for their own safety. Returning to the *Concert*-system was not an option as the recent wars had deteriorated several of their mutual relations and, thus, mistrust and rivalries were dominant among some of the great powers.[89] The alliance agreements offered the option to establish provisions in the relationship between the powers, through which they guaranteed one another mutual military assistance against attacks by other nations. This practice was mastered by the German chancellor Otto von Bismarck (1815–1898), who led the newly established German Empire into alliances with Austria-Hungary and Russia, the so-called *League of the Three Emperors* (1873–1887). When he resigned in 1890, German foreign policy, as well as the European system, changed once more. The Russian-German alliance was not renewed. Russia turned to France instead, resulting in the formation of the *Entente* between Russia and France, on the one hand, and the *Triple Alliance* on the other, consisting of Germany, Austria-Hungary, and Italy. For the time being, this alliance system secured peace and stability in Europe by forming power blocs that were capable of deterring any actions being taken against the other bloc. After 1871, Europe enjoyed a period of another 43 years of ongoing peace as both the greater and smaller European powers avoided armed conflicts within Europe. Instead, they re-located their rivalries and conflicts to battlegrounds outside of the European continent. Their competition in other world regions deepened their mutual conflicts and animosities. Furthermore, increasingly influential ideologies such as Social-Darwinism, *realpolitik*, nationalism, and racism fueled the states' rivalries as well.

During the last third of the 19th century, European countries (and the United States) entered into open competition with one another for global influence, territory, and power. They incorporated millions of square miles, and people in Africa, Asia, and in the Pacific, into their empires in order to satisfy their imperialist aspirations.[90] Since the 1870s, *imperialism* became one – if not *the* – leading foreign political approach among European great powers, and in the United States. Instead of focusing entirely on national or regional con-

88 Gordon A. Craig, *Geschichte Europas 1815–1980* (n 47 in Chapter 2) 257–261.

89 Ibid 200–203.

90 Matthew Craven, 'Colonialism and Domination' in Bardo Fassbender and Anne Peters (eds.), *The Oxford Handbook of the History of International Law* (n 28 in Chapter 1) 879.

siderations, their endeavors for power also developed a global perspective. Until today, the precise causes of the emergence of imperialism remain rather unclear. But it seems – according to Matthew Craven (*'Colonialism and Domination'* from 2012) – as if an

> [...] over-accumulation of capital in Europe had encouraged the speculative interest in overseas investment (in trade, mining, manufacturing, railways, telegraph systems etc) which had, in turn, fed through into a self-reinforcing logic of acquisition: colonies and territories had to be acquired in order to 'protect' overseas trade and investment from dangers posed by the monopolist or protectionist policies of rival colonial powers.[91]

On the other hand, it stands to reason that the emergence of ideological worldviews focusing on the competition between nations also played a decisive role in this regard. Social-Darwinism, in particular, encouraged the belief in the existence of an eternal struggle between nations and of the principle of the survival of the fittest within the international community. According to radical interpretations of this approach, the struggle had to be waged by all available means because only three or four superpowers could prevail in the end, while all other powers would be absorbed by the victorious states.[92] Hence, global empires had to be established in order to strengthen the motherland and not to be outcompeted by the other nations. The consequences of these developments were the *Scrambles for Africa, for Asia,* and *for the Pacific*. From 1870 onwards, European states took control over great shares of these regions.

The enormous (and quickly increasing) speed of the European colonialization of Africa soon narrowed down the amount of obtainable territories; and, already by 1900, almost the entire African continent was under European control.[93] Therefore, the colonial empires bordered on each other and restricted the colonial ambitions of their opponents. Border disputes, opposing territorial claims, the striving for influence, and a series of other issues caused tensions and resentments, and deepened the already existing rivalries between the colonial powers even more. Some of these tensions were serious enough to bear the potential of the resulting actual wars, which could have even spread

91 Ibid 880.

92 Paul Kennedy, *Aufstieg und Fall der großen Mächte* (Fischer 1991) 303. See also: Fritz Fischer, *Krieg der Illusionen* (Droste 1969) 65–66; G Gordon A. Craig, *Geschichte Europas 1815–1980* (n 47 in Chapter 2) 319.

93 Gordon A. Craig, *Geschichte Europas 1815–1980* (n 47 in Chapter 2) 321 et seq.

from the colonies to the European homelands. One prominent example of this is the *Fashoda Incident* (1898) between Great Britain and France, which brought the two states to the brink of war.[94] Consequently, imperialism and the struggle for colonies evoked new and even more potential for conflicts between the great powers after 1870, further deteriorating their relations.

In conclusion, states strove ruthlessly for colonies, influence, and power by the turn of the 20th century. Wars were regarded by many governments as suitable instruments for the achievement of the goals of their own nation. This practice had already prevailed in Europe between 1848 and 1871 when the continent was dominated by open struggles for power, and even by actual wars between the great powers. During the period from 1871 to 1899, peace was re-established and secured in Europe. But the great powers did not simply put their differences aside. They moved them to the global level and competed fiercely with one another for colonies, influence, and universal domination.

Moreover, *ius ad bellum* took a turn in the 19th century state practice, which resulted in a considerably broader understanding of it. Numerous international lawyers claimed that states were not bound by any restrictions of *ius ad bellum* any longer. Some of these scholars even postulated the thought that the decision to go to war was a purely political one, whereas legal considerations were – according to them – not supposed to play a role in this regard. However, analyzing the state practice from these years leads to the conclusion that most states continued to provide justification when they went to war (even if the invoked arguments were many a time, mere pretexts). Despite opposing approaches in legal scholarship, this tradition (stemming from the *Just War Doctrine*) still prevailed during the 19th century. However, this aspect only concerned the reasoning of the use of force. States were – *de facto* – free to use force by simply bringing forward pretexts that claimed that the respective wars were to be fought for defensive reasons.

2 Arbitration and Adjudication

Today, international law offers a variety of instruments for the peaceful settlement of international disputes, given the case that diplomatic attempts did not result in suitable solutions. A (non-enumerated) list of those measures is provided in Article 33 of the UN Charter, according to which parties to any dis-

94 Susan Peterson, *Crisis Bargaining and the State: The Domestic Politics of International Conflict* (University of Michigan Press 1996) 95–132. See also: Christoph Marx, *Geschichte Afrikas: Von 1800 bis zur Gegenwart* (UTB 2004) 128.

pute, which, if continued, would likely lead to threat to international peace and security, shall, "[...] first of all, seek a solution by negotiation, enquiry, mediation, conciliation, arbitration, judicial settlement, resort to regional agencies or arrangements, or other peaceful means of their own choice."

Charles H. Brower II (*'Arbitration'* from 2007) divides the listed instruments into two categories: diplomatic and legal procedures.[95] Negotiation, mediation, enquiry, and conciliation fall into the former category, whereas arbitrations and adjudications belong to the latter.[96] Arbitration and adjudication are regarded today as the most suitable and effective means for the achievement of peaceful and long-lasting settlements of international conflicts.[97] Moreover, both instruments are characterized by the fact that they involve a third party that decides the conflict,[98] and that they result in legally binding decisions that are issued on the basis of law.[99] The major difference between them is that judicial settlements are carried out through formal legal procedures before standing international courts,[100] while arbitration happens through *ad hoc* panels. According to Gary Goertz, Paul F. Diehl, and Alexandru Balas (*'The Puzzle of Peace'* from 2016), arbitration is, therefore,

> [...] an adversarial process with presentation of cases by two states, but there are several notable differences [to adjudication; *added by the author of the present book*]. First, the 'tribunal' might be ad hoc and created by the disputants, or it could be institutionalized as in the Permanent Court of Arbitration. Second, the arbiters could be a single individual or set of individuals, often chosen by the disputants. Third, the rules of procedure and the bases on which a decision is made by the arbiter(s) might be determined by the disputants and might include some nonlegal elements.[101]

---

95 Charles H. Brower II, 'Arbitration', *Max Planck Encyclopedia of International Law (online)*.

96 Compare: Alf Ross, *A Textbook of International Law: General Part* (The Lawbook Exchange 2006) 275.

97 Stephen E. Gent, 'The Politics of International Arbitration and Adjudication' (2013) 2 Penn State Journal of Law & International Affairs 66.

98 Franz Cede, 'The Settlement of International Disputes by Legal Means – Arbitration and Judicial Settlement' in Jacob Bercovitch (ed.), *The SAGE Handbook of Conflict Resolution* (SAGE Publications 2009) 358.

99 Stephen E. Gent, 'The Politics of International Arbitration and Adjudication' (n 97 in Chapter 2) 67.

100 Gary Goertz, Paul F. Diehl, and Alexandru Balas, *The Puzzle of Peace: The Evolution of Peace in the International System* (Oxford University Press 2016) 171.

101 Ibid.

Finally, arbitral decisions are not necessarily based on judicial independence or impartiality due to the fact that the conflict parties may have a say in the selection procedure of the arbitrators or that they may be entitled to determine the scope of the arbitration procedure (or the procedural rules).[102] That being said, arbitration is still considered a legal instrument under current international law.[103]

While these definitions of arbitration refer to the modern understanding of arbitration, the here-presented concept stands in sharp contrast to the one that prevailed during the 19th (and early 20th) century. Back then, arbitration used to be a method for the peaceful settlement of international conflicts in which a third party compromised the conflicting states' interests in accordance with the principle *ex aequo et bon.*[104] Today, this principle (*ex aequo et bono*) means that arbitrators are entitled to push international law aside in order to find a fair solution for a conflict on the base of equity, but without leaving the general framework of the international legal order.[105] Or, to quote Markus Kotzur (*'Ex Aequo et Bono'* from 2009), conflicts are to be settled "[…] 'in good conscience' and notwithstanding the written law".[106] In the 19th century, however, the principle had a very different meaning. According to it, arbitrators could completely refrain from taking into consideration prevailing law when deciding on a dispute. Instead, they usually focused on compromising the interests of the opposing parties in order to find a solution that was suitable and agreeable to them both.[107] But notwithstanding the fact that cases were decided by arbitration in a non-judicial way, the issued awards were still legally binding for the participating states, so long as the decision complied with the scope of the arbitral procedure, as defined in the (underlying) *compromis.*[108]

---

102 Anja Seibert-Fohr, 'International Judicial Ethics' in Cesare P.R. Romano, Karen J. Alter & Yuval Shany (eds.), *The Oxford Handbook of International Adjudication* (Oxford University Press 2014) 774.

103 Charles H. Brower II, 'Arbitration' (n 95 in Chapter 2).

104 Compare, e.g.: Nils Börnsen, *Nationales Recht in Investitionsschiedsverfahren* (Mohr Siebeck 2016) 10 et seq. See also: Hersch Lauterpacht, *The Function of Law in the International Community* (Oxford University Press 2000) 318 et seq.

105 Alain Pellet, 'Article 38' in Andreas Zimmermann, Christian Tomuschat, Karin Oellers-Frahm, and Christian J. Tams (eds.), *The Statute of the International Court of Justice: A Commentary* (Oxford University Press 2012) 796. See also: Markus Kotzur, 'Ex Aequo et Bono', *Max Planck Encyclopedia of International Law* (*online*).

106 Markus Kotzur, 'Ex Aequo et Bono' (n 105 in Chapter 2).

107 Compare, e.g.: Heinrich Lammasch, *Die Lehre von der Schiedsgerichtsbarkeit in ihrem ganzen Umfange* (W. Kohlhammer 1913) 9.

108 Ibid 176, 187.

2.1 *Initial Remarks*

Before coming to a detailed definition of arbitration, it is necessary to look at the terminology that will be used in the subsequent sections. In particular, the term *traditional arbitration* plays a key role in this regard. This phrase will be used in the following in a specific sense, and with a particular meaning. The term *traditional arbitration* will refer to the concept of arbitration in the period between the *Jay-Treaty* in 1794 and the middle of the 19th century. During this time, a certain understanding and practice of arbitration prevailed, which will be used as a starting point for outlining the course of the further development of this concept, and for identifying the changes that this concept underwent during the subsequent years.

However, certain conceptual and ideological changes already took place between 1794 and the middle of the 19th century. It is therefore a bit simplistic to speak of a settled and stable concept of *traditional arbitration*, and to claim that this concept prevailed unchanged over the entire period. But the purpose of the following paragraph is to provide a brief introduction of the concept, and of the situation in the first half of the 19th century. Besides, the most important alterations and conceptual changes took place in the later parts of the century. It was only then that arbitration became more professional and that lawyers took the decisions in arbitral procedures.[109] Therefore, it appears reasonable and tenable to make this distinction along the afore-mentioned dates, and in accordance with these conceptual lines.

2.2 *The Legal Nature of Arbitration*

After having clarified this point, two definitions of (voluntary) arbitration will be taken into consideration. This will be done in order to reveal the most important characteristics of this instrument and to demonstrate the basic concept of arbitration. The first definition stems from Hans-Jürgen Schlochauer (*'Arbitration'* from 1992). Neither Schlochauer nor Henry Wager Halleck, who will be quoted hereafter, was a scholar from the concerned period, the first half of the 19th century.[110] But both studies have given very clear, fundamental definitions of the term *arbitration*. Their remarks shall demonstrate the basic conceptual framework of arbitration. Afterwards, these definitions will be placed in context with the basic characteristics and the legal nature of arbitration in the first half of the 19th century in order to determine

109 Both quotes stem from: Christian J. Tams, *World Peace Through International Adjudication?* (2016) 3; available online <https://papers.ssrn.com/sol3/papers.cfm?abstract_id=2733307> uploaded: February 15, 2016.

110 For example, Henry Wager Halleck's treatise *'International Law; Or, Rules Regulating the Intercourse of States in Peace and War'* was published in 1861 (by D. Van Nostrand).

the specific meaning of the term *traditional arbitration*. According to Jürgen Schlochauer, arbitration is "[...] the process of resolving disputes between states by means of an arbitral tribunal appointed by the parties".[111] Halleck held a very similar approach, defining arbitration as a procedure "[...] where the decision of a dispute is left to arbitrators chosen by common agreement".[112] In both of these short but very telling quotes, it becomes apparent that the authors considered the most important and crucial characteristics of arbitration to be (1) that the states took the decision to refer their cases to a third party for peaceful settlement, (2) that they appointed arbitrators of their own choice, and (3) that they established the tribunal in accordance with nothing but their own preferences.

This means two things. Firstly, it follows that the composition of arbitral tribunals falls into the exclusive competence of the parties themselves and, secondly, the parties' explicit consensus is always required for initiating an arbitral settlement of a certain conflict. The *Permanent Court of International Justice* (hereinafter the *PCIJ*) affirmed this requirement in a judgement dated 1923, declaring that (voluntary) arbitration was based on the *principle of consent.* According to the court, "[...] no state can, without its consent, be compelled to submit its disputes [...] to arbitration, or any other kind of pacific settlement".[113] As it will be shown in the following paragraph, this ruling applied to all kinds of voluntary arbitration, regardless of whether it was *traditional* or *modern* arbitration.

2.3 *Traditional Arbitration*

During the first half of the 19th century (the times in which *traditional arbitration* prevailed in state practice), states generally kept control over arbitrations and remained the sole masters of their arbitral procedures. This arrangement basically meant that whenever states decided to settle a conflict by arbitration, they alone took every single decision, ranging from whether to even refer a case for arbitration to the establishment, functioning, and working procedures of the tribunals. This step usually took place in either of the following two ways:

---

111 Hans-Jürgen Schlochauer, 'Arbitration' in Rudolf Bernhardt, *The Encyclopedia of Public International Law*, vol. 1 (Elsevier 1992) 215–216.

112 Henry Wager Halleck, *International Law* (n 110 in Chapter 2) 292.

113 The quote stems from: Cesare P.R. Romano, 'The Shift from the Consensual to the Compulsory Paradigm in International Adjudication: Elements for a Theory of Consent' (2006/07) 39 New York University Journal of International Law and Politics 792. According to him, the original source is the following one: Advisory Opinion, 1923 P. C. I. J. (ser. B) No. 5, at 19 (Jul. 23).

(1) *ad hoc* (in cases in which a conflict does not fall within scope of an obligatory arbitration agreement between the conflicting states, these states need to conclude a so-called *compromis*; a joint decision to arbitrate the respective conflict in which they establish the procedural framework for the arbitration),
(2) *ante hoc* (in cases in which there exists an obligatory arbitration agreement between the conflicting states and the conflict at stake falls within the scope of this treaty; if these conditions are fulfilled, the conflicting states are obliged to arbitrate the case in accordance with the provisions determined in the underlying agreement).[114]

In the first half of the 19th century, obligatory arbitration commitments were rare.[115] Hence, the focus of the present section is on *ad hoc* tribunals. To provide a small summary of the most important characteristics of *ad hoc* tribunals, it is to say that these bodies did not have any pre-determined procedural rules. They had to be established anew for every case arising, and were only competent to settle the case at hand. Unlike international judicial courts, they were not permanent institutions and, therefore, ceased to exist once they had settled the conflict at hand.[116] Accordingly, it used to be common practice that once two (or more) states had taken the decision to settle a conflict via arbitration (*principle of consent*), they created a new arbitral court in their mutual relationship for the settlement of this one dispute. This procedure made it necessary to determine anew for each case the procedural rules, the exact question which the parties wanted the court to settle, the board of arbitrators, and the mode for their appointment.[117] The parties usually did so through a bilateral agreement (the *compromis*), in which they affirmed the decision to take the case to arbitration, in which they codified the mentioned points and which also served as the legal base for the subsequent arbitral procedures.[118]

The way in which states used to handle arbitration, in practice, during this period becomes apparent by looking at the common approach to appointing arbitrators. Throughout most of the 19th century, states did not usually choose independent experts of public international law (such as impartial judges or trained lawyers). States usually established either commissions that were

---

114 Ibid 804.
115 Ibid.
116 Manley O. Hudson, *A Treatise on the Permanent Court of International Justice* (The Macmillan company 1934) 3.
117 George B. Davis, *The Elements of International Law* (Harper & Brothers 1915) 255.
118 William Edward Hall, *A Treatise on International Law* (Clarendon Press 1909) 354.

equally filled with candidates nominated by both conflicting parties, or they chose together a neutral third party to arbitrate the conflict; in such cases, they tended to nominate rulers or political leaders of their own preference (usually a head of state of a befriended country).[119] It seems as if states followed this practice because, on the one hand, they hoped that by doing so, they could keep as much influence on the outcome of arbitrations as possible.[120] While, on the other hand, *traditional arbitration* had a lot in common with diplomatic procedures.[121] In certain aspects, arbitration at the time resembled diplomacy, more than judicial procedures. To appoint heads of states as arbitrators, instead of legal experts, is a telling example of this approach. States seem to have expected the former to award a higher level of sincerity, standing, and integrity to arbitral rulings because of their own reputation and prestige.[122] However, this practice became less common towards the end of the 19th century. In the literature of these years, the fact that heads of states were favored as arbitrators over legal experts was harshly criticized. By the end of the century, this practice was even regarded as risky, in that it could lead to unwanted results. A prominent example of this risk can be found in the arbitration of a dispute between Great Britain and the United States, which was decided by the king of the Netherlands. He was supposed to render his decision in accordance with a *compromis* from September 29, 1827. But – according to international legal scholars – he exceeded his powers and the scope of the question referred to him.[123] Other arguments raised against this practice were based on the ques-

119 Arthur Nussbaum, *Geschichte des Völkerrechts* (C. H. Beck 1960) 244–245. Also: Wilhelm G. Grewe, *Die Epochen der Völkerrechtsgeschichte* (n 49 in Chapter 2) 610.

120 Tomasz Milej, *Entwicklung des Völkerrechts: Der Beitrag internationaler Gerichte und Sachverständigengremien* (De Gruyter 2014) 40.

121 Heinrich Lammasch, *Die Lehre von der Schiedsgerichtsbarkeit in ihrem ganzen Umfange* (n 107 in Chapter 2) 116 et seq.; Wilhelm G. Grewe, *Die Epochen der Völkerrechtsgeschichte* (n 49 in Chapter 2) 609.

122 Wilhelm G. Grewe, *Die Epochen der Völkerrechtsgeschichte* (n 49 in Chapter 2) 610.

123 Compare: Charles Cheney Hye, 'Legal Problems Capable of Settlement by Arbitration' in Charles Edward Beales, *Proceedings of the Second National Peace Congress* (Peterson Linotype Co. 1909) 225. Also: J.H.W. Verzijl, *International Law in Historical Perspective, Part VIII – Inter-State Disputes and their Settlement* (A.W. Sijthoff 1976) 87; Hersch Lauterpacht, *The Function of Law in the International Community* (Oxford University Press 1933) 136. See also: Hans Wehberg, *The Problem of an International Court of Justice* (Clarendon Press 1918) 17. According to Wehberg, the famous Argentinian jurist Carlos Calvo criticized the award in 1880 as follows: "In place of determining, in his award, the true points at issue, this sovereign left the question of law in suspense and confined himself to suggesting a basis of settlement of an entirely new and contingent character." Original source: Carlos Calvo, *Le Droit International Théorique et Practique 2* (Guillaumin 1880) 575.

tion of the impartiality of heads of states, the possibility that their own interests could affect their decision in the arbitral procedure and, among other things, the fact that they were usually unskilled in legal science.[124] All of the aforementioned considerations and the criticism stemmed from the later parts of the 19th century. During the first half, the instrument of arbitration was still used in its *traditional* understanding, namely, as an instrument widely shaped in accordance with diplomatic practices and habits.

Probably the most important difference between the *traditional* conception of arbitration and the *modern* one is that, in the past, arbitral tribunals were not regarded to be obliged to rule in accordance with law. The parties of an arbitration could (of course) determine that the settlement of their dispute was to be issued on the basis of the prevailing legal rules, just as they could determine basically everything regarding the procedures and the institutional framework of the arbitral tribunal.[125] From time to time, arbitrators certainly appeared to have made reference to laws.[126] Authors like, e.g., Johann Ludwig Klüber (*'Europäisches Völkerrecht, Vol. 1'* from 1821) even claimed that arbitrators were generally obliged to decide cases in accordance with the prevailing international law.[127] But this was, in fact, neither the common practice during most of the 19th century, nor was there any kind of obligation for arbitrators to do so. States were completely free to decide on what basis arbitral decisions were to be taken. Consequently, arbitral tribunals settled most cases in accordance with the principle *ex aequo et bono*.[128] At that time, the main objective of arbitrations remained the settlement of conflicts in a way that was satisfactory for both parties involved. Hans Wehberg (*The Problem of an International Court of Justice'* from 1918) stated the following in this regard:

> The parties desire from an arbitrator a decision satisfactory to both sides, not one based upon the greater right, since their object is to dispose of the dispute. In consequence, they attach no importance to the point that the judges be jurists in the highest sense of the word, but choose any person at all in whom they have confidence. On the con-

124 Compare. e.g.: Heinrich Lammasch, *Die Lehre von der Schiedsgerichtsbarkeit in ihrem ganzen Umfange* (n 107 in Chapter 2) 116 et seq. See also: John Westlake, *International Law – Part 1: Peace* (Cambridge University Press 1910) 363.

125 J.H.W. Verzijl, *International Law in Historical Perspective, Part VIII* (n 123 in Chapter 2) 86.

126 Compare, e.g.: Charles Cheney Hye, *Legal Problems Capable of Settlement by Arbitration* (n 123 in Chapter 2) 223 et seq.

127 Johann Ludwig Klüber, *Europäisches Völkerrecht*, vol. 1 (Cotta 1821), page 511.

128 For further details, see: Markus Kotzur, 'Ex Aequo et Bono' (n 105 in Chapter 2).

> trary, in judicial settlement [...], there must be a permanent tribunal with permanent judges, because only such an institution can guarantee a decision according to strict law.[129]

Lassa Oppenheim (*'The Future of International Law'* from 1921) applied a very similar approach in his work, in which he declared that

> [...] an arbitral tribunal is not a court in the real sense of the word, for its decisions are not necessarily based on rules of law, and it does not necessarily deal with legal matters. An arbiter, unless the terms of the reference otherwise provide, decides *ex aequo et bono*, whilst a judge founds his decision on rules of law and is only applied to on legal issues.[130]

This distinction between arbitrators and judges is a very ancient one. It was already known among learned scholars from Ancient Greece such as Aristotle (384–322 BC), who declared that "[...] the arbiter looks to what is fair, the judge to what is law."[131] The fact that this distinction prevailed means that compliance with prevailing law was not the foremost goal of an arbitration under the *traditional* understanding of it.[132] Arbitrators were not bound by the rule of law and the goal of arbitration was not the re-establishment of peace under law. Instead, arbitration (in the *traditional* sense of it) had to offer solutions to the conflicts at hand. These solutions were supposed to settle conflicts in a way that satisfied both parties, and to which both could agree without losing face.[133] The *traditional* understanding of the concept of arbitration – according to which arbitration was only supposed to provide equity-based solutions between the parties – was only challenged from the late 19th century onwards. As it will be shown in Chapter 3, during these years, several scholars of international law began to argue that arbitral decisions should comply with international law. Soon, this approach was also adopted and realized in state practice through the conclusion of conventions and treaties containing such clauses. Arguably, the most important and prominent of these agreements was the *Convention for the Peaceful Settlement of International Conflicts*, concluded in 1899 at the *First Hague Peace Conference*. According to its Article 15,

129 Hans Wehberg, *The Problem of an International Court of Justice* (n 123 in Chapter 2) 14.

130 Lassa Oppenheim, *The Future of International Law* (Clarendon Press 1921) 46.

131 Cited in: James Brown Scott, *The Hague Peace Conferences of 1899 and 1907*, vol. 1 (The John Hopkins Press 1909) 189. An English translation of Artistotle's work is available, e.g., in: Lane Cooper (ed.), *The Rhetoric of Aristotle* (D. Appleton and Co. 1932), 1374a.

132 Hans Wehberg, *The Problem of an International Court of Justice* (n 123 in Chapter 2) 22.

133 Ibid 14. See also: Lassa Oppenheim, *The Future of International Law* (n 130 in Chapter 2) 47.

"[i]nternational arbitration has for its object the settlement of differences between States by judges of their own choice, and on the basis of the respect for law." Hence, arbitration went through a phase of transformation: From an instrument for conflict settlement based on equity and compromises to a method under which legal aspects were taken into consideration on a growing scale.

In this regard, it must also be borne in mind that Wehberg's and Oppenheim's above-quoted remarks stemmed from the period between the turn of the century and the early 1920s. At this time, many international lawyers had already distinguished very clearly between arbitration and adjudication. But the latter, the concept of adjudication, had not yet been realized in many cases. Therefore, their contributions must be understood, at least to a certain extent, as an approval of (and propaganda for) the idea to create international courts of law. Contrasting arbitration with adjudication in such absolute terms was probably necessary for them in order to argue convincingly in favor of the need to establish such an institution (of purely judicial nature) on the global level. In the state practice for the majority of the 19th century, however, such a distinction, between arbitration (leading only to compromises) and adjudication (decisions based on law), had not yet existed.[134] As it will be shown in more detail in the later parts of this work, this was mainly due to the fact that adjudication remained a very utopian concept throughout the 19th century, which was only discussed by the peace movement and among international lawyers (but not yet among states). Arbitration, on the other hand, was the only instrument at that time that states took actual recourse to for the peaceful settlement of their mutual conflicts. Arbitration used to be regarded as having a (*quasi-*) judicial nature and it was invoked for the settlement of all sorts of international disputes, regardless of whether they were legal or political. This was because states were, in most cases, not striving for definite decisions of their mutual disputes that were taken in sole accordance with law but rather aimed for having them settled through compromises that complied with and respected the interests of both parties.[135] Consequently, there was no need for states, politicians, and most international scholars (outside the

134 Hans Wehberg, *The Problem of an International Court of Justice* (n 123 in Chapter 2) 7 et seq.

135 Francis Anthony Boyle, *Foundations of World Order* (n 28 in Chapter 1) 38. He adds in this regard that states also preferred arbitration over adjudication in these years because "[...] a subjective cost-benefit analysis indicates that it is politically better to sustain a high probability of not losing everything and only winning something by means of arbitration than to run a substantially greater risk of losing everything [...] by means of adjudication."

peace movement) to differentiate between these two concepts and to deal with adjudication.

Hans Wehberg demonstrated that the tendency stemming from *traditional arbitration* – to favor compromises over law-based decisions in arbitrations – still prevailed in state practice between 1899 and 1914.[136] Despite the trend to include clauses in international arbitration agreements that determined that decisions were to be taken with respect for law, equity and compromises seem to have remained the decisive factors in arbitral procedures. Wehberg based this claim on an evaluation of the awards issued during that time by the PCA. Furthermore, he also studied 170 arbitral decisions from the 19th century that he found in the works of authors such as Henri La Fontaine or A.G. de Lapradelle.[137] According to Wehberg, only six of these decisions were based on sufficient (judicial) grounds.[138] Especially in the first half of the 19th century, the decisive factor in arbitrations used to be the fact that they settled a dispute, whereas reasonable (judicial) grounds were attributed merely secondary importance in this context.[139] Or (again) in Wehberg's words: "The parties desire from the arbitrator a decision satisfactory to both sides, not one based on the greater right, since their object is to dispose the dispute."[140]

Wehberg's contemporaries – for example, authors such as James Brown Scott (*'The Evolution of a Permanent International Judiciary'* from 1912) or James L. Tryon ('*Proposals for an International Court*' from 1914) – also criticized arbitration and drew the following conclusions concerning the nature of this instrument. According to Scott, arbitration stood "[…] midway between self-redress, whose excess it has stayed, and judicial decision, whose disinterestedness and impartial determination it foreshadowed".[141] Tryon, on the other hand, regarded arbitration to be "[…] more like an adjustment by diplomatists, each thinking of his own country's interests, than a decision by impartial judges deciding upon principles of international law".[142]

136 Hans Wehberg, *The Problem of an International Court of Justice* (n 123 in Chapter 2) 29–41.

137 Ibid 17. According to Wehberg, the original sources of their works are the following: Henri La Fontaine, *Pasicrisie Internationale: Histoire documentaire des arbitrages internationaux* (Impr. Stämpfli & cie 1902). A.G. de Lapradelle, *Recueil des arbitrages internationaux*, vol. 1 1798–1855 (A. W. Sijthoff's Publishing Co. 1905).

138 Ibid 19.

139 Ibid 18.

140 Ibid 14.

141 James Brown Scott, 'The Evolution of a Permanent International Judiciary' (1912) 6 The American Journal of International Law 318.

142 James L. Tryon, 'Proposals for an International Court' (1914) 23 The Yale Law Journal 424.

To summarize, arbitration, in the *traditional* understanding, can best be described as an instrument for the settlement of isolated cases in the exclusive relationship between the involved states or, in James Brown Scott's words, as their "private courts."[143] Arbitral tribunals were established *ad hoc*, in accordance with the respective *compromis*, and decisions were taken by *ad hoc* arbitrators who were nominated by the parties (but they only held this office for the settlement of the specific case in question). The arbitral awards only bound the respective parties and they did not have any further external effects. Disputes were usually settled by compromising the involved parties' interests, with legal considerations not playing a decisive role or being completely ignored altogether.

2.4 *International Adjudication*

To approach the concept of international adjudication in more detail and to emphasize the concrete differences between arbitration and judicial settlements at the international level, reference is first made to Christian Tomuschat (*'International Court and Tribunals'* from 2011). According to him,

> [i]nternational courts and tribunals are permanent judicial bodies made up of independent judges which are entrusted with adjudicating international disputes on the basis of international law according to a predetermined set of rules of procedure and rendering decisions which are binding on the parties.
>
> [...] The basic idea underlying the creation of international courts and tribunals is for them to function as permanent bodies, less subject to considerations connected with the issues at stake in the case at hand, and capable of ensuring a certain degree of continuity of legal reasoning.[144]

Unlike in arbitral procedures, adjudicative tribunals are permanent courts of law that have a standing bench of judges, appointed for a determined tenure, and which settle conflicts in strict accordance with law and based on predetermined procedural rules. This practice ensures continuous and consisting legal rulings. Hence, the most important and fundamental characteristics of international adjudication are the following:

---

143 James Brown Scott, 'The Evolution of a Permanent International Judiciary' (n 141 in Chapter 2) 336.

144 Christian Tomuschat, 'International Courts and Tribunals', *Max Planck Encyclopedia of Public International Law (online)*.

- *On the base of law:* The PCIJ proclaimed in 1929 that "[…] the true function of the Court is to decide disputes between states […] on the basis of international law".[145] Instead of striving for compromises, in accordance with the principle *ex aequo et bono* as in arbitrations, international courts of law decide cases by the interpretation and application of legal rules.
- *Permanence*: Unlike arbitral *ad hoc* tribunals, international adjudicative bodies are permanent. They are established for an indefinite, or at least a pre-determined, tenure, and are, therefore, set up for the settlement of an unlimited number of cases.
- *Independence*: Judges are not chosen for the settlement of single cases by the conflicting parties, as in arbitration. Instead, they are appointed for standing benches of judges which serve for pre-determined tenures. Furthermore, the salaries of the judges are usually not paid by the conflicting parties, or their home countries, but from the budget of the court. All these points serve the goal of guaranteeing the impartiality and independence of judges and to enable them to rule on nothing else other than the sole base of law.[146]
- *Compulsoriness and Consent*: While procedures before national courts can usually be initiated by the unilateral action of one person, this is a comparably rare phenomenon in international law.[147] In most cases, mutual consent is – even today – still required from the involved parties to initiate the settlement of a conflicts before an international court.[148] Even the *International Court of Justice* (hereinafter the ICJ) does not possess general obligatory jurisdiction. Instead, states must ratify a separate declaration to recognize the jurisdiction of the ICJ as compulsory.[149] Therefore, there does not exist a general distinction to arbitration in this point.

---

145 Case Concerning the Payment of Various Serbian Loans Issues in France, published in: Publications of the Permanent Court of International Justice, Series A., No 20 (1929), page 19.

146 Tomasz Milej, *Entwicklung des Völkerrechts* (n 120 in Chapter 2) 41. See also: Karin Oellers-Frahm, 'International Courts and Tribunals, Judges and Arbitrators', *Max Planck Encyclopedia of Public International Law* (*online*)

147 Alain Pellet, 'Judicial Settlement of International Disputes', *Max Planck Encyclopedia of Public International Law* (*online*).

148 Ibid.

149 According to Article 36, para 2 UN Charter, member states of the Statute of the ICJ may "[…] at any time declare that they recognize as compulsory *ipso facto* and without special agreement, in relation to any other State accepting the same obligation, the jurisdiction of the Court". See also: Stephan Hobe, *Einführung in das Völkerrecht* (10th ed., UTB 2014) 329–330.

In conclusion, judicial decisions are taken in accordance with prevailing international law by permanent and independent courts of justice. Their decisions result into a consecutive and steadily developing body of case law and, therefore, into an on-going advancement and specification of international law.

2.5 *The Difference between* Isolated *and* Institutional *Arbitration*

Having dealt with the differences between (*traditional*) arbitration and adjudication, it is also necessary to differentiate between *isolated* and *institutional* arbitration.[150] These terms were coined by Heinrich Lammasch (*'Die Lehre von der Schiedsgerichtsbarkeit in ihrem ganzen Umfange'* from 1913). Lammasch argued that *isolated* arbitration was an instrument for the settlement of individual disputes between states which had not yet entered any obligatory arbitration agreements in their mutual relationship. Hence, isolated arbitration relates to an individual conflict that has already arisen and which the conflicting states refer to arbitration (under full awareness of its scope) within the framework of a set of rules exclusively established for this particular case.[151] Moreover, cases of *isolated* arbitration were settled before *ad hoc* tribunals, and after the conclusion of a *compromis* between the involved parties.

In *institutional* arbitration, on the other hand, the states had already concluded an obligatory arbitration treaty in the past, which stipulated that (certain types of) mutual conflicts had to be submitted to obligatory arbitration.[152] Therefore, these treaties were concluded for an indefinite number of future cases.[153] If a conflict arose between two states which adhered to such an agreement, they did not have to negotiate whether they wanted to refer the case to arbitration. They merely had to settle the conditions (the composition of the court, etc.), if those were not already provided for in the treaty. Therefore, the major conceptual difference between *isolated* and *institutional* arbitration concerned consent. Consent for *ad hoc* – or *isolated* – arbitrations had to be reached anew between (even the same) two states for every new case arising. In *institutional arbitration,* the exact opposite was the case. States declared

150 Heinrich Lammasch, *Die Lehre von der Schiedsgerichtsbarkeit in ihrem ganzen Umfange* (n 107 in Chapter 2) 8–10, 51. In this context also: J.H.W. Verzijl, *International Law in Historical Perspective, Part VIII* (n 123 in Chapter 2) 177–179.

151 J.H.W. Verzijl, *International Law in Historical Perspective, Part VIII* (n 123 in Chapter 2) 178. Hans J. Morgenthau, *Politics among Nations* (Knopf 1949) 220.

152 Heinrich Lammasch, *Die Lehre von der Schiedsgerichtsbarkeit in ihrem ganzen Umfange* (n 107 in Chapter 2) 8–10.

153 Hans J. Morgenthau, *Politics among Nations* (n 151 in Chapter 2) 221.

their mutual consent to arbitrate future disputes before the actual emergence of the conflict by entering obligatory arbitration treaties.[154]

As it will be shown in the following Chapters, obligatory arbitration treaties were regularly concluded from the later parts of the 19th century onwards.[155] However, that does not mean either that *isolated* arbitration began to disappear entirely from international relations after 1850, or that it was about to be replaced by *institutional* arbitration. States continued to take recourse to it during the entire 19th century, and beyond, because it had the clear advantage that the procedures and outcomes of an *isolated* arbitration were comparably predictable. The concerned states only referred clearly determined questions and individual cases to the decision of arbitral *ad hoc* tribunals, wherefore the resulting awards could only cover previously foreseeable topics and sums. As a result, the decision to refer a conflict to *isolated* arbitration bore a relatively low risk for the parties of resulting in unwanted or unpredictable outcomes.[156] This predictability of *ad hoc* arbitrations lowered the reluctance of the states against this instrument. By referring only isolated cases to arbiters, and by not establishing any kind of obligation for the future use of arbitration in the relationship between the involved parties, states kept the undisputed control over their external affairs. They remained the sole masters over the arbitral procedures and did not have to give up on parts of their sovereignty rights by subjecting themselves to obligatory arbitration clauses.

This set up also explains the reluctance of some of the states to enter into obligatory arbitration treaties throughout the 19th and early 20th centuries. They were highly concerned with preserving the full control over their sovereignty rights, and their freedom to act in international affairs. *Institutional* arbitration bore the potential of constituting limitations in this regard, as obligatory arbitration clauses stipulated that states had to settle (certain types of) their mutual conflicts through arbitration. Consequently, such provisions would have ruled out the use of force in situations in which a conflict arose between two states that were bound by an obligatory arbitration treaty. Moreover, the level of commitment in *institutional* arbitration was considerably higher than in *isolated* arbitration because it covered an indefinite number of cases (instead of dealing only with one particular conflict).[157]

---

154 Manley O. Hudson, *A Treatise on the Permanent Court of International Justice* (n 116 in Chapter 2) 3. See also: Helen May Cory, *Compulsory Arbitration of International Disputes* (Columbia University Press 1932) IX.

155 Manley O. Hudson, *A Treatise on the Permanent Court of International Justice* (n 116 in Chapter 2) 3.

156 J.H.W. Verzijl, *International Law in Historical Perspective, Part VIII* (n 123 in Chapter 2) 74.

157 Ibid 178.

The unwillingness of certain states to enter into obligatory arbitration agreements in the 19th century will be dealt with in Chapter 3 in more detail. For now, the preceding remarks shall suffice, and the view is to be turned back to the terminology and differentiation of (different types of) obligatory arbitration, which was (also) introduced by Heinrich Lammasch. According to him, there were *special* and *general compromissory* agreements.[158] Both kinds of treaties have in common the fact that they provide for the compulsory use of arbitration. However, they differ decisively from one another in certain aspects. The parties of treaties that contain *special compromissory* clauses commit themselves to settle only specific categories of their mutual conflicts through arbitration. Hence, this commitment to arbitration is limited. According to Lammasch, the types of cases that are supposed to fall under special obligatory arbitration clause are usually explicitly listed in the respective treaties.[159] This means that states could provide catalogues of cases that they were willing to subject to compulsory arbitration in their mutual relations. This practice allowed them to keep control over the scope of the arbitration commitment, and to make sure that the agreement did not cover any topics that they did not want to be obliged to arbitrate in the future. Hence, *special compromissory* arbitration was the mildest form of obligatory arbitration. Treaties containing *general compromissory* clauses, on the other hand, constituted a general and unlimited obligation to arbitrate disputes in the mutual relationship of the adhering states. Consequently, all differences between the two states that have concluded a general obligatory arbitration treaty with each other must be arbitrated (if they cannot be solved by diplomatic means).[160] Therefore, *general compromissory* clauses establish the most extensive form of obligatory arbitration commitments.

As a last point in this regard, it must also be emphasized that hardly any obligatory arbitration treaties were without exceptions. Exemption clauses were usually introduced to these treaties in order to provide the adhering states the opportunity to avoid the arbitration obligatorium in cases that concerned the involved nations' vital interests, their independence, or their honor

158 These terms were widely universal. Compare, e.g.: Heinrich Lammasch, *Die Lehre von der Schiedsgerichtsbarkeit in ihrem ganzen Umfange* (n 107 in Chapter 2) 51 et seq. Lammasch used the term "allgemeine oder beschränkte kompromissorische Klausel" in German and in French Henri La Fontaine (*Pasicrisie Internationale* (n 137 in Chapter 2) x–xv) referred to "clauses compromissoires spéciales ou générales".

159 Heinrich Lammasch, *Die Lehre von der Schiedsgerichtsbarkeit in ihrem ganzen Umfange* (n 107 in Chapter 2) 51.

160 Ibid 52. See also: J.H.W. Verzijl, *International Law in Historical Perspective, Part VIII* (n 123 in Chapter 2) 227.

(as well as cases involving third states).[161] In some cases, however, the exemption clauses were so extensive that they undermined the entire purpose of the treaty and turned it into a mere illusion, since the contracting parties allowed themselves too much room for outmaneuvering the obligatorium.[162]

2.6 *Conclusion*

To summarize the present section in a few words, the following is to be said:

First, throughout the 19th century, arbitration was the only available and known (*quasi-*)judicial instrument for the peaceful settlement of international disputes (once diplomacy had failed to provide a solution). In its *traditional* understanding, arbitration had a diplomatic rather than judicial nature. Its decisions were based on equity and compromises between the involved parties' interests, with legal considerations hardly playing a role. Only by the end of the 19th century, voices were raised to call for arbitral decisions to pay more respect to the law. Although this trend was even written into numerous treaties and conventions, the concentration on compromises, and decisions based on the principle *ex aequo et bono,* remained to be a dominant factor in state practice concerning arbitrations, even during the early 20th century.

Second, arbitration differed from judicial procedures, in particular, on the point that courts of law had standing benches of judges, who were supposed to be impartial and independent, and who took their decisions in accordance with law. Arbitral tribunals, on the other hand, used to be established only for the settlement of one particular case, i.e., on an *ad hoc* basis, after which they ceased to exist. Furthermore, states were the sole masters of arbitral procedures. They determined every single detail of the arbitrations; chose the arbitrators, defined the exact questions that were to be decided by the arbitral tribunals, and even determined the procedural rules.

Third, obligatory arbitration only became more prominent during the second half of the 19th century (as it will be shown in the subsequent chapters). It constituted a second form of appearance of arbitration: *Isolated* arbitration was invoked by states that had not stipulated in advance how to deal with future disputes between them. *Institutional* arbitration, on the other hand, was the exact opposite. States concluded obligatory arbitration treaties in their mutual relationship in order to determine that (certain types of) their future mutual conflicts had to be submitted to arbitration.

---

161 David J. Hill, 'The Second Peace Conference at the Hague' (1907) 1 The American Journal of International Law 681–682.

162 J.H.W. Verzijl, *International Law in Historical Perspective, Part VIII* (n 123 in Chapter 2) 76.

CHAPTER 3

Conflict Settlement in the North Atlantic World before 1899

> We make great improvements in nature daily. There is one I wish to see in moral philosophy: the discovery of a plan that would induce and oblige nations to settle their disputes without first cutting one another's throats.
>
> When will human reason be sufficiently improv'd to see the advantage of this! When will men be convinc'd that even successful wars do at length become misfortunes to those who unjustly commenc'd them, and who troumph'd blindly in their success, not seeing all its consequences.[1]
>
> BENJAMIN FRANKLIN, in *The Autobiography of Benjamin Franklin, Vol. 2*

∴

1 The Historical Outset of Arbitration

Arbitration was already invoked on a regular base by ancient Greek city-states for the settlement of their mutual conflicts.[2] Evidence of this practice can be found, e.g., in the works of authors such as Thucydides (*c.*460–*c.*400 BC). According to him "[…] it is wicked to proceed against him who is ready to refer the question to an arbitrator."[3] On another occasion, Thucydides recalled the words of the King of Sparta, who had uttered the following during the *Peloponnesian War* (431–404 BC): "[…] it is impossible to attack as a trans-

1 Republication by: Mark Skousen (ed), *The Autobiography of Benjamin Franklin,* vol. 2 (Regnery History 2007) 196.

2 John Bassett Moore, 'Historical Notes on International Arbitration,' *The American Conference on International Arbitration held in Washington D.C. April 22 and 23 1896* (Baker & Taylor 1896) 170.

3 Cited in English in: John Watson Foster, *Arbitration and the Hague Court* (Houghton, Mifflin and Company 1904) 6.

 | DOI:10.1163/9789004754126_004

gressor him who offers to lay his grievance before a tribunal of arbitration."[4] In contrast with ancient Greece, arbitration was hardly ever invoked by the Roman Empire for the settlement of its conflicts with others.[5] The Romans strove for universal dominion, and their foreign policy was dedicated, by a large extent, to this goal.[6] Consequently, they were not willing to submit themselves, and their foreign policy, to the ruling or judgement of any – independent – third power, entity, or person.

It was not until the Middle Ages that arbitration re-appeared as a regularly used instrument for the settlement of international disputes. At this time, new kingdoms and lordships emerged all over the Europe (from the residues of the Roman Empire), which were inter-connected with each other through a feudal system. While power had been centralized in the hands of the Roman Empire in the past, the situation was decisively different in the Middle Ages. Europe was fragmented in a multitude of different entities, often (loosely) united under the roof of greater kingdoms or empires. However, despite their feudal relations, the seigniors of these entities enjoyed a *de facto* high level of independence; also concerning the right to wage war.[7] Countless armed struggles and feuds were the consequence and war became a regular phenomenon of medieval times. But despite the commonness of war, arbitration went through a revival in these years because of the ongoing Christianization of Europe. Large portions of the continent converted to Christianity and, regardless all bellicose attempts to conquer each other's territories, their common Christian faith established, at least to a certain level of, attachment and solidarity between them. According to Randall Lesaffer (*'The Grotian Tradition Revisited'* from 2002), modern and Renaissance Europe even "[...] defined itself as a religious, cultural and to a certain extent, political and juridical unity, often referred to as the *respublica christiana.*"[8] Furthermore, this development also resulted into the growth of the power of church dignitaries, especially of the pope. Since the declaration of Gregory VII (*c.*1015–1085) in 1075, popes con-

4 Cited in English in: John Bassett Moore, 'Historical Notes on International Arbitration' (n 2 in Chapter 3) 172.

5 Hanns Göhler, *Freies Kriegsführungsrecht und Kriegsschuld* (Noske 1931) 25. However, the principle was not unknown to Ancient Rome either; compare: Erich S. Gruen, *The Hellenistic World and the Coming of Rome*, vol 1 & 2 (University of California Press 1984).

6 John Bassett Moore, 'Historical Notes on International Arbitration' (n 2 in Chapter 3) 173.

7 Cornelis G. Roelofsen, 'International Arbitration and Courts' in Bardo Fassbender and Anne Peters (eds.), *The Oxford Handbook of the History of International Law* (n 28 in Chapter 1) 152.

8 Randall Lesaffer, 'The Grotian Tradition Revisited: Change and Continuity in the History of International Law' (2002) 73 The British Yearbook of International Law 112.

sidered themselves to be placed above all secular sovereigns because of their status as the sole representative of God on earth.[9] Based on their self-proclaimed superiority, popes used to consider themselves to hold the divinely ordained jurisdiction over all international conflicts between Christian rulers. This approach was officially proclaimed by Innocent III (1160/1161–1216) in the decree *Novit ille* in 1205.[10] The popes only lost their position as the ultimate and sole instance for the ruling over conflicts in the Christian world when the power of the Catholic Church was questioned in the 16th century due to the emergence of absolutism and the *Reformation*.[11] Furthermore, the occurrence of the concept of modern states (and of the *Westphalian System*) turned the principle of sovereignty into an increasingly crucial issue in international relations. The growing importance, which was attached to this concept, resulted into a decreasing willingness of the European powers to refer their mutual disputes to arbitration, or to any form of judicial settlement by a third power/institution.[12]

A series of prominent authors argued that arbitration was scarcely invoked in the period between the 16th and 18th centuries.[13] However, this conclusion appears to be questionable, especially if the findings of other authors are taken into consideration. Cornelis G. Roelofsen, Karl-Heinz Lingens, or James Brown Scott – to name only a few but very telling examples – proved that arbitration did not vanish completely from state practice during these years but that only the frequency of its use decreased. To prove the correctness of this claim, they listed numerous (types of) cases in which states continued to take recourse to

---

9 Wilhelm G. Grewe, *The Epochs of International Law* (n 28 in Chapter 2) 93.

10 Wilhelm G. Grewe (ed.), *Fontes Historiae Iuris Gentium*, vol. 1 (De Gruyter 1995) 219.

11 Cornelis G. Roelofsen, 'International Arbitration and Courts' (n 7 in Chapter 3) 152.

12 Compare in this regard: Randall Lesaffer, 'The Grotian Tradition Revisited' (n 8 in Chapter 3) 113. There, he stated that "[…] until the end of the seventeenth century, the Pope was often invited to arbitrate between sovereign rulers." This finding shows that until the end of the 17th century, the pope remained a highly respected authority and a decisive factor within the European state system. However, it also shows that the sovereigns invited him to arbitrate their disputes and that the pope could not simply insist on taking charge of the respective conflict anymore. This shows that he must have suffered a loss of influence and power due to the named reasons.

13 Compare for example: Wilhelm G. Grewe, *Die Epochen der Völkerrechtsgeschichte* (n 49 in Chapter 2) 606; Hanns Göhler, *Freies Kriegsführungsrecht und Kriegsschuld* (n 5 in Chapter 3) 25; Guerra Everett, 'International Arbitration in the Americas' (1939/1940) 17 New York University Law Quarterly Review 618; Heinz-Gerhard Justenhoven, *Internationale Schiedsgerichtsbarkeit: Ethische Normen und Rechtswirklichkeit* (Kohlhammer 2006) 189; Hans-Jürgen Schlochauer, 'Die Entwicklung der internationalen Schiedsgerichtsbarkeit' (1962/1963) 10 Archiv des Völkerrechts 6; Manley O. Hudson, *International Tribunals: Past and Future* (Rumford Press 1944) 3.

arbitration; among them *special compromissory* arbitration treaties, cases of naval disputes settled by regular tribunals or prize courts, and territorial disputes, which states continued to refer to arbitration for settlement.[14]

Apart from the application of arbitration in state practice, the instrument also became increasingly more popular with educated and informed circles in Europe,[15] at least since the beginning of the 17th century. Hugo Grotius, for example, repeatedly referred to arbitration in his highly influential treatise on the laws of war and peace (*'De Jure Belli ac Pacis'* from 1625).[16] Later scholars followed Grotius in this approach and his interest in arbitration, such as Georg Friedrich von Martens (1756–1821)[17] or Emer de Vattel (1714–1767).[18] Therefore, it can be concluded that even though the frequency of the use of arbitration did, in fact, decrease to a certain extent in state practice during these years, it did not, however, completely disappear.[19] Moreover, a growing number of legal and philosophical scholars dealt with the issue during that time as well and praised it for its usefulness and effectiveness in matters of peace.[20] They launched several initiatives for the preservation of peace through international organizations, and these plans often provided for the establishment of mechanisms for the settlement of international conflicts through arbitration, or other means of peaceful conflict settlement. The most utopian of these concepts even advocated for the establishment of permanent arbitral bodies, and some of them even did so during times in which voluntary arbitration was only occasionally invoked. Examples of such approaches (for world organizations and permanent arbitral tribunals) can be found in the writings of authors such as Pierre Dubois (1255–1321). He proposed already in 1306 the establishment of an assembly of princes and of a permanent court of arbitration for the settlement of international disputes.[21] In addition to that, numerous scholars

14 Cornelis G. Roelofsen, 'International Arbitration and Courts' (n 7 in Chapter 3) 158; Karl-Heinz Lingens, *Internationale Schiedsgerichtsbarkeit und Jus publicum europaeum 1648–1794* (Duncker & Humblot 1988) 21; James Brown Scott, *The Hague Peace Conferences of 1899 and 1907*, vol. 1 (n 131 in Chapter 2) 205.

15 Cornelis G. Roelofsen, 'International Arbitration and Courts' (n 7 in Chapter 3) 156.

16 Compare: Warren F Kuehl, *Seeking World Order: The United States and International Organization to 1920* (Vanderbilt University Press 1969) 6–7.

17 Georg Friedrich von Martens, *Précis du droit des gens moderne de l'Europe fondé sur les traités et l'usage* (n 72 in Chapter 2) 270.

18 Emer de Vattel, *The Law of Nations or Principles of the Law of Nations* (printed and sold by Samuel Campbell 1858; first published in French in 1758) 277 et seq.

19 Cornelis G. Roelofsen, 'International Arbitration and Courts' (n 7 in Chapter 3) 159.

20 Warren F. Kuehl, *Seeking World Order* (n 16 in Chapter 3) 3–21.

21 Ibid 4. See also: Robert Jones and S. S. Sherman, *The League of Nations from Idea to Reality: Its Place in History and in the World of To-Day* (Pitman 1927) 43.

from the early modern period worked on similar topics: for example, Émeric Curcé (1590–1648) and Maximilien de Béthune, duc de Sully (1560–1641). The former was a French monk and presented a plan for a world organization in 1623.[22] According to him, a "[…] permanent congress composed of all the sovereigns […] should regulate the differences between them […and the…] gravest questions touching sovereignty and independence were to be referred to arbitration."[23] Moreover, Sully published in 1638 his so-called *Great Design*[24] in which he provided for a very comparable concept.[25] By the end of the 17th century and during all the 18th century, a large volume of plans for international organization and the establishment of mechanism for the preservation of peace were presented (probably driven by the experiences of the *Thirty Years' War*).[26] Authors, such as William Penn (1644–1718),[27] Charles Irénée de Saint-Pierre (1658–1743),[28] Jean-Jacques Rosseau (1712–1778),[29] Jeremy Bentham (1748–1832),[30] and Immanuel Kant (1724–1804), with his inspiring *Perpetual Peace,*[31] contributed to this development and were particularly influential.[32]

Kant, for example, advocated for the establishment of an international organization based on the principle of law. Due to the popularity of his writings, he contributed a lot to the spread of these ideas. They were particularly

22 Émeric Crucé, *Le nouveau Cynée ou discours d'Estat représentant les occasions et moyens d'establir une paix génerallе et la liberté de commerce par tout le monde* (J. Villery 1623).

23 Jackson Harvey Ralston, *International Arbitration from Athens to Locarno* (Stanford University Press 1929) 118.

24 In the literature, there is disagreement as to whether Sully was the actual author of this text. Compare: Warren F. Kuehl, *Seeking World Order* (n 16 in Chapter 3) 5 (footnote 8).

25 See also: Charlotte Lennox (ed.), *Maximilien de Béthune, duc de Sully, The memoirs of the Duke of Sully, prime-minister to Henry the Great* (Printed by W. Bulmer and co. 1817).

26 Warren F. Kuehl, *Seeking World Order* (n 16 in Chapter 3) 8.

27 William Penn, *Essay Towards the Present and Future Peace of Europe* (printed and sold by Randal Taylor 1693).

28 Charles Irénée de Saint-Pierre, *Projet pour rendre la paix perpétuelle en Europe* (Chez A. Schouten 1713).

29 Jean-Jacques Rousseau, *A Lasting Peace through the Federation of Europe and the State of War* (Constable 1917, originally published in French in 1761).

30 John Bowring (ed.), *The Works of Jeremy Bentham, vol. 2: Judicial Procedure, Anarchical Fallacies, works on Taxation* (William Tait 1843). Regarding Bentham's work, see also: James Brown Scott, *The Hague Peace Conferences of 1899 and 1907*, vol. 1 (n 131 in Chapter 2) 513 et seq.; William Evans Darby, *International Arbitration; International Tribunals: A Collection of the various Schemes which have been produced; and of Instances in the Nineteenth Century* (J.M. Dent 1904) 147.

31 Immanuel Kant, *Zum Ewigen Frieden* (Friedrich Nicolovius 1795).

32 Jackson Harvey Ralston, *International Arbitration from Athens to Locarno* (n 23 in Chapter 3) 120–127.

well received in the United States and influenced advocates of peace, supporters of arbitration, and lawyers who strove for the codification of international law in the 19th century. The reason for the interest of many U.S.-Americans in his writings can be found in the fact that his idea for an international world federation followed the concept of a constitutional republic;[33] a highly popular notion in the United States around the turn of the 19th century. Furthermore, Kant managed to turn the discussions on peace from a merely political one into a rational, ethical, and moral question. Since peace became a generally very decisive and fundamental topic in U.S.-American political thinking in these years, this constellation provided the perfect basis for a widespread and favorable reception of Kant's writings and U.S.-Americans were very receptive for them at that time.[34] Thereby, he and the other aforementioned authors contributed to the emergence of the idea of the achievement of peace through law, and to the rise of the cause of peace to a prominent idea in U.S.-American political and ethical thinking.

Another characteristic which many of the concepts proposed by the aforementioned authors had in common was that they considered world organizations as the most suitably means for establishing long-lasting peace; and many of the proposed plans for international organizations provided for the creation of assemblies or congresses, for joining forces, and/or for the formation of permanent arbitral tribunals. It is, however, essential to note that the creation of such tribunals was only taken into consideration (in these proposals) in the context of world organizations. None of these plans provided for the creation of independent courts.

2 Arbitration in the First Half of the 19th Century

In several contributions on this topic, the beginning of the history of modern arbitration is dated to the *Jay-Treaty* from 1794.[35] By taking into consideration some of the more recent literature – such as contributions from Cornelis G. Roelofsen, Miloš Vec, or Karl-Heinz Lingens – it appears rather debatable

33 Warren F. Kuehl, *Seeking World Order* (n 16 in Chapter 3) 10.

34 Ibid.

35 Compare, e.g.: Karl-Heinz Ziegler, 'Zur Entwicklung von Kriegsrecht und Kriegsverhütung im Völkerrecht des 19. und frühen 20. Jahrhunderts' (2005) 42 Archiv des Völkerrechts 280–281; Wilhelm G. Grewe, *Die Epochen der Völkerrechtsgeschichte* (n 49 in Chapter 2) 606–607; J.H.W. Verzijl, *International Law in Historical Perspective, Part VIII* (n 123 in Chapter 2) 72–73; Tobias Lock, *Das Verhältnis zwischen dem EuGH und internationalen Gerichten* (Mohr Sibeck 2010) 5.

whether this claim can be upheld.[36] However, it is not of the foremost importance for the present book to determine the exact starting point of this development. Instead, it is enough to refer to the early 19th century as the period in which the states began to, once again, take recourse to arbitration on a significantly higher rate than during most of the 18th century. The *Jay-Treaty* will, nevertheless, be dealt with in more detail in the following because it serves as a telling example for the special relationship between the United States and Great Britain in the 19th century. This is especially the case with regards to the two states' affinity for arbitration and on the U.S.-American approach towards arbitration and adjudication.

The *Jay-Treaty* was concluded between the United States and Great Britain to resolve conflicts originating from the *American War of Independence* (1775–1783). In accordance with this agreement, mixed commissions were established to deal with claims for compensations and to determine by arbitral means the exact course of the border between Canada, still a British colony at that time, and the United States.[37] Over a period of ten years, between 1794 and 1804, the *Jay-Treaty* then served as the framework for the award of 536 arbitral decisions.[38] Furthermore, the United States concluded arbitration treaties shaped in accordance with the *Jay-Treaty*, especially for the settlement of border disputes, at several other occasions throughout the 19th century; for example, with Great Britain (in 1814, 1853, and 1854),[39] Spain (in 1795, 1819, and 1834),[40] and with several states from North, Central, and South America.[41] Thereby, the practice of settling boundary disputes by arbitration was further spread, especially since the other American nations also started to adopt this

---

36 Cornelis G. Roelofsen, 'International Arbitration and Courts' (n 7 in Chapter 3) 160; Miloš Vec, 'From the Congress of Vienna to the Paris Peace Treaties of 1919' (n 28 in Chapter 1) 673; Karl-Heinz Lingens, 'Der Jay-Vertrag (1794) als Geburtsstunde der modernen internationalen Schiedsgerichtsbarkeit? Zur Entstehung eines undifferenzierten Geschichtsbildes' in Miloš Vec & Serge Dauchy (eds.), *Les Conflits entre Peiples* (Nomos 2011) 65–82.

37 William Evans Darby, *International Arbitration; International Tribunals* (n 30 in Chapter 3) 271–276. Also: Hans-Jürgen Schlochauer, 'Die Entwicklung der internationalen Schiedsgerichtsbarkeit' (n 13 in Chapter 3) 6. John Bassett Moore, 'Historical Notes on International Arbitration' (n 2 in Chapter 3) 181 et seq.

38 Mary Ellen O'Connell and Lenore Vanderzee, 'The History of International Adjudication' in Cesare P.R. Romano, Karen J. Alter & Yuval Shany (eds.), *The Oxford Handbook of International Adjudication* (n 102 in Chapter 2) 44.

39 Hans-Jürgen Schlochauer, 'Die Entwicklung der internationalen Schiedsgerichtsbarkeit' (n 13 in Chapter 3) 9 (*footnote 50*).

40 Ibid 9 (*footnote 52*).

41 Ibid 9 (*footnote 51*). According to him, the United States concluded such treaties with Mexico (in 1839, 1848, and 1868), Costa Rica (1860), Brazil (1842), Chile (1858), Ecuador (1862), Peru (in 1862 and 1868), and Venezuela (1866).

practice after the achievement of independence in 1825 and applied it in their mutual relations too.[42]

At first glance, it may appear rather astonishing that Great Britain and the United States agreed on the peaceful settlement of their mutual disputes by arbitration so soon after the end of the war for independence. Some of the reasons they took this decision are as follows: firstly, strong relations, interlinkages, and cultural, as well as linguistic, commonalities existed between Great Britain and the United States because of their long common history. This resulted in a great amount of mutual understanding and cultural proximity. Secondly, the war against Napoleonic France bound most of Great Britain's military forces in Europe, wherefore they (probably) preferred to refer border disputes to arbitration instead of settling them by a costly war across the Atlantic. Thirdly, Great Britain and their North American colonies had lived under the same legal system during colonial times. Thus, they had a common legal background and shared the same legal tradition. Fourthly, certain types of disputes between the British colonies in North America and the British motherland had already been settled in colonial times by judicial means before the *British Privy Council*[43] (since 1833 known as *Judicial Committee of the Privy Council*). Hence, both states were already used to taking recourse to peaceful methods for the settlement of their mutual conflicts. Despite the previous war, it, therefore, appears reasonable to assume that the long and shared history, as well as their linguistic, cultural, and legal commonalities, were strong enough to allow them to strive for the peaceful resolution of their current conflict and to conclude the *Jay-Treaty*.

In addition to that, another factor must be taken into consideration, which exclusively concerned the United States. It explains why the United States showed so much openness to arbitration for the settlement of international conflicts at that time. For this purpose, it is necessary to focus on the procedure of turning the thirteen founding states of the later United States into one nation. A transitional constitution was concluded in 1777, the so-called *Articles of Confederation and Perpetual Union*,[44] which provided for the peaceful settlement of the mutual disputes of its member states through an *ad hoc* institution called the *American Court of Arbitration*.[45] This tribunal was supposed to substitute war between the founding states by peaceful means of conflict settle-

42 Ibid.

43 J.H.W. Verzijl, *International Law in Historical Perspective, Part VIII* (n 123 in Chapter 2) 73.

44 *Articles of Confederation and Perpetual Union* <https://www.govinfo.gov/content/pkg/SMAN-107/pdf/SMAN-107-pg935.pdf> accessed December 13, 2016.

45 Compare: James Brown Scott, *The Hague Peace Conferences of 1899 and 1907*, vol. 1 (n 131 in Chapter 2) 460–464.

ment in form of arbitration.[46] Only a few years later, the United States went even further and established the *U.S. Supreme Court*. It was introduced through the enactment of the U.S. Constitution in 1789 and replaced the *American Court of Arbitration*. Unlike the previous institution, the *Supreme Court* is a purely judicial and permanent tribunal composed of a standing bench of judges who decide public legal disputes (and those between the state and individuals) on the sole basis of law.[47] Therefore, the United States first established an arbitral *ad-hoc* tribunal for their internal relations, which was later replaced with a purely judicial and truly permanent court. This development already indicates the existence of a high affinity for judicial means in the United States, and for the willingness to take recourse to peaceful means for the solution of disputes on the inter-state level. It also shows that the development from arbitral to judicial means was an integral part of the U.S.-American unification process, of becoming an independent nation, and for the further advancement and strengthening of the governmental system of the United States. At least parts of the United States seem to have considered this course of development – from the establishment of arbitral towards judicial institutions – as an essential element of the achievement of peaceful relations and, possibly, also as a blueprint for the replacement of war with law (and arbitration) on the international level.

In this regard, it should also be noted that the special conditions and characteristics of the relationship between the United States and Great Britain did not prevent the two states from getting into conflicts with one another on multiple occasions during the 19th century. The unilaterally declared *Monroe-Doctrine* (1823) directed against European annexations of American soil,[48] the *Caroline Incident* (1837),[49] the *Aroostook War* (1838/1839),[50] the *Pig War* (1859), and the British conduct during the *American Civil War* (1861–1865; e.g., the *Trent Affair*[51] or the selling of warships to the Confederate States[52]) are

46 Georg Stadtmüller, *Rechtsidee und Machtpolitik in der amerikanischen Geschichte* (Isar 1957) 15–16. Also: James Brown Scott, 'The Proposed Court of Arbitral Justice' (1908) 2 The American Journal of International Law 776–777.

47 Compare: Michla Pomerance, *The United States and the World Court as a 'Supreme Court of the Nations': Dreams, Illusions and Disillusion* (Springer Netherland 1996) 10.

48 Please compare pages 115–117 and 139–142 of the present book.

49 Frederica Paddeu, *Justification and Excuse in International Law: Concept and Theory of General Defenses* (Cambridge University Press 2018) 351.

50 Howard Jones, 'Anglophobia and the Aroostook War' (1975) 48 The New England Quarterly 519–539.

51 Kenneth Bourne, *Britain and the Balance of Power in North America 1815–1908* (University of California Press 1967) 206 et seq.

52 Compare pages 85 et seq. of the present book.

telling examples of the existence of strong tensions between them. Although none of these situations escalated into severe wars, they all bore the potential of doing so, or they heavily burdened – at least – the relationship between the two nations. Therefore, the U.S.-American–British relationship during the 19th century was not free of conflicts either. Despite the fact that the two states settled multiple mutual conflicts through arbitration, other cases could still have easily escalated into wars. Consequently, it is hard to consider the *Jay-Treaty* as the starting point for a period of complete dedication to the preservation of peace in their bi-lateral relation.

On the other hand, however, it should also be acknowledged that, when it comes to arbitration, the relationship between the United States and Great Britain differed decisively from the ones between other nations. To understand this claim, it is necessary to consider the total number of isolated arbitrations, which were conducted at the time. According to the data provided in A.M. Stuyt's *'Survey of International Arbitrations 1794–1970'* (from 1972), William E. Darby's *'International Arbitration; International Tribunals'* (from 1904), and Henri La Fontaine's *'Histoire Sommaire et Chronologique des Arbitrages Internationaux'* (from 1902),[53] recourse was taken to arbitration in a total of 25 cases between 1817 and 1853. This period has been chosen for (the first phase of) further consideration because the year 1817 marks the end of the arbitral procedures on pecuniary and territorial claims, which took place in the aftermath, and as a consequence of, the *Napoleonic Wars*.[54] The period ends in 1853 with of the outbreak of the *Crimean War*, in the aftermath of which substantial changes took place concerning the European order. Breaking down the numbers in Table 3.1 shows that settling 25 cases in 37 years only accounts for a frequency of 0.68 cases per year. These figures seem to indicate that arbitration was invoked only on occasion. Furthermore, the vast majority of arbitrations in the first half (but also during most of the rest) of the 19th century concerned conflicts of somewhat secondary importance. Eduard Descamps (*'Die Organisation eines internationalen Schiedsgerichts'* from 1897) listed several types of disputes which were usually referred to arbitration during that century. According to him, most of these conflicts were of an

53 A.M. Stuyt, *Survey of International Arbitrations 1794–1970* (A.W. Sijthoff. Dobbs Ferry, N.Y. Oceana 1972) 26–233; William Evans Darby, *International Arbitration; International Tribunals* (n 30 in Chapter 3) 769 et seq.; and Henri La Fontaine, *Histoire Sommaire et Chronologique des Arbitrages Internationaux (1794–1900)* (Revue de Droit International et de Législation Comparée 1902) 344 et seq.

54 A.M. Stuyt, *Survey of International Arbitrations 1794–1970* (n 53 in Chapter 3) 18–25.

> [...] economic or commercial nature, disputes over territorial delimitations, infringements of neutrality rights, obligations to indemnify other states or citizens of the latter, differences concerning fishing rights or prize law, [or] conflicts between the states' different legal regimes in civil and/or penal law.[55]

While most states referred only a few cases to arbitration during these years, Great Britain and the United States pursued a decisively different approach. They were the forerunners, and the major advocates, of isolated arbitration between 1817 and 1853. Either Great Britain, the United States, or both, were involved in 17 out of the 25 cases of arbitration. This accounts for a share of no less than 68%. To go into a bit more detail: Great Britain participated in 13 out of these 25 arbitrations while the United States was involved in 8 of them (4 arbitrations took place in their mutual relations).[56] Therefore, arbitration was only invoked in 8 cases in which neither of the two states participated. Arbitrations between European states (hereinafter: *inter-European arbitrations*) – not involving Great Britain – even only took place twice during this period.[57] Consequently, the United States and Great Britain had a particular approach to, and a clear affinity for, arbitration, whereas the other European states usually preferred to abstain from taking recourse to this instrument. Moreover, it seems that the increase in the number of arbitrations between 1817 and 1853 (in comparison to earlier periods) can primarily be traced back to the initiative of the United States and Great Britain. Nevertheless, the trend to invoke arbitration on an increasing frequency for the settlement of international conflicts was already recognizable but not yet universal.

One reason for the reluctance of the continental European states to invoke arbitration for the settlement of their conflicts can be found in the political situation in Europe in the period between 1817 and 1853. As described above,

---

55 Translated analogously by the author of the present book from: Eduard Descamps, *Die Organisation des internationalen Schiedsgerichts* (A. Schupp 1897) 35 et seq. Compare also: Otfried Nippold, Die Fortbildung des Verfahrens in völkerrechtlichen Streitigkeiten (Duncker & Humblot 1907), 214. Or: Wilhelm G. Grewe, *Die Epochen der Völkerrechtsgeschichte* (n 49 in Chapter 2) 613.

56 See also: Arthur Nussbaum, *Geschichte des Völkerrechts* (n 119 in Chapter 2) 242.

57 Those took place between Austria and Sardinia in 1845 and between France and Spain in 1851; compare: A.M. Stuyt, *Survey of International Arbitrations 1794–1970* (n 53 in Chapter 3) 44 and 47.

TABLE 3.1 Isolated arbitrations

	1817–1853 (37 years)	1854–1870 (17 years)	1871–1899 (29 years)
Total amount	25	43	139
Ø per year	0.68	2.53	4.79
Increase by factor	/	3.72	1.89
Inter-European	9	7	26
Share in the total amount	36%	16.3%	18.7%
Ø per year	0.24	0.41	0.9
Increase by factor	/	1.71	2.2
Inter-American	5	13	40
Share in the total amount	20%	30%	29%
Ø per year	0.16	0.76	1.38
Increase by factor	/	4.75	1.82
European/American	9	18	55
Share in the total amount	36%	42%	40%
Ø per year	0.24	1.06	1.9
Increase by factor	/	4.42	1.79
Others	1	5	18
Share in the total amount	4%	11.6%	13%
Ø per year	0.03	0.29	0.62
Increase by factor	/	9.67	2.14

The data stems from the following publications: A.M. Stuyt, Survey of International Arbitrations 1794–1970 (n 53 in Chapter 3) 26–233. William Evans Darby, International Arbitration; International Tribunals (n 30 in Chapter 3) 769 et seq. Henri La Fontaine, Histoire Sommaire et Chronologique des Arbitrages Internationaux (1794–1900) (n 53 in Chapter 3) 344 et seq.

the *Congress of Vienna* 1814/1815) had established a system of political and territorial standstill on the continent. This system followed more than 20 years of ongoing wars against France (1792–1815). However, this construct was based, to a large extent, on political and sovereign inequality.[58] The

58 Miloš Vec, 'From the Congress of Vienna to the Paris Peace Treaties of 1919' (n 28 in Chapter 1) 659.

great powers could interfere in the concerns of other countries whenever they wished (if they acted together), whereas smaller states were widely suppressed and subjected to the dominance of the *Concert*. This arrangement, and the privileged position of the great powers, were probably among the major reasons for the great powers to avoid arbitrations. They held the necessary power to enforce their will on smaller nations and did not have to rely on peaceful instruments of conflict settlement, which would compromise their own interests with those of the less powerful states. Recourse to arbitral means would have meant that the great powers forfeited their politically and militarily dominant position towards smaller nations (since they would meet the smaller states on an equal footing in such procedures) and that they had to hand over control over the disputes to an arbitrator or court. Consequently, congress diplomacy was the preferred means of the continental great powers for conflict settlement and there remained little room for arbitrations at that time.[59]

Regarding the situation of institutional arbitration between 1817 and 1853, it should be emphasized that isolated arbitration was by far the more common form of arbitration. Obligatory arbitration treaties were already being concluded from time to time, although very occasionally. At least, this was the case when it came to obligatory arbitration between European states or to those concerning the relationships between European and American countries (hereinafter: *American/European relations*).[60] Little importance was attached by European states to obligatory arbitration in the period under present review. In fact, they concluded only two treaties between 1817 and 1853, which entailed for *special compromissory* clauses. The first was an agreement between France and Argentina in 1840,[61] and the second was between France and Chile in 1852.[62] Regarding treaties providing for *general compromissory* arbitration commitments, the situation was not much different. Only three agreements of that type were concluded; namely between Belgium and Mex-

59 The conservative great powers Prussia, Russia, and Austria-Hungary only showed little (if any) willingness to refer conflicts to arbitral settlements. Austria-Hungary only took recourse to this instrument once between 1817 and 1853; in the case of a dispute with Sardinia. The other two states did not make any attempt in this direction at all.

60 The corresponding developments in the mutual relations of the American states will be dealt with in Chapter 4.

61 *Convention between Buenos Aires and France, signed at Buenos Aires*, 29 October 1840 (available: Oxford Historical Treaties; OUP reference: 91 CTS 111).

62 *Additional Articles to the Treaty of Commerce of 15 September 1846 between Chile and France*, signed at Santiago, 30 June 1852 (available: Oxford Historical Treaties; OUP reference: 108 CTS 213).

ico in 1839,[63] Belgium and Peru in 1850,[64] and Spain and Peru in 1853.[65] One of the reasons for the reluctance of European states to enter obligatory arbitration treaties was certainly the fact that isolated arbitration was not yet invoked on such a regular basis as in the second half of the 19th or during the early 20th century. Before this background, it is only logical that states which still held reservations against isolated arbitration would only conclude very few (if any) obligatory arbitration agreements either. Furthermore, in those cases, in which European states actually participated in an isolated arbitration, either the United States or Great Britain was usually the other involved party. But not even the United States and Great Britain joined obligatory arbitration treaties at that time. Hence, obligatory arbitration lacked a similarly potent driving force as the one fulfilled in the context of isolated arbitration by the two Anglo-American nations. Finally, European states seemed to be more willing to enter obligatory arbitration treaties with Latin American nations than with other European ones. The reasons behind this approach might be found in the fact that Latin American/European relations were usually not as thematically wide reaching as inter-European ones. They generally concerned issues relating to trade, financial concerns, or commercial matters. Therefore, conflicts between a European and a Latin American state hardly ever bore the same potential of affecting critical aspects of the states' interests, as it used to be the case in inter-European conflicts. The latter, conflicts in inter-European affairs, could easily concern matters of life and death, the independence of the involved states, or other crucial topics. Concluding obligatory arbitration treaties with Latin American countries, however, was considerably less incisive and less far-reaching for the European states as it only entailed limited obligations, mostly towards non-vital issues, and affected the states' sovereignty rights to a comparably limited extent.

Surprisingly, however, the most advanced and far-going initiative to introduce obligatory arbitration into an (multi-lateral) inter-European treaty was taken at the *Congress of Paris* in 1856, on a meeting attended only by representatives of the great powers. The congress was held to bring an end to the

---

63 Compare: Alfred H. Fried, *Handbuch der Friedensbewegung*, vol. 1 (Friedens-Warte 1911) 174. According to him, the treaty was put into effect whereas J.H.W. Verzijl mentioned that it was never ratified (compare: J.H.W. Verzijl, *International Law in Historical Perspective, Part VIII* (n 123 in Chapter 2) 75). It was not possible to find a definite answer in this regard.

64 *Treaty of Friendship, Commerce and Navigation between Belgium and Peru,* signed at London, 16 May 1850 (available: Oxford Historical Treaties, OUP reference: 104 CTS 103).

65 *Treaty of Peace and Friendship between Peru and Spain* from 1853 (available: <https://archive.org/stream/colecciondelost06peru#page/116/mode/2up> accessed January 7, 2015). But it remains unclear whether this treaty was actually put in force.

Crimean War (1853–1856), which was the first armed clash between European great powers since the *Napoleonic Wars*. The *Crimean War* was the nail in the coffin of the *Concert*-system,[66] which had already been severely weakened by the revolutions in 1848. Politicians and statesmen, such as the Austrian Prince Klemens von Metternich (1773–1859), had maintained the system for more than 30 years. However, they were muscled out of their offices during the riots in 1848 and were replaced with politicians who preferred to pursue nationalist approaches, pure power policies, and *realpolitik*.[67] In spite of the tense situation (the *Crimean War*), the great powers worked together at the *Congress of Paris* to re-established peace and a stable balance of power after the war.[68] To achieve these goals, Article 8 of the *Treaty of Paris* provided that, in the event of the emergence of a dispute between any of the signatory states and the Ottoman Empire, the parties of this dispute were supposed to give one another (and also the other signatory states) the opportunity to mediate the conflict before taking recourse to the use of force.[69] The provision was voluntary and was limited to the special event of the emergence of a conflict between the Ottoman Empire and any of the great powers. Nevertheless, despite all these conceptual shortcomings and its limitedness, it was still the first time that any kind of multi-lateral provisions was adopted by the great powers which served the purpose of encouraging the parties of a conflict to avoid the use of force and to settle it peacefully instead. Furthermore, a British representative, George Villiers, 4th Earl of Clarendon (1800–1870), proposed "[…] to make this recommendation more general, if not universal, and thus avoid 'impulsive' wars."[70] Thereby, he aimed for expanding the signatory states' right to recommend mediation to one another as an alternative to war, and to apply it to all kinds of conflicts. His initiative was, eventually, successful. At a follow-up conference between the contracting parties, they expressed the wish in their 23rd protocol (on April 14, 1856) that "[…] all States, between which any serious misunderstanding might arise, should as far as possible have recourse to the good offices of a friendly Power before appealing to arms, and that the

66 Bob Reinalda, *Routledge History of International Organizations* (n 59 in Chapter 2) 26, 51. See also: Gordon A. Craig, *Geschichte Europas 1815–1980* (n 47 in Chapter 2) 134.

67 Compare pages 30 et seq. of the present book.

68 Gordon A. Craig, *Geschichte Europas 1815–1980* (n 47 in Chapter 2) 134.

69 Compare: Article 8, *General Treaty of Peace between Great Britain, Austria, France, Prussia, Russia, Sardinia, and Turkey*, signed at Paris, 30th March, 1856 (available: Augustus Oakes & R.B. Mowat (eds.), *The Great European Treaties of the Nineteenth Century* (Clarendon Press 1930) 176 et seq.). See also: Charles H. Stockton, 'The Declaration of Paris' (1920) 14 The American Journal of International Law 356.

70 Harold Temperley, 'The Treaty of Paris of 1856 and Its Execution' (1932) 4 The Journal of Modern History 413.

Governments not represented at the congress should unite in the sentiment that inspired this wish."[71] Despite this success and the pioneering character of these provisions, it must not be forgotten that the protocol amounts to a mere expression of 'wish.' It did not have any (legal) binding power. While its conclusion must have seemed promising for advocates of peace, these provisions soon proved to be insufficient to prevent any of the wars, which broke out between the great powers during the subsequent years (1856–1871).

3 Peace Societies

State practice is only one side of the development of international arbitration in the 19th century. States were – beyond a doubt – the most important and impactful actors in this regard. They were the only ones entitled to make international law, and to refer cases to arbitration. Without their willingness to pursue a more progressive attitude towards arbitration, and to arbitrate more cases, no development would have been possible. Nevertheless, states were not the only actors in this regard. A quickly growing number of non-governmental associations, pressure groups, and organizations were created during the 19th century. They advocated for an increased use of arbitration, which further developed the conceptual framework of mechanisms of conflict settlement, and which had a remarkable impact on political decisions (in favor of arbitration) in several countries, (at the latest) by the end of the century.[72] Peace societies played a key role in this regard.

Before their emergence, authors such as William Penn, Charles Irénée de Saint-Pierre, Jean-Jacques Rousseau, Jeremy Bentham, and Immanuel Kant had been the driving forces, and the main contributors, regarding the further development of the idea to both establish and preserve peace at the international level (as shown above).[73] When the peace movement emerged, its members took up these concepts and implemented them into their own agenda. Meaning, the peace societies cannot be considered to be the creators of many of these ideas, but they can be credited for having turned them from intellectual considerations into proposals, which were introduced to the polit-

71 Coleman Phillipson, *Termination of War and Treaties of Peace* (The Lawbook Exchange 2008) 79.

72 Alfred H. Fried, *Handbuch der Friedensbewegung*, vol. 2 (Friedens-Warte 1913) 96. Also: David Cortright, *Peace: A History of Movements and Ideas* (Cambridge University Press 2008) 38–40.

73 Heinrich Lammasch, *Die Lehre von der Schiedsgerichtsbarkeit in ihrem ganzen Umfange* (n 107 in Chapter 2) 37.

ical discourse. Peace activists were capable of taking this step because they joined forces. Instead of striving for the realization of their goals on an individual basis, they formed societies. Thereby, the cause of peace was given an institutional framework. Formerly separated, and individually operating peace activists, were united within an organizational network, which allowed them to work together, to communicate, and to exchange ideas. By co-ordinating their actions, and by finding a common agenda, they appeared more consistent to the outside world. Furthermore, they could speak with a common and considerably more powerful voice. Therefore, the cause of peace was significantly strengthened and became politically more influential with the emergence of the peace movement.

In order to focus on the actual origin of peace societies, it is necessary to look at the years around 1815, and on developments in Great Britain and the United States. Tendencies towards peace had already existed in the United States for a long time.[74] Among religious groups like the Quakers and Mennonites, the commitment to pacifism and non-violence was particularly strong. Unsurprisingly, the first peace societies (in 1815 in Massachusetts, Ohio, and New York, and only a year later also in Great Britain) were created by members of these religious groups. They took this step as a reaction to the suffering and losses of human lives during the *Anglo-American War* from 1812 and the *Napoleonic War*.[75]

Until 1828, the number of peace societies grew to between 36 and 50 groups.[76] All of which had in common a clearly shared religiously motivated approach. They were convinced that war was incompatible with the *New Testament*, therefore, international conflicts were to be settled peacefully.[77] In the early years of the peace movement, the newly established societies even con-

74 Mary Ellen O'Connell, 'Arbitration and Avoidance of War: The Nineteenth-Century American Vision' in Cesare P.R. Romano (ed.), *The Sword and the Scales: The United States and International Courts and Tribunals* (Cambridge Univ. Press 2009) 30.

75 Arthur Charles Frederick Beales, *The History of Peace: A Short Account of the Organised Movements for International Peace* (Bell 1931) 45.

76 Bob Reinalda, *Routledge History of International Organizations* (n 59 in Chapter 2) 43. According to him, there were 36 peace societies at that time, whereas Jacob Ter Meulen mentioned 50 of them (compare: Jacob Ter Meulen, *Der Gedanke der Internationalen Organisation in seiner Entwicklung*, vol. 2.1 (M. Nijhoff 1929) 237).

77 Mark Weston Janis, *The American Tradition of International Law: Great Expectations 1789–1914* (Oxford University Press 2004) 98–101. Also: David Cortright, *Peace: A History of Movements and Ideas* (n 72 in Chapter 3) 26. Sandi E. Cooper, 'The Origins and Development of European Peace Movements: From Vienna to Frankfurt' in Gernot Heiss and Heinrich Lutz (eds.), *Friedensbewegungen: Bedingungen und Wirkungen* (Oldenbourg Wissenschaftsverlag 1984) 76.

sidered themselves to be exclusively religious organizations.[78] Thus, they abstained from attempting to influence everyday politics, and from associating with political parties. It was only when significantly more, and less religious, people started to support the cause of peace and join the ranks of these societies that the situation changed. A quickly growing, and increasingly better organized, peace movement emerged during the 1820s and 1830s, and, then, the peace societies also began to strive for political influence.[79]

The advocacy of an increased use of arbitration for the peaceful settlement of conflicts as an alternative to war was an essential part of the agenda of the peace movement since the very beginning.[80] Besides the writings of progressive thinkers from the 17th and 18th centuries, it was, in particular, the success of the *Jay-Treaty* that encouraged both the British and the U.S.-American branches of the peace movement to support arbitration. They hoped that this instrument was the key to the establishment of a stable state of peaceful coexistence between the nations.[81] However, the peace movement did not continue to focus on arbitration alone. New concepts and ideas were developed by some of its most progressive members. One of them was William Ladd (1778–1841), the author of the treatise *'Essay on a Congress of Nations'* (from 1840). Later authors referred to him as the 'leading light'[82] of the Anglo-American peace movement (Marks Weston Janis) or as the 'advocate of peace' (Elihu Burritt).[83] And, indeed, Ladd's ideas broke new ground. They gave the agenda of the American peace movement a new shape, as he was the first to publish a concept for the introduction of international adjudication.

In 1828, Ladd united the individual U.S.-American peace societies under the roof of the *American Peace Society*. He also served as the first executive officer of this new organization, and later as its president.[84] Moreover, he vastly contributed to the enormous growth of the importance of the peace movement, of its political influence, and its public acceptance by contributing decisively to the transformation from an entirely religious society to one which was also

---

78 David Cortright, *Peace: A History of Movements and Ideas* (n 72 in Chapter 3) 28.

79 Compare: Michla Pomerance, *The United States and the World Court as a 'Supreme Court of the Nations'* (n 47 in Chapter 3) 7.

80 David Cortright, *Peace: A History of Movements and Ideas* (n 72 in Chapter 3) 28.

81 Bob Reinalda, *Routledge History of International Organizations* (n 59 in Chapter 2) 44.

82 Mark Weston Janis, *The American Tradition of International Law* (n 77 in Chapter 3) 103.

83 According to James Brown Scott, Elihu Burritt referred to Ladd as such. Compare: James Brown Scott (ed.), *An Essay on a Congress of Nations by William Ladd* (Oxford University Press 1915), page iii; re-print from the original: William Ladd, *An Essay on a Congress of Nations* (Whipple and Damrell 1840).

84 Mark Weston Janis, *America and the Law of Nations 1776–1939* (Oxford University Press 2010) 79.

involved in politics, and which publicly lobbied for the peace cause. For example, Ladd himself made sure that three motions were introduced to the Massachusetts State Legislature (in 1835, 1837, and 1838),[85] in which he advocated for an increased use of peaceful methods of conflict settlement and for the creation of a congress of nations. According to him, the object of the *American Peace Society* was the increase and promotion of the practice already begun, "[...] of submitting national differences to amicable discussion and arbitration, and finally of settling all national controversies by an appeal to reason, as becomes rational creatures, and not by physical force, as is worthily only of brute beasts, and this shall be done by a Congress of Christian Nations."[86] Moreover, Ladd convinced the majority of the participants at the annual meeting of the American Peace Society in 1835 of adopting the demand for the creation of a congress and a court of nations as an essential element of the general agenda of the society.[87] In the following years, Ladd, and the American Peace Society, further developed this approach and came up with a clearer conceptual structure for the international order, which they wanted to propose. These efforts resulted in the changing of the society's agenda in such a way that it started to demand the establishment of an international code of law, as well as the creation of a congress *and* of a court of nations.[88] Therefore, Ladd did not only demand the complete abolition of war (cf., e.g., his second motion from 1837). But he also stated that "[...] a Congress or Court of Nations appears to be, at present, the best practical method by which disputes between nations can be adjusted, and the appeal to arms avoided."[89] In Ladd's third motion (from 1838), corresponding to the named conceptual changes and adaptions, Ladd then demanded the creation of "[...] a Congress of Nations for the purpose of framing a code of international law, and a high court of arbitration for the settlement of controversies between nations."[90]

Against this background, it should be emphasized that the predominant understanding of arbitration was still in accordance with its *traditional* concept. Correspondingly, most people still regarded arbitration as the only opt-

---

85 Arthur Deerin Call, 'The War Has Not Destroyed x: The Will to End War' (1920) 82 Advocate of Peace through Justice 272. According to him, the American Peace Society submitted similar motions also to the Congress of the United States in 1837, 1838, 1840, 1841, and 1849.

86 William Ladd, *An Essay on a Congress of Nations* (n 83 in Chapter 3) 78–79.

87 W.H. van der Linden, *The International Peace Movement 1815–1874* (Tilleul Publications 1987) 136–137.

88 Ibid.

89 Published in: William Ladd, *Prize Essays on a Congress of Nations* (Whipple and Damrell 1840) 659.

90 Ibid 660.

ion available for the peaceful settlement of international conflicts in a (*quasi-*) judicial way. Actual judicial decisions – on the pure basis of law – did not yet exist at the international level. Even the idea for such (purely judicial) procedures under international law was not yet discussed. The reason for the neglect of this option must be found in the very nature of judicial procedures – as their results would have been rulings in favor of one of the parties involved, with the respective other party declared as having been in the wrong. Hence, this approach stood in sharp contrast to the prevailing *traditional* understanding, which used to aim for compromising the interests of the participating states instead of explicitly determining which side of a conflict was right and which was wrong. Moreover, there did not yet exist a conceptual differentiation between arbitral and adjudicative procedures in international legal scholarship; and such a differentiation only became common in the later parts of the 19th century and in early 20th century.

Although the *traditional* concept of arbitration continued to prevail in most academic works, as well as in state practice, Ladd's above-mentioned proposal already differed decisively from this concept. In the subsequent years, he then developed his concept for a future peace-driven world order (under the roof of a world organization) even further. In his '*Essay on a Congress of Nations*,' he demanded "[…] a regular system of arbitration, and the organization of a board of arbitrators, composed of the most able civilians in the world, acting on well-known principles, established and promulgated by a Congress of Nations."[91] As mentioned, it was very common to mix terms belonging to arbitration and adjudication at the time and to not distinguish clearly between the two concepts just yet. As it becomes apparent, in the quoted paragraph, Ladd was also not an exception in this regard. According to the quote, he proposed the introduction of a 'system of arbitration.' However, he also wanted the arbitrators to decide cases on the pure base of the (legal) principles established by the congress of nations. Due to the great differences between the prevailing (*traditional*) understanding of arbitration and Ladd's approach, it appears questionable whether he actually aimed for the creation of an arbitral tribunal. In fact, he might actually have been proposing a judicial court, although he was still relying on the terminology of arbitration. Evidence for the correctness of this assumption can be found in further passages of his '*Essay*' in which he concentrated first on the *Congress of Nations*, which was supposed to consist of "[…] ambassadors from all those Christian and civilized

91 William Ladd, *An Essay on a Congress of Nations* (n 83 in Chapter 3) 124; on 90 and 96–97, he referred to the court, which he was about to propose, and mentioned 'arbitration' and 'judicial bodies' synonymously.

nations who should chose to unite in this measure."[92] According to him, the mission of the congress was to "[…] fix the fluctuating and various points of international law, by the consent of all the parties represented, making the law of nations so plain that a court […] could easily apply those principles to any particular case brought before [it]."[93] The *Court of Nations* was, therefore, supposed to rule on the basis of the code of international law established by the congress and to "[…] act as a conservator of the peace of Christendom and watch over the welfare of mankind."[94] To enable the court to fulfill this task, Ladd wanted it to consist of "[…] the most eminent jurists of the countries represented at the Congress"[95] who "[…] shall hold their places according to the tenure previously agreed on."[96] In addition, he proposed that these judges were to decide international conflicts "[…] by the true interpretation of existing treaties and by the laws enacted by the Congress."[97] None of the quoted notions concerning the structure, shape, and function of the proposed court of nations complied with the prevailing concept of *traditional arbitration*. Instead, Ladd wanted the court to be composed of trained jurists who were appointed for a previously determined tenure (but not only for single cases) and who ruled on conflicts on the sole basis of international law. The typical characteristics of *traditional arbitration* – such as compromises, the nomination of heads of states as arbitrators, or the enormous influence of the conflicting parties – simply did not occur in Ladd's writings. Because his proposal resembles considerably more the characteristics of judicial procedures,[98] it stands to reason that he actually aimed for the establishment of a permanent, and truly judicial, court at the international level.

Ladd's ideas, and his turn to judicial (instead of arbitral) measures for the settlement of international conflicts, were not made by chance and did not come out of nowhere. They were probably inspired by the U.S.-American domestic experiences since 1790, in which all kinds of public legal conflicts were decided by the *Supreme Court*. The submission (even of the government and state authorities) to the rule of law, and to the ruling of a high court, preserved peace in U.S.-American domestic affairs and effectively banned war from them. The notion that Ladd wanted to transfer these developments

92 William Ladd, *An Essay on a Congress of Nations* (n 83 in Chapter 3) 8.
93 Ibid.
94 Ibid 36.
95 Ibid 8.
96 Ibid 34.
97 Ibid 35.
98 Compare pages 45–47 of the present book.

to the international level, and expected to achieve similar results, can also be deduced from the following quote from Ladd's *'Essay'*:

> The ascending scale of justice, from the mayor's or justice's courts, to the inferior and the superior courts, and finally to the Supreme Court of the United States, wants but one step more to complete the system and that is a court which shall settle disputes between sovereign and independent nations in the same manner as the Supreme Court of the United States [...].[99]

It should not be forgotten either that Ladd's ideas were still highly utopian. The creation of a world organization comprising as much nations as possible was practically inconceivable at that time. The *Concert of Europe* dominated European affairs, and it is highly doubtful whether the great powers were willing to give up on their influential and powerful positions. Therefore, it can be concluded that although Ladd laid the conceptual foundations for international adjudication in his works (not yet in form of an independent and autonomous international court of law, but only in form of an organ of a world organization), the time was not yet ripe for the realization of his ideas.

While it seems as if Ladd's enormous influence and reputation were among the main reasons why the peace movement adopted these ideas to the agenda, most members of the American Peace Society still considered it to be an unrealistic approach. The correctness of this assumption becomes apparent when taking into consideration the sudden conceptual and strategic change, which took place within the peace movement right after William Ladd's death in 1841.[100] Soon after he had passed away, voices were raised to question Ladd's approach, and to propose alternative strategies. For example, William Jay (1789–1858), who was another influential peace activist at that time, was convinced that, in the long term, a congress and a court of nations would be created.[101] But he considered this concept as too utopian to be realized at that point of time. Instead, Jay wanted to advocate for a gradual change of the international order because he was sure that this strategy would be more suitable and promising to lead – in the end – to the realization of Ladd's ideas. One possible measure proposed by Jay, to initiate such a stepwise development,

---

99 James Brown Scott (ed.), *An Essay on a Congress of Nations by William Ladd* (n 83 in Chapter 3) 94. See also: Warren F. Kuehl, *Seeking World Order* (n 16 in Chapter 3) 17.

100 W.H. van der Linden, *The International Peace Movement 1815–1874* (n 87 in Chapter 3) 136–143.

101 Ibid 145.

concerned the conclusion of an obligatory arbitration treaty between the United States and France. This agreement was supposed to contain the following clause:

> It is agreed between the two contracting parties that if, unhappily, any controversy shall hereafter arise between them in respect to the true meaning and intention of any stipulation in this present treaty, or in respect to any other subject, which controversy cannot be satisfactorily adjusted by negotiations, neither party shall resort to hostilities against the other; but the matter in dispute shall, by a special convention, be submitted to the arbitrament of one or more friendly parties.[102]

The idea behind the conclusion of such a treaty was to set a good example, which Jay expected many other nations to follow suit. In this regard, he seemed to have hoped to stipulate a development, which would result in the conclusion of numerous bi-lateral, general obligatory arbitration treaties between countries from all over the world. Through this development, he wanted to gradually ban war from international law through the creation of a growing network of bi-lateral agreements, each of which should prohibit the use of force in the respective bi-lateral relations.

In the end, both fractions within the peace movement strove for the same objective: The establishment of a system capable of preserving peace, and of settling international conflicts pacifically. They both even believed that this could best be achieved by the creation of a world organization, and of a world court. However, they differed in the approaches through which they wanted to achieve this goal. Those who supported Jay's concept seem to have evaluated the prevailing international situation in a considerably more realistic way and sought to achieve their goals through gradual steps since they did not believe that their ultimate goal – the creation of a world organization – could be achieved all at once. H.T.J. Macnamara expressed this notion in a speech at the *First General Peace Convention in London* (1843) by declaring that the creation of a world organization "[…] will obviously be the work of ages; and meanwhile we need, as a temporary substitute for wars, the expedient of Judge Jay, which might […] be adopted at once by all the nations of Christendom."[103] Most members of the American Peace Society supported the demand for a stepwise development as well, whereas Ladd's supporters

102 The quote stems from: ibid 146.

103 H.T.J. Macnamara, 'The Second Paper' in Peace Society Office, *The Proceedings of the First General Peace Convention* (Ward and Co 1843) 65–66.

persisted in preferring a considerably more radical solution. They did not regard the current practice of occasional arbitration and arbitral decisions issued by heads of states as an actual alternative to the establishment of a completely new system, which based on a congress and a court of nations.[104] Although the more realistic approach prevailed in the end, Ladd's ideas and concepts did not fall into oblivion either. But they were pushed to the second rank in the agenda of the peace movement,[105] as they were henceforth regarded as long-term goals, not immediately achievable results.

Only some of the most radical peace activists continued to uphold and to publicly promote Ladd's ideas. One of them was Elihu Burritt (1810–1879). According to one of his articles, published in May 1848 in the journal *'Bond of Brotherhood,'* he continued to strive for the creation of a 'Congress and Supreme Court of Nations'[106] which were to be shaped in accordance with Ladd's concepts. But Burritt did not only uphold Ladd's ideas but he also developed them further. This becomes particularly apparent in the context of the conceptual differentiation between arbitration and adjudication. While Ladd used the term *arbitration* for referring to arbitral and judicial procedures, Burritt took a more elaborate stand in this regard and criticized the *traditional* understanding of arbitration as being too arbitrary. Furthermore, he argued that arbitral clauses could easily be ignored by states, and that conflicts should be submitted to the decision of judges, which ruled on the sole base of law rather than appointing heads of states as arbitrators who could be prejudiced.[107] He used even clearer terminology. At the peace congress in London in 1843, for example, he demanded that a court of nations should be established which was shaped in form of a 'high court of adjudication.'[108] Additionally, he further elaborated on this demand by declaring to believe "[...] it indispensable for the order and peace of nations, that there should not only be established a court of equity or arbitration, but also a well-defined authoritative code of international law, which should govern the decisions of the tribunal, in settling the disputes referred to it."[109] Hence, while Ladd had introduced

---

104 Both quotes stem from: W.H. van der Linden, *The International Peace Movement 1815–1874* (n 87 in Chapter 3) 146.

105 Ibid 368.

106 Elihu Burrit, 'Congress and Supreme Court of Nations' (May 1848) Bond of Brotherhood 37–39.

107 W.H. van der Linden, *The International Peace Movement 1815–1874* (n 87 in Chapter 3) 368–369.

108 Henry Richard and Elihu Burritt (eds.), *Report of the Proceedings of the Second General Peace Congress held in Paris on the 22nd, 23rd and 24th of August 1849* (Gilpin 1849) 57.

109 Ibid 57.

the idea for the establishment of an international court of law to the discussions, and to the agenda of the peace movement, the final steps towards a clearer conceptual differentiation between arbitration and adjudication were taken by his successors, by peace activists such as Elihu Burritt.

At the *First General Peace Convention* in London (1843), however, the majority of the members of the peace movement kept supporting William Jay and concentrated almost entirely on the concept of arbitration.[110] But apart from determining the conceptual strategy of the peace movement, the London conference also pursued a second goal. It was held to spread the aim for peace beyond the Anglo-American context. Before that day, the peace movement had been strong only in Great Britain and the United States, where it had already developed into an influential and important reformation movement. But there did not exist any comparable initiative in the rest of Europe.[111] To change this situation and to further spread their ideas and to win additional supporters, the Anglo-American peace activists decided to encourage continental Europeans to join their efforts in favor of the preservation of peace[112] by hosting a set of peace congresses in Europe.

The first of these meetings was the conference in London. However, it was primarily attended by British peace activists (292 out of 325 participants). Apart from them, 26 representatives from the U.S.-American branch and only six participants from the rest of Europe joined the event.[113] Despite the failure of bringing together numerous continental Europeans in London who were all interested in the cause of peace, the British and U.S.-American peace movements did not give up. They organized follow-up conferences in Brussels (1848), Paris (1849), Frankfurt/Main (1850), and again in London (1851), and these meetings were far bigger successes. Most participants of the Brussels conference still came either from Great Britain or from the United States (and only few participants were from France, Belgium, or Spain).[114] But the fact that it was held in continental Europe raised a lot of attention and aware-

110 Ibid 151.

111 Compare: Ramaa Prasad Dhokalia, *The Codification of Public International Law* (Manchester University Press 1970) 21. Also: Jacob Ter Meulen, *Der Gedanke der Internationalen Organisation in seiner Entwicklung*, vol. 2.1 (n 76 in Chapter 3) 238. David Cortright, *Peace: A History of Movements and Ideas* (n 72 in Chapter 3) 28.

112 Sandi E. Cooper, 'The Origins and Development of European Peace Movements: From Vienna to Frankfurt' (n 77 in Chapter 3) 77.

113 Mark W. Janis, 'North America: American Exceptionalism in International Law' in Bardo Fassbender and Anne Peters (eds.), *The Oxford Handbook of the History of International Law* (n 28 in Chapter 1) 537; in this context, he cites from: Arthur Charles Frederick Beales, *The History of Peace* (n 75 in Chapter 3) 66–67.

114 David Cortright, *Peace: A History of Movements and Ideas* (n 72 in Chapter 3) 34.

ness for the cause of peace all over Europe and paved the way for the congress in Paris. The meeting in the French capital, in 1849, was a remarkable success then. It was attended by more continental Europeans than any of the previous meetings. The overwhelming majority of the 840 delegates still came from Great Britain (670 of them) but there were also 100 French participants, 12 Belgians, 20 U.S.-Americans, and 38 attendants from other European countries.[115] Additionally, the congress was presided by the famous French author Victor Hugo (1802–1885). His participation not only attracted lots of public attention but he also delivered a speech on the need to establish the 'United States of Europe.'[116] Despite the success of the Paris conference,[117] this meeting also constituted the peak of the mid-centurial enthusiasm for peace in Europe, as well as in the Anglo-American sphere. The two follow-up meetings, in Frankfurt and London, were significantly smaller and less influential.

The years around the middle of the 19th century stood, therefore, for two opposing developments. On the one hand, the first peace societies were founded in Europe, which not only considerably strengthened the cause of peace on the continent but also universally. But, on the other hand, the peace movement also had to face serious throwbacks resulting from the emergence of fundamental problems on the national, as well as international, levels. These developments negated most of the successes made during the previous years and almost resulted into the entire collapse of the peace movement. Three of the most important developments in this regard were the following: *firstly*, there arose a severe panic in Great Britain of being invaded by France after Napoleon III's *coup d'état* (in 1851).[118] The members of the *British Peace Society* decided to cancel plans for further international peace congresses, and, instead, held two exclusively British meetings in 1852 and 1853.[119] At these occasions, they discussed measures to prevent a mobilization of the British forces and to convince the British population of abandoning its warlike mentality.

115 Ibid.

116 Victor Hugo, 'Inaugural Address,' in: Henry Richard and Elihu Burritt (eds.), *Report of the Proceedings of the Second General Peace Congress held in Paris on the 22nd, 23rd and 24th of August 1849* (n 108 in Chapter 3) 11. At this occasion, Hugo declared: "A day will come when bullets and bomb-shells will be replaced by votes, by the universal suffrage of nations, by the venerable arbitration of a great Sovereign Senate, which will be to Europe what the Parliament is to England, what the Diet is to Germany, what the Legislative Assembly is to France."

117 Bob Reinalda, *Routledge History of International Organizations* (n 59 in Chapter 2) 46.

118 W.H. van der Linden, *The International Peace Movement 1815–1874* (n 87 in Chapter 3) 448.

119 David Nicholls, 'Richard Cobden and the International Peace Congress Movement, 1848–1853' (1991) 30 Journal of British Studies 354 (footnote 6).

The British government, however, showed a very hostile attitude,[120] which a lot of the population followed. Anti-French and anti-British attitudes arose on the respective sides of the British Channel, and, thus, washed away the enthusiastic attitude for peace, which had prevailed at the conference in Paris in 1849. When mutual mistrust and hostility dominated the British–French relations, and when people adopted a more bellicose attitude towards the other nation, the peace movements in both countries lost both members and influence. *Secondly*, the outbreak of the *Crimean War* (1853–1856) was a shock for many peace activists and severely weakened the peace movement in the countries involved in this conflict. In Great Britain, for example, all of the Welsh branches of the peace movement had ceased to exist by the end of the war, the London Peace Society only consisted of a handful of people at that point, and the number of subscribers to its journal, *The Herald of Peace*, was at a low point as well.[121] *Finally*, the *U.S.-American Civil War* (1861–1865) caused a (temporary) downfall of the peace movement in the United States. The U.S.-American society was highly divided over the question of slavery,[122] and the American Peace Society was also internally torn.[123] Many of its members considered themselves to be absolute pacifists, due to a deep Christian faith. However, when they realized that the liberation of slaves was only possible by applying force to break the resistance of the Southern States, they faced a moral dilemma. Furthermore, the American Peace Society feared that it would split into supporters and opponents of slavery if the situation should escalate. And indeed, this assumption was correct. When the *American Civil War* broke out, the American peace movement eroded and was devastated for many years.

4 Arbitration between 1854 and 1870

The period of peace and territorial immutability, but also of political standstill, which had prevailed under the *Concert*-System after 1815, was brought to an end by the revolutions in 1848 and the outbreak of the *Crimean War* in 1853. Due to these events, Europe, once again, experienced times of imbalanced relations

120 Bob Reinalda, *Routledge History of International Organizations* (n 59 in Chapter 2) 46.

121 W.H. van der Linden, *The International Peace Movement 1815–1874* (n 87 in Chapter 3) 463. Also: Alexander Tyrrell, 'Making the Millennium: The Mid-Nineteenth Century Peace Movement' (1978) 21 The Historical Journal 94.

122 David Cortright, *Peace: A History of Movements and Ideas* (n 72 in Chapter 3) 35.

123 Cecilia Lynch, 'Peace Movements, Civil Societies, and the Development of International Law' in Bardo Fassbender and Anne Peters (eds.), *The Oxford Handbook of the History of International Law* (n 28 in Chapter 1) 208.

between the great powers, and the re-emergence of war as a common phenomenon. Pure power policy, Social Darwinism, and nationalism were the driving forces behind these changes and manifested in open competition between the European powers.[124] These developments also resulted in a power shift within the European system. Italy was united (in 1870), and emerged as a new great power, while the foundation of the German Empire (in 1871) created a new (power) political fix point in continental Europe.

Both unifications were realized by the application of *realpolitik*, and the ruthless use of force by the Germans and Italians against their respective opponents. Numerous wars occurred – for example, during the Italian *Risorgimento* (1861–1870), the *Second Schleswig War* (1864) fought by Prussia and Austria-Hungary against Denmark, the *Austro-Prussian War* (1866), or the *Franco-German War* (1870–1871). The cessation of the *Concert of Europe*, and the re-organization of the European political order, also enabled smaller states to (re-)gain more sovereignty and independence from the great powers. The hegemony of the *Concert* was, therefore, abolished and the great powers could not maintain the practice anymore of controlling all Europe by compromising their interests at conferences. Instead, the door was opened for smaller states to choose their own preferred means of conflict settlement and the great powers had to consider other options for dealing with disputes. This development paved the way for a significant increase in the use of arbitration.

The data provided in Table 3.1 demonstrate that between 1854 and 1870, states referred significantly more often to isolated arbitration than before. Worldwide, 43 cases were settled by arbitration during these 17 years, which accounts for an increase by the factor 3.72 in comparison to the earlier period (2.53 cases were arbitrated per year between 1854 and 1870). However, this does not mean that every state suddenly embraced arbitration. The pure numbers only provide a general overview and do not throw individual lights on any of the various countries. In fact, only few European states participated in the trend to take recourse to arbitration more regularly. Great Britain, for example, continued to be the main practitioner of isolated arbitration, as they participated in 18 out of the 43 arbitrations worldwide (42%). Sardinia (later Italy), Spain, and especially Portugal and France were other European states that took recourse to this instrument comparably often. To give but one example: Portugal and France each took part in four arbitrations, which made them the states which used arbitration second most in Europe in that period, after Great Britain. However, to speak of a general trend in favor of arbitration among European states would be misleading. France and Portugal only took recourse

124 Gordon A. Craig, *Geschichte Europas 1815–1980* (n 47 in Chapter 2) 194–195, 200.

to this instrument once every four years. The three conservative great powers Prussia, Russia, and Austria-Hungary, as well as most of the other European states, hardly ever invoked arbitration at all.[125] Outside of continental Europe, the United States remained the most frequent user of arbitration, after Great Britain. Surprisingly, the *American Civil War* hardly affected them in this regard. They continued to take recourse to arbitration before, after, and even during the war. The United States had 17 cases (out of 43 arbitrations worldwide) settled by arbitration between 1854 and 1870, which accounts for a share of 40%. The data show that the United States and Great Britain continued to participate in most of the arbitrations in this period. Either one, or both, were involved in 33 out of 43 cases, which corresponds to a share of almost 77% of all arbitrations worldwide (this share even increased by around 9% in comparison to the previous period). These figures seem to indicate that arbitration was still primarily an Anglo-American instrument. It should, nevertheless, be noted that also a raising number, and also a broader variety of Latin American and European states, participated in isolated arbitrations. Smaller (European) states, in particular, played a pioneering role in this regard. It is correct that they primarily referred to arbitration in cases of conflicts with the United States or Great Britain. However, they also began to invoke it, albeit on a low but gradually growing scale, for the settlement of disputes with Latin American states, and occasionally even with other European countries.

Against this background, it should also be acknowledged that most of the arbitrated conflicts were still of secondary importance. Only a few countries – such as Great Britain – toyed with the idea of expanding its scope to more critical issues. Every attempt to convince conflicting parties between 1854 and 1870 to arbitrate cases concerning matters of peace and war failed; for example, the British proposals to arbitrate both German-Danish wars (in 1848 and again in 1864).[126] In conclusion, arbitration was invoked significantly more often and seems to have enjoyed greater acceptance in the period under present review. However, it was still evolving and had not yet developed into an instrument, which most states were familiar enough with to take recourse to in the case of the emergence of conflicts.

125 Prussia was the only one of the three conservative great powers that had any case settled by arbitration in this period; namely a conflict between them and Bavaria in 1866. Compare: A.M. Stuyt, *Survey of International Arbitrations 1794–1989* (M. Nijhoff 1990) 81.

126 Concerning the first German-Danish War from 1848, see: Inge Adriansen and Jens Ole Christensen, *The Second Schleswig War 1864* (Museum Sønderjylland 2013) 21. Concerning the second German-Danish War from 1864, compare also: William Carr and Harry Hearder, *The Wars of German Unification 1864–1871* (Routledge 1999) 83.

Turning the view now to institutional arbitration, it becomes apparent that the number of concluded agreements containing obligatory arbitration commitments also grew significantly between 1854 and 1870.[127] The conclusion of the *Cobden-Treaty* (1860) between Great Britain and France played a crucial role in this regard.[128] The agreement provided for the signatory states to grant one another the status of most-favored nations, better trade conditions, and lower custom duties. Inspired by the *Cobden-Treaty*, lots of states followed the example of France and Great Britain and entered similar agreements. In general, it can be observed that a remarkable number of international trade agreements were concluded during these years. This development enhanced free trade, abolished trade barriers, and reduced custom duties. This wave of conclusions of bi-lateral treaties both contributed to and strengthened the already on-going process of globalization, and the deepening of international economic relations.[129] Moreover, many of these treaties contained obligatory arbitration clauses.

In comparison to the years between 1817 and 1853, when 13 treaties containing *general compromissory* clauses (0.76 treaties per year) had been concluded, the numbers rose to 21 treaties of that kind between 1854 and 1870 (1.24 treaties/year). This constitutes an increase by the factor 1.63. Furthermore, five *special compromissory* arbitration treaties were concluded during both periods, between 1817 and 1853, as well as between 1854 and 1870. Because of the longer duration of the first period, the frequency of conclusions of this type of agreements accounted for 0.14 treaties per year between 1817 and 1853, whereas it increased after 1853 by the factor 2.1 to 0.29 treaties per year. Although these numbers must appear rather low in comparison to the subsequent interval (1871–1899), the growth rates indicate, nevertheless, that a re-thinking took place and that (not all, but a growing amount of) states followed the trend of concluding obligatory arbitration treaties on a more regular scale. This tendency seems to have constituted the origin – i.e., the early stage – of the developments taking place regarding obligatory arbitration after 1871. Furthermore, it should be noted in this context that the majority of *general compromissory* arbitration treaties were concluded in the mutual relations of American nations (in the figures referred to as '*Between American Nations*'). This had already been the case for 77% of the treaties of that kind during the period 1817–1853, and – with 57% – the respective numbers remained to be on a comparably high level between 1854 and 1870. In fact, introducing *general compromissory*

127 Arthur Nussbaum, *Geschichte des Völkerrechts* (n 119 in Chapter 2) 226.

128 Ibid.

129 Ibid.

TABLE 3.2 Obligatory arbitration agreements

A) Treaties containing general compromissory arbitration clauses

	1817–1853 (37 years)	1854–1870 (17 years)	1871–1899 (29 years)
Total amount	13	21	42
General Ø per year	0.76	1.24	1.45
General increase by factor	/	1.63	1.17
Inter-European	0	0	1
Share	0%	0%	2%
Ø per year	0	0	0.03
Increase by factor	/	/	/
Between American nations	10	12	27
Share	77%	57%	64%
Ø per year	0.27	0.57	0.93
Increase by factor	/	2.11	1.63
European/American	3	5	10
Share	23%	24%	24%
Ø per year	0.08	0.29	0.34
Increase by factor	/	3.63	1.19
Europe and other countries	0	4	4
Share	0%	19%	10%
Ø per year	0	0.24	0.14
Increase by factor	0	/	0.58

TABLE 3.2 Obligatory arbitration agreements

B) Treaties containing *special compromissory* arbitration clauses

	1817–1853 (37 years)	1854–1870 (17 years)	1871–1899 (29 years)
Total amount	5	5	49
General Ø per year	0.14	0.29	1.69
General increase by factor	/	2.1	5.83
Inter-European	0	0	21
Share	0%	0%	43%
Ø per year	0	0	0.72
Increase by factor	/	/	/
Between American nations	3	2	11
Share	60%	40%	22%
Ø per year	0.08	0.12	0.38
Increase by factor	/	1.5	3.17
European/American	2	3	10
Share	40%	60%	24%
Ø per year	0.05	0.18	0.34
Increase by factor	/	3.6	1.19
Others	0	0	7
Share	0%	0%	14%
Ø per year	0	0	0.24
Increase by factor	/	/	/

clauses into treaties of peace, alliance, and commerce seems to have been a widespread practice in the mutual relations of the American states.[130] European countries, on the other hand, were still rather hesitant to enter into such agreements with their direct neighbors. As a result, no such agreements were concluded in inter-European relations. The European nations continued to pursue the strategy of only concluding general obligatory arbitration treaties

130 Helen May Cory, *Compulsory Arbitration of International Disputes* (n 154 in Chapter 2) 6–7.

with American (24%) respectively with other non-European states (19%). The increase in the amount of obligatory arbitration treaties in the American/European relations, as well as between European and other non-European countries, nevertheless, provides reason to assume that – at least some of – the European states became more receptive to these kinds of agreements. In particular, smaller European states, such as Belgium, Portugal, Denmark, Switzerland, and Italy, showed a grown willingness in this regard. They concluded several obligatory arbitration agreements with Latin American states between 1854 and 1871.[131] As mentioned above, the European countries probably showed more openness to establish these types of obligations with distant (trade) partners, with whom they had rather limited relations,[132] than with other European states, with whom they shared hundreds of years of common experiences (including feuds, struggles for power, and wars). The risk arising from entering into such agreements with Latin American states was comparably small and did not bear the same potential of constituting any inestimable impact on the states' vital interests. The great powers, on the other hand, continued to abstain from entering general obligatory arbitration treaties. The reason for them rejecting these types of commitment can be found in the fact that great power used to have interests in all parts of the world and considered their global political approaches to be of the utmost importance for their survival in the on-going struggle for domination and influence. Hence, none of them wanted to risk being bound by any kind of unpredictable, generally applicable, and unrestricted arbitration obligations, which bore the potential of limiting their options in foreign political affairs.

Some of the great powers, just as the smaller European nations, developed, nevertheless, an increasingly more favorable approach towards obligatory arbitration between 1854 and 1870. But, instead of concluding general obligatory arbitration agreements, they preferred special obligatory ones. This kind of agreement only bound the adhering states to a limited, previously determined extent. Entering this kind of treaty bore significantly less risk of being obliged to arbitrate cases, which the states did not want to be settled this way. Hence, the great powers preferred special arbitration over general obligatory arbitration. Evidence in support of this claim can be found in the data provided in Table 3.2. It shows that five special obligatory arbitration treaties were concluded between 1817 and 1871 in American/European relations. None of them involved smaller European nations. Instead, all of these agreements were con-

131 Furthermore, Norway, Sweden, Belgium, and Austria/Hungary (as the only great power) concluded general obligatory arbitration agreements with Siam in 1868/1869.

132 Compare page 64 of the present book.

cluded between a European great power and a Latin American nation.[133] Therefore, it stands to reason that those European great powers, which were open to concluding obligatory arbitration agreements, did so by entering into special obligatory ones. Smaller European states, on the other hand, were rather willing to conclude general obligatory arbitration agreements. However, despite the increased number of obligatory arbitration treaties between 1854 and 1871, it constituted only a first step in the development of obligatory arbitration into a regularly used tool in international relations.[134] Obligatory arbitration did not become a common phenomenon among European states until, at least, 1870. In fact, not a single obligatory arbitration agreement was concluded in the inter-European context before 1880 (neither of a special nor of a general nature). Hence, Europe embraced obligatory arbitration, so far, only to a very limited extent.

5 Arbitration between 1871 and 1899

Several authors describe the year 1871 as a turning point in the history of arbitration,[135] as well as in history in general.[136] Coming first to the general changes, which took place during this period. 1871 marked the end of a period of inter-European wars. The subsequent period of peace in Europe lasted until the outbreak of the *World War I*. But, unlike the years between 1815 and 1853, the new system was not based on any form of institutionalized hegemony of the great

---

133 Great Britain, Sardinia, France, and Prussia concluded such treaties with Chile and – in the case of France – also with Argentina.

134 Johan H.W. Verzijl, *International Law in Historical Perspective, Part VIII* (n 123 in Chapter 2) 74.

135 Mark Weston Janis, *America and the Law of Nations 1776–1939* (n 84 in Chapter 3) 132, 134; at this occasion, he referred to the *Alabama*-Case from 1871 as "[...] probably the most influential event of nineteenth-century American international law [... because...] it was an exceptionally encouraging development for American international law enthusiasts." See also: Randall Lesaffer, 'The Temple of Peace: The Hague Conferences, Andrew Carnegie, and the Building of the Peace Palace 1898–1913' in *Mededelingen van de Koninklijke Nederlandse Vereniging voor Internationaal Recht, Preadviezen*. vol. 140 (2013) 20. Alfred H. Fried, Handbuch der Friedensbewegung (Oesterreichische Friedensgesellschaft 1905) 243–244. Warren F. Kuehl, *Seeking World Order* (n 16 in Chapter 3) 29–30. Francis Anthony Boyle, *World Politics and International Law* (Duke University Press 1985) 44. Hans Wehberg, *The Problem of an International Court of Justice* (n 123 in Chapter 2) 21.

136 Compare, e.g., Gordon A. Craig, *Geschichte Europas 1815–1980* (n 47 in Chapter 2) 192–200. See also: David G. Williamson, *Bismarck and Germany: 1862–1890* (Longman 2011), Chapter 11. Ann Goldberg, *Honor, Politics and the Law in Imperial Germany: 1871–1914* (Cambridge University 2010) 194.

powers. There were no more *Concert*-like organizations, which maintained peace, territorial order, and the balance of power. Furthermore, the relations between the great powers were dominated by mistrust and insecurities after 1871 due to the previous wars.[137] Nationalism, and the protection of their vital interests, moved into the focus of the governments' concerns with co-operation and the preservation of peace were only attached as a secondary importance. Because the second half of the 19th century was also the age of *Imperialism*, and of the *Scramble for Africa and Asia*, competition for colonies and global influence became crucial in the great powers' foreign policies. Several open rivalries arose over conflicting colonial interests. While the situation in Europe remained peaceful, competition between the great powers outside of Europe became harsh and, sometimes, even shaped by violence and aggression. This resulted in severe tension between the great powers, which was even further fueled by tariff wars, competition for new markets, and armament races.[138]

Turning back to arbitration, the period between 1871 and 1899 was characterized by a steadily advancing internationalization of the societies, the emergence of a global public opinion, and the re-appearance of the universal peace movement. After the heydays of the peace movement in the 1840s, and early 1850s, it had suffered a severe setback due to the wars in Europe and the *American Civil War*. Following the end of these conflicts, peace activists managed to revive the movement and their strive for peace picked up fresh movement in the United States, as well as in many of the greater and smaller European states. This success was achieved, *inter alia*, due to the signal effect of the arbitral settlement of one particular case, the *Alabama*-Arbitration (1871). The underlying dispute of this case concerned the relationship between the United States and Great Britain during the *American Civil War*. During this domestic U.S.-American conflict, Great Britain recognized the belligerent status of the Confederate States, the secessionist Southern states of the United States. The Union, the Northern parts of the United States, regarded this step as deeply unfriendly and encroaching.[139] Additionally, Great Britain also permitted the Confederate States to buy ships from a British shipyard. One of them was the *Alabama*, the name giver of this case. The ships were used to prey and capture merchant vessels from the Union. As a result of this transaction, the relations between the United States and Great Britain were severely damaged. The idea to re-normalize them by arbitrating this conflict had

137 Gordon A. Craig, *Geschichte Europas 1815–1980* (n 47 in Chapter 2) 200.

138 Ibid 196–200.

139 Tom Bingham, 'The Alabama Claims Arbitration' (2005) 54 The International and Comparative Law Quarterly 3.

already arisen during the war. However, the atmosphere between the two states had been too toxic to come to an acceptable solution before 1871.[140] When the award was finally issued, it ordered Great Britain to compensate the United States with $15.5 million. Today, this sum would correspond to, at least, £160 million.[141] Therefore, the award constituted a huge financial burden for Great Britain, a sum that was high enough to be regarded as of crucial concern for the country's vital interests.

The fact that the two countries had come to an agreement to arbitrate the case, and that Great Britain accepted the award, was regarded as a huge success by the peace movement. Moreover, the settlement resulted into a wave of enthusiasm for arbitration in Europe and in the United States, caused lots of political activity on behalf of arbitration, and dominated the agenda of the peace movement until the outbreak of *World War I*.[142] In addition to that, with the *Alabama*-Arbitration, Great Britain and the United States entered new judicial ground. It was the first time in history that a conflict was solved by arbitration, which deeply affected the national interests of two great powers, and which was serious enough that it could have escalated into war.[143] Hence, the *Alabama*-Arbitration case proved that the instrument of arbitration was capable – not only in theory but in practice – of solving even those problems which affected the states' national honor and vital interests.[144] In other words, the case proved the suitability of (isolated) arbitration in the avoidance of war.[145]

5.1 *The Societal Perspective on International Law*

After the *Alabama-Settlement* in 1871, the European peace societies not only regained previously lost members and influence but they also managed to attract so far unattained popularity in significantly wider parts of the popula-

140 Mark Weston Janis, *America and the Law of Nations 1776–1939* (n 84 in Chapter 3) 134. Also: Jonathan Parry, *The Politics of Patriotism: English Liberalism, National Identity and Europe, 1830–1886* (Cambridge University Press 2006) 294.

141 Tom Bingham, 'The Alabama Claims Arbitration' (n 139 in Chapter 3) 1. At this point, Bingham cited Roy Jenkins and his findings (compare: Roy Jenkins, *Gladstone* (England Papermac 1995) 359). According to Jenkins, this sum would correspond to even higher numbers today if it was set in relation to Great Britain's GDP (in this case, it would be equivalent today to £4 billion). If Great Britain's state budgets from 1871 and the one from today were taken into consideration, the award would even correspond today to £150 billion.

142 Randall Lesaffer, 'The Temple of Peace' (n 135 in Chapter 3) 20. David Cortright, *Peace: A History of Movements and Ideas* (n 72 in Chapter 3) 36.

143 Alfred H. Fried, *Handbuch der Friedensbewegung*, vol. 2 (n 72 in Chapter 3) 82.

144 Arthur Nussbaum, *Geschichte des Völkerrechts* (n 119 in Chapter 2) 242.

145 Mark Weston Janis, *America and the Law of Nations 1776–1939* (n 84 in Chapter 3) 134.

tions, and among a growing number of politicians.[146] In comparison to the situation in Europe, it took significantly longer in the United States to re-establish the peace movement. In fact, this process was only completed in the late 1870s/early 1880s when a new generation of peace activists took over the leadership and re-organized it. Only then could a similar development take place as in Europe. As a result, the membership numbers of the U.S.-American peace movement increased significantly again (from that point onwards), its political influence grew quickly, and more importance was attached the cause of peace, in the United States, than ever before.[147]

Aside from the *Alabama Settlement*, the recent experiences of the horrors of modern warfare also played a key role in the re-emergence of the peace movement in Europe, as well as in the United States.[148] Especially the *Franco-Prussian War* had demonstrated the dangers of lawless international relations (only driven by pure power politics and force), which resulted into a radical re-thinking among leading international lawyers and peace activists, but also among politicians.[149] Furthermore, peace societies did not only re-appear in Europe. But they quickly grew in France, in Scandinavia, the Latin countries, as well as in the German Empire and Austria-Hungary.[150] Thereby, a new impetus was given to the striving for peace, even though the peace movement never developed into a mass movement.[151] While most peace societies only had a comparably small rosters of members,[152] the movement, nevertheless, succeeded in developing a steadily growing political influence after 1871 and lobby for its cause among politicians and governments, just as well as among intellectuals, members of parliaments, and leading industrials.[153] Thereby, the

146 Alfred H. Fried, *Handbuch der Friedensbewegung*, vol. 2 (n 72 in Chapter 3) 82.

147 David S. Patterson, *Towards a Warless World: The Travail of the American Peace Movement 1887–1914* (Indiana University Press 1976) 1–2. See also: Warren F. Kuehl, *Seeking World Order* (n 16 in Chapter 3) 38.

148 The Advocate of Peace (March 1907) 69 (issue 3) 67; the following reference to the Franco-German War is made: "In the Franco-Prussian war of 1870 and 1871, one of the swiftest and most terrible conflicts of modern times, the aggregate losses on both sides amounted to not less than 225,000 men […]."

149 Irwin Abrams, 'The Emergence of the International Law Societies' (1957) 19 The Review of Politics 363; according to him, the quote stems from: Anon., 'The German Empire' (April 1871) CXXXIII Edinburg Review 459–484.

150 David Cortright, *Peace: A History of Movements and Ideas* (n 72 in Chapter 3) 36.

151 David S. Patterson, *Towards a Warless World* (n 147 in Chapter 3) 2.

152 Warren F. Kuehl, *Seeking World Order* (n 16 in Chapter 3) 38. See also: Merle Eugene Curti, *Peace or War: The American Struggle 1636–1936* (Garland Pub. 1972) 76.

153 David Cortright, *Peace: A History of Movements and Ideas* (n 72 in Chapter 3) 36.

peace movement managed to achieve support from some of the most influential members of the societies.

Numerous members of national legislative assemblies (in Europe and in the United States) were war-weary and deeply impressed by the *Alabama*-Settlement as well. Consequently, they started to show interest in the cause of peace following 1871. They did so, in particular, by adopting a series of motions in national parliaments all over Europe, which advocated for the conclusion of obligatory arbitration treaties. One of these motions was introduced to the *British House of Commons* in 1873 by Henry Richards (1812–1888), a Member of Parliament, peace activist, and the secretary of the *British Peace Society* for forty years. He proposed the establishment of a general and permanent system of arbitration, which the parliament accepted with 98 votes to 88.[154] Over the following years, several other legislatures followed the British example, and adopted similar resolutions. The Italian parliament did so already in the same year (1873), the Dutch one followed in 1874, the Belgians in 1875, the Danish and Spanish in 1890, the Austrians adopted in 1896, and the Norwegian parliament in 1897.[155] By taking these steps and supporting the preservation of peace through the promotion of obligatory arbitration treaties, members of parliaments stopped focusing on exclusively national initiatives. Instead, they broadened their views and strove for international co-ordination.

An Austrian peace activist, Adolf Fischhof (1816–1893), provided then the catalyst for an initiative in the direction of international (inter-parliamentary) co-ordination by proposing that parliamentarians from all over the world should periodically come together for consultations, discussions, and sharing of ideas. He hoped that this step would result in the development of a common concept for the effective preservation of peace, and for the persuasion of their respective governments of such a plan.[156] Fischhof's proposal was well received by numerous peace activists, but it took until 1887 that a series of national parliaments finally made efforts to realize his idea.[157] One of the most important initiatives in this regard was taken by the *British House of Commons* when they decided to send a delegation of ten of its members to the United States. They were entrusted with the task of negotiating terms for a general, and permanent, Anglo-American obligatory arbitration treaty.[158]

154 Heinrich Lammasch, *Die Lehre von der Schiedsgerichtsbarkeit in ihrem ganzen Umfange* (n 107 in Chapter 2) 39.

155 Ibid.

156 Sandi E. Cooper, *Patriotic Pacifism: Waging War on War in Europe 1815–1914* (Oxford University Press 1991) 49.

157 Alfred H. Fried, *Handbuch der Friedensbewegung*, vol. 2 (n 72 in Chapter 3) 92.

158 Ibid.

This step resulted in an enormous increase of sympathy for the cause of peace, and obligatory arbitration in the United States. The *U.S. Senate*, as well as the *House of Representatives*, even adopted several resolutions in favor of the conclusion of similar treaties with all the countries with which the United States maintained diplomatic relations.[159] An Anglo-American treaty (the so-called *'Olney-Pauncefote Treaty'*) was negotiated over the following years, however, its conclusion failed in the end. Nonetheless, the work put into this project had not been in vain as the projected agreement served as an example for similar attempts. For example, only a year later (in 1888), the French *Chamber of Deputies* called for general, and permanent, obligatory arbitration treaties with the United States and Great Britain. To advance the project with the latter, the French government supported a plan of Frédéric Passy (1822–1912), one of the members of the *Chamber of Deputies*, to bring French and British parliamentarians together in order for them to discuss the conclusion of such an agreement. That very same year, 9 British and 24 French delegates met in Paris[160] – and they invited parliamentarians from other countries to come to a follow-up meeting, which took place in 1889 in the context of the *Exposition Universelle* in Paris. Members of Parliament from Italy (five), Belgium, Denmark, Hungary, Liberia, Spain, and the U.S. (one each)[161] followed this invitation and discussed at this occasion how to advance the cause of peace through obligatory arbitration, to convince their respective governments of supporting their efforts on behalf of obligatory arbitration, and to introduce obligatory arbitration clauses into trade and commercial treaties.[162] Furthermore, they also decided to hold regular conferences. Over the following years, these meetings were attended by a quickly growing number of influential participants; most of them parliamentarians, but also ministers, diplomats, and legal scholars.[163] Due to this success, the conferences were institutionalized in the form

---

159 Ibid.

160 Ibid 94. Compare also the discrepancies of Fried's description of the process with the writings of the following two authors: Bob Reinalda, *Routledge History of International Organizations* (n 59 in Chapter 2) 6. Paul Laity, *The British Peace Movement 1870–1914* (Clarendon 2001) 123. According to Reinalda, "[...] it was Cremer who in 1888 took the initiative by bringing a group of British members of parliament to Paris."

Paul Laity, on the other hand, mentioned 25 French members and points out that the first meeting could not be considered as having led to an immediate success of the idea of inter-parliamentary meetings as "[...] this initial meeting was badly attended."

161 Bob Reinalda, *Routledge History of International Organizations* (n 59 in Chapter 2) 63.

162 Ibid.

163 David Cortright, *Peace: A History of Movements and Ideas* (n 72 in Chapter 3) 40.

of an international organization, which was referred to from 1899 onwards as the *Inter-Parliamentary Union* (hereinafter IPU).[164]

The IPU advocated for the preservation of peace through the conclusion of a network of obligatory arbitration agreements, binding a growing number of states and, thereby, banning war from international law through the stepwise replacement of the use of force with arbitration.[165] As shown above, this approach was not new. It had already been pursued by peace activists in the 1840s and 1850s. However, following its re-emergence during the 1870s/1880s, it was given new spin. The aim of peace was no longer limited to the bourgeois and very religious parts of the societies, the parts, which had traditionally formed the core of the peace societies.[166] The belief in the suitability of arbitration for the peaceful settlement of conflicts, in the need for better measures to preserve peace, and in the replacement of war by arbitral means was now shared by politicians, statesmen, and legal scholars – as well as by significantly greater (and still growing) shares of the populations. Although the IPU relied on established concepts, the innovativeness of its attempts derived from the fact that it was composed of a new group of supporters of the cause of peace. Individual parliamentarians had already been among the members of the peace movement in the past; however, the IPU formed an organized, and co-ordinated, association in the framework of which parliamentarians could work together for the cause of peace across borders and national sensitivities. Therefore, the establishment of the IPU serves as a telling example for the developments after 1871, which resulted in the opening of the peace movement to greater shares of the populations, to a better cross-border co-ordination between its national branches, and to the achievement of greater influence on decision-makers within national governments and parliaments.

164 The Inter-Parliamentary Union seems to have been a first and foremost European project until 1900 (despite one U.S.-American delegate who participated in the 1889-meeting). Compare: David S. Patterson, *Towards a Warless World* (n 147 in Chapter 3) 114. According to him, before that date "[…] most American congressmen had never heard of it. Even in American peace circles the union was known before 1900 only to those peace workers who had regularly attended the Lake Mohonk and international peace congresses."

165 Compare: Alfred H. Fried, *Handbuch der Friedensbewegung*, vol. 2 (n 72 in Chapter 3) 92. Kurt Ed. Imberg, *Die Stellung der Vereinigten Staaten von Nordamerika zur internationalen Schiedsgerichtsfrage* (F. Vahlen 1914) 17. Frederick W. Holls, *The Peace Conference at The Hague and its Bearings on International Law and Policy* (Macmillan 1900) 232. According to them, the major object of Inter-Parliamentary Union was the conclusion of bi- and multi-lateral obligatory arbitration agreements, the implementation of commitments to arbitration into national constitutions, and the creation of a permanent tribunal of arbitration.

166 David S. Patterson, *Towards a Warless World* (n 147 in Chapter 3) 3–6. David Cortright, *Peace: A History of Movements and Ideas* (n 72 in Chapter 3) 36–37.

A development, which was very similar to the organization of parliamentarians within the framework of the IPU, can also be observed among international legal scholars, as well as among advocates of a strengthening of international law for the preservation of peace. The *Institut de Droit International* and the *International Law Association*[167] were created in 1873 as the result and manifestation of these developments.

The impulse for the creation of the *Institut* was given by Gustave Rolin-Jaequemyns (1835–1902), a Belgian international lawyer and the editor of the *'Revue de Droit international et de Législation comparée'* (the first journal for international law, published since 1869).[168] In a *note confidentielle* sent to a number of international lawyers from several different countries, he proposed to establish an institution dedicated to the advancement of international law.[169] As a result, eleven of them – to whom Alfred H. Fried (*'Handbuch der Friedensbewegung, Vol. 2'* from 1913) later referred as "[…] the most outstanding legal scholars of this time"[170] – met in Ghent in 1873 and created the *Institut de Droit International.* According to Article 1 of its foundation statue, its central object was determined to be the following: "De favoriser le progrès du droit international, en s'efforçant de devenir l'organe de la conscience juridique du monde civilisé."[171] Moreover, Rolin-Jaequemyns himself stated that the intention (behind the *Institut*) was "[…] to found a permanent institution, purely scientific, which, without proposing the realization of far distant Utopias or an immediate reform, can nevertheless aspire to serve as the organ, in the realm of the law of nations, of the legal conscience of the civilized

167 The International Law Association was initially founded under the name 'Association for the Reform and Codification of the Law of Nations.' Compare: Wilhelm G. Grewe, *The Epochs of International Law* (n 28 in Chapter 2) 517. See also: Mark W. Janis, 'North America: American Exceptionalism in International Law' (n 113 in Chapter 3) 542.

168 Fritz Münch, 'Das Institut de Droit international' (1990) 28 Archiv des Völkerrechts 77.

169 Arthur Eyffinger, *Dreaming the Ideal, Living the Attainable – T.M. C. Asser [1838–1913]: Founder of The Hague Tradition* (TMC Asser Press, 2011) 25.

170 Alfred H. Fried, *Handbuch der Friedensbewegung*, vol. 2 (n 72 in Chapter 3) 83. Also: Irwin Abrams, 'The Emergence of the International Law Societies' (n 149 in Chapter 3) 375. Fritz Münch, 'Das Institut de Droit international' (n 168 in Chapter 3) 77. According to Münch, the founding members of the *institut* were: T.M.C. Asser (Netherlands), Vl. P. Besobrasof (Russia), Joh. Caspar Bluntschli (Germany), Carlos Calvo (Argentina), David Dudley Field (USA), E. de Laveleye (Belgium), James Lorimer (England), P.S. Mancini (Italy), Gustave Moynier (Switzerland), Aug. Pierantoni (Italy), and G. Rolin-Jaequemyns (Belgium).

171 As quoted in: Martti Koskenniemi, *The Gentle Civilizer of Nations: The Rise and Fall of International Law 1870–1960* (n 56 in Chapter 2) 41; broadly translated: "To further the progress of international law in order to turn it into the judicial conscience of the civilized world."

world."[172] Following this premise, the institute became an exclusively scientific body,[173] which was composed of only a handful of experts in public international law. Membership was initially limited to 50 persons who were dedicated to the study and further development of international law.

A second private international organization was created the very same year in form of the *International Law Association*. It was founded on the initiative of American peace activists and lawyers[174] who wanted the association to promote and advance international law. Membership of the association was neither limited to a certain number of persons, nor did it exclusively focus on scholars of international law. Instead, it welcomed "[…] representatives from a wide range of spheres, covering the worlds of commerce, banking, and industry as much as the law, arbitration, and peace studies."[175] Hence, it was not a purely academic institution (unlike the *Institut*). But it was supposed to serve, according to its own premise, as a forum for "[…] all who, from whatever point of view, are interested in the improvement of international relations."[176] These two non-governmental organizations, the *Institut* and the *Association*, both contributed to the furtherance of international law. They did, however, apply decisively different approaches, as it becomes apparent from a quote of the report of an IPU meeting in 1905:

> The Institute has applied itself to the scientific study of the various branches of International Law, and has adopted series of resolutions or drafted model Codes on a great number of subjects […].
>
> [The] Association, without attempting this purely scientific treatment of questions of international law, has occupied itself in popularizing such questions by public discussion, in bringing to bear on their solution the suggestions of practical men – ship-owners, merchants, and practicing lawyers of different nationalities – and in formulating recommendations likely to have practical effect.[177]

---

172 Gustave Rolin-Jaequemyns, 'De la nécessité d'organiser une institution scientifique permanente pour favoriser l'étude et le progrès du droit international' (1873) 1 Revue de Droit Internationale et de Législation Comparée 480, 487.

173 Fritz Münch, 'Das Institut de Droit international' (n 168 in Chapter 3) 76, 79.

174 International Law Association, *Report of the Twenty-Second Conference held at Christiania, September 1st–4th 1905* (West, Newman & Co. 1906) VII. According to it, Elihu Burritt and James B. Miles, two U.S.-American peace activists, convinced David Dudley Field, an U.S.-American scholar of international law, of the necessity to create the association.

175 Arthur Eyffinger, *The 1899 Hague Peace Conference* (n 28 in Chapter 1) 210.

176 International Law Association, *Report of the Twenty-Second Conference held at Christiania, September 1st–4th 1905* (n 174 in Chapter 3) VIII.

177 Ibid VIII–IX.

Arnulf Becker Lorca (*'Mestizo International Law'* from 2014) remarked that the foundation of these two institutions "[...] marked the beginning of international law as a liberal reformist project"[178] whose supporters and participants "[...] believed in an international community governed by law."[179] Furthermore, the formation of these two institutions (the *Institut* and the *Association*) also contributed to the emancipation of international law from state practice.

This becomes particularly clear with the – simultaneous – establishment of international law as an independent scientific discipline.[180] Only after 1870, international law was distinctively separated from other areas of law, from philosophy, or from diplomacy, and it was conceived as an autonomous science.[181] This process went along with the positivization of international law,[182] since international legal scholars henceforth sharply distinguished between natural legal (moral) approaches and scientific (positivist) ones.[183] Francis Anthony Boyle (*'World Politics and International Law'* from 1985) concluded this development as follows: "[...] international legal studies had to step irrevocably forward into the twentieth century by developing an actual science of public international law based upon a positivist approach that was antithetical to the content and methodology of outmoded natural law and natural rights theories."[184] Hence, a sharp line was drawn after 1870 between international legal scholarship and other disciplines.[185] Furthermore, the discipline of international law was now understood – in accordance with the views of positivist scholars – as an exact and precise science based on a set of clearly determined rules, derived from customary law or international treaties. Philosophical or moral considerations, on the other hand, were banned.[186] This development corresponded with, and can be traced to a great extent to, the general trend for

178 Arnulf Becker Lorca, *Mestizo International Law: A Global Intellectual History 1842–1933* (Cambridge University Press 2014) 1.

179 Ibid.

180 Miloš Vec, 'From the Congress of Vienna to the Paris Peace Treaties of 1919' (n 28 in Chapter 1) 667.

181 Martti Koskenniemi, *The Gentle Civilizer of Nations: The Rise and Fall of International Law 1870–1960* (n 56 in Chapter 2) 28, 112. See also: Arthur Nussbaum, *Geschichte des Völkerrechts* (n 119 in Chapter 2) 258.

182 Miloš Vec, 'From the Congress of Vienna to the Paris Peace Treaties of 1919' (n 28 in Chapter 1) 668.

183 Francis Anthony Boyle, *World Politics and International Law* (n 135 in Chapter 3) 18.

184 Ibid.

185 Miloš Vec, 'From the Congress of Vienna to the Paris Peace Treaties of 1919' (n 28 in Chapter 1) 671–672.

186 Francis Anthony Boyle, *World Politics and International Law* (n 135 in Chapter 3) 18.

Positivism in science, the secularization of international relations, and the *Scientification* of many Western societies during the 19th century.[187] Moreover, international law lost its idealistic approach when it was put on a scientific base. It no longer aimed at re-modeling the international order in a single strike. Instead, scholars of international law now attempted to attain a better world in which the frequency of wars was reduced by the gradual improvement, and further development of international law.[188] They hoped that this (presumably long-lasting) process would ultimately result in the outlawing of war.

Consequently, the importance, and standing, of international law, as well as of international legal scholarship, increased significantly during this time. International legal scholarship became an independent academic discipline (with an increased importance and standing), whose scholars started to co-operate internationally (under the framework of the *Institut de Droit International*). Furthermore, the IPU and the *International Law Association* also aimed for the further development and strengthening of international law, and advocated for an increased use of (obligatory) arbitration. The immensely growing support for international law, and the substantial increase of attention, which was attached to it during the years by scholars, members of parliament, politicians, and also within the general public, shows that international

187 Compare: Rainer Liedtke, *Die industrielle Revolution* (Böhlau Verlag 2012) 23 et seq.; Günter Vogler, *Europas Aufbruch in die Neuzeit 1500–1650* (Ulmer 2003) 51–61; Jörg Fisch, *Europa zwischen Wachstum und Gleichheit 1850–1914* (n 84 in Chapter 2) 311 et seq.; Beate Althammer, *Das Bismarckreich 1871–1890* (Ferdinand Schöningh 2009), 180–182; John Stuart Mill, *Auguste Comte and Positivism* (Trübner 1866); Michael Stinger, *The Legacy of Positivism* (Palgrave Macmillan 2005) 3–32; Heinrich Honsell and Theo Mayer-Maly, *Rechtswissenschaft: Eine Einführung in das Recht und seine Grundlagen* (Springer 2015) 179 et seq.; Friedrich Ebel and Georg Thielmann, *Rechtsgeschichte: Von der Römischen Antike bis zur Neuzeit* (C.F. Muller 2003) 354 et seq.; Dietrich Tripp, Der *Einfluß des naturwissenschaftlichen, philosophischen und historischen Positivismus auf die deutsche Rechtslehre im 19. Jahrhundert* (Duncker & Humblot 1983) 21 et seq. According to Jörg Fisch (*Europa zwischen Wachstum und Gleichheit*, 312), the 19th century – in particular the second half – even "[…] became the age of science par excellence."

188 Francis Anthony Boyle, *Foundations of World Order* (n 28 in Chapter 1) 12. Boyle added the following in this context: "The purpose of international law not yet perceived by Americans to be the outlawing of these manifestations of interstate violence [war, imperial conquest, and the threat and use of force; *added by the editor*], but more simply to reduce their incidence, mitigate their fury, and limit their scope so as to protect neutrals – especially the United States […]. The institution of a more just condition in relations between states would further the maintenance of world peace and thus contribute to the promotion of all human values."

law developed into a considerably more important and crucial factor in international relations after 1871.

5.2 *International Law in Practice*

Growing importance was not only attached to international law by scientists, peace activists, and lawyers, but governments began to recognize its relevance in the second half of the 19th century too. Their representatives met at several international conferences during that time, in the framework of which they not only focused on purely political situations (as they had under the *Concert*-system), but also, turned more and more towards concluding legally binding conventions in order to regulate their mutual relations. Telling examples of this development can be found, *inter alia*, in the humanitarization of international law (e.g., in the conclusion of the *Geneva Convention* from 1864), in the establishment of norms for the colonialization of new territories (e.g., by the *General Act of the Berlin Conference* from 1885), and in the creation of international organizations (e.g., the *Universal Postal Union* in 1874). It can generally be noted that states began to rely on international law significantly more after 1870. The accuracy of this findings also becomes apparent in the example of the quickly growing number of bi-lateral treaties, which were concluded from the 1860s onwards. These agreements dealt with trade, free navigation, and amity[189] and regulated the respected topics through a binding set of detailed rules. Thereby, they governed the states' mutual relations to depth so far unknown. In the early years of this development, the treaties primarily concerned free trade, the abolishment of import duties, the mutual award of most-favored-nation clauses, and free navigation. However, they became broader over time and soon concerned other fields of the contracting parties' relations as well. The consequence of this development was a gradual juridification of international relations. Through this stepwise conclusion of a growing number of, as well as thematically increasingly broader, bi-lateral treaties, a network of such agreements was established among states.

The juridification of international relations can best be described as an ongoing process which took place over most the 19th century, but which reached its peak only in the second half. The creation of the first international governmental organizations serves as another telling example in this regard. The very first organization of that type was the *Central Commission for the Navigation of the Rhine*. Several European states agreed on its creation at the *Congress of*

189 Arthur Nussbaum, *Geschichte des Völkerrechts* (n 119 in Chapter 2) 226 et seq.

Vienna (1815), but it was only brought into existence in 1832.[190] In the subsequent years, a number of organizations dealing with a wide range of different topics were also founded, such as the *Superior Council of Health* in 1838 (which was established to avert the spread of cholera from Asia to Europe),[191] the *International Telegraph Union* in 1865, and the *Universal Postal Union* in 1874. These organizations were established to provide the states with multi-lateral fora for co-operation in questions of common concern. Hence, they were designed as international administrative unions, and had the purpose to create legal frameworks for, and to regulate the common handling of, specific cross-border topics of international importance. As mentioned above, states were generally very reluctant to limit, or even to transfer, parts of their sovereignty rights during the 19th century. By entering into international unions, however, they had to subordinate themselves to binding legal rules, which naturally limited their freedom of action. The fact that they, nevertheless, took this step, cannot only be reasoned with the simple necessity of having to do so because of practical considerations and necessities (due to the on-going globalization).[192] But this change of mind can also be traced back to the emergence of a general tendency among states in the second half of the 19th century of attaching more importance to international law. Both the conclusion of numerous bi-lateral agreements, and the creation of international administrative unions, were, therefore, expressions of the on-going juridification of international relations at that time.

Another factor, which must be taken into consideration in the context of the *Universal Postal Union,* is the following: the founding treaty of this organization provided for a, so far, unique characteristic, which constituted a major difference to other international organizations and treaties from that time. Article 16 of this agreement, the *Treaty of Bern* (1874), stipulated that, in the case of the emergence of a "[...] disagreement between two or more members of the Union as to the interpretation of the present treaty, the question in

190 Bob Reinalda, *Routledge History of International Organizations* (n 59 in Chapter 2) 28. Also: Leo J. Bouchez, 'The Netherlands and the Law of International Rivers' in H.F. van Panhuys, W.P. Heere, J.W. Josephus Jitta, Ko Swan Sik, and A.M. Stuyt (eds.), *International Law in the Netherlands*, vol. 1 (Sitjhoff & Noordhoff 1978) 253. J.H.W. Verzijl, *International Law in Historical Perspective, Part III – State Territory* (A.W. Sijthoff 1970) 131 et seq.

191 Ramses A. Wessel, 'Towards a United Europe? A Legal Perspective on European Institutionalization and Integration' in Jaap de Wilde and Hakan Wilberg (eds.), *Organized Anarchy in Europe: The Role of States and Intergovernmental Organizations* (Tauris Academic Studies 1996) 45.

192 Compare: Bob Reinalda, *Routledge History of International Organizations* (n 59 in Chapter 2) 86–89.

dispute shall be decided by arbitration."[193] Hence, the treaty contained a special obligatory arbitration clause according to which the adhering states had to refer their mutual conflicts to arbitration, if they concerned the *Treaty of Bern*. The implementation of this provision was a remarkable development. As mentioned above, European countries had not yet concluded any kind of obligatory arbitration agreement in their mutual relations. However, all founding members of the *Universal Post Union* stemmed from Europe (with the sole exception of the United States). Therefore, this agreement provided for the first (special) obligatory arbitration commitment in inter-European relations, and it took only until 1880 that a second one followed in form of special obligatory arbitration treaty between Italy and Romania.[194]

With the conclusion of the *Treaty of Bern* and the Italian-Romanian agreement, the ice was finally broken, and the way was paved for obligatory arbitration in inter-European relations. This becomes evident due to the fact that another 20 bi-lateral special obligatory arbitration treaties were concluded between European states in the subsequent years (between 1880 and 1899). These numbers account for a frequency of slightly more than one conclusion of special obligatory arbitration treaties per year (1.05 treaties/year), and they constituted a remarkable increase in comparison to the years before (during which, none of the agreements concluded in inter-European relations were of this kind). Furthermore, the number of conclusions of obligatory arbitration treaties between 1871 and 1899 not only increased in the inter-European context but also on a global level. The data from Table 3.2 show that 42 general obligatory arbitration treaties and 49 special obligatory ones were concluded globally during these years. These numbers account for an increase of the frequency of conclusions of general obligatory arbitration treaties by the factor 1.17, when compared with the previous period. In comparison, 1.24 agreements of that kind had been concluded per year between 1854 and 1870, whereas the frequency rose to 1.45 treaties per year between 1871 and 1899. In the context of special obligatory arbitration treaties, a more drastic increase took place. The frequency of conclusions of such agreements rose by the factor 5.83. 1.69 special obligatory arbitration agreements were concluded per year; in comparison to 0.29 treaties per year between 1854 and 1870. In this regard, it is even more striking to note that the share of inter-European agreements (in the total amount of conclusions of such agreements) rose from 0% to 43%, which

193 *Treaty Concerning the Formation of a General Postal Union*, concluded on October 9, 1874, <http://avalon.law.yale.edu/19th_century/usmu010.asp> accessed August 3, 2016.

194 *Consular and Establishment and Extradition Conventions between Italy and Romania, signed at Bucharest, 5 August 1880*, available online: Oxford Historical Treaties.

equals 21 out of the 49 special obligatory arbitration treaties concluded worldwide at that time. This data shows that the frequency of conclusions of special obligatory arbitration treaties increased significantly between 1871 and 1899. In particular, European countries now had a great share in this development since they did not only enter into such agreements in their relations to Latin American or other non-European countries any longer. But, from the 1880s onwards, they did so in the inter-European context as well.

At first glance, it appears as if the European countries had finally overcome their reluctance to obligatory arbitration in their mutual relations. However, a closer look at these numbers reveals that only certain states – namely (mostly) smaller European states, Italy, and Great Britain – followed this trend. They continued to pursue their positive approach towards obligatory arbitration from the earlier period[195] and concluded a substantial number of bi-lateral inter-European obligatory arbitration treaties between 1871 and 1899.[196] Other European (great) powers, on the other hand, maintained their reluctant attitude towards obligatory arbitration in inter-European relations, as well as obligatory arbitration in general. This becomes apparent by taking into account the figures regarding the conclusions of obligatory arbitration treaties in European/American relations, as well as between European and non-European countries during the same period. Between 1871 and 1899, European states concluded 12 special obligatory arbitration agreements with American or other non-European countries. Italy participated in 7 of them, Great Britain in 3, and Norway (respectively: Norway/Sweden) in 2. A similar development also took place in the context of general obligatory arbitration treaties – although only one of the 42 agreements of that type which came into force between 1871 and 1899 was an inter-European one (namely a treaty between Portugal and the Netherlands from 1894).[197] Regarding the 14 general obligatory arbitration treaties which were concluded between European and American (or with other non-European) states during these years, however, it can be noticed that smaller European states participated in 13 out of these 14 treaties (Spain: 5 treaties, Switzerland: 4 treaties, and Belgium: 4 treaties). France was the only

195 Compare pages 83–84 of the present book.

196 Italy participated in 10 (out of 21) special obligatory arbitration treaties during these years. Belgium was involved in 5 of them, Greece in 4, Spain, Norway, and Switzerland in 3 (each), Romania, Montenegro, Great Britain and Portugal in 2 (each), and Sweden and Denmark in 1 (each).

197 *Convention between the Netherlands and Portugal relative to Commerce, Navigation, Boundaries and Mutual Rights of Pre-emption in the Timor and Solor Archipelago*, signed at Lisbon, June 10, 1893; available in: Heike Krieger (ed.), *East Timor and the International Community: Basic Documents* (Cambridge University Press 1997) 2–3.

great power following this trend too. Therefore, there was no general trend among the European countries towards obligatory arbitration just yet. Only a group of smaller European states, Italy, and Great Britain (as well as France in one case) to have changed their minds regarding obligatory arbitration, while the other European states – and especially the conservative great powers (Russia, Austria-Hungary, and Germany) – did not follow this trend. They abstained from concluding any special obligatory arbitration treaty (apart from the mentioned *Treaty of Bern*) before 1899.

Apart from this trend, two more remarkable developments took place regarding arbitration during this period. Firstly, European states referred a quickly growing number of cases to isolated arbitration. Secondly, the concept of arbitration changed substantially. Coming first to the increased use of isolated arbitration, Table 3.1 shows that 139 cases were settled by this instrument between 1871 and 1899. These numbers account for an increase by the factor 1.89 in comparison to the earlier period, and for a frequency of 4.79 settlements of conflicts by isolated arbitration per year. Thereby, isolated arbitration developed – at the latest during these years – into a widely accepted, regularly invoked, and common phenomenon in international relations. This also becomes apparent by taking a closer look at the role of the United States and Great Britain when it comes to their use of isolated arbitration. These two nations had participated in most arbitrations during the two previous periods. However, the situation changed after 1871. Great Britain remained the country, which referred more cases to arbitration than any other European nation. But a growing number of states – and among them also several great powers – now began to act likewise. For example, France participated in 21 cases of arbitration while Germany and Italy were each involved in 10 arbitral settlements in this period. Therefore, Italy not only held a pioneering role with regards to obligatory arbitration but the country was also among the nations, which took regular recourse to isolated arbitration. Furthermore, out of the 22 European countries existing during these days,[198] 17 of them participated, at least once, in an isolated arbitration between 1871 and 1899. All the five great powers were among them as well. A similar observation can also be made with regards to the global level. 41 out of the 50 states (existing worldwide in 1900)[199] invoked arbitration, at least once, during these years. This accounts for a share of 82% of all independent countries, including all of the most powerful nations. Countries abstaining from participating in this trend were mostly rather small nations or microstates, such as Lichtenstein, Luxembourg, or San Marino.

---

198 According to: Egbert Jahn, Politische Streitfragen, Band 4: Weltpolitische Herausforderungen (Springer VS 2015) 13–31.

199 Ibid.

Turning the view now to the second topic mentioned above, the important conceptual change. Before 1870, the *traditional* understanding of arbitration had widely prevailed. But with the rise of legal positivism in state practice in the second half of the 19th century and the growing importance, which was attached to international law, as well as the juridification of international relations, the approach towards arbitration was adapted in line with these changes. These conceptual modifications concerned, first and foremost, the understanding of the role of arbitration and its application for the settlement of certain types of cases. During the first half of the 19th century, *traditional* arbitration had been regarded as applicable to all kinds of conflicts, regardless of whether they were of a political or judicial nature.[200] Although arbitration was considered as a (quasi-)judicial instrument in these days, arbitral awards were seldom taken in accordance with legal rules.[201] Instead, arbitrations had usually been decided on the basis of equity, and by compromising the interests of the parties involved. However, this understanding of arbitration changed (gradually) during the second half of the 19th century. Apart from the above-named reasons, these changes were also driven by the on-going globalization process, and the intensification of international trade. These factors resulted in closer international relations and, consequently, also in more sources for potential conflicts. Some of these conflicts fell in what states considered to be their exclusive sphere of sovereignty, which they wanted no other nation to interfere with.[202] The great powers, in particular, were hardly ever willing to subject (the full range of) their international affairs to legal regulations, or to accept limitations of their freedom to act in foreign affairs. Hence, obligatory arbitration treaties often provided for exception clauses, which excluded conflicts from their scope that bore the potential of affecting the parties' vital interests, honor, sovereignty, or other crucial aspects.[203] The great powers insisted on this practice, regarding conflicts of major political importance, because they considered them as non-judiciable but purely political matters.[204] Even the

200 Otfried Nippold, *Die Fortbildung des Verfahrens in völkerrechtlichen Streitigkeiten* (n 55 in Chapter 3) 171. Compare also pages 38 et seq. of the present book.

201 Hans Wehberg, *The Problem of an International Court of Justice* (n 123 in Chapter 2) 16 et seq.

202 David Dudley Field, *Outline of an International Code*, vol. 1 (Baker 1872) 9.

203 Hans Wehberg, 'Restrictive Clauses in International Arbitration Treaties' (1913) 7 The American Journal of International Law p. 310.

204 Thomas Balch, *International Courts of Arbitration* (Allen, Lane, and Scott 1912; first published 1874), 29. He stated the following: "In cases where the real object of a war is to determine the relative strength of two nations, and where an unquestioned supremacy is to be the prize of victory, it is clear that arbitration is hopeless [...]."

prominent *Alabama-Settlement* could not change the mind of these states in this regard.[205]

Nevertheless, a crucial conceptual change of arbitration took place during this time, a change which soon manifested in the composition of many obligatory arbitration treaties. Since the 1870s, the scope of these agreements was considerably narrowed and became more limited by the introduction of clauses, which provided that only conflicts of a judicial nature were to fall within the scope of the obligatory arbitration commitment.[206] Several international scholars supported this step and argued accordingly that arbitration was only suitable for the settlement of judicial conflicts, whereas political ones had to remain subjects of the states' exclusive and non-restrictable sphere of sovereignty.[207] This notion soon became dominant in legal scholarship,[208] although certain dissenting views existed as well.[209] But most scholars, at that time, rejected the extension of the scope of arbitration beyond purely judicial disputes.[210] Thus, they regarded crucial aspects of foreign affairs as political and, consequently, non-arbitrable. Emanuel Ullmann (*'Völkerrecht'* from 1908), for example, described this approach as follows:

> Conflicts between states arise because of collisions of interests; but these collisions are often the result of traditional and, so far, latent differences between the concerned peoples, which now emerge because of the execution of the sovereign rights of the states. [...] as a last consequence it is the enforcement of the personality of the state as a factor of

205 John Westlake, *International Law – Part 1: Peace* (n 124 in Chapter 2) 359.

206 According to J.H.W. Verzijl, *International Law in Historical Perspective, Part VIII* (n 123 in Chapter 2) 86.

207 Compare, e.g.: Friedrich Adolf Trendelenburg, *Lücken im Völkerrecht: Betrachtungen und Vorschläge aus dem Jahre 1870* (Hirzel 1870) 21. Also: Dr. Goldschmidt, 'Ein Reglement für internationale Schiedsgerichte' (1875) 2 Zeitschrift für das Privat- und Öffentliche Recht der Gegenwart 716. John Westlake, *International Law – Part 1: Peace* (n 124 in Chapter 2) 357.

208 Otfried Nippold, *Die Fortbildung des Verfahrens in völkerrechtlichen Streitigkeiten* (n 55 in Chapter 3) 168–178. There, he provided a detailed overview on these pages on the existing literature concerning this topics.

209 Compare, e.g.: William W. Thayer, 'International Arbitration of Justiciable Disputes' (1913) 26 Harvard Law Review 424. Thomas Baty, *International Law* (John Murray 1909) 2. Heinrich Lammasch, *Die Lehre von der Schiedsgerichtsbarkeit in ihrem ganzen Umfange* (n 107 in Chapter 2) 62. Also: J.H.W. Verzijl, International Law in Historical Perspective, Part VIII (n 123 in Chapter 2) 7–8. Paul S. Reinsch, 'The Concept of Legality in International Arbitration' (1911) 5 The American Journal of International Law 604–614.

210 Otfried Nippold, *Die Fortbildung des Verfahrens in völkerrechtlichen Streitigkeiten* (n 55 in Chapter 3) 171 et seq.

> pure power within the international community of states. In the case of such conflicts of interests, legal and moral considerations have to stand back; those are factual actions, which cannot be subjected to judicial review.[211]

Scholars of international law were hesitant to extend the scope of arbitration to all aspects of state actions, but preferred to restrict it to non-political (and, therefore, non-vital) ones. At the same time, they accepted the need to establish new international rules and procedures for the organization, and regulation, of the on-going globalization, steadily increasing international trade relations, and the phenomenon of intensifying interconnections and cross-border linkages between their societies. The enormously growing number of potential points of contacts between states made it necessary to establish legal regimes, and normative frameworks, to regulate them and to be able to handle them effectively. Furthermore, states accepted arbitration as an integral part of international relations over the course of the second half of the 19th century. The frequency at which they invoked isolated arbitration to settle their mutual conflicts rose steadily, even though they continued to refer to arbitration in most cases for the settlement of questions of minor importance.

5.3 *The Peace Movement's Plans for the Future*

For the members of the peace movement, these developments were, after all, remarkable successes. They considered them as crucial steps in the right direction, towards the fulfillment of their dream of substituting war with obligatory arbitration. Although states now accepted arbitration as a viable option for the settlement of, at least minor, conflicts, it still remained a long way to go until the establishment of purely judicial and arbitral obligatory modes of conflict settlement on the international level. Instead of attempting to achieve this goal by only demanding the creation of a close network of bi-lateral arbitration treaties, peace activists often pursued other plans for the reduction – and the prohibition – of the use of force under international law too. To replace it by a structured mode of conflict settlement, they also made the following two proposals.

First, they proposed the establishment of an international court of arbitration. As mentioned above, the concept was not entirely new. Philosophers, thinkers, and advocates of peace were already dealing with this idea for centuries. Furthermore, it was an integral (even though secondary) part of the agenda

211 Analogously translated by the author of the present book from: Emanuel Ullmann, *Völkerrecht* (J.C.B. Mohr 1908) 430.

of the U.S.-American peace movement since the 1830s. But the idea to create an international court of arbitration had, so far, always been part of concepts for world organizations. This approach posed the problem that its realization would have required the complete re-structuring of the international order. Because most peace activists considered this plan as too utopian to be realized in the prevailing situation, they placed the idea to one side. Nevertheless, they never stopped working on the concept for an international court of arbitration. Until the 1880s, most of those who dealt with this idea continued to think of an international court of arbitration only in form of an organ of a world organization;[212] for example, Émile de Laveleye from 1873,[213] J. de Strada[214] or J.M. de la Codre.[215] Other scholars, however, such as David Dudley Field (1804–1894), a U.S.-American international lawyer who called for the creation of a *High Tribunal of Arbitration* in 1872,[216] or Leone Levi (1821–1888), an English jurist who promoted the establishment of a *Permanent Council of International Arbitration* in 1904,[217] thought in another direction. Their concepts did not differ much from earlier proposals for international courts of arbitration but in one crucial point: they aimed now for the creation of an autonomous international court. Hence, since the 1870s, (first) proposals were made, which did not longer perceive it as only an organ of a potential world organization. Instead, they wanted the court to be a completely independent and truly autonomous institution. Thereby, these authors set out on a new – and more realistic – path. The introduction of an autonomous tribunal would have still been a highly progressive development. But it was decisively more realistic and feasible.[218] Hence, it did not take long until the approach towards the creation of an independent international court of arbitration found growing support

---

212 The quote stems from: Warren F. Kuehl, *Seeking World Order* (n 16 in Chapter 3) 33.

213 Émile de la Laveleye, *Des Causes Actuelles de Guerre in Europe et de l'Arbitrage* (C. Muquardt 1873) 206. There he presented his ideas concerning the establishment of an international court: "1° Nommer une conférence composée de délégués des différents pays – juristes et diplomates – afin de fixer les principes du droit des gens aujourd'hui contestés. 2° Décider qu'en cas de dissentiment sur l'application de ces principes, on s'en référera à la décision d'une haute cour composée des juristes représentant les parties contractantes."

214 J. de Strada, *L'Europe sauvée, et la Fédération* (A. Le Chevalier 1868).

215 J.M. de la Codre, *L'Opinion Publique et l'Extinction de la Guerre* (Dentu 1867). See also: Jacob ter Meulen, *Der Gedanke der Internationalen Organisation in seiner Entwicklung*, vol. 2.1 (n 76 in Chapter 3) pp. 335–337.

216 David Dudley Field, *Outline of an International Code*, vol. 1 (n 202 in Chapter 3) 370–373.

217 Leoni Levi, 'Draft Project of a Council and High Court of International Arbitration,' reprinted in: William Evans Darby, *International Arbitration; International Tribunals* (n 30 in Chapter 3) 216 et seq.

218 Compare: Warren F. Kuehl, *Seeking World Order* (n 16 in Chapter 3) 33.

among peace activists and international lawyers. In addition, states showed (as demonstrated above) a considerably more favorable, and benevolent, attitude towards arbitration in general (and towards obligatory arbitration as well) in this period. Therefore, the time must have seemed right to the proponents of this approach to call for the next step. Even if states were not completely ready to take it, the introduction of concepts for an independent international court of arbitration into public discussion bore the potential of attracting the attention of government officials, parliamentarians, politicians, and also of the general public. By raising awareness for their idea, the peace movement, and international lawyers, hoped to familiarize the latter with the concept, and to initiate a development, which would result in the realization of this concept in the long run.

Second, a less realistic and considerably more progressive concept was discussed at the same time by authors such as Frederic Seebohm, Guillaume Pays, James Lorimer, and Patrice Larroque.[219] They all advocated for the introduction of the rule of law in international relations.[220] For example, Seebohm (*'On International Reform'* from 1871) called for

> [...] the establishment of, not necessarily of any fixed judicial tribunal, but of some kind of really judicial international machinery for interpreting international law, for giving such an impartial and authoritative decision of what is the law as it should be stain upon a nation's honor either to sue for or obey.[221]

On numerous points, his ideas resembled the above-mentioned plans for world organizations, as he also proposed the creation of such an institution.[222] But, unlike other authors, he aimed for the establishment of an international judiciary,[223] which took decisions exclusively on the basis of law, instead of referring this task to an arbitral institution. According to Seebohm, this concept did

219 Compare: James L. Tryon, 'Proposals for an International Court' (n 142 in Chapter 2) 415–436.

220 Surprisingly, none of these authors referred directly to Ladd and his writings. Compare in this regard: James Truslow Adams, *The History of New England*, vol. 3 (Little, Brown 1927) 376. According to him Ladd's "[...] name is probably unknown to all but a few specialists [...although...] few men in the New England of his day have had a more lasting influence throughout the whole world."

221 Frederic Seebohm, *On International Reform* (Longmans, Green and Co. 1871) 122–123.

222 Compare pages 54 et seq. of the present book. Also: Leonid Kamarowsky, 'De l'idée d'un tribunal international' (1883) 15 Revue de Droit International et de Législation Comparée 45.

223 Frederic Seebohm, *On International Reform* (n 221 in Chapter 3) 122–123.

not have to be realized in form of a permanent international tribunal; in fact, he remained rather silent regarding the potential structure and shape of the projected judiciary. He also did something else that was quite remarkable, as he distinguished, very clearly, between arbitration and adjudication and demanded that the proposed system for conflict settlement was to be exclusively based on the latter. According to him, the international system required a purely judicial mechanism, which was capable and competent to interpret international law impartially and authoritatively – which basically means: in accordance with the rule of law. Several scholars shared his ideas and developed them further in the upcoming years.[224] They drew up elaborate concepts for the creation of institutionalized judicial tribunals, capable of enforcing the rule of law on the international level. Furthermore, these scholars also combined this concept with the above-mentioned approach, which envisioned international courts of arbitration as independent institutions. Accordingly, they proposed to create an international court of law, outside the framework of a world organization, but in the form of an autonomous body. For them, such a judicial institution would have been perfectly capable of guaranteeing peace through law in international affairs, thus, replacing war with law. James L. Tryon (*'Proposals for an International Court'* from 1914) stated the following in this regard:

> [...] the value of an international court is [...] that a nation would not be justified by public opinion in going to war if there were an impartial tribunal to judge its case [... and ...] that many disputes would be quashed at the outset if the parties knew that the point disputed was likely to become subject of an impartial investigation by able judges.[225]

Another scholar, James B. Miles (*'Le Tribunal International'* from 1874), also suggested the creation of an independent international tribunal that "[...] doit avoir un caractère essentiellement juridique."[226] Unlike most of the

---

224 Jacob ter Meulen named in this regard, e.g., James Lorimer, a British lawyer, and Leonid Kamarowsky, a Russian scholar. Compare: Jacob ter Meulen, *Der Gedanke der Internationalen Organisation in seiner Entwicklung*, vol. 2.2 (M. Nijhoff 1940) 181 et seq., 212–213. See also: Leonid Kamarowsky, *Le Tribunal International* (A. Durand et Pedone-Lauriel 1887) 503 et seq. Johann Caspar Bluntschli, *Gesammelte kleine Schriften*, vol. 2 (C.H. Beck 1881) 292 et seq.

225 James L. Tryon, 'Proposals for an International Court' (n 142 in Chapter 2) 421.

226 James B. Miles, *Le Tribunal International* (Debons et Ce 1874) 7. Analogously translated by the author of the present book: "[...] that should have an essentially judicial character."

other scholars and peace activists from these years, Seebohm, Miles, and like-minded international lawyers regarded arbitration and adjudication as two decisively different concepts. For example, Seebohm expressed the following in this regard:

> What is really required is, not the decision of an *umpire* but the decision of a *judge* – not the decision of arbitrators, one chosen by each of the disputants, with a special view to the particular dispute, and therefore liable to some extent to the suspicion of being more or less partial, but a decision, given under the authority of the whole society of nations, deciding *what is law* without reference to who may be the disputants; – a decision which shall be binding upon other nations in like cases as well as upon the disputants, and which must, to a large extent, be placed by that very fact beyond suspicion of favoring either party.[227]

These progressive scholars preferred judicial settlement over arbitration because of its impartiality and compliance with the rule of law, while they claimed that arbitration based on equity and arbitrariness. Thereby, the concept of purely judicial settlement of conflicts developed from a utopian long-term, secondary, goal of the peace movement (which it used to be during the time following William Ladd's presidency of the *American Peace Society*) into a well determined and elaborate concept (during the later parts of the 19th century), which was a seriously discussed scheme in international legal scholarship. Hence, adjudication found its way into international legal scholarship during this time, raising awareness among a quickly growing number of international lawyers and peace activists.

Despite the success of adjudication, arbitration still remained the most prominent and renowned principle for conflict settlement in international legal scholarship. The number of advocates for adjudication was comparably small, which was also the case because the idea to create an international court of law was far more utopian than the one concerning the institutionalization of arbitration in a comparable institution. This was the case because arbitration had (already) developed in the second half of the 19th century into a widely accepted principle of conflict settlement, while adjudicative procedures remained a purely theoretical concept so far. This arrangement resulted into a situation, around the turn of the century, in which supporters of adjudication already distinguished between the concepts of arbitration and adjudication, while most of the less progressive scholars did not do. The latter continued to uphold their rather vague and imprecise understanding of arbitration, which

227 Frederic Seebohm, *On International Reform* (n 221 in Chapter 3) 123.

was, many a time, a mixture of rather modern considerations, *traditional* conceptions, and sometimes even of adjudicative elements. For example, at the *Fifth Universal Peace Congress* held on August 1893 in Chicago, arbitration was referred to in many different ways. On one occasion, it was defined as a voluntary instrument through which international controversies were settled "[...] according to just and equitable principles" and "[...] on economic as well as on moral grounds."[228] While in another address, delivered by William Allen Butler, Dorman B. Eaton, and Cephas Brainerd under the title *'International Court of Arbitration,'* the following was postulated: "[...] any successful and adequate method of establishing a permanent Court of Arbitration of an international character must be the result of special treaty stipulations between nations willing to adopt such a judicial method of settling their disputes."[229] These three authors also referred to the idea to create a court of arbitration. They wanted it to be "[...] constituted and organized as to form an International Court of supreme and final jurisdiction";[230] whereby they mixed adjudicative and arbitral terminology as well. A similar approach was taken by Belva A. Lockwood who declared at the very same conference that "[t]he question of an International Arbitration Court, by which all difficulties between nations may be settled judicially, without recourse to arms, has absorbed the attention of the most learned jurists of our time."[231] Hence, it is difficult to clearly determine what was precisely meant by the participants of this congress when they referred to arbitration or judicial procedures, especially because the event was attended by both supporters of arbitration and adjudication. One of the advocates of judicial procedures, C.C. Bonney, for example, proposed "[...] the establishment of a permanent International Court of Justice to declare the law and the right [...]" because

> [a]s in private life, the courts of justice have actually and successfully taken the place of personal conflict, as in the American Republic, the supreme court of the nation has for more than a century successfully decided controversies between powerful States, so we believe it to be

228 Both quotes stem from: 'Preliminary Address of the Committee of Arrangements of the World's Congress Auxiliary on a Congress of Arbitration and Peace' (1893) 55 American Advocate of Peace 75.

229 American Peace Society, *Official report of the Fifth Universal Peace Congress held at Chicago, United States of America, August 14 to 20, 1893, under the auspices of the World's congress auxiliary of the World's Columbian exposition* (American Peace Society 1893) 161.

230 Ibid.

231 Ibid 172.

> entirely practical for civilized nations to establish an International Court of Justice for the determination of differences between them.[232]

Similar observations regarding the vagueness and indistinctiveness of the participants' conceptual approaches towards arbitration (and adjudication) can also be made in the context of the *First Lake Mohonk Conference on International Arbitration* from 1895. Benjamin F. Trueblood proposed at this event the establishment of a "[…] great international tribunal of arbitration, which shall be to the nations of the world what the United States Supreme Court is to the States of the Union."[233] Although Trueblood seems to have intended to advocate for the creation of an international court of law, his terminology still remained ambitious and inconclusive (by referring to the proposed institution as a 'tribunal of arbitration'). His colleague Austin Abbott, on the other hand, chose plainer words. He demanded that all future conflicts were to be settled in accordance with "[…] what is right" and by "[…] judicial reason and judicial power."[234] To achieve this goal, he suggested to "[…] carry out the same system between civilized nations"[235] as between individuals; a clear reference to adjudication. Finally, Edward Everett Hale referred to the remarkable success of the U.S. Supreme Court by stressing that "[…] in one hundred and five years there have been thirty or forty conflicts between States in the American Union which, under any other circumstances, would have been adjusted by shock of arms."[236] But, all of these disputes had been peacefully settled by the court; a fact which, according to Hale, took Europeans "[…] entirely by surprise."[237] Hale argued that steps should be taken in order to transfer the experience made with the U.S. Supreme Court to the international level by creating an international court, shaped in accordance with the example of the U.S. Supreme Court, consisting of twelve judges, and ruling on the sole base of international law.[238] Each of the six great powers would have the right to appoint one "[…] jurist of the highest rank in jurisprudence,"[239] the other six judges were to be named by smaller countries. Furthermore, the judges were supposed to sit so long as their health permits, or until they asked

232 Ibid 10, 24–25, 71 (with a direct reference to the work of William Ladd), 166–167.

233 Martha D. Adams, *Report of the First Annual Meeting of the Lake Mohonk Conference on International Arbitration in 1895* (The Lake Mohonk Arbitration Conference 1895) 9.

234 Both quotes stem from: ibid 12.

235 Ibid.

236 Ibid 22.

237 Ibid.

238 Ibid 23–25.

239 Ibid 24.

for retirement. By introducing the latter rule, he aimed for guaranteeing the impartiality of the judges, another characteristic of a court of law.

To conclude the above-said: around the turn of the century, arbitration and adjudication were still continuously inter-mixed and there did not exist a clear and established terminology yet, neither within the peace movement, nor among international lawyers. As a result, the discussions on the cause of peace were in a phase of transition, with many new ideas emerging. Due to the peace activists' growing political and social influence, these ideas soon made their way into the discussions on the inter-governmental level too.

6 Conclusion

The world achieved a level of globalization during the second half of the 19th century, which turned bi-lateral relations into increasingly more complex and challenging matters. Distances shrined due to technological innovations. Greater markets developed, and global trade became an essential element for the states' economies. Therefore, countries were more significantly interconnected, on the governmental level just as much as on the economic, financial, political, and social level. Due to the increased points of contact – and consequently, points of potential conflicts – more and more states turned towards arbitration in order to settle (mostly minor) mutual conflicts on this way. By doing so, isolated arbitration developed into a common, integral, and regularly used instrument in international relations. Additionally, a growing number of states also began to conclude bi- and multi-lateral obligatory arbitration commitments; and, by the later parts of the 19th century, they even started doing so in inter-European relations. Therefore, by the end of the century (obligatory as well as isolated), arbitration was considered to be of significantly more importance than ever before.

The peace movement (which arose during the early 19th century) welcomed these developments. It considered them to be the first steps towards the implementation of a system based on the principle of *peace through law*; by which its members meant: a system under which (obligatory) arbitration, respectively adjudication, replaced war and banned it from international law. However, despite the already made progress during these years, peace activists, and international lawyers, did not rest and were not yet satisfied with what they had achieved so far. They held multiple congresses, organized themselves internationally in numerous organizations, and continuously developed their ideas further.

Among the most prominent concepts discussed in this context were the calls for the establishment of an autonomous international court of arbitration, or in few cases, also for an autonomous international court of law, and the demand for the introduction of the rule of law in international relations. These topics set the framework for the upcoming discussions on the inter-state level, which were about to take place between 1899 and 1914. So far – before 1899 – they were primarily dealt with by peace activists, in international legal scholarships, and in the above-mentioned non-governmental private organizations which were dedicated to the furtherance of peace and international law. Therefore, they remained as theoretical concepts at that time. From 1899 onwards, however, they managed to make their way into the discussions between states on multi-lateral conferences and, thereby, lost their primarily theoretical character.

CHAPTER 4

The Situation in Latin America

> After fifteen years of sacrifices devoted to the liberty of America to secure a system of guaranties that in peace and war shall be the shield of our new destiny, it is time the interests and relations uniting the American Republics, formerly Spanish colonies, should have a fundamental basis that shall perpetuate, if possible, those Governments.[1]
>
> SIMÓN BOLÍVAR, *December 7, 1824*

∴

1 Historical Outset

At the turn of the 18th century, the whole of Latin America was still under the colonial control of Spain and Portugal, and, to a smaller extent, a few other European countries. Portugal ruled over the territories that were to become Brazil, and Spain did so for most of the rest of Central and South America. The Spanish colonial Empire consisted of four viceroyalties (New Spain, Peru, New Granada, and Río de la Plata), which were spread over a territory around twice the size of Europe.[2] The political power in these regions was in the hands of the Spanish colonial administrators and the Creole elites, who owned most of the agricultural land and wealth.[3] At the end of the 18th century, a simultaneous development took place in all four viceroyalties, which fundamentally altered the prevailing situation. Great shares of the Creole elites were influenced by the *Enlightenment* and were stirred up by the French and U.S.-

1 'Circular Invitation addressed by Simón Bolívar to the Governments of Colombia, Mexico, Central America, The United Provinces of Buenos Aires, Chile, and Brazil,' available in: James Brown Scott (ed.), *The International Conferences of American States 1889–1928* (Carnegie Endowment for International Peace 1931) XIX.

2 George Pendle, *A History of Latin America* (Penguin Books 1963) 51.

3 Gerhard Mauser, 'Der Vergessene Kontinent: Lateinamerika zwischen Diktatur und Demokratie' (1959) 7 Vierteljahreshefte für Zeitgeschichte 25.

 | DOI:10.1163/9789004754126_005

American revolutions.[4] In conjunction with an upcoming sense of Spanish-American nationalism,[5] an increasing dissatisfaction with the subordination to Spain, and a growing desire for independence,[6] a revolutionary spirit arose all over Spanish-America.[7] When Napoleon Bonaparte attacked Spain and launched the *Peninsular War* (1807–1814), it must have seemed to the Spanish-American Creoles that independence was finally within reach. Spain was busy defending themselves against France, wherefore many of their forces were bound in Europe. Hence, revolutionary movements began to oppose the Spanish colonial rule in all four viceroyalties from 1810 onwards. However, despite initial successes, it would take until 1824/25 that the revolutionary forces around José San Martin (1778–1850), Simón Bolívar (1773–1830), Antonio José de Sucre (1795–1830), and Francisco de Paula Santander (1792–1840)[8] could deal fatal blows against the Spanish royalists, driving them out of Latin America, and deciding the war in their favor. In the end, these victories allowed the former Spanish colonies to accomplish independence. Because of the long distances between their regional centers, and because of their individual regional personalities, the four viceroyalties then split into seven separate states:[9] Mexico, the United Provinces of Central America, Colombia, Peru, Chile, Paraguay, and the Provinces of the Río de la Plata.[10] Not long after, around 1830, Ecuador and Venezuela seceded from Colombia, and, as a result, the number of Spanish-American states grew to nine.

Despite the victory against Spain, peace did not come easily for most Spanish American countries, neither internally nor internationally. The long years of the war for independence had undermined the stability in the region and had caused serious economic problems in most of the new republics.[11] Former

---

4 Simon Collier, 'Nationality, Nationalism, and Supranationalism in the Writings of Simón Bolívar' (1983) 63 The Hispanic American Historical Review 38.

5 Lynn V. Foster, *A Brief History of Central America* (Facts on File Inc. 2007) 129. Also: John Lynch, *The Spanish American Revolutions 1808–1826* (Weidenfeld and Nicolson 1973) 24–36.

6 Arthur P. Whitaker, 'The Origin of the Western Hemisphere Idea' (1954), 98 Proceedings of the American Philosophical Society 324.

7 John Edwin Fagg, *Latin America: A General History* (Macmillan 1963) 303.

8 Gerhard Mauser, 'Der Vergessene Kontinent' (n 3 in Chapter 4) 25.

9 See: George Pendle, *A History of Latin America* (n 2 in Chapter 4) 84–86. Or: Marcelo G. Kohen, 'La Contribución de América Latina al Desarrollo progresivo del Derecho Internacional en Materia territorial' (2001) 17 Anuario Español de Derecho Internacional 55–77.

10 R.A. Humphreys, 'Chapter XXV: The States of Latin America' in John Patrick Tuer Bury (ed.), *The New Cambridge Modern History, vol. 10: The Zenith of European Power 1830–70* (Cambridge University Press 1960) 659.

11 Ibid.

colonial structures had vanished due to the war, and the Spanish administrators, royal agents, and colonial officers had been driven out of the continent. The newly created republics attempted to re-introduce effective administration and, thus, to re-establish social order. But their efforts failed in many cases. Political chaos, instabilities in the new systems, and civil wars were the consequences, and troubled their domestic affairs for many years.[12] This situation resulted in the emergence of countless unrests and revolutions in Spanish America (at least until the 1860s). A special case in this regard was the United Provinces of Central America. Their political situation was particularly unstable. Domestic struggles for power and influence between the church, the central government, and the regions perpetually unsettled the country. There was a civil war between 1827 and 1829, followed by a second one between 1837 and 1840. Anarchy ruled the isthmus during these years, finally leading to the disintegration of the United Provinces of Central America into five independent states in 1841: Guatemala, Nicaragua, Costa Rica, El Salvador, and Honduras.[13]

In the first decades following their independence, not only were the domestic affairs of most Spanish American countries constantly unstable and troubled, but the same could also be said for the mutual relations of the Latin American countries. Border disputes, struggles for power, and wars were common phenomena in Latin America at the time. Consequently, both internal conflicts and troubled inter-Latin American relations were two key reasons for the constant instability in Latin America, as they repeatedly threw the unstable (Spanish) American states into chaos.[14]

The main causes for the steady (re-)emergence of conflicts between the Latin American states were unresolved problems from colonial times and their growing greed for power. There did not yet exist a stable equilibrium of power among the newly established states (yet) which could have restricted their hegemonic approaches. It first had to be developed through state practice. However, doing that took a lot of time and a long series of economic and political disputes, as well as armed conflicts, which claimed tens of thousands of lives. For example, Brazil and Argentina competed for the position as the dominant regional force in Latin America, and the relationship with Chile, Peru, and Bolivia was also highly conflictual. The situation between the three last-named nations alone escalated into several wars (in the 1830s, 1840s, and

12 Ibid 667.

13 Lynn V. Foster, *A Brief History of Central America* (n 5 in Chapter 4) 136–142.

14 Alejandro Alvarez, 'Latin America and International Law' (1907) 3 The American Journal of International Law (1907) 290–292.

1870s), all of which were won by Chile. Furthermore, Chile competed with Argentina over territories in Patagonia for several years. The conflict resulted in a financially crippling armament race between the two countries.[15] These examples, which by no means constitute an exhaustive list, show that the Latin American countries used to settle most of their mutual conflicts in the 19th century by war and with the help of brute force.

In addition to that, the United States also provoked several conflicts and wars on the American continent at that time – against Great Britain because of border disputes (and other reasons)[16] and also against Latin American states. Especially, a harsh dispute between the United States and Mexico, the *Mexican-American War* (1846–1848), must be mentioned in this context. The war had its roots in Texas' separation from Mexico in 1835, and in 1846 the conflict escalated to open hostilities. Two years later (in 1848), it ended with the defeat of Mexico and in the loss of enormous parts of their territory to the United States. This development alarmed the other Latin American countries. The war was a first, but very clear, sign of the imperialistic policy of the United States towards Latin America,[17] a policy which the United States upheld for the rest of the century.

In conclusion, Latin America suffered from constant political instability, internal as well as external conflicts, and huge economic problems in the years between the accomplishment of independence (in 1825) and the 1860s. The newly founded states engaged in numerous struggles, rivalries, and, above all else, border disputes in their mutual relations, which repeatedly escalated into conflicts and even open wars. Consequently, the use of force between Latin American states was a common phenomenon of their mutual relations in this period.

2 Legal Background

Notwithstanding the numerous wars in their mutual relations, the constant, fierce competition and struggles for territory, dominance, and power, the Spanish American countries claimed, on countless occasions throughout the

---

15 Peter Birle, 'Zwischenstaatliche Konflikte in Südamerika vom 19. Jahrhundert bis heute. Ursachen, Lösungsansätze, Perspektiven' in Lothar Mark and Erich G. Fritz (eds.): *Lateinamerika im Aufbruch. Eine kritische Analyse* (Athena 2009) 128.

16 For example, the British-American War (1812–1815) or the Aroostook War (1838–1839).

17 F. Llewellyn Jones, 'The Concert of America: The New World's League of Nations' in (1925) 11 Transactions of the Grotius Society 119.

19th century, to have a special relationship between them which was based on their overwhelming spirit of solidarity and togetherness.

2.1 *An Overwhelming Spirit of Solidarity and Togetherness*

These two aspects of inter-Spanish American relations – the belligerent attitude in practice and the claim for solidarity and brotherhood – appear to contradict one another at first sight. But they both formed integral parts of the development of the Spanish American states into independent countries, of their consolidation process, and of the procedure of creating an equilibrium of power among Latin America.

The idea of the existence of a spirit of solidary and togetherness between the Spanish-American countries had already arisen at the beginning of the 19th century due to the fact that the American peoples considered their mutual relationship to have a special nature, which distinguished them from the rest of the world.[18] They regarded all American states to belong to an American system (independent from the European one).[19] This notion was based on the common experience of the American peoples that they used to be colonies of European empires in the past and (except for Brazil) had to fight long and costly wars to achieve independence,[20] which connected them with each other. However, Latin American countries and the United States seem to have drawn decisively different conclusions from these experiences. In 1823, the United States had already begun to pursue a possessive attitude towards the rest of the Western hemisphere[21] and claimed supremacy over the other

18 Gordon Connell-Smith, *The Inter-American System* (Oxford University Press 1966) 1. There, he refers also to: A. P. Whitaker, *The Western Hemisphere: its Rise and Decline* (Cornell University Press, 1954), 1.

19 However, this approach was not universally shared in all the United States. Others regarded the Latin American countries with a lot of skepticism, under the assumption of their own superiority. When the administration of President James Buchanan (1791–1868), e.g., sent William Churchwell, a former member of the House of Representatives to a special mission to Mexico in 1858, the latter characterized in his report Mexicans as degenerated and the condition of the Mexican state as pure anarchy; compare: Lars Schoultz, *Beneath the United States: A History of U.S. Policy toward Latin America* (Harvard University Press 1998) 45.

20 Gordon Connell-Smith, *The Inter-American System* (n 18 in Chapter 4) 7. See also: Arthur P. Whitaker, 'The Origin of the Western Hemisphere Idea' (n 6 in Chapter 4) 323. According to him, "[p]aradoxically, the roots of this anti-European idea lie deep in America's European past, for it grew out of the conception of America as a New World."

21 Gordon Connell-Smith, *The Inter-American System* (n 18 in Chapter 4) 3.

American states.[22] One result of this possessive and hegemonic approach of the United States was the so-called *Monroe*-Doctrine. U.S. President James Monroe (1758–1831) proclaimed it in 1823 by declaring that the United States would interfere in favor of any American state that was attacked by a European power.[23] This policy should not, however, be understood as a mere promise to protect. It also constituted a limitation of the Latin American states' freedom of action.[24] Furthermore, Latin American states were not invited to establish an American system together with the United States. Instead, the United States attempted to subject them to an order (based on inequality) which they themselves exclusively dominated.[25] Thus, cooperation among the American states was not the purpose for the United States behind this policy. They rather strove for driving out the European powers from America. Internationalism and cooperation were fostered instead in Spanish America.[26] Consequently, the

22 Ibid 2. According to Connell-Smith, Henry Clay, an U.S.-American politician, proposed the creation of a system in America "[…] of which we shall be the centre, and in which all South America will act with us."

23 The following excerpt is taken from: Elihu Root, 'The Real Monroe Doctrine' (1914) 199 The North American Review 841. According to him, Monroe declared that he considered it necessary "[…] to declare that we should consider any attempt on their [the European powers'; *added by the author of the present book*] part to extend their system to any portion of this hemisphere as dangerous to our peace and safety. With the existing colonies or dependencies of any European Power we have not interfered and shall not interfere. But with the Governments who have declared their independence and maintained it, and whose independence we have on great consideration and on just principles acknowledged, we could not view any interposition for the purpose of oppressing them, or controlling in any other manner their destiny, by any European power, in any other light than as the manifestation of an unfriendly disposition towards the United States."

24 Gordon Connell-Smith, *The Inter-American System* (n 18 in Chapter 4) 2–3. According to him "[…] the United States has always opposed attempts by Latin American governments to enter into relations with countries outside the western hemisphere which might threaten her interests."

25 Joseph Smith, *The United States and Latin America: A History of American Diplomacy, 1776–2000* (Routledge 2005) 16. See also: Henry P. de Vries, *The Law of the Americas: An Introduction to the Legal Systems of the American Republics* (Oceana Publications 1965) 16; Juan Pablo Scarfi, 'In the Name of the Americas: The Pan-American Redefinition of the Monroe Doctrine and the Emerging Language of American International Law in the Western Hemisphere, 1893–1933' (2016) 40 Diplomatic History 193.

26 Gordon Connell-Smith, *The Inter-American System* (n 18 in Chapter 4) 4. Compare also: Juan Pablo Scarfi, 'In the Name of the Americas' (n 25 in Chapter 4) 193. On this page, Scarfi describes (in accordance with: Jay Sexton, *The Monroe Doctrine: Empire and Nation in the Nineteenth-Century America* (Hill & Wang 2011) 5–8; and with: William Appleman Williams, *The Tragedy of American Diplomacy* (W.W. Norton, cop. 2009) 18–57) the Monroe Doctrine as follows: "The doctrine was anti-colonial since it set limits to Euro-

subsequent pages will mainly focus on the internationalist (and cooperativist) approach of the Spanish American countries. It will only be directed to the U.S.-American relations and interconnections with the rest of the continent when it comes to the concept of *Pan-Americanism* and its development into a prominent topic in North America in the end of the 19th century.

Pan-Americanism is an ideological concept resting on the belief in the existence of a geographic, economic, and historical order encompassing both North and South America.[27] Its supporters strove for the organization of the countries of the Western Hemisphere into an international cooperative body.[28] The first attempts in this direction took place in 1881[29] and culminated in the *First Pan-American Conference* in 1889. However, long before this, the Spanish American states began to pursue an approach for peace in their mutual relations which will be referred to in the following as *Spanish-Americanism*. Under the roof of this notion, the Spanish American states sought cooperation and – in its most far-reaching form – the establishment of an international (political) body uniting all Spanish-America.[30] These nations were, therefore, the first ones on the continent actually attempting to establish closer regional cooperation. The common experience of having defeated their colonial rulers in a bloody war appears to have played a key role in this regard.[31] Together the Spanish American states had evolved from colonies into independent states, wherefore – according to the influential Chilean international lawyer Alejandro Alvarez (*'Latin America and International Law'* from 1909) – "[i]n the struggle for freedom, the Spanish-American colonies looked upon one another as brothers and gave military aid to one another in this common cause."[32] Moreover, the Spanish American states were also closely connected to one another because they spoke the same language, were all culturally influenced by Spain, and were

pean imperialism and intervention in the Western Hemisphere. It was imperial in the sense that it was applied, especially by President James Polk in the 1940s, and an expansionist principle over the Americas and associated with the 'manifest destiny' of the United States."

27 Carlos J. Alonso, 'The Criollista Novel' in Roberto González Echevarría and Enrique Pupo-Walker (eds.), *The Cambridge History of Latin American Literature, vol. 2: The Twentieth Century* (Cambridge University Press 1996) 198.

28 David Sheinin, 'Rethinking Pan Americanism: An Introduction' in David Sheinin (ed.), *Beyond the Ideal: Pan Americanism in Inter-American Affairs* (Greenwood Press 2000) 1.

29 Carlos J. Alonso, 'The Criollista Novel' (n 27 in Chapter 4) 198. Also: David Sheinin, 'Rethinking Pan Americanism' (n 28 in Chapter 4) 1.

30 Peter Blanchard, 'Pan Americanism and Slavery in the Era of Latin American Independence' in David Sheinin (ed.), *Beyond the Ideal* (n 28 in Chapter 4) 9.

31 Ibid.

32 Alejandro Alvarez, 'Latin America and International Law' (n 14 in Chapter 4) 272.

generally in very similar situations. Therefore, they felt bond together and seem to have regarded one another as belonging to the same family of states. But the claim for the existence of solidarity and of a feeling of togetherness between these countries did not remain a solely philosophical and subliminal phenomenon. It soon resulted in actual attempts to put this notion into practice.

Símon Bolívar, the first president of Gran Colombia, took the first steps in this regard. He is often referred to as the "father of Pan-Americanism."[33] Not only because he was one of the leaders during the wars for independence but, very soon after the end of these wars, he was also the first to make serious efforts to convince the other Latin American states of establishing mechanisms for closer regional cooperation.[34] To achieve this goal, he proposed in the so-called *Jamaica Letter* (1815)[35] to unite the emerging Latin American states under the roof of a confederation. Furthermore, after 1822, Gran Colombia concluded several bi-lateral treaties under his reign with Peru, Chile, Mexico, and Central America. Through these agreements, he intended to achieve the maintenance of peace between the adhering states and to pave the way for a general alliance.[36] Additionally, he organized a multi-lateral conference in Panama in 1826, the so-called *First Congress of American States*. It was attended by representatives from Gran Colombia and the four above-named countries (Peru, Chile, Mexico, and Central America). Delegates from the United States, Bolivia, Brazil, and Argentina were also invited to attend, but they did not reach Panama in time.[37] At this occasion, the participating states discussed topics which were of an absolutely astonishing nature for this era as the participating states strove for ideological, as well as actual, revolutions at this occasion by setting up a new international system in America. Several treaties were concluded at the congress, among them the *Treaty of Perpetual Union, League, and Confederation*[38] which aimed for the creation of an American union and at the common defense of "[...] the sovereignty, independence, and territorial integrity of all and each of the Confederated Republics of Amer-

33 For example: Gordon Connell-Smith, *The Inter-American System* (n 18 in Chapter 4) 4.

34 Inter-American Institute of International Legal Studies, *The Inter-American System: Its Development and Strengthening* (Oceana Publications 1966) xv.

35 *Jamaica Letter*; <http://www.oas.org/sap/peacefund/VirtualLibrary/CongressofPanama%2FJamaicaLetter.pdf> accessed February 8, 2017.

36 Helen May Cory, *Compulsory Arbitration of International Disputes* (n 154 in Chapter 2) 5.

37 Inter-American Institute of International Legal Studies, *The Inter-American System* (n 34 in Chapter 4) xvi.

38 *Treaty of Perpetual Union, League, and Confederation*; <http://www.oas.org/sap/peacefund/VirtualLibrary/CongressofPanama/Treaties/TreatyPerpetualUnion.pdf> accessed September 26, 2016.

ica, against all foreign domination."[39] Aside from collective security mechanisms, the union was also given a very progressive political agenda. According to it, *inter alia*, the slave trade was to be prohibited, the citizens of the adhering states were to enjoy equal rights in the territory of the other adhering states, and a general assembly was supposed to be established. The last of these points is particularly interesting in the present context, as the general assembly was not only intended to function as the governing body of the union but also to contribute to the maintenance of a friendly and unalterable peace between the confederate powers.[40] This was to be achieved through the compliance of the adhering states with Article 16 of the pact, which provided that

> [...] contracting parties solemnly oblige and bind themselves to amicably compromise between themselves all differences now existing or which may arise in the future, and in case no settlement can be reached between the disagreeing powers the question shall be taken for settlement to the judgment of the assembly.[41]

War against any fellow member of the union was – according to Article 17 – only permitted after the respective dispute had been submitted to the general assembly and a decision had been issued on it.[42] Hence, the union had the objective to (1) guarantee and secure peace among its member states (*internal purpose*) and (2) to form a common front against outer aggressors (*external purpose*).[43]

There are good reasons to assume that the *internal purpose* of the union, to establish peace and security among its member states, derived from the above-mentioned claim for the existence of some kind of spirit of solidary among the Spanish American states as well as from their feeling of belonging to one family of states.[44] In Panama, the participating nations attempted to prevent all

39 Alejandro Alvarez, 'Latin America and International Law' (n 14 in Chapter 4) 277–278.

40 *Treaty of Perpetual Union, League, and Confederation. Article 13, 2nd paragraph* (n 38 in Chapter 4).

41 Article 16, ibid.

42 Article 17, ibid.

43 Simon Collier, 'Nationality, Nationalism, and Supranationalism in the Writings of Simón Bolívar' (n 4 in Chapter 4) 50–51.

44 Compare: Preamble of the *Treaty of Perpetual Union, League, and Confederation* (n 38 in Chapter 4): "The Republics of Colombia, Central America Peru, and the United States of Mexico, desiring the more firmly to bind their present intimate relations and to cement in the most solemn and stable manner those which should hereafter exist between them, which well becomes nations having a common origin, that have fought in unison to secure the benefits of liberty and independence, [...]."

future wars in their mutual relations by introducing an obligatory system of peaceful conflict settlement, to which recourse should be taken when diplomacy failed to provide suitable solutions. Thereby, they tried to ban war, at least to a great extent, from their mutual relations. The participating states would have had the obligation, under this legal regime, to refer their disputes to an assembly that was to be equipped with the competence to settle the issue. This mechanism widely equated to the concept of arbitration by state leaders. But, unlike in European relations, it was supposed to have an obligatory nature. Hence, the participating countries showed a very peace-oriented approach at the *First Congress of American States*. Thereby, they would have limited their *ius ad bellum* in cases of mutual conflicts (through a system of obligatory dispute settlement). This peaceful orientation of the union also becomes apparent in Article 2 of the treaty which determined the following:

> The object of this perpetual compact will be to maintain in common, defensively and offensively, should occasion arise, the sovereignty and independence of all and each of the confederated powers of America against foreign subjection, and to secure to themselves from this time forward the enjoyment of unalterable peace, and to promote in this behalf better harmony and good understanding as well between the countries, citizens, and subjects, respectively, as with the other powers with which they should maintain or enter into friendly relations.[45]

It becomes clear from this article that, besides striving for internal peace, the pact also had an *external purpose*. During the first decades following the accomplishment of Spanish America's independence, the European powers had posed the greatest threat to the Spanish American states, since the Europeans openly considered plans to reconquer their former colonies.[46] Therefore, the idea to create a union between the Spanish American states was not only meant to establish peace in their mutual relations but also, and probably

45 *Article* 2, ibid.

46 At the Congress of the Concert of Europe in 1818 in Aix-la-Chapelle, the conservative European great powers already seriously discussed the option of restoring the rebelling Spanish American colonies' allegiance to the Spanish crown by force. Compare, e.g.: Simon Collier, *Chile: The Making of a Public 1830–1865* (Cambridge University Press 2003) 174. Gordon S. Brown, *Latin American Rebels and the United States: 1806–1822* (McFarland et Company 2015) 147; Javier Corrales and Richard E. Feinberg, 'Regimes of Cooperation in the Western Hemisphere: Power. Interests, and Intellectual Traditions' (1999) 43 International Studies Quarterly (1999) 4.

this constituted its first and most important purpose, it was directed against the European powers and their plans to re-colonize the continent.[47]

Despite all progressive initiatives, favorable statements, and conclusions of agreements, the participating states refused, in the end, to ratify the Panama treaties and, thereby, to transfer the claimed spirit of solidarity and togetherness into a reality. Hence, the regional integration of Spanish America, the (far-reaching) limitation of war in their mutual relations, and the establishment of a common (military) front against outer enemies were not realized in Panama. Nevertheless, it should be acknowledged that the ideas and concepts which had been discussed at the *Panama Conference* were not without use. They played a key role in future developments as they prevailed in Spanish American thinking,[48] influenced inter-Spanish American policies over the course of the 19th century and thereafter, and built the foundation for the further development of *Pan-Americanism*.

The aim of putting the spirit of Spanish-American togetherness into practice did not remain limited to the single occasion of the *Congress of Panama*. It was further pursued on several follow-up meetings over the course of the next decades. Mexico took a leading role in this regard as they called for similar conferences in 1831, 1838, 1839, and 1840.[49] In the end, all such initiatives failed, and until the middle of the century, Spanish-American states seemed to have been hesitant to come together again for another conference in order to work on similar agendas. It was only in 1847 when another congress was finally held, this time in Lima, Peru. The conference aimed, once again, at the creation of a Spanish American union, the establishment of a defensive alliance against potential non-American aggressors, and the implementation of mechanisms for the peaceful settlement of conflicts in the mutual relations of the participating states.[50] The so-called *Congress of Lima* was attended by representatives from Bolivia, Chile, Ecuador, New Granada, and Peru. The fact that all of these countries were again showing a willingness to deal with the idea of regional integration can be traced back – just as in the case of the *Panama Conference* – to another outer-American danger which had just arisen and which threatened the existence of all participating countries. This threat was posed by the former

47 Alejandro Alvarez, 'Latin America and International Law' (n 14 in Chapter 4) 275.

48 Gordon Mace, 'Regional Integration in Latin America: A Long and Winding Road' (1988) 43 International Journal 406.

49 Alejandro Alvarez, 'Latin America and International Law' (n 14 in Chapter 4) 280.

50 Compare: *Tratado de Confederación entre las Republicas del Perú, Bolivia, Chile, Ecuador y Nueva Granada,* firmado en Lima a 8 de Febrero de 1848; <http://www.oas.org/sap/peacefund/VirtualLibrary/CongressofLima1847/Treaty/TratadoConfederacionPeruBoliviaChileEcuadorNuevaGranada.pdf > accessed October 12, 2016.

Ecuadorian president Juan José Flores (1800–1864), who aimed for the establishment of a monarchy in his country under Spanish or French aegis.[51] Furthermore, the United States had just waged war against Mexico,[52] resulting in the Spanish American countries fearing further imperialistic attempts from the United States.[53] Due to this situation, the five participating states decided to meet in order to revive the idea of *Spanish-Americanism* and to form an alliance for preserving their independence, sovereignty, and territorial integrity.[54]

The congresses in Panama and Lima had in common that they were both held because of the emergence of threats of North Atlantic countries for the independence of the Spanish American states. But this constellation did not only apply for these two congresses. The subsequent two major Spanish American gatherings (in Santiago de Chile in 1856 and again in Lima in 1864) at which the introduction of alliances as well as of systems of collective security were seriously discussed again were all preceded by outer-American threats against the independence and territorial integrity of Spanish American states.[55] Hence, it seems Spanish American countries felt the need to meet up,

---

51 Lawrence A. Clayton, *Peru and the United States: The Condor and the Eagle* (University of Georgia Press 1999) 35. Also: Alejandro Alvarez, 'Latin America and International Law' (n 14 in Chapter 4) 280.

52 Compare: Bronwyn Mills, *U.S.-Mexican War* (Chelsea House 2003). Christopher Conway (ed.), *The U.S.-Mexican War: A Binational Reader* (Hackett Publishing Company 2010). Colin M. Maclachlan and William H. Beezley, *Mexico's Crucial Century, 1810–1910* (University of Nebraska Press 2010).

53 Lawrence A. Clayton, *Peru and the United States* (n 51 in Chapter 4) 35.

54 Gonzalo Quesada, *Arbitration in Latin America* (Wyt 1907) 8.

55 *The first one*, the Congress of Santiago (1856), was held by Chile, Ecuador, and Peru.
- due to another Spanish treat to re-occupy Spanish American territory,
- due to the imperialist policy of the United States towards Mexico, and
- due to William Walker, an U.S.-American soldier of fortune, who used the confusion of a civil war in Nicaragua in order to capture the town Granada and to declare himself as (one of several rivaling) president of the country.

Compare also: R.A. Humphreys, 'Chapter XXV: The States of Latin America' (n 10 in Chapter 4) 681; Gustave A. Nuermberger, 'The Continental Treaties of 1856: An American Union "Exclusive of the United States"' (1940) 20 The Hispanic American Historical Review 40. G. Pope Atkins, *Encyclopedia of the Inter-American System* (Greenwood Press 1997) 302.

The second one, the Congress of Lima (1864), was "provoked by the French occupation of Mexico, the Spanish reoccupation of the Dominican Republic, and the Spanish war with Peru and Chile" (see: G. Pope Atkins, Encyclopedia of the Inter-American System (1997), page 302). It was attended by Bolivia, Chile, Colombia, Ecuador, El Salvador, Guatemala, Peru, and Venezuela. Compare also: Georg Stadtmüller, *Rechtsidee und Machtpolitik in der amerikanischen Geschichte* (n 46 in Chapter 3) 49–53.

and discuss these kinds of topics, only in situations in which non-(Spanish-) American aggressors threatened their existence.

On various occasions throughout the 19th century, these threats appear to have been pressing enough that the Spanish American states forgot about their mutual conflicts, closed ranks, and demonstrated unity to deter the outer aggressors. Therefore, it cannot be claimed that it was (only) their sense of unity and togetherness which brought them together. Rather, it was (also) their fear of being re-colonized. However, what must also be noted in this regard is the following: Although the primary reason for the Spanish American states to come together for holding these conferences, might have been external dangers, they never limited their discussions to the topic of collective security. Among other topics, they also always dealt on these occasions with the creation of mechanisms for the peaceful settlement of their mutual conflicts. For example, in the (unratified) *Treaty of Confederation* concluded by Peru, Bolivia, Chile, Ecuador, and New Granada at the *Congress of Lima* in 1847/48, Article 9 provided the following: "Las Repúblicas Confederales [...] establecen que cualesquiera cuestiones ó diferencias que entre ellas su suseiten, se arreglen siempre por vías pacíficas. [...] En consecuencia, jamás se emplearán las fuerzas de unas contra otras [...]."[56] The treaties concluded at the conferences in 1856 and 1864 contained similar provisions.[57] In the *Treaty on the Preservation of Peace* from 1864, the commitment to Spanish American peace was explicitly renewed in Article 1: "Las Altas Partes contratantes se obligan solemnemente á no hostilizarse, ni aun por vía de apremio, y á no ocurrir jamás al empleo de las armas como medio de terminar sus diferencias."[58] Therefore, the contracting states intended, by concluding this treaty, to abandon the right to wage war in their mutual relations. In addition to that, they determined in Article 2 that each of their mutual conflicts was to be

56 Analogously translated by the author of the present book: "The confederated republics determine that every question or difference which arises among them shall be settled by peaceful means. Consequently, they will never use force among each other." Source: *Tratado de Confederación entre las Republicas del Peru, Bolivia, Chile, Ecuador y Nueva Granada, firmado en Lima a 8 de Febrero de 1848* (n 50 in Chapter 4).

57 Compare: Article 19 of the *Continental Treaty of Alliance and Reciprocal Assistance* (concluded at the Congress of Santiago in 1856); <http://www.oas.org/sap/peacefund/VirtualLibrary/ContinentalCongressofSantiago/TratadoContinental1856.pdf> accessed January 30, 2017.

58 Analogously translated by the author of the present book: "The high contracting parties commit themselves not to settle their mutual differences by coercive measures or force." Source: *Treaty on the Preservation of Peace* from 1864; <http://www.oas.org/sap/peacefund/VirtualLibrary/SecondCongressofLima/TratadoSobreConservacionPazEntreEstadosdeAmericaContratantes.pdf> accessed January 30, 2017.

referred to peaceful settlement by an "[....] Asamblea especial de Plenipotenciarios nombrados por las Naciones contratantes."[59] This case serves a perfect example for the tendency of the Spanish American nations to meet external threats to independence and their territorial integrity by closing ranks against external dangers and – at the same time – by creating modes for the peaceful settlement of conflicts in inter-Spanish American relations.[60] Since they regarded themselves as forming a distinct family of nations, they also aimed for improving their mutual (Spanish American) relations at all of these conferences. For example, in the preamble to the *Treaty of Confederation* from 1848, the adhering states even explicitly affirmed this point by declaring that they were

> [...] bound together by origin, language, religion and customs, by geographical position, by the common cause they have defended, and by the analogy of their institutions, and, above all, by common necessity and reciprocal interests, cannot be considered but as parts of the same nation, which should unite their forces and resources to remove all the obstacles opposing the destiny offered them by nature and civilization.[61]

A similar view was also expressed in the preamble of the *Continental Treaty of Alliance and Reciprocal Assistance*, which was concluded at the *Continental Congress of Santiago* in 1856. According to this provision, the signing powers strove to cement a "[...] unión que entre ellas existe, como miembros de la grande familia Americana, ligados por intereses comunes, por un común origen, por la analogía de sus instituciones, y por otros muchos vínculos de fraternidad."[62]

---

59 Analogously translated by the author of the present book: "[...] a special assembly of plenipotentiaries nominated by the contracting nations." Source: ibid Article 2.

60 Carolyn M. Shaw, *Cooperation, Conflict, and Consensus in the Organization of American States* (Palgrave Macmillan 2004) 44. See: Marcelo G. Kohen, 'La Contribución de América Latina al Desarrollo Progresivo del Derecho International en Materia Territorial' (n 9 in Chapter 4) 59–63.

61 Preamble of the *Tratado de Confederación entre las Republicas del Peru, Bolivia, Chile, Ecuador y Nueva Granada*, firmado en Lima a 8 de Febrero de 1848 (n 50 in Chapter 4). Originally, the text is in Spanish, the translation derives from: Alejandro Alvarez, 'Latin America and International Law' (n 14 in Chapter 4) 281.

62 Analogously translated by the author of the present book: "[...] union which exists between them, the members of the great American family, interconnected through common interests, a common origin, the analogy of their institutions, and several more bonds of brotherhood." Compare: *Continental Treaty of Alliance and Reciprocal Assistance* (n 57 in Chapter 4).

Even though none of the measures which had been discussed in the context of any of these conferences were ever realized in the end, the participating Spanish American states showed – just by discussing these topics (which already constituted a development which was highly unlikely to happen at that time in inter-European relations) – that there existed a common and underlying conviction among them of belonging to one family of states. This assumption was based on their common history, shared culture, close bonds, as well as on the fact that they shared a series of interests, concepts, ideas, and values.[63] The work done at the *Congress of Panama*, and at the subsequent meetings of the Spanish American states, therefore, established a line of thinking concerning regional integration which was later expanded to the other American states.[64] The special relationship between the Spanish American countries and their attempts to establish close connections among each other, to join (defensive) unions, and to engage in regional integration were the origin of what was to develop over the next 100 years into a continental movement aiming for closer cooperation, regional integration, and the preservation of peace in all of America.[65] In the course of this process, the aspect of facing external dangers and of establishing defensive unions retreated more and more, while other topics, such as economic and trade-related questions, regional cooperation, and the settlement of disputes between the adhering states,[66] moved into the focus of Spanish American, respectively *Pan-American*, considerations.

---

63 Javier Corrales and Richard E. Feinberg, 'Regimes of Cooperation in the Western Hemisphere' (n 46 in Chapter 4) 3–4. According to them, the "Western Hemisphere Idea" provided that "[…] the societies of the hemisphere share more than a geographic location; they also share common political values that go beyond a preference for nontyrannical, republican institutions free from the vestiges of European feudalism."

64 Simon Collier, 'Nationality, Nationalism, and Supranationalism in the Writings of Simón Bolívar' (n 4 in Chapter 4) 48, 52.

65 Javier Corrales and Richard E. Feinberg, 'Regimes of Cooperation in the Western Hemisphere' (n 46 in Chapter 4) 4. Also: Liliana Obregón, 'Regionalism Constructed: A Short History of "Latin American International Law"' (2015) 5 European Society of International Law – Conference Paper Series 9–10.

66 Compare: Andrés Rivarola Puntigliano, 'Geopolitics and Integration: A South American Perspective' in Andrés Rivarola Puntigliano and José Briceño-Ruiz (eds.), *Resilience of Regionalism in Latin America and the Caribbean: Development and Autonomy* (Palgrave Macmillan 2013) 29. There, he remarked the following concerning the inter-American congresses: "No doubt external threat was a trigger for these Hispanic American gatherings, but these issues discussed there went beyond that. The agenda of the Anfictionic Congress remained, and was complemented by new issues such as obligatory arbitration, consular treaties and conflict preventive measures. Moreover, in the discussions around the third Congress, in Santiago, the economic item started to receive more attention."

2.2 *The Instrument of Arbitration*

The character of the mutual relations of the Spanish American states during the 19th century seemed to have been very distinctive, especially when compared to the relations between European nations. In conjunction with their tendency to meet for conferences to discuss the establishment of Spanish American unions, one of the (other) main characteristics of this approach can be found in their highly favorable attitude towards the instrument of arbitration.

Gonzalo de Quesada (*'Arbitration in Latin America,'* 1907) claimed that the American states had held an indubitable affinity for (obligatory) arbitration as a measure to restrict *ius ad bellum*, and to establish peace in their mutual, as well as general, international relations. According to him, Latin America "[...] has been animated, from the first years of its emancipation, at the beginning of the last century, by a humanitarian spirit which has favored and advocated Arbitration as the means of settling all disputes arising not only among themselves but between them and other Governments."[67] To prove the correctness of his claim and show that arbitration played, in fact, a key role in Spanish American (international) relations, it is necessary to examine the actual approach of these countries towards voluntary and obligatory arbitration. Thereby, it will be possible to identify particularities as well as differences between their understanding (and use) of arbitration and the European one. The thereof resulting findings will allow conclusions to be drawn regarding the influence of the Spanish American states on the further development of the instrument of arbitration during the 19th century.

In the previous chapter, the approach of European states during the 19th century towards obligatory arbitration was examined. These findings have proven the hesitance of many European nations to enter into obligatory arbitration treaties in their mutual relations. But it has also become apparent that (special and general) obligatory arbitration had – despite this hesitance – already been a well-known, comparably common, phenomenon among European states in their relations to Latin American (and other non-European) countries since 1839.[68] However, as shown by the numbers provided in *Table 2*, obligatory arbitration was considerably more prominent in Latin America. According to it,

---

67 Gonzalo Quesada, *Arbitration in Latin America* (n 54 in Chapter 4) 2.

68 Compare pages 63–66, 80–84, 98 et seq. of the present book.

- between 1817 and 1853,
  - 2 special and 3 general obligatory arbitration treaties were concluded in European/American relations (0.05 respectively 0.08 treaties per year) and
  - 3 special and 10 general obligatory ones were entered in the Latin American context (0.08 respectively 0.27 treaties per year);
- between 1854 and 1870, the number of concluded obligatory arbitration treaties increased to
  - 5 special and 3 general obligatory ones in European/American relations (0.18 respectively 0.29 treaties per year) and to
  - 2 special and 12 general obligatory arbitration treaties in Latin American ones (0.12 respectively 0.57 treaties per year);
- between 1871 and 1899, the above-described development[69] began in Europe, which resulted in the conclusion of
  - 21 special and 1 general obligatory arbitration treaties in inter-European relations (0.72 respectively 0.03 treaties per year);

  additionally, in the same period
  - another 10 special and 10 general obligatory arbitration treaties were concluded in European/American relations (0.34 treaties per year in both categories) and
  - 11 special and 27 general obligatory ones were entered in the mutual relations of American countries (0.38 respectively 0.93 treaties per year).

Given these numbers, it can be concluded that American states showed a particular attachment to obligatory arbitration agreements throughout the 19th century; and that it was considerably greater than the interest in obligatory arbitration which prevailed among European states. At that time, Latin American countries concluded more obligatory arbitration agreements than their European counterparts (although the European states were even more numerous). The first obligatory arbitration treaty in inter-Latin American relations was even entered into before the end of the wars for independence against Spain, namely between Chile and Peru in 1823. In doing so, these two states took the first step in a long series of conclusions of obligatory arbitration treaties between Latin American countries (as well as in their relations with European countries) which endured for the rest of the 19th, and even parts of the 20th century.[70] Therefore, the assumption seems to be correct that the Latin American states were particularly dedicated to this instrument.

---

69 Compare pages 96 et seq. of the present book.

70 Gonzalo de Quesada, *Arbitration in Latin America* (n 54 in Chapter 4) 74.

Looking at the practice of obligatory arbitration treaties during the 19th century, furthermore, reveals that most of these agreements were concluded by, and between, Spanish American states. Concentrating only on the period between 1823 and the early 1860s even shows that, at least one of the treaty parties of every single obligatory arbitration agreement which was concluded (worldwide) in this period stemmed from the ranks of the Spanish American nations. The United States, on the other hand, concluded only one general obligatory arbitration treaty in the entire 19th century, namely with Mexico in 1848. Brazil also showed severe reluctance in this regard having only concluded one special and one general obligatory arbitration treaty until the end of the century.

Although the numbers seem to provide a very clear picture of the use of obligatory arbitration in the 19th century and they appear to indicate an absolute affection of the Spanish American states for this instrument, the situation can also be interpreted in a different way. For example, Helen May Cory (*'Compulsory Arbitration of International Disputes'* from 1932) claimed that "[…] before 1880, the actual practice of arbitration between the Latin American countries was almost unknown."[71] According to her, hardly any of the obligatory arbitration treaties concluded among Latin American countries before 1880 were devoted to arbitration alone. Usually, these agreements primarily dealt with the establishment of peace, alliances, or better commercial relations and obligatory arbitration clauses were only introduced in the form of secondary functions. Because these treaties primarily dealt with topics of high political importance and, thus, affected the parties' vital interests and sovereignty rights in many cases, Cory argued that they were often infringed or ignored after a while. When they were abandoned because of their primary regulations, the arbitration clauses lapsed as well.[72] In addition to that, Alfred H. Fried (*'Pan-Amerika: Entwicklung, Bedeutung und Umfang der pan-amerikanischen Bewegung'* from 1910), an Austrian pacifist, author, and Nobel Peace Prize laureate (awarded in 1911), also dealt with the topic of obligatory arbitration agreements in the American context.[73] He reviewed the astonishingly high amount of conclusions of such treaties among Latin American states before 1880 and concluded that these numbers could only result from the fact that most of the treaties had, first and foremost, a theoretical character and were

71 Helen May Cory, *Compulsory Arbitration of International Disputes* (n 154 in Chapter 2) 10.

72 Ibid 10 et seq.

73 Alfred H. Fried, *Pan-Amerika: Entwicklung, Bedeutung und Umfang der pan-amerikanischen Bewegung* (Maritima 1910) 25.

barely enforced in state practice.[74] Otherwise, it would be inexplicable why the same states would continue to conclude similar treaties again and again.[75] Gaston Moch (*'Histoire Sommaire de l'Arbitrage permanent.'* From 1905), a French pacifist, also remarked, in this context, that the Spanish American states might have tried to follow the example of Bolívar[76] in his striving for the preservation of peace in Spanish America.[77] However, they were still too unstable – both internally and externally – to establish a reliable and peaceful international system amongst themselves. Finally, similar criticisms were also expressed by Jost Dülffer (*'Regeln gegen den Krieg?'* from 1981). According to him, between 1822 and 1889, Latin American countries concluded 118 obligatory arbitration treaties and another 100 between 1890 and 1910.[78] But many of those treaties could not have amounted to anything more than sole declarations of intent because they lacked the necessary level of liability for introducing lasting commitments to arbitration and peace. Instead, these agreements often lapsed when the government of one of the parties, or both, changed their political course or were overturned and replaced.[79] Dülffer regarded the numerous conclusions of obligatory arbitration treaties in the Spanish American context as some kind of mutual assurance of one another's good-will and friendly intentions. He did not, however, understand them to be judicially binding commitments. Regarding these criticisms, the following two points should be taken into consideration:

First, it is doubtlessly correct that, despite their repeated conclusion of obligatory arbitration agreements, Spanish American States seldom referred to arbitration prior to 1870 for the actual settlement of their mutual differences. This indicates that, in many cases, they did not draw practical consequences from the concluded obligatory arbitration treaties. Looking at the number of cases (Table 3.1) which were actually settled through the use of

---

74 Ibid.

75 Ibid 24.

76 Gaston Moch, *Histoire Sommaire de l'Arbitrage permanent* (Institut international de la paix 1905) 17. Also quoted in: Alfred H. Fried, *Pan-Amerika* (n 73 in Chapter 4) 24–25.

77 Compare also: Gonzalo Quesada, *Arbitration in Latin America* (n 54 in Chapter 4) 2. He quotes Bolívar as follows: "May it be granted that some day we be happy enough to install an august body of the representatives of republics, kingdoms, and empires, to consider and discuss the weighty questions of peace and war with the nations of other parts of the world."

78 Jost Dülffer, *Regeln gegen den Krieg?* (n 20 in Chapter 1) 229. There, he mentions also that these numbers only refer to treaties which were actually ratified. He estimates that the number of similar treaties which were signed but never ratified during these years is comparably high.

79 Ibid.

arbitration during the 19th century, and which involved Latin American countries, confirms this assumption. The numbers reveal that, between 1817 and 1853, only two cases were settled by arbitration in European/American relations (in which neither Great Britain nor the United States were involved).[80] The same can be found for the relations between American states. Almost all arbitrations between them took place between the United States and a Latin American country. There were only two exceptions from this trend: A case between Canada and New Brunswick (in 1851) and another between Ecuador and Peru (in 1853).[81] Between 1854 and 1870, the situation was quite similar. Only three cases were settled by arbitration in European/American relations which did not involve either the United States or Great Britain; during these years, the two Anglo-Saxon countries participated in 83% of European/American arbitrations.[82] In the mutual relations of the American states, there wasn't even a single case which was settled by arbitration in which the United States was not involved. Remarkably, the British and U.S.-American dedication to arbitration did not spread among the Latin American states. They were closely related with Great Britain and the United States, used arbitration repeatedly in their relations with the two nations, and concluded numerous obligatory arbitration agreements among themselves. However, until the 1870s, the Latin American states widely, or almost entirely, abstained from taking recourse to this instrument in their mutual relations, or in relations to European countries other than Great Britain.

One possible explanation for the disinterest of the Latin American states in the effective use of (isolated) arbitration could be found in the fact that their mutual relations still suffered from the chaos caused by continuous conflicts and power struggles, which many a time escalated into wars. It took many years until the Spanish American economies fully recovered from the damages suffered during the wars for independence.[83] Such factors hindered their

80 They took place in 1839 and 1840 between France and Mexico, respectively, between France and Argentina; compare: A.M. Stuyt, *Survey of International Arbitrations 1794–1989* (n 125 in Chapter 3) 34, 36.

81 Ibid 48, 50.

82 They took place between the Netherlands and Venezuela in 1857, Argentina and France in 1860, and France and Venezuela in 1864; compare: ibid 56, 68.

83 The Latin American countries suffered from the consequences of the wars for independence and the therewith linked fragmentation of political power among the newly established states, the militarization of the societies, which happened under the rule of the *caudillos*, and the mobilization for wars. This influenced the economic strength of Latin America to such an extent that it did not reach the level of *per capita* income until the middle of the 19th century, which it had had before the revolutions. See: Leandro Prados de la Escosura, 'The Economic Consequences of Independence in Latin America' in

mutual trade, and it delayed the appearance of that kind of minor (often trade-related) disputes between them, which were often settled by arbitration at that time. Furthermore, the Latin American economies were still largely shaped in accordance with the former colonial structures. Meaning, they were primarily directed towards exporting resources, basic products, and food (especially coffee and sugar). Therefore, their economies focused to a great extent on trade with Europe and the United States.[84] This set up maintained that trade among Latin American states was at a low level,[85] especially because most of the countries offered comparable products. The lack of train and steamboat connections was another factor which hindered their mutual trade before the 1870s/1880s.[86] It was only in the late 19th century that the region experienced an economic growth spurt, which intensified Latin American trade. Consequently, it was also only at this time that Latin American countries began to resort more often to arbitration for the settlement of their mutual conflicts.[87] This conclusion can be drawn from the number of isolated arbitrations in the Latin American context between 1871 and 1899 (Table 3.1) which shows that in European/American relations, recourse was now taken to the instrument of isolated arbitration for 55 times, which constituted an enormous increase in comparison to the years before. Moreover, the share of cases in which either the United States or Great Britain, or both, were involved decreased significantly as well. Now, it accounted for 'only' 49% (representing 27 out of 55 cases). Regarding the mutual relations of American states, the picture is very similar to the one concerning European/American relations at that time. The total number of arbitrations increased significantly in the American context – with the amount of arbitrations involving the United States decreasing to 'only'

Victor Bulmer-Thomas, John Coatsworth, and Roberto Cortes-Conde (eds.), *The Cambridge Economic History of Latin America* (Cambridge University Press 2005) 465.

84 Kenneth L. Sokoloff and Stanley L. Engerman, 'History Lessons: Institutions, Factors Endowments, and Paths of Development in the New World' (2000) 14 The Journal of Economic Perspectives 221–222.

85 Robert H. Bates, John H. Coatsworth, and Jeffrey G. Williamson, 'Lost Decades: Postindependence Performance in Latin America and Africa' (2007) 67 The Journal of Economic History 927. According to them, intercolonial trade was already "relatively modest, largely due to imperial trade monopolies and high transportation costs."

86 This was especially the case because civil wars, border disputes, and struggles for power made it necessary to invest huge shares of the states' budgets in the military. See: ibid 924. According to them, the Latin American states spend around 77% of their budgets on military expenditures between 1822 and 1860. Therefore, there remained little money for anything else.

87 Whether or not this development can really be traced back to the grown inter-Latin American trade, remains unclear and would require further research which cannot be done in the context of the present book.

13 out of 40 cases (representing 32.5% in comparison to 100% in the earlier period). All the other cases of (isolated) arbitrations (in the American context) took place between Latin American countries. In conclusion, the Latin American countries only began to invoke isolated arbitration on a regular base in the later parts of the 19th century. The instrument does not seem to have been a 'genuine' element of their mutual relations beforehand. They only began to use it more frequently after they had experienced a strong economic growth which intensified their mutual relations. As a consequence of this development, more (minor) trade-related conflicts emerged among them which were typically settled by arbitration at that time.

Second, before the 1870s, a great number of bi-lateral obligatory arbitration agreements between Latin American countries seem as if they had, first and foremost, been of a political/theoretical nature.[88] They were hardly ever invoked, and the Latin American states apparently did not regard them as binding. This assumption is based on the fact that in the case of conflicts, Latin American states did not usually take recourse to their compulsory arbitration clauses. Instead, they preferred to settle the cases through the use of force. Hence, Helen May Cory's, Alfred H. Fried's, and Jost Dülffer's (above-mentioned) remarks, concerning the primarily theoretical character of these treaties, appear to be well-founded. It stands to reason that Latin American states concluded obligatory arbitration treaties, first and foremost, for assuring one another of their benevolence and friendship, especially when the obligatory arbitration commitments were part of peace agreements. This finding does not, however, automatically have to result in a negative view of obligatory arbitration in Latin America, nor does it necessarily have to mean that obligatory arbitration was futile in this context. Alfred H. Fried argued it had to be regarded as a failure that the above-mentioned projects for the establishment of systems of conflict settlement (discussed at the Spanish American congresses) were not realized in the end and that obligatory arbitration treaties were concluded, but hardly invoked. However, at the same time, he also stressed the fact that Latin American states were "[…] the first and only ones to conclude obligatory arbitration treaties"[89] in these years. Thereby, they broke new (judicial) ground. Fried tended to mark the initial problems and failures of obligatory arbitration and of the Spanish American

88 Alfred H. Fried, *Pan-Amerika* (n 73 in Chapter 4) 24. He remarked in this regard the following [*broadly translated by the author of the present book*]: "[A]t least in the first period of the Latin American independence – the efforts for the introduction of [obligatory] arbitration was a primarily theoretical character; just as it used to be in the case of the attempts to establish a Spanish American union."

89 Ibid 25.

congresses as "teething troubles,"[90] but, at the same time, considered Latin America as "the cradle of [obligatory] arbitration."[91]

His arguments are convincing. Especially because the Spanish American states had already concluded obligatory arbitration agreements before their final accomplishment of independence in 1825 and continued to do so over the course of the 19th century. Hence, obligatory arbitration was a common feature of Spanish American relations since their independence. In the second half of the 19th century, between 1864 and 1902, the number of Latin American obligatory arbitration agreements increased even more and reached new heights. In these years, the Latin American states entered into 143 agreements of that type in their mutual relations.[92] This wave of obligatory arbitration treaties, and their attempts at establishing systems for peaceful conflict settlement (pursued at the Spanish American congresses), are proof of their great interest in the matter, and their dedication to obligatory arbitration (although they seldom invoked the concluded compulsory arbitration clauses).

By concluding obligatory arbitration agreements so frequently in their mutual relations, and, to a lesser extent, also in their relations to European countries, the Latin American states were the first to deal with obligatory arbitration on a regular basis and to establish it as a key instrument in state practice and in international law. Taking into account their pioneering role in this context, and the (initial) hesitation of European states to follow their example, the conclusion seems plausible that it was the Latin American states that spread, introduced, and embedded obligatory arbitration in international relations. The Latin American states seem to have gotten European countries in touch with the concept of obligatory arbitration and, thus, gradually familiarized them with it. Especially the smaller European countries took this practice over and, by the late 19th century, implemented it in their inter-European relations as well. Therefore, the Latin American dedication to obligatory arbitration was probably (one of) the main reason(s) for the global spread of this instrument in the second half of the 19th century.

2.3 *International Law in Latin America*

Before turning to the last decades of the 19th century and *Pan-Americanism*, the Latin American understanding of international law needs to be addressed.

---

90 Ibid.

91 Ibid 24.

92 Gaston Moch, *Histoire Sommaire de l'Arbitrage permanent* (n 76 in Chapter 4) 25 et seq. Also: Alfred H. Fried, *Pan-Amerika* (n 73 in Chapter 4) 25. According to Fried, 127 out of the 142 treaties were concluded in inter-Latin American relations.

This will serve the purpose of providing a comprehensive picture of how Latin American scholars dealt with international law and its Eurocentric approach at that time, identifying characteristics of the Latin American understanding of international law, and showing which initiatives for changing the international legal order stemmed from Latin America.

From the mid-19th to the mid-20th century, the existence or non-existence of an independent *American International Law* was enthusiastically discussed[93] by many U.S.-American and Latin American scholars.[94] Today, Liliana Obregón (*'Latin American International Law'* from 2009) argues that the emergence of the concept of a Latin American International Law in the 19th and early 20th centuries was a manifestation of a particular regional understanding of international law.[95] In this regard, Jorge L. Esquirol (in the *'Oxford Handbook of the History of International Law'* from 2012) mentioned that – in its strongest expression – Latin American International Law was supposed to "[...] apply to relations among American states as well as between European and American states"[96] and to "[...] rank equal to, and in case of conflict, trump general or European international law."[97]

The historical origin of the idea for an independent international legal sphere in (Latin) America can be traced back to Amancio Alcorta's reply to Carlos Calvo's treatise *'Derecho 'Internacional teórico y práctico de Europa y América'* (from 1868).[98] Alcorta criticized in 1887 Calvo's omission to mention the possibility of the existence of such an autonomous international legal order in Latin America.[99] From 1868 onwards, a quickly growing number of treatises were published then by Latin American scholars in which they argued in favor of the existence of a separate (Latin) American system in international law. This included Rafael F. Seijas' treatise *'El derecho internactional Hispano-Americano'* (1884), Amancio Alcorta's *'Cours de droit international public'*

93 Arnulf Becker Lorca, 'International Law in Latin America or Latin American International Law? Rise, Fall, and Retrieval of a Tradition of Legal Thinking and Political Imagination' (2006) 47 Harvard International Law Journal 285.

94 Compare, e.g.: Jorge L. Esquirol, 'Latin America' in Bardo Fassbender and Anne Peters (eds.), *The Oxford Handbook of the History of International Law* (n 28 in Chapter 1) 563–566.

95 Liliana Obregón, 'Latin American International Law' in James D. Armstrong (ed.), *Routledge Handbook of International Law* (Routledge 2009) 154.

96 Jorge L. Esquirol, 'Latin America' (n 94 in Chapter 4) 563–564.

97 Ibid.

98 Liliana Obregón, 'Regionalism Constructed' (n 65 in Chapter 4) 2.

99 Amancio Alcorta, 'La ciencia del derecho internacional. A propósito de la obra de Calvo' (1883) 7 Nueva Revista. Compare also: Liliana Obregón, 'Regionalism Constructed' (n 65 in Chapter 4) 2–3.

(1887), and Alejandro Alvarez' article *'Latin America and International Law'* (1909),[100] to name but a few. Opposing views were also held, for example, by Manuel de Sá Vianna, a Brazilian jurist, who strongly rejected these concepts at the *First Pan American Scientific Congress* in Santiago de Chile in 1908.[101] According to Jorge L. Esquirol, an autonomous (Latin) American international law had the following particular characteristics:

> Non-intervention by third-party States; compulsory international arbitration for State to State disputes; territorial limits based on *uti possidetis iuris* of 1810; third party right to recognition of internal belligerents; right of diplomatic asylum; the principle of *ius soli* in nationality laws; freedom of national rivers and navigation; coastal security jurisdiction; freedom of neutral trade in times of wars, and a few others.[102]

Whether these particularities of the mutual relations of (Latin) American states actually constituted an individual and separate international legal sphere in (Latin) America is hard to determine. It would require an in-depth analysis, which would easily exceed the limitations of the present chapter. This issue must, nevertheless, be brought up at this particular point because of one of the listed characteristics of the (Latin) American approach to international law: the so-called *Calvo Doctrine*.[103] This doctrine originated from the pen of Carlos Calvo (1824–1906), the above-mentioned Argentinian scholar.[104] In order to deal with his ideas in a bit more detail, it is necessary to recall the fact that the Latin American states were confronted with European and U.S.-American interventions, attacks, blockades, and wars since the accomplish-

100 Amancio Alcorta, *Cours de Droit International Public*, vol. 1 (Lajouane 1887). Rafael F. Seijas, *El derecho internacional Hispano-Americano* (El Monitor 1884). Alejandro Alvarez, 'Latin America and International Law' (n 14 in Chapter 4) 269–353.

101 Manuel de Sá Vienna, *De la Non-Existence d'un Droit International Américain* (L. Figueredo 1912) 3–6.

102 Jorge L. Esquirol, 'Latin America' (n 94 in Chapter 4) 564. On page 554–557, Esquirol elaborates on the 'Recognition of Belligerency' in Latin America and on pages 558–559 on the 'Right of Diplomatic Asylum.' On pages 566–570, he deals with the principle of 'Non-Intervention.'

103 The list of topics stems from: ibid 564. According to Esquirol, the *Calvo Doctrine* can be summarized under the title 'non-intervention by third-party States.'

104 In this regard, it should be noted that some authors, such as Santiago Montt, questioned the general assumption of Calvo's authorship of the doctrine. Instead, they claim that it was Andrés Bello, a Venezuelan jurist, who wrote "[...] the first treatise on the subject in the region" in 1832 ('Derecho de Jentes'). Compare: Santiago Montt, *State Liability in Investment Treaty Arbitration: Global Constitutional and Administrative Law in the BIT Generation* (Hart 2009) 42.

ment of their independence. Over the course of the entire 19th century, they were repeatedly threatened with the prospect of being re-colonized, or at least widely dominated, by outer-Latin American powers. They were also often forced to comply with extensive demands on the part of the North Atlantic powers. For example, the United States alone deployed 68 military interventions in Latin American countries between their independence and 1945. European states often acted in a very similar way as well through gunboat diplomacy, port blockades, the open use of force, or occupations.[105] As a response to these threats and interventions, Latin Americans insisted on the principle of non-intervention, according to which, all countries had to refrain from intervening in one another's respective internal affairs.[106] An (early) attempt to put this principle into practice, and to ensure compliance with it, can be found in the above-described efforts to establish Spanish American unions. The *Calvo Doctrine* was another, albeit later, attempt to respond to the European and U.S.-American interventions and threats.

As described above, the Latin American economies grew strongly in the second half of the 19th century, and globalization resulted in closer connections between Latin America and the North Atlantic states. This intensified contact also led to an increase in the potential for frictions between the trade partners. However, at the same time, Latin America depended heavily on loans from European and U.S.-American investors (often private) for the construction of its infrastructure and industries. In several cases, these loans could not be re-paid in a timely manner and, as a result, nationals of European countries, or the United States, were (financially) harmed or had to suffer losses in Latin America. In such instances, the foreign citizens (the credit grantors or the injured persons) often turned to the governments of their respective home countries in order to call for help in the settlement of the issue.[107] Their governments responded to these calls in many cases by putting pressure on the Latin American states, on behalf of their citizens, and urged the Latin American states to repay debts, reimburse for losses, or to compensate damages.[108] This pressure was applied in a number of ways, and several escalation steps can be identified in this regard. The actions taken ranged from

105 Jorge L. Esquirol, 'Latin America' (n 94 in Chapter 4) 566.

106 Gordon Connell-Smith, *The Inter-American System* (n 18 in Chapter 4) 9.

107 Jorge L. Esquirol, 'Latin America' (n 94 in Chapter 4) 567.

108 Compare: Lionel Morgan Summers, 'The Calvo Clause' (1933) 19 Virginia Law Review 459. Frank Griffith Dawson, 'Contributions of Lesser Developed Nations to International Law: The Latin American Experience' (1981) 13 Case Western Reverse Journal of International Law 47.

sending protest notes to the application of brute force.[109] The latter happened, for example, in the form of gunboat diplomacy[110] or temporary occupations of the Latin American states' territories. Since the European countries and the United States were economically and militarily considerably stronger than their Latin American counterparts, their threat to impede further loans, put an embargo on them, block their harbors, or apply gunboat diplomacy forced the Latin American nations to comply with the European/U.S.-American demands. This often-invoked practice resulted in a sort of extraterritorial justice for foreigners in Latin American countries. They enjoyed the protection of their governments and could claim the reimbursement of damages without having to take recourse to the local judicial systems in which they would have had to prove the correctness of their claims.[111] Thereby, they avoided judicial means and, instead, relied on diplomatic pressure which even allowed them to invoke unfounded claims. Consequently, nationals of North Atlantic countries were enormously favored, due to the military and economic superiority of their home countries, in the settlement of pecuniary claims against Latin American debtors and states. The Latin American countries strongly resented this practice – but they could not resist it, either militarily or economically, due to their financial dependence on the North Atlantic countries. A first attempt to change this situation was made in 1868 by the introduction of a new legal regime in Latin American international law in form of the *Calvo Doctrine.*[112] According to Horacio A. Grigera Naón (*'Arbitration and Latin America'* from 2005), the doctrine was aimed at establishing the following:

> The general principle postulated by Carlos Calvo is that foreign aliens may not claim or enjoy rights, treatment or protection superior to or different from those afforded to nationals. A central and complementary

109 Jorge L. Esquirol, 'Latin America' (n 94 in Chapter 4) 567.

110 The term *'gunboat diplomacy'* describes the practice of (usually) North Atlantic states enforcing their will and demands on militarily inferior nations by coercive diplomacy or measures short of war. Compare: James Cable, *Gunboat Diplomacy 1919–1979: Political Applications of Limited Naval Force* (Macmillan 1981) 39. He defined gunboat diplomacy as follows: "[…] the use or threat of limited naval force, otherwise than an act of war, in order to secure advantage or to avert loss, either in the furtherance of an international dispute or else against foreign nationals within the territory of the jurisprudence of their own state."

Compare also: Robert Mandel, 'The Effectiveness of Gunboat Diplomacy' (1986) 30 *International Studies Quarterly* 59–76.

111 Lionel Morgan Summers, 'The Calvo Clause' (n 108 in Chapter 4) 459.

112 Carlos Calvo, *Derecho Internacional Teórico y Práctico de Europa y América*, vol. 1 (D'Amyot 1868).

> part of the Calvo doctrine is that, together with asserting the submission of foreign aliens to the laws and jurisdiction of the host country where they reside, it excludes the threat or use of force by their home country in support of their claims or grievances against the host country.[113]

Broadly speaking, Calvo proposed to abandon the system of extraterritorial justice for foreigners. He wanted them to take recourse to the domestic courts of the Latin American countries and for the practice of imbalanced diplomatic protection of the interests and goods of foreign nationals by their powerful home countries to be ended.[114] Therefore, this was an attempt to introduce new legal norms, through Latin American international law, in order to stop the North Atlantic countries from intervening, or threatening to intervene, in Latin America.

In Europe and in the United States, the *Calvo Doctrine* was not supported by governments or (the majority of) international lawyers.[115] However, this setback did not prevent the Latin American countries from further attempting to equip legally binding force to the underlying principle behind the *Calvo Doctrine*. For example, they tried introducing so-called *Calvo Clauses* into their agreements with foreign investors. In such clauses, the signing foreign (private) parties agreed to take disputes arising out of their contractual relationships to local courts instead of relying on diplomatic protection by their home countries.[116] But the concept of *Calvo Clauses* bore the difficulty that if an individual is harmed in or by a foreign country, the individual's home country (but not the individual himself/herself) is assigned the right to demand redress under international law. The respective citizen cannot effectively wave the state's right in this regard.[117] Therefore, the introduction of *Calvo Clauses* did not result in a generally accepted legal prohibition of interventions either. The North Atlantic powers were simply not yet willing, in the 19th century, to give up on their power to impose their will on Latin American countries through

---

113 Horacio A. Grigera Naón, 'Arbitration and Latin America: Progress and Setbacks' (2005) 21 Arbitration International 134. According to Grigera Naón, the origin of his remarks is: Carlos Calvo, *Derecho Internacional Teórico y Práctico de Europa y América*, vol. 1 (n 112 in Chapter 4) 294, 392.

114 Patrick Juillard, 'Calvo Doctrine/Calvo Clause,' *Max Planck Encyclopedia of Public International Law (Online)*.

115 Kate Miles, *The Origins of International Investment Law: Empire, Environment and the Safeguarding of Capital* (Cambridge University Press 2013) 51.

116 Jeswald W. Salacuse, *The Law of Investment Treaties* (Oxford University Press 2015) 76.

117 Kate Miles, *The Origins of International Investment Law* (n 115 in Chapter 4) 51. Concerning the receipt and acceptance of the Calvo Clauses under international law, please see also: Patrick Juillard, 'Calvo Doctrine/Calvo Clause' (n 114 in Chapter 4).

(the threat of) force.[118] Instead, threats of forceful interventions continued to be a popular tool in European and U.S.-American relations to Latin America, and a welcome opportunity for them to establish their dominance in the region. Moreover, the North Atlantic powers were not willing to abandon this practice, or restrict their influence over Latin America, because of their imperialist tendencies. In these years, they sought to gain as many territories and as much, direct as well as indirect, control over other countries and world regions as possible. Although the North Atlantic powers no longer questioned the independence of the Latin American countries by the end of the 19th century, they still aimed for dominance over them.

2.4 *Imperialism in America*

During most of the first half of the 19th century, the United States showed little interest in the rest of the continent. Other states, such as Great Britain, France, or Portugal, had far closer political relations to Latin America at that time than the United States did.[119] In fact, the major initiative taken by the United States during these years regarding Latin America was the proclamation of the *Monroe-Doctrine* in 1823 whereby they took a clear stand against the re-occupation and re-colonialization of Latin America.[120] However, they did not invoke the doctrine in state practice for many years. They abstained from doing so, for example, when Great Britain occupied the Falkland Islands in 1833, when France intervened in the Republics of River Plate in 1838, and when Spain occupied the Chincha Islands in 1865.[121] The decision not to intervene in any of these cases was based, to a great extent, on the fact that the U.S.-American interest in Latin America during these years was neither political nor hegemonic, just yet, but, rather, predominantly economic and trade-oriented. Furthermore, during the first decades after the proclamation of the *Monroe-*

---

118 Mark Eric Williams, *Understanding U.S.-Latin American Relations: Theory and History* (Routledge 2012), 123. According to him, "[...] the lack of international consensus kept the Calvo Clause outside the canons of international law." Compare also: Edward McWhinney, *The International Court of Justice and the Western Tradition of International Law* (Martinus Nijhoff Publishers 1987) 10.

119 Gregory B. Weeks, *U.S. and Latin American Relations* (Wiley-Blackwell 2015) 29.

120 Compare: Edward Renehan, *The Monroe Doctrine: The Cornerstone of American Foreign Policy* (Chelsea House 2007) 90–91. He praised the doctrine and described its great influence on the Latin America as follows: "Without the existence of the Monroe Doctrine, the history of Latin America, not to mention the history of world, would have been completely different, just as the map of contemporary South America would be completely different as well."

121 Carlos Castro-Ruiz, 'The Monroe Doctrine and the Government of Chile' (1917) 11 The American Political Science Review 231.

Doctrine, the United States did not have the necessary military power yet to enforce it against the European states.[122]

While Latin America was of rather secondary importance for the United States,[123] Great Britain managed to become the dominant power in the region and held on to this position until the early 1880s.[124] The United States, on the other hand, focused on the colonialization of the North American West. In the first decades of the 19th century, the United States' territorial aim was, therefore, first and foremost directed at the expansion to the Pacific coast.[125] It was only in the 1840s when a (first) significant change can be observed in the U.S.-American attitude towards Latin America; namely, when they proclaimed the concept of *Manifest Destiny*, annexed Texas (both in 1845), and declared war on Mexico in 1846.[126] The concept of *Manifest Destiny* was a doctrine that aimed for the justification of the further territorial expansion of the United States. It was first coined by John O'Sullivan (1813–1895), a U.S.-American journalist, who declared that the United States had "[…] the right of our manifest destiny to overspread and to possess the whole continent which Providence has given us for the development of the great experiment of liberty and federated self-government."[127] For him, further territorial acquisition was indispensable to the United States. It guaranteed them success and the continued existence of their governmental system. According to him, the superiority of the U.S.-American federal and democratic state structure justified the claim for more territory.[128] Furthermore, O'Sullivan considered it legitimized to take

---

122 Thomas C. Wright, *Latin America since Independence: Two Centuries of Continuity and Change* (Rowman & Littlefield Publ. 2017) 140.

123 Don M. Coerver and Linda B. Hall, *Tangled Destinies: Latin America & The United States* (The University of New Mexico Press 1999) 3. Compare also: Joseph Smith, 'The First Conference of American States (1889–1890) and the Early Pan American Policy of the United States' in David Sheinin (ed.), *Beyond the Ideal* (n 28 in Chapter 4) 19. According to him, the United States regarded Latin America for the greatest part of the 19th century as "geographically remote, economically backward, politically unstable, and unworthy of much attention."

124 Robert T. Buckman, *Latin America* (Stryker-Post Publications 2015) 24. Also: Howard J. Wiarda, *American Foreign Policy Toward Latin America in the 80s and 90s: Issues and Controversies from Reagan to Bush* (New York: University Press 1992) 81. According to Wiarda, the dominance even lasted "well into the twentieth" century.

125 Laurel Clark Shire, *The Threshold of Manifest Destiny: Gender and National Expansion in Florida* (University of Pennsylvania Press 2016) 13 et seq.

126 Thomas C. Wright, *Latin America since Independence* (n 122 in Chapter 4) 141.

127 John O'Sullivan, 'Annexation' (1845) 17 United States Magazine and Democratic Review 5–10.

128 Thomas R. Hietala, *Manifest Design: American Exceptionalism and Empire* (Cornell University Press 1985) 256.

land from Native Americans and Mexico because of the superiority of the 'Anglo-Saxon race.'[129] Due to this claim, he held it to be the U.S.-American right to make territorial gains on other peoples' costs. In the 1840s, the concept of *Manifest Destiny* developed into a very influential and pervasive approach in the United States.[130] It reached the highest political decision-making levels and even influenced officials such as U.S. President James K. Polk (1795–1849).[131] Furthermore, the United States did not confine their imperialist efforts to the annexation of Texas. They also attempted, during these years, to buy Cuba from Spain and to acquire Oregon. Alejandro Álvarez commented on this situation and the U.S.-American policy towards Latin America from the 1840s onwards as follows: "While the territorial history of the Latin states reduces itself to a struggle over boundaries, that of the United States is that of the extension of territory. In this growth, Latin countries on the south and west were absorbed."[132]

The *Mexican-American War* from 1846 was the first eruption of the new U.S.-American imperialism. But such actions taken during the 1840s were still directed to the acquisition of new territories (as part of the process of the United States spreading over great shares of North America). In later years, however, the United States also started to strive for establishing and expanding their sphere of influence over further parts of the American continent, not only Mexico but also over the Caribbean and Central America.[133] Until the end of the 19th century, the United States managed to establish themselves as the uncontested hegemonic power in this region and also dominated (most of) the rest of the continent.[134]

The South American countries were (mostly) exempt from being invaded by U.S.-American troops and, therefore, from the physical presence of the United States on their territories. Economically, however, they were also strongly dependent on the United States and their investments. It meant, in the end,

129 Compare: Thomas C. Wright, *Latin America since Independence* (n 122 in Chapter 4) 141.

130 John Hope Franklin, 'The Southern Expansionists of 1846' (1959) 25 The Journal of Southern History 323. Also: Richard Griswold del Castillo, *The Treaty of Guadalupe Hidalgo: A Legacy of Conflict* (University of Oklahoma Press 1990) 4.

131 Rodney P. Carlisle and J. Geoffrey Golson, *Manifest Destiny and the Expansion of America* (ABC Clio 2007) 49.

132 Alejandro Alvarez, 'Latin America and International Law' (n 14 in Chapter 4) 308 (in footnote 48).

133 Thomas L. Karnes, *The Failure of Union: Central America 1824–1975* (Tempe Arizona State University 1976) 177. Also: Lynn V. Foster, *A Brief History of Central America* (n 5 in Chapter 4) 161.

134 Antony Best, Jussi M. Hahimäki, Joseph A. Maiolo, and Kirsten E. Schulze, *International History of the Twentieth Century and Beyond* (Routledge 2004) 379.

that they could not avoid being subject to their dominance either.[135] The United States justified the establishment of hegemony over Latin America – and particularly over Central America and the Caribbean – by taking recourse to the *Monroe Doctrine.* According to Gordon Connell-Smith (*'The Inter-American System'* from 1966), the United States invoked this doctrine in the second half of the 19th century to prevent "[…] extra-hemispheric powers from intervening to challenge [their] hegemony,"[136] and to justify their own interventions in Central America.

Hence, the United States pursued an imperialistic approach towards Latin America since the 1840s and especially during the second half of the 19th century. They strove for hegemony over the entire continent and attempted to drive European countries out of the region, as they considered Latin America to fall within their exclusive sphere of influence. Consequently, their approach towards other states from the Western Hemisphere was not a peace-oriented neighborhood policy but, rather, they aimed for dominance over them, gained benefits on their costs, and, by invoking their superior military and economic capacities, they made sure that the Latin American states complied with their demands.

3 The *First Pan-American Conference* (1889/90)

The U.S.-American policy towards Latin America before the 1870s/1880s, as well as their imperialist approach, formed the basis for the emergence of *Pan-Americanism* in the last two decades of the century. This approach resulted, at least as an initial development, in the *First Pan-American Conference* in 1889/90.

As illustrated above, the United States had initially shown little interest in regional integration or cooperation with Latin American countries.[137] They had abstained from participating in any attempt for continental cooperation and showed a rather imperialist attitude towards the rest of the continent. From the side of the Spanish American countries, there did not seem, any-

---

135 Ibid 379.

136 Gordon Connell-Smith, *The Inter-American System* (n 18 in Chapter 4) 10. Also: Mark T. Gilderhus, 'The Monroe Doctrine: Meaning and Implications' (2006) 36 Presidential Studies Quarterly 9. According to Gilderhus, the United States invoked the *Monroe Doctrine*, e.g., in 1845 "[…] as a warning against British and French meddling in Texas and California."

137 Joseph Smith, 'The First Conference of American States (1889–1890) and the Early Pan American Policy of the United States' (n 123 in Chapter 4) 19.

more, to have been much hope or interest in the participation of the United States in efforts for closer regional cooperation. This point becomes clear when taking into consideration the following example. Colombia and Chile signed a treaty for general arbitration in 1880, the so-called *Treaty of Bogota.*[138] After its conclusion, they invited the other Spanish American republics, but not Brazil or the United States,[139] to a meeting in Panama in 1881 to have them join the agreement. This initiative had the potential to result in a general arbitration agreement which would have covered all of Spanish America. In the end, the meeting could not be realized due to a war between Chile on the one side, and Peru and Bolivia on the other. The Colombian-Chilean treaty was not ratified, but the point which, nevertheless, becomes apparent in this regard is that the United States and Brazil were excluded from this initiative;[140] unlike in the case of the *Congress of Panama* from 1826, where they had received an invitation. It can also be concluded that the attempt to unite the Spanish American states under one common general arbitration agreement once more demonstrated their high affection for this particular instrument and for regional organization. In this context, Alfred H. Fried (*'Pan-Amerika'* from 1910) cited several of the reactions of the Spanish American states to the Chilean-Colombian invitation.[141] They were all, except Mexico, very positive and welcomed the initiative. For example, Uruguay declared that "[...] every kind of conflict and problem should be subordinated to and settled by arbitration; even border disputes or those affecting the states' territorial integrity."[142]

Despite the then-prevailing indifference among the Spanish American states regarding potential U.S.-American participation in this kind of initiatives, a remarkable development took place in the beginning of the 1880s. The former lack of interest in regional integration faded away in the United States and gave way to a more open attitude towards Latin America. Soon after the inauguration of James G. Blaine (1830–1893) as U.S. Secretary of State, he launched an initiative for a *Pan-American* conference which was supposed to be held in 1881, and which would not only include Spanish America but the entire continent. Blaine claimed to have proposed the conference "[...] for the purpose of considering and discussing the methods of preventing war between

138 Compare: Alfred H. Fried, *Pan-Amerika* (n 73 in Chapter 4) 31.

139 Only Brazil was excluded. Compare: ibid 32. See also: Alejandro Alvarez, 'Latin America and International Law' (n 14 in Chapter 4) 301.

140 A. Curtis Wilgus, 'James G. Blaine and the Pan American Movement' (1922) 5 The Hispanic American Historical Review (1922) 667.

141 Alfred H. Fried, *Pan-Amerika* (n 73 in Chapter 4) 32–35.

142 Analogously translated by the author of the present book; source: ibid 34.

the nations of America."[143] Juan Pablo Scarfi (*'El Imperio de la Ley'* from 2014) and David Healy (*'James G. Blaine and Latin America'* from 2001) added that he hoped to introduce a "[…] system of hemispheric arbitration to stop the cycle of inter-American wars that had disturbed Latin America from the 1860s to the 1880s."[144] In late 1881, Blaine was replaced as U.S. Secretary of State by Frederick T. Frelinghuysen (1817–1885), who withdrew the U.S. invitation to a *Pan-American* conference by August 1882.[145] However, the idea for such a conference remained a factor in U.S.-American policies and kept attracting lots of attention from the public as well as from politicians – in particular, because the original peace-focused concept was later joined by the idea for a hemispheric customs union and a sphere of free trade.[146] The support in U.S.-American policies for the intensification of relations with Latin America grew so strongly over the course of the 1880s, that, in 1888, the U.S. Congress explicitly authorized the president to invite the Latin American states to a conference.[147] When Blaine became the U.S. Secretary of State once more in 1889, he realized the plan in the very same year and re-invited all of Latin America to Washington and, apart from Santo Domingo, every Latin American state accepted the invitation.[148] On October 2, 1889, the conference was officially opened by Blaine, and it was attended by 16 Latin American countries and the United States.[149]

Although economic and trade-related considerations seem to have been crucial too, apparently, they were not the only reasons for the United States to launch this initiative. They also aimed to establish enduring peace in (Latin)

---

143 James Gillespie Blaine, 'Note of the Secretary of State of the United States Inviting the Republics of America to a Pan-American Congress' (1910) 4 The American Journal of International Law, Supplement: Official Documents 253.

144 David Healy, *James G. Blaine and Latin America* (Missouri: University of Missouri Press 2001) 144. Also: Juan Pablo Scarfi, *El Imperio de la Ley: James Brown Scott y la Construcción de un Orden jurídico interamericano* (Fondo de Cultura Económica de Argentina 2014) 55.

145 Compare: David Healy, *James G. Blaine and Latin America* (n 144 in Chapter 4) 144. Furthermore, one reason for Frelinghuysen's decision to withdraw the invitation was the Pacific War (1879–1884) between Chile on the one side and Peru and Bolivia on the other. Compare: 'Frederick Theodore Frelinghuysen to Osborn, 9 Aug. 1882' in *Papers Relating to the Foreign Relations of the United States, Year: 1882* (United States Government Printing Office 1883) 4.

146 David Healy, *James G. Blaine and Latin America* (n 144 in Chapter 4) 144. Also: Juan Pablo Scarfi, *El Imperio de la Ley* (n 144 in Chapter 4) 55.

147 Samuel Guy Inman, *Inter-American Conferences 1826–1954: History and Problems* (Washington University Press 1965) 33–34.

148 Ibid 34.

149 David Healy, *James G. Blaine and Latin America* (n 144 in Chapter 4) 146.

America and for the creation of a system of obligatory arbitration. Furthermore, the United States seems to have held the time to be ripe to change the general situation in the Americas – a situation in which the continent's Northern and Southern parts were politically divided and both had closer relations to Europe than with one another.[150] The United States did not intend to change this arrangement by establishing an All-American union but, instead, by closer regional cooperation. The Spanish American states were also no longer interested in the creation of international unions since the European countries had given up on the idea of re-colonizing Latin America. Because this threat to the independence of the Latin American states had vanished, enthusiasm for substantial changes to the international order on the American continent also faded away.[151] This situation resulted into the following agenda at the *First Pan-American Conference*:

> [T]he conclusion of treaties of commercial reciprocity; the routes of communication between the American states by way of the Pacific, the Atlantic, or the Gulf of Mexico and the Caribbean Sea; the navigation of American international rivers; the construction of a Pan-American railroad; the establishment of an American International Bank; the adoption of a common silver currency for all the nations of America; the establishment of a Commercial Office of the American Republics; and, finally, the prevention of conquests and grants of territory in America.[152]

The last point – the prevention of conquests and grants of territory in America – is particularly important in the present context. The issue was introduced to the conference agenda because of a joint Argentine-Brazilian initiative (from January 15, 1890), in which they called for arbitration and opposed all acquisition of territory by conquest.[153] Hence, the proposal to ban territorial conquest from the mutual relations of American states was a first attempt to extend the Latin American legal principle of non-intervention to the United States. Even though it would not have forced the United States to completely abstain from interventions, as it did not cover gunboat diplomacy, for example, it would have contributed to the limitation of U.S.-American imperialism, and the two states hoped to achieve this goal with the help of legal provi-

---

150 Friedrich Wilhelm von Rauchhaupt, *Völkerrechtliche Eigentümlichkeiten Amerikas, insbesondere Hispano-Amerikas* (H. Sack 1924) 24.

151 Alfred H. Fried, *Pan-Amerika* (n 73 in Chapter 4) 29.

152 Alejandro Alvarez, 'Latin America and International Law' (n 14 in Chapter 4) 327.

153 Samuel Guy Inman, *Inter-American Conferences 1826–1954* (n 147 in Chapter 4) 43.

sions. By the end of the conference, both propositions of the Argentine-Brazilian declaration were adopted in the form of the limitation of conquest and the introduction of an American code of arbitration.[154] According to Samuel Guy Inman (*'Inter-American Conferences'* from 1965), the resolution on the right of conquest "[…] called for the elimination of the principle of conquest from American public law and the nullification of any surrender of territory made under the threat of war or the pressure of armed force."[155] With regards to arbitration, the represented states concluded an agreement according to which (in Article 1) "[t]he Republics of North, Central, and South America hereby adopt Arbitration as a principle of American international law for the settlement of the differences, disputes, or controversies that may arise between two or more of them."[156] In the subsequent articles of this agreement, it was further specified that arbitration should be obligatory in all cases, except of those which had the potential of imperiling the parties' independence.[157] Consequently, the concluded treaty would have constituted a general arbitration obligation covering (almost) all American countries, even the United States, had it been ratified.

For the Latin American countries, striving for such an agreement was the logical continuation of their above-described positive approach to obligatory arbitration. The fact that arbitration was even referred to as "a principle of American international law" and, therefore, as an integral part of the American states' mutual relations shows how much importance they attached to it. Because of this treaty, conflicts, in which diplomacy had failed to lead to a peaceful solution, would have been settled by arbitration and no longer by the use of or threat of force. Furthermore, its conclusion would have resulted in a wide-reaching (legal) limitation of military interventions by the United States. The United States, on the other hand, pursued the goals at this occasions of creating an American market and establishing themselves as the uncontested hegemonic power in all America (under the exclusion of Europe from this region).[158] Although the concluded agreements would have legally limited their interventionist policy, their plan was to make up for that by gaining profound influence over the Latin American countries through economic and political means – which the United States seems to have expected to result

---

154 The resolution on the right of conquest was unanimously adopted by all states represented, except for Chile which abstained from voting.

155 Samuel Guy Inman, *Inter-American Conferences 1826–1954* (n 147 in Chapter 4) 44.

156 James Brown Scott (ed.), *The International Conferences of American States 1889–1928* (n 1 in Chapter 4) 41.

157 Article 4 of the said 'Plan for Arbitration'; see: ibid.

158 David Healy, *James G. Blaine and Latin America* (n 144 in Chapter 4) 156, 157.

in a considerably higher degree of dominance over the rest of the continent than what would have been possible through an interventionist policy.

With regards to these considerations, it can be concluded that the *First Pan-American Conference* was a continuation of the U.S.-American striving for hegemony over the American continent, and of their imperialist policy. The Latin American countries, however, strongly opposed the U.S.-American attempts to realize these goals. They did not want to be turned into sole tributaries and they also did not intend to cut their relations with Europe.[159] Therefore, the U.S.-American plan failed to turn all of America into its exclusive sphere of dominance. The United States could not simply impose their imperialistic approach on the Latin American states, as this would have hampered the negotiations at the conference.

In the end, the represented states concluded the two aforementioned declarations on the right of conquest and arbitration and regulated several other issues concerning trade, civil rights, etc. Furthermore, they also agreed on the foundation of the *International Union of the American Republics* (later *Pan American Union*). This organization was to be represented by the *International Bureau of American Republics*, was to be situated in Washington, D.C., and should be responsible for "[…] the collection, tabulation and publication […] of information as to productions and commerce and as to the customs, laws and regulations of their respective countries."[160] However, only the *Union* was established. All the other resolutions were never put into practice. For example, the general obligatory arbitration treaty was signed by the United States, Haiti, Guatemala, El Salvador, Honduras, Nicaragua, Ecuador, Bolivia, and Brazil – but none of the countries ever ratified it.[161]

---

159 Ibid 156–157.

160 'Report of the Committee on Custom Regulations' in James Brown Scott (ed.), *The International Conferences of American States 1889–1928* (n 1 in Chapter 4) 36.

161 Alejandro Alvarez, 'Latin America and International Law' (n 14 in Chapter 4) 329. See also: Shirley V. Scott, *International Law, US Power: The United States' Quest for Legal Security* (Cambridge University Press 2012) 59. There, she cited from Secretary of State James Blaine's words on the closure of the conference as follows: "We hold up this new Magna Carta, which abolishes war and substitutes arbitration between the American republics, as the first and great fruit of the International American Conference". But, as Scott showed in the following, neither Blaine's words nor the support by the U.S.-American president (according to whom the ratification of the conventions would have resulted in "[…] one of the happiest and most hopeful incidents in the history of the Western Hemisphere") convinced the U.S.-American Senate of taking any actions on it. Furthermore, Scott argued that the United States "[…] was not alone. Only half of the states signed the convention and none ratified it". For further details: Helen May Cory, *Compulsory Arbitration of International Disputes* (n 154 in Chapter 2) 16.

Even though the results of the conference were rather limited, the event cannot be dismissed as unimportant or as a failure. It heralded a new era in the mutual relations of the American states. Former initiatives on regional integration had always been limited to Spanish America and used to have a primarily defensive character. Although they had also involved plans for the introduction of mechanisms for obligatory arbitration, the impulses for considering the creation of Spanish American unions had always derived from external threats. In the case of the *First Pan-American Conference*, the conference was finally covering all of America, as it also included the United States and Brazil. The meeting was not initiated for closing ranks against a common enemy but by the U.S.-American invitation to the Latin American countries to discuss regional integration, the preservation of peace, and the expansion of trade relations. The simple fact that this initiative could be realized, and that the American states actually came together, already constituted an important novelty in their mutual relations.

The motives of the United States were surely not as noble as they had pretended them to be. As shown above, they wanted to use to the conference for consolidating their position as the hegemonic power in America. They showed a broad willingness to support the Latin American initiative for banning the right of conquest and for introducing obligatory arbitration, while they also integrated themselves into the mutual relations of American states; a step which they had abstained from taking during most of the 19th century. By bringing together Latin American representatives in Washington, they finally abandoned this isolationist approach and initiated closer co-operation among the countries of the Western hemisphere. All in all – and despite the lack of any actual consequences in the form of ratified resolutions – the conference can still be regarded as a commitment to more peaceful American relations, to arbitration as the preferred instrument for the settlement of the represented states' mutual disputes, and to the prohibition of conquest, as all of these topics were seriously discussed at the conference and general consent could be achieved. Finally, the *First Pan-American Conference* also set the precedent for further *Pan-American* meetings – even though it would take another 11 years until the next one was held in Mexico City in 1901/02.[162]

162 David Healy, *James G. Blaine and Latin America* (n 144 in Chapter 4) 159.

4 Conclusion

Right after, and before, the achievement of independence, the Spanish American states already began to show a strong commitment to obligatory arbitration. They concluded treaties among themselves which contained obligatory arbitration clauses, and soon after, they also began to do the same with European countries. They even came together for a series of Spanish American conferences to discuss the creation of unions, which would have provided obligatory mechanisms for the settlement of the mutual relations of the union's member states. At the *First Pan-American Conference* in 1889/90, the American states, furthermore, declared arbitration to be an element of American international law and, thereby, stressed again its importance for American relations and their dedication to it.

However, as also shown in this chapter, the Latin American countries never really invoked the obligatory arbitration clauses entailed in their bi-lateral treaties and, before the 1870s/1880s, only very occasionally used the instrument of arbitration at all. The obligatory arbitration clauses often seem to have been concluded to appease the other treaty party, to show benevolence, and to promise peace for the future. But, in the end, these treaties often had a rather political, instead of a legally binding, nature. War, on the other hand, remained a common phenomenon in American relations. This contradictory arrangement can be traced back to the fact that the Latin American states were still very young. They had not yet established a stable equilibrium of power. However, it cannot be negated either that – besides the wars – there are convincing indications for the existence of a strong spirit of togetherness among the Spanish American states. They seem to have felt closely connected to one another and to have considered themselves as belonging to one family of states, due to their common history, shared common experiences, and similar cultures. Unlike in Europe and in the United States, where arbitration became more and more prominent primarily because of the successful lobbying of private (international) pressure groups and initiatives, the driving factor behind the spread of (obligatory) arbitration in Spanish America were the governments themselves. They seem to have followed Bolívar's demand for closer cooperation and friendly relations (and for the creation of a confederation) among the newly established Spanish American nations. One approach for fulfilling this demand, was to create peace-oriented relations which were based on the principle of (obligatory) arbitration, instead of war. In the first decades after their independence, this approach did not fully work out in state practice. As the above-discussed figures have shown, the Latin American countries only took recourse to isolated arbitration (on an increasing basis) during the later parts of the 19th century.

The findings also indicate that the Latin American countries influenced European states with regards to obligatory arbitration. Obligatory arbitration was prominent in Spanish American relations first, was later introduced to European/American relations, and finally found its way into inter-European relations in the last decades of the 19th century. Although it remains an assumption for now,[163] that the European countries were influenced by their Latin American counterparts (as a second major factor besides the peace movement and other pressure groups) to integrate obligatory arbitration into their foreign policy, the given numbers and invoked arguments seem to point in this direction. Apart from that, it is also noteworthy that the Spanish American countries gave up on the attempt to establish Spanish American unions during the later parts of the 19th century, opting instead to strive for regional cooperation, and the conclusion of a Spanish American obligatory arbitration treaty. At the *First Pan-American Conference* in 1889/1890, they almost succeeded in this regard, as an obligatory arbitration treaty (covering almost all America) was concluded, but never ratified.

Therefore, it is one of the most crucial findings of this chapter that the Spanish American countries showed a very benevolent and favorable attitude towards obligatory arbitration. They seem to have played a key role in establishing obligatory arbitration as an element of international law on the global level. While, on the other hand, it remained uncommon for Latin American countries to refer cases, even those of minor importance, to isolated arbitration before the 1870s/1880s. It was only due to the intensification of trade relations with Europe, with the United States, and among themselves that the Latin American countries took over this practice and began to refer a quickly growing number of cases to isolated arbitration.

Hence, the situation in Latin America concerning international law, and arbitration, was decisively different than the one which prevailed in the North Atlantic context at that time. While the countries from the latter region used isolated arbitration for the settlement of conflicts of secondary importance on a regular basis and widely abstained for most parts of the 19th century from concluding obligatory arbitration agreements, the Spanish American countries pursued an approach to arbitration which was the exact opposite.

163 It cannot be determined with certainty whether this assumption is correct or not because of a research gap in the existing literature in this regard. The thematical limitation of the scope of this book leaves no room for a detailed study on this issue either. Therefore, it only remains to identify the gap and to continue working on the basis of the made assumption.

During the last decades of the 19th century, the two approaches – the North Atlantic and the Latin American one – started to draw considerably closer. Apart from that, regarding international law (as a whole), it was also not possible to speak of a globally coherent, and homogenous, approach to it by the turn of the 20th century. While the North Atlantic powers strove for the realization of their imperialist goals and upheld the hegemonic structure of the international order from which they benefitted a lot and which put them in a very favorable position against the vast majority of other countries, the Latin American states attempted to change the prevailing order. They hoped that their efforts would result in a better standing under international law, and into more protection from the striving for dominance by the North Atlantic powers.

CHAPTER 5

Arbitration (1899–1905)

> A careful study of history, he [James Brown Scott] maintained, showed the development of improved methods of maintaining peace. These stages ranged from anarchy to diplomacy through arbitration, and eventually, to an International Court of Justice.[1]
>
> RALPH NURNBERGER, *'James Brown Scott: Peace through Justice'*

1 The Outset in 1899

Organizations such as the *International Law Association*, the *Inter-Parliamentary Union*, or the manifold national peace societies in North America and Europe emerged (as shown above) as important players on the international scene during the 19th century. They fought for the enhanced use of peaceful methods of conflict settlement, for the institutionalization of these instruments, for the codification and further development of international law, and – as an ultimate goal – for the replacement of war through justice. In the following, the view will be turned to the second of the named issues, the institutionalization of arbitration. This topic became increasingly prominent among peace activists and international lawyers in the late 19th century. This is evidenced by the fact that a high number of plans and concepts were published at this time.[2] While some of them have already been mentioned in Chapter 3,[3] two additional concepts will be dealt with on the subsequent pages to provide a telling insight into the history of the idea of institutionalizing arbitration right before the *First Hague Peace Conference*.

The first of these attempts can be dated back to a meeting of the *Inter-Parliamentary Union* in Brussels in 1894 at which the idea to establish an independent and permanent court of arbitration was discussed; an approach which differed from earlier concepts because (as shown above) they con-

1 Ralph Nurnberger, *James Brown Scott: Peace through Justice* (Georgetown University 1975) 3.
2 Mark Weston Janis, *The American Tradition of International Law* (n 77 in Chapter 3) 144.
3 Compare pages 102 et seq of the present book.

 | DOI:10.1163/9789004754126_006

sidered such courts only in the context of world organizations.[4] The concept presented in Brussels in 1894 for the creation of the so-called *Cour permanente d'arbitrage* fulfilled exactly this condition. It promoted only the establishment of an autonomous permanent court of arbitration and did not call for the creation of any other organization or association. Furthermore, it also paid attention to the aversion of many (greater European) states to obligatory arbitration commitments and limitations of their sovereignty rights.[5] National sovereignty was to be maintained to the fullest extend since the court was conceptualized as an entirely voluntary institution, and all nations were to enjoy full equality.[6] By abstaining from demanding any obligatory arbitration commitment, proposing the institutionalization of the so far prevailing practice of isolated arbitration in from of an autonomous, permanent, and only facultative international court of arbitration, the *Inter-Parliamentary Union* offered a realistic option for the creation of such an institution. The proposal soon gained prominence within the peace movement and attracted the attention of several governments. For the subsequent *First Hague Peace Conference*, it even served as an inspiration and point of reference;[7] especially because it was further developed by the Belgian Senator Edouard Descamps (1847–1933) who also served as a delegate at the *First Hague Peace Conference*. Based on this proposal, he formulated a model treaty for an independent tribunal and sent it to numerous governments to raise awareness for the project.[8]

A second influential proposal was made in 1896, this time by the *New York State Bar Association*. Its members were dedicated to the cause of peace, and they were highly discontent with the prevailing situation on the international level. They demanded for more impartiality in arbitrations and for binding arbitral decisions to law.[9] These claims had arisen more frequently during the 1890s among progressive peace activists and international lawyers, especially in the United States. In order to address the issue, the members of the *New York State Bar Association* appointed a committee in 1896. In its final report, it recommended the creation of an autonomous and permanent court of arbitration which was to be composed:

4 Alfred H. Fried, *Handbuch der Friedensbewegung*, vol. 2 (n 72 in Chapter 3) 8 et seq.

5 Compare: Heinrich Lammasch, *Die Lehre von der Schiedsgerichtsbarkeit in ihrem ganzen Umfange* (n 107 in Chapter 2) 40.

6 Jackson Harvey Ralston, *International Arbitration from Athens to Locarno* (n 23 in Chapter 3) 140.

7 Ibid. See also: Heinrich Lammasch, *Die Lehre von der Schiedsgerichtsbarkeit in ihrem ganzen Umfange* (n 107 in Chapter 2) 41.

8 Jost Dülffer, *Regeln gegen den Krieg?* (n 20 in Chapter 1) 81. See also: Sandi E. Cooper, *Patriotic Pacifism* (n 156 in Chapter 3) 103.

9 David S. Patterson, *Towards a Warless World* (n 147 in Chapter 3) 102.

> […] of nine members, one each from nine independent states or nations, such representative to be a member of the Supreme or Highest Court of the nation he shall represent, chosen by a majority vote of his associates, because of his high character as a publicist and judge and his recognized ability and irreproachable integrity.[10]

Hence, the committee strove to replace arbitrators with trained judges in the settlement of state-to-state disputes. The appointment of competent and experienced judges (selected by the highest courts of their home countries) was proposed to ensure impartiality, independence, and legal competence in the decisions of the court, and to achieve a better compliance with the principle of the rule of law. Consequently, the establishment of such a court would have been a first step in the direction of adjudication. By sending the proposal to members of the U.S.-American government, to the State Department, and even to U.S. President Stephan Grover Cleveland (1837–1908), the *New York State Bar Association* managed to garner a lot of attention for its plan. According to David S. Patterson (*'Towards a Warless World'* from 1976), the concept even "[…] had some influence on the […] personnel who drafted the American proposal for a permanent court"[11] for the *First Hague Peace Conference*. Therefore, the draft of the *New York State Bar Association* exerted substantial influence on the U.S.-American government and even foreshadowed its policy in the subsequent years.

During the 1890s, the idea to create an autonomous and permanent court of arbitration was already prominently discussed by peace activists and international lawyers. They detached the concept for such a court from the plan to establish a world union and were, thereby, able to turn it into a considerably more realistic and acceptable option for states. Nevertheless, it is astonishing that it only took until 1899 for this idea to make its way into the highest political levels, and onto the agenda of a major international conference, the *First Hague Peace Conference*.

2 The *First Hague Peace Conference* (1899)

The initiative for holding the *First Hague Peace Conference* stemmed from the Russian Czar Nicholas II (1868–1918) who, in 1898, ordered his foreign minister

10 New York State Bar Association, *Address of Congratulation and Commendation of the New York State Bar Association to His Imperial Majesty, Nicholas II, Emperor of all Russians, on the Occasion of the Peace Congress at The Hague and Recommending the Creation of an International Court* (New York State Bar Association 1899) 11.

11 David S. Patterson, *Towards a Warless World* (n 147 in Chapter 3) 103.

Vladimir N. Murav'ev (1845–1900) to deliver a memoir to the delegates and ambassadors accredited to the Court in Saint Petersburg. The so-called *Czar's Rescript* was an outstanding, but rather untypical, step for that time. Against the prevailing trend of constant imperialistic struggles and great power rivalries which dominated the international scene,[12] the Czar suggested to address the problems of world peace and disarmament in the context of a multi-lateral conference.[13] Furthermore, he launched his initiative publicly which guaranteed him a lot of attention by the media and the public. The public interest in the event was particularly high because the Czar's initiative matched with a certain spirit of that time which regarded the warmongering tendencies in Europe with skepticism and anxiety. Concerns were widespread about the threat of war and the horrors of modern military technology. In addition, there was growing support for the cause of peace and for the conviction that the instrument of international arbitration, optimally combined with the establishment of an international court, represented the best possible chance for lasting peace.[14]

Because of the uniqueness of the *Czar's Rescript*, and its unusual nature for this period, Arthur Eyffinger (*'The 1899 Hague Peace Conference'* from 1999) referred to it as "[...] one of the most remarkable and at the same time enigmatic products of diplomacy over the whole period between the French-Prussian War and the roaring of the Guns of August."[15] Describing the *First Hague Peace Conference* as "[t]he Dawn of a New Era"[16] – as again Eyffinger did it in the very same publication – is certainly an ambitious claim. However, the conference was indeed of a unique character. It not only brought together representatives of 26 countries, but it also made them discuss topics some of which had not yet played any role in international politics. New political ground was broken merely by putting the question of the establishment of an autonomous and permanent court of arbitration on the conference agenda. As described on the previous pages, the idea to create such a tribunal had

12 Jost Dülffer, *Regeln gegen den Krieg?* (n 20 in Chapter 1) 19.

13 Bob Reinalda, *Routledge History of International Organizations* (n 59 in Chapter 2) 65. According to the Czar's Rescript, the purpose of the conference was the following: "The maintenance of general peace, and a possible reduction of the excessive armaments which weigh upon all nations, present themselves in the existing condition of the whole world, as the ideal towards which the endeavors of all Governments should be directed." Compare: Arthur Eyffinger, *The 1899 Hague Peace Conference* (n 28 in Chapter 1) 17.

14 David D. Caron, 'War and International Adjudication: Reflections on the 1899 Peace Conference' (2000) 94, The American Journal of International Law 5–6.

15 Arthur Eyffinger, *The 1899 Hague Peace Conference* (n 28 in Chapter 1) 16.

16 Ibid 15.

already been dealt with by peace activists and international lawyers in recent years. However, it had not yet been a point of discussion in any bi- or even multi-lateral conference so far.[17] On the *First Hague Peace Conference*, representatives from all major North Atlantic countries and from several other (non-European) states dealt with the idea. Thereby, the concept reached the stage of big politics.

The *First Hague Peace Conference* was a remarkable and ground-breaking event which had a significant effect not only on (the institutionalization of) the instrument of arbitration but also on several other areas of international law. It left a lasting impression on the peace movement, legal scholarship, and the participating states and marked a first climax of the trend for international conferences dealing more and more regularly with juridical topics. In the first half of the 19th century, international conferences had been primarily political events. They had been held for the settlement of pressing conflicts through negotiations between the most powerful countries. In the second half of the 19th century, after the end of the *Concert of Europe*, the trend shifted. A growing number of international conferences were held to deal with legal topics such as the laws of war or the foundation of international administrative organizations. The *First Hague Peace Conference* continued this tradition, however, with a more general character than the former law-related meetings. At the same time, it should also be born in mind that even though 26 countries were represented in The Hague, the conference cannot be regarded as a world congress. It remained a primarily North Atlantic event; no African countries and very few Asian and America countries (the United States, Mexico, and Brazil) were invited.[18]

---

17 At the inter-American conferences of the 19th century, the issue of creating a permanent court of arbitration was also addressed. However, this option was always discussed in the greater framework of the establishment of an inter-American union/federation. Plans for independent courts were not dealt with on these occasions.

18 Those were China, Japan, Persia, Siam, and Turkey. For further explanations on (the reasons for) the invitation of Asian countries to the First Hague Peace Conference, please see: Vitit Muntarbhorn, 'The 1899 Hague Peace Conference and the Development of the Laws of War: Asia's Contribution to the Quest for Humanitarianism?' in Timothy L.H. McCormack, Michael Tilbury, and Gillian D. Triggs (eds.), *A Century of War and Peace: Asia-Pacific Perspectives on the Centenary of the 1899 Hague Peace Conference* (Kluwer Law International 2001) 113 et seq. Regarding the American states, it should be noted that only the former two accepted the invitation. Brazil rejected it and did not participate in the First Hague Peace Conference. Compare: Peter Calvert, *The International Politics of Latin America* (Manchester University Press 1994) 190.

2.1 *The* Czar's Rescript

The rescript did not mention the establishment of a permanent international court of arbitration yet. But it addressed two other important goals: World peace and disarmament.[19] However, the vagueness, which inhered the Czar's note, left the other countries in a state of uncertainty about the precise content of his proposal and his motivations for having launched it.[20] Several peace activists, newspapers, and politicians openly expressed their doubts about the Czar's motives.[21] Arthur Eyffinger concluded contemporary reactions and current views as follows:

> To this day, the riddle of the exact drift and tenor, its immediate rationale and ultimate purport baffles scholarship. In a way, the mixture of disbelief, skepticism, blank amazement and pleasant surprise which prevailed among ambassadors and ministers of the first moment of delivery still holds critics divided.[22]

It was only when the Czar published a *Second Circular Note* in late 1898 that his initiative took a more concrete shape. This note provided a draft agenda for the proposed conference and brought relief to the other governments. They became more comfortable with the initiative, especially because the note explicitly excluded questions which concerned "[…] the political relations of States, and the order of things established by treaties, as in general all questions which do not directly fall within the program adopted by the cabinets."[23] Murav'ev introduced this paragraph to the note in order to convince the other governments that Russia did not strive for fundamental changes to the international order, only for adaptions. For this purpose, he also added topics to the agenda which were less controversial and political, but which had a rather technical nature.[24] In the end, the *Second Circular Note* contained the following eight topics:

> 1. An understanding stipulating the non-augmentation, for a term to be agreed upon, of the present effective armed land and sea forces, as well

---

19 Arthur Eyffinger, *The 1899 Hague Peace Conference* (n 28 in Chapter 1) 15.

20 Compare: Jost Dülffer, *Regeln gegen den Krieg?* (n 20 in Chapter 1) 22 et seq.

21 Alfred H. Fried, *Handbuch der Friedensbewegung* (n 135 in Chapter 3) 164–165.

22 Arthur Eyffinger, *The 1899 Hague Peace Conference* (n 28 in Chapter 1) 16.

23 'Russian Circular Note Proposing the Program of the First Conference from 30 December 1898', published, e.g., in James Brown Scott (ed.), *Instructions to the American Delegates to The Hague Peace Conferences and their Official Reports* (Oxford University Press 1916) 4–5.

24 Jost Dülffer, *Regeln gegen den Krieg?* (n 20 in Chapter 1) 53.

> as the war budgets pertaining to them; preliminary study of the ways in which even a reduction of the aforesaid effectives and budgets could be realized in the future.
> 2. Interdiction of the employment in armies and fleets of new firearms of every description and of new explosives, as well as powder more powerful than the kinds used at present, both for guns and cannons.
> 3. Limitation of the use of field fighting of explosives of a formidable power, such as are now in use, and prohibition of explosive from balloons or by similar means.
> 4. Prohibition of the use in naval battles of submarine or diving torpedo boats, or of other engines of destruction of the same nature; agreement not to construct in the future war-ships armed with rams.
> 5. Adaption to naval war of the stipulations of the Geneva Convention of 1864, on the base of the additional articles of 1868.
> 6. Neutralization, for the same reason, of boats or launches employed in the rescue of the shipwrecked during or after naval battles.
> 7. Revision of the declaration concerning the laws and customs of war elaborated in 1874 by the Conference of Brussels, and not yet ratified.
> 8. Acceptance, in principle, of the use of good offices, mediation, and voluntary arbitration, in cases where they are available, with the purpose of preventing armed conflicts between nations; understanding in relation to their mode of application and establishment of a uniform practice in employing them.[25]

These issues were considerably more concrete and tangible for the other governments than the initial invitation. But at the same time, they fell short regarding the Czar's original goal of achieving universal peace. Only the first point still dealt with disarmament,[26] whereas points 2–7 focused on the laws of war and the use and ban of certain weapon systems (*ius in bello*).[27] Because the present book is primarily concerned with limitations of the *ius ad bellum*, the following pages will mainly deal with the eighth point. This point refers to the further development of methods for the peaceful settlement of conflicts

---

25 'Russian Circular Note Proposing the Program of the First Conference from 30 December 1898' (n 23 in Chapter 5) 4.

26 Andrew Webster, 'Reconsidering Disarmament at the Hague Peace Conference of 1899, and after', in Maartje Abbenhuis et al. (eds.), *War, Peace and International Order?* (n 25 in Chapter 1) 69–86.

27 David D. Caron, 'War and International Adjudication' (n 14 in Chapter 5) 14. According to him: "The new agenda items on the laws of war in the Russian circular of January 1899 were more amenable to producing agreement, but for opponents of war these proposals were anathema, making war less horrific rather than peace more likely."

and formed the basis for discussions on the establishment of a permanent court of arbitration in The Hague.

That the second circular note contained a point about peaceful conflict settlement can be traced back to the fact that the Russian government had to realize that the topic of disarmament was too delicate, too political, and too controversial to expect discussions at a multi-lateral conference to result in actual progress. Therefore, additional topics (such as point 8) were introduced to the agenda of the conference. They seemed to be more promising in that they would result in presentable successes and, therefore, prevent the conference from failing.[28] According to David D. Caron (*'War and International Adjudication'* from 2000), the Russian government had to have realized that the Czar's initial "[…] proposals for disarmament were nonstarters from the outset."[29] In order to prevent the conference from failing and to disguise the failure of the original proposal,[30] Russia moved the focus towards the laws of war and the methods for the peaceful settlement of international conflicts. Thereby, the attention was turned to topics which were less utopian, less controversial, and less fundamental.[31] According to Randall Lesaffer (*'The Temple of Peace'* from 2013), this step turned "[…] the disarmament conference into a broad peace conference."[32]

Other authors have named further possible reasons for the introduction of the eighth point to the agenda. For example, Eyffinger mentioned that "[…] in all likelihood, it was probably introduced as ballast to lend more weight to the rather meagre initial programme and without any clear expectations on its own account."[33] Some authors also referred to the influence of Mr. Bazili, a Russian diplomate who had attended several meetings of the *Universal Peace Congress* before 1899. At these occasions, he seems to have been exposed to ideas to increase the use of methods for peaceful conflict settlement and to establish a permanent court of arbitration.[34] When he was promoted in 1898, to the prestigious position of head of the Asiatic division in the Russian foreign office,[35] he

28 Karl von Stengel, *Die Haager Friedenskonferenz und das Völkerrecht* (J.C.B. Mohr 1900) 189.

29 David D. Caron, 'War and International Adjudication' (n 14 in Chapter 5) 14.

30 Arthur Eyffinger, *The 1899 Hague Peace Conference* (n 28 in Chapter 1) 38.

31 Compare also: Vladimir V. Pustagarov and William Elliott Butler, *Our Martens: F.F. Martens, International Lawyer and Architect of Peace* (Simmonds & Hill 2000) 162–169.

32 Randall Lesaffer, 'The Temple of Peace' (n 135 in Chapter 3) 23.

33 Arthur Eyffinger, *The 1899 Hague Peace Conference* (n 28 in Chapter 1) 38.

34 Dan L. Morrill, 'Nicholas II and the Call for the First Hague Conference' (1974) 46 The Journal of Modern History 304.

35 Thomas K. Ford, 'The Genesis of the First Hague Peace Conference' (1936) 51 Political Science Quarterly 360.

would have been able to introduce some of these ideas to the agenda of the upcoming conference.[36] Moreover, none of the invited countries raised objections to the addition of the eighth point to the conference agenda, even though it had not been included in the first note.[37] But despite its late introduction, the peaceful settlement of international disputes did not remain a side issue in The Hague. Instead, it developed into one of the major topics of the entire conference.

2.2 *The Proceedings of the Conference*

The *First Hague Peace Conference* opened on May 18, 1899. Already on its second plenary meeting, Baron Georges de Staal (1822–1907), president of the conference and head of the Russian delegation, explicitly stressed the importance of the peaceful settlement of conflicts. He referred to the purpose of the conference as follows:

> [...] we shall devote ourselves especially to the generalization and codification of arbitral practice, and of mediation or good offices. These ideas are, so to speak, the very essence of our task, the general goal toward which we are to direct our efforts: *the prevention of conflicts by peaceful means.*[38]

Staal, as a member of the nation which had initiated the conference, now attached the greatest importance to this topic.[39] This can be taken as a telling sign that the focus of the conference had changed since the submission of the rescript. Instead of disarmament, the further development of methods for peaceful conflict settlement stood in the center of attention at The Hague. This finding is further substantiated by the fact that Staal declared that one of the major tasks of the conference was the following:

> Diplomacy long ago admitted them [arbitration and other means of peaceful conflict settlement] in its practice, but diplomacy has not laid down definite rules for applying them; it has not specified the cases to which they may be applied. That is the noble work upon which we are

---

36 Dan L. Morrill, 'Nicholas II and the Call for the First Hague Conference' (n 34 in Chapter 5) 304.

37 Jost Dülffer, *Regeln gegen den Krieg?* (n 20 in Chapter 1) 67.

38 James Brown Scott (ed.), *The Proceedings of The Hague Peace Conferences: The Conference of 1899* (Oxford University Press 1920) 18.

39 William I. Hull, *The two Hague Conferences and their Contributions to International Law* (Ginn & Company 1908) 46.

> about to direct our energies, sustained by the conviction that we are labouring for the good of all mankind along the road which former generations have laid out for us.[40]

Soon after the opening of the conference, the actual work began. On May 20, 1899, the plenum took the decision to create three commissions to address the topics of the second circular note.[41] The first one dealt with points 1–4 of the agenda, the second one with 5–7, and the third one was dedicated solely to point 8. However, contrary to the actual wording of point 8, the third commission quickly started dealing with issues in a way that went beyond its given work scope. Initially, its mission had been to discuss the improvement of the practice of good offices, mediation, and voluntary arbitration and the creation of a uniform practice for employing these means. But, already by its second meeting (on May 26, 1899), Léon Bourgeois (1851–1925),[42] president of the third commission, questioned this thematic limitation by asking the other members of the commission whether they all agreed "[…] to try to establish relations between nations preferably according to law, and to regulate them, in case of dispute, according to justice? In other words, is it more desirable to have recourse to peaceful means rather than to force in settling disputes between nations?"[43] Instead of only dealing with the tasks initially given, he therefore strongly advocated for the extension of the scope of the third commission by also addressing the following topics:

> We shall […] ask ourselves whether there are cases where nations can agree in advance that this recourse [to arbitration] shall be obligatory.
>
> It will then be necessary to establish in advance an *arbitral procedure* accepted by all.
>
> […]

---

40 James Brown Scott (ed.), *The Proceedings of The Hague Peace Conferences* (n 38 in Chapter 5) 19.

41 Ibid.

42 Léon Bourgeois was the head of the French delegation, served as prime minister from 1895 to 1896, was president of the Chamber of Deputies from 1902 to 1904, and held several ministerial positions before and during World War I. After the war, he became the president of France (between 1920 and 1923). Additionally, he advocated for international solidarity and for the peaceful settlement of international conflicts through arbitration; compare, for example: Léon Bourgeois, *Solidarité* (A. Colin et cie 1896). In 1920, he received the first post-war Nobel Peace Prize. For further details, see: Arthur Eyffinger, *The 1899 Hague Peace Conference* (n 28 in Chapter 1) 140.

43 James Brown Scott (ed.), *The Proceedings of The Hague Peace Conferences* (n 38 in Chapter 5) 583.

> Will it be preferable to proceed by extending the system of *permanent arbitration* treaties by introducing the arbitration clause in international acts?
>
> Or, on the contrary, shall there be established a permanent *international institution* to act:
>
> 1. as an intermediary, to remind the parties of the existence of the conventions, of the possible application of arbitration, and to offer to set the procedure in motion;
> 2. as a means of conciliation previous to any judicial discussion; and
> 3. finally, as a court in the form of an international tribunal.[44]

In the following weeks, the last point – the introduction of an international tribunal – quickly moved into the central focus of the commission's work and became the most critical issue. The enormous growth of importance and attention which were attached to the court project resulted from the fact that it soon became apparent to conference participants and observers that the discussions on disarmament would most likely not lead to any substantial results.[45] As a consequence, the focus of public attention moved to the third commission. The expectations in its work grew, putting pressure on its members to achieve far-going results. Furthermore, Edouard Descamps, who had already dealt with the above-mentioned plan of the *Inter-Parliamentary Union* for a permanent court of arbitration,[46] represented Belgium in the third commission and provided all the other participating states with the afore-mentioned plan.[47] The British delegate Sir Julian Pauncefote (1828–1902)[48] received it particularly favorably and was one of the strongest supporters of the creation of such an institution. In a speech delivered at the second meeting of the third commission, he made this point clear by declaring the following:

> [...] the subject which I believe to be the most important, that is, the establishment of a permanent international court of arbitration [...].

---

44 Ibid 583–584.

45 Jost Dülffer, *Regeln gegen den Krieg?* (n 20 in Chapter 1) 80.

46 Compare pages 152–154 of the present book.

47 Jost Dülffer, *Regeln gegen den Krieg?* (n 20 in Chapter 1) 81.

48 Sir Julian Pauncefote was a diplomat and politician who had an important impact on the development of arbitration. He was involved in an arbitration of fishing rights in the Bering Sea (in 1892) between the United States and Great Britain, he paved the way for an arbitral settlement of the Venezuela-British Guyana case, and he served as the British negotiator for the above-mentioned British-American Treaty of Arbitration. Compare: Arthur Eyffinger, *The 1899 Hague Peace Conference* (n 28 in Chapter 1) 152–153.

> [...]
>
> If we want to make a step forward, I believe that it is absolutely necessary to organize a permanent international tribunal, which may be able to assemble at once upon the request of the disputing nations.[49]

He concluded his remarks with the announcement to submit a proposal for the establishment of a permanent court of arbitration.[50] Russia did not intend to stand back in this regard and brought two documents to the attention of the third commission (already at its second meeting). The first one provided an *Outline of a Draft Convention*[51] and concerned good offices and mediation, arbitration, and commissions of inquiry. In the context of arbitration, the Russian draft even provided for a limited obligatory arbitration commitment in the form of a list of topics which were supposed to be subjected to compulsory arbitral settlement.[52] Although this was a progressive steps (compared to the previous attitude of most European nations towards obligatory arbitration), the proposed obligatory commitment would have been fairly limited. The listed topics primarily concerned administrative aspects and pecuniary claims. Some of the issues – such as the international and intergovernmental administration of telegraphs and posts – were even already subject to obliga-

49 James Brown Scott (ed.), *The Proceedings of The Hague Peace Conferences* (n 38 in Chapter 5) 584.

50 Ibid.

51 Ibid 797–800.

52 Article 10 of the Russian *Outline of a Draft Convention* (in: ibid 799) listed the following topics:

I. [...] differences or disputes relating to pecuniary damages suffered by a State, or its nationals, as a consequence of illegal actions or negligence on the part of another State or its nationals.

II. [...] disagreements relating to the interpretation or application of treaties and conventions mentioned below:

- Treaties and conventions relating to the posts and telegraphs, railroads, and also those bearing upon the protection of submarine telegraph cables; regulations concerning methods to prevent collisions of vessels on the high seas; conventions relating to the navigation of international rivers and interoceanic canals.
- Conventions concerning the protection of literary and artistic property as well as industrial property (patents, trademarks, and trade names); conventions relating to money and measures; conventions relating to sanitation and veterinary surgery, and for the prevention of phylloxera.
- Conventions relating to inheritance, exchange of prisoners, and reciprocal assistance in the administration of justice.
- Conventions for marking boundaries, so far as they concern purely technical and non-political questions.

tory arbitration through other regulations.[53] Furthermore, the outline also included a clause according to which states were to be exempt from the arbitration obligation if the case at stake concerned the parties' vital interests or national honor.[54] The second document was a *Draft of an Arbitral Code,*[55] proposing a set of rules for the performance of arbitral procedures.

The main purpose of both Russian proposals seemed to be the codification of the already established practice of arbitration.[56] However, codifying it in a multi-lateral agreement would have resulted in significant simplification (and standardization) of the initiation process and of the general procedures of arbitration. The adoption of such a framework would have enabled the contracting powers to enter into arbitral procedures without first having to compromise over questions concerning the composition of the tribunal, arbitral rules, or other (rather administrative) aspects; as it used to be the case so far in individual arbitrations.[57] Hence, the implementation of the Russian drafts would have enhanced the prevailing situation and would have provided for a better preservation of peace through a facilitated use of arbitration. However, it would not have resulted in far-going conceptual changes of international law.

The third commission decided to subject both concepts – the British as well as the Russian one – to a preliminary examination by a special committee, the so-called *Comité d'Examen.* Apart for Bourgeois and Paul Henri d'Estournelles (1852–1924),[58] all other members of that special committee were experts in international law.[59] Most of them had even been appointed to their respective delegations as technical or legal advisers.[60] With their nomination to the committee, they were assigned a role of utmost importance in the conference, since they were chosen to address the very sensitive issues of obligatory arbitration and of the establishment of a permanent court of arbitration. They had to deal with topics which stood in the center of attention of the global public. Regarding their political and legal opinions, it can be observed that several of

---

53 Compare pages 96–99 of the present book.

54 James Brown Scott (ed.), *The Proceedings of The Hague Peace Conferences* (n 38 in Chapter 5) 799.

55 Ibid 801–804.

56 Jost Dülffer, *Regeln gegen den Krieg?* (n 20 in Chapter 1) 82.

57 Compare pages 38–45 of the present book.

58 Arthur Eyffinger, *The 1899 Hague Peace Conference* (n 28 in Chapter 1) 142. According to him, d'Estournelles was by "[…] no doubt one of the most influential advocates of arbitration and arms limitation in the decades around the turn of the century."

59 Jost Dülffer, *Regeln gegen den Krieg?* (n 20 in Chapter 1) 89.

60 Ibid.

them were open supporters of the cause of peace and of an increased use of arbitration.[61] For example, D'Estournelles[62] and Bourgeois[63] were influential members of the peace movement while Tobias Asser (1838–1913) was a founding member of the *Institut de Droit International*. According to Eyffinger, Asser was also a "[…] great advocate of arbitration and of the Permanent Court of Arbitration."[64] Moreover, most of the governments (represented in the committee) encouraged their delegates to strive for progress in the field of arbitration and regarding the establishment of a permanent court. Only Heinrich Lammasch, the Austrian delegate (though he personally supported arbitration),[65] and Philipp Zorn, the German representative, received contrary instructions from their governments.

The nomination of peace activists and experts in international law to the committee of examination turned out to be a crucial and extremely momentous decision for the entire conference. They dealt very carefully with the topics which had been assigned to them while at the same time incorporating progressive ideas of the peace movement and from legal scholarship into the discussions, showing a benevolent attitude for changes and modifications of the prevailing practice of arbitration. Throughout the course of the conference, the committee met more often than any other panel of the *First Hague Peace Conference*. They came together at least eighteen times. Due to the importance, which was attached to their discussions, the committee soon became "[…] the heart and soul of the whole Conference."[66]

Throughout the work of the committee, it focused on (a) the Russian proposals for an arbitral code and for the creation of regulations for methods of conflict settlement, (b) the introduction of arbitration obligations, and (c)

61 The committee of examination was composed of Count Constantino Nigra, Sir Julian Pauncefote, Tobias Asser, Chevalier Descamps Baron D'Estournelles de Constant, Frederick W. Holls, Heinrich Lammasch, Frédéric de Martens, Edouard Odier, and Philipp Zorn. Compare: James Brown Scott (ed.), *The Proceedings of The Hague Peace Conferences* (n 38 in Chapter 5) 687. Also: Arthur Eyffinger, *The 1899 Hague Peace Conference* (n 28 in Chapter 1) 124 et seq.

62 Henri Paul d'Estournelles de Constant (1852–1924) was a French politician (senator and member of parliament), peace activist, and Nobel Peace Prize laureate (1909). He dedicated much of his political work to the cause of peace and arbitration and was the founder and president of the French parliamentary group for obligatory arbitration. Furthermore, he represented France at both Hague Peace Conferences and served as a member of the Permanent Court of Arbitration from 1900 onwards.

63 Compare *footnote 42* of the present chapter.

64 Arthur Eyffinger, *The 1899 Hague Peace Conference* (n 28 in Chapter 1) 168.

65 Ibid; Eyffinger referred at this page to Lammasch as an 'idealistic pacifist,' as 'a champion of arbitration,' and as someone who looked 'upon war as an antiquated relic.'

66 Ibid 381.

the creation of a permanent court of arbitration.[67] When the committee started its work, it did so by concentrating first on the articles of the Russian *Outline of a Draft Convention* concerning mediation and good offices. Though some crucial aspects were to be settled and had to be clarified in this regard, a common view was quickly reached. Even when the discussion moved to the more sensitive topic of obligatory arbitration, the situation did not change much. The members of the committee and of the third commission showed an astonishing level of readiness to work together. The obligatory arbitration commitment, which the committee recommended to enter as a result of its first negotiations on the Russian proposal, was supposed to be restricted to a limited set of cases[68] (and was therefore of a special compromissory nature). In all other cases, arbitration was to remain optional.[69] Despite the limitedness, this first step towards a multi-lateral obligatory arbitration commitment clearly demonstrated the representatives' willingness to adopt changes. They overcame the still prevailing hesitations towards obligatory arbitration which were particularly widespread among the European great powers. As shown above,[70] (at least special compromissory) obligatory arbitration had already become more common in inter-European policies during the 1890s. However, the trend was so far limited to a set of (mostly smaller) nations, whereas others – and especially the conservative great powers Austria-Hungary, Germany, and Russia – had widely abstained from concluding agreements of that type with other (European) states. Negotiations in the committee of examination for concluding obligatory arbitration commitments, however, were going surprisingly well.

Nonetheless, this progressive mood of collaboration quickly came to an end when discussions were started at the sixth meeting of the committee on the proposal to establish a permanent court of arbitration. At this point, the German delegate Professor Philipp Zorn expressed "[…] the sincere hope that the day will come when […] conflicts between States may be regulated, at least in

67 The decision to use the British plan as the basis for the discussions of the committee on the establishment of a permanent court of arbitration was taken in accordance with the Russian and the U.S.-American representatives. Compare: James Brown Scott (ed.), *The Proceedings of The Hague Peace Conferences* (n 38 in Chapter 5) 708. Also: William I. Hull, *The two Hague Conferences and their Contributions to International Law* (n 39 in Chapter 5) 370–371.

68 Article 10 of the Russian *Outline of a Draft Convention.*

69 James Brown Scott (ed.), *The Proceedings of The Hague Peace Conferences* (n 38 in Chapter 5) 596.

70 Compare pages 96 et seq. of the present book.

the great majority of cases, [...] by a permanent international court."[71] However, at the same time, he also declared that the German government could not agree to the establishment of a permanent court of arbitration at the present conference. According to Zorn, it would require more experience in the field of occasional arbitration before a permanent court could be created. Additionally, he also stressed that the German government had never agreed to deal with the topic in The Hague, as the issue "[...] has not [...] been foreshadowed in the initial program of the Russian Government."[72] Andrew Dickson White (1832–1918),[73] head of the U.S. delegation, had the following to say about the German stance: "At our arrival there was general skepticism; shortly afterward, and especially when the organization of the arbitration committee was seen to be so good, there came a great growth of hope; now comes the usual falling back of many."[74] White provided further insights into the German position by reporting about talks outside the scope of official meetings. According to him, Count Georg Herbert zu Münster (1820–1902), head of the German delegation, declared in a private discussion with White that he (Münster) was:

> [...] entirely opposed to it [the subject of arbitration], or, at least, entirely opposed to any well-developed plan. He did not say that he would oppose a moderate plan for voluntary arbitration, but he insisted that arbitration must be injurious to Germany; that Germany is prepared for war as no other country is or can be; that she [Germany] can mobilize her army in ten days; and that neither France, Russia, nor any other power can do this. Arbitration, he said, would simply give rival powers time to put themselves in readiness, and would therefore be a great disadvantage to Germany.[75]

The German opposition to the initiative for the establishment of a court of arbitration brought the project to a (temporary) end. The other delegates of the committee tried to convince Zorn of the projected court by referring to

71 James Brown Scott (ed.), *The Proceedings of The Hague Peace Conferences* (n 38 in Chapter 5) 712–713.

72 Ibid 713.

73 For a more detailed study of Andrew D. White's role at the First Hague Peace Conference, please see: Randall Lesaffer, 'Peace through law' (n 25 in Chapter 1) 31–52.

74 Andrew Dickson White, *Autobiography of Andrew Dickson White*, Vol II (Century 1905) 265.

75 Ibid; compare also: Venera Steller, *Diplomatie von Angesicht zu Angesicht: Diplomatische Handlungsformen in den deutsch-französischen Beziehungen 1870–1919* (Schöningh 2011) 247–248. Herbert von Nostiz, *Bismarcks unbotmäßiger Botschafter Fürst Münster von Derneburg, 1820–1902* (Vandenhoeck & Ruprecht 1968) 246.

concrete experiences with the instrument of occasional, respectively isolated, arbitration, pointing to the purely voluntary character of the proposed tribunal, and recalling the great expectations of the public in the work of the third commission.[76] In the end, Zorn agreed to continue participating in the negotiations of the committee on the topic while still upholding the strict German opposition to the court project.[77] This approach put Germany in an isolated position. Instead of rethinking this policy, the German government insisted on its rejection and even summoned its delegates to openly threaten to withdraw from the committee.[78] The German delegation, however, feared the negative consequences of a withdrawal. Such a step would have risked resulting in highly negative publicity for Germany and severe damage for the country's relations to those nations which supported the projected court. Furthermore, keeping up the opposition to the prestigious project of a permanent court of arbitration could have resulted in the failure of the entire conference. This had to be regarded as a plausible consequence because majority decisions were deemed impossible in crucial questions. Important decisions could not be made against the explicit dissenting vote of any of the great powers.[79] Therefore, such powers held a (unofficial) veto right in the most crucial decisions – which resulted in the dilemma that Germany's opposition could not simply be ignored or outvoted. Münster himself did not support the court project either, but he was well aware of the dangers and potential consequences which would have followed if Germany had upheld their unrelenting position. The German foreign minister Bernhard von Bülow and the German emperor, on the other hand, seem to have tended more towards rejecting any kind of measure taken with regards to arbitration in The Hague and, thereby, to completely block the work of the committee. The German government seem to have been convinced that it would be necessary to reject arbitration to preserve their freedom to act in foreign affairs and to guarantee their independence.[80] The situation only changed when Zorn was called back to Berlin to settle the issue directly with Bülow, and when the U.S.-American delegation also sent an envoy to Berlin, Frederick W. Holls. It is not clear who – Zorn or Holls – was able to persuade the German government of making concessions, and maybe this decision was only taken because the German government feared an inter-

76 James Brown Scott (ed.), *The Proceedings of The Hague Peace Conferences* (n 38 in Chapter 5) 713–714.

77 Ibid 714.

78 Jost Dülffer, *Regeln gegen den Krieg?* (n 20 in Chapter 1) 92.

79 Ibid.

80 Ibid 131.

national isolation if it caused a failure of the conference.[81] But, regardless of the reasons for the change of mind, the German government agreed in the end to the institutionalization of arbitration in form of a permanent court. When Zorn returned to The Hague and resumed his participation in the committee, he declared that "[h]is Government recognizes the importance and the magnitude of this new institution."[82]

But the consent came at a price. The German government required the committee to preserve the principle of the free choice of arbitrators within the framework of the new court. Thus, each party of a dispute (dealt with before the court) was to be entitled to nominate two arbitrators for their individual case from a pre-determined list of potential candidates.[83] In addition, the German government demanded further concessions in exchange for its consent. Firstly, Zorn wanted the name of the institution to be changed from *tribunal* to *court*,[84] and, secondly, he declared that "[…] the German Government is not in a position to accept compulsory arbitration."[85] Although the pre-existing compulsory arbitration treaties were to remain in force, he strictly rejected any attempt to introduce references to obligatory arbitration in the acts of The Hague.[86] Instead, he believed that the extension of the competences of the court (through obligatory arbitration commitments) had to be postponed to a later time when the states had each developed their own individual experiences with (occasional and obligatory) arbitration.[87] The other delegates had to realize that it was highly unlikely that the German position would change.[88] Therefore, they agreed to withdraw the provision which contained the (already concluded) list of topics which were to be subjected to obligatory arbitration. Thereby, one of the most important achievements of the committee was undone. However, the delegates were aware of the necessity to present tangible results by the end of the conference. Paul Henri d'Estournelles concluded the need to achieve presentable accomplishments

---

81 Ibid 93.

82 James Brown Scott (ed.), *The Proceedings of The Hague Peace Conferences* (n 38 in Chapter 5) 755.

83 William I. Hull, *The two Hague Conferences and their Contributions to International Law* (n 39 in Chapter 5) 384; James Brown Scott (ed.), *The Proceedings of The Hague Peace Conferences* (n 38 in Chapter 5) 718–721, 755.

84 Arthur Eyffinger, *The 1899 Hague Peace Conference* (n 28 in Chapter 1) 395.

85 James Brown Scott (ed.), *The Proceedings of The Hague Peace Conferences* (n 38 in Chapter 5) 755.

86 Ibid 767.

87 Ibid 768.

88 Jost Dülffer, *Regeln gegen den Krieg?* (n 20 in Chapter 1) 94.

regarding the establishment of a permanent court of arbitration by declaring the following in the thirteenth meeting of the committee (on July 3, 1899):

> We are approaching the end of our labours, we are going to create a court, a code of international arbitration. That is something when we recall that nothing of its kind existed before our meeting at The Hague. It is but little when we think of all that humanity expects from us.[89]

After another five meetings, the committee of examination concluded its work and presented a plan for the creation of a permanent court of arbitration which was adopted by the third commission and the plenum of the conference. However, this plan remained a compromise which did not really satisfy any of the parties. The German government regarded it as too far going, while several other states had wished for decisively more progressive and innovative achievements. This was particularly the case with regards to the conclusion of a list of topics subjected to compulsory arbitration which had held a prominent position on the agenda of several nations.[90] The U.S.-American delegation – more than anyone else – had had to depart from its initial goals. But, since it had proven to be impossible to realize them against the German opposition, the U.S.-American delegates agreed on a 'trimmed-down version' of a permanent court of arbitration.

The court which was created in the end as a result of the *First Hague Peace Conference* – the *Permanent Court of Arbitration* (PCA) – definitely constituted a huge novelty and a unique step in the history of international law. According to Eyffinger, it was even "[…] the signal success of the Conference."[91] The PCA was the first permanent international institution dedicated to the peaceful settlement of international conflicts by arbitral means. Furthermore, its creation represented a decisive change in the mindset of the participating states. They had come together in The Hague to discuss the issue of peace and the creation of mechanisms for its preservation (as well as of laws of war). But before the conference began, they still had had serious doubts and had regarded the conference with a lot of skepticism.[92] But during the conference itself, many of the represented states showed a very benevolent attitude towards progressive ideas. This approach allowed them to discuss issues at

89 James Brown Scott (ed.), *The Proceedings of The Hague Peace Conferences* (n 38 in Chapter 5) 759.

90 Compare: ibid 768–772.

91 Arthur Eyffinger, *The 1899 Hague Peace Conference* (n 28 in Chapter 1) 441.

92 Helen May Cory, *Compulsory Arbitration of International Disputes* (n 154 in Chapter 2) 41.

The Hague which had so far been very uncommon on the international stage, and which had sometimes even been deemed unrealistic and utopian. Special as well as general obligatory arbitration clauses had already found their way into multiple bi-lateral (trade) treaties before 1899. But the states did not only discus at The Hague to aggregate the already existing clauses and practice in form of a multi-lateral treaty. The majority of the represented states accepted extending these clauses by introducing obligatory arbitration for a list of certain topics. This attempt only failed because of the German opposition. Nevertheless, the sole fact that the majority of participating states agreed on it and strove for its realization[93] proves that obligatory arbitration found support (if not even acceptance) among most of their governments.

The same can also be said for the PCA. Its establishment broke new ground in international relations and was also the result of a change in the mindset of many states. Later critics were right to point out that the concession to Germany of replacing obligatory by voluntary arbitration was a missed opportunity to achieve more striking and further-reaching results.[94] But, on the other hand, the establishment of the first permanent international institution for the peaceful settlement of state-to-state disputes still constituted a major accomplishment. Although the creation of such an institution had already been discussed by peace activists and international scholars before the conference, it still constituted a major change of the so far prevailing attitude of many countries. Furthermore, it seems as if this development was only possible because the participating states were pushed to do so by the media, by public opinion, and by the fact that they wanted to prevent the conference from becoming a failure. Thereby, a window of opportunity was opened which allowed the realization of these ideas in the form of the creation of the PCA. It remains highly dubious whether a similar result could have been achieved without the initiative of the Czar.

2.3 *The* Convention for the Peaceful Settlement of International Disputes

The PCA was based on the *Convention for the Peaceful Settlement of International Disputes* and coincided to a great extent with the (above-mentioned) British proposal. According to Article 20 of the convention, it had "[…] the object of facilitating an immediate recourse to arbitration for international

93 James Brown Scott (ed.), *The Proceedings of The Hague Peace Conferences* (n 38 in Chapter 5) 769–770.

94 Arthur Eyffinger and Arthur Witteveen, *The International Court of Justice 1946–1996* (Kluwer Law International 1996) 47. Also cited in: Bob Reinalda, *Routledge History of International Organizations* (n 59 in Chapter 2) 68–69.

differences."[95] This goal was supposed to be achieved through the creation of the PCA and the introduction of a number of procedural rules for arbitrations (and other methods of peaceful conflict settlement).

Looking first at the court itself, it was "[…] competent for all arbitration cases, unless the parties agree to institute a special Tribunal"[96] (Article 21). Therefore, taking recourse to the court was – in conformity with the German demands – a completely optional (respectively voluntary) decision. Whenever states decided to submit cases to the PCA, each of the parties was entitled to appoint two arbitrators from a list of potential candidates in order to form the bench of the PCA for their specific case. Together the four chosen arbitrators determined a fifth candidate that would serve as an umpire (Article 24).[97] The list of potential arbitrators was to be composed of a maximum of four individuals from each adhering state and the potential candidates were appointed for membership in the list for six years. According to Article 23, they had to be "[…] of known competency in questions of international law, of the highest moral reputation, and disposed to accept the duties of Arbitrators."[98] By allowing the states to pick their arbitrators from this list of pre-determined candidates, the convention preserved the principle of free choice of arbitrators – which was an essential element of *traditional* arbitration (in the sense described in Chapter 2). Article 15 explicitly stressed this point by providing that "[i]nternational arbitration has for its object the settlement of differences between States by judges of their own choice, and on the basis of respect of law."[99] Any attempt to change this particular point (the free choice of arbitrators) and to introduce a standing panel of arbitrators (as the United States had proposed)[100] had failed in The Hague because of the objection of several other countries.[101]

Hence, the PCA cannot be described as a truly permanent institution. Its panels had to be composed anew for each case and each of them was only competent to settle the one specific case for whose settlement it had been appointed. Consequently, the term *permanent* did not refer to the panels

95 *Convention for the Peaceful Settlement of International Disputes* (*1899*); <http://avalon.law.yale.edu/19th_century/hague01.asp> accessed June 1, 2017.

96 Ibid Article 21.

97 Ibid Article 24.

98 Ibid Article 23.

99 Ibid Article 15. Regarding the requirement to take decisions 'on the basis of respect of law,' compare also: Hans Wehberg, *The Problem of an International Court of Justice* (n 123 in Chapter 2) 15 et seq.

100 Compare pages 177–184 of the present book.

101 Compare, e.g., James Brown Scott (ed.), *The Proceedings of The Hague Peace Conferences* (n 38 in Chapter 5) 718 et seq.

respectively the bench of arbitrators of the PCA.[102] The truly *permanent* factors of the PCA were (apart from the permanency of the overall institution) only the International Bureau and the list of potential arbitrators.[103] The PCA provided only a framework under which the adhering states could settle their mutual conflicts in accordance with a set of pre-determined procedural rules. Therefore, it can be observed that the states did not change much in the fundamental and prevailing conception of arbitration. Key characteristics of the *traditional* approach were kept, and the outmost respect was paid to the principle of national sovereignty by avoiding interferences with the states' freedom of decision in foreign political matters.[104]

On the other hand, a decisively different development took place in those provisions which dealt with the nature of arbitrations under the *Hague Convention*. Article 15 provided that "[i]nternational arbitration has for its object the settlement of differences between States by judges of their own choice, and on the basis of respect for law."[105] Furthermore, Article 16 determined the following:

> In questions of a legal nature, and especially in the interpretation or application of International Conventions, arbitration is recognized by the Signatory Powers as the most effective, and at the same time the most equitable, means of settling disputes which diplomacy has failed to settle.[106]

On these points, the convention clearly departed from the *traditional* concept of arbitration. Instead of continuing the practice of dealing with disputes through arbitrations on the basis of equity, compromises, and arbitrariness, the drafters of the convention followed the recent developments in the field of arbitration (as addressed in Chapter 3).[107] In the decades prior, the focus of arbitration had shifted. Many international lawyers no longer regarded it as applicable to all kinds of cases (legal and political ones). Instead, they argued

102 In this regard: Hans Wehberg, *The Problem of an International Court of Justice* (n 123 in Chapter 2) 148. Wehberg argued that "[...] the formation of a permanent list of judges is merely the preliminary step to a truly permanent court of justice."

103 Article 22, *Convention for the Peaceful Settlement of International Disputes* (n 95 in Chapter 5).

104 Compare: Arthur Eyffinger, *The 1899 Hague Peace Conference* (n 28 in Chapter 1) 441–442.

105 Article 15, *Convention for the Peaceful Settlement of International Disputes* (n 95 in Chapter 5).

106 Ibid Article 16.

107 Compare pages 96 et seq. of the present book.

that arbitration was only suitable for the settlement of purely legal disputes as well as those which were eligible for judicial decisions any longer. This trend in legal scholarship corresponded to the recent state practice in which the scope of a quickly growing number of obligatory arbitration treaties was limited to legal questions as well.

This development has decisively changed the prevailing understanding of arbitration – at least in theory. However, what could have been a starting point for a juridification of arbitration and a gradual process of turning it into a (more and more) judicial procedure failed in practice. Hans Wehberg demonstrated (as shown in Chapter 2)[108] in his treatise *'The Problem of an International Court of Justice'* (from 1918) that equity, compromises, and arbitrariness remained decisive factors in the decision-making of arbitrations between 1899 and 1914 (regardless of whether cases were decided by the PCA or outside of its framework).[109] In this regard, he even came to the following conclusion:

> We see, therefore, that in the prevailing system theory and practice are in complete opposition. Arbitral awards are so unanimously recognized as a compromise [...] that the words of the Hague Convention which speaks of a decision 'on the basis of respect for law' must be regarded as a delusion.[110]

Despite the failure of realizing this aspect in state practice, the *Hague Convention* constituted, nevertheless, a great achievement. The determination of procedural rules for arbitrations and for other mechanisms of peaceful conflict settlement bore, at least in theory, the potential for paving the way for significant changes in the practical application of arbitration. For example, Article 1 contained a clear commitment to peace and to conflict settlement by peaceful means:

> With a view to obviating, as far as possible, recourse to force in the relations between States, the Signatory Powers agree to use their best efforts to insure the pacific settlement of international differences.[111]

---

108 Compare pages 41–45 of the present book.

109 Hans Wehberg, *The Problem of an International Court of Justice* (n 123 in Chapter 2) 29–41.

110 Ibid 38–39.

111 Article 1, *Convention for the Peaceful Settlement of International Disputes* (n 95 in Chapter 5).

Here, it becomes clear that although the convention did not amount to an obligatory arbitration commitment, it still endorsed arbitration. It emphasized on several occasions the usefulness of this instrument for the settlement of state-to-state disputes. According to Eyffinger, the convention, therefore, "[…] marks the first acceptance on principle by all civilized nations of the concepts of mediation and arbitration as such as a recommendable means of settling disputes."[112] Additionally, he stated that "[f]rom now on, the pacific settlement of disputes, by whatever mechanism, was to be the rule."[113] This claim is supported by the U.S.-American delegates to *the First Hague Peace Conference* who argued in a report that the convention expressed "[…] a general moral duty for the performance of which each State is accountable only to itself."[114]

Apart from this point and the establishment of the PCA, the convention was basically a collection of prevailing practice and of the most acknowledged and conventional procedural rules of arbitration (and of the other means for peaceful conflict settlement).[115] Consequently, arbitration was not decisively further developed in a conceptual sense by the decisions taken at The Hague.[116] However, the adoption of the convention still added a lot of value to the cause of (the preservation of) peace, to the furtherance of arbitration, and to the process of replacing war by peaceful methods of conflict settlement.

By enacting the convention, states found themselves in a new situation. If they decided to settle their disputes under the *Hague Convention*, taking recourse to arbitration would have been considerably facilitated. Beforehand, it would have taken two major decisions for initiating arbitration; the *compromis* (the agreement to arbitrate the case) and the determination of the procedural rules for the arbitration of the specific case.[117] The *Hague Convention* allowed states to skip the second point because cases settled before the PCA followed the procedural rules contained in the convention. Hence, the parties

---

112 Arthur Eyffinger, *The 1899 Hague Peace Conference* (n 28 in Chapter 1) 441.

113 Ibid.

114 'Report of Messrs. White, Low and Holls to the American Delegation to the First Hague Conference, regarding the Work of the Third Commission of the Conference' in James Brown Scott (ed.), *Instructions to the American Delegates to The Hague Peace Conferences and their Official Reports* (n 23 in Chapter 5) 57.

115 In the following, the focus will be on arbitration while good offices, mediation, and commission of inquiry will be spared out since the former is of a considerably higher importance for the present book.

116 Hans Wehberg, e.g., criticized The Hague Conference for not having taken the step from international arbitration to judicial settlement; see: Hans Wehberg, *The Problem of an International Court of Justice* (n 123 in Chapter 2) 140–154.

117 Compare pages 38–45 of the present book.

only had to come to an agreement on the *compromis*. Negotiations on the constitution of individual arbitral courts, on the nomination of arbitrators, and on procedural rules had always been the source for a lot of conflict and had involved the risk that the parties did not come to terms. Since disagreement on any of these points could have prevented the arbitration from taking place, the initiation of arbitral procedures was considerably facilitated by the introduction of established procedural rules through the convention. Thereby, the *Hague Convention* added remarkable value to international law by offering states a way to initiate arbitration which was free from difficult negotiations over the constitution of the court and the determination of procedural rules.

Finally, despite the conventions purely voluntary character, it also contained a norm which kept the door open for the extension of the competences of the PCA by concluding bi-lateral obligatory arbitration treaties. Article 19 provided that all:

> [...] Powers reserve to themselves the right of concluding, either before the ratification of the present Act or later, new Agreements, general or private, with a view to extending obligatory arbitration to all cases which they may consider it possible to submit to it.

At the time of the adoption of this article, little importance was attached to it.[118] The German opposition against obligatory arbitration had dealt a severe setback to any aspiration in The Hague to the introduction of the principle on the global stage. But Article 19 enabled the contracting states to extend the competences of the PCA through bi-lateral obligatory arbitration treaties. The respective parties of these agreements could simply subject all or some of their future mutual conflicts to the jurisdiction of the PCA.[119] James Brown Scott (*'The Hague Peace Conferences of 1899 and 1907, Vol. 1'* from 1909) stressed that "[t]he article did not seem at the time to be of any special importance and it was generally looked upon as useless."[120] However, in the coming years, many states would take recourse to this option thereby reviving the discussion on obligatory arbitration.[121]

---

118 Francis Anthony Boyle, *Foundations of World Order* (n 28 in Chapter 1) 31. See also: 'Editorial Comment: Treaties of Arbitration since the First Hague Conference' (1908) 2 The American Journal of International Law 823–824.

119 Francis Anthony Boyle, *Foundations of World Order* (n 28 in Chapter 1) 31.

120 James Brown Scott, *The Hague Peace Conferences of 1899 and 1907*, vol. 1 (n 131 in Chapter 2) 813.

121 Compare pages 214 et seq. of the present book.

2.4 *The U.S.-American Plan for an International Tribunal*

Before focusing on the developments in the aftermath of the conference, one last point will be dealt with regarding the *First Hague Peace Conference*. It concerns the U.S.-American *Plan for an International Tribunal* which was presented to the committee of examination of the third commission on May 31, 1899. Discussions about this initiative were short and shallow. The proposal seems to have been too far-reaching and too progressive for most delegates. The German opposition against any concept of a permanent court of arbitration, which exceeded a pure list of arbitrators, was instrumental in causing a quick rejection of the U.S.-American plan. However, due to its innovativeness and because it foreshadowed later developments, it will, nevertheless, be dealt with here.

Already in his instructions to the U.S.-American delegation, Secretary of State John Hay (1838–1905) declared his support for the creation of an international court by stating the following:

> The proposed conference promises to offer an opportunity thus far unequalled in the history of the world for initiating a series of negotiations that may lead to important practical results. The long-continued and widespread interest among the people of the United States in the establishment of an international court [...] gives assurance that the proposal of a definite plan of procedure by this Government for the accomplishment of this end would express the desires and aspirations of this nation. The delegates are, therefore, enjoined to propose, at an opportune moment, the plan for an international tribunal [...] and to use their influence in the conference in the most effective manner possible to procure the adaption of its substance or of resolutions directed to the same purpose.[122]

The U.S.-American plan for an international tribunal differed greatly from the final shape of the PCA and from the British and Russian/Italian[123] plans for

---

122 'Instructions to the American Delegates to The Hague Conference of 1899' in James Brown Scott (ed.), *Instructions to the American Delegates to The Hague Peace Conferences and their Official Reports* (n 23 in Chapter 5) 8–9.

123 At the first meeting of the committee of examination, Count Constantino Nigra (1828–1907), first delegate of Italy, launched a proposal for an Amendment to the Russian Draft extending it by provisions for the establishment of a court of arbitration. Compare: 'Amendment to the Russian Draft regarding Mediation and Arbitration submitted by his Excellency Count Nigra', in: James Brown Scott (ed.), The Proceedings of The Hague Peace Conferences (n 38 in Chapter 5) 817.

permanent courts of arbitration. The other proposals all had in common that they attached great importance to the preservation of some of the fundamental principles of *traditional* arbitration, *inter alia* to the free choice of arbitrators. In contrast to this, the U.S.-American delegation strove for the establishment of a tribunal whose structure rather resembled the U.S. Supreme Court[124] and which differed decisively from the common conception of individual arbitral courts at that time. In a report to Secretary of State John Hay, the U.S.-American delegates summarized the main conceptual differences between their plan and the PCA as follows:

> The American plan contained a carefully devised project for such a tribunal, which differed from that adopted mainly in contemplating a tribunal capable of meeting in full bench and permanently in the exercise of its functions, like the Supreme Court of the United States, instead of a Court like the Supreme Court of the State of New York, which never sits as a whole, but whose members sit from time to time singly or in groups, as occasion demand.[125]

In another report of the U.S.-American delegation, which focused on the work of the third commission and of its committee of examination, the point was further elaborated on: "The fundamental idea of the American plan was a court which should not only be permanent but continuous in its functions."[126] In order to realize this goal, the projected tribunal was supposed to be composed of a standing panel of judges. Furthermore, Article 1 of the U.S.-American plan provided that these judges were to be "[…] chosen on account of their personal integrity and learning in international law by a majority of the members of the highest court now existing in each of the adhering States."[127] Even in relation to the points listed so far, the resemblance with the structure of the U.S. Supreme Court is already apparent. In addition to that, the U.S.-American proposal aimed for breaking with the principle of free choice of arbitrators. It provided that the judges were to be appointed by the highest courts of justice of all

124 Arthur Eyffinger, *The 1899 Hague Peace Conference* (n 28 in Chapter 1) 440.

125 'General Report of the Commission' in James, Brown Scott (ed.), *The Hague Peace Conferences 1899 and 1907, vol. II: Documents* (Oxford University Press 1909) 22.

126 'Report of Messrs. White, Low and Holls to the American Delegation to the First Hague Conference, regarding the Work of the Third Commission of the Conference' (n 114 in Chapter 5) 53.

127 'Plan for an International Tribunal' in James Brown Scott (ed.), *Instructions to the American Delegates to The Hague Peace Conferences and their Official Reports* (n 23 in Chapter 5) 15.

adhering states for a pre-determined tenure, whereas the *Hague Convention* entitled the governments of the conflicting parties to nominate the bench of arbitrators anew for each case. If the U.S.-American plan had been adopted, the consequence would have been the creation of an actual permanent institution.

This prospect resulted in strong opposition from multiple sides. Some states were afraid of a continuously sitting tribunal which would – according to a U.S.-American report – "[…] assume a dignity and importance for which the nations were not yet prepared."[128] Hence, these countries feared that a standing tribunal could develop a continuous jurisprudence and create precedents; a constellation which bore the risk of resulting in further development of international law through continuous case law by the tribunal (detached from the consent of states). This would have collided with the interests of many states which were keen to maintain their full sovereignty rights as well as their position as the sole and exclusive legislators of international law. Hence, these states strove for preserving the prevailing concept and rejected the idea of a truly permanent international court at the time of the *First Hague Peace Conference*.

Other objections raised against the U.S.-American plan were less fundamental. For example, they concerned the question of whether there would be enough cases to keep a truly permanent tribunal busy or whether a continuously sitting and permanent court would result in excessive costs.[129] The latter point stands in close connection to another important particularity of the U.S.-American proposal in which it resembled the U.S. Supreme Court and other domestic courts of law. According to Article 6 of the U.S.-American plan, the expenses for the remuneration of the judges and for the maintenance of the international court were to be divided among all adhering states.[130] Whereas the costs for arbitral settlements (and the salaries of the arbitrators) were usually paid by the parties, the U.S.-American government aimed for introducing a structure which detached the judges and the tribunal from the (financial) control of the member states. Since the remuneration and maintenance of the tribunal were supposed to be paid from a common budget, the individual judges would have been financially independent from their home countries. This setup was expected by the U.S.-American delegation to result in a higher

128 'Report of Messrs. White, Low and Holls to the American Delegation to the First Hague Conference, regarding the Work of the Third Commission of the Conference' (n 114 in Chapter 5) 53.

129 Ibid.

130 'Plan for an International Tribunal' (n 127 in Chapter 5) 15.

degree of impartiality and neutrality of the judges. In this regard, it should also be noted that the demand for detaching the tribunal from the influence of the adhering states can be considered to be a general characteristic of the U.S.-American proposal. The *Plan for an International Tribunal* provided for a standing panel of judges (appointed for long term tenures instead of individual cases), did not uphold the principle of free choice of arbitrators, and aimed for a remuneration of the judges through the institutional system of the court. The implementation of these points would have given the court and its judges an enormous degree of independence, especially since the judges were supposed to be appointed by the highest court of their respective home countries. By establishing this system, the respective governments would have lost any direct influence on the nomination procedure. Finally, the U.S.-American delegates also aimed (in accordance with Article 5 of their plan) to exclude judges from cases in which their home countries were either directly involved or in which they had strong interests.[131]

The proposal to turn away from the principle of the free choice of arbitrators, and to detach the court from the parties by granting it a great level of independence,[132] marked a distinct difference between the U.S.-American plan and the PCA. The former, the U.S.-American plan, provided the structure for a widely independent court which differed decisively from the *traditional* conception of arbitration. Its realization would have resulted in the foundation of a tribunal which was independent, impartial, and truly permanent. The PCA, on the other hand, offered the adhering states the opportunity to appoint their preferred arbitrators. Hence, it complied, to a great extent, with the prevailing state practice concerning arbitration. Thus, it would not be an exaggeration to say that the PCA failed to fulfill the highest dreams and hopes of progressive peace activists and international lawyers. For them, the creation of the Hague court constituted a step into the right direction. But they did not consider it to be the final stage of the institutionalization process of international justice or towards preserving peace through law.[133] In this regard, the U.S.-American proposal would have gone much further. The projected tribunal resembled a court of law with regards to its permanency, impartiality, and independence. The U.S. plan even provided for a general obligatory arbitration commitment in Article 3. According to it, all adhering states had to "[…] submit

131 Ibid 15.

132 So far, the parties of arbitrations determined the precise question at stake, provided the procedural rules, and nominated the arbitrators which appeared most suitable to them. They were the undisputed masters of the proceedings. Compare: pages 38–45 of the present book.

133 Arthur Eyffinger, *The 1899 Hague Peace Conference* (n 28 in Chapter 1) 440.

to the international tribunal all questions of disagreement between them, excepting such as may relate to or involve their political independence or territorial integrity."[134]

Despite the obligatorium, and the other above-named characteristics which the projected international tribunal had in common with courts of law, it remains dubious whether the U.S.-American delegation intended to propose the creation of an international court of law or of arbitration. The U.S.-American project was definitely inspired by the U.S. Supreme Court.[135] Furthermore, U.S. Secretary of State John Hay stressed the importance of international justice and of the adherence to law (on the international level) in his instructions to the Hague Conference delegates; and he did so right at the point in his text where he also referred to the *Plan for an International Tribunal*.[136] Annexed to the instructions, John Hay also provided a *Historical Resumé*[137] covering the U.S.-American experiences with arbitration over the preceding decades. In this text, the terms *adjudication* and *arbitration* were used as synonyms. For example, John Bassett Moore (1860–1947), a U.S.-American scholar of international law, was praised in the *resumé* for having placed "[…] beyond controversy the applicability of judicial methods to a large variety of international disagreements which have been successfully adjudicated by individual arbitrators or temporary boards of arbitration."[138] Furthermore, U.S. President William McKinley (1842–1901) was quoted in this text with a paean on arbitration. According to it, he claimed that "[a]rbitration is the true method of settlement of international as well as local or individual differences."[139] The fact that *arbitration* and *adjudication* were used as synonyms, and that they were not regarded as two distinctively different concepts, complied with the prevailing state practice and the dominant opinion in legal scholarship.

The projected structure, impartiality, independence, and permanency of the institution indicate that it is not unlikely that the United States strove for

134 'Plan for an International Tribunal' (n 127 in Chapter 5) 15.

135 Arthur Eyffinger, *The 1899 Hague Peace Conference* (n 28 in Chapter 1) 440.

136 James Brown Scott (ed.), *The Hague Peace Conferences 1899 and 1907, vol. II: Documents* (n 125 in Chapter 5) 8. According to it, Secretary of State John May declared the following: "Nothing can secure for human government and for the authority of law which it represents so deep a respect and so firm a loyalty as the spectacle of sovereign and independent States, whose duty it is to prescribe the rules of justice and to impose penalties upon the lawless, bowing with reverence before the august supremacy of those principles of right which give to law its eternal foundation."

137 'Historical Resumé' in James Brown Scott (ed.), *Instructions to the American Delegates to The Hague Peace Conferences and their Official Reports* (n 23 in Chapter 5) 9–14.

138 Ibid 13.

139 Ibid 12.

a truly adjudicative court. However, it must also be taken into consideration that the indifference between the terms *adjudication* and *arbitration* suggests that the U.S.-American government did not clearly distinguish between the two concepts just yet. Although reference is made in the *resumé* to vocabulary from *adjudication*, the terminology remained ambiguous on multiple occasions and was still intermixed with terms from *arbitration*. Moreover, in 1899, even the majority of peace activists and international lawyers still regarded adjudication as highly utopian. As shown by the example of the proposal of the *New York Bar Association* (which is likely to have influenced the U.S.-American *Plan for an International Tribunal*),[140] it was international courts of arbitration that stood in the focus of attention during these years. Only a minority of very progressive scholars went further and discussed the idea of international courts of law. Before this background, it would have been a very progressive step if the U.S.-American delegation had actually proposed the creation of a true international court of law (shaped in full accordance with the example of the U.S. Supreme Court). Nevertheless, this possibility cannot be ruled out either.

All attempts to interpret the U.S.-American intensions behind this proposal are highly speculative. There is not enough information to determine the exact nature of the proposed tribunal. The only thing which can be said with certainty is that the U.S.-American *Plan for an International Tribunal* went far beyond the scope of the other proposals for courts which were discussed at the *First Hague Peace Conference*. It would have had several essential criteria in common with domestic courts of law and it would have even provided for obligatory arbitration. But whether this tribunal was really intended to take decisions in sole accordance with law (and whether the proposal was not only supposed to result, for example, into a modification of the prevailing understanding and practice of arbitration through the introduction of judicial elements), cannot be finally and reliably determined.

The last issue which must be dealt with in the context of the U.S.-American *Plan for an International Tribunal* concerns the question of the motivation that drove the United States to propose this progressive project. A possible answer can be found in the (predominantly) positivist and legalist understanding of international law which prevailed in the United States at the beginning of the 20th century.[141] This approach provided that international

---

140 Compare pages 185 et seq. of the present book.

141 Francis Anthony Boyle, *Foundations to World Order* (n 28 in Chapter 1) 11. Also: Lassa Oppenheim, 'The Science of International Law: Its Task and Method' (1908) 2 The American Journal of International Law 313–356.

law was only based on established and recognized rules (of customary and written law) while ethical, moral, or philosophical considerations no longer played a crucial role. But, according to Francis Anthony Boyle (*'Foundations of World Order'* from 1999),

> [t]his positivist methodology did not preach that international law should never concern itself with the promotion of moral values. Rather, it was premised on the forthrightly admitted assumption that international legal positivism [...] constituted the superior means to progress toward the Aristotelian 'final cause' of international legal studies: preservation of peace among nations to the greatest degree possible under the given historical circumstances.
>
> [...]
>
> The purpose of international law was not yet perceived by Americans to be the outlawing of [...] manifestations of interstate violence, but more simply to reduce their incidence, mitigate their fury, and limit their scope so as to protect neutrals.[142]

Therefore, the belief that it was the greater purpose of international law to maintain peace was particularly common in the United States. Peace activists and progressive international lawyers engaged in the attempt to realize it. Moreover, international lawyers did not only uphold this approach in theory, in their writings, and in legal scholarship but they were also recruited on a quickly increasing scale by the U.S.-American government. Around the turn of the century, several international lawyers were appointed to influential positions (especially in the State Department). These offices allowed them to exert "[...] increasing influence upon the government"[143] and its policies. Furthermore, this development allowed such lawyers to bring "[...] their unique perspective on international relations directly to bear upon the policy formulation process."[144] Finally, between 1898 and 1910, even the majority of Secretaries of State were trained lawyers.[145] Several of them, such as John Hay or his successor Elihu Root (1845–1937), were moreover enthusiastic "advocates of

142 Francis Anthony Boyle, *Foundations to World Order* (n 28 in Chapter 1) 12. At this point, Boyle stated the following: "International legal positivism was said to be more conducive to interstate agreement on current and proposed rules of international behavior than was the dogma of Grotian natural-law morality, whose reputed tenets invariably tried to mask perceived national interests and received national prejudices."

143 Mark Weston Janis, *America and the Law of Nations 1776–1939* (n 84 in Chapter 3) 144.

144 Francis Anthony Boyle, *World Politics and International Law* (n 135 in Chapter 3) 22.

145 Ibid 23. According to Boyle: "[O]f the eight U.S. Secretaries of State who held office from 1898 until 1920 [...], only Bacon was not a lawyer."

international adjudication."[146] Consequently, the policy of the State Department was highly influenced by U.S.-American international lawyers, their legal positivist considerations, and their dedication to the preservation of peace through the juridification of international relations.[147] According to Boyle, "[…] it was during the interim between the Spanish-American War and World War I that American international lawyers exercised a more profound influence upon the formation of American foreign policy than they have as a group at any time before or since."[148]

The U.S.-American international lawyers' profound influence on the State Department, in conjunction with their strong interest in the further development of international arbitration and in the creation of better mechanisms for the preservation of peace, resulted in a high degree of sympathy for these issues within the U.S.-American government. The U.S.-American affection for the establishment of a progressive and independent permanent court of arbitration could, therefore, have rested on the dominant positivist approach to international law which prevailed among U.S.-American international lawyers at that time. Civil initiatives (such as the peace movement) further encouraged the United States to follow this approach. Driven by the *New York State Bar Association*'s proposal,[149] and by their domestic experiences with the Supreme Court,[150] the United States developed the *Plan for an International Tribunal* which resembled in several points with domestic courts of law. This project clearly exceeded the other proposals at The Hague for the introduction of international courts because of its progressiveness and its detachment from the *traditional* understanding of arbitration. That being said, these points were also its major downfall. Because the plan departed from the prevailing understanding in so many ways, most states rejected it straight away.

3 The Years between the Two Hague Conferences

The U.S.-American *Plan for an International Tribunal* was, as just shown, considerably more progressive than the PCA, the institution whose establishment

146 Martti Koskenniemi, 'The Ideology of International Adjudication and the 1907 Hague Conference' (n 30 in Chapter 1) 135.

147 Mark Weston Janis, *America and the Law of Nations 1776–1939* (n 84 in Chapter 3) 144.

148 Francis Anthony Boyle, *World Politics and International Law* (n 135 in Chapter 3) 22.

149 Compare: David S. Patterson, *Towards a Warless World* (n 147 in Chapter 3) 103. According to him, the plan "[…] had some influence on the […] personnel who drafted the American proposal for a permanent court".

150 Compare pages 58 et seq. of the present book.

had been concluded at the *First Hague Peace Conference*. The United States had to accept that it was impossible at that point to overcome the opposition of the other countries against their proposal, especially trying to convince the Germans to give up on their rejection of any further going commitments. Taking into consideration the complicated situation in The Hague, the U.S. delegates were satisfied with the accomplishments made and declared the following in a report to their Secretary of State:

> As to the results thus obtained from as a whole regarding arbitration, in view of all circumstances and considerations revealed during the sessions of the Conference, it is our opinion that the 'Plan for the pacific settlement of international disputes,' which was adopted by the Conference, is better than that presented by any one nation. We believe that, though it will doubtless be found imperfect and will require modification as times goes on, it will form a thoroughly practical beginning, it will produce valuable results from the outset, and it will be the germ out of which a better and better system will be gradually evolved.[151]

The U.S. delegates had striven for further going results in The Hague. But although the PCA did not suffice their progressive aspirations, they had decided not to reject it despite its imperfections. Instead, they considered it as a step in the right direction. Moreover, they expected the court to prove its practicality and usefulness for the prevention of war by providing a suitable and easily accessible option for peaceful conflict settlements. The U.S. delegates expressed this hope as follows in the same report:

> As questions arise threatening resort to arms it may well be hoped that public opinion in the nations concerned, seeing in this great international court a means of escape from the increasing horrors of war, will insist more and more that the questions at issue be referred to it. As times goes on such reference will probably more and more seem to the world at large natural and normal, and we may hope that recourse to the tribunal will finally, in the great majority of serious differences between nations, become a regular means of avoiding the resort to arms.[152]

---

151 'Report to the Secretary of State of the Delegates to the First Hague Conference' in James Brown Scott (ed.), *Instructions to the American Delegates to The Hague Peace Conferences and their Official Reports* (n 23 in Chapter 5) 23.

152 Ibid 24.

Despite the shortcomings of the PCA, the United States intended to put it to regular use and to try to convince the more hesitant states of joining them as soon as possible. They seem to have expected that rich experiences with this voluntary court, and an increased use of arbitration in the upcoming years, would result in a gradual familiarization of the other states with institutionalized arbitration. Based on this procedure of stepwise accustomization, the United States hoped to win other states over for supporting further going plans and institutional advancements of the PCA. Therefore, the United States seems to have regarded the PCA as a suitable starting point for further going developments which might ultimately result in the creation of a court shaped in accordance with their *Plan for an International Tribunal.*

However, before the provisions of the *Convention for the Peaceful Settlement of International Disputes* could even be invoked for the first time, contrasting trends arose at the international level which were, once again, driven by imperialist and nationalist considerations. They diametrically opposed the spirit of togetherness, progress, and peace which had dominated at The Hague. In October 1899, little more than two months after the end of the *First Hague Peace Conference*, the *Second Boer War* (1899–1902) broke out. Of all the countries, it was Great Britain that waged this war against two independent republics in Southern Africa with the aim of colonization; against the South African Republic and the Orange Free State (the so-called *Boer Republics*).[153] Yet, it had also been Great Britain that had launched the first and most noted proposal for a permanent court of arbitration at The Hague. Their plan had formed the basis for the negotiations on institutionalized arbitration which later resulted in the establishment of the PCA. Thus, Great Britain can be considered as one of the main founders of the institution. However, when the Boer Republics offered to arbitrate the conflict, Great Britain rejected it.[154] They would only have agreed to establish a joint commission of inquiry.[155] This peaceful alternative to avoid the war was also rejected, this time by the Boer Republics. In the end, the war could not be prevented by peaceful means.

The pacific spirit and the overwhelming support for arbitration which had dominated in The Hague seems to have been forgotten soon after the end of the conference, and this was not only the case for Great Britain. It was a general phenomenon that the peaceful settlement of conflicts quickly faded into the

153 Compare: Christoph Marx, *Geschichte Afrikas: Von 1800 bis zur Gegenwart* (n 94 in Chapter 2) 120 et seq.

154 Steffen Bender, *Der Burenkrieg und die deutschsprachige Presse* (Brill 2009) 52. Also: Alfred Fried, *Handbuch der Friedensbewegung* (n 135 in Chapter 3) 312.

155 Compare: Robert Granville Campbell, Neutral Rights and Obligations in the Anglo-Boer War (The Johns Hopkins Press 1908) 49.

background. It was only attached secondary importance once more when the great powers turned back their focus on the scramble for Africa and Asia, on their mutual rivalries, and on their constant struggles for superiority. Another example of the trend to return to the pre-Hague situation marked the second German *Flottengesetz* (Naval Law) from 1900 which was concluded with the intention to enable Germany to challenge Great Britain's naval superiority.[156] The law caused a German–British naval armament race, a serious deterioration of the German–British relations, and the emergence of a harsh rivalry between the two countries. A series of other conflicts arose between 1899 and 1914 as well, all of which gave evidence to the fact that the great powers did not intend to give up on their imperialistic policies. They continued to fiercely compete with one another, placing their individual goals over the greater common goods of peace and stability. The formation of two opposing great power blocks – the *Triple Entente* (Great Britain, France, and Russia) and the *Triple Alliance* (Austria–Hungary, Germany, and Italy) – was another important example of this tendency. But before it came to an open clash between these two alliances, and the outbreak of *World War I* in 1914, another conflict escalated in 1904/05 which resulted in a crucial incident: The *Russo-Japanese War*. It is considered today as the first 'modern' war, and this brutal fight in East Asia between Russia and Japan gave the world a bitter taste of the horrors of the upcoming world war.[157] At some point, the conflict even bore the risk of spreading further and involving Europe too. Russia was closely allied with France and Japan was so with Great Britain.[158] Since Germany and the United States were also highly interested in the conflict and toyed with the idea of intervening, the war was about to develop global dimensions.[159] However, an expansion beyond East Asia could be prevented in the end and the war remained limited to the two original conflict parties. Against most expectations, the conflict was dominated by Japan which dealt a series of grave

156 Moritz Ritter, 'Deutschland und der Ausbruch des Weltkrieges' (1919) 121 Historische Zeitschrift 43. Michael Epkenhans, *Der Erste Weltkrieg* (Ferdinand Schöningh 2015) 13 et seq.

157 Rotem Kowner, 'Preface' in Rotem Kowner (ed.), *The Impact of the Russo-Japanese War* (Routledge 2007) xvi. Also: John W. Steinberg, 'Was the Russo-Japanese War World War Zero?' (2008) 67 The Russian Review (2008) 1–2.

158 Paul W. Doerr, 'Anglo-Japanese Alliance' in Spencer C. Tucker (ed.), *World War I: The Definite Encyclopedia and Document Collection*, vol. 1 (ABC Clio 2014) 102.

159 Compare: Edward B. Parsons, 'Roosevelt's Containment of the Russo-Japanese War' (1969) 38 Pacific Historical Review 21–44. Also: Winston B. Thorson, 'American Public Opinion and the Portsmouth Peace Conference' (1948) 53 The American Historical Review 439–464. Ian Nish, *The Origins of the Russo-Japanese War* (Routledge 2014) 2.

defeats to the Russian Empire.[160] In 1905, the war could finally be ended through the conclusion of a peace treaty[161] at the *Portsmouth Peace Conference* in the United States. The initiative for the meeting stemmed from an address of the Japanese government to Theodore Roosevelt (1858–1919) in which the former asked the president of the United States to negotiate between the conflicting parties.[162] Roosevelt complied with the inquiry and brought Russia and Japan together to settle conditions for peace. In 1906, he received the Nobel Peace Prize for this achievement.[163]

Overall, the *Russo-Japanese War* can be described as a result of a conflict between two nations striving for expansions of their spheres of influence in the same area. Due to its imperialist nature, it can be put on par with the other above-mentioned incidents, all of which arose because of imperialism, great power policy, and nationalism and were rooted in the pre-1899 understanding of war as a political instrument for the enforcement of the interests of the states.[164] By only taking into consideration the aforementioned aspects, it cannot be observed that immediate changes derived from The Hague regarding the states' willingness to abstain from pursuing their interests by force and to preserve peace. However, a closer examination of the developments between the two *Hague Peace Conferences* provides different and more specific insights. In this regard, Douglas Howland (*'Sovereignty and the Laws of War'* from 2011) argued, for example, that the *Russo-Japanese War*:

160 Reinhard Zöllner, *Geschichte Japans: Von 1800 bis zur Gegenwart* (Ferdinand Schöningh 2013) 290–293. Raymond A. Esthus, 'Nicholas II and the Russo-Japanese War' (1981) 40 The Russian Review (1981) 397 et seq. David Schimmelpenninck van der Oye, 'Rewriting the Russo-Japanese War: A Centenary Retroperspective' (2008) 67 The Russian Review 79.

161 *The Treaty of Portsmouth and the Russo-Japanese War, 1904–1905*; <https://history.state.gov/milestones/1899-1913/portsmouth-treaty> accessed February 9, 2016.

162 Robert K. Godwin, 'Russia and the Portsmouth Peace Conference' (1950) 9 The American Slavic and East European Review 279.

163 It was the first time that the prize was awarded to an acting head of state. Compare in this regard the information given at the homepage of the Nobel Prize Committee (<http://www.nobelprize.org/nobel_prizes/peace/laureates/1906/roosevelt-facts.html> accessed February 9, 2016).

164 Douglas Howland, 'Sovereignty and the Laws of War: International Consequences of Japan's 1905 Victory over Russia' (2011) 29 Law and History Review 54. In this article, Howland also stated the following: "In the absence of rules, a state was largely free to pursue its will, and Japan's aggressive assertion of sovereignty forced the family of nations to reexamine several issues at the Second Hague Peace Conference in 1907. Japan's commencement of the war, for example, persuaded international delegates to advocate a declaration of war prior to hostilities [...]."

> […] was the first war in which both belligerents pledged to adhere to the international laws of war. In that regard, the Russo-Japanese War marks a culmination of the tireless international diplomacy to secure legal limitations on warfare in the nineteenth century. In 1904, both Russia and Japan justified their operations according to international law, for the benefit of an international audience who had five years earlier celebrated some progress with the signing of The Hague Conventions of 1899.[165]

According to Howland, Russia and Japan made a great deal of effort in proving before the global public, and the international community, that their actions taken during the war complied with international law. This behavior illustrates their respect for international legal rules and that compliance with those norms played a significant role in international politics at the time. It is perhaps excessive to refer to this development as a clear sign for a general change of mind concerning the role of international law and for a juridification of international relations. But it does show that the states attached significantly more importance to international law than they had done before the turn of the century and that international law had grown into a crucial factor in international politics.

Roosevelt's initiative to invite the disputing parties of the *Russo-Japanese War* to Portsmouth and encouraging them to settle their conflict by peaceful means was also praised as to have been "[…] absolute in accord with the new and nobler ideas solemnly sanctioned by The Hague Conference of 1899."[166] This quote stems from the article *'The Portsmouth Peace Conference'* written by Frédéric de Martens (1845–1909) in 1905. De Martens was a famous Russian international lawyer and had represented his country in the committee of examination on arbitration at the *First Hague Peace Conference*. At this occasion, he had significantly contributed to the conclusion of the *Convention for the Peaceful Settlement of International Disputes*. In the quoted article, he referred to Article 8 of said convention according to which all adhering states had the right to recommend mediating disputes between other adhering states without infringing the sovereignty rights of the disputing parties.[167]

165 Ibid.

166 Frédéric de Martens, 'The Portsmouth Peace Conference' (1905) 181 The North American Review 642.

167 Article 8, *Convention for the Peaceful Settlement of International Disputes* (n 95 in Chapter 5).

According to de Martens, it was at the *First Hague Peace Conference* from 1899 that:

> [...] twenty-five Powers of Europe, America and Asia took upon themselves the moral engagement not to rebuff the good offices of a neutral State in the case of international conflicts. [...] [T]he generous action of President Roosevelt ought to be applauded, not only by the American people, but by the whole universe.[168]

President Roosevelt's initiative was induced by Japan, warmly welcomed by Russia, and indeed supported by several other nations.[169] The approval of his offer to mediate the conflict was, therefore, widely spread although, in earlier years, interferences of this nature could have been regarded as infringements of the sovereignty rights of the affected states. After the conclusion of the *Hague Convention*, however, this notion seems to have changed. Such initiatives were now considered as legal[170] and appear to have been welcomed by the concerned parties as well as by a great number of other nations, at least in this particular case.

3.1 *The* Second Pan-American Conference (*1901/1902*)

Roosevelt's initiative to hold the *Portsmouth Peace Conference* in order to end the *Russo-Japanese War* was neither the only nor the first crucial action which the United States took between the *First* and the *Second Hague Peace Conferences* in order to support the further development of (institutionalized, obligatory, as well as voluntary) conflict settlement. Due to the chronology of events, attention will first be drawn to the *Second Pan-American Conference* in 1901/1902 before focusing on other developments and initiatives which took place in this regard in the subsequent years.

On December 5, 1899, only a few months after the end of the *First Hague Conference*, U.S. President McKinley proposed in a *State to the Union*-Address to hold as soon as possible a *Second Pan-American Conference*.[171] In the frame-

168 Frédéric de Martens, 'The Portsmouth Peace Conference' (n 166 in Chapter 5) 642–643.

169 Ibid.

170 Ibid 642. According to de Martens, Roosevelt's initiative was "[...] perfectly correct, based as it was not only on moral grounds, but also on solid legal grounds."

171 Ecuador had already proposed to hold a second Pan-American Conference in Mexico City in 1896. However, only delegates from Mexico, Venezuela, Central America, and the United States were present wherefore the conference was postponed. Compare: Samuel Guy Inman, *Inter-American Conferences 1826–1954* (n 147 in Chapter 4) 50. A second attempt (which was just as unsuccessful as the first one) was made by Colombia in 1898.

work of such a meeting, he wanted to address questions which had been considered at the *First Pan-American Conference*, but which had not been "[...] finally settled, and others which have since then grown into importance."[172] On February 8, 1900, Secretary of State John Hay responded on his President's initiative and sent an official communication to the representatives of the Latin American countries accredited in Washington, D.C., in order to get the project for a second conference off the ground.[173]

The conference took place only a year and a half later in Mexico City. It was opened on October 22, 1901, and representatives from nineteen American nations participated in it.[174] In the inaugural address, the Mexican Secretary of State Ignacio Mariscal (1829–1910) declared that the conference was "[...] a friendly gathering of sister republics [...] whose results may be perhaps the adoption of practical means for the general peace and progress to which we all aspire."[175] Furthermore, he praised the successes of The Hague (and the *Madrid Conferences*)[176] and proclaimed that there was a clear tendency towards the submission of force to law.[177] In order to achieve similar goals in the inter-American context, the conference agenda comprised the following issues:

> I. Points studied by the previous Conference, which the new Conference may decide to reconsider
> II. Arbitration
> III. International Court of Claims
> IV. Means of protection to industry, agriculture, and commerce. Development of communications between the countries of the Union. Consular regulations of ports and custom-houses. Statistics

---

See: Alejandro Alvarez, *Le Droit International Américan* (Institut américain du droit international 1910) 218.

172 State of the Union Address of President William McKinley to the Senate and the House of Representatives on December 5, 1899, <http://www.thisnation.com/library/sotu/1899wm.html> accessed June 14, 2017.

173 John Vavasour Noel, *History of the Second Pan-American Congress* (Guggenheimer, Weil & Co. 1902) 18.

174 Ibid 83.

175 The quote stems from: ibid 85–86.

176 Alfred H. Fried, *Pan-Amerika* (n 73 in Chapter 4) 100. According to him, the Madrid Conferences were held to celebrate the fourth centenary of the discovery of America. Within the context of these conferences, a congress of lawyers dealt with arbitration and the question of the further development of this instrument.

177 Ibid 108.

v. Reorganization of the International Bureau of the American Republics[178]

Especially the second and third issues are of particular interest here, and they also played key roles at the *Second Pan-American Conference*.[179] Additionally, John Vavasour Noel (*'History of the Second Pan-American Conference'* from 1902) remarked that he found it:

> […] indeed, stirring to think that the young nations of America, breaking the fetters of tradition and setting an example to effete Europe, should, by mutual consent, agree to dispense with savage warfare and in one stroke of the pen accomplish that which has been a utopic dream for centuries.[180]

Noel, along with other progressive peace activists from the United States, seem to have shared the dream that their country would take a leading role by contributing to the accomplishment of far-reaching results in the field of obligatory and institutionalized arbitration in Mexico City.[181] But, unlike at The Hague or at the *First Pan-American Conference*, the United States pursued a comparably conservative policy. Several Latin American countries, on the other hand, stepped in and advocated for the realization of highly progressive concepts. They showed an open-minded attitude towards obligatory and institutionalized arbitration, which is hardly surprising when their above-described relationship towards these instruments during the 19th century is taken into consideration.[182] Two of the most recent examples of this practice were the conclusions of two obligatory arbitration treaties in 1898, one between Spain and Peru[183] and another one (of an even general nature) between Argentina and Italy. The latter agreement is particularly remarkable because it did not contain any exceptions and, therefore, provided for unrestricted and general arbitration of all cases of mutual conflicts between these two nations. Furthermore, several Latin American countries had introduced

178 John Vavasour Noel, *History of the Second Pan-American Congress* (n 173 in Chapter 5) 21.

179 Kurt Ed. Imberg, *Die Stellung der Vereinigten Staaten von Nordamerika zur internationalen Schiedsgerichtsfrage* (n 165 in Chapter 3) 66. Also: Alejandro Alvarez, *Le Droit International Américan* (n 171 in Chapter 5) 220. Alfred H. Fried, *Pan-Amerika* (n 73 in Chapter 4) 110.

180 John Vavasour Noel, *History of the Second Pan-American Congress* (n 173 in Chapter 5) 110.

181 Ibid 111.

182 Compare Chapter 4 of the present book.

183 Alfred H. Fried, *Pan-Amerika* (n 73 in Chapter 4) 101.

provisions to their constitutions in the 1890s according to which they were only entitled to wage war after having taken recourse to arbitration to attempt to settle the respective conflict peacefully.[184]

At the *Second Pan-American Conference*, it was clear from the beginning that all participating states favored the conclusion of arbitral agreements in inter-American relations.[185] Consequently, they did not have to discuss the question whether a multi-lateral arbitration treaty was to be concluded. They only had to come to terms on the scope and shape of the agreement.[186] From the subsequent discussions, the following three views can be identified as those most frequently invoked:

- The first one was in favor of "[o]bligatory arbitration, covering all questions pending or future when they did not affect either the independence or the national honor of a country."
- The second approach advocated for "[o]bligatory arbitration, covering future questions only and defining what questions shall constitute those to be excepted from arbitration."

184 Ibid 100; according to Fried, Brazil introduced such a provision to their constitution in 1891 (Article 34), Venezuela in 1893 (Art. 141), and a union of Nicaragua, Honduras and Salvador in 1894 (Article IV 2). Ecuador had already done so before in 1878 (Article 116). The same also happened in the Dominican Republic, since arbitration was given the rank of a constitutive principle. Article 97 of the (1880 adopted) constitution provided the following:

"Art. 97. Los Poderes encargados por esta Constitución de declarar la guerra, no deberán hacerlo sin antes proponer el arbitramiento de una o más potencias amigas.

Para afianzar este principio, deberá introducirse en todos los tratados internacionales que celebra la República, esta cláusula: 'Todas las diferencias que pudiesen suscitarse entre las partes contratantes, deberán ser sometidas al arbitramiento de una ó más naciones amigas, antes de apelar á la guerra.'"

Compare: *Constitución de la República Dominicana* (1880), Art. 97, <http://www.consultoria.gov.do/constituciones%201844-2008/Constitucion%201880.pdf> accessed June 5, 2016.

185 Kurt Ed. Imberg, *Die Stellung der Vereinigten Staaten von Nordamerika zur internationalen Schiedsgerichtsfrage* (n 165 in Chapter 3) 66. Also: Alfred H. Fried, *Pan-Amerika* (n 73 in Chapter 4) 112.

186 In the context of the Second Pan-American Conference, Jost Dülffer referred to an attempt to establish a general court of arbitration in the inter-American context. Other authors did not mention such a project regarding this conference. They only dealt with attempts to introduce compulsory arbitration and to create an international court of claims. Because no supporting evidence could not be found regarding Dülffer's claim, the project for a general court will be spared from the subsequent considerations. Compare: Jost Dülffer, *Regeln gegen den Krieg?* (n 20 in Chapter 1) 235.

– The third position preferred "[f]acultative or voluntary arbitration, as best expressed by The Hague convention."[187]

These extremely divergent views resulted, to a great extent, from differences in the current situations of the participating states and from political considerations (general ones as well as those regarding arbitration). For example, Chile was involved at that time in a long-standing dispute with Peru over the national affiliation of two provinces.[188] Because their economic and military superiority guaranteed them the role of the dominant party in this conflict, Chile had little interest in arbitrating the issue. Therefore, in Mexico City, they rejected any form of obligatory arbitration. Brazil held a very similar situation regarding outstanding boundary questions with Bolivia and France (in Guyana).[189] Furthermore, even the United States, the nation which had shown one of the most progressive attitudes concerning institutionalized and obligatory arbitration at the *First Hague Peace Conference*, rejected obligatory arbitration in Mexico City. According to the instructions for the U.S.-American delegates to the *Second Pan-American Conference*, the government of the United States was "[…] favorable to the pacific settlement of international disputes."[190] But all arbitration "[…] should be voluntary" and "[…] the choice of judges should be left to mutual agreement."[191] Hence, the United States pursued a policy in Mexico City which differed greatly from the one in The Hague in 1899.[192] Mexico, on the other hand, proposed a plan which would have constituted – according to the U.S.-American delegation – "[…] the furthest possible step in the direction of compulsory arbitration."[193] Article 15 of the Mexican proposal determined that arbitration was to become a fundamental principle of American international law and that all adhering states

187 All three quotes stem from: United States Congress, *Second International Conference of American States: Message from the President of the United States, transmitting a Communication from the Secretary of State, submitting the Report, with accompanying Papers, of the Delegates of the United States to the Second International Conference of American States, held at City of Mexico from October 22, 1901 to January 22, 1902* (United States Government Printing Office 1902) 9.

188 Samuel Guy Inman, *Inter-American Conferences 1826–1954* (n 147 in Chapter 4) 55.

189 Ibid. See also: Alfred H. Fried, *Pan-Amerika* (n 73 in Chapter 4) 111.

190 'Instructions to the United States Delegates' in John Vavasour Noel, *History of the Second Pan-American Congress* (n 173 in Chapter 5) 371.

191 Both quotes stem from: ibid.

192 Kurt Ed. Imberg, *Die Stellung der Vereinigten Staaten von Nordamerika zur internationalen Schiedsgerichtsfrage* (n 165 in Chapter 3) 68–69. Also: Alfred H. Fried, *Pan-Amerika* (n 73 in Chapter 4) 120.

193 United States Congress, *Second International Conference of American States* (n 187 in Chapter 5) 10.

were to be obliged to refer their mutual conflicts to arbitral settlement (if they were not able to settle them by diplomatic means).[194] The only cases which were to be excluded from the arbitral clause were those which concerned their national honor or independence. Mexico's progressive plan was supported, for example, by Argentina whose delegates declared that their country was strongly determined to put an end to international conflicts through arbitration, regardless of whether it was done through treaties or without them.[195] A number of other countries, such as Peru and Bolivia, also supported a general obligatory arbitration agreement.[196] However, it seems as if Peru's motivation to support this plan not only derived from their dedication to peace and their belief in the usefulness of obligatory arbitration. Peru also wanted to "[…] bring up indirectly the question of her dispute with Chile […] and to secure some expression of censure or rebuke"[197] against their Southern neighbor. Therefore, political considerations and pending conflicts also tended to play decisive roles in this regard.

It soon became apparent that no agreement could be reached on the Mexican plan. Even a number of the states which generally supported obligatory arbitration demanded that "[…] exceptions as broad as practically"[198] possible were introduced into the agreement. As a result of these overwhelming differences, the participating states quickly decided to refrain from dealing with the Mexican proposal any longer. Instead, they began to discuss the accession of the participating states to *The Hague Convention* of 1899 for voluntary arbitration.[199] This proposal can be considered to be a minimum consensus and a concession to the positions of Brazil, Chile, and the United States. In the end, the participating states agreed on a resolution in Mexico City, according to Article 1 of which the adhering states recognized the principles of the *Hague Convention* as American international law. Furthermore, the participating states requested Mexico and the United States (in Article 3 of this agreement) to negotiate terms for their admission to the *Hague Convention* with the signatory states of this agreement.[200]

194 Alfred H. Fried, *Pan-Amerika* (n 73 in Chapter 4) 113.

195 Ibid 114.

196 Ibid 116–119.

197 John Vavasour Noel, *History of the Second Pan-American Congress* (n 173 in Chapter 5) 11.

198 United States Congress, *Second International Conference of American States* (n 187 in Chapter 5) 10.

199 Samuel Guy Inman, *Inter-American Conferences 1826–1954* (n 147 in Chapter 4) 56.

200 'Translation of the Protocol of Adherence to the Conventions of The Hague' in United States Congress, *Second International Conference of American States* (n 187 in Chapter 5) 36–37.

The conclusion of this resolution did not mean that obligatory arbitration was completely off the table in Mexico City. Argentina, Bolivia, San Domingo, Salvador, Guatemala, Mexico, Paraguay, Peru, Uruguay, and Venezuela drew up and signed a treaty which was widely modeled after the Mexican proposal, and went even further in certain points. The first article corresponded to (the above-mentioned) Article 15 of the Mexican plan. But Article 2 was already shaped decisively differently in an important aspect. In certain cases, it restricted the right of the adhering states to invoke exemption clauses from the treaty. Usually, they were entitled to reject an arbitration of cases if their national honor or independence would have been affected. Contrary to the Mexican proposal, however, the new treaty provided that its adhering states were not empowered to invoke such clauses in cases concerning diplomatic privileges, boundaries, shipping and navigations laws, and the interpretation, applicability, and validity of treaties and conventions. Thereby, it constituted a limitation of the statutory exceptions – or, in other words, it introduced an unrestricted and fully compulsory obligation to arbitrate cases from the above-listed fields. Furthermore, Article 3 determined that the PCA was the competent body for the settlement of disputes between the adhering states (if the parties did not create an individual tribunal for the arbitration of their conflicts).[201]

Apart from obligatory arbitration, the creation of an international court of claims constituted another significant point of discussion at the *Second Pan-American Conference*. The idea to establish such an institution stood in the intellectual tradition (and was supposed to function as an extension of) the *Calvo Doctrine*[202] according to which pecuniary claims of aliens had to be settled before domestic courts. It opposed the right of the home countries of the aggrieved foreigners to intervene, either diplomatically or militarily, in the debtor states on behalf of their nationals in order to enforce these claims.

It was the Chilean delegation which proposed to establish an international court of claims.[203] According to this plan, appeal to this tribunal was only to be opened for the settlement of pecuniary claims if access to justice was denied, or abnormally delayed, by a domestic court or if the decision of a domestic court constituted an evident violation of the principles of international law. Therefore, the international court of claims was intended to function as a *catch-all element* (or in other words: as a subsidiary court). It

201 Compare: Alfred H. Fried, *Pan-Amerika* (n 73 in Chapter 4) 122–123.

202 Compare pages 134–139 of the present book.

203 John Vavasour Noel, *History of the Second Pan-American Congress* (n 173 in Chapter 5) 133–134.

meant that cases concerning pecuniary claims usually had to be settled before domestic courts, a step which would have constituted an acknowledgement of the *Calvo Doctrine* in inter-American terms. It was only if this practice did not result in suitable outcomes, or if pecuniary claims were not properly settled by domestic courts, that the case could be referred to the international court of claims. By attempting to introduce a mechanism for the settlement of pecuniary claims before domestic and international courts (through the *Calvo-Doctrine* and the establishment of the projected tribunal), the Latin American states sought to prohibit the use of force for the enforcement of such claims in inter-American relations.

The discussions in Mexico City concerning the creation of the proposed court were complex and challenging. Very divergent opinions had to be brought together. For example, the United States supported the creation of an international court of claims in general, but they did not want it to have an obligatory character, or to restrict the free choice of judges.[204] Hence, the U.S.-American delegates proposed an institution shaped in accordance with the model of the PCA.[205] Several Latin American countries, on the other hand, seem to have striven for further going results because they would have been the greatest profiteers of the creation of such an institution. According to John Vavasour Noel,

> [t]here is scarcely one of the American republics which does not feel that it has been subjected at some time or another to a peculiar injustice by the superior force of some more powerful country making a demand upon it for indemnity for damages sustained by some one of its citizens or subjects residing within their territory.[206]

However, due to conceptual differences, the participating states did not come to terms in Mexico City on the exact shape of the projected court of claims. Instead, they decided to take recourse to the solution which had already been employed in the context of obligatory arbitration; the introduction of a clause subjecting their disputes to the jurisdiction of the PCA. Accordingly, the participating states determined in Article 2 of the *Treaty of Arbitration of Pecuniary Claims* "[…] to submit to the decision of the permanent Court of Arbitra-

---

204 'Instructions to the United States Delegates' in John Vavasour Noel, *History of the Second Pan-American Congress* (n 173 in Chapter 5) 374.

205 Ibid. Also: Kurt Ed. Imberg, *Die Stellung der Vereinigten Staaten von Nordamerika zur internationalen Schiedsgerichtsfrage* (n 165 in Chapter 3) 70.

206 John Vavasour Noel, *History of the Second Pan-American Congress* (n 173 in Chapter 5) 132.

tion [...] all controversies which are the subject matter of the present Treaty, unless both Parties should prefer that a special jurisdiction be organized."[207] By consenting to the conclusion of this treaty, the U.S.-American delegates complied with an essential part of their instructions, the non-restriction of the free choice of arbitrators. However, they could not uphold their opposition against obligatory arbitration commitments for pecuniary claims. In the end, the United States agreed to the treaty even though they had to concede on this point.

Article 1 of the treaty stated that the signatory states "[...] agree to submit to arbitration all claims for pecuniary loss or damage which may be presented by their respective citizens, and which cannot be amicably adjusted through diplomatic channels and when said claims are of sufficient importance to warrant the expenses of arbitration."[208] Furthermore, the treaty neither provided restrictions of the extent of the claims nor exceptions from the obligatory arbitration commitment. Therefore, it constituted an unrestricted obligatory arbitration commitment for all cases of conflicts concerning pecuniary claims between the adhering nations. All participating states of the *Second Pan-American Conference* – except Brazil – signed the treaty in the end[209] and nine of them also ratified it (namely: Colombia, Costa Rica, Ecuador, Guatemala, Honduras, Mexico, Peru, El Salvador, and the United States).[210]

Overall, the American states accomplished a series of innovative and far going results in Mexico City. They concluded an agreement for adherence to the *Hague Convention* and decided to apply for admission to it. Moreover, they even entered an obligatory arbitration treaty for pecuniary claims which determined the PCA as the competent body for the settlement of conflicts of that kind. A similar provision was also implemented in another treaty concluded in Mexico City, the aforementioned general obligatory arbitration agreement to which a group of 10 Spanish American countries entered at this occasion. According to this agreement, the PCA was supposed to act as the competent body for the settlement of their mutual disputes (falling within the scope of the agreement). These two treaties, containing the provisions to submit cases to the jurisdiction of the PCA, were in complete accordance with the *Hague*

207 'Treaty of Arbitration for Pecuniary Claims' in James Brown Scott (ed.), *The International Conferences of American States 1889–1928* (n 1 in Chapter 4), page 105.

208 Ibid 104.

209 Ibid *footnote 1*. James Brown Scott pointed out that Venezuela had signed the treaty but that their "[...] withdrawal from the conference invalidated its adherence."

210 Jorge E Viñuales and Magnus Jesko Langer, 'Foreign Investment in Latin America: Between Love and Hatred' in Claude Auroi and Aline Helg (eds.), *Latin America 1810–2010: Dreams and Legacies* (Imperial College Press 2012) 325, footnote 8.

Convention since the PCA was competent to settle cases submitted by any state.[211] Therefore, even those American states, which were not yet members of the convention, were fully entitled to subject their disputes to the court for settlement. With regards to their attempt to be admitted to the *Hague Convention*, however, they underwent an application procedure which took until 1907. Probably, it was so lengthy because the convention did not provide a settled mode for handling requests for admission.[212] The receipt of the first applications from El Salvador and Argentina – the first two Latin American applicants for admission – and later also from other Latin American countries and Korea, resulted in discussions among the adhering states whether, and how, new members were to be approved.[213] These negotiations remained inconclusive at first, with the Latin American countries only being admitted in 1907, right before the beginning of the *Second Hague Peace Conference*.[214]

Although it took some time for the Latin American states to become members of the convention, the sole fact that they had decided to apply for admission and, more importantly, that they had appointed the PCA in two obligatory arbitration treaties as the competent institution for the settlement of their mutual conflicts, reveals an astonishing finding: After the *First Hague Peace Conference*, the European countries – which had accounted for the majority of participants at the conference and of the founding states of the PCA – were not the ones to take the leading role when it came to making use of the court and the convention in practice. Instead, it was the Latin American countries and the United States – most of whom were not even members of the convention (yet) – that further developed the Hague system during the initial years following 1899, even extending the competencies of the PCA through the conclusion of obligatory arbitration treaties. Thereby, they went considerably further than any of the European signatory powers. This leads to the conclusion that the American states once again became the pioneers and took the leading role in arbitration and in its further development.[215] The *Second Pan-American Conference* can, therefore, be considered as a success for the American states. They had had to handle an abundance of conceptual

211 A.G. de Lapradelle and Ellery C. Stowell, 'Latin America at the Hague Conference' (1908) 17 The Yale Law Journal 270.

212 Apart from Article 59 which provided that those non-signatory states were entitled to join The Hague Convention which had participated in the First Hague Peace Conference. Compare: *Convention for the Peaceful Settlement of International Disputes* (n 95 in Chapter 5).

213 Jost Dülffer, *Regeln gegen den Krieg?* (n 20 in Chapter 1) 236.

214 Ibid 238.

215 Compare also: ibid 236.

differences and disputes over important aspects regarding international law, the proposed international court of claims, and arbitration. That being said, they were able to come to an agreement concerning the conclusion of progressive measures for the preservation of peace and for the pacific settlement of their conflicts. But the conference can also be considered as a major success for the Hague system. Due to the resolutions taken in Mexico City, the system gained global dimensions – as several Latin American states subjected themselves to it (and did so even before joining the convention). In doing so the American states decided to abstain from establishing a separate American court of arbitration and instead referred their cases to the PCA. This step prevented the emergence of double structures and uncertain or overlapping competences on the international level. It concentrated the entire system in just one institution. Hence, the *Second Pan-American Conference* extended the Hague system to Latin America and significantly strengthened it at this occasion.

The claim that no parallel institutions were established on the American continent, by way of the creation of another court of arbitration, is only correct, however, for the *Second Pan-American Conference* itself. While the conference was ongoing, and the participating states could not agree in Mexico City on the establishment of an inter-American court of claims or arbitration, four Central American republics (Costa Rica, Nicaragua, Honduras, and El Salvador)[216] followed a different path in Corinto, Nicaragua. As a result of their negotiations, they decided (on January 20, 1902) to determine general obligatory arbitration to be the fundamental principle for conflict settlement in their mutual relations and agreed to create the so-called *Central American Arbitration Tribunal*.[217]

According to Article 2 of the *Treaty of Corinto*, the contracting states "[...] establish the principle of obligatory arbitration, in order to adjust every difficulty or question that might present itself between the contracting parties,

---

216 Manley O. Hudson, 'The Central American Court of Justice' (1932) 26 The American Journal of International Law 760. According to him, the treaty was ratified by Costa Rica, Honduras, and El Salvador in 1902. He does not mention whether Nicaragua followed their example or abstained from doing so. See also: *Papers relating to the Foreign Relations of the United States, with the annual message of the president transmitted to Congress December 2, 1902* (United States Government Printing Office 1902) 881. There, William Laurence Henry (a member of the U.S.-American legation in San José, Costa Rica), reported to Secretary of State John Hay that "[...] the president of Guatemala has also agreed to sign it."

However, it was not possible to find any proof that Guatemala followed this announcement and actually ratified the treaty in the end.

217 Manley O. Hudson, 'The Central American Court of Justice' (n 216 in Chapter 5) 759.

binding them in consequence to submit them to a tribunal of Central American arbitrators."[218] Furthermore, Article 11 of the same agreement provided that the signatory states would not "[...] execute any hostile act, warlike preparations, or mobilization of forces, with the object of not impending the arrangement of the difficulty or question through the means established by the present agreement."[219] Consequently, the effective implementation of the treaty would have resulted in a prohibition of war in the mutual relations of the four Central American treaty parties. They would have been obliged to subject all of their disputes to arbitral settlement by a regional court of arbitration. This would have been the so far most far-reaching realization of the principle of *peace through law* and the replacement of war with (quasi-)legal remedies in history.[220] Many peace activists and international lawyers dreamt of accomplishments like this on the global level during these days. However, even though the tribunal was actually set up on October 2, 1902, it was not a success, remaining irrelevant in practice.[221] In another Central American peace treaty, concluded only a year later between Guatemala, Nicaragua, El Salvador, and Honduras (on November 9, 1903), the *Treaty of Corinto* was not even mentioned anymore despite remaining in force.[222] Furthermore, the only time that the treaty was invoked, and a case was referred to the regional court, was in 1907 when a conflict broke out between Honduras and Nicaragua. Costa Rica appealed to the court for settlement of this dispute – but when the court issued a decision, only Honduras accepted it. Due to Nicaragua's decision not to comply with the judgment, Honduras and El Salvador declared the treaty void. Thereby, they brought the agreement itself, as well as the court, to an end.[223]

Despite its failure, the attempt of the four Central American countries to introduce a second permanent court of arbitration, and to subject all their

218 *Papers relating to the Foreign Relations of the United States, with the annual message of the president transmitted to Congress December 2, 1902* (n 216 in Chapter 5) 882. According to Article 10 of the treaty, only those conflicts were not to be settled by the Central American court of arbitration which concerned boundaries. Instead, these disputes were supposed to be submitted to a "[...] foreign arbitrator of American nationality."

219 Ibid.

220 Cesare P.R. Romano, 'Trial and Error in International Judicialization' in Cesare P.R. Romano, Karen J. Alter, and Yuval Shany (eds.), *The Oxford Handbook of International Adjudication* (n 102 in Chapter 2) 127.

221 Cameron A. Miles, *Provisional Measures before International Courts and Tribunals* (Cambridge University Press 2017) 33.

222 Manley O. Hudson, 'The Central American Court of Justice' (n 216 in Chapter 5) 760.

223 Cameron A. Miles, *Provisional Measures before International Courts and Tribunals* (n 221 in Chapter 5) 34.

mutual conflicts to compulsory arbitration, allows drawing two essential conclusions: Firstly, this episode provides clear proof of the difficult and unstable situation in Central America which repeatedly resulted in wars and struggles. Secondly, it shows, nevertheless, that the Central American states had an affection for (obligatory) arbitration, that they were generally willing to settle their mutual relations peacefully, and that they were receptive to progressive arbitral concepts. The correctness of this claim becomes apparent when taking a look at the shape of the court. It had a truly permanent bench of judges (Article 3), its impartiality was guaranteed (Article 4),[224] and the general obligatory arbitration commitment from Article 2 turned the court into the competent institution for the settlement of all kinds of conflicts between the signatory states. Hence, the court was designed to be far more progressive and far-reaching than the PCA.

Following these supplementary remarks, the focus will once again be on the *Second Pan-American Conference* in order to emphasize one more point, an aspect of the conference which remains unclear until today. It is the fact that the United States pursued an approach towards obligatory arbitration at this occasion which differed decisively from their policy in The Hague. J. Lloyd Mecham (*'The United States and Inter-American Security'* from 1961) provides a possible explanation for this point. He argued that the United States rejected general obligatory arbitration in Mexico City because they believed that this instrument "[…] could more profitably be applied to restricted subjects – pecuniary claims, for example."[225] According to Mecham,

> [i]t felt that if any type of dispute was susceptible of arbitral settlement it would be claims for damages by individual citizens of one state against the government of another, since these controversies are usually free of the emotional factor which makes recourse to arbitral procedure so difficult in the settlement of political questions. Moreover, it is felt that a multi-lateral treaty on the compulsory arbitration of pecuniary claims not only would give the American states opportunity to prove their attachment to the principle but would be valuable preparation for extending the scope of compulsory arbitration.[226]

224 *Papers relating to the Foreign Relations of the United States, with the annual message of the president transmitted to Congress December 2, 1902* (n 216 in Chapter 5) 882. According to it, "[t]he arbitrators of those states among whom exists the disagreement shall not form part of the tribunal for the consideration of the concrete case."

225 J. Lloyd Mecham, *The United States and Inter-American Security 1889–1960* (University of Texas Press 1961) 61.

226 Ibid.

Contrary to this view, it can be seen that Secretary of State John Hay had explicitly ordered his delegates in Mexico City to oppose any form of general as well as special obligatory arbitration commitments.[227] Since it does not seem as if the United States had pursued two different approaches towards obligatory arbitration (one for general questions, the other fur pecuniary claims), it appears reasonable to assume that Hay's order to reject such commitments had applied to pecuniary claims as well. A possible explanation for the fact that the United States yielded in the end to an obligatory arbitration commitment for pecuniary claims was the fact that their delegates seem to have realized that they had to compromise on this particular point in order not to risk the success of the conference. Hence, it remains doubtful whether J. Lloyd Mecham's explanations are correct.

Another conceivable explanation was given by William I. Buchanan (in *'Latin America and the Mexican Conference'* from 1903). He argued that the differences between the positions of the U.S. delegations towards obligatory arbitration pursued at the *First Hague Peace Conference* in comparison to the one from the *Second Pan-American Conference* could be tracked back to the fact that the U.S.-American government had come to the political conviction in the years between these two events:

> [...] that while obligatory arbitration might be a blessing to the world if carried out, that it is impracticable between nations owing to the absence of any motive power to bring about its use outside the two countries interested, since no matter what the character of the obligatory clause might be, there exists no power to force a country to carry out a general treaty obligation to arbitrate a case when it is believed its independence, its national life or interests would be jeopardized by such a recourse.[228]

His argument surely touches on a fundamental aspect of the international legal order (at that time just as today): The lack of an executive power to enforce international law. Compliance with treaties and obligations depended, to a wide extent, on the goodwill of the contracting parties. However, this had already been a very well-known fact at the turn of the century, but it had not hindered the United States in proposing the conclusion of an obligatory arbitration commitment in The Hague in 1899. Furthermore, Buchanan

227 'Instructions to the United States Delegates' in John Vavasour Noel, *History of the Second Pan-American Congress* (n 173 in Chapter 5) 374.

228 William I. Buchanan, 'Latin America and the Mexican Conference' (1903) 22 The Annals of the American Academy of Political and Social Science 53.

did not mention the obligatory arbitration agreement on pecuniary claims which the United States signed in Mexico City despite their – as he claimed – general aversion to obligatory arbitration. Therefore, his arguments are not fully convincing either.

A third possible explanation for the existence of the differences between the approaches of the United States in The Hague and in Mexico City could be found in the U.S.-American relations to the participating countries. The *First Hague Peace Conference* was primarily composed of European countries, which the United States considered as equals. At the *Second Pan-American Conference*, however, all the participating states were from America. As previously mentioned, during the second half of the 19th century, the United States had developed an imperialist approach towards the South of the continent, especially towards Central America and the Caribbean.[229] Between the *First* and the *Second Pan-American Conferences*, two important developments plainly demonstrated that the United States continued to pursue a hegemonic policy to Latin American states and that they considered them as belonging to their exclusive sphere of influence. Firstly, the United States had openly pursued this approach in 1895 in the context of a boundary dispute between Great Britain (British Guiana) and Venezuela. Secondly, they also did so by intervening in the war for Cuban independence in 1898.[230] The former incident concerned a long-lasting boundary controversy which Venezuela asked the United States to settle in 1894 after Great Britain had refused to arbitrate the case. U.S. Secretary of State Richard Olney (1835–1917) responded to the Venezuelan request by sending a strongly worded note to the British government. He not only demanded arbitration of the case but also laid down what was to become known as the *Olney Doctrine* by issuing the following statement:

> Today, the United States is practically sovereign on this continent, and its fiat is law upon the subjects to which it confines its interposition. Why? [...] It is because, in addition to all other grounds, its infinite resources combined with its isolated position render it master of the situation and practically invulnerable as against any or all other powers.[231]

229 Compare pages 139–142 of the present book.

230 Samuel Guy Inman, *Inter-American Conferences 1826–1954* (n 147 in Chapter 4) 49.

231 'Message from US Secretary of State Richard Olney to US Ambassador to the United Kingdom Thomas F. Bayard' in Jeffrey F. Taffet and Dustin Walcher, *The United States and Latin America: A History with Documents* (Routledge 2017) 53–55.

Furthermore, the United States argued that Great Britain had violated the *Monroe Doctrine* by trying to expand their territories at the expense of Venezuela. The United States would not tolerate this action and Olney explicitly emphasized the U.S.-American claim for exclusive hegemony over Latin America by issuing this doctrine. At first, Great Britain raised some objections to it but soon they gave in and agreed to arbitration.[232] Great Britain did not want to risk a war and hoped for the United States' support (in exchange) in other affairs of global importance.[233] By ousting Great Britain from Latin America, the United States finally achieved the status of the undisputed hegemon in Latin America – and they openly declared their willingness to defend this position before the rest of the world.[234] The second case concerns the U.S. reaction to the Cuban war for independence in 1895.[235] The United States had already intervened in Latin American countries on multiple occasions during the 1890s in order to secure their influence and to enforce their political goals, for example, in Haiti in 1888/1889, in Chile in 1891, in Brazil and Nicaragua both in 1893/1894, and in Venezuela in 1895/1896.[236] But, when the United States decided to interfere in the Cuban war for independence (which led to the *Spanish-American War* in 1898), they reached a new phase. They had already been a regional power and their strong economic and financial resources had guaranteed them influence in the world. But by defeating Spain in this conflict, the United States achieved the status of a great power. Furthermore, they also became a colonial power by annexing the Philippines, Guam, Hawaii, and Puerto Rico[237] from Spain as a result of this war and by occupying Cuba.[238] These two incidents demonstrate that the United States continued to pursue an expansionist policy towards Latin America (and beyond) at the turn of the 20th century. On the one hand, they did so by striving for direct imperialism, for example, in the form of annexations of islands in the Pacific. While, on the other hand, in Latin America, they aimed for a rather indirect form of imperi-

232 Lars Schoultz, *Beneath the United States* (n 19 in Chapter 4) 115 et seq.

233 Samuel Guy Inman, *Inter-American Conferences 1826–1954* (n 147 in Chapter 4) 49.

234 Compare pages 139–142 of the present book.

235 Compare, e.g.: John L. Offner, 'McKinley and the Spanish-American War' (2004) 34 Presidential Studies Quarterly 50 et seq.

236 Volker Depkat, *Geschichte Nordamerikas* (UTB GmbH 2008) 263.

237 Justin D. Murphy, 'Insular Cases' in Spencer C. Tucker (ed.), *The Encyclopedia of the Spanish-American and Philippines-American Wars* (ABC Clio 2009) 304–305.

238 Mark Peceny, 'A Constructivist Interpretation of the Liberal Peace: The Ambiguous Case of the Spanish-American War' (1997) 34 Journal of Peace Research 425. The U.S.-American occupation of Cuba lasted until 1902, then the power was turned over to an elected government (but the United States kept a lot of influence on the island).

alism. They wanted to bring the entire continent under their hegemony by making use of their dominant economic power, of the financial dependency of the Latin American states on U.S.-American loans and investments, and (from time to time) of military interventions.[239] The U.S.-American imperialism was particularly strong under President McKinley (in office: 1897–1901) and during the first years of the presidency of his successor Theodore Roosevelt (in office: 1901–1909). Thus, the United States pursued a policy of 'cooperation among equals' with regards to the European countries, while they regarded Latin American countries as standing under their hegemony and subordinated to their power and will.

Taking all of this into consideration, it can reasonably be assumed that the United States considered themselves to be superior to the Latin American states. An obligatory system of arbitration, however, would have severely questioned this superiority since it would have allowed all American states to refer cases to an arbitral settlement, regardless of their political, economic, and military power. This arbitration would be before an arbitral tribunal whose arbitrators were equally nominated by both parties (not even to speak of the situation before a permanent, independent, and impartial tribunal with a standing panel of judges as the one which the United States had proposed in The Hague). In this situation, the United States would have lost their superior position and would have been subjected to the same treatment by the court as the Latin American countries. By preventing the establishment of an inter-American system of obligatory arbitration, and of such a court, the United States could have aimed to preserve their dominant – power-based – position over the Latin American states. Thereby, they could still have imposed their will on them and could have maintained the option to enforce their goals through firm diplomacy or the use of force whenever it pleased them. Hence, the U.S.-American imperialistic policy appears to be a probable – and realistic – cause for their rejection of plans for the introduction of systems of obligatory arbitration in the inter-American context. It would also explain the differences between the U.S.-American approaches in The Hague and Mexico City because the United States seem to have regarded the (mostly European) participants of the *Hague Conference* as equals, whereas they aimed for preserving their hegemonic power over the (American) participants of the meeting in Mexico City.

However, the fact that the U.S.-American delegation in Mexico City gave in and agreed to an obligatory arbitration treaty for pecuniary claims does not

239 Dominick Jenkins, *The Final Frontier: America, Science, and Terror* (Verso 2002) 174. Also: Susan A. Brewer, *Why America Fights: Patriotism and War Propaganda from the Philippines to Iraq* (Oxford University Press 2009) 16–18.

seem to comply with this assumption, at least not at first glance. But it should be borne in mind that the initial instructions had provided the order to reject any form of obligatory arbitration commitments. It was only when the United States were confronted with a strong majority of supporting votes for this treaty from the side of the Latin American countries, that they gave in and showed goodwill towards the other conference participants. Furthermore, by doing so, they only took an insignificant risk. This was the case as when it came to the granting of credits, the United States was usually the creditor, and the Latin American countries were the debtors. Therefore, the United States would only have to deal with a small (and calculable) probability of being sued on the basis of this treaty. In the majority of cases of (potentially arising) pecuniary claims, however, it would have been the United States that held the position of the plaintiff. Finally, pecuniary claims were very technical questions of (at most) secondary importance. Therefore, their subjection to obligatory arbitration for pecuniary claims did not bear a high risk of substantially affecting the U.S.-American freedom to act in foreign affairs. The United States were only stripped of the option of using force for the collection of such claims. But they did not have to limit their general imperialist strivings in Latin America. Instead, concluding this treaty was a great opportunity for the United States to openly prove their pacific orientation and benevolence towards the Latin American nations.

Despite all these reflections on the U.S.-American attitude towards obligatory arbitration and its imperialist aspirations towards Latin America, it should not be forgotten that the results of the *Second Pan-American Conference* were of a truly outstanding nature. On that occasion, the American states (including the United States) concluded treaties of key importance for the further development of (obligatory) arbitration in the inter-American, as well as in the global context. They took the first steps to extend the competences of the PCA by conferring obligatory jurisdiction, in general or for certain types of case, to this institution. Thereby, the Hague system was significantly strengthened, and an example was set for the other states.

3.2 *A Wave of Conclusions of Obligatory Arbitration Treaties*

Between 1902 and 1905, the above-described situation did not change much. The imperialistic attitude of the United States continued to be a dominant factor in their relations to Latin America. It became even stronger during the first years of Theodore Roosevelt's presidency, which began in 1901. In 1904, U. S.-American imperialism became particularly visible and was even raised to the level of a fundamental principle of the country's foreign policy when Roosevelt announced an addendum to the *Monroe Doctrine*, the so-called

Roosevelt Corollary. It constituted an important shift in the relations between the United States and Latin America, as well as in those between the United States and Europe. The corollary provided that the United States were entitled to act as a police force in Central and Latin America for guaranteeing peace and stability, e.g., by ensuring that countries from this region repaid their debts.[240] Roosevelt announced his new foreign political approach in his annual message to the United States Congress on December 6, 1904:

> Chronic wrongdoing, or an impotence which results in a general loosening of the ties of civilized society, may in America, as elsewhere, ultimately require intervention by some civilized nation, and in the Western Hemisphere the adherence of the United States to the Monroe Doctrine may force the United States, however reluctantly, in flagrant cases of such wrongdoing or impotence, to the exercise of an international police power.[241]

According to Francis Anthony Boyle ('*World Politics and International Law*' from 1985), "[…] the essence of this precept meant that the U.S. government would exercise an alleged right of preemptive intervention into the domestic affairs of Central American and Caribbean countries delinquent in the payment of their public debts to private creditors in European countries."[242] One reason for the United States to impose this policy on Latin America was that they aimed to prevent European countries from applying political pressure on Latin American states on behalf of private creditors, from using gunboat diplomacy against them, and – especially – from waging war for the enforcement of claims of their citizens. Instead, the United States sought exclusive control and hegemony over Latin America and wanted to limit Europe's influence on the region as much as possible, even more than they already had. According to Boyle, the United States therefore imposed "[…] upon Latin American debtor countries a formal regime for proper administration of their public finances and the retirement of their public debts under direct U.S. supervision."[243] Effective supervision required enforcement tools and the United States considered themselves to be entitled to intervene in Latin American debtor states

240 Kris James Mitchener and Marc Weidenmier, 'Empire, Public Goods, and the Roosevelt Corollary' (2005) 65 The Journal of Economic History 658–659.

241 *State of the Union Address delivered by U.S. President Theodore Roosevelt before the United States Congress on December 6, 1904*, <http://www.presidency.ucsb.edu/ws/index.php?pid=29545> accessed June 28, 2017.

242 Francis Anthony Boyle, *World Politics and International Law* (n 135 in Chapter 3) 269.

243 Ibid.

whenever they deemed them not to comply with their obligations. Thereby, the *Monroe Doctrine* was turned from a (originally) protective policy against European intervention into a justification for U.S.-American interventions in Latin American states.[244] This policy did not violate the wording of the just signed *Treaty of Arbitration of Pecuniary Claims*, although it clearly obstructed its spirit and the underlying reason for its conclusion. While this agreement only banned the use of force for the collection of claims of the citizens of the respective countries, the *Roosevelt Corollary* was supposed to entitle the United States to intervene in Latin American countries whenever they did not comply with European claims. Thereby, the United States bypassed the prohibition of the use of force in cases of pecuniary claims by simply adopting a different focus. Even though they did not violate the respective treaty, this step was a clear manifestation of the U.S.-American imperialistic approach towards Latin America. Furthermore, it shows that the United States were not willing, at least in Roosevelt's early presidency, to give up on the practice of imposing their will on the Latin American countries (if also necessary) by force.

However, the foreign policy of the United States towards Latin America between 1902 and 1906 can best be described as 'ambivalent'. The country sent very different, sometimes even openly opposing signals, and took actions which ran counter to the aforementioned imperialistic approach. Reviewing these actions supports the assumption that (also) a very peace-oriented trend existed in U.S.-American foreign policy towards Latin America and towards the rest of the world which rang alongside the imperialist attitude. Besides numerous (military) interventions in Latin America, the United States remained one of the pioneers in the field of arbitration and in strengthening the PCA.[245] Evidence in support of his claim can be found in the fact that, despite the initial enthusiasm for the establishment of the PCA, the court was widely ignored until 1902 by all adhering states. Alfred H. Fried (*'Handbuch der Friedensbewegung'* from 1905) even held the suspicion that most European states hoped that they could simply return to their usual imperialistic and nationalist policies after the end of the *First Hague Peace Conference* without having to pay much attention to the resolutions adopted at this event.[246] No govern-

244 Thomas A. Bailey, *A Diplomatic History of the American People* (Prentice-Hall 1974, 9th ed.) 505.

245 Calvin DeArmond Davis, The United States and the Second Hague Peace Conference (n 28 in Chapter 1) 19.

246 Alfred H. Fried, *Handbuch der Friedensbewegung* (n 135 in Chapter 3) 309.

ment showed any willingness to submit cases to the court and several of them even seem to have tended to let the PCA fall into oblivion.[247]

Only in 1902, the situation finally changed when the United States convinced Mexico, the only other American member of the *Hague Convention* so far, to refer the first case in history to the PCA, the so-called *Pious Fund Case*.[248] This case was only of secondary importance in political terms, but it concerned a dispute which had pended between the United States and Mexico for years. The United States demanded the annuities generated by the name giving fund from Mexico for "the benefit of the Archbishop of San Francisco and the Bishop of Monterey."[249] By convincing Mexico to bring the case before the PCA, the United States hoped to kill two birds with one stone. On the one hand, they wanted to bring the PCA into existence and inspire other signatory states of the *Hague Convention* to follow their example. While, on the other hand, the United States had, as just shown, taken a leading role at the *Second Pan-American Conference* in the task of convincing the Latin American countries of submitting membership requests for the *Hague Convention*, of appointing the PCA as the competent institution for the settlement of their mutual pecuniary claims, and of abstaining from the establishment of a separate American court of arbitration. Following the *Second Pan-American Conference*, the United States seems to have felt the need to demonstrate the workability and functionality of the PCA to the other American states in order to prove to them that they had been right to follow the U.S.-American lead in Mexico City.[250] Regarding the second point, this attempt soon backfired severely on the United States. Instead of building trust among the Latin American countries in the Hague system and strengthening their dedication to it, the *Pious Fund Case* resulted in the exact opposite. When the PCA decided the case in favor of the United States, it caused a lot of anger, indignation, and even rejection of the decision and of the PCA as a whole both in Mexico and the rest of Latin America.[251]

---

247 Ibid.

248 Howard S. Levie, 'Final Settlement of the Pious Fund Case' (1969) 63, The American Journal of International Law 791–792.

249 Compare: *Award of the Permanent Court of Arbitration in the matter of the Pious Fund of the Californias, rendered on October 14, 1902*, <http://www.pca-cpa.org/The%20Pious%20Funde37e.pdf?fil_id=1820>, accessed December 11, 2015. Also: William E. McDonald, 'The Pious Fund of the Californias' (1934) 19 The Catholic Historical Review 427–436.

250 Jost Dülffer, *Regeln gegen den Krieg?* (n 20 in Chapter 1) 237.

251 Ibid; according to Dülffer, the award was regarded as an affront and as an offence to Mexico.

The *Pious Fund Case* did not remain the only issue which dealt a huge setback to the trust of the Latin American states in the functioning of the prevailing system of arbitration, in the PCA, and especially in the United States. A dispute between Great Britain, Italy, and Germany on the one hand and Venezuela on the other hand, the so-called *Venezuela Preferential Case*, was referred to the PCA in 1904.[252] It arose in 1902 because of unremunerated debts and pecuniary claims for losses and injuries of nationals of the complainant parties in Venezuela[253] and escalated into (first a pacific and later) a belligerent blockade of the Venezuelan coast by Great Britain and Germany. Due to U.S.-American pressure, the two European great powers agreed to lift the blockade, to settle the case peacefully, and to refer it to the PCA. The court was ordered to decide whether the complainant parties deserved preferential treatment in the fulfillment of their demands before other states which held similar claims against Venezuela.[254]

The *Venezuela Preferential Case* was one of the most, if not the single most important decision of the PCA before 1914.[255] It touched upon a topic which was important enough that it ran the risk of resulting in open war. But "[...] all those who had hoped the court would be a great agency for peace"[256] were sorely disappointed. The PCA decided the case in favor of the complainant parties and, therefore, granted preferential treatment to those states which had taken recourse to arms in order to enforce their claims. Many peace activists and international lawyers did not regard this award as a peace-oriented

252 *Award of the Permanent Court of Arbitration in the matter of the Venezuela Preferential Case, rendered February 22, 1904*, <http://legal.un.org/riaa/cases/vol_IX/99-110.pdf> accessed August 23, 2017.

253 Calvin DeArmond Davis, *The United States and the Second Hague Peace Conference* (n 28 in Chapter 1) 73–82.

254 Arthur Eyffinger, *The 1899 Hague Peace Conference* (n 28 in Chapter 1) 445. Also: Rudolf Bernhardt, 'Preferential Claims against Venezuela Arbitration' in Rudolf Bernhardt, Rudolf L Bindschedler, and Rudolf Dolzer (eds.), *Encyclopedia of Public International Law, vol. 2: Decisions of International Court and Tribunals and International Arbitrations* (North-Holland Publ. Co. 1981) 234. W.L. Penfield, 'The Anglo-German Intervention in Venezuela' (1903) 177 The North American Review 86.

255 Calvin DeArmond Davis, *The United States and the Second Hague Peace Conference* (n 28 in Chapter 1) 71. According to Davis, "[o]nly in this instance did the court touch upon a matter of first importance." Compare also: Francis Anthony Boyle, *World Politics and International Law* (n 135 in Chapter 3) 32. According to Boyle, "[f]rom the perspective of maintaining international peace and security, the most significant of the Hague Court's arbitrations proved to be the Venezuela Preferential Case and the Casablanca Case."

256 Calvin DeArmond Davis, *The United States and the Second Hague Peace Conference* (n 28 in Chapter 1) 88.

decision, and it did not acquire strong approval from the United States[257] or any Latin American country either. John Watson Foster (*'Arbitration and the Hague Court'* from 1904), for example, referred to manifold criticism in legal scholarship against the award.[258] But despite the frustration of the American states, peace activists, and international lawyers regarding the Venezuela-decision, the award actually seems to have strengthened the global acceptance of arbitration. No less than 10 European powers (plus three non-European nations) participated in the settlement of this dispute either as claimants, arbitrators, or interested parties.[259] Therefore, Foster concluded the following:

> The importance of the Venezuela case at The Hague can scarcely be exaggerated. The thirteen nations there represented, embracing a population of more than four hundred and fifty millions, the most enlightened as well as the most powerful of the world in military establishment, are a striking object lesson of the wisdom and efficacy of arbitration.[260]

These numbers are certainly impressive, especially when taking into account that the entire world population at the time was approximately 1.7 billion people.[261] Hence, the populations of the thirteen nations participating in the dispute (450 million people) accounted for around 26% of the world population. Furthermore, the case involved some of the most powerful European countries. The global importance of the case, and the fact that it was referred to the PCA, suggests that the popularity and importance of the PCA had increased significantly. This was especially the case regarding Europe,[262] as it was the first dispute settled by the court which involved European states. In the aftermath of the Venezuela-decision, acceptance (slowly) grew among European nations for the PCA and its function as a central mechanism for international conflict settlement. This trend was further continued by two more cases which were both decided by the PCA in 1905 and which also involved European countries. First, the *Japanese House Tax Case*, which was settled by the PCA between Japan on the one hand and France, Germany, and

---

257 Ibid 89.

258 John Watson Foster, *Arbitration and the Hague Court* (n 3 in Chapter 3) 72.

259 Ibid 71–72.

260 Ibid 74.

261 'The World at Six Billion' 4; by the Population Division, Department of Economic and Social Affairs at United Nations Secretariat (ESA/P/WP.154) from 12 October 1999.

262 See also: Calvin DeArmond Davis, *The United States and the Second Hague Peace Conference* (n 28 in Chapter 1) 89.

Great Britain on the other,[263] and, second, the so-called *Muscat Dhows Case* between France and Great Britain.

Notwithstanding the slowly increasing number of cases brought before the PCA, it should also be noticed that the court only settled four cases between 1900 and 1907, or 14 cases in total between 1900 and 1914.[264] The reason for the comparably low frequency with which states referred cases to the PCA can, *inter alia,* be found in the fact that statesmen, legal scholars, and the public considered the court to function too intricate, too slowly, and to be too costly.[265] The still prevailing reluctance against the PCA becomes also apparent when comparing the number of cases settled by the PCA with the total amount of arbitrations in these years (although it should also be born in mind that very different figures can be found in the literature regarding these numbers). To give just three examples: (1) According to Neil Hollander (*'Elusive Dove'* from 2013), at least 200 arbitrations were carried out between 1900 and 1915.[266] (2) A.M. Stuyt (*'Survey of International Arbitrations 1794–1989'* from 1990) lists 58 arbitrations for the period between the *First* and the *Second Hague Peace Conference* (1899–1907), respectively, 90 arbitrations between the *First Hague Peace Conference* and the outbreak of *World War I* (1899–1914).[267] (3) Andrew Webster (*'Internationalism'* from 2007), finally, referred to 114 cases of arbitration between 1900 and 1914.[268] It cannot be determined which of these authors provided the most accurate numbers in this regard. Arbitrations were carried out among countries from all over the world in their bi-lateral relations, with no obligation to publish details on the procedures. Therefore, inaccuracies are unavoidable – but regardless of whether 90, 114, or over 200 arbitrations took place between 1899 and 1914, the figures show that the share of cases settled by the PCA was fairly low. It accounted for somewhere between 7% and 15.5% of all arbitrations.

The figures provide a telling picture not only of the PCA but also of the general situation concerning arbitration in this period. As shown in Chapter 3, 139 disputes were settled by arbitration between 1871 and 1899, which accounts for 4.79 cases per year. The 200 arbitrations listed by Neil Hollander

263 *Award of the Permanent Court of Arbitration in the matter of the Japanese House Tax Case, rendered May 22, 1905*, <https://pca-cpa.org/en/cases/69/> accessed August 11, 2017.

264 Compare: https://pca-cpa.org/en/cases/ (accessed: August 11, 2017).

265 Hans Wehberg, *The Problem of an International Court of Justice* (n 123 in Chapter 2) 51–52.

266 Neil Hollander, *Elusive Dove: The Search for Peace during World War I* (McFarland & Company, Inc., Publishers 2013) 10.

267 A.M. Stuyt, *Survey of International Arbitrations 1794–1989* (n 125 in Chapter 3).

268 Andrew Webster, 'Internationalism' in Gordon Martel (ed.), *A Companion to International History 1900–2001* (Blackwell 2007) 41.

for the period between 1900 and 1915 would correspond to 13.3 cases per year – which would equate to quite an enormous increase (by the factor 2.78). Dealing with the lower numbers given by Stuyt and Webster, the increase would of course be lower, but still impressive. For Stuyt, it would mean that 5.63 cases were settled by arbitration per year during this period (a growth by the factor 1.17) while Webster's numbers correspond to 7.6 arbitrations per year (an increase by the factor 1.59). Therefore, (isolated) arbitration was still on the rise. Moreover, it was continuously used in international relations for the settlement of pending conflicts and was already an integral part of the states' set of instruments in their bi-lateral relations before *World War I*.

Even though only 14 cases were referred to the PCA between 1899 and 1914 (which only corresponds to around one case per year), it cannot be claimed either that the court was entirely rejected by the international community. In fact, it even seems as if the acceptance of the PCA grew continuously after 1902 and that the states integrated the court more and more into international relations and state practice. This assumption is also supported by the fact that a wave of obligatory arbitration treaties was concluded in the aftermath of the *First Hague Peace Conference*. This development had its roots (again) outside inter-European relations . The situation in Europe was as such at that time that several European powers had shown a very benevolent attitude towards obligatory arbitration in The Hague. But, in the years directly after the conference, they did not pay much attention to it anymore. Latin American states, on the other hand, upheld their favorable approach to obligatory arbitration. They concluded a multi-lateral obligatory arbitration treaty for pecuniary claims (with the United States) at the *Second Pan-American Conference* (in 1901/1902) and some of them had even gone further by entering a general obligatory arbitration agreement which did not contain any exemption clauses.[269] Both of these (inter-American) treaties provided that the PCA was the competent body for the settlement of those disputes which fell within their scopes. By doing so, the adhering states broke new judicial ground and were the first ones to make use of the option provided in Article 19 of the *Hague Convention* (indirectly and without explicit mentioning this article though). Moreover, the Latin American states had never stopped concluding bi-lateral obligatory arbitration agreements in their mutual relations. After the *First Hague Peace Conference*, they even extended this practice once more and, between 1899 and 1906, Spanish American countries also began to enter similar agreements with Spain. These were the following:

---

269 Compare pages 196–199 of the present book.

- Mexico in January 1902
- Bolivia in February 1902
- Argentina in January 1902[270]
- Columbia in February 1902
- San Domingo in January 1902
- Guatemala in February 1902
- San Salvador in January 1902
- Nicaragua in October 1904
- Uruguay in January 1902
- Honduras in May 1905[271]

One aspect which all of these treaties had in common was that they determined the competent arbitral instance to settle conflicts between the signatory parties to be either a "Spanish-American head of state or a Spanish-American tribunal";[272] while in exceptional cases, it was also permissible to invoke the PCA. The role of the court was, therefore, not really expanded through these treaties, but at least included (in some instances) as a *fallback* instrument.

Only a year later, in 1903, however, a development set in which caused an enormous increase in the importance that was attached to the PCA. A new wave of enthusiasm for obligatory arbitration and for the PCA arose at that time. But this time, the development had its origin in Europe. The number of bi-lateral obligatory arbitration treaties which were concluded confirm that a ground-breaking change happened in these years. Between 1871 and 1899, 91 (special and general) obligatory arbitration treaties had been concluded worldwide – which accounts for 3.1 treaties per year. In comparison to earlier years, this was an exceptionally high figure. Already during the later decades of the 19th century, increased importance was attached to obligatory arbitration. However, between 1903 and 1905, obligatory arbitration treaties were concluded on such a massive scale that the numbers from earlier periods were easily surpassed. This development constituted a substantial change in the so far prevailing practice.

The origin of this development can be found in the conclusion of a bi-lateral obligatory arbitration treaty between Great Britain and France in 1903. The agreement enshrined many aspects of the prevailing practice of bi-lateral treaties of that kind (so far, a mostly European/American, and inter-Spanish

---

270 Alfred H. Fried, *Pan-Amerika* (n 73 in Chapter 4) 152. According to him, the treaty was never put into force but was replaced by another treaty in September 1903.

271 Ibid 153.

272 Ibid 154.

American phenomenon). But it was also different from previous treaties on a number of key points. For example, it was the first bi-lateral agreement of that type concluded between two European great powers. Thereby, it contributed to the spread of obligatory arbitration in the inter-European context. But before France and Great Britain were able to take this step, they first had to overcome their pending mutual disputes and their rivalries over colonial issues in Egypt (especially the *Fashoda Incident*)[273] and in other regions.[274] It was only after having found suitable compromises to end their conflicts that their relations improved. The conclusion of the British-Franco obligatory arbitration treaty in 1903 was a crucial step in this regard; a development which, in 1904, also resulted in the creation of the *Entente Cordiale*.[275] Their rapprochement was enthusiastically supported by wide parts of the populations from both sides of the English Channel (including numerous peace activists).[276] For example, Sir Thomas Barclay, president of the British chamber of commerce in Paris, and Baron d'Estournelles, a famous peace activist and advocate for arbitration, took leading roles in this movement and sought to win wide support for it in both countries.[277] They managed to link the Franco-British rapprochement process with the idea of new-found stability and importance of their countries' relationship by concluding a treaty of obligatory arbitration.[278] This step was aimed at building trust and friendship between their nations,[279] but they also used the opportunity to strive for the realization of their pacifist goals. According to Helen May Cory ('*Compulsory Arbitration of International Disputes*' from 1932), the situation was such in Great Britain and France that "[…] the movement in favor of a general treaty of arbitration was so widespread that the government could not refuse to consider it of great importance."[280] On October 14, 1903, the Franco-British obligatory arbitration treaty (which was shaped in accordance with the model of the unratified

273 See, e.g.: Gordon A. Craig, *Geschichte Europas 1815–1980* (n 47 in Chapter 2) 329–330.

274 Alfred H. Fried, *Handbuch der Friedensbewegung* (n 135 in Chapter 3) 321.

275 John Keiger, 'How the Entente Cordiale Began' in Richard Mayne, Douglas Johnson, and Robert Tombs (eds.), *Cross Channel Currents: 100 Years of the Entente Cordiale* (Routledge 2004) 3 et seq. See also: Jörg Fisch, *Europa zwischen Wachstum und Gleichheit 1850–1914* (n 84 in Chapter 2) 355.

276 Alfred H. Fried, *Handbuch der Friedensbewegung* (n 135 in Chapter 3) 322.

277 Jost Dülffer, *Regeln gegen den Krieg?* (n 20 in Chapter 1) 260–261.

278 Alfred H. Fried, *Handbuch der Friedensbewegung* (n 135 in Chapter 3) 323.

279 Jost Dülffer, *Regeln gegen den Krieg?* (n 20 in Chapter 1) 260.

280 Helen May Cory, *Compulsory Arbitration of International Disputes* (n 154 in Chapter 2) 51. According to her, the original quote stems from Lord Lansdowne (see: Archives Diplomatiques (1903) 88, no. 10, 49–53).

Olney-Pauncefote Treaty from 1897)[281] was put into force. Regarding its exact content and scope, Article 1 provided the following:

> Differences which may arise of a legal nature, or relating to the interpretation of treaties existing between the two contracting parties, and which it may not have been possible to settle by diplomacy, shall be referred to the Permanent Court of Arbitration, [...] provided, nevertheless, that they do not affect the vital interests, the independence, or the honor of the two contracting states and do not concern the interest of third parties.[282]

Hence, the treaty constituted the obligation to refer all conflicts to arbitral settlement by the PCA which had a purely legal nature, or which concerned the interpretation of treaties (if they did not fall under the exception clauses). The fact that the provision focused exclusively on legal questions, excluding political ones, complied with the above-described practice of European countries concerning (obligatory) arbitration and with their understanding of arbitration as an instrument for the settlement of legal issues.[283] Consequently, it cannot be claimed that the scope of the treaty was exceptionally wide in comparison to other obligatory arbitration treaties which had been concluded in inter-Spanish American or European/American relations in these years.[284] But while the majority of its points complied with the prevailing practice the treaty was, nevertheless, anything else but remarkable. It marked the beginning of a development which massively changed the status of obligatory arbitration as well as of the PCA under international law and in state practice. Firstly, it was the first agreement which explicitly referred to Article 19 of the *Hague Convention* and permanently subjected parts of the two states' bi-lateral relations to the court's jurisdiction. At the time of the adoption of Article

281 Calvin DeArmond Davis, *The United States and the Second Hague Peace Conference* (n 28 in Chapter 1) 97. See also pages 88–89 of the present book.

282 Helen May Cory, *Compulsory Arbitration of International Disputes* (n 154 in Chapter 2) 51–52.

283 Compare pages 41 et seq. of the present book.

284 Alfred H. Fried, *Handbuch der Friedensbewegung*, vol. 1 (n 63 in Chapter 3) 175, 180–181. According to him, the above-mentioned trade treaty between Portugal and the Netherlands (from July 5, 1894) contained a general obligatory arbitration commitment which was fairly wide. Furthermore, regarding European/American relations, he referred to two treaties which Italy concluded with Argentina and Mexico in the direct aftermath of the First Hague Peace Conference (on September 18 and October 16, 1899). Both treaties established general obligatory arbitration commitments in the contracting parties' mutual relations and hardly contained any restrictions or limitations.

19, little importance had been attached to this provision[285] and no state had made (explicit) reference to it prior to 1903. This situation only changed when France and Great Britain concluded the aforementioned agreement. Secondly, the Franco-British agreement initiated an entire wave of conclusions of similar treaties during the following years. Regarding this development, and especially regarding Article 19 of the *Hague Convention*, James Brown Scott (*'The Hague Peace Conferences of 1899 and 1907, Vol. 1'* from 1909) concluded that "[...] this article, insignificant and useless as it may seem, marks, one may almost say, an era in the history of arbitration. The existence of the article has called attention on the subject of arbitration and by reference to it many States have negotiated arbitration treaties."[286] In the following years, dozens of obligatory arbitration treaties were concluded worldwide and almost all of them followed the model of the Franco-British agreement. Helen May Cory stated in this regard:

> About forty treaties based on this model were concluded by European countries before the World War, and an equal number by the United States and Brazil after the Second Hague Conference [...]. Of the European countries, England, France, Portugal, Italy and Switzerland were foremost in encouraging this type of arbitration convention.[287]

Both James Brown Scott and Francis Anthony Boyle counted the conclusion of 77 obligatory arbitration agreements of that type between 1899 and 1908;[288] and Boyle also added in this regard that "[...] all but twelve provided for some sort of reference to the Permanent Court of Arbitration".[289] Alfred H. Fried even referred to 111 obligatory arbitration treaties for the same period (147 of such agreements for the years between the end of the *First Hague Peace Conference* and the end of the year 1910).[290] Finally, Neil Hollander came to the conclusion that "[w]hen war broke out in 1914, 209 arbitration treaties were in

285 Francis Anthony Boyle, *Foundations of World Order* (n 28 in Chapter 1) 31. Also: 'Editorial Comment: Treaties of Arbitration since the First Hague Conference' (n 118 in Chapter 5) 823–824.

286 James Brown Scott, *The Hague Peace Conferences of 1899 and 1907*, vol. 1 (n 131 in Chapter 2) 813.

287 Helen May Cory, *Compulsory Arbitration of International Disputes* (n 154 in Chapter 2) 53.

288 James Brown Scott, *The Hague Peace Conferences of 1899 and 1907*, vol. 1 (n 131 in Chapter 2) 815–817.

289 Francis Anthony Boyle, *Foundations of World Order* (n 28 in Chapter 1) 31.

290 Alfred H. Fried, *Handbuch der Friedensbewegung*, vol. 1 (n 63 in Chapter 3) 185–188.

force. Many of these agreements were well reported in the press, each regarded as a benchmark on the road to world peace."[291]

Again, it is fairly impossible to determine which of these figures is most accurate. However, all of them demonstrate that a development was initiated in 1903 which resulted in the creation of a rapidly increasing number of obligatory arbitration treaties, a trend which soon involved countries from all over the world. On the one hand, Helen Mary Cory also claimed that these treaties were rather vague and that they left lots of room for political maneuvers and for avoiding arbitration obligation due to wide exception clauses.[292] But, on the other hand, it also cannot be negated that the conclusion of these agreements brought obligatory arbitration back on the agenda for the entire community of states, not only on the one of the Spanish American nations. Even the German Empire participated in the movement,[293] wherefore, it can reasonably be assumed that obligatory arbitration lost its stigma as an impracticable measure in international relations and that it was turned instead into a fully accepted element of state practice.

These agreements concluded between 1903 and 1905 further extended the work of the *First Hague Peace Conference*. Article 19 had initially been nothing but a concession to all those countries which had sought obligatory arbitration in The Hague but whose endeavors had been thwarted by the German resistance. By taking recourse to obligatory arbitration in 1903, Great Britain and France initiated a wave of obligatory arbitration treaties which grew beyond the wildest dreams of many peace activists. While obligatory arbitration had still been deemed incompatible with the dogma of the inviolability of state sovereignty before 1903,[294] this wave of agreements washed the hesitations away. It turned obligatory arbitration into an integral and commonly accepted part of international relations; also, in inter-European relations and even between the great powers.

The United States also concluded a series of eleven obligatory arbitration treaties with other nations (shaped in accordance with the Franco-British agreement) between November 1904 and February 1905. However, the so-called *Hay Arbitration Conventions* (named after U.S.-Secretary of State John Hay who had negotiated them) were signed but never ratified by the United

291 Neil Hollander, *Elusive Dove* (n 266 in Chapter 5) 10.

292 Helen May Cory, *Compulsory Arbitration of International Disputes* (n 154 in Chapter 2) 53.

293 Germany concluded obligatory arbitration treaties with Great Britain on July 12, 1904 and the United States on November 22, 1904 (although the latter was not ratified by the United States). Compare: Alfred H. Fried, *Handbuch der Friedensbewegung*, vol. 1 (n 63 in Chapter 3) 186.

294 Ibid 179.

States. They failed to be enacted because of domestic struggles between the Senate and the President.[295] Despite their practical irrelevance (due to their non-ratification), it is indispensable to mention them in this context because of their influence on the subsequent developments. In the course of public discussions on the pros and cons of the conclusion of the *Hay-treaties*, several (private) conferences were held in the United States in 1903 and 1904. These events were often attended by many well-respected and influential persons who showed open support for the cause of peace and arbitration.[296] Public awareness for the cause of obligatory arbitration was thereby raised in the U.S.-American public mind. But it must also be noticed that the agendas of these meetings were never restricted to just obligatory arbitration and always embraced other peace-related topics as well. For example, on the *Second American Conference on International Arbitration*, held in January 1904 in Washington, D.C., the role of the PCA was discussed. Andrew Carnegie (1835–1919), an industrialist and enthusiastic advocate of peace, declared at this occasion his affection for this institution by referring to it as "[...] the supreme court of the world [...] to settle international disputes."[297] Another event was held in 1905 in St. Louis by the *Inter-Parliamentary Union*. It dealt with obligatory arbitration but also addressed "[t]he establishment of an international congress which shall meet at sated periods to discuss international questions."[298] This issue was a very often discussed topic among U.S.-American peace activists.[299] But it was only when it was addressed in St. Louis that this trend spread beyond the U.S.-American context and influential parliamentarians from all over the world began to deal with it as well. By the end of the conference, the *Inter-Parliamentary Union* launched a resolution in

295 Francis Anthony Boyle, *Foundations of World Order* (n 28 in Chapter 1) 31–32.

296 Calvin DeArmond Davis, *The United States and the Second Hague Peace Conference* (n 28 in Chapter 1) 100–101. Also: Helen May Cory, *Compulsory Arbitration of International Disputes* (n 154 in Chapter 2) 53.

297 *The Second American Conference on International Arbitration held in Washington, D.C., January 12, 1904* (Gibson Bros. 1904) 93. Also published in Calvin DeArmond Davis, *The United States and the Second Hague Peace Conference* (n 28 in Chapter 1) 101.

298 Published in Calvin DeArmond Davis, *The United States and the Second Hague Peace Conference* (n 28 in Chapter 1) 107.

299 Bob Reinalda, *Routledge History of International Organizations* (n 59 in Chapter 2) 78. Reinalda mentioned at this point that already in 1903 "[...] the American Peace Society urged politicians to present a resolution to Congress to authorize the president 'to invite the governments of the world to join in establishing ... a regular international congress to meet at stated periods to deliberate upon the various questions of common interest to the nations and to make recommendations thereon to the governments.'" According to Reinalda, the quoted parts originally stem from: Arthur Eyffinger and Arthur Witteveen, *The International Court of Justice 1946–1996* (n 94 in Chapter 5) 57.

which it declared its strong support for periodic follow-up meetings of the *First Hague Peace Conference*.[300] This resolution did not go unheard. According to Samuel J. Barrows (*'The Tour of the Interparliamentary Union'* from 1904), President Roosevelt responded to it by declaring that he "[...] shall at an early date ask the other nations to join in a second congress at The Hague,"[301] and Roosevelt took this pledge to the heart.[302] Already on October 21, 1904, the United States launched an initiative to implement the resolution. They invited the participating countries of the *First Hague Peace Conference* for a second meeting.[303] Thereby, holding a follow-up meeting of this conference became a seriously discussed idea on the diplomatic level.

But, although Roosevelt complied with this request of the *Inter-Parliamentary Union*, he did not pursue a very peace-oriented agenda in general. For example, he was not willing to give up on his imperialist aspirations.[304] However, his concessions and actions in support of the cause for peace were, according to the findings of Jost Dülffer (*'Regeln gegen den Krieg?'* from 1981), not purely tactical maneuvers either.[305] Instead, Roosevelt regarded arbitration as an instrument capable of settling some, but not all, state-to-state conflicts.[306] For him, war and the use of force were (at least for the near future) still necessary elements of the current international order, which was an attitude often dominating the U.S.-American foreign policy during these years.[307] For example, Roosevelt's administration intervened:

300 Bob Reinalda, *Routledge History of International Organizations* (n 59 in Chapter 2) 78.

301 Samuel J. Barrows, *Tour of the Interparliamentary Union Tendered by the Government of the United States* (United States Government Printing Office 1904) 225. Also published in: Calvin DeArmond Davis, *The United States and the Second Hague Peace Conference* (n 28 in Chapter 1) 110.

302 Kurt Ed. Imberg, *Die Stellung der Vereinigten Staaten von Nordamerika zur internationalen Schiedsgerichtsfrage* (n 165 in Chapter 3) 83.

303 Calvin DeArmond Davis, *The United States and the Second Hague Peace Conference* (n 28 in Chapter 1) 112. See also: 'Editorial Comment: The Second Peace Conference of The Hague' (1907) 1 The American Journal of International Law 432–433.

304 Jost Dülffer, *Regeln gegen den Krieg?* (n 20 in Chapter 1) 228.

305 Ibid 243.

306 Ibid 244.

307 Oliver Stone and Peter Kuznick, *The Untold History of the United States* (Ebury Press 2012), xxx (*Introduction*). According to them, "[b]etween 100 and 1925, the United States repeatedly intervened militarily in Latin America. It send troops to Honduras in 1903, 1907, 1911, 1912, 1919, 1924, and 1925; to Cuba in 1906, 1912, and 1917; to Nicaragua in 1907, 1910, and 1912; to the Dominican Republic in 1903, 1914, and 1916; to Haiti in 1914; to Panama in 1908, 1912, 1918, 1921, and 1925; to Mexico in 1914; and to Guatemala in 1920. The only reason it didn't intervene more frequently was that it often stayed, occupying countries for extended periods of time: Nicaragua from 1912 to 1933, Haiti from 1914 to

- in Panama in 1903 by sending warships to back separatist movements against Colombia, a step that allowed the United States to further pursue their plans for building the *Panama-Canal*;[308]
- in Santo Domingo in 1904 by sending troops and by 'convincing' the Dominican authorities to allow U.S.-American agents to collect customs at Dominican ports to serve foreign debts;[309] or
- in Cuba in 1906 as a reaction to the collapse of the Cuban political system and as an attempt to protect U.S.-American interests there.[310]

These actions complied with Roosevelt's aforementioned imperialist attitude, and the president would have even intervened more often in Latin America in these years if he had been sure of being fully backed by the U.S.-American public in such initiatives.[311] Hence, the United States upheld, on the one hand, an imperialist approach in their foreign policy (especially towards Latin America). On the other hand, they also pursued a peace-oriented attitude, particularly in global terms (outside the exclusive American context). By taking the initiative for a *Second Hague Peace Conference* and negotiating peace terms in the *Russo-Japanese War*, the Roosevelt administration proved its favorable attitude for arbitration and international justice. This approach formed a fundamental part of the U.S.-American foreign policy at that time, even in spite of the president's reluctant and doubting attitude towards it.[312] It follows from these considerations that the U.S.-American foreign policy was very ambivalent during these years. The support for peace and justice was just as real and constituted just as much a part of the U.S.-American foreign policy as the imperialist one.

In this regard, it should also be noticed that the United States was not the only great power which pursued two disparate and inconsistent foreign polit-

---

1933, the Dominican Republic from 1916 to 1924, Cuba from 1917 to 1922, and Panama from 1918 to 1920."

308 Alan McPherson, *A Short History of U.S. Interventions in Latin America and the Caribbean* (John Wiley & Sons, Inc. 2016) 56 et seq.

309 Sidney Lens, *The Forging of the American Empire: From the Revolution to Vietnam: A History of U.S. Imperialism* (Pluto Press 2003) 206.

310 Lester D. Langley, *The Banana Wars: United States Intervention in the Caribbean, 1898–1934* (SR Books 2002) 27 et seq.

311 Benjamin Allen Coates, *Legalist Empire: International Law and American Foreign Relations in the Early Twentieth Century* (Oxford University Press 2016) 107. According to him, Roosevelt declared the following: "I would have interfered in some similar fashion in Venezuela, in at least one Central American State, and in Haiti already … if I could have waked up our people so that they would back a reasonable and intelligent foreign policy which should put a stop to crying disorders at our very doors."

312 Jost Dülffer, *Regeln gegen den Krieg?* (n 20 in Chapter 1) 243–244.

ical approaches at the same time. Their attitude did, however, very clearly reflect the overall situation in the years between the two *Hague Conferences*. Great powers continued to regularly engage in struggles for dominance, power, and colonial possessions while also showing a growing sympathy for obligatory arbitration and the PCA. The *Boer-War* (1899–1902) and the *First Moroccan Crisis* (1905/06)[313] are two examples for the prevalence of imperialism and for the continuance of colonial struggles between the great powers. At the same time, the PCA became (as shown above) significantly more accepted and was quickly integrated into foreign political considerations of all states. Although the number of cases grew slowly, the wave of obligatory arbitration treaties which were being concluded among European and American states between 1903 and 1905 provides a clear sign for the globally increasing acceptance of the court. Due to this wave of agreements, obligatory arbitration gained considerably in terms of importance; and this development was not only limited to American or smaller European states but also involved the European great powers. Finally, also the number of cases of isolated arbitrations increased substantially in these years. Therefore, it can be concluded that both the use and acceptance of arbitration was at an all-time peak between 1899 and 1906. Never before in history were so many obligatory arbitration treaties concluded, and so many international disputes arbitrated. The PCA, although seldom referred to, stood out as a beacon of light for the peaceful settlement of state-to-state disputes and as a reminder of the promise of the states to raise arbitration to the regular instrument for the settlement of international disputes.[314]

In the case of the United States, another factor contributed to the emergence of the aforementioned ambivalent approach in their foreign affairs as well. This ambivalence was the strongest in their policy towards Latin America. They continued pursuing imperialist goals and strove for dominance over the rest of the continent, but, at the same time, also tried to act as an advocate on behalf of the Latin American countries and to improve their situation on the global level.[315] Peace-oriented policies generally enjoyed a lot of support in the United States at that time. However, it was also a settled fact in U.S.-American foreign policies that the United States considered Central America and

313 The term 'Morocco-Crisis' describes a conflict between France and Germany in 1905/06 over the status of Morocco. The conflict bore an actual risk of escalating into open war. Compare: John Lowe, *The Great Powers, Imperialism, and the German Problem 1865–1925* (n 29 in Chapter 1) 166 et seq.

314 Compare pages 171–176 of the present book.

315 Compare: Kurt Ed. Imberg, *Die Stellung der Vereinigten Staaten von Nordamerika zur internationalen Schiedsgerichtsfrage* (n 165 in Chapter 3) 85.

the Caribbean as their exclusive sphere of influence[316] and they did not hesitate to periodically intervene in these countries. Furthermore, their imperialist approach towards Latin America was accompanied in many cases by the belief that Latin Americans were 'racially inferior'.[317] Even leading U.S.-American politicians such as President Roosevelt or Francis B. Loomis, the ambassador of the United States in Venezuela (between 1897–1901) and later Assistant Secretary of State (between 1903–1905), held such views.[318] The claim for racial superiority seems to have formed the justification for some U.S.-American politicians to claim dominance over the entire American continent and, therefore, also for military interventions in the region. As described above, since the middle of the 19th century, the United States had pursued a policy called *Manifest Destiny* which provided for an idea according to which "[...] it was America's God-given right and duty to expand its borders across the North American continent."[319] The doctrine implied that the interests of other states – for example, the ones of Mexico whose territories in Northern America the United States had annexed as a result of the *Mexican-American War* (1846–1848)[320] – which got in the way of the U.S.-American striving for the fulfillment of their destiny were rightfully to be ignored. In the course of the second half of the 19th century, concepts of biological racism and Social-Darwinism arrived from Europe, deeply influenced the U.S.-American attitude towards Latin America. They reinforced the U.S.-American claim for dominance over territories in America. According to Thomas F. O'Brien (*'The Century of U.S. Capitalism in Latin America'* from 1999), the situation in the United States was such that "[m]any Americans at all different levels of society believed that Latin Americans were inherently inferior."[321] Furthermore, O'Brien also stated the following:

316 Compare pages 139–142 of the present book.

317 Compare: Lars Schoultz, *Beneath the United States* (n 19 in Chapter 4) 176 et seq., and in particular 181–182.

318 Ibid.

319 J.T. Moriarty, *Manifest Destiny: A Primary Source History of America's Terrestrial Expansion in the 19th Century* (Rosen Publications Group 2005) 4.

320 Compare pages 114, 140 of the present book. Also: Thomas F. O'Brien, *The Century of U.S. Capitalism in Latin America* (University of New Mexico Press 1999) 11. There he claimed the following: "Although such views did not necessarily represent the perspective of all or even most Americans at this time, racism did provide the ideological justification for the American assault on Mexico."

321 Thomas F. O'Brien, *The Century of U.S. Capitalism in Latin America* (n 320 in Chapter 5) 11.

> Influenced by European thinkers, and anxious to justify their displacement of Native Americans and enslavement of Africans, a growing number of Americans accepted racialist interpretations of humanity.
>
> […] As the abolitionist movement clearly demonstrated, not all Americans harbored racist views. But a growing number of Americans assured themselves that they comprised an important part of the superior Anglo Saxon race as opposed to the degenerate Indian and African races with whom they shared North America. These fortunate Anglo Saxons soon drew a similar distinction between themselves and Latin Americans, particularly their closest Latin neighbors, the Mexicans.[322]

By categorizing Latin Americans as 'inferiors', and by arguing that their unstable political systems were the result of their 'racial insufficiency', U.S.-Americans granted themselves the right to compensate these 'insufficiencies' by interfering in Latin American domestic affairs. According to Lynn V. Foster (*'A Brief History of Central America'* from 2007), the United States considered themselves to be the "[…] natural protector of the Western hemisphere."[323] This paternal, as well as racist, approach played a key role in justifying the U.S.-American imperialist approach towards Latin America and their interventions in the region for the enforcement of their interests. The fact that the imperialist attitude of the United States towards Latin America was, nevertheless, accompanied by benevolent actions and a peace-oriented approach whereby they strove for the creation of a (voluntary) system of arbitration in America, and advocated for the admission of Latin America to the *Hague Convention*, can be found explained in the following two points. Firstly, as Juan Pablo Scarfi (*'In the Name of the Americas'* from 2016) pointed it out, the United States was already in a period of transition; a "[…] difficult and slow transition from interventionism to multilateral Pan-Americanism"[324] which they should further pursue and intensify in the following years. But at the same time, they had not abandoned the interventionist attitude towards Latin America yet. Secondly – and at least as important as the first point – the United States also seems to have striven for increasing the use of arbitration in their relations with other American states and for integrating the Latin American nations into the established and institutionalized Hague system to encourage peace and stability in the region. This point also seems to have been an important economic factor for the United States. Unrests, riots, and wars bore the risk of endangering the U.S.-American citizens' manifold (and quickly

322 Ibid.

323 Lynn V. Foster, *A Brief History of Central America* (n 5 in Chapter 4) 193.

324 Juan Pablo Scarfi, 'In the Name of the Americas' (n 25 in Chapter 4) 192.

growing)[325] investments in the region and could have hampered their control over it. This attitude had already become apparent on both *Pan-American Conferences* at which the United States had been eager to conclude trade agreements and to encourage regional integration; two measures which would have both allowed them to create closer economic relations with Latin America, to facilitate access to foreign markets, and to remove trade barriers.

Therefore, one of the primary goals of the United States behind *Pan-Americanism* – besides purely imperialist considerations – was to gain influence in Latin America to further increase trade with the region, to open new markets for U.S.-American companies and investments, and to secure U.S.-American investments. Accordingly, David Sheinin (*'Beyond the Ideal'* from 2000) described *Pan-Americanism* as "[...] the friendly face of U.S. dominance in the hemisphere."[326] Through (racially justified) interventions, the United States secured these investments and ensured that their economic and political interests were not interfered with.[327]

3.3 *A Different Attitude towards Latin America*

The fact that the United States decided in 1905 to perform a change in their foreign political approach, to shift away, at least a little, from their imperialist attitude, and to pursue a different policy towards Latin America, can, *inter alia*, be traced back to the death of John Hay in this very year. He was replaced as Secretary of State by Elihu Root who – according to Juan Pablo Scarfi – "[...] was an outstanding figure of a new style of U.S. foreign policy promoted by the Republican Party, based on legal diplomacy and the promotion of peace and international law."[328] In the beginning of his career, Root was a corporate lawyer[329] who played a leading role "[...] in New York State Republication politics through the 1890s."[330] He was appointed as Secretary of War in 1899, a position which he held until 1904. After a year back in private business, Roosevelt appointed Root as Hay's successor (1905). Root, in turn, nominated

325 Thomas F. O'Brien, *The Century of U.S. Capitalism in Latin America* (n 320 in Chapter 5) 116. Also: Lynn V. Foster, *A Brief History of Central America* (n 5 in Chapter 4) 192. According to her, "U.S. capital invested in Central America was growing at a phenomenal rate, from $11,5 million in 1897 to $76.9 million in 1914."

326 David Sheinin, 'Rethinking Pan Americanism' (n 28 in Chapter 4) 1,

327 Juan Pablo Scarfi, 'In the Name of the Americas' (n 25 in Chapter 4) 196.

328 Ibid.

329 Calvin DeArmond Davis, 'Elihu Root' in Edward S. Mihalkanin (ed.), *American Statesmen: Secretaries of State from John Jay to Colin Powell* (Greenwood Press 2004) 430–431.

330 Jonathan Zasloff, 'Law and the Shaping of American Foreign Policy: From the Gilded Age to the New Era' (2003) 78 NYU Law Review 244.

James Brown Scott (1866–1943) as his legal advisor.[331] Scott was a leading scholar in international law at that time but, so far, he was completely unexperienced in governmental work.[332]

These two men, Root and Scott, changed U.S.-American (foreign) policy during the subsequent years. Both were supporters of the U.S.-American peace movement,[333] lawyers,[334] and strict legalists. They believed that international law held a crucial function in international relations and that "[…] justice should be the determining factor in each foreign political decision."[335] For them, international law was the most capable means for dealing with international disputes because of its neutral nature and non-political character.[336] Hence, they deemed international law to be capable of effectively organizing international relations and the community of states.[337] According to Francis Anthony Boyle ('*Foundations of World Order*' from 1999), they regarded the underlying cause of international law to be "[…] the preservation of peace among nations to the greatest degree possible under the given historical circumstances."[338] Therefore, it can be concluded that Root and Scott pursued a foreign political approach which was driven by legal(ist) considerations and attached the highest importance to the function of (the rule of) law in international relations. Through the influence which they, in particular Root, exerted on the U.S.-American foreign political agenda, they were able to shape it in accordance with their legalist considerations soon after Root's inauguration.[339]

Root's and Scott's work did not remain limited to governmental activities. In 1905/06, they founded the *American Society of International Law*, a private organization dedicated to the further development and promotion of inter-

331 Christopher R. Rossi, *Broken Chain of Being: James Brown Scott and the Origins of Modern International Law* (Kluwer Law International 1998) 6–7.

332 For a detailed study of James Brown Scott's work and his background, see: Ralph D. Nurnberger, *James Brown Scott: Peace Through Justice* (n 1 in Chapter 5).

333 Juan Pablo Scarfi, 'In the Name of the Americas' (n 25 in Chapter 4) 197.

334 Calvin DeArmond Davis, *The United States and the Second Hague Peace Conference* (n 28 in Chapter 1) 119. According to him, "[…] Root brought to the State Department a greater knowledge of law, both national and international, than Hay had possessed."

335 Ralph D. Nurnberger, *James Brown Scott: Peace Through Justice* (n 1 in Chapter 5) 137.

336 Tuomas Lihr, 'Elihu Root and International Legalism: Legalist Remarks on Collective Security and American Realism' (2014) 1 Helsinki Law Review 66.

337 Martha Finnemore, *The Purpose of Intervention: Changing Beliefs about the Use of Force* (Cornell University Press 2003) 33.

338 Francis Anthony Boyle, *Foundations of World Order* (n 28 in Chapter 1) 12.

339 Tuomas Lihr. 'Elihu Root and International Legalism' (n 336 in Chapter 5) 66.

national law.[340] Root presided over it and Scott acted as its secretary. According to the prospectus of the society, it should "[...] count for much in the formation of a sound and rational body of doctrine concerning the true principles of international relations."[341] Right from its beginning, the society also published a journal, the *American Journal of International Law*, the purpose of which was to "offer a ready and valuable means of communication between jurists and students of international law on the one hand, and the scientific and lay public on the other."[342] A central element of the society was, therefore, the education and the furtherance of the expertise of the American people with regards to international law.[343] Consequently, the society was conceived – according to Frederic L. Kirgis (*'The American Society of International Law's First Century'* from 2006) – "[...] not primarily as a scholarly society, but as an instrument for peace in the world. Those who conceived it were brought together by their faith in arbitration as a means of avoiding war and serving American interests, but they broadened their focus to encompass the spectrum of international relations and to promote justice as well as peace."[344] According to Mark Weston Janis (*'America and the Law of Nations'* from 2010), the second mission of the society and its journal was "[...] the legalization of international disputes. They saw international courts and arbitral tribunals as likely ways to world peace."[345]

Indeed, the latter point played a distinct role in both Root's and Scott's thinking. They were pioneers in this regard and took steps which resulted in decisive achievements in the introduction of adjudicate instruments into the international legal order. As described above, the concept of adjudication had remained, so far, a topic of secondary importance (at best) in the agenda of the U.S.-American peace movement. However, adjudication was never completely forgotten since the days of William Ladd. For example, some of its elements could be recognized in the proposal for an international court of arbitration made by the *New York State Bar Association* (in 1896) or in the plan for an international tribunal presented by the U.S.-American delegation at the *First Hague Peace Conference*.[346] Nevertheless, most legal scholars and governmen-

340 Mark Weston Janis, *America and the Law of Nations 1776–1939* (n 84 in Chapter 3) 150.

341 'Prospectus: The Aim and Scope of the American Society of International Law' (1907) 1 The American Journal of International Law 130–131.

342 Ibid.

343 Mark Weston Janis, *America and the Law of Nations 1776–1939* (n 84 in Chapter 3) 150.

344 Frederic L. Kirgis, *The American Society of International Law's First Century: 1906–2006* (Nijhoff 2006) 16.

345 Mark Weston Janis, *America and the Law of Nations 1776–1939* (n 84 in Chapter 3) 151.

346 Compare pages 177 et seq. of the present book.

tal officers did not distinguish between arbitration and adjudication just yet. They continued to refer to both concepts under the general term 'arbitration'. But, due to Scott's and Root's influence, this situation was about to change from 1906 onwards; *inter alia* because of the foundation of the *American Society for the Judicial Settlement of International Disputes* in 1910.[347]

According to Jonathan Zasloff (*'Law and the Shaping of American Foreign Policy'* from 2003), Root's position in the U.S.-American government was outstanding and he effectively served "[...] as Roosevelt's prime minister."[348] Furthermore, Roosevelt empowered him to re-orient the U.S.-American policy towards Latin America,[349] and Root utilized this opportunity. Over the following years, he substantially changed the prevailing U.S.-American foreign political approach towards the other American nations. Root strove for the establishment of the rule of law in international relations,[350] aimed for the strengthening of international law, and for making sure that Latin American states were finally awarded full sovereignty and the status of equals under international law. In particular, his efforts made in relation to the last point promptly led to practical results. After Roosevelt had condemned the political instability and reliability of Latin American states in the announcement of his corollary in 1904, he already held a decisively adjusted position in 1905 (only a few months after Root's inauguration). This fact became apparent, for example, in the Roosevelt's annual message to the Congress in 1905:

> [...] there are certain republics to the south of us which have already reached such a point of stability, order, and prosperity that they themselves, though as yet hardly consciously, are among the guarantors of the doctrine [the *Monroe Doctrine*]. These republics we now meet not

347 'The American Society for the Judicial Settlement of International Disputes' (1910) 4 The American Journal of International Law 930–932.

348 Jonathan Zasloff, 'Law and the Shaping of American Foreign Policy' (n 330 in Chapter 5) 244.

349 Benjamin Allen Coates, *Legalist Empire* (n 311 in Chapter 5) 107.

350 On the role of the rule of law in international relations respectively on the history of the process of introducing this rule into international law, compare: Antônio Augusto Cançado Trindade, 'Reflections on a Century of International Justice and Prospects for the Future' in Giorgia Gaja and Jenny Grote Stoutenburg (eds.), *Enhancing the Rule of Law through the International Court of Justice* (Brill – Nijhoff 2012) 1–32. Also: Ian Brownlie, *The Rule of Law in International Affairs* (Nijhoff 1998). Mónica García-Salmones Rovira, *The Project of Positivism in International Law* (Oxford University Press 2013) 110. Spencer Zifcak (ed.), *Globalisation and the Rule of Law* (Routledge 2005).

> only on a basis of entire equality, but in a spirit of frank and respectful friendship, which we hope is mutual.[351]

The origins of his sharp policy change can – according to Lars Schoultz (*'Beneath the United States'* from 1998) – be traced back to Root's influence.[352] Beforehand, Roosevelt had applied pure power policy on a regular basis to have the Latin American states follow his orders. Root, on the other hand, strove for an improvement of the U.S.-American relations to the Southern neighbors.[353] However, Root's approach was not entirely altruistic either. He cannot be considered to have shared the strong imperialist approach pursued by many of the other U.S.-American politicians and members of government.[354] But the reasons for his legalism and the attempt to strengthen international law in inter-American relations also rested in his striving for the preservation or even extension of U.S.-American control over Latin America. Benjamin Allen Coates (*'Legalist Empire'* from 2016) argued in this regard that "[…] the United States would seek to extend control over other states that were in principle equal and sovereign by insisting that all conform to certain behavioral norms – norms that include the protection of foreign capital and submission to particular forms of international oversight."[355] By binding themselves to these norms, the United States lent a lot of credence to these regulations. Thereby, they put up persuasive arguments for Latin American states to comply with them too. Moreover, under Root's legalist diplomacy the United States finally recognized the Latin American states as equals, at least formally. This step was an achievement which these countries had sought for a long time.[356] Furthermore, it promised to result in a substantial change of the relations with the United States in favor of the Latin American states because U.S.-American

351 'State of the Union Address delivered by U.S. President Theodore Roosevelt before the U.S. Congress on December 5, 1905' in Theodore Roosevelt, *Presidential Addresses and State Papers* (P.F. Collier & Son 1905), 604. Also published in: Lars Schoultz, *Beneath the United States* (n 19 in Chapter 4) 190.

352 Lars Schoultz, *Beneath the United States* (n 19 in Chapter 4) 190.

353 Robert E. Hannigan, *The New World Power: American Foreign Policy, 1898–1917* (University of Pennsylvania Press 2002) 66.

354 Samuel Guy Inman, *Inter-American Conferences 1826–1954* (n 147 in Chapter 4) 63.

355 Benjamin Allen Coates, *Legalist Empire* (n 311 in Chapter 5) 110.

356 Ibid 24. See also: Arnulf Becker Lorca, *Mestizo International Law* (n 178 in Chapter 3). Louise Fawcett, 'Between West and non-West: Latin American Contributions to International Thought' (2012) 34 The International History Review (2012) 679–704. Liliana Obregón, 'Between Civilisation and Barbarism: Creole interventions in international law' (2006) 27 Third World Quarterly 815–832.

pure power and imperialist policies would have been substituted by law if these changes had been fully realized.[357]

Root chose to change the U.S.-American approach towards Latin America in this particular way for two reasons. Firstly, he understood that guaranteeing stability in Latin America was crucial for the protection of the interests and investments of his country in the region.[358] Secondly, he noticed – according to Lars Schoultz – that

> […] the public's enthusiasm for conquest had deteriorated into frustration over expensive time-consuming efforts at colonial consolidation, particularly in the Philippines.
>
> […] For nearly two decades, U.S. policy toward Latin America had been impelled by the public's lusty surge of imperial ambition. The electorate had embraced leaders committed to acquiring an empire – and then, about halfway through the first decade of the century, the fickle public disappeared over a different political horizon.[359]

Therefore, Root aimed, on the one hand, for adapting the U.S.-American policy towards Latin America to the new (political) situation and to the then prevailing mood in the U.S.-American public. But, on the other hand, he also wanted to improve U.S.-American relations with Latin America to overcome 'anti-Yankee sentiments' in the South of the continent. Such sentiment had arisen in Latin America over the past decades and put severe strains on the relationship between the United States and countries from this region.[360] Furthermore, Root also aimed for strengthening international law and international legal institutions in Latin America in order to preserve stability and growth. He hoped this would also stimulate trade and better relations with the United States.[361] Finally, Root was convinced that "[i]t will be, from the most selfish point of view, for our interests to have peaceful, prosperous, and progressive republics in Central"[362] and South America. The Southern Latin American

357 Benjamin Allen Coates, *Legalist Empire* (n 311 in Chapter 5) 117–118.

358 Ibid 118.

359 Lars Schoultz, *Beneath the United States* (n 19 in Chapter 4) 191–192.

360 Joseph Smith, *Unequal Giants: Diplomatic Relations between the United States and Brazil, 1889–1930* (University of Pittsburgh 1991) 35. Also: Jeffrey W. Meiser, *Power and Restraint: The Rise of the United States, 1898–1941* (Georgetown University Press 2015) 109. Martha Finnemore, *The Purpose of Intervention* (n 337 in Chapter 5) 32.

361 Martha Finnemore, *The Purpose of Intervention* (n 337 in Chapter 5) 32.

362 'Address of the Hon. Elihu Root, Secretary of State of the United States, when calling the conference to order on November 14, 1907' in *Papers relating to the Foreign Affairs of the United States with the Annual Message of the President transmitted to Congress December*

states in particular, as well as Mexico, moved into the center of attention of Root's foreign policy. According to Schoultz, several of these states had managed to fundamentally change their economic structures over the past years and were experiencing an enormous economic growth.[363] These developments made them particularly interesting for the United States with regards to trade, investments, and economic cooperation – good relations were a necessary requirement for all these. However, despite these considerations, it seems as if Root also followed a "strong moral compass,"[364] which drove him to draw conclusions concerning arbitrations with smaller states such as the following: "We must always be careful, and especially so in our relations with the small states, that we never propose a settlement which we would not be willing to accept if the situation were reversed."[365]

Hence, the United States did not give up on their imperialist approach towards Latin America under Root's term as Secretary of State. They persisted in considering the entire continent, especially Central America and the Caribbean, as their exclusive sphere of influence and intervened in the internal affairs of states from these regions whenever they regarded it necessary. Sometimes they even did so militarily.[366] Nonetheless, U.S.-American foreign policy towards Latin America changed a lot during these years. Root pursued a new and particular approach in this regard as a result of which the South American states enjoyed significantly more freedom and were spared from (direct) imperialist charges of the United States for now. These steps bore the risk of limiting the U.S.-American influence in the region. However, during Root's

---

3, 1907, vol 2 (United States Government Printing Office 1910) 688. Also published in: Benjamin Allen Coates, *Legalist Empire* (n 311 in Chapter 5) 119.

363 Lars Schoultz, *Beneath the United States* (n 19 in Chapter 4) 192–193. Also: Joseph Smith, *Unequal Giants: Diplomatic Relations between the United States and Brazil, 1889–1930* (n 360 in Chapter 5) 35. According to Smith, "[t]he booming American economy was also eager to take advantage of commercial opportunities on its doorstep. Between 1900 and 1910 trade and investment with Latin America more than doubled and grew at a faster rate than with other regions of the world."

364 Lars Schoultz, *Beneath the United States* (n 19 in Chapter 4) 191.

365 James Brown Scott, 'Elihu Root – An Appreciation' (1939) 31 Proceedings of the American Society of International Law at its Annual Meeting 7–8. Also: Ralph D. Nurnberger, *James Brown Scott: Peace Through Justice* (n 1 in Chapter 5) 139.

366 Compare: Oliver Stone and Peter Kuznick, *The Untold History of the United States* (n 307 in Chapter 5) xxx (*Introduction*). There, they name a series of interventions as well as occupations of Central American territories. In this regard, they listed the following incidents: "The only reason it [the United States] didn't intervene more frequently was that it often stayed, occupying countries for extended periods of time: Nicaragua from 1912 to 1933, Haiti from 1914 to 1933, the Dominican Republic from 1916 to 1924, Cuba from 1917 to 1922, and Panama from 1918 to 1920."

tenure the United States seems to have regarded the maintenance of good relationships with Latin American countries as one of their primary foreign political premises, even subordinating other considerations to this goal.[367]

The reason for the change of their foreign political approach towards Latin America can, therefore, not only be found in the attempt to improve their relations with Latin America because of economic considerations and trade interests but also because Root and Scott considered it as an essential necessity to juridify international relations in general, to establish the rule of law in international law, and to replace war by justice and law. For them, these steps promised stability in international relations (and especially in those between American nations) which they were convinced to be an indispensable necessity for a prosperous, peaceful, and wealthy future. Hence, the *good-neighbor-policy* which Root initiated in these years[368] was regarded as beneficial for both, the United States and Latin America. It was based to a huge extent on Root's legalist considerations and beliefs, and reflected very well the then prevailing non-imperialist mood in (wide parts of) the U.S.-American public.

4 Conclusion

Between 1899 and 1905, arbitration and international law underwent distinctive developments. This can be said from the time of the *First Hague Peace Conference* through to the subsequent years. Before the conference in The Hague, isolated arbitration had already been a common instrument for the settlement of state-to-state conflicts on both sides of the Atlantic. Obligatory arbitration, on the other hand, used to enjoy popularity first and foremost in inter-Spanish American and – to a certain extent also – in European/American relations. It was only during the last decades of the 19th century that (predominantly special) obligatory arbitration commitments had been concluded (on a then quickly growing scale) among a series of (mostly) smaller European countries as well. Because of the *First Hague Peace Conference*, and due to the subsequent developments in its aftermath, this constellation changed considerably. Isolated Arbitration remained to be an often-invoked instrument. But its use was institutionalized in form of the (voluntary) *Permanent Court of Arbitration* – which henceforth stood out in international relations and international law as a beacon of light for arbitration and for the commitment of

367 Calvin DeArmond Davis, *The United States and the Second Hague Peace Conference* (n 28 in Chapter 1) 266.

368 Lars Schoultz, *Beneath the United States* (n 19 in Chapter 4) 190.

the adhering states to this instrument. Far-reaching results were also achieved regarding obligatory arbitration. Between 1903 and 1905, a wave of obligatory arbitration treaties were concluded in American, European/American, as well as inter-European relations (including even those between great powers) in which the parties used to appoint the PCA as the competent body for conflict settlement. Thereby, the position of the PCA was significantly strengthened, and obligatory arbitration finally became a fundamental element of international relations all over the world as well, and not only in Latin America.

Spanish America was the origin of the movement for obligatory arbitration. But it took many years before European (great) powers were finally willing to integrate similar commitments into their mutual relations as well. Hence, the Spanish American countries held a pioneering role in this regard since the 19th century – and the *Second Pan-American Conference* (1901/02) constituted just another, particularly remarkable, step in this development. The American countries took innovative, progressive, and, so far, unique steps at this conference for the further development of international law and arbitration. They did so by subjecting their mutual pecuniary claims to obligatory arbitral settlement by the PCA with some Spanish American countries going even further by also doing the same for all of their mutual conflicts. Thereby, they paved the way for the aforementioned global wave of obligatory arbitration treaties, acting as a shining example for the European states, and attaching a lot of importance and prominence to the PCA. By doing so and by filing applications for the admission to the Hague system, the Latin American countries drew closer to the European legal system and strengthened the PCA as well as the instrument of (obligatory) arbitration.

Despite all progresses and changes made between 1899 and 1905, it should also be born in mind that imperialism and great power policies remained decisive factors in international relations. The great powers in particular had little interest in changing this situation. Nevertheless they also contributed to the progressive developments in favor of the establishment of arbitration as a suitable, well-recognized, and regularly applied instrument for the peaceful settlement of state-to-state disputes. By doing so, and in particular by creating the PCA and assigning it with a quickly increasing compulsory jurisdiction (by referring to Article 19 of the *Hague Convention* in bi-lateral agreements), states turned arbitration – at least on paper – into a functional alternative to war for the settlement of disputes. They contributed more and more to the furtherance of international law, showed more willingness to comply with international legal norms and obligations, and settled more conflicts by arbitration than during the 19th century. Yet, these states also made sure to include far-reaching exception clauses in their obligatory arbitration agreements which provided them with ample room for political maneuvers and for avoiding arbitration whenever it pleased them. Moreover, the belief prevailed, especially but not exclusively, among the great powers that they had to rely on their military and economic strength in order to guarantee their survival in the struggle for existence and the constant competition among themselves. Therefore, peaceful methods for conflict settlement were largely reserved for cases of secondary importance, seldom being invoked for the solution of crucial questions. Cases of primary concern were only occasionally dealt with by these instruments. Nevertheless, arbitration took a great step forward between 1899 and 1905 in particular with regards to its institutionalization and integration as an obligatory and functional element in international relations and international law. States from all over the world showed a substantially grown (and still growing) willingness to establish a closer, more developed, and considerably more legalist system on the international level. Therefore, the conclusion that can be drawn from this chapter is that decisive steps were taken towards the achievement of the goal of peace movements to replace war by justice (*peace through law*) between 1899 and 1905, although it remained a long way to go until its realization.

CHAPTER 6

Adjudication (1906–1914)

> I feel that peace between nations can only come by the slow and gradual development of the system of law, and by the creation of agencies for its interpretation and administration, just as permanent peace has come within national lines by the growth of the system of law and judicial agencies.[1]
>
> JAMES BROWN SCOTT to NEWTON D. BAKER; July 27, 1915

1 The Period before the *Second Hague Peace Conference* (1906/1907)

The situation described in the previous chapter changed after 1906. Beforehand, (obligatory) arbitration had stood at the heart of international discussions. It had been among the most important and controversially discussed points at several prominent international conferences, and it had developed into the main instrument for the peaceful settlement of international conflicts. Thereby, arbitration had become an indispensable part of state practice. By 1905, many states had already referred numerous disputes (of secondary importance) for arbitration on a regular basis. Between 1906 and 1914, however, adjudication became the new focal point (not necessarily of state practice but) of many peace activists, international lawyers, and even some government officials.

In order to analyze the process of the emergence of adjudication as a seriously discussed topic on the international level in greater detail, it is necessary to concentrate first on the origin of the initiative for the *Second Hague Peace Conference*. As mentioned above, U.S. President Theodore Roosevelt and his Secretary of State John Hay called for a second meeting in The Hague on October 21, 1904, "[…] in order to take up and advance the work so auspiciously inaugurated by the conference of 1899."[2] According to Hay, the first conference

1 'James Brown Scott to Newton D. Baker, July 27, 1915' in *The Papers of James Brown Scott, box 1*.

2 'Editorial Comment: The Second Peace Conference of The Hague' (n 303 in Chapter 5) 432.

 DOI:10.1163/9789004754126_007

had left certain topics "[…] to the discussion by another conference in the near future, such as questions affecting the rights and duties of neutrals, the inviolability of private property in naval warfare, and the bombardment of ports, towns, and villages by a naval force."[3] Apart from these issues, Hay also proposed to "[…] consider and adopt a procedure by which States non-signatory to the original Acts of the First Hague Conference may become adhering parties."[4]

The governments (among them all the great powers) that were invited responded very favorably to the initiative for a follow-up conference. Some reservations were made, however, primarily concerning the date of the event.[5] In particular, Russia considered the time not yet ripe for a second peace conference since the country was engaged at that time in a war with Japan over territories in the Far East (the *Russo-Japanese War* in 1904/05).[6] It was only following the end of this conflict that Russia took the initiative to send a memorandum to President Roosevelt (on September 13, 1905)[7] proposing a second conference in July 1906.[8] But since the American states had already scheduled the *Third Pan-American Conference* for this date, Secretary of State Elihu Root ensured that the *Second Hague Peace Conference* was postponed to 1907. In fact, convincing the other (European) governments to move the event to 1907 was a terrific opportunity for Root as it allowed him to step in for the other American countries and to act in their favor. According to Juan Pablo Scarfi (*'The Hidden History of International Law in the Americas'* from 2017), this move "[…] gave him and his country more credentials

3 'The Secretary of State of the United States to the American Diplomatic Representatives Accredited to the Governments signatory to the Acts of the First Hague Conference (October 21, 1904)' in James Brown Scott (ed.), *The Hague Conventions and Declarations of 1899 and 1907* (Oxford University Press 1915) XIX.

4 Ibid XXIII.

5 'The Secretary of State of the United States to the American Diplomatic Representatives Accredited to the Governments signatory to the Acts of the First Hague Conference (December 16, 1904)' (n 3 in Chapter 6) XXIV.

6 Ibid. Compare also pages 187–189 of the present book.

7 'Memorandum from the Russian Embassy handed to the President of the United States, September 13, 1905, proposing a Second Peace Conference at The Hague' in Ibid xxv. See also: Calvin DeArmond Davis, *The United States and the Second Hague Peace Conference* (n 28 in Chapter 1) 123.

8 Juan Pablo Scarfi, *The Hidden History of International Law in the Americas: Empire and Legal Networks* (Oxford University Press 2017) 23. Also: Stephanie Dennson, *Joaquim Nabuco: Monarchism, Pan-Americanism and Nation-Building in the Brazilian Belle Epoque* (P. Lang 2006) 175.

and legitimacy as a continental hegemonic power in the eyes of the South American elites."[9]

The first Russian circulars concerning a second peace conference were only distributed to the signatory states of the acts of the first conference. U.S.-American initiatives for also inviting non-signatory states to the second conference and letting them join the Hague system,[10] were widely ignored by the Russian government. Furthermore, the request of the Latin American countries for admission to The *Hague Convention* still remained unanswered at this time.[11] According to James Brown Scott (as cited in Samuel Flagg Bemis *'The American Secretaries of State and their Diplomacy'* from 1963), it was even "[…] an open secret that Europe was not then anxious to have the American republics invited."[12] The Latin American states were, nevertheless, invited to the *Second Hague Peace Conference* in the end and they were also invited to sign the convention. This can mainly be traced back to further interferences by the United States and to the political pressure that they applied on the other adhering states.[13] Thereby, Root and the United States secured themselves the goodwill of the Latin American countries – a result which Root had been striving for and on which he intended to prosper at the *Third Pan-American Conference* in 1906. According to Calvin DeArmond Davis, Root "[…] was especially anxious that the United States take a conspicuous stand for hemispheric harmony at the conference, for there had been much criticism of the administration's actions in the Caribbean and of the Roosevelt Corollary."[14]

The Latin American critique of the U.S.-American hegemonic behavior in the Caribbean was certainly not unfounded. Root was convinced that this policy had to be changed (at least gradually) to improve relations with Latin America. But to achieve this goal, he was also aware that the United States had to take the first step and to prove their goodwill to overcome the Latin American mistrust.[15] In order to do so, Root put U.S.-American relations with Latin America on a new footing; and he did so especially by juridifying them. Along with his legal advisor James Brown Scott, he strove for the creation of a reso-

---

9 Juan Pablo Scarfi, *The Hidden History of International Law in the Americas* (n 8 in Chapter 6) 23.

10 Compare page 195 of the present book.

11 Bob Reinalda, *Routledge History of International Organizations* (n 59 in Chapter 2) 78.

12 James Brown Scott, 'Elihu Root' in Samuel Flagg Bemis (ed.), *The American Secretaries of State and their Diplomacy*, vol. IX (Cooper Square Publishers 1963) 220.

13 Ibid 220–221. Also: Calvin DeArmond Davis, 'Elihu Root' (n 329 in Chapter 5) 435.

14 Calvin DeArmond Davis, 'Elihu Root' (n 329 in Chapter 5) 435.

15 María del Rosario Rodríguez Díaz, 'La misión diplomática de Elihu Root en América Latina y el Caribe, 1906' (2004) 9 Revista Mexicana del Caribe 139.

lute, consistent, and objective science of public international law. They also sought to spread the U.S.-American (in particular, their own) conception of it all over the world, but especially in Latin America.[16] Juan Pablo Scarfi (*'El Imperio de la Ley'* from 2014) showed that essential points of their understanding of international law concerned arbitration, the use of judicial methods for peaceful conflict settlement, and the creation of international (legal) tribunals (institution building).[17] It was their profound view that international disputes could be better (and more efficiently) settled without resorting to the use of force.[18] Maintaining peace and avoiding war formed part of their supreme goals, and those goals were closely linked with their striving for *Pan-Americanism* and the improvement of U.S.-American relations with Latin America. Consequently (and following again Scarfi's argumentation), during Root's term in office the Roosevelt administration became "[…] more moderate about U.S. intervention in the Americas, for Root promoted cooperative and friendly relations with Latin America."[19]

Several authors rightfully claimed that Root's and Scott's rule-of-law-oriented approach was, nevertheless, still dominated by imperialism, aimed at maintaining hegemony over the Western hemisphere, and was primarily pursued to establish better and more lucrative commercial relations with Latin America.[20] For example, María del Rosario Rodríguez Díaz (*'La misión diplomática de Elihu Root en América Latina y el Caribe, 1906'* from 2004) argued that the United States gave up on their *Big Stick policy* and applied a more benevolent, but still imperialist, approach towards Latin America.[21] Better relations with Latin America were supposed to enable the United States to control the entire continent (*"conocerla para dominarla"*).[22] Of course, this claim is correct in as much as it concerns the fact that, under Root and Scott, law played a key role in U.S.-American efforts to exercise hegemonic control over the rest of the continent.[23] The civilizational mission of the United States

16 Juan Pablo Scarfi, *El Imperio de la Ley* (n 144 in Chapter 4) 25.

17 Ibid 26, 47.

18 Ibid 26; originally in Spanish, translated into English by the author of the present book.

19 Juan Pablo Scarfi, 'In the Name of the Americas' (n 25 in Chapter 4) 203. Also: Lars Schoultz, *Beneath the United States* (n 19 in Chapter 4) 193.

20 For example: Lars Schoultz, Beneath the United States (n 19 in Chapter 4) 209 et seq. Also: María del Rosario Rodríguez Díaz, 'La misión diplomática de Elihu Root en América Latina y el Caribe, 1906' (n 15 in Chapter 6) 146. Benjamin Allen Coates, *Legalist Empire* (n 311 in Chapter 5) 110.

21 María del Rosario Rodríguez Díaz, 'La misión diplomática de Elihu Root en América Latina y el Caribe, 1906' (n 15 in Chapter 6) 146.

22 Ibid.

23 Juan Pablo Scarfi, *El Imperio de la Ley* (n 144 in Chapter 4) 209.

and Root's and Scott's striving for creating networks between Latin American politicians, academics, and members of the elites with their U.S.-American counterparts formed fundamental aspects of this approach and contributed to the subjection of Latin American thinking to U.S.-American policy and (intellectual) hegemony.[24] But nonetheless, it should also be noted that Root's and Scott's less imperialist and more cooperation-oriented approach had (at least) a considerably friendlier face than the pure power policy, i.e., *Big Stick policy*, which had dominated Roosevelt's early presidency. This would therefore explain why Maria del Rosario Rodriguez Diaz described Root and Scott's policy as "benevolent imperialism".[25] Root and Scott not only strove for establishing U.S.-American dominance over Latin America, but they also aimed to improve the situation of the Latin American states and their international standing.

1.1 *The* Third Pan-American Conference

Further steps in this regard were taken at the *Third Pan-American Conference*. The event took place between July 25 and August 27, 1906, in Rio de Janeiro and was as well organized as it was pompous.[26] In particular, the host country Brazil made every effort to present themselves at their best (not only in the eyes of the United States but also before the entire world).[27] According to Ori Preuss (*'Bridging the Island: Brazilian's Views of Spanish America and Themselves, 1865–1912'* from 2011), the conference was "[…] to a large degree a well-orchestrated spectacle destined for foreign eyes […] to enhance the image of Brazil as a highly civilized nation."[28] Unlike previous Pan-American conferences, which served as fora for discussing topics of high political and legal importance (especially regarding arbitration), the *Rio Conference* avoided most of the controversial topics.[29] Instead, it functioned as a preparatory

24 Ibid 210.

25 María del Rosario Rodríguez Díaz, 'La misión diplomática de Elihu Root en América Latina y el Caribe, 1906' (n 15 in Chapter 6) 146.

26 Ori Preuss, *Bridging the Island: Brazilian's Views of Spanish America and Themselves, 1865–1912* (M. Vervuert 2011) 159.

27 Calvin DeArmond Davis, *The United States and the Second Hague Peace Conference* (n 28 in Chapter 1) 132.

28 Ori Preuss, *Bridging the Island* (n 26 in Chapter 6) 159.

29 Jost Dülffer, *Regeln gegen den Krieg?* (n 20 in Chapter 1) 243. Also: Paul S. Reinsch, *Public International Unions: Their Work and Organization* (Boston Ginn 1911) 92–93. Samuel Guy Inman, *Inter-American Conferences 1826–1954* (n 147 in Chapter 4) 68–69. According to Inman, the most remarkable act taken at the Third Pan-American Conference was to issue a recommendation that "[…] the treaty on pecuniary claims, drawn up at the

meeting for the subsequent *Second Hague Peace Conference*.[30] No spectacular obligatory arbitration treaties or court projects were dealt with on this occasion. The participating states only issued a resolution according to which all American states were recommended to strive (together) for the conclusion of a general arbitration convention in The Hague.[31] The conference is, nevertheless, of immense importance because it shaped the future relationship between the United States and Latin America and paved the way for the upcoming developments in The Hague. U.S.-American Secretary of State Elihu Root took a key role in this regard; not only because of statements made in the context of the conference but also because of his sole presence in Rio de Janeiro. His attendance at this conference (and his subsequent tour through Latin America) was the first occasion in which an acting Secretary of State left the United States in an official capacity.[32] Thereby, Root reinforced the key importance that the United States attached to (the improvement of) their relations with the other American nations during his term in office.

The Latin American states seem to have welcomed this initiative and embraced the new U.S.-American policy with open arms. Proof for this can be found in the heartwarming reception that Root received not only in Rio de Janeiro but in all South American countries that he visited during his journey.[33] In order to further his agenda even more, he used one of these occasions, a special session of the *Rio Conference*, which was held in his honor, to announce new principles and proclaiming a new approach in U.S.-American relations towards Latin America,[34] by issuing the following statement:

> I believe it to be true that, viewed against the background of conditions a century, a generation, a decade ago, government in my own country has advanced, in the intelligent participation of the great mass of people, in the fidelity and honesty with which they are represented, in respect for

---

Second Conference, should continue in force, both for those nations which had ratified and for those which might subsequently do so."

30 Courtney Johnson, 'Understanding the American Empire: Colonialism, Latin Americanism, and Professional Social Science, 1898–1820' in Alfred W. McCoy and Francisco A. Scarano (eds.), *Colonial Crucible: Empire in the Making of the modern American State* (University of Wisconsin Press 2009) 184.

31 F. Llewellyn Jones, 'The Concert of America. The New World's League of Nations' (n 17 in Chapter 4) 121. Also: Alfred H. Fried, *Pan-Amerika* (n 73 in Chapter 4) 158–159.

32 Richard Graham, *Britain & the Onset of Modernization in Brazil 1850–1914* (Cambridge University Press 1972) 312.

33 Juan Pablo Scarfi, *El Imperio de la Ley* (n 144 in Chapter 4) 61.

34 James Brown Scott, 'Elihu Root' (n 12 in Chapter 6) 217.

law, in the obedience to the dictates of a sound morality, and in effectiveness and purity of administration.

Nowhere in the world has this progress been more marked than in Latin America. Out of the wreck of Indian fighting and race conflicts and civil wars, strong and stable governments have arisen. Peaceful secession in accord with the people's will has replaced the forcible seizure of power permitted by the people's indifference. Loyalty to country, its peace, its dignity, its honor, has risen above partisanship for individual leaders. The rule of law supersedes the rule of man."[35]

With these words, Root publicly recognized that the Latin American states had developed from crises-ridden and widely unstable entities to fully functioning nations.[36] He even abandoned the (earlier) U.S.-American claim according to which Latin American countries were – at best – 'half-civilized';[37] a claim that had been posed by the *Roosevelt Corollary* and that had been further perpetuated in the writings of several U.S.-American authors. Moreover, in the 19th century, the *standard of civilization* had been used by European countries and the United States to marginalize and exploit Latin America.[38] The *standard* had functioned as an argumentative justification for the maintenance of a strict hierarchic system under international law. The then prevailing system had clearly favored the North Atlantic states, in particular the great powers, and had deprived (most) non-European countries of equal rights. Only at the *Third Pan-American Conference* in 1906 did the United States, in person of Elihu Root, take the step to recognize the sovereign equality (at least in formal terms) of the Latin American nations. Root did so by declaring the following:

We wish for no victories but for peace; for no territory but for our own; for no sovereignty except the sovereignty over ourselves. We deem the

35 'Elihu Root's Address at the Proceedings of the Special Session held in Honor of the honorable Elihu Root, Secretary of State of the United States of America, and honorary Vice President of the Conference (July 31, 1906)' in *Report of the Delegates of the United States to the Third International Conference of the American States held at Rio de Janeiro, July 21, to August 26, 1906* (United States Government Printing Office 1907) 63.

36 Compare in this regard Roosevelt's earlier statement on page 208 of the present book.

37 Compare: Carsten-Andreas Schulz, 'Civilisation, Barbarism and the Making of Latin America's Place in the 19th Century International Society' (2014) 42 Millennium Journal of International Studies 853. There, he cites Lord Palmerston, British prime minister (1855–1858 and 1859–1865), who referred to the Chinese, Spanish American, and Portuguese American governments as "half-civilized." Also: Matthew Brown, *Informal Empire in Latin America: Culture, Commerce and Capital* (Blackwell 2008) 19.

38 Benjamin Allen Coates, *Legalist Empire* (n 311 in Chapter 5) 24.

> independence and equal rights of the smallest and weakest members of the family of nations entitled to as much respect as those of the greatest empires, and we deem the observance of that respect the chief guaranty of the weak against the oppression of the strong. We neither claim nor desire any rights or privileges, or powers that we do not freely concede to every American Republic. We wish to increase our prosperity, to expand our trade, to grow in wealth, in wisdom, and in spirit, but our conception of the true way to accomplish this is not to pull down others and to profit by their ruin, but to help all friends to a common prosperity and a common growth, that we may all become greater and stronger together.
>
> Within a few months, for the first time the recognized possessors of every foot of soil upon the American continent can be, and I hope will be, represented with the acknowledged rights of equal sovereign States in the great World Congress at The Hague.[39]

As it is apparent from this statement, Root aimed at granting sovereign equality to the Latin American countries and encouraged other states to follow suit. He even promised that the United States would henceforth abstain from oppressing their Latin American neighbors and would respect their independence to the fullest extent. Of course, these words were – at least in part – a hollow promise. Later developments showed that the United States continued to pursue an imperialist attitude towards Latin American states and intervened repeatedly (also militarily) in their internal affairs.[40] But by officially issuing this statement and declaring it to be the new policy of the United States, Root sent a clear signal, which went far beyond the scope of only attempting to improve U.S.-American relations with Latin America. Instead, he made the United States the first country out of the group of so-called 'civilized' nations to admit the long-pursued claim of the Latin American nations for being recognized as equally and fully 'civilized' and, therefore, for enjoying sovereign equality under international law.[41] Thereby, Root made a major

39 'Elihu Root's Address at the Proceedings of the Special Session held in Honor of the honorable Elihu Root, Secretary of State of the United States of America, and honorary Vice-President of the Conference (July 31, 1906)' (n 35 in Chapter 6) 64.

40 Compare *footnote* 307 in Chapter 5 of the present book.

41 Emer de Vattel, *The Law of Nations or Principles of the Law of Nature* (T.&J.W. Johnson 1853; originally published in 1758) LXII. According to him, nations "[...] are naturally equal, and inherit from nature the same obligations and rights". Counter to Vattel's view, it should be held that the international system was highly hierarchic until the end of World War II; compare in this regard: Jessica Whyte, "Always on Top?" The "Responsi-

contribution to ending the marginalization and oppression of Latin American states.[42] Furthermore, through this statement Root also took a first step towards a general change of the international order. By proclaiming that the United States granted full equality to the Latin American states, making sure that they were invited to the *Second Hague Peace Conference,* ensuring that they enjoyed the very same rights at this occasion as any other country, and convincing the nations adhering to the *Hague Convention* to admit the Latin American countries to this agreement, the Roosevelt administration went significantly further than granting only some advantages, or a better status, to the Latin American countries on a bi-lateral basis. Instead, the U.S.-American government attempted to set an example and it did its best to achieve recognition of the sovereign equality of the Latin American nations from the entire international community. By issuing these statements in Rio de Janeiro, Root aimed for a paradigm shift in international law and for overcoming the systematic discrimination of the Latin American states. According to James Brown Scott, one of the consequences of these efforts was that "[m]any of the Americans to

---

bility to Protect" and the persistence of colonialism' in Jyotsna G. Singh and David D. Kim (eds.), *The Postcolonial World* (Routledge 2017) 308–325. According to Whyte, the differences in the treatment of states were justified at that time by the so-called 'standard of civilization.' In the beginning, this concept had been closely linked with Christianity. However, the on-going positivization and secularization of international law during the 19th century ousted religious reasoning from (most) international legal thinking. Instead, other factors were introduced, which would justify the categorization of European countries as 'civilized' and of non-European ones as 'uncivilized.' It referred to a set of minimum features of 'civilization' and to European value standards. See also: Gerry Simpson, *Great Powers and Outlaw States: Unequal Sovereigns in the International Legal Order* (n 51 in Chapter 2) 234.

The concept of an exclusively European international law (which excluded non-European states because of their 'savageness') was a manifestation of the European states' sense of superiority, which they felt in regards to other nations at that time. Its creation was an attempt to justify the European hegemonic and colonial approach to other parts of the world. Compare: Wilhelm G. Grewe, *Die Epochen der Völkerrechtsgeschichte* (n 49 in Chapter 2) 521, 533. See also: Carsten-Andreas Schulz, 'Civilisation, Barbarism and the Making of Latin America's Place in the 19th Century International Society' (n 37 in Chapter 6) 838. Defining the term 'civilization' in sole accordance with their own value concepts enabled the European states to disrespect international law in their relations with countries which they deemed 'uncivilized' and, therefore, put them at systematic disadvantage. See in this regard: Liliana Obregón, 'The Civilized and the Uncivilized' in Bardo Fassbender & Anne Peters (eds.), *The Oxford Handbook of the History of International Law* (n 28 in Chapter 1) 918.

42 Lars Schoultz, *Beneath the United States* (n 19 in Chapter 4) 194.

the south of the Rio Grande look[ed] upon Secretary Root's pronouncement as the Magna Carta of the Americas."[43]

However, this was not the only remarkable result of Root's tour through South America. According to Lars Schoultz, "[e]ach stop was a diplomatic success, but none was greater than Root's reception in Buenos Aires."[44] The enthusiastic response to his visit in Argentina was the result of a particular speech which Root delivered on August 17, 1906, in the *Teatro Colón* in Buenos Aires. At this occasion, in front of 600 guests, he gave special attention to the *Drago Doctrine*. In Rio de Janeiro, the participating states had decided not to tackle the issue concerning the introduction of this doctrine just yet but, instead, to postpone it to the *Second Hague Peace Conference*.[45] In Buenos Aires, however, Root took the initiative and declared the following:

> The United States of America has never deemed it to be suitable that she should use her army and navy for the collection of ordinary contract debts of foreign governments to her citizens [...] We deem it to be inconsistent with that respect for the sovereignty of weaker powers which is essential to their protection against the aggression of the strong [...] We consider that the use of the army and navy of a great power to compel a weaker power to answer to a contract with a private individual, is [...] an infringement upon the sovereignty of those countries, and we are now, as we always have been, opposed to it; and we believe that, perhaps not today nor tomorrow, but through the slow and certain process of the future, the world will come to the same opinion.[46]

With these words, Root (and with him the United States) seems to have given full backing for the *Drago Doctrine*,[47] a Latin American maxim (existing since the Venezuelan blockage in 1902) that strongly opposed the forceful collections of pecuniary claims. It was based on the above-mentioned *Calvo Clause*, a provision that had never found universal recognition.[48] But the *Calvo Clause*

---

43 James Brown Scott, 'Elihu Root' (n 12 in Chapter 6) 217.

44 Lars Schoultz, *Beneath the United States* (n 19 in Chapter 4) 193.

45 Alfred H. Fried, *Pan-Amerika* (n 73 in Chapter 4) 181–182. Also: Paul S. Reinsch, *Public International Unions* (n 29 in Chapter 6) 94.

46 'Elihu Root's Reply to Luis Drago's Speech at the Banquet at the Opera House in Buenos Aires, August 17, 1906' in Robert Bacon and James Brown Scott (eds.), *Latin America and the United States: Addresses by Elihu Root* (Harvard University Press 1917) 98–99.

47 Jorge L. Esquirol, 'Latin America' (n 94 in Chapter 4) 567–568.

48 Mark Eric Williams, *Understanding U.S.-Latin American Relations: Theory and History* (n 118 in Chapter 4) 90.

had paved the (intellectual) way for the *Drago Doctrine*. According to this doctrine, public debt cannot result into the right or into any kind of justification for non-American nations to intervene in American states or to occupy (parts of) their territory.[49] In Buenos Aires, Root expressed the hope that this doctrine would become globally recognized. The reason for this initiative was that Root wanted the United States to accept the *Drago Doctrine* (at least as far as possible) in order to show goodwill to the Latin American countries.[50] By doing so, Root appears to have been in line with his president; as Roosevelt declared in late 1905 that "[o]ur own Government has always refused to enforce such contractual obligations on behalf of its citizens by an appeal to arms. It is much to be wished that all foreign governments would take the same view."[51] Lars Schoultz, however, raised strong arguments against the reliability of Root's declaration in Buenos Aires and referred to it as "pure diplomatic legerdemain."[52] For him, the hollowness of Root's declaration was proven by the simple fact that the United States continued to intervene militarily in Central America in the subsequent years.

With regards to Root's declaration, Lester D. Langley (*'America and the Americas'* from 2010) pointed out that especially the greater South American powers focused primarily on the development of closer relations with the United States instead of paying too much attention to the unity of Latin America.[53] For South Americans, it seems to have been more important to secure U.S.-American support in order to achieve global recognition as sovereign equals than it was to stand up against U.S.-American domination over the Caribbean region.[54] Schoultz took these thoughts into consideration too and

49 Edward McWhinney, *The International Court of Justice and the Western Tradition of International Law* (n 118 in Chapter 4) 10.

50 Calvin DeArmond Davis, 'Elihu Root' (n 329 in Chapter 5) 435.

51 'Annual Message of the President to Congress, December 5, 1905' in: *Papers relating to the Foreign Relations of the United States, with the annual message of the president transmitted to Congress December 5, 1905* (United States Government Printing Office 1906) xxx.

52 Lars Schoultz, *Beneath the United States* (n 19 in Chapter 4) 194.

53 Lester D. Langley, *America and the Americas: The United States in the Western Hemisphere* (University of Georgia Press 2010) 107.

54 Lars Schoultz, *Beneath the United States* (n 19 in Chapter 4) 194. Moreover, Schoultz cited from a letter written by Henry White, an U.S.-American diplomat, to his Secretary of State. White described the prevailing political opinion in the greater South American countries concerning the U.S.-American striving for hegemony in Central America as follows: "I ascertained from talks with their representative men, that they have a contempt for the Central American countries, which they consider a disgrace of the very name of America, and anything which we can do, whether by occupation, protection or otherwise, to improve existing conditions in those countries will meet with their sympathy and approval." According to Schoultz, the original source is: 'White to Knox,

concluded from them that "[t]his willingness of 'developed' South America to accept U.S. hegemony in the Caribbean was encouraged by Root's proposal that the Drago Doctrine [...] be placed on the agenda of the upcoming second Hague Conference."[55] Following Schoultz' argumentation and taking into consideration the manifold U.S.-American interventions in the region (and especially in Central America and the Caribbean), there was plenty of room for doubt on the seriousness of the United States' commitment to the *Drago Doctrine*. That being said, the United States did, however, support the Latin American states' claim to put the topic on the agenda at the *Second Hague Peace Conference*. This again suggests that Root's declaration was more than just an act of mere courtesy. The United States seems to have actually been willing to discuss the issue with the Latin American and European states in The Hague,[56] but without giving up on their hegemony over Central America.

In the end, it appears to be highly difficult to come to a clear conclusion concerning the nature of Root's declaration. He was in favor of rule of law-based international relations, and the implementation of the *Drago Doctrine* would have constituted another step in this direction. However, his past political agenda had not been free from imperialist considerations either.[57] Therefore, there existed a lot of contradictoriness regarding these points, and also regarding the subsequent U.S.-American actions taken in the Latin American countries (interventions in the Caribbean region on the one hand, but support for the recognition of their sovereign equality on the other). The most convincing conclusion of this situation seems to be that the United States was especially interested in improving their relations with the greater South American states. They were even willing to make concessions in order to reduce the resistance of these countries against the U.S.-American attempt for establishing hegemony over Central America and the Caribbean.

Nonetheless, the objective to improve their relations with Latin America (without pursuing primarily imperialist intentions) seems to have been the

---

22 October 1910' (available in form of a microfilm in the United States' Nation Archives; reference number: 710.11/46, NA M1276/R1).

55 Lars Schoultz, *Beneath the United States* (n 19 in Chapter 4) 195.

56 'Report to the Secretary of State of the Delegates of the United States to the Second Hague Conference' in James Brown Scott (ed.), *Instructions to the American Delegates to the Hague Peace Conferences and their Official Reports* (n 23 in Chapter 5) 87. According to this report, "[t]he United States, however, reserved the right to bring to discussion two matters of great importance not included in the program, namely, [...] and restrictions or limitations upon the use of force for the collection of ordinary public debts arising out of contracts". It becomes apparent that the United States played a crucial role in introducing the topic to the discussions/the agenda of the Second Hague Peace Conference.

57 Compare pages 238–240 of the present book.

predominant goal of the United States at the *Third Pan-American conference.* This point generally appears to have been a guiding and fundamental principle of U.S.-American foreign policy since Root's inauguration and he managed to bring the entire Roosevelt administration in line with it. For its realization, Root took steps that were so far unprecedented in order to win the Latin American states' favor. For example, traveling in person to the *Rio Conference*, making lots of full-bodied promises, and – which is quite exceptional – advocating for full global recognition of the Latin American states' equal sovereignty, especially in the run-up to and at the *Second Hague Peace Conference* in 1907.

1.2 *Adjudication*

Before turning the view to the proceedings of the *Second Hague Peace Conference*, another issue of crucial importance should be addressed first: adjudication. Unlike in previous years, adjudication began to play a significant role in the period between 1906 and 1914. During the 19th century and early years of the 20th century, it had only been a matter of interest among progressive and utopian peace activists and public international lawyers. It had not yet exercised any practical impact, nor had it not developed into a leading view so far. As mentioned above,[58] the idea to settle state-to-state conflicts on a purely judicial basis before a permanent and international court of law played a role in the thinking of the peace movement since the days of William Ladd in the 1830s and 1840s. But in the meantime, it was deemed to be more of a secondary importance, and only few peace activists and international lawyers kept the idea of international adjudication alive. Only towards the end of the 19th century and the beginning of the 20th century, the interest in adjudication grew again. At that time, arbitrariness in the existing mechanisms for peaceful methods of conflict settlement was critically addressed by a growing number of scholars, peace activists, and politicians. They demanded that arbitrations be based on purely legal considerations. For example, John Westlake ('*International Law, Vol. 1*' from 1910) proclaimed that only "[l]egal questions are suitable for arbitration; political questions are generally not so."[59] Furthermore, there existed a continuously increasing tendency in state practice at that time to limit arbitration to the settlement of legal problems and to spare out political conflicts from its scope of application.[60] Hence, the focus of arbitration was shifted towards legal issues in these years.

58 Compare pages 68 et seq. of the present book.

59 John Westlake, *International Law – Part 1: Peace* (n 124 in Chapter 2) 357.

60 Compare pages 100–102, 173–174 of the present book.

Alongside this development, scholars also began to argue for basing the decision-making procedure of arbitrations on legal rather than political considerations. Hans Wehberg (*'The Problem of an International Court of Justice'* from 1918), a German peace activist and international lawyer, commented on this trend. According to him, a growing number of international agreements already provided that arbitral decisions had to be taken in conformity with the law (or at least with respect for law).[61] But the prevailing state practice did not yet correspond to this approach, nor did the PCA's decision-making practice.[62] Instead, the element of arbitrariness prevailed, political considerations were still taken into account, and the arbitrators sought compromises, which suited both parties but did not (necessarily) correspond to prevailing legal rules. Consequently, in the early 20th century, arbitration was still in the midst of a development into a 'more legal instrument.' The trend was advanced by leading legal scholars and it was also realized, at least theoretically, in numerous bi-lateral international agreements.

In his treatise *'Seeking World Order'* (from 1969), Warren F. Kuehl mentioned two peace activists in particular who took leading roles in this development; namely Hayne Davis (1868–1942), an attorney from New York City, and Raymond L. Bridgman (1848–1925), a journalist from Massachusetts. Both were dominant figures in the striving for the conceptual extension and further development of the Hague system after 1899, a period which Kuehl described as "unusually quiet" for the American peace movement.[63] Davis and Bridgman breathed new life into the movement by proposing to take the PCA as only a starting point for establishing a new international system based on the concept of a world union. They both argued since around 1903 – in the beginning independently and without knowing one another[64] – for a congress of nations (functioning as a world legislature), for an extension of the competences of the PCA, and for the creation of an executive branch at the global level.[65] Both wanted the international system to be modeled after the example of the United States. Especially Bridgman went even so far as to propagate the conversion of the PCA into, according to Kuehl, "[...] a genuine court [...]. The arbitral body created at The Hague in 1899 was generally unrelated to international law and should be transformed into a 'supreme court of the world'."[66]

61 Hans Wehberg, *The Problem of an International Court of Justice* (n 123 in Chapter 2) 15.

62 Ibid 29–41.

63 Warren F. Kuehl, *Seeking World Order* (n 16 in Chapter 3) 57.

64 Ibid 62.

65 Ibid 63 et seq. See also: David S. Patterson, *Towards a Warless World* (n 147 in Chapter 3) 111.

66 Warren F. Kuehl, *Seeking World Order* (n 16 in Chapter 3) 65.

The peace movement did not adopt all their ideas. However, several activists joined Bridgman and Davis at least to that extent that they also began to endorse and to propagate the creation "[...] of a regular international congress, to meet at stated periods, to deliberate upon such questions as concern the nations jointly, and to make recommendations thereon to the governments."[67] For them, the most obvious way to realize this idea was to turn the Hague conferences into a series of periodic and successive events. The resumption of the *First Hague Conference* through a second event in 1907 was, therefore, regarded as a first step in this direction.

Unlike them, most members of the international peace movement were still convinced that the furtherance of peace could best be achieved through the conclusion of far-reaching obligatory arbitration agreements.[68] They aimed to improve the existing (arbitration-based) system by extending the competences of the PCA and by introducing additional multi-lateral obligatory arbitration agreements. To achieve these goals, they placed their hope above all on the *Second Hague Peace Conference*. According to Amos S. Hershey (in 1906), an U.S.-American professor, "[...] the best service which the Conference could perform at the present time would be to agree upon a general treaty of arbitration, or, if that prove impracticable, to extend the jurisdiction of the Hague Tribunal and furnish the nations with a model treaty of arbitration together with a recommendation for its general adoption."[69] However, the concentration on obligatory arbitration was a rather moderate approach at the beginning of the 20th century.[70] A growing number of U.S.-American scholars and peace

---

67 'A Stated International Congress' (1903) LXV Advocate for Peace page 21. Also: David S. Patterson, *Towards a Warless World* (n 147 in Chapter 3) 112. According to him, Benjamin Trueblood, leader of the American Peace Society, aimed for a federation which gradually (but inevitably) developed into the "unity of the human race" instead of striving for a radical change of the entire international order.

68 Compare: 'A Programme for The Hague' (October 7, 1905) The Outlook 297–298. Also: Calvin DeArmond Davis, *The United States and the Second Hague Peace Conference* (n 28 in Chapter 1) 165.

69 Amos S. Hershey, 'The Coming Peace Conference at The Hague' (1906) LXI The Independent 611. Compare also: 'Emile Arnaud's report of the work of *'Commission B'* of the 15th Meeting of the Universal Peace Congress (1906)' in *Bulletin Officiel du 15. Congrès Universel de la Paix tenu à Milan du 15 au 22 septembre 1906* (Impr. Büchler & Co. 1906) 75–78.

70 Sandi E. Cooper, *Patriotic Pacifism* (n 156 in Chapter 3) 106–107. But he also pointed out the following: "Given the initial program of the Interparliamentary Conference of 1889–1890, this model treaty [for Arbitration from 1906 which was presented at the meeting of the Inter-Parliamentary Union in London (1906); *added by the author of the present book*] was an immense leap forward. Governments were invited to use The Hague machinery for a vast array of issues that would largely accustom nations to a

activists began instead to support the idea of a truly judicial and permanent court of justice at the international level. For them, this notion even became the key to world peace.[71] In addition to that, they continuously stressed the defects and weaknesses of arbitration and the imperfection of the PCA. For example, John B. Henderson declared the following at the 10th annual meeting of the Lake Mohonk Conference in 1904:

> If arbitration cannot prevent all wars, nor even relieve the nervous tension which the possibility of war endangers, it shows that arbitration, as well as human nature, is defective in some essential particular.
>
> [...] Mr. Chairman, is it still too revolutionary for us to urge something more immediate, more substantial, more binding, more reliable than a mere arbitration agreement? May we not agitate for a permanent international court, always in session and always ready – a permanent, dignified, wise and confidence-inspiring tribunal into which a nation may immediately and without the loss of a precious moment bring legal actions against another?
>
> [...] The Hague Tribunal marks an epoch in the evolution of peace, but it does not go far enough.[72]

Henderson's words are just one example of this trend. Regarding the years right before the beginning of the *Second Hague Peace Conference*, it can be noticed that the opposition and criticism against the PCA and its design grew substantially in the United States. U.S.-American scholars called, in particular, for impartiality of the arbitrators.[73] William L. Penfield (*'International Arbitration'* from 1907), for example, declared that the success of the instrument of arbitration "[...] has also been retarded by the inveterate practice of withholding from arbitral tribunals their proper judicial character through the appointment by governments of their own nationals [...] as arbitrators to hear and decide controversies to which they were parties."[74] To remedy this short-

---

new routine. Such issues would automatically go to The Hague without specific government review. For Continental parliamentarians, this project reflected real changes in European politics."

71 Ralph D. Nurnberger, *James Brown Scott: Peace Through Justice* (n 1 in Chapter 5) 93–94.

72 John B. Henderson, 'The Hague Tribunal does not go far enough' in William J. Rose (ed.), *Report of the Tenth Annual Meeting of the Lake Mohonk Conference on International Arbitration 1904* (Lake Mohonk arbitration conference 1904) 76–77.

73 Jackson H. Ralston, 'Some Suggestions as to the Permanent Court of Arbitration' (1907) 1 The American Journal of International Law 322.

74 William L. Penfield, 'International Arbitration' (1907) 1 The American Journal of International Law 332. Compare also: R. Floyd Clarke, 'A Permanent Tribunal of International

coming, he proposed to appoint neutral and independent arbitrators, which decided cases in conformity with the law, and to change the nature of the PCA from an arbitral to a purely legal institution.[75]

Several critical articles addressing the shortcomings and deficiencies of the PCA were published in April 1907 in the first volume of the *American Journal of International Law*.[76] The journal was the flagship publication of the *American Society of International Law*[77] and gave (mostly American) international lawyers room to express their progressive and sometimes challenging views on international law. The issue from April 1907 was the last one published before the opening of the *Second Hague Peace Conference* and James Brown Scott, the editor of the journal, seems to have chosen this thematic focus for the issue in order to create a mood for progressive and far-reaching steps to be taken at The Hague in favor of the further development of international law as a guarantor of peace. In this regard, it should be emphasized that James Brown Scott was a leading figure in these endeavors. He aimed for considerably deeper changes than the sole extension of the jurisdiction of the PCA through the introduction of (a list for types of cases being subjected to) obligatory arbitration. Instead, his main objective was the creation of an actual international court of law.[78] For him, arbitration was merely "[…] a transitional stage before the world would finally accept an international court."[79] But he did not hope to create an entire world union. Instead, he wanted the court to function as an autonomous institution, existing side by side with the PCA and outside the framework of any (higher) institution. Furthermore, Scott held international law and purely judicial conflict settlements to be the actual keys to world

---

Arbitration: Its Necessity and Value' (1907) 1 The American Journal of International Law 343.

75 William L. Penfield, 'International Arbitration' (n 74 in Chapter 6) 332.

76 American Journal of International Law (April 1907, Vol. 1, No. 2) 321–329, 330–341, and 342–408.

77 Frederic L. Kirgis, *The American Society of International Law's First Century 1906–2006* (n 344 in Chapter 5) 6. Also: Juan Pablo Scarfi, 'Excepcionalismo Estadounidense y Hegemonia Legal Hemisferica: La Corte Suprema de Estados Unidos como Modelo Imperial de Justicia Internacional para Contramerica y America Latina, y su Inlufjo en el Sistema Interamericano (1906–1938)' (2016) 4 Revista Latinoamericana de Derecho Internacional 4.

78 Ralph D. Nurnberger, *James Brown Scott: Peace Through Justice* (n 1 in Chapter 5) 94. According to him, Scott argued that "[…] if the Court could settle only a proportion of the disputes that arose between the nations, it would be beneficial to create it. […] Scott claimed that merely preventing one war would justify the efforts expended in setting it up."

79 Ibid 100. But Nurnberger also stressed the fact (on page 106) that "[…] Scott was willing to accept diplomacy, arbitration, and mediation to achieve peaceful solutions" too.

peace. He assumed that nations would prefer to submit their disputes to judicial settlements rather than to have them settled by arbitration because adjudication relied on established legal principles and precedents whereas arbitration was based on arbitrariness.[80] However, he was also aware that an international court of law could not handle conflicts of all possible natures either. Therefore, he wanted it to concentrate on justiciable problems whereas arbitration should best be used if political questions are at stake.[81] Consequently, Scott concluded that the PCA would retain its reason for existence even after the creation of an international court of law. Scott's view on and his arguments for the establishment of an international court are best summarized by his own words (from 1910):

> We hope that an international court will lessen the causes of public war, just as national courts have abolished private war; that a less frequent resort to force will destroy the justification for and therefore the burden of armament; that disarmament will be a condition consequent, not a condition precedent, to the peaceful settlement of international differences, and that the resultant peace will be permanent because it is just and based, as it will be, upon law and its judicial interpretation.[82]

Between 1905 and *World War I*, a group of progressive legalistic-thinking international lawyers around James Brown Scott and Elihu Root shaped the agenda of the U.S.-American peace movement in accordance with their ideas. Due to their prominent and influential positions in the U.S.-American government (especially in the State Department), they also managed to shape the foreign policy of the United States in accordance with their progressive legalist and peace-oriented approach.[83] Through this way, the idea to create a court at the international level which was modeled after the U.S.-American Supreme Court not only spread within the U.S.-American peace movement and among international lawyers but also became part of the official foreign policy of

80 Ibid 110.

81 Ibid 108.

82 'Address of President James Brown Scott' in American Society for Judicial Settlement of International Disputes, *Proceedings of the International Conference under the Auspices of the American Society for Judicial Settlement of International Disputes, December 15–17, 1910 in Washington, D.C.* (Waverly Press 1911) 4.

83 David S. Patterson, *Towards a Warless World* (n 147 in Chapter 3) 160. Also: Benjamin Allen Coates, *Legalist Empire* (n 311 in Chapter 5) 87–88.

the United States and their agenda at the *Second Hague Peace Conference.*[84] Elihu Root even mentioned this fact explicitly in his instructions to the U.S.-American delegates to the *Second Hague Peace Conference*:

> If there could be a tribunal which would pass upon questions between nations with the same impartial and impersonal judgment that the Supreme Court of the United States gives to questions […], there can be no doubt that nations would be much more ready to submit their controversies to its decision than they are now to take the chances of arbitration. It should be our effort to bring about in the Second Conference a development of the Hague tribunal into a permanent tribunal composed of judges who are judicial officers and nothing else, who are paid adequate salaries, who have no other occupation, and who will devote their entire time to the trial and decision of international causes by judicial methods and under a sense of judicial responsibility.[85]

It was apparent from the works and contributions of Scott and other U.S.-American scholars that the U.S.-American approach at the *Second Hague Peace Conference* would decisively differ from the ones of several of the European countries and that it would entail some progressive (if not utopian) points. Furthermore, President Roosevelt publicly joined the group of supports of the implementation of an international judiciary by sending a message to the *'National Arbitration and Peace Congress'* taking place in New York in April 1907. In his address, Roosevelt declared the following:

> More important than reducing the expense of the implements of war is the question of reducing the possible causes of war which can most effectually be done by substituting other methods than war for the settlement of disputes. Of those other methods, the most important which is now attainable is arbitration. I do not believe that in the world as it actually is, it is possible for any nation to agree to arbitrate all difficulties which may arise between itself and other nations; but I do believe that there can be at this time a very large increase in the classes of which it is agreed shall be arbitrated, and that provision can be made for greater facility and certainty of arbitration. I hope to see adopted a general arbitration treaty

84 Compare: Juan Pablo Scarfi, *El Imperio de la Ley* (n 144 in Chapter 4) 69. Also: Ralph D. Nurnberger, *James Brown Scott: Peace Through Justice* (n 1 in Chapter 5) 93 et seq.

85 'Instructions to the American Delegates to The Hague Conference of 1907' in James Brown Scott (ed.), *Instructions to the American Delegates to The Hague Peace Conferences and their Official Reports* (n 23 in Chapter 5) 79–80.

> among the nations; and I hope to see the Hague Court greatly increased in power and permanency, and the judges in particular made permanent and given adequate salaries, so as to make it increasingly probable that in each case that may come before them, they will decide between the nations, great or small, exactly as a judge within our own limits decides between the individuals, great or small, who come before him.[86]

Roosevelt used the term 'arbitration' in this context. But he also made clear that he strove for transforming the PCA into a permanent and considerably more powerful institution with (special) obligatory competences. Moreover, he wanted the arbitrators of the PCA to become actual judges who decided cases in the same way as domestic courts used to do it; in other words: on the pure basis of law. Consequently, there are strong reasons to presume that the court, which he had in mind was no longer to be arbitral in nature but judicial instead. This assumption is further supported by the fact that his address complied greatly with a statement made by Elihu Root at the same occasion:

> What we need for the further development of arbitration is the substitution of judicial action for diplomatic action, for the substitution of judicial sense of responsibility for diplomatic sense of responsibility. We need for arbitration, not distinguished public men concerned in all the international questions of the day, but judges who will be interested only in the question appearing upon the record before them. Plainly this end is to be attained by the establishment of a court of permanent judges who will have no other occupation and no other interest but the exercise of the judicial faculty under the sanction of that high sense of responsibility which has made the courts of justice in the civilized nations of the world the exponents of all that is best and noblest in modern civilization.[87]

Root strove for the establishment of a purely judicial court, despite using the term 'arbitration.' Apparently, Roosevelt and Root were still sticking to the *traditional* terminology (at this occasion). However, they clearly distinguished between the concept of arbitration and judicial decisions. They both rejected the former as they deemed it too arbitrary and defective because of the inherent partiality of arbitrators. But just as James Brown Scott, Root did not want to

86 Robert Erskine Ely, *Proceedings of the National Arbitration and Peace Congress, New York, April 14th to 17th, 1907* (National Arbitration and Peace Congress 1907) 33–34.

87 Ibid 45.

replace or to abolish arbitration. Instead, he wanted it to function as a means for finding compromises for political disputes whereas justiciable ones should be referred to judicial and purely law-based procedures.[88]

Roosevelt's and Root's statements (as well as James Brown Scott's ideas) complied very well with the prevailing views at that time within the U.S.-American (political) establishment and the U.S.-American striving for judicialism (respectively legalism) in international relations.[89] Although Roosevelt supported Root's and Scott's legalist considerations and their endorsement for the establishment of a truly permanent international court of law, he himself held a quite distinct approach to international law. In several cases, he had openly recommended legal remedies for the settlement of international conflicts (for example, in the *Venezuela Preferential Case* from 1903).[90] But in the end, he did not consider international law as 'real' law because of the lack of sanctions and effective execution.[91] According to him, "[a]s yet, there is only a partial and imperfect analogy between international law and internal or municipal law, because there is no sanction of force for executing the former while there is in the case of the latter."[92] Instead, he upheld a power-based political approach and did not want to appear as a "professional peace advocate."[93] Therefore, he maintained a quite skeptical approach towards Root's and Scott's project for an international court of law and it surely was not him who introduced this topic (or – more generally speaking – the turn to legalism) to the agenda of the U.S.-American government for the *Second Hague Peace Conference*. However, Roosevelt endorsed Root and supported him in his attempt to realize this project, which was one of Root's main political goals. Consequently, it was not Roosevelt but Elihu Root, James Brown Scott, and other legalists from

88 Benjamin Allen Coates, *Legalist Empire* (n 311 in Chapter 5) 88–89. There, Coates cited Root as follows: "[T]he great objection to obligatory arbitration was not to the principle of the thing but was to a fear that the arbitration would not really be impartial." Root thought that arbitrations "[…] too often involved diplomats, resulting in 'negotiation, not judicial decision'" and that nations "[…] feared that 'politics may well enter into the question, and that political bias rather than the evidence actually submitted will determine the decision'" in arbitral procedures.

89 Benjamin Allen Coates, *Legalist Empire* (n 311 in Chapter 5) 88.

90 Compare pages 211–212 of the present book.

91 Benjamin Allen Coates, *Legalist Empire* (n 311 in Chapter 5) 89. Also: Calvin DeArmond Davis, *The United States and the Second Hague Peace Conference* (n 28 in Chapter 1) 166–167.

92 'Annual Message of the President to the Congress' in *Papers relating to the Foreign Relations of the United States, with the Annual Message of the President transmitted to Congress December 5, 1905* (n 51 in Chapter 6) xxx.

93 Benjamin Allen Coates, *Legalist Empire* (n 311 in Chapter 5) 90.

the rows of the State Department who were the driving forces behind the U.S.-American attempt to establish a truly permanent international court of law.

The success of their efforts became apparent in the shaping of the *'Instructions to the* U.S *–American Delegates to The Hague Conference of 1907'*.[94] But Elihu Root did not leave it at that. He also decided to compose the U.S.-American delegation to a great extent of supporters of his cause to ensure that his legalist goals – and above of all of them: the creation of an international court of law – were pursued the best possible way in The Hague.[95] Against the tradition to appoint diplomats and statesmen, most of Root's delegates to the *Second Hague Peace Conference* were lawyers.[96] Root's legal advisor James Brown Scott, who was appointed as a technical expert to the delegation, played a crucial role in this regard. Calvin DeArmond Davis (*'The United States and the Second Hague Peace Conference'* from 1975) described Scott's approach and his role in the delegation as follows:

> He [Scott] believed that the nations of the world formed a society, and insisted on their equality in that society. Not for him was any elaborate plan for the organization of the world, but he believed a genuine world court could dispense justice and eliminate causes of war. Root could have appointed no one better qualified to speak for the United States in any negotiation to found a court.[97]

Francis Anthony Boyle (*'Foundations of World Order'* from 1999) argued that Scott was also closely involved in the preparation of the draft for the *Court of Arbitral Justice*, which the United States proposed at the *Second Hague Peace Conference*.[98] Benjamin Allen Coates went even further and claimed that Scott

94 'Instructions to the American Delegates to The Hague Conference of 1907' (n 85 in Chapter 6) 69–85. Also: Calvin DeArmond Davis, *The United States and the Second Hague Peace Conference* (n 28 in Chapter 1) 167–168.

95 Benjamin Allen Coates, *Legalist Empire* (n 311 in Chapter 5) 87.

96 For example, the head of the delegation, Joseph Hodges Choate, was a former U.S. ambassador to the United Kingdom and an international lawyer. Several of his delegates plenipotentiary were also trained lawyers or peace activists – such as Uriah M. Rose (an influential lawyer), David J. Hill (former Assistant Secretary of State and "staunch advocate of international arbitration," or George B. Davis (acting Judge Advocate General of the U.S. Army). Origin of the quote: Benjamin Allen Coates, *Legalist Empire* (n 311 in Chapter 5) 87.

97 Calvin DeArmond Davis, *The United States and the Second Hague Peace Conference* (n 28 in Chapter 1) 168–169.

98 Francis Anthony Boyle, *Foundations of World Order* (n 28 in Chapter 1) 43.

was the one who had drafted the plan.[99] However, it does not really matter at this point whether the main initiative and input for the court project came from Root or Scott. They both played crucial roles in shaping the U.S.-American agenda for The Hague, whereas Roosevelt does not appear to have really interfered with their work.[100] Therefore, it was possible for them to instruct the U.S.-American delegates in accordance with their goals and ideas. This allowed them to turn the plan for a permanent international court of law into one of the fundamental elements and most important issues of the U.S.-American agenda in The Hague. Their success in this regard also becomes apparent when looking at the instructions to the delegates. In this document, Root first recalled the agenda of the *Second Hague Peace Conference* set by the Russian government and admitted by the participating countries. According to it, the main topics of the conference were the following:

> 1. Improvements to be made in the provisions of the Convention relative to the peaceful settlement of international disputes as regard the court of arbitration and the international commissions of inquiry.
> 2. Additions to be made to the provisions of the Convention of 1899 relative to the laws and customs of war on land – among others, those concerning the opening of hostilities, the rights of neutrals on land, etc. [...]
> 3. Framing of a convention relative to the laws and customs of maritime warfare, concerning
> [...]
> The private property of belligerents at sea.
> The rights and duties of neutrals at sea; among others, the questions of contraband, the rules applicable to belligerent vessels in neutral ports; destruction, in cases of *vis major*, of neutral merchant vessels captured as prizes
> 4. Additions to be made to the Convention of 1899 for the adaption to maritime warfare of the principles of the Geneva Convention of 1864.[101]

In this context, Jost Dülffer (*'Regeln gegen den Krieg?'* from 1981) pointed out that the agenda set by the Russians for the *Second Hague Peace Conference*

---

99 Benjamin Allen Coates, *Legalist Empire* (n 311 in Chapter 5) 90.

100 Ibid. See also: Calvin DeArmond Davis, *The United States and the Second Hague Peace Conference* (n 28 in Chapter 1) 162 et seq.

101 'Instructions to the American Delegates to The Hague Conference of 1907' (n 85 in Chapter 6) 69–70.

was rather "macabre and unrealistic".[102] Although the term 'The Hague' had become a synonym for world peace since 1899, the agenda for the second conference primarily concerned restrictions on the conduct in war. Instead of focusing on new initiatives towards the limitation of the *ius ad bellum*, the conference was supposed to deal, first and foremost, with the *ius in bello*. Only the first point allowed discussions on methods for the peaceful settlement of international conflicts. But, despite the limited and little progressive thematic focus of the agenda, Elihu Root did not hesitate to instruct his delegation to present additional topics at The Hague. Apart from the court project, those concerned "[…] the reduction or limitation of armaments and the attainment of an agreement to observe some limitations upon the use of force for the collection or ordinary debts arising out of contracts."[103] With regards to the first issue, Root seems to have striven for taking up the goal of Nicolas II's initial proposal for the *First Hague Peace Conference* once more, the so-called *Czar's Rescript* from 1898. In this circular, the Russian czar had proposed to limit armament to guarantee peace.[104] With the second point, Root responded to his promises made during his trip through Latin America in 1906. He let actions follow his words after he had publicly expressed his support for the *Drago Doctrine* in Buenos Aires. In the instructions to the U.S.-American delegation, he further emphasized this point and argued that the established practice of forceful collection of debts was "[…] injurious in its general effect upon the relation of nations and upon the welfare of weak and disordered States, whose development ought to be encouraged in the interests of civilization; that it offers frequent temptation to bullying and oppression and to unnecessary and unjustifiable warfare."[105] Thus, he wanted the practice of forceful collections of claims to be limited, or even completely abandoned, although he also admitted in his instructions that it was highly unlikely that all governments (and in particular the European ones) would immediately agree to take such steps and to limit their *ius ad bellum* in this way. Due to the expected resistance against the proposed (far going) limitations, he presented the following compromise formula to the members of his delegation:

102 Jost Dülffer, *Regeln gegen den Krieg?* (n 20 in Chapter 1) 280.

103 'Instructions to the American Delegates to The Hague Conference of 1907' (n 85 in Chapter 6) 70.

104 Compare pages 157–160 of the present book. Regarding Root's reasons for ordering his delegates to present the topic of armament at the Second Hague Peace Conference, see: 'Instructions to the American Delegates to The Hague Conference of 1907' (n 85 in Chapter 6) 75.

105 'Instructions to the American Delegates to The Hague Conference of 1907' (n 85 in Chapter 6) 76.

> The use of force for the collection of a contract debt alleged to be due by the Government of any country to a citizen of any other country is not permissible until after
>
> 1. The justice and amount of the debt shall have been determined by arbitration, if demanded by the alleged debtor.
> 2. The time and manner of payment, and the security, if any, to be given pending payment, shall have been fixed by arbitration, if demanded by the alleged debtor.[106]

As it becomes apparent, he did not expect that it would be possible to realize Drago's plan to the widest possible extent. He supported the concept in general, but he was also aware that a majority could not be reached in The Hague for a complete prohibition of forceful collections of debts.[107] Even the compromise formula risked being met with harsh resistance from Europe. Nevertheless, Root decided to have his delegates propose it. He was convinced that "[...] forcible debt collection encouraged speculators and thought that speculators were promoting revolution in Latin America by advancing money for arms and ammunition and making contracts with weak governments which were trying to avoid overthrow."[108] However, supporting the Latin American demand for better protection from forcible collections of debts was not just an altruistic gesture for the United States. Root was first and foremost pursuing vested U.S.-American interests by doing so. Forceful interferences by European states in Latin America bore the danger of challenging the U.S.-American hegemony over the region and of infringing the *Monroe Doctrine*. By instructing his delegates to introduce the topic to the discussions in The Hague, he could therefore kill two birds with one stone. On the one hand, he proved his reliability and support for the cause of the Latin American countries (as he had promised to do so in Buenos Aires and Rio de Janeiro) and, on the other hand, this initiative also aimed at restricting the influence of European countries in Latin America and – as a consequence – strengthening the U.S.-American hegemonic position in the region.

The most important topical fields in the context of which the United States strove for achieving considerable changes to the prevailing legal order rem-

106 Ibid 77.

107 Ibid. Also: Calvin DeArmond Davis, *The United States and the Second Hague Peace Conference* (n 28 in Chapter 1) 170.

108 Calvin DeArmond Davis, *The United States and the Second Hague Peace Conference* (n 28 in Chapter 1) 170.

ained, nevertheless, obligatory arbitration and adjudication. In this regard, Root's instructions provided for the following:

> In the general field of arbitration two lines of advance are clearly indicated. The first is to provide for obligatory arbitration as broad in scope as now appears to be practicable, and the second is to increase the effectiveness of the system so that nations may more readily have recourse to it voluntarily.[109]

Under Root's guidance, the United States returned, therefore, to a favorable policy towards obligatory arbitration on major international conferences; a policy that they had already pursued at the *First Pan-American Conference* in 1889/90 and at the *First Hague Peace Conference* in 1899. At the *Second Pan-American Conference* in Mexico City (1901/02), however, they had initially opposed any form of obligatory arbitration agreements. At the *Second Hague Peace Conference*, they now held a considerably more favorable position towards the instrument once more; an approach that complied with the generally very positive mood for obligatory arbitration at that time, not only in the United States but also internationally. But it was not the public mood alone that motivated Elihu Root to introduce obligatory arbitration into the U.S.-American agenda for the conference. He was also convinced that a general treaty for obligatory arbitration was (one of) the natural next step(s) in the process of striving for *peace through law*. Because of the above-described developments in favor of obligatory arbitration, and especially because of the wave of obligatory arbitration treaties, which were concluded between 1903 and 1905,[110] he held the time to be ripe to conclude a multi-lateral obligatory arbitration treaty.[111]

Apart from obligatory arbitration, Root also aimed for increasing the effectiveness of the system for peaceful conflict settlement, which had been established in 1899. In this regard he declared that

---

109 'Instructions to the American Delegates to The Hague Conference of 1907' (n 85 in Chapter 6) 77.

110 Compare pages 207 et seq. of the present book.

111 'Instructions to the American Delegates to The Hague Conference of 1907' (n 85 in Chapter 6) 77–78. But it should also be noted that Root instructed his delegates to only sign an obligatory arbitration treaty in The Hague if the following was added to it (compare page 79): "In signing the general arbitration treaty the delegates of the United States desire to have it understood that the special agreements provided for in article _ of said treaty will be subject to submission to the Senate of the United States." By pursuing this approach, Root hoped to avoid a rejection of the treaty by the Senate (like in the case of the Hay-Treaties).

> [t]here can be no doubt that the principal objection to arbitration rests not upon the unwillingness of nations to submit their controversies to impartial arbitration, but upon the apprehension that the arbitration which they submit may not be impartial. It has been a very general practice for arbitrators to act, not as judges deciding questions of fact and law upon the record before them under a sense of judicial responsibility, but as negotiators effecting settlements of questions brought before them in accordance with the traditions and usages and subject to all the considerations and influences which affect diplomatic agents.[112]

He continued his argumentation by stressing that arbitral and judicial settlement of conflicts differed decisively from one another and that they led to completely different results. Against this background, he claimed that "[i]t very frequently happens that a nation which would be very willing to submit its differences to an impartial judicial determination is unwilling to subject them to this kind of diplomatic process."[113] Though there was probably no reliable data that supported, or even proved, this claim he was deeply convinced that more states would be more willing to refer their disputes for settlement to judicial procedures than to arbitration. Because of this belief, he ordered his delegates to present a plan for the establishment of an international court of law in The Hague. Or in his words, he wanted them to propose the creation of a

> [...] tribunal which would pass upon questions between nations with the same impartial and impersonal judgment that the Supreme Court of the United States gives to questions arising between citizens of the States, or between foreign citizens and the citizens of the United States [...]. It should be your effort to bring about in the Second Conference a development of the Hague tribunal into a permanent tribunal composed of judges who are judicial officers and nothing else, who are paid adequate salaries, who have no other occupation, and who will devote their entire time to the trial and decision of international causes by judicial methods and under a sense of judicial responsibility.[114]

Consequently, it was his aim to realize the above-described concepts for the introduction of a truly permanent and autonomous international court of law.

112 Ibid 79.
113 Ibid.
114 Ibid 79–80.

In this regard, numerous similarities can be identified between this approach and the U.S.-American plan for an international tribunal presented at the *First Hague Peace Conference*. Therefore, it can be claimed that the initiative to propose the creation of an international court of law stood in the tradition of the U.S.-American foreign policy from the end of the 19th century onwards. However, it was up to Root and Scott to introduce a concept for such a tribunal into the agenda of the U.S.-American government for the *Second Hague Peace Conference*, which not only aimed for a court that resembled a domestic tribunal but one that would be shaped in a way that did not leave any doubts concerning its nature. In fact, they distinguished very clearly between judicial and arbitral procedures. Hence, Root and Scott did not only want the competences of the PCA to be extended, but they aimed for the creation of an international court of law, which was a permanent and judicial institution and did not decide cases on anything but the pure basis of law and by judicial methods.[115] The judges of this court were supposed to be independent, of the highest reputation, and to fairly represent "[...] the different systems of law and procedure and the principal languages."[116] Consequently, Root rejected arbitration as the dominant instrument for the settlement of international conflicts and preferred adjudication instead.

Therefore, Root and Scott must be attributed the honor of having been the first to initiate the presentation of a clear conceptual differentiation between arbitration and judicial settlements before (almost the entire) world community; and, thereby, Root and Scott introduced this new view on arbitration (and adjudication) to the discussions among states.[117] Because these ideas were still rather utopian and they had not found any support among government officials and state leaders outside the United States yet, it was a high-risk decision to address them at the *Second Hague Peace Conference*. It was only in the United States that a strong and very influential peace movement as well as a group of state officials shared these ideas due to their legalist worldviews.[118]

---

115 Compare in this regard: William Cullum (ed.), *The Second International Peace Conference, held at The Hague from June 15 to October 18, 1907* (United States Government Printing Office 1908) 22–23.

116 'Instructions to the American Delegates to The Hague Conference of 1907' (n 85 in Chapter 6) 80.

117 Warren F. Kuehl, *Seeking World Order* (n 16 in Chapter 3) 102. Kuehl mentioned in this regard that Roosevelt had considered a multi-lateral obligatory arbitration treaty as the most important goal for the conference. However, Root and Choate instead aimed for the establishment of a judicial tribunal and therefore moved this issue to the center of attention of the U.S.-American delegation.

118 Michla Pomerance, *The United States and the World Court as a 'Supreme Court of the Nations'* (n 47 in Chapter 3) 55. There he quotes Joseph H. Choate as follows: "Let us,

The reaction of the other states, on the other hand, could hardly be estimated in advance and by introducing the topic to the discussions in The Hague, Root and Scott risked its immediate rejection.

By presenting the conceptual differentiation between arbitration and adjudication as well as the plan for a permanent international court of law at the *Second Hague Peace Conference* – despite any misgivings and the prospect of having to face the immediate opposition of the other states – Root and Scott set the agenda for one of the most important points in the discussions on the further development of methods for the pacific settlement of international conflicts in The Hague. They were striving for the implementation of innovative changes and for turning the prevailing international legal system – which so far considered arbitration as the most suitable means for the settlement of conflicts – into a rule-of-law based one; and, thereby, they aimed for a full juridification of the system for the peaceful settlement of international conflicts. Besides, their agenda also involved the idea to implement the *Drago Doctrine* (at least in a trimmed-down version) into international law in order to limit the states' *ius ad bellum* and to subject the settlement of pecuniary claims to peaceful methods.

2 The Second Hague Peace Conference

Unlike the United States, most European countries did not primarily focus on the further development of the system for peaceful conflict settlement or on a reform of the PCA in their preparatory works for the *Second Hague Peace Conference*. For them, issues concerning the laws of wars and the avoidance of having to deal with disarmament at a major international conference were far more important. For example, the German emperor Wilhelm II even threatened not to send a delegation to the conference if disarmament was not completely banned from its agenda.[119] Jost Dülffer (*'Regeln gegen den Krieg?'* from 1981) argued in this regard that topics concerning the relations between the great powers in cases of war and the laws of war had moved into

---

then, seek to develop [....] a Permanent Court which shall hold regular and continuous sessions, which shall consist of the same judges, which shall pay due heed to its own decisions, which shall speak with the authority of the united voice of nations, and gradually build up a system of international law, definite and precise, which shall command the approval and regulate the conduct of nations." According to Pomerance, the quote stems from: James Brown Scott (ed.) *The Hague Peace Conferences of 1899 and 1907*, vol. 2 (The John Hopkins Press 1909), page 24.

119 Compare: Jost Dülffer, *Regeln gegen den Krieg?* (n 20 in Chapter 1) 291.

the focus of the European great powers in the years right before the conference.[120] This was the case because wars between them had become plausible events once more. Such wars had not been completely unrealistic at the time of the *First Hague Peace Conference* (or before it) either. But in 1906/07, this option appeared considerably more probable again since the world had just experienced the horrors of modern warfare in the *Russo-Japanese War* (1904/05).[121] Additionally, the formation of two opposing power blocks in Europe – the *Triple Entente* (France, Great Britain, and Russia) on the one hand and the *Triple Alliance* (Austria-Hungary, Germany, and Italy) on the other – in combination with the ongoing armament race among the European great powers resulted in the common conviction that Europe was right in the middle of an escalation process.[122] The discussion about the enactment of new laws and restrictions in the field of the *ius in bello* was, therefore, widely welcomed. Disarmament, on the other hand, remained a highly disputed topic among the European great powers. Because of the uncompromising position of the German (as well as the Austrian and Russian) government(s) in this regard, the participating states agreed not to deal with the topic in the framework of the *Second Hague Peace Conference*;[123] against Root's initial plan to bring it up at this occasion.

Peace activists, internationalists, and progressive international lawyers, nevertheless, put a lot of hope into the *Second Hague Peace Conference*. They expected the event to result in significant progress in the further development of the *ius in bello*.[124] Furthermore, they also hoped for the conclusion of a multi-lateral obligatory arbitration treaty and – at least the U.S.-American peace activists and international lawyers – also the conversion of the PCA into a truly permanent and judicial institution. The United States had already attached the greatest importance to these (last) two issues before the beginning of the conference and their representatives were aware – Root warned about it repeatedly[125] – that it would be very difficult to achieve all their goals at once. Therefore, he put his hopes into a potential continuation of the *Hague Conferences* and in their conversion into a series of periodic meetings.

120 Ibid 281.
121 Compare pages 187–189 of the present book.
122 Jost Dülffer, *Regeln gegen den Krieg?* (n 20 in Chapter 1) 281.
123 Ibid 296–299.
124 Warren F. Kuehl, *Seeking World Order* (n 16 in Chapter 3) 101.
125 'Instructions to the American Delegates to The Hague Conference of 1907' (n 85 in Chapter 6) 69 et seq. Also: Warren F. Kuehl, *Seeking World Order* (n 16 in Chapter 3) 102. Kurt Ed. Imberg, *Die Stellung der Vereinigten Staaten von Nordamerika zur internationalen Schiedsgerichtsfrage* (n 165 in Chapter 3) 88.

He hoped that subsequent conferences would gradually adapt further steps towards the realization of the U.S.-American goals.[126]

Other countries did not travel to The Hague with expectations as hopeful and optimistic as the United States. In particular, Germany regarded the conference with lots of suspicion. However, their representatives put a good face on the matter since they wanted to avoid further international isolation at all costs; as, for example, during the *First Moroccan Crisis* (1904–06) when German and French colonial ambitions had clashed or as during the *First Hague Peace Conference* when the German resistance against obligatory arbitration and their (initial) rejection of an arbitral tribunal had raised severe irritations among the other countries. But regardless their expectations of the conference, all major European countries, several Asian nations, and most of the Latin American states participated in the *Second Hague Peace Conference*. Calvin DeArmond Davis, therefore, characterized the *Second Hague Peace Conference* as follows: "The first conference included only the independent powers of Europa and Asia, the United States, and Mexico. The second conference included most of the other American states, and came closer to being a conference of the world than any other international meeting up to that time."[127] Apart from Costa Rica and Honduras, which were not present,[128] the participating delegates in the *Second Hague Peace Conference* represented (almost) all states being recognized as independent nations at that time. Consequently, the conference could be called the first universal congress in history.[129] The great number of participants and representatives from so many countries also shows the great importance that was attached to the meeting. As mentioned above, 'The Hague' had become a synonym for world peace

126 Kurt Ed. Imberg, *Die Stellung der Vereinigten Staaten von Nordamerika zur internationalen Schiedsgerichtsfrage* (n 165 in Chapter 3) 88.

127 Calvin DeArmond Davis, *The United States and the Second Hague Peace Conference* (n 28 in Chapter 1) 4.

128 Betsy Baker, 'The Hague Conferences (1899 and 1907)' in *Max Planck Encyclopedia of Public International Law* (*online*) paragraph 22. According to her: "All of the Latin American States received invitations and 19 attended. Honduras and Costa Rica responded to the invitation by appointing delegates and reserved seats, but neither country took the seats."

129 Compare: Jonkheer van Tets van Goudriaan's (Dutch Minister of Foreign Affairs) address on the opening meeting of the Second Hague Peace Conference; available in: James Brown Scott (ed.), *The Proceedings of the Hague Conferences: The Conference of 1907*, vol. 1 (Oxford University Press 1920) 45–46. He referred to the Second Hague Peace Conference as a "world conference" and as the "the most completely representative of the States of the world which has met up to our own day." Furthermore, he pointed out that "[…] for the greater number of States participating in the Conference, the more certain will be the general and undisputed observance of the provisions upon which they agree."

since 1899[130] and the first conference had received extensive media coverage.[131] The second meeting was also closely observed by the media, by peace activists, and by the public in general. Especially in the beginning, it was hitting the headlines on an almost daily basis.[132] Due to the crucial importance of the event and high expectations of the public, there was hardly any state that would have voluntarily opted not to attend. The loss of face, of influence on the discussed matters, and the international isolation would have been too extensive. The great powers in particular were keen to attend the event and they put a lot of effort in preparatory works and consultations with other states to protect their interests in The Hague.

The number of participating states increased from 26 nations in 1899 to 44 in 1907 and the majority of the new states came from Latin America. Mexico had been the only participant from this region present at the *First Hague Peace Conference*,[133] wherefore the number of Latin American states participating in the conference grew from 1 in 1899 to 18 nations in 1907. Latin American countries now accounted for around 40% of all participants at the *Second Hague Peace Conference*[134] and, therefore, became a highly influential factor. A.G. de Lapradelle and Ellery C. Stowell (*'Latin America at the Hague Conference'* from 1908) claimed in this regard that the *Second Hague Peace Conference* was, furthermore, the first occasion that "[...] Europe found itself face to face with Latin America"[135] at a multi-lateral gathering. But since the Latin American countries were invited to this event as well, they were set on an equal footing with their North Atlantic counterparts, at least formally, for example, with regards to voting rights.[136] Moreover, because the Latin American states accounted for such a great share of the participating countries, it was simply impossible to ignore them and their influence on the course of the conference. Nevertheless, the Europeans (governments as well as newspapers) treated the Latin American representatives with lots of caution and suspicion.[137] By reviewing a series of German and French journals, and by referring to the general mood at the conference, Alfred H. Fried (*'Pan-Amerika'* from 1910) concluded that the Latin

130 Compare page 259 of the present book.

131 Jost Dülffer, *Regeln gegen den Krieg?* (n 20 in Chapter 1) 71.

132 Ibid.

133 Compare page 156 and *footnote* 18 in Chapter 5 of the present book.

134 Compare: Arnulf Becker Lorca, *Mestizo International Law* (n 178 in Chapter 3) 152 et seq.

135 De Lapradelle, A.G. and Ellery C. Stowell, 'Latin America at the Hague Conference' (n 211 in Chapter 5) 271.

136 James Brown Scott, *The Hague Peace Conferences of 1899 and 1907*, vol. 1 (n 131 in Chapter 2) 100.

137 De Lapradelle, A.G. and Ellery C. Stowell, 'Latin America at the Hague Conference' (n 211 in Chapter 5) 271.

American delegates were (at least in the beginning of the conference) often regarded as 'rastaquouères,' slackers, and impostors.[138] But the longer the conference went on, the Latin American delegates were respected more and seen with different eyes. Fried quoted William T. Stead, a British journalist and peace activist, who even referred to the *Second Hague Peace Conference* as the "[...] second discovery of South America."[139] Without going as far as Stead, it seems, however, as if the Latin American countries did in fact experience an enormous growth of prestige and standing in The Hague. The United States had taken the pioneering role in this regard by declaring their full recognition of the Latin American countries' sovereign equality and exerted their enormous influence in order to get the other North Atlantic countries in line. However, in The Hague, the Latin American countries themselves also did their best to prove – on the global scale – that they were equally capable and respectable members of the international community.

According to Gerry Simpson (*'Great Powers and Outlaw States'* from 2004), the great powers tried to change the decision-making procedures – in comparison to the first conference – in their own favor (although they no longer enjoyed veto rights).[140] But these attempts did not hinder the Latin American states in the pursuit of their goals in The Hague; and some of these goals even stood in stark contrast to the policy of the United States. This situation was a surprise for most of the European countries. Before the beginning of the conference they had expected the Latin American countries to serve as mere instruments of the United States.[141] However, the Latin American representatives acted very self-confidently and independently in The Hague;[142] they even did so vigorously in some respects, without much willingness to compromise.

---

138 Alfred H. Fried, *Pan-Amerika* (n 73 in Chapter 4) 208.

139 Ibid.

140 Gerry Simpson, *Great Powers and Outlaw States: Unequal Sovereigns in the International Legal Order* (n 51 in Chapter 2) 139. Simpson argued that unanimity had been required to pass resolutions at the First Hague Peace Conference. On the second conference, however, "[...] there was a majority rule in the plenary and commissions and quasi-unanimity in the adoption of the Second Conference resolutions and Acts." Quasi-unanimity was applied in cases in which the opposing state(s) agreed to the use of the concept of quasi-unanimity or in which "[...] the number of dissenting states was small and their status low." By linking the use of quasi-unanimity with the status of the dissenting countries, the great powers made sure they were not outvoted (not even by a great majority of smaller countries). Therefore, the privileged status of the great powers not only prevailed at the Second Hague Peace Conference, but it was also strengthened.

141 Compare: Adolf Baron Marschall von Bieberstein, *Die Gruppierung der Staaten auf der Haager Konferenz* (accessible at: Politisches Archiv des Auswärtigen Amts, R 172).

142 Jost Dülffer, *Regeln gegen den Krieg?* (n 20 in Chapter 1) 301.

2.1 *The Proceedings*

Led by manifold and very different considerations, goals, and approaches, the representatives of the 44 participating countries came together in The Hague on June 15, 1907, for the opening session of the conference. In order to review the proceedings of the *Second Hague Peace Conference* with regards to the subject of the present book, the following three topics will be taken into consideration:

- The proposal for a multi-lateral obligatory arbitration treaty,
- The establishment of international courts of law, the projected *International Prize Court*, and the *Court of Arbitral Justice*, and
- The implementation of the *Porter Doctrine.*

Topics concerning the laws of war, neutrality, and other issues were also dealt with in The Hague in 1907 and were not of any less importance. However, they will not form part of the following considerations due to their limited significance for the topic under present review.

Regarding the most important topics dealt with in The Hague, conference president Aleksandr Nelidow (1838–1910) declared already at the first conference meeting that "[...] it was the idea of peace, which brought the Governments to delegate from every quarter of the globe the most eminent men of their countries to discuss together the most cherished interest of mankind – conciliation and justice."[143] The attitude in favor of peace and justice was also dominant in the discussions of the three above-listed topics, which all took place in the framework of the first commission. In the opening address at the first meeting of this commission on June 22, 1907, Léon Bourgeois, its president and head of the French delegation, re-emphasized the achievements of the *First Hague Peace Conference* regarding the institutionalization of arbitration and the introduction of established procedures for its use within the framework of the PCA.[144] He also did not fail to stress one of the greatest defects of the convention from 1899, and a major failure of the first conference, by recalling its incapacity to produce a resolution on obligatory arbitration.[145] He then continued by not only proposing to extend the competences of the PCA and to facilitate its procedures at the *Second Hague Peace Conference* but also called attention to the wave of obligatory arbitration treaties concluded in recent years and to the role of Article 19 of the *Hague Convention* from 1899

143 James Brown Scott (ed.), *The Proceedings of the Hague Conferences: The Conference of 1907*, vol. 1 (n 129 in Chapter 6) 47.

144 James Brown Scott (ed.), *The Proceedings of the Hague Conferences: The Conference of 1907*, vol. 2 (Oxford University Press 1921) 2.

145 Ibid.

in this context.[146] While he did not believe that the *Second Hague Peace Conference* would already result in the conclusion of a treaty of unrestricted and general obligatory arbitration, he still stressed that since "[…] *obligatory* arbitration had widely been introduced into international practice in the last years, owing to the signature of a large number of special treaties,"[147] the majority of states already accepted obligatory arbitration in 1907, at least in general and with regards to special obligatory arbitration. Then, he recalled the words of Dr. Philipp Zorn, a German delegate, from the first conference. In 1899, he had turned down all attempts to introduce obligatory arbitration by declaring that "[w]hen the Permanent Court shall be established and when it shall function, the opportune moment will come when, in virtue of special experience, it may be possible to enumerate certain cases of obligatory arbitration for all."[148] Before this background, Bourgeois found the second conference to be this opportune moment. He asked the other delegates whether – in the light of recent developments in favor of obligatory arbitration and the far-reaching changes of the attitude of numerous governments towards it – the time was ripe to conclude a multi-lateral (special) obligatory arbitration treaty.[149] Thereby, Bourgeois set the tone for the upcoming discussions[150] and turned obligatory arbitration into one of the dominant topics of the first commission, of the first sub-commission (dealing with the pacific settlement of international disputes), and of the *Committee of Examination A*. The last body was created "to study the modifications proposed to the Convention of 1899"[151] in a smaller group of experts in international law.

2.2 *A General Treaty of Obligatory Arbitration*

On August 3, 1907, the '*Committee of Examination A*' began its work and negotiated – right at the beginning – a proposal from the Dominican Republic for a

146 Ibid 3.

147 Ibid 5.

148 Ibid.

149 Ibid.

150 Additionally, Baron Guillaume, a Belgian delegate, stressed (at the 4th meeting of the First Sub-Commission) the leading role of smaller countries in this regard and declared the willingness of his delegation to agree that "[…] arbitration might be made obligatory between the Powers represented at the Conference, for certain classes of disputes […]. However, it does not regard it as superfluous to remark, even now, that it would accept the principle of obligatory arbitration – reserving the disputes affecting the essential interests of the States – for all cases of controversies of a juridical nature arising from the interpretation and the application of treaties, concluded or to be concluded, between the contracting parties." Compare: ibid 213.

151 Ibid 375.

multi-lateral general treaty of obligatory arbitration. Their representatives suggested introducing unlimited and general obligatory arbitration for all kinds of conflicts.[152] While the Netherlands and Denmark supported this initiative, the overwhelming majority of participants soon agreed that the projected plan was too utopian to be realized at the present point in time. Consequently, the idea for an unlimited general treaty was quickly taken off the table. Instead, the committee turned to other initiatives for the introduction of obligatory arbitration. One such proposition was made by Brazil. It also provided for general obligatory arbitration but, unlike the Dominican proposal, it contained broad exemption clauses.[153] Other plans were introduced by the Swedish, Portuguese, and U.S.-American delegations. They resembled each other in a lot of points and basically aimed for the same outcome, wherefore they will be dealt with in the following under one umbrella. The most striking thing, which they all had in common, was that all of them provided for the introduction of obligatory arbitration only for "[...] questions of a legal nature, and especially in the interpretation or application of international conventions."[154] Furthermore, all these proposals contained exemption clauses (applicable in cases affecting the states' vital interests, honor, or independence). But they also included lists of types of conflicts in which the exemption clauses were not invokable.[155] The representative of Sweden, Mr. Hammarskjöld, declared in this regard that similar limitations of exemption clauses were "[...] already inscribed in something like twenty international treaties."[156] According to him, these clauses were widely identical to the just-quoted formula.[157] The Swedish delegates wanted to transfer the structure of these treat-

152 Ibid 406, 879–880. According to this proposal "[...] it is necessary to give arbitration the greatest scope, so that it may include all differences which might arise among States."

153 Ibid 406 et seq., 879.

154 The quote stems from the Swedish proposal; compare ibid 878. The Portuguese and U.S.-American plans resemble the Swedish one a lot as they both want states to bind themselves "[...] to submit to arbitration differences of a legal nature or relating to the interpretation of treaties existing between the signatory Powers." Compare: 'Proposition of the Portuguese Delegation,' ibid 874.

155 Ibid 875, 878, 892–893. Besides the named proposals, there were also a greater number of other approaches but all of them had quite similar shapes and differed only in details. See: ibid 412–415.

156 Ibid 417.

157 Compare earlier made remarks on the Franco-British obligatory arbitration treaty from 1903; further reference to this agreement is available at pages 215 et seq. of the present book. According to Article 1 of this agreement, "[d]ifferences which may arise of a legal nature, or relating to the interpretation of treaties existing between the two contracting parties, and which it may not have been possible to settle by diplomacy, shall be referred to the Permanent Court of Arbitration [...]."

ies onto the global level; by concluding an agreement of – as they called it – "conditional general obligation for recourse to arbitration."[158]

The international *zeitgeist* and public opinion were very favorable of obligatory arbitration in these years and its acceptance had grown significantly among states as well. Strong and popular arguments could, therefore, be put forward in favor of the adoption of plans such as the Swedish, Portuguese, and U.S.-American ones. Consequently, these initiatives were not only supported by Latin American states or the United States but also by a great number of smaller European countries as well as several great powers. France, Italy, and Austria-Hungary showed a welcoming attitude towards the conclusion of an agreement[159] shaped in accordance with the proposed plans. Great Britain had held quite a negative view on them in the beginning, but they changed their mind during the conference and joined the group of supporters of an obligatory arbitration agreement.[160] Germany, Brazil, Rumania, and Turkey,[161] on the other hand, were the only countries opposing it completely and which could not be convinced to make any concessions in this regard throughout the entire conference. Baron Marschall von Bieberstein, head of the German delegation, even did his best to win support from other delegates for his position. That being said, although he steadily objected proposals and compromises in favor of obligatory arbitration and attempted to raise doubts concerning the functionality of a universal treaty of obligatory arbitration,[162] he did not openly declare the rejection of the conclusion of such a treaty right away. For him, participating in the negotiations and pretending to be willing to compromise for the good of all countries was diplomatically necessary in order to avoid an isolation of the German Empire (as it had been the case at

158 James Brown Scott (ed.), *The Proceedings of the Hague Conferences: The Conference of 1907*, vol. 2 (n 144 in Chapter 6) 417.

159 Ibid 416 et seq. Compare also: Jost Dülffer, *Regeln gegen den Krieg?* (n 20 in Chapter 1) 313–314. According to Dülffer, more than 30 proposals concerning the introduction of obligatory arbitration were presented (primarily by smaller states) at the Second Hague Peace Conference.

160 Jost Dülffer, *Regeln gegen den Krieg?* (n 20 in Chapter 1) 314–316. Dülffer argued that the British change of mind based on the object not to isolate herself by rejecting this popular project. Compare also: James Brown Scott (ed.), *The Proceedings of the Hague Conferences: The Conference of 1907*, vol. 2 (n 144 in Chapter 6) 466. Adolf Baron Marschall von Bieberstein, *Die Verhandlung der zweiten Haager Friedenskonferenz 1907: Allgemein* (accessible at: Politisches Archiv des Auswärtigen Amtes, R 176).

161 Adolf Baron Marschall von Bieberstein, *Die Verhandlung der zweiten Haager Friedenskonferenz 1907: Allgemein* (n 160 in Chapter 6).

162 Ibid.

the *First Hague Peace Conference*).[163] Johannes Kriege, Germany's second delegate plenipotentiary, however, showed less reticence. He declared – very bluntly – that Germany rejected any universal obligatory arbitration commitment by stating that "[…] the German delegation cannot give its adhesion to any one of the projects directed to the establishment of obligatory and world arbitration for all matters of a juridical nature, or relative to the interpretation of treaties. The German delegation will vote against these propositions."[164] Marschall von Bieberstein was little pleased by his colleague's undiplomatic pronouncement and tried to appease the other delegations by showing a more amiable attitude in the committee of examination.[165] However, he could not simply take back Kriege's statement. It would not only have resulted into a loss of face for the German Empire, but Kriege's declaration corresponded to an order from Berlin that directed its delegates to reject any obligatory arbitral commitment.[166] Von Bieberstein would have preferred to pursue a less absolute way in communicating Germany's opposition[167] as he regarded the German isolation at *the First Hague Peace Conference* as a horrible debacle. For the second conference, he had hoped to be able to prevent the recurrence of a similar situation.[168] Hence, once Kriege had declared this to be the German position, von Bieberstein tried to remedy the situation somewhat. He wanted to show the goodwill of his country and its readiness to contribute to the success of the conference by showing a (surprisingly) progressive and benevolent attitude regarding other crucial issues on the conference agenda, such as the establishment of international courts of law. As it will become apparent in the following, Germany even took a leading role in this regard. But against von Bieberstein's hopes, the other participants did not consider this newly arisen German support for courts of law as reason enough to give up on their demand for a global obligatory arbitration treaty.[169] Since they felt the need to come to presentable results concerning obligatory arbitration at The Hague, they

163 Jost Dülffer, *Regeln gegen den Krieg?* (n 20 in Chapter 1) 317.

164 James Brown Scott (ed.), *The Proceedings of the Hague Conferences: The Conference of 1907*, vol. 2 (n 144 in Chapter 6) 420.

165 Jost Dülffer, *Regeln gegen den Krieg?* (n 20 in Chapter 1) 317.

166 Ibid.

167 Baron Marschall von Bieberstein, *Die Verhandlung der zweiten Haager Friedenskonferenz 1907: Allgemein* (n 160 in Chapter 6). According to Bieberstein, he was afraid that Germany would be blamed for having put the plan for a universal obligatory arbitration treaty to an end – since this project would have been "[…] such a pretty child but the big German killed it with a mace" [analogously translated by the author of the present book].

168 Jost Dülffer, *Regeln gegen den Krieg?* (n 20 in Chapter 1) 316–317.

169 Ibid 313.

exerted more and more pressure on the German delegates. They tried to win their support by offering compromises and by adapting their proposals. Léon Bourgeois asked von Bieberstein for the acceptance of only a very limited list of topics to be subjected to obligatory arbitration and the Russian delegation even proposed to establish a commitment to obligatory arbitration for only "[…] four, three, or even one" type of rather unimportant cases in order to stipulate at least the slightest progress.[170] However, the Germans rejected these offers – and, thereby, chose to isolate themselves.

Due to the close alliance between Germany and Austria-Hungary, von Bieberstein was able to win the Austrians over and to make them vote against the conclusion of an obligatory arbitration treaty as well.[171] In this regard, von Bieberstein mentioned in an internal paper that he and his Austrian counterpart agreed on several key issues. For example, it was essential for them to make sure that the great powers kept their outstanding position in the international order. Sovereign equality was a thorn in their side, especially because they expected the introduction of a universal obligatory arbitration agreement to result in severe losses of influence and power for the great powers. The role of pure strength would have been diminished in the international system[172] because an obligatory arbitration treaty would have allowed all states, regardless of their size or standing, to invoke arbitration whenever it pleased them. Consequently, the great powers would not be able anymore to enforce their will easily through the (threat of the) use of force. This scenario was a veritable nightmare for the German government. It strove for the extension of its influence and territory (*Weltpolitik*),[173] if necessary, also by force. Due to this, Germany was not willing to agree to the conclusion of a general treaty of obligatory arbitration at the *Second Hague Peace Conference*. It would have restricted their colonial and power political aspirations and – according

170 Ibid 318. See also: James Brown Scott (ed.), *The Proceedings of the Hague Conferences: The Conference of 1907*, vol. 2 (n 144 in Chapter 6) 463. There, Scott reproduced Tobias Asser's remark according to which "[…] the list of cases that may be adopted is not in itself of great importance, and that the essential value lies in the moral effect which might result from the adoption of obligatory arbitration without reservations. It is for the principle that we must fight, and it is the triumph of the principle that we must applaud. By limiting ourselves to the conclusions of the subcommittee, we would secure but a restricted list; but this was foreseen from the beginning, and in spite of that fact, the list would remain an interesting one; it would certainly mark a beginning."

171 Jost Dülffer, *Regeln gegen den Krieg?* (n 20 in Chapter 1) 319.

172 Adolf Baron Marschall von Bieberstein, *Die Verhandlung der zweiten Haager Friedenskonferenz 1907: Allgemein* (n 160 in Chapter 6).

173 F.R. Bridge and Roger Bullen, *The Great Power and the European States System 1814–1914* (Pearson Longman 2005) 255 et seq.

to F.R. Bridge and Roger Bullen (*'The Great Powers and the European States System 1814–1914'* from 2005) – it would have hampered Germany in their striving for transforming "[...] from a European into a world power, on par with Great Britain, Russia, and the United States."[174]

Surprisingly, the committee of examination did not stop working on the plan for a global obligatory arbitration treaty, despite the clear rejection by the German delegation (and its supporters). Instead, the other members of the committee continued to discuss the issue and emphasized their dedication to (obligatory) arbitration. Following Kriege's declaration, the committee met a further eleven times and continued to develop its ideas and concepts.[175] This happened in spite of the fact that the other members of the committee agreed, at the same time, not to enter a global obligatory arbitration treaty against the explicit opposition of any of the great powers and, therefore, not to conclude it without Germany.[176] Hence, the project was doomed to failure. The uncompromising attitude and the total rejection of any kind of obligatory arbitration agreement by the Germans led to strong irritations, especially among countries such as France, Great Britain, and the United States.[177] They simply could not understand the German stance. Although Germany was not the only country that rejected obligatory arbitration, they had taken the lead in this regard and had voiced their rejection in the most undiplomatic and maladroit

174 Ibid 255.

175 James Brown Scott (ed.), *The Proceedings of the Hague Conferences: The Conference of 1907*, vol. 2 (n 144 in Chapter 6) 432–591.

176 Compare in this regard: Jost Dülffer, *Regeln gegen den Krieg?* (n 20 in Chapter 1) 319.

177 Ibid 319–321. See also: James Brown Scott (ed.), *The Proceedings of the Hague Conferences: The Conference of 1907*, vol. 2 (n 144 in Chapter 6) 74. The U.S.-American representative Joseph H. Choate even publicly expressed his anger about the German position as follows: "I should like to say a few words in reply to the important discourse delivered by the first delegate of Germany, with all the deference and regard to which he is justly entitled because of the might empire that he represents, as well as for his own great merits and his unfailing personal devotion to the consideration of the important subjects that have arisen before the Conference. But which all his deference it seems to me that either there are, in this conference, two first delegates of Germany, or, if it be only the one whom we have learned to recognize and honor, he speaks with two different voices. Baron Marschall is an ardent admirer of the abstract principle of arbitration and even of obligatory arbitration, and even of general arbitration between those with whom he chooses to act. But when it comes to putting this idea into concreate forms and practical effect he appears as our most formidable adversary. He appears like one who worships a divine imagine in the sky, but when it touches the earth it loses all charm for him. He sees as in a dream a celestial apparition which excites his ardent devotion, but when he wakes and finds her by his side he turns to the wall, and will have nothing to do with her." See also: Calvin DeArmond Davis, *The United States and the Second Hague Peace Conference* (n 28 in Chapter 1) 282.

way. Therefore, the other countries blamed the failure of the project for an obligatory arbitration treaty on Germany.

In the final voting at the fifth meeting of the First Commission (on October 5 and 7, 1907), it became apparent that the Germans (and their supporters) were in a clear minority in this point. In the end, 35 (out of 44 participating) countries voted for the adoption of the following provision:

> Differences of a legal nature, and especially those relating to the interpretation of treaties existing between two or more of the contracting States, which may in future arise between them and which it may not have been possible to settle by diplomacy, shall be submitted to arbitration, provided, nevertheless, that they do not affect the vital interests, the independence or the honor of any of the said States, and do not concern the interests of other States not involved in the dispute.[178]

Among the states supporting obligatory arbitration, were all the participating Latin American states, the United States, France, Great Britain, Italy, and Russia (as well as a number of smaller European and few Asian states). Only Germany, Austria-Hungary, Greece, Rumania, and Turkey voted against it.[179] But, regardless of the overwhelming majority in its favor, the initiative still failed. The group of opposing states may have been rather small, but it comprised of two great powers (Austria-Hungary and Germany). Therefore, it constituted more than a negligible minority and could not simply be overcome by declaring the vote in favor of obligatory arbitration as to comply with the requirements for a *'quasi-unanimous'*-decision.[180] The German international lawyer and peace activist Walther Schücking (*'Die Organisation der Welt'* from 1909) commented on the result of this voting and on the failure of the projected agreement as follows:

> The population of the 32 countries (including their colonies) voting in favor of the principle of obligatory arbitration accounts for around 1200 million people, whereas the population of the 9 opposing states only equates 220 million (for the most part from the Balkans). The popula-

178 James Brown Scott (ed.), *The Proceedings of the Hague Conferences: The Conference of 1907*, vol. 2 (n 144 in Chapter 6) 92.

179 Ibid; apart from the mentioned states, Japan, Luxemburg, Montenegro, and Switzerland abstained from voting.

180 Compare: Gerry Simpson, *Great Powers and Outlaw States: Unequal Sovereigns in the International Legal Order* (n 51 in Chapter 2) 139. Also: Jost Dülffer, *Regeln gegen den Krieg?* (n 20 in Chapter 1) 319.

> tion of those states abstaining from voting finally accounted for around 95 million.[181]

With these words, Schücking concluded the result of the negotiations at the *Second Hague Peace Conference* on the implementation of a universal treaty of obligatory arbitration very plainly. According to him, the realization of the project was prevented by a small, but not uninfluential, group of nations against the will and the open support for obligatory arbitration by the majority of states. Therefore, obligatory arbitration must, in fact, be considered as a widely accepted and recognized instrument at that time, which many states regarded as to be of key importance for the further development of international law, for the preservation of peace, and for the maintenance of good relations.

2.3 *The International Prize Court*

Already in the first meeting of the First Commission on June 22, 1907, a proposition was introduced to its discussions concerning the jurisdiction of prizes,[182] which also contained the idea for the establishment of an international prize court. Surprisingly, the topic was brought up by von Bieberstein. Amos S. Hershey (*'An International Prize Court'* from 1907) remarked in this regard that "[t]he extreme desirability, if not the absolute need for an International Prize Court has long been admitted on all sides."[183] The importance of prize law had increased significantly and had become widely apparent during the *'Russo-Japanese War'* in 1904/05.[184] Due to this development, prizes and their legal treatment held key points on the agendas of many states in 1907. Nevertheless, it remains astonishing that it was the German delegation that made a proposition in this regard, especially when taking into account the content of its proposal.[185] According to it, "[t]he validity of the capture of a merchant ship or its cargo shall be decided by a price court. Such jurisdiction is exercised in the first

---

181 Walther Schücking, *Die Organisation der Welt* (A. Kröner 1909) 73. Originally, the text is in German, the (analogous) translation was produced by the author of the present book.

182 James Brown Scott (ed.), *The Proceedings of the Hague Conferences: The Conference of 1907*, vol. 2 (n 144 in Chapter 6) 6.

183 Amos S. Hershey, 'An International Prize Court' (1907) 19 The Green Bag 652.

184 Natalino Ronzitti, 'International Prize Court (IPC)' in *Max Planck Encyclopedia of Public International Law (online)*.

185 Compare in this regard: Jost Dülffer, *Regeln gegen den Krieg?* (n 20 in Chapter 1) 313. According to him, the German delegation showed a lot of readiness for conciliation regarding the establishment of a general international court of law in order to secure benevolence from the other participating states and to cushion their outrage towards the German opposition to a universal treaty of obligatory arbitration. Concerning the intro-

instance by the national prize court of the belligerent captor; in the second instance by a High International Prize Court."[186] Therefore, the German delegation proposed the introduction of an international prize court, which was intended to function as an international court of appeal and which was to be equipped with superior jurisdiction over national tribunals.[187] Despite this highly progressive approach, it should also be noted that the German delegation did not intend to outright introduce a permanent institution. Instead, international prize courts (in the German sense) were to be "[...] organized upon the outbreak of a naval war and shall pass upon all prize cases arising out of the war."[188] Hence, the so called 'courts' would have only held jurisdiction over the respective relationship between the two participating states in one particular naval war. In the event of any subsequent naval war between the same countries (or in the case of the emergence of conflicts between other countries involved in the same naval war), other *'High International Prize Courts'* would have had to be created.[189] However, even though the prize courts were not meant to be permanent (in which the concept resembled the one of the PCA), the German proposal was still exceptional.

In addition to the German plan, the British delegation introduced an initiative for an international judiciary on prize law to the discussions of the First Commission as well. The British advocated for a number of "[...] propositions relative to the Creation of an International Prize Court"[190] and thereby strove in a similar direction as the Germans. By having two major European powers arguing in the same way, a lot of attention was drawn to the project. According to Henry B. Brown (*'The Proposed International Prize Court'* from 1908), judge at the U.S. Supreme Court, it was, furthermore,

> [...] the opinion of the entire conference, that there was a clear distinction between land and sea operations, in the fact that the former are carried on against the enemy alone, and require no judicial authoriza-

---

duction of an international prize law, the Germans' apparent willingness to make concessions seems to have been motivated by the same reasons.

186 James Brown Scott (ed.), *The Proceedings of the Hague Conferences: The Conference of 1907*, vol. 2 (n 144 in Chapter 6) 1051.

187 Henry B. Brown, 'The Proposed International Prize Court' (1908) 2 The American Journal of International Law 476.

188 James Brown Scott (ed.), *The Proceedings of the Hague Conferences: The Conference of 1907*, vol. 2 (n 144 in Chapter 6) 1051.

189 Ibid.

190 Ibid 1058–1059. Later the British delegation also introduced a more detailed and elaborated proposal in form of the 'Draft Convention relative to a Permanent International Court of Appeal'; compare: ibid 1056–1058.

> tion; while the latter, dealing as they do with the property of neutrals who are alleged to have violated their neutrality, require a judicial determination both of the question of violation and of the fact of neutral ownership.[191]

Furthermore, Brown pointed out that it was necessary for leading naval powers (such as Great Britain and Germany) to come to terms on an international treaty, which settled prize law-related questions. Otherwise, captures and damages of goods of neutral states done during times of war could easily result in severe consequences for international trade relations, or lead to other serious conflicts. As it seems, most of the participating countries in The Hague agreed on these points. Consequently, it was soon decided to take the German and British proposals as a basis for further discussions in the second sub-commission (of the first commission).

Already at the second meeting of this sub-commission, von Bieberstein made the following very telling statement regarding the nature of the projected international prize court:

> According to the principle universally admitted in the law of nations, every maritime prize must be confirmed by a judicial decision. At present, this decision proceeds exclusively from the jurisdiction of the belligerent captor. It is the captor who establishes the tribunals and regulates their procedure. Whatever may be the organization of this jurisdiction in the various countries, it cannot be denied that this state of things is not satisfactory and is associated with grave inconveniences from the point of view both of the principles of justice and equity, and of the interests of individuals, as well as from that of the interests of neutral States and of the belligerents themselves.[192]

Furthermore, he stressed the necessity to create an impartial international court of law deciding cases of prize law by declaring that "[i]t is, then, highly desirable that an international jurisdiction be established, whose impartiality cannot be doubted."[193] Hence, the German delegation strove for the establishment of an international prize court, which had a purely judicial nature. This constituted a huge novelty, not only for German foreign politics but also for

191 Henry B. Brown, 'The Proposed International Prize Court' (n 187 in Chapter 6) 476.

192 James Brown Scott (ed.), *The Proceedings of the Hague Conferences: The Conference of 1907*, vol. 2 (n 144 in Chapter 6) 783–784.

193 Ibid.

the entire international system. So far, there only existed a (non-permanent) court of arbitration at the international level (the PCA), which was equipped with purely voluntary competences.[194] Therefore, the establishment of an international prize court composed in accordance with the plan of the German delegation would have led to the constitution of the first international court of law ever.

At the beginning, this prospect seems not to have attracted much attention and enthusiasm among the delegates and the conference observers. One reason for the rather unagitated reaction could have been the fact that the public opinion, and probably also numerous delegates, had put their hopes on other projects. Negotiations on the establishment of a general international court of law and on the conclusion of a universal treaty of obligatory arbitration took place at the very same time. These projects were considerably more prestigious due to their general and universal characters. Nevertheless, it should also be born in mind what Henry B. Brown wrote regarding the projected international prize court. He emphasized the importance of this proposal, its novelty, and its innovative character and declared the initiative to be of great significance "[…] because of its potentiality in the possible creation of other courts of more enlarged powers, which may ultimately go far toward the peaceful settlement of all international disputes which do not involve the integrity of the territory or the vital interests or honor of particular powers."[195] Despite the initially low interest in the topic, some of the delegates in The Hague still seem to have recognized the potential of the projected international prize court, and several more followed them very soon. The notion of the realization of the projected court raised hopes for causing a lighthouse effect and, therefore, bore the potential to pave the way for further and more far-going court projects once the states had become used to the (thematically and jurisdictional limited) international prize court. It was also not only the Germans who made clear that they wanted the international prize court to have a purely judicial nature. The British voiced that intention too by declaring that the court "[…] shall render its decisions by applying the principles of international law."[196] Hence, questions concerning the legal nature were quickly settled and did not result in any further discussions or objections.

194 Compare pages 171–176 of the present book.

195 Henry B. Brown, 'The Proposed International Prize Court' (n 187 in Chapter 6) 476.

196 Article 6 of the British 'Draft Convention relative to a Permanent International Court of Appeal'. It provided for the following procedural rules: "If the legal question to be decided has already been settled by a convention to which the Powers in dispute are signatories, the decision of the Court shall be in conformity with the stipulations of the convention. In the absence of a convention, if all civilized nations are in agreement upon

A point that caused considerably more difficulties was the one concerning the nomination of judges. The British proposal provided for a high degree of impartiality and freedom from prejudices while the Germans proposed to grant the adverse parties the right to nominate the judges *ad hoc* for each case (comparably to the system of the PCA).[197] Moreover, the British did not want the court to be established anew every time a naval war occurred. According to them, the lack of permanency would have turned the international prize court into an institution which was just as inconsistent as the PCA. The British also objected to the German idea to create the court only in the bi-lateral relationship of two belligerent parties. They wanted it to be a permanent decision-making body, which was universally competent to settle all cases of appeal in the field of prize law. The British representative Henry Howard concluded this position by declaring that the court proposed by the Germans "[...] would be organized only at the beginning of the war, and by the belligerents. It would, therefore, be created *ad hoc*, with no element of stability, with no tradition, and the transitory nature of which would not fail to harm its prestige and rob its decisions of any and all moral worth."[198] Due to that, the British strove for

> [...] the creation of a permanent court which will have a regular system of procedure and a continuity of principles. The court will be organized in time of peace and not at the beginning of hostilities: its members will be appointed, not by the belligerents as such, but by the States largely interested in maritime commerce. One of the principal objects of the project will be to insure the impartiality of the decisions by the exclusion, in each case, of the judges appointed by the parties in dispute.[199]

---

a legal point, the court must likewise render a decision in conformity with this general opinion. Where these conditions do not exist, the Court shall render its decision by applying the principles of international law." Compare: James Brown Scott (ed.), *The Proceedings of the Hague Conferences: The Conference of 1907*, vol. 2 (n 144 in Chapter 6) 1057.

197 According to article 4 of the 'Proposition of the German Delegation regarding the Prize Court', "[t]he High International Prize Court shall be composed of five members: two admirals and three members of the Permanent Court of Arbitration of The Hague." Each of the opposing parties were supposed to choose an admiral whereas the nomination of the other judges shall lay in the hands of neutral powers selected by the parties (except of the third judge who was to be nominated by another neutral power chosen by the appointed two neutral states). Compare: ibid 786, 1051.

198 Ibid 793.

199 Ibid 794.

Despite these conceptual differences between the German and the British plans, the generally similar goal that underpinned both propositions – the creation of an international judiciary for prize law – seems to have been one of the reasons for the German delegation to show willingness to compromise. Another reason was probably the fact that the German representative Johannes Kriege – when reasoning the German preference for a non-permanent institution and for a nomination of the judges in the above-described way – also admitted that a permanent court would "[…] have the advantage of offering more guarantees with the continuity of jurisdiction."[200] He added, however, that he just could not imagine a fair way of choosing the judges for a permanent tribunal.[201] The Swedish representative publicly drew the conclusion from these explanations that "[…] the German delegation is not opposed, in principle, to the constitution of a more or less permanent tribunal for maritime prizes, but that it has certain doubts regarding the possibility of organizing it satisfactorily."[202] Even though the Russian and Austrian delegations took sides with the Germans,[203] Kriege had to realize that the Swedish arguments were outmaneuvering him. He had not immediately objected the Swedish conclusions, wherefore the German delegation found itself under immense pressure. The Swedes had challenged Germany to follow Kriege's words with deeds and their delegates could not simply ignore this openly exerted pressure. Backtracking was also not an option since it would have resulted in another public loss of face and open self-humiliation, especially since the initiative for an international prize court had come from the German delegation. Consequently, the Germans were forced to act.

When the second sub-commission decided to establish a committee of examination, the German representatives, therefore, showed a lot of willingness to compromise. They worked productively together with the U.S.-American, French, and British delegates and created a new proposal for an international prize court.[204] Regarding the permanency of the projected institution, the new plan followed the British concept: The court was supposed to be established as a permanent body composed of judges who were to be "[…]

200 Ibid 795.

201 Ibid 796. In this regard, Kriege declared the following: "It is, of course, agreed that it would not be possible for each distinct State to designate a member of the court. The court composed of so many judges would scarcely be able to perform any practical work. On the other hand, by restricting the number of States authorized to designate the members, one would avoid with difficulty, the reproach of failing in equity."

202 Ibid 799.

203 Ibid 799–800, 807–808.

204 Ibid 813.

jurists of known proficiency in questions of international maritime law"[205] and to be appointed by the signatory states for tenures of six years.[206] Hence, the new proposal aimed at the establishment of a truly permanent and judicial court. It was to have independent and impartial judges and was not supposed to follow the *traditional* concept of arbitration any longer.

Coming to this progressive proposal had only been possible because the fiercest opponent of a truly permanent international prize court, the German Empire, had changed its mind in this regard. Structural and conceptual problems seemed to have been settled and the way appeared to have been paved for the establishment of this court. However, another problem was waiting just around the corner: The question concerning the method for nominating judges. In Article 12 of the new proposal, the aforementioned four great powers suggested the following method for composing the court:

> The Court is composed of fifteen judges; nine judges constitute a quorum.
> The judges appointed by the following signatory Powers: Germany, Austria-Hungary, the United-States of America, France, Great Britain, Italy, Japan, and Russia, shall always be summoned to sit.
> The judges and deputy judges appointed by the other Powers shall sit by rota as shown in the table hereto annexed.[207]

Apart from the preferential treatment of the great powers, the mentioned table[208] provided (for total tenure periods of six years each) that Spain would have been entitled to nominate a judge as well as a deputy judge for terms of office of four years, the Netherlands would have been awarded the same right but for terms of three years, and the majority of other European states (and China) would have been assigned seats for judges and deputy judges for two years each. Only few European (and some Asian) countries were granted shorter terms than two years. In total, smaller states from Europe (and Asia) would have held seats in the prize court (and the right to nominate deputy judges) for 30 years per period. Because tenures of 6 years and a bench constituted of 15 judges accounted for a total amount of 90 one-year seats per tenure, these smaller and medium-sized European (together with some Asian) states were entitled to a third of the total amount of seats of the court per period.[209]

205 Ibid 817.
206 Ibid 818.
207 Ibid.
208 Available at: ibid 817.
209 However, the underrepresentation of Asian countries should not be spared at this point either. China was supposed to be entitled for tenure of 2 years for each judge and a

Furthermore, the great powers enjoyed the right of permanent representation, which accounted for another 48 years of the tenure. Due to this setup, little was left for the Latin American countries. Only Argentina, Brazil, Chile, and Mexico were supposed to be represented by judges for terms of two years, but not by deputy judges. All the other Latin American countries would have been granted nomination rights on an even lesser scale. In total, the share of the Latin American states would have accounted for 12 years in each office (judges and deputy judges) per tenure and none of them was supposed to be among the permanently represented powers.

This setup caused enormous discontent among the Latin American representatives and especially Ruy Barbosa (1849–1923), a Brazilian delegate, excelled in his elaborated opposition against the proposed nomination procedure. On August 17, 1907, he expressed his view on the matter by declaring that

> [t]he constitution of the International Prize Court [...] affects only those States that have interests upon the seas, that is to say, it affects almost exclusively those States owning a merchant fleet. Therefore, it is in proportion to the value of such a fleet that their rights should be measured in this matter [... and that...] the rôles of each of the interested parties in this common judicature [should be distributed] according to the respective importance of their merchant fleet.
>
> In consequence, we should have nothing to object to the bases themselves of the Franco-Anglo-German-American project. We consider its principles as reasonable. But the application of it seems to us sometimes unjust, unequal, contradictory.[210]

In the following, he reasoned his claim for better representation of his country by questioning the general fairness of the distribution of nomination rights, and especially by challenging the ones of some of the great powers.[211] He referred in this context to the "flagrant injustice of the project in regard to Brazil."[212] According to him, his home country had a merchant fleet of a considerably bigger size than the ones of several smaller European countries. However, these smaller countries were to be entitled to nominate judges and

deputy judge. Persia, on the other hand, should hold seats for a judge and a deputy judge for 1 year each; whereas Siam was only to be represented by a judge for 1 year. Compare: ibid 817.

210 Ibid 827.

211 Ibid 828–830.

212 Ibid 827.

deputy judges for periods of two years each whereas Brazil was only supposed to have a judge (but no deputy) for the same time span.[213] Furthermore, Barbosa also argued that the proposed categorization not only constituted a disadvantage to Brazil but to all Latin American countries. According to him, Mexico, Argentina, and Chile would have had to be assigned the same rights of representation as smaller European states (such as Belgium, Portugal, or Rumania) if the same standard of measurement had been equally applied to all countries.[214] Due to this constellation, he "[…] would never deprive any of the other nations of the place assigned to it in the project. We claim for ourselves only a place proportionately equal to that of the rest. […] In consequence, the project should be modified along that line."[215]

The implementation of the principle of sovereign equality had already stood in the center of Latin American politics for a long time. In fact, the Latin American states had continuously argued for their full recognition as sovereign equals since the days of the achievement of their independence. But, so far, it had been (mostly) withheld from them.[216] It was only at the *Third Pan-American Conference* in 1906 that the tide had turned, and the United States had taken an initiative for the full recognition of their sovereign equality.[217] In The Hague, the Latin American states openly demanded equal rights and treatment; only to experience that they were put at an obvious disadvantage once again when it came to the distribution of seats in the discussion on the establishment of the first international court of law in history, the *International Prize Court* (*hereinafter* IPC). For this reason, and because of the indignation of the Latin American countries for being disadvantaged (once again), Brazil did not remain the only country from this region to object to the proposal. Other Latin American diplomats rose to speak as well and aligned themselves with Barbosa. They shared his outrage and declared the proposed method for the nomination of judges to be "unequal, unjust and inequitable."[218] For example, the Mexican delegation published a statement according to which it

213 Ibid 827–828.

214 Ibid 828.

215 Ibid.

216 Compare pages 238 et seq. of the present book.

217 James Brown Scott (ed.), *The Proceedings of the Hague Conferences: The Conference of 1907*, vol. 2 (n 144 in Chapter 6) 828.

218 Ibid 830; the quote summarizes the statement of Gonzalo A. Esteva, a member of the Mexican delegation.

> [...] cannot adhere to any convention in which all the States invited to the Peace Conference, large or small, strong or weak, are not considered as upon the most absolute and the most perfect footing of equality. In the present project anent an International Prize Court, the Mexican delegation does not find that just and desirable equality, and, in consequence, it will cast its vote against the project.[219]

The Venezuelan delegation joined the opposition against the projected structure of the IPC as well (although it generally supported the idea of "a really universal court")[220] and declared the following: "Believing that the project of the committee of examination is in evident contradiction with the principle of equal representation of the States, the Venezuelan delegation declares that it will abstain from voting upon the whole of this project [...]."[221]

Argentina, on the other hand, was also well aware that the plan for the IPC did not provide for equal representation in the court on their behalf,[222] but their representatives were "[...] yet willing to make this small sacrifice as a homage to this great work of right and of justice."[223] They believed that "[...] the prize court will constitute an important progress, for the two-fold fact that, so to speak, it will superpose decisions of an impartial tribunal on the more or less interested decisions of the belligerents, and furthermore, it will be the first international jurisdiction created by the civilized world."[224]

The IPC indeed bore the potential to substantially improve the prevailing international legal order by introducing the rule of law in international prize law through the creation of an international court of appeal for this particular field of law. Judicial settlement of cases concerning prize law and the detachment of this kind of questions from the exclusive jurisdiction of the capturing parties would have allowed countries and individuals (whose cargo was seized) to take recourse to an international, permanent, and impartial decision-making body. Hence, despite unequal representation rights, the Latin American countries would also probably have benefited from the introduction of the IPC because they were usually not the ones capturing ships. Instead, they were among those countries whose vessels were captured. Therefore, they would have enjoyed better judicial protection in cases of seizures. Due to this constellation, and because the Latin American countries eventually decided not to

219 Ibid 833.
220 Ibid 19.
221 Ibid.
222 Ibid 13.
223 Ibid.
224 Ibid 11.

block progress by voting against the creation of the IPC, most of them gave up on their resistance in the end (despite their discontent over the method of nomination). Only Brazil and Turkey voted against the creation of the IPC, whereas 27 states supported this initiative (the remaining 16 participating nations abstained from voting). Among the countries voting in favor of the project, there were mostly European countries and the United States, but also Argentina, Bolivia, Cuba, the Dominican Republic, Haiti, Peru, and Uruguay. On the other hand, Chile, Colombia, Ecuador, Guatemala, Mexico, Nicaragua, Panama, Paraguay, El Salvador, and Venezuela did not vote. Their abstention from voting allowed the other states to conclude the convention for the establishment of the IPC.

This step was of great importance for the further development of international law as the states had proven their willingness and ability to come to a conclusion regarding the creation of the first international court of law ever. They overcame hesitations and worked together for the common good as well as for the juridification of international relations. Prize law was only a rather small and not-too-important area of international law, and it should also be borne in mind that the court was not designed to prevent wars from breaking out. It would only have been able to settle questions of prize law in a peaceful and judicial manner, which arose during naval conflicts. The IPC was, therefore, not supposed to function as a peace-keeping instrument and could not really contribute to the realization of the ideal of the peace movement to prevent wars from breaking out by having all conflicts settled through an international judiciary (at best even on an obligatory base). However, the decision to establish the IPC was still groundbreaking because of its novelty, because new judicial ground was broken by this decision, and because a (small) first step was taken towards the implementation of an international judiciary. Furthermore, the discussions and negotiations on the creation of this institution were also important because they foreshadowed what was about to take place in the context of the other proposal made in The Hague for the establishment of an international court of law, the one concerning the creation of the *Court of Arbitral Justice*.

2.4 *The Court of Arbitral Justice*

Court of Arbitral Justice (hereinafter CAJ) was the term used to refer to an institution whose creation was also discussed at the *Second Hague Peace Conference* and which was supposed to be shaped in the form of a general, permanent, and autonomous international court of law. The initiative for this topic came from Joseph H. Choate, first delegate of the United States, who launched the proposal at the 9th meeting of the First Sub-Commission (of the First Commission) on August 1, 1907.

James Brown Scott's text collection *'American Addresses at the Second Hague Peace Conference'* (from 1916)[225] allows us to take a detailed view behind the scenes as well as into the thinking and the motivations of the U.S.-American government for having its delegation file this proposal. According to these texts,

> [...] it is evident that there is no permanent court; at most there is a permanent panel, from which a temporary tribunal can be constituted for each case as it arises. The American delegation to the Second Conference sought to make arbitration a judicial remedy by establishing a court truly permanent, composed of judges acting under a sense of judicial responsibility, representing the various languages and judicial systems of the world, and ready at all times to receive and to decide a case pursuant to the principles of law and justice. Accepting the declaration of the First Conference that arbitration is at once the most equitable and the most efficacious method of settling controversies, the American delegation endeavored by the establishment of a court to make it judicial.[226]

Elihu Root had already expressed a similar concept for a truly international court at the *National Arbitration and Peace Congress* in New York on April 15, 1907. At this occasion, he had declared the following:

> It has seemed to me that the great obstacle to the universal adoption of arbitration is not the unwillingness of civilized nations to submit their disputes to the decision of an impartial tribunal; it is rather an apprehension that the tribunal selected will not be impartial.
>
> [...] Arbitration too often acts diplomatically rather than judicially; they [the arbitrators] consider themselves as belonging to diplomacy rather than to jurisprudence; they measure their responsibility and their duty by the traditions, the sentiments, and the sense of honorable obligation which has grown up in the centuries of diplomatic intercourse, rather than by the traditions, the sentiments, and the sense of honorable obligation which characterizes the judicial department of civilized nations.

---

225 James Brown Scott (ed.), *American Addresses at the Second Hague Peace Conference* (World Peace Foundation 1916).

226 Ibid 77.

> [...] What we need for the further development of arbitration is the substitution of judicial action for diplomatic action, the substitution of judicial sense of responsibility for diplomatic sense of responsibility. We need for arbitrators not distinguished public men concerned in all the international questions of the day, but judges who will be interested only in the question appearing upon the record before them. Plainly this end is to be attained by the establishment of a court of permanent judges, who will have no other occupation and no other interest but the exercise of the judicial faculty under the same sanction of that high sense of responsibility which has made the courts of justice in the civilized nations of the world the exponents of all that is best and noblest in modern civilization.[227]

When Choate presented the U.S.-American proposal for the CAJ at the *Second Hague Peace Conference*, he commenced his speech by praising the successes of the first conference. In addition to that, he stressed that arbitration used to serve as a substitute for wars and that its role in settling international conflicts peacefully had advanced decisively over the last years.[228] According to Choate, especially the creation of the PCA had been a great step ahead. But it could not be ignored that the PCA had been an experiment – and that its creation had been closely linked with the hope that it would later serve as a basis for further advancement in the same direction.[229] In the light of the developments over the previous years, Choate then proposed to carry the work of the *First Hague Peace Conference* to its logical conclusion by extending the competences of the PCA, by adapting its structure, and by turning it into a truly permanent court.[230] With regards to one particular point, however, the U.S.-American government preferred to stick with the prevailing conception of the PCA. They wanted the CAJ to have a voluntary nature. Refraining from proposing the conclusion of any obligatory competences for the projected court must have appeared highly recommendable to the U.S.-American delegates at that time in order to secure reasonable chances of success for their project. The heated discussions regarding the introduction of a general treaty of obligatory arbitration, and the failure of finding a compromise on this

---

227 Quoted in: James Brown Scott (ed.), *The Proceedings of the Hague Conferences: The Conference of 1907*, vol. 2 (n 144 in Chapter 6) 316–317.

228 Ibid 313.

229 Ibid.

230 Compare pages 248 et seq. of the present book.

point[231] had proven that any step in this direction would have resulted in a quick end to the proposed court.

Nevertheless, the proposed CAJ was of a more than revolutionary nature. James Brown Scott emphasized the particularity of the proposal when he rose to deliver a speech right after Choate had finished his explanations. From the beginning of his address to its very end, Scott stressed the fact that the proposed court was supposed to be entirely judicial (despite still referring to it as a 'court of arbitration'). The CAJ was to be permanent, impartial, and composed of judges who were nominated for long-term tenures (instead of on an *ad-hoc* basis for individual cases). Furthermore, Scott declared that "[t]o decide as a judge, and according to law, it is evident that a court [...] should sit as a judicial, not as a diplomatic or political, tribunal."[232] By presenting the concept for the CPA with these detailed explanations on its judicial character, and by distinguishing clearly between judicial and arbitral procedures, it must be acknowledged – according to Hans Wehberg (*'The Problem of an International Court of Justice'* from 1918) – that it was

> [...] Scott's chief service to have been the first to lay down clearly at a great gathering of states that we have, on the one hand, international arbitration for the equitable settlement of disputes which the parties regard as strictly political in character, and that on the other hand, we have international judicial settlement for strictly legal decision of disputes regarded by the parties as legal in character.[233]

By presenting the concept for an international court of law at the *Second Hague Peace Conference*, Scott closed the gap between the academic thinkers and peace activists, who had already dealt with progressive approaches for such tribunals in the past, on the one hand, and the realm of international politics, on the other. The movement for an international and truly judicial court was very influential in the United States but still rather marginal in

231 Compare pages 270–277 of the present book.

232 James Brown Scott (ed.), *The Proceedings of the Hague Conferences: The Conference of 1907*, vol. 2 (n 144 in Chapter 6) 319.

233 Hans Wehberg, *The Problem of an International Court of Justice* (n 123 in Chapter 2) 41. See also: Robert C. Smith, 'The Need and Advantages of an International Court of Justice' in James Brown Scott (ed.) *Proceedings of the Third National Conference of the American Society for Judicial Settlement of International Disputes, December 20–21, 1912* (Williams & Wilkins Company 1913) 33; Walther Schücking, *The International Union of The Hague Conferences* (H. Milford 1918) 41, 95; Ralph D. Nurnberger, *James Brown Scott: Peace Through Justice* (n 1 in Chapter 5) 148–149.

Europe; wherefore most European countries must have entered unknown territory when they were confronted with the U.S.-American proposal. The *Plan for an International Tribunal*, proposed by the United States at the *First Hague Peace Conference*, had already had several characteristics in common with domestic courts (such as a truly permanent nature or impartial judges). Nevertheless, the initiative for the creation of the CAJ went considerably further than the U.S.-American plan from 1899. The CAJ was supposed to be a truly judicial court instead of an arbitral one. This was a great step ahead and constituted a fundamental conceptual difference. Consequently, Scott and Choate forced the other states to enter widely unknown and new territory by presenting this differentiation between legal and arbitral procedures and by bringing up the idea for a purely judicial international court.[234]

The concept for this permanent international court of law was laid down in the so-called *'Proposition of the Delegation of the United States of America'*, which was introduced to the discussions of the First Sub-Commission on August 1, 1907. The text provided a provisional draft code for the creation of such a tribunal and its preamble determined that the court was supposed to "[…] facilitate the immediate reference to judicial determination of international differences that cannot be settled through the diplomatic channel".[235] Furthermore, according to Article 1 of the proposition, the court was "[…] to consist of fifteen judges of the highest moral standing and of recognized competency in questions of international law. They and their successors […] shall be chosen from the different countries that the various systems of law and procedure and the principal languages shall be suitably represented."[236] The draft also determined that the judges of the court were to be nominated for a clearly defined tenure (Article 1), that the court had the competence to draw up its own regulations (Article 2), that it was to be composed of impartial and independent judges (Articles 2 and 3), and that it should have a voluntary nature; unless other bi- or multi-lateral treaty determined it to be any different and constituted an obligation to refer cases to it (Article 4).[237]

Following Choate's and Scott's speeches, the other members of the committee raised their voices. For example, von Bieberstein stated that "[…] the German Government considers the establishment of a permanent court of arbi-

234 Calvin DeArmond Davis, *The United States and the Second Hague Peace Conference* (n 28 in Chapter 1) 261.

235 James Brown Scott (ed.), *The Proceedings of the Hague Conferences: The Conference of 1907*, vol. 2 (n 144 in Chapter 6) 1015.

236 Ibid 1015–1016.

237 Ibid 1016.

tration as a real step in the line of progress."[238] Jost Dülffer (*'Regeln gegen den Krieg?'* from 1981) referred to von Bieberstein's instantly declared support for the project of a permanent international court as 'surprising'.[239] The German reaction stood in clear contrast to the one held at the *First Hague Peace Conference*. At this occasion in 1899, the Germans had fiercely rejected the idea to provide the PCA with any kind of permanency that went further than the creation of a mere list of potential arbitrators.[240] But Germany did not remain the only country which immediately rose to declare its support for the creation of an institution of the proposed nature. The British representative Edward Fry followed von Bieberstein's example and gave full support to the U.S.-American proposal.[241] Similar views were expressed by many of the other countries as well, at this and the following meeting;[242] for example, by the Bulgarian delegate Ivan Karandjouloff who declared that only "[...] an international jurisdiction and not the present armed peace [...] could prevent wars."[243] Others, such as the French representative Léon Bourgeois already thought about how to implement such a court of law in the existing international legal system. He held it to be the best solution to establish it side by side with the PCA. In this case, the main task of the PCA would have been to deal with controversies of a political nature, wherefore the parties' freedom to choose arbitrators should be preserved within its framework. According to him, "[...] no nation, big or small, will consent to go before a court of arbitration until it takes an active part in the appointment of the members composing it."[244] Regarding an international court of law dealing only with questions of a purely legal nature, on the other hand, Bourgeois asked whether everyone would not "[...] realize that a real court, composed of real justices, may be

238 Ibid 328.

239 Jost Dülffer, *Regeln gegen den Krieg?* (n 20 in Chapter 1) 308. Despite his surprise, Dülffer provided a possible explanation for the German position. According to him, merely tactical reasons had driven von Bieberstein to show goodwill and support for the project. Germany had already isolated themselves at the conference by uncompromisingly rejecting any attempt to create an obligatory arbitration agreement. They were keen not to worsen the situation even more; therefore, the German delegates supported this project (just as in the case of the international prize court).

240 Compare pages 166–169 of the present book.

241 James Brown Scott (ed.), *The Proceedings of the Hague Conferences: The Conference of 1907*, vol. 2 (n 144 in Chapter 6) 329.

242 Ibid 325–354.

243 Ibid 347.

244 Ibid 351.

considered as the most competent organ for deciding controversies of this character and for rendering decisions on pure questions of law?"[245]

Besides the European representatives, the Latin American delegates also expressed their general consent and support for the U.S.-American project. For example, the Mexican delegate Francisco L. de la Barra declared that his country "[…] will enthusiastically concur in any proposition whose object it is to give greater luster to the Permanent Court and to facilitate access thereto."[246] The Argentinian representative Carlos Rodriguez Larreta stated that "[…] the present resolution would indicate an important advance in the work accomplished by the First Conference"[247] and, furthermore, showed a lot of support for the proposed court. The delegates from Panama, Venezuela, and Uruguay expressed similar views as well,[248] and Mr. J.N. Léger, a delegate from Haiti, issued even a highly enthusiastic statement in favor of the proposed court by declaring that "[…] to-day it is possible to take another forward step and to consolidate, by perfecting it, an institution that the common conscience of the peoples demands more and more as one of the best guarantees of universal peace and fraternity."[249] Some of the other Latin American states made reservations or expressed doubts about the court project, especially against the proposed method for nominating its judges.[250] But when the members of the First Sub-Commission (of the First Commission) had to decide on August 3, 1907, whether they wanted to take the U.S.-American proposition into further consideration, all the Latin American states answered in the affirmative.[251] Only 12 (out of 44) states abstained from voting, whereas the rest of them endorsed the U.S.-American proposal. To provide a forum for further going discussions on this topic, the request was filed to establish another subcommittee exclusively dedicated to this purpose.[252] The request was satisfied wherefore the *Committee of Examination B* was created. It met eight times between August 13 and September 18, 1907.

The United States, Germany, and Great Britain played a crucial role in the first meeting of the new committee as they presented an adapted and more elaborated draft for the creation of a permanent international court of law at

245 Ibid.
246 Ibid 329.
247 Ibid 330.
248 Ibid 337–338, 341–342, 353.
249 Ibid 339.
250 Venezuela and Haiti did so for example; compare: ibid 339, 341.
251 Ibid 354.
252 Ibid 1015.

this occasion.[253] The new code provided in Article 1 for coexistence of the projected court of law and the PCA.[254] The implementation of this provision probably paid tribute to Bourgeois' above-cited declaration according to which the French delegation preferred two separate institutions. This step was presumably accompanied by the expectation that although states would have been free to choose between these two institutions, they would gradually begin to prefer adjudication over arbitration once both institutions had entered into force.[255] The only point that was considered controversial by the members of the committees with regards to Article 1 concerned the proposed name of the new court. The institution was referred to as "an International High Court of Justice"; but this term corresponded too much to the idea of a world federation or of a 'United States of the World.'[256] The states wanted to avoid the impression that the court was supposed to serve as some kind of world court of appeal (according to Louis Renault and Ruy Barbosa).[257] It was only during the subsequent (additional) drafting works and discussions that the term *Court of Arbitral Justice* was introduced.[258]

The subsequent articles of the draft did not result in any highly remarkable discussions. However, it should be noted that the Brazilian delegate Ruy Barbosa already wanted to comment on the method for nominating judges. Although the discussion on this topic was postponed to a later date, his interjection already provided a telling insight as to the importance that was later attached to it by the Latin American nations. Barbosa even considered the nomination procedure to be the key issue that would decide whether the court would be established in the end.[259] This notion was probably driven by the fact that the plan for how to nominate judges for the *International Prize Court* had only been published on the previous day.[260] This draft (for

253 Ibid 1019. Compare also: Jost Dülffer, *Regeln gegen den Krieg?* (n 20 in Chapter 1) 309.

254 James Brown Scott (ed.), *The Proceedings of the Hague Conferences: The Conference of 1907*, vol. 2 (n 144 in Chapter 6) 599.

255 Francis Anthony Boyle, *Foundations of World Order* (n 28 in Chapter 1) 39.

256 James Brown Scott (ed.), *The Proceedings of the Hague Conferences: The Conference of 1907*, vol. 2 (n 144 in Chapter 6) 599.

257 Ibid 599–600.

258 It would take until the Sixth Meeting of the Committee of Examination B (First Commission, First Sub-Commission) on September 2, 1907, that the term 'Court of Arbitral Justice' (respectively 'International Court of Arbitral Justice') was used for the first time. It was the Austrian delegate Heinrich Lammasch who proposed it and thereby introduced it as an alternative to the term 'International High Court of Justice.' Compare: ibid 659.

259 Ibid 603.

260 Ibid 817.

the IPC) caused severe concerns among the Latin American countries as they felt highly underrepresented in it. In the present meeting (of the *Committee of Examination B* on August 13, 1907), a similarly disadvantageous table was introduced as well for the CAJ[261] and the Latin American countries were – again – severely concerned about it. But Choate asked the members of the committee to "[…] reserve the consideration and determination of the question of judges until the end."[262] The United States, Germany, and Great Britain were well aware that this topic was highly contentious.[263] On this ground, James Brown Scott did his best to convince the other states of a solution, which he found most suitable. According to him, it follows from the principle of the equality of states that a correct system of international law did not differentiate between great and smaller states.[264] Furthermore, he noted that under ideal conditions and by paying the fullest respect to the principle of sovereign equality "[e]ach State – be it large or small, an empire of one hundred million or a republic of a few hundred thousand – should possess the right to appoint, and should actually appoint, a judge of its own choice for the full period contemplated by the Convention, namely twelve years."[265] However, should each country actually have the right to nominate one judge for the full period, this would lead to the problem that the court would comprise 46 judges.[266] In order to create a functional court, he preferred to reduce its bench to 15 or 17 judges.[267] This conclusion sounds logical and plausible at first glance. But it soon turned out to be a very difficult task to bring together the principle of legal equality and the wish for a small and functional court. Scott admitted that his solution for the problem was not perfect either, but he hoped that the states would accept it unless a better plan was found.

According his plan, the most feasible and fair method for the nomination of judges for the CAJ had to be"[…] based, in general, upon the principle of population, for we believe it self-evident that large aggregations of people have large interests, and that there is, in general, a relation between population on the one hand and industry and commerce on the other."[268] As it can be concluded from these words, it was a logical assumption for Scott that greater powers (states with greater populations, industry, and commerce) required

261 Ibid 1024–1025.
262 Ibid 596.
263 Ibid 609.
264 Ibid.
265 Ibid.
266 Ibid 609.
267 Ibid.
268 Ibid 610.

more extensive representation rights in the court than smaller nations. He reasoned this claim by declaring that the interests of greater states are usually more widespread and universal (than those of smaller nations).[269] In order to take this aspect into account in the composition of the court, he proposed not to push the principle of legal equality to its logical extreme but to take into consideration other points as well.[270] According to Scott, it was the best possible solution "[...] to assign to certain States a permanent representation in the court, and with due regard to populations, industry, commerce, system of law, and language, to permit each State representation for a longer or shorter period by system of rotation."[271] Hence, the proposed mode favored great powers and put smaller (particularly Latin American) ones to a systematic and obvious disadvantage (again).

At first glance, this proposal must appear as if its drafters – Germany, Great Britain, and the United States – intended to secure their status as dominant states and great powers in this way. Nevertheless, it should also be kept in mind that smaller states would potentially have been the major beneficiaries of the introduction of such a court. According to Francis Anthony Boyle, the smaller states "[...] would obtain greater protection from the [great powers] than otherwise would be the case, while a great power would receive no additional protection from other great powers by means of a world court alone."[272] In other words, the great powers would have had to voluntarily surrender parts of their dominant power-based positions (as the introduction of an international judiciary constituted, at least, a moral obligation to actually make use of it by referring disputes to the court for peaceful settlement instead of taking up arms). But unlike the smaller states, the introduction of the CAJ would not have resulted in any immediate advantages for the great powers (not even in their mutual relations). Consequently, the drafters of the proposal wanted to offer something in exchange to the great powers to win their support, namely preferential representation in the court. Furthermore, since smaller states would have gained so much from the establishment of this institution, Scott and his colleagues seem to have expected them to accept lesser representation rights in exchange for the sole creation of the CAJ (and, therefore, to agree to the non-compliance with the principle of legal sovereignty). Accordingly, Scott proposed to establish "[...] a perfect nucleus of the court; that each nation is, within the period chosen, represented within the court, and

269 Ibid 322.
270 Ibid 610.
271 Ibid.
272 Francis Anthony Boyle, *Foundations of World Order* (n 28 in Chapter 1) 44.

that each nation, in a larger or smaller degree, contributes to the judicial determination of the cases and to the development of international law."[273]

Just as in the case of the IPC, great powers were supposed – according to Scott's plan – to be entitled to full representation (by one judge and a deputy judge) for the entire period of tenure (of twelve years).[274] Furthermore, Spain, the Netherlands, and Turkey should have the right to nominate judges (and deputy judges) for ten years each, while the greater Latin American states were set on a level with most of the rest of the European (smaller) nations. Argentina, Brazil, Chile, and Mexico were only supposed to be entitled to nominate judges (and deputy judges) for four years each – just as (considerably smaller) nations such as Belgium, Norway, Denmark, or Portugal. China also fell into this category.[275] All the other countries were either restricted to terms of 2 or 1 year(s) of representation through their own judges (and deputy judges) in the new court.[276] In total, a court of 17 seats for judges with tenures of twelve years would have accounted for 204 one-year seats in the court over the entire period. According to the proposed list,

- the eight great powers would have occupied 96 of these seats (47%);
- the smaller European states (including Turkey) would have held 66 of them (32%);
- the Asian states (without Japan) would have had 10 seats (5%); and
- the Latin American states should hold 32 (15%).[277]

After the conclusion of the second meeting of the committee (at which Scott had held his speech on the advantages of the proposed mode for the rotation schedule for the judges of the new court), the discontented delegates gave up on the initially shown caution and restraint. For example, Ruy Barbosa expressed a great deal of anger about the systematic disadvantage of his and the other Latin American countries already in the afternoon of the same day (on August 17, 1907) in the context of the discussions on the IPC in the second sub-commission. At this occasion, he made it particularly clear that Brazil was

273 James Brown Scott (ed.), *The Proceedings of the Hague Conferences: The Conference of 1907*, vol. 2 (n 144 in Chapter 6) 611.

274 Ibid 611–612. Scott considered the following states as great powers: Germany, the United States, Austria-Hungary, France, Great Britain, Italy, Japan, and Russia.

275 Just as mentioned above in the context of the international prize court (compare pages 283–287 and *footnote 209* of the present chapter), Asia would have been highly underrepresented in the proposed mode too. According to it, Persia and Siam were entitled to nominate a judge and a deputy judge for 2 years each; China for 4 years (for both judges and deputy judges), and only Japan would have enjoyed full representation (12 years).

276 James Brown Scott (ed.), *The Proceedings of the Hague Conferences: The Conference of 1907*, vol. 2 (n 144 in Chapter 6) 612–613.

277 Ibid.

highly unsatisfied with the shape of the proposed rotation schedule.[278] Delegates from many Latin American countries followed him in his arguments and soon began to raise similar objections as well. The heated atmosphere in the context of the discussions on the creation of the IPC also affected the mood of the Latin American delegates in the upcoming meeting of the *Committee of Examination B* (on August 20, 1907). At this occasion, similar developments took place as in the context of the discussions on the IPC in the second subcommission.

After Barbosa had already clearly expressed his objections against the proposed system for the nomination of judges for the IPC, he did not intend to beat around the bush regarding the CAJ either. He immediately took the word after the opening of the session in order to refer to the rotation schedule as a "the proclamation of the inequality of national sovereignties."[279] Furthermore, he declared that Brazil rejected any proposal that did not fully comply with the principle of sovereign equality among all states.[280] He even preferred not to set up the court at all if it based on "[...] creating among States through a contractual stipulation categories of sovereignty that humiliate some to the profit of others, by sapping the bases of the existence of all, and by proclaiming with a strange lack of logic the legal predominance of might over right."[281] After this absolute statement, Barbosa returned to more moderated tones. He proposed to reform the existing PCA instead of setting up a second court alongside it. According to him, the PCA could be turned into a truly permanent institution and the adhering states could have the right to appoint a judge (and a deputy judge) each for the entire tenure of the court.[282] Barbosa's proposal provided for the parties of a dispute to be "[...] free to either to submit their controversy to the full court or to choose from the court [...] the number of judges that they agree upon."[283] Unlike the previously discussed proposal from Germany, Great Britain, and the United States, the Brazilian draft com-

---

278 Compare pages 283–287 of the present book.

279 James Brown Scott (ed.), *The Proceedings of the Hague Conferences: The Conference of 1907*, vol. 2 (n 144 in Chapter 6) 619.

280 Ibid. Furthermore, Barbosa also criticized the apparent imbalance in the proposed nomination system, which favored European countries and put the Latin American states on a systematic disadvantage. According to him (compare: ibid 620), the U.S.-American proposal "[...] scattered variously among the different States according to a scale of importance which has nothing to do with the subject and which, noticeably partial in favor of certain European countries, does not correspond to the obvious reality of the facts."

281 Ibid 620–621.

282 Ibid 622.

283 Ibid.

plied – according to Barbosa – with the principle of equality and did not sacrifice it for the benefit of the great powers.

In the following discussions, Barbosa was supported by the Romanian delegate whereas the representatives of the great powers either questioned the competence of the committee to deal with a new proposal (and thereby completely ignored Barbosa's proposition and his concerns) or defended the draft for the CAJ by invoking cursory arguments. For example, James Brown Scott answered Barbosa very curtly by stating that "[…] the project of the appointment of judges was established upon the principle of absolute equality and that this fact cannot be overlooked. As it was impossible to organize a court of forty-six judges, it was indeed necessary to resort to a system of rotation."[284] The attempt to palm him off with empty phrases and without seriously discussing his objections did not satisfy Barbosa at all. He rose again and extensively – and sometimes polemically – addressed the issue of equality of states. According to him, the proposed rotation mode for the CAJ satisfied, indeed, the principle of equality when it came to the sole right to nominate judges. Since all states were to be entitled to appoint a judge, all of them were equal in this point. But, according to Barbosa, with regards to the proposed nomination mode, smaller states would be treated absolutely unequally, which violates the principle of sovereign equality.[285] He reasoned this claim by referring to the differences between the proposed terms of service of the judges of the participating countries:

> There are men here who dare say that those condemned to receive only a more or less small fraction of the total period enjoy the same right as those to whom is given the privilege of the entire period. Spain with ten years of service, Mexico and Brazil with four, Serbia with two, Bolivia with only one, enjoy a right equal to that of Great Britain, Germany, or the United States with twelve years of service. Is there any sense to this?[286]

Despite his fierce criticism,[287] his rather undiplomatic diction, and the fact that he put his finger on a highly disputable point, Barbosa's objections con-

284 Ibid 625.

285 Ibid 628.

286 Ibid 627–628.

287 In the following (compare: ibid 645), Barbosa even added the following: "Under the preoccupation of removing war, we are tending to shake the most solid basis of peace by attacking that equality of right which was the last brake to the ambition and to the pride of the peoples. We would inject into their relations the basis of a justice whose

tinued to be widely ignored. The great powers did not care too much about complying with the Brazilian objections and ensured that the committee moved its attention quickly back to the study of the other articles of the draft code. The fact that Gonzalo A. Esteva, the Mexican representative in the committee, expressed his explicit support for Barbosa's position and that "[...] the Mexican delegation must not acquiesce in any convention in which all the States invited to the Peace Conference are not treated on the basis of the most absolute and most perfect equality", did not change anything either.[288] That being said, Mexico's decision to join ranks with Brazil and protest against the nomination procedure already foreshadowed the following events.

In following meetings of the *Committee of Examination B*, the great powers continued with the reading of the draft. At the seventh meeting, Choate even expressed the following view on the progress, on the work of the commission, and on its success with regards to the projected court:

> The committee has now reached a stage in its deliberations which marks a most important advance towards the creation of a permanent court of arbitration which shall satisfy the universal demand that presses upon us. We have decided with practical unanimity that there shall be such a court, and have adopted a constitution for its organization and powers with equal unanimity.[289]

He did mention in this speech that some countries were still upholding concerns against the project but the fact that he mainly spoke of 'practical unanimity' shows how little importance he attached to the critical, if not to say rejective, positions of the Brazilian and Mexican delegates. Instead of taking up their points of criticism and instead of trying to find a compromise, Choate praised the progressive character, so-far unique nature, and contribution of the CAJ to the further development of international law.[290] Indeed, the realization of the court project would have constituted an enormous step forward regarding the creation of an international judiciary, to the replacement of war

---

nature would be characterized by a judicial distinction of values between States, according to their greatness and their power. The Powers would then no longer be formidable only by the weight of their armies and their fleets. They would also have a superiority of right in the international magistracy, by arrogating unto themselves a privileged position in the institutions to which we pretend to entrust the meting out of justice to the nations."

288 Ibid 653.

289 Ibid 683.

290 Ibid 684.

with justice, and to the idea of *peace through law*. The court would have been a (widely) independent and autonomous institution of a purely judicial nature. Its judges would have been appointed for long-time tenures, been remunerated from a common budget, and decided cases (of a judiciable nature) based on law instead of arbitrariness. Although the court was supposed to be voluntary, its constitution would have resulted in the emergence of the first general purely judicial court of law on the international level. By settling cases in an exclusively judicial manner, the court could have contributed to the strengthening of the rule of law in international relations. Moreover, this institution had the potential to constitute an actual alternative to waging war by providing the option of judicial settlements of state-to-state conflicts. But, despite all these positive aspects and its potential for contributing to a considerable strengthening of international law, the sole fact that Choate and the other representatives of the great powers ignored the Latin American objections against the rotation system for the nomination of judges of the court so systematically, and for so long, resulted in the failure of the entire project.

The representatives of the great powers had shrugged off objections against the non-compliance with the principle of sovereign equality for almost the entire length of the negotiations in the *Committee of Examination B*. They simply kept claiming that the proposed nomination procedure would guarantee absolute and equal sovereignty of each of the participating states.[291] Only in the end of the negotiations were the great powers starting to look for alternative modes for the appointment of judges when they finally began to realize that Brazil was not alone in their opposition against the court project. Ruy Barbosa succeeded to unite the other Latin American states behind him on this particular point. Some of them had even already expressed their explicit opposition to any kind of non-compliance with the principle of sovereign equality in the context of the discussions about the creation of the IPC.[292] In one of his reports on the *Second Hague Peace Conference*, von Bieberstein noted in this regard that the Latin American countries were just about to follow Barbosa right on the heels in his harsh critiques of the proposed system.[293] However, it seems as if the great powers underestimated the willingness of the Latin American countries to fight for equal representation. They did not expect the Latin American delegates to be willing to risk the complete failure of the court. This could have been the case because the Latin Ameri-

291 Ibid.

292 Compare pages 283–287 of the present book.

293 Adolf Baron Marschall von Bieberstein, *Die Gruppierung der Staaten auf der Haager Konferenz* (n 141 in Chapter 6).

cans had caved in the end in the discussions on the IPC. But, as it turned out, they were not willing to do so again regarding the general international court of law. When the representatives of the great powers finally became aware of this fact, it was not only Choate who began to list a number of possible alternatives to the proposed rotation system.[294] Even an entire sub-committee was established before the last meeting of the *Committee of Examination B*. It was composed of the eight first delegates of Russia, France, the United States, Germany, Brazil, Austria-Hungary, Italy, and Great Britain. Due to the prominence and political importance of its members, the sub-committee can be regarded as an earnest attempt of the great powers to change Barbosa's mind and to win him over with regards to the project. They discussed another method for appointing judges for the projected court. Instead of granting every country the right to choose a qualified candidate for the court (and having the candidates' turns in office depend on a previously determined 'importance' of the nominating countries), the great powers proposed to elect the members of the court from a list of potential judges by all the adhering states to the PCA.[295] According to them, the problem concerning the non-compliance with the principle of sovereign equality would be off the table if all countries held the same voting rights in this procedure.

But Barbosa seems to have put an end to the discussions about the possible shape of these elections very quickly. According to him, "[a]nimated by a spirit of conciliation which it never forsakes [....], the Brazilian Government thought at one time that it might accept a compromise by accepting this [...] plan in order to succeed in constituting the projected court."[296] But this willingness to compromise did not seem to have prevailed for long in Brazil. The correctness of this claim becomes clear in his subsequent explanations. According to them, a clearly-shaped public opinion had arisen in Brazil, which strongly opposed the establishment of the projected court. It had manifested due to the hitherto shown attitude of the great powers, which had been completely uncompromising and relentless regarding the Brazilian objections and con-

---

294 James Brown Scott (ed.), *The Proceedings of the Hague Conferences: The Conference of 1907*, vol. 2 (n 144 in Chapter 6) 683–687. There, he referred, e.g., to the proposition to assign "[...] four judges [...] to America, as a unit, trusting to that cordial and friendly relation which exists [...] between the United States and all the other nations of Central and South America [...] to enable them to make a distribution among themselves of the four judges so assigned, in a manner that should be satisfactory to all."

295 According to the Russian delegate Aleksandr Nelidow, "[e]ach Government should nominate four candidates; the list thus established would be submitted to the members of the present court who would choose therefrom" the judges of the new court. Compare: ibid 690.

296 Ibid 691.

cerns.[297] Therefore, he declared that his government was convinced "[…] that the equality of the States through any means whatever apart from the system of real participation of all nations in the court, each with its own representative, can never be realized."[298] He further supported this statement by expressing the following:

> Election from among the subjects of one and the same State is the best means of selection; for the reason that it is the members of the same family who know each other best. An international election, of all methods of selection, is the most unreliable, for being entrusted to strangers, it is carried out precisely by those who are least acquainted with the eligible persons.[299]

The argument does not appear completely convincing especially if Barbosa's earlier proposal for a reform of the PCA is taken into consideration, which did not comply with this point either. But there is good reason to assume that the aspect of logic or comprehensibility no longer played a role. The negotiations had simply reached a deadlock. The great powers must have realized that they could not win the Latin American countries over for supporting their project anymore and that the CAJ, therefore, was in danger of failing. Consequently, they suddenly showed more openness for other ideas and even put up the

297 Benjamin Allen Coates, *Legalist Empire* (n 311 in Chapter 5) 92. Also: Adolf Baron Marschall von Bieberstein, *Die Gruppierung der Staaten auf der Haager Konferenz* (n 141 in Chapter 6).

298 James Brown Scott (ed.), *The Proceedings of the Hague Conferences: The Conference of 1907*, vol. 2 (n 144 in Chapter 6) 691–692. Barbosa's unforgiving and uncompromising position can also be traced back to the fact that he furiously opposed the idea of a true international judiciary. He was a supporter of the use of the instrument of arbitration; wherefore he also declared that "[…] there is, juridically speaking, a difference between judicial magistracy and arbitral magistracy. […] The juridical form of justice is permanent and inalterable. It is the law that established it. With regard to arbitration, the juridical form is variable and casual. It is the agreement between the parties which decides that form. Justice emanates from sovereignty and imposes itself upon obedience. Its organs are created by power. The parties must submit to it. Arbitration, on the contrary, has its source in liberty. It is the work of a convention; it has no other authority except that admitted by the contractants, and its magistrates are those voluntarily chosen. This is the reason why the judicial form of justice it that which is preferable in regard to the relations between individuals, and why the arbitral form is the only one applicable between the nations. The latter submit only to the authorities that they have constituted among themselves. To substitute justice in the place of arbitration would, so far as they are concerned, be to replace voluntary consent with constraint." Source: ibid 661 (see also: 692).

299 Ibid 692.

mentioned sub-committee to appease Barbosa. But while the great powers had egoistically – and, as it seems, inconsiderately – pursued their goals during the earlier discussions, insurmountable divides had emerged between them and the Latin American countries. The latter states felt strongly affronted because of the proposed rotation system, the arrogant attitude towards Barbosa's objections, and the fact that they had been supposed to be put at a systematic disadvantage. Hence, public opinion probably not only turned in Brazil against the idea for a permanent international court of law but due to the course of the negotiations in The Hague, it appears to be likely that similar developments took place in other Latin American countries as well.

In The Hague, the Latin American delegates proved that they were determined not to give in concerning their claim for equal representation and to submit their interests to the wishes of the great powers for a second time (as they had already done so in the case of the IPC).[300] Against the initial expectations of several European participants, the Latin American countries had not come to The Hague to play the role of mere supporters and providers of votes for the United States.[301] Instead, they felt the time to be ripe to stand their ground and decided to do so in the context of the question on equal representation in the framework of the proposed CAJ.

On the last meeting of the *Committee of Examination B* (on September 18, 1907), its members took a decision about the adoption of the code for the establishment of the CAJ. Articles 6, 7, and 8 – which concerned the nomination procedure of its judges – were, however, spared out from the voting because a final compromise had not been reached in this regard. In the end, only 8 out of the 15 members of the committee voted for the creation of the projected court. Among them there were all the Western great powers except Austria-Hungary which abstained from voting, as did Luxemburg.[302] Greece, Peru, Brazil, Romania, and Belgium, on the other hand, voted against its realization. Therefore, the committee of examination adopted the draft with the

---

300 Compare pages 283–287 of the present book.

301 Adolf Baron Marschall von Bieberstein, *Die Gruppierung der Staaten auf der Haager Konferenz* (n 141 in Chapter 6). In this report, he expressed his honest surprise about the behavior of the Latin American countries in The Hague. He had expected them to promptly comply with any request and demand of the United States, but he had to admit that his assumption – which, according to him, he had shared with all the representatives of the European great powers – was false. The Latin American countries did not only do what the United States wanted them to, but they also pursued their individual policies – even against the explicit will of the United States.

302 The Netherlands, Germany, Great Britain, the United States, Italy, Portugal, Russia, and France voted in favor of the project. Compare: James Brown Scott (ed.), *The Proceedings of the Hague Conferences: The Conference of 1907*, vol. 2 (n 144 in Chapter 6) 705.

narrowest majority possible. It then forwarded the code for discussions to the First Commission and recommended also the adoption of the following resolution (the so-called *'Vœu voted by the Commission'*): "The Conference recommends to the signatory Powers the adoption of the project it has voted for the creation of a Court of Arbitral Justice, and putting it into force as soon as an agreement has been reached respecting the selection of the judges and constitution of the Court."[303]

The fierce discussions and unbridgeable differences concerning the proposed method for the nomination of the judges of the CAJ resulted, therefore, in a failure of coming to terms for a complete code for a (general) permanent international court of law. Instead, the members of the committee decided to only submit the less controversial articles to the voting by the First Commission and to spare points concerning the nomination procedure of judges (Articles 6, 7, and 8). Hence, the submitted draft was rather a declaration of intent. It promoted the realization of the project, but it did not provide functional regulations for all relevant aspects. Due to the mentioned differences, the delegates had to choose this way and could only add the *'vœu'* to the submitted draft in order to keep the court project alive and to provide a perspective for its future realization. In this regard, von Bieberstein declared that "[i]n the present conditions of our labors, we are not at all in position to adopt this project, because it is incomplete. How then could we recommend its adoption to the Governments? We must confine ourselves to expressing the hope that a solution will be found."[304] Apparently, most of the members of the committee of examination shared this view. Therefore, they soon agreed that issuing this *'vœu'* was the best suitable way of dealing with the project and all its differences and complications. In the end, it was recommended to the First Commission "[…] to include the project for a court of arbitral justice into the final act by *subordinating* its putting into force to the organization of the recruiting of judges."[305]

After the *Committee of Examination B* had concluded its work, the dealing with the topic of the establishment of the proposed CAJ rested until October 9, 1907. It was only then, and on the subsequent meeting on October 10, 1907, that the First Commission finally addressed it before the entire conference. At these two meetings, another discussion took place about the creation of the CAJ. The Romanian representative Alexandru Beldimann stood out on these occasions because he did not withhold his criticism against the behavior of the

303 Ibid 1050.

304 Ibid 702.

305 Ibid 703.

great powers in the committee of examination regarding the nomination procedure for the judges of the court. According to him, they "[…] have not even dared to face within the Commission a discussion of the various solutions that had been suggested."[306] Furthermore, he considered the court project having failed entirely and regarded the conclusion of the *'vœu'* as the burial of the project for an international permanent court of law.[307] Other countries – particularly the Latin American states – persisted in their critical approaches towards the project as well. They were, however, less absolute than Beldimann and did not generally reject the idea of such a court. Instead, they insisted primarily on what they claimed to be the project's major defect – the non-compliance with the principle of sovereign equality – and rejected it due to this reason.

Ruy Barbosa had already led the opposition against the court project in the committee and had, thereby, exasperated the Western great powers. He did not fail to criticize the project once more before the First Commission. Barbosa was among the first to speak on October 9, 1907, repeating his former points of critique on the projected court,[308] and, thereby, set the agenda for the other Latin American delegations. They followed him in his approach and also justified their rejection of the proposed CAJ in the same way. The representative of Chile, Augusto Matte, declared that his delegation generally supported the idea to establish an international court of law, but it could not agree to the proposed draft because it did not comply with the principle of sovereign equality.[309] Francisco Henriquez i Carvajal[310] (representative of the Dominican Republic), José Gil Fortoul (head of the Venezuelan delegation), and Pierre Hudicourt (delegate of Haiti) held very similar views. Hudicourt even declared that he had "[…] the honor to reiterate the acceptance of the principle of the institution of a permanent court of arbitral justice, upon the express and formal condition that the constitution of this court rest on the absolute principle of the juridical equality of the States."[311] The Venezuelan representative Fortoul stated that he "[…] will vote for the *vœu* of the British delegation, provided it is understood that in the constitution of the Court of

306 Ibid 179.

307 Ibid 180.

308 Ibid 147–156.

309 Ibid 180–182.

310 According to Francisco Henriquez i Carvajal, "[s]till while voting in favor of the convention project for the establishment of an international Court of Arbitral Justice the delegation from the Dominican Republic cannot accept the plans hitherto proposed for the composition and choice of the judges of the said court." Compare: ibid 146.

311 Ibid 182–183.

Arbitral Justice and in the selection of the judges the principle of the juridical equality of the State will, at all events, be expressly recognized."[312] The other Latin American delegates issued similar declarations as well[313] and, thereby, rejected the realization of the CAJ in the proposed form. In the light of this constellation, the decision to submit only a truncated, i.e., incomplete, version of the draft in conjunction with the *'vœu'* to the voting of the First Commission must have appeared to be the wisest solution. Otherwise, the Latin American countries would have jointly rejected the creation of the CJA straight away. Because 18 out of the 44 participating countries at the *Second Hague Peace Conference* were from Latin America (which accounts for around 40%), their combined disagreement would have had a serious impact and could not simply have been considered as to be of minor or insignificant importance. Instead, it would have brought the court project to an end (at least temporarily). In effect, the only way to keep the project alive was the *'vœu.'* It offered the possibility to conclude the conference with a positive message regarding the establishment of a (general) international permanent court of law and kept options open for its realization in the future; although the discussions about this topic had reached a dead-end in The Hague and no compromise could be found to overcome it.

In the end, the dispute over the nomination procedure for the judges of the proposed court, the insistence of the Latin American countries on the compliance with the principle of full equality of all states, and the non-willingness of the great powers to take the Latin American concerns into consideration resulted in the failure of the project of a permanent international court of law. Its establishment would have marked a great step forward for the cause of *peace through law*, the establishment of the rule of law on the international level, and for the juridification of international relations. However, the Latin American states were not willing to give in a second time and to step back regarding their demand for full equality (as they had already done it in the case of the IPC). The great powers had only realized that the Latin American resistance was so fierce and inescapable that it would cause a failure of the entire court project when it was already too late. At this point, they could not

312 Ibid 189.

313 Compare the statements of José Batlle y Ordoñez (a delegate for Uruguay; ibid 156–158), José Tible Machado (Guatemala; compare: ibid 158–161), Gonzalo A. Esteva (Mexico; compare: James Brown Scott (ed.), *The Proceedings of the Hague Conferences: The Conference of 1907*, vol. 1 (n 129 in Chapter 6) 327), Santiago Perez Triana (El Salvador and Colombia; compare: ibid), Eusebi Machain (Paraguay, compare: ibid 328), Belisario Porras (Panama; compare: ibid), Enrique Dorn y de Alsiia (Ecuador; compare: ibid), Claudio Pinilla (Bolivia; compare: ibid), or Crisanto Medina (Nicaragua; compare: ibid).

do a thing anymore to change the opinion of the Latin American delegates in favor of the project. Even the proposition of another nomination method – by general election of all the adhering states of the *Hague Convention* (and while abandoning the proposed nomination mode on base of national quotas) – could not hold up matters anymore either.[314] The fronts had hardened, public opinion in Latin America had turned against the project, and the differences were already too insurmountable to be overcome.

Secretary of State Elihu Root had warned his delegation in an internal paper against granting preference to European countries and to the great powers over the interests of the Latin American nations. According to him,

> [t]he enumeration of European powers without regard to the population and including Spain seems to assume superiority over non-European powers which would be very distasteful to South America. We must not on any account sacrifice our position of asserting the national equality of American States with the other powers of the earth. It is far more important to us than the whole court scheme.[315]

In order not to risk all the achievements that Root had made during his trip through Latin America regarding the improvement of U.S.-American relations with the countries from this region, he ordered his delegates to abstain from enforcing the realization of the CAJ against the explicit will of the Latin American states. Therefore, he gave preference to the maintenance of good relations with Latin America and for the preservation of the unique position of the United States as the leader and advocate of the Western hemisphere; and he ranked these points even higher than the court project. The proposed plan and its non-compliance with the principle of full equality had – probably – already damaged the U.S.-American reputation in Latin America and Root was not willing to risk falling back to relations marked by distrust and suspicion.

Consequently, the above-mentioned reasons prevented the CAJ from being created at the *Second Hague Peace Conference*. Hence, the participating states missed a great opportunity to substantially change the international system. Since the overwhelming majority of states had agreed – at least in general – on

314 Compare: James Brown Scott (ed.), *The Proceedings of the Hague Conferences: The Conference of 1907*, vol. 2 (n 144 in Chapter 6) 694 et seq.

315 Quoted in: Calvin DeArmond Davis, *The United States and the Second Hague Peace Conference* (n 28 in Chapter 1) 266.

the creation of such a court in the beginning of the conference,[316] there seems to have existed an actual chance to achieve this goal. However, the states' unwillingness to compromise and to aim for a solution suitable to all the parties involved prevented it from happening. Apart from a sole *'vœu'* in favor of this project, the states left The Hague empty-handed when it comes to the establishment of a (general) permanent international court of law.[317]

2.5 *The Porter Doctrine*

The last point of the *Second Hague Peace Conference*, which is important in the context of the present analysis concerns the so-called *Porter Doctrine*. The *Drago Doctrine* postulated the prohibition of armed interventions against American countries or the occupation of their territories for the recovery of private contract debts by non-American powers (in the name of their nationals).[318] At the *Third Pan-American Conference* in Rio de Janeiro in 1906, Elihu Root had expressed the hope that the *Drago Doctrine* would be universally recognized in the future and had declared the United States' open support for this principle.[319] According to Lars Schoultz (*'Beneath the United States'* from 1998), the Latin American states regarded the support of the U.S.-American Secretary of State for turning the provision into a universally applicable principle as part of a trade-off between them and the United States; he stated the following in this regard: "The willingness of 'developed' South Americans to accept U.S. hegemony in the Caribbean was encouraged by Root's proposal that the Drago Doctrine – a Latin American initiative – be placed on the agenda of the upcoming second Hague Conference."[320] But, while the Latin American states seem to have expected full support of the United States for the implementation of the *Drago Doctrine* into international law at the *Second Hague Peace Conference*, Root ordered his delegation to pursue a modified policy at this occasion. In accordance with Root's instructions, General Horace Porter, a member of the U.S.-American delegation, proposed the adoption of a provision

316 In the end, 36 countries voted in favor of the adoption of the *'vœu'* and only 6 countries abstained from voting. Compare: James Brown Scott (ed.), *The Proceedings of the Hague Conferences: The Conference of 1907*, vol. 1 (n 129 in Chapter 6) 328–329.

317 However, the states in The Hague could at least agree on the establishment of the International Prize Court. Compare pages 286–287 of the present book.

318 Antônio Augusto Cançado Trindade, 'The Presence and Participation of Latin America at the Second Hague Peace Conference of 1907' in Yves Daudet, *Actualité de la Conférence de La Haye de 1907, deuxième Conférence de la paix: colloque, La Haye, 6–7 septembre 2007* (Nijhoff 2008) 56. Also: Edward McWhinney, *The International Court of Justice and the Western Tradition of International Law* (n 118 in Chapter 4) 10.

319 Compare pages 245–246 of the present book.

320 Lars Schoultz, *Beneath the United States* (n 19 in Chapter 4) 195.

at the conference according to which – under certain conditions – wars would have been prohibited if the underlying conflicts had had purely pecuniary origins.[321] According to the U.S.-American proposal (in the version of September 3, 1907), the following should be concluded:

> In order to prevent armed conflicts between nations of a purely pecuniary origin growing out of contract debts claimed from the Government of one country by the Government of another country as due to its nationals, the signatory Powers agree not to resort to armed force for the collection of such contract debts.[322]

The limitation of the use of force in pecuniary cases was supposed to stand under the condition that "[t]his stipulation, however, shall not apply when the debtor State rejects or ignores a proposal of arbitration, or, in the case of acceptance, makes it impossible to establish the *compromis*, or after arbitration, fails to comply with the award."[323] In other words, the United States intended to establish a prohibition of the use of force for the collection of debts for cases in which the debtor state agreed to arbitration and complied with the award filed by an arbitral court. Otherwise, if the debtor state rejected the request for arbitration, or it did not comply with the award, the creditor state would still have been entitled to use force to employ the pecuniary claims.[324] Root made sure that this condition was implemented to keep the option of intervening in states, which were openly and persistently refusing to pay their debts.[325] Furthermore, Root also had to keep in mind his president's view on the issue since Roosevelt did not support yet an unequivocal prohibition of the use of force.[326]

In one of his speeches delivered in support of the conclusion of such a doctrine (on July 16, 1907), General Porter criticized the established practice of

---

321 James Brown Scott (ed.), *The Proceedings of the Hague Conferences: The Conference of 1907*, vol. 2 (n 144 in Chapter 6) 555. The U.S.-American delegation had already introduced two proposals for the conclusion of such a limitation of the use of force to the discussions of the First Sub-Commission at The Hague before (on July 2, 1907, compare: ibid 214, 906; and at July 16, 1907, compare: ibid 226). But these drafts attracted lots of criticism wherefore they were reworked several times before being re-introduced to discussions on September 3, 1907.

322 Ibid 913.

323 Ibid.

324 Mark C. Weidmaier, 'Contracting for State Intervention: The Origins of Sovereign Debt Arbitration' (2010) 73, no. 4 Law and Contemporary Problems 340.

325 Lars Schoultz, *Beneath the United States* (n 19 in Chapter 4) 195.

326 Ibid.

Western private creditors to appeal to the foreign offices of their home countries whenever they felt mistreated by (in many cases Latin American) debtor states. In these cases, the foreign offices often responded by putting political pressure on the debtor states, by threatening them with the use of force, or even by applying force to collect the debts for the private creditors. Porter considered this system as unfair and unjudicial because there was "[…] no jury to ascertain the facts, no competent and impartial court to guide it as to the law, no tribunal to promote upon the equity of the claim."[327] Instead of settling the case on the basis of law and by taking into consideration the rights of both parties, the decisive factor in such cases was the power of the creditors' home countries and the willingness of their governments to help their nationals.

Porter supported Calvo and Drago in their demand for abstaining from invoking force for the settlement of this type of conflict. But, unlike Calvo who had aimed for subjecting these demands to the national jurisdictions of the creditor states, Porter wanted to introduce the duty to refer the conflict to arbitration. Therefore, the draft resembled the obligatory arbitration treaty from the *Second Pan-American Conference* in Mexico City (1901/02). At this occasion, an agreement had been concluded, which prohibited the use of force for the collection of pecuniary claims among the adhering states. But, while the treaty from Mexico City applied without any further conditions or restrictions (except the necessity that the underlying claims were important enough to justify the costs of an arbitration),[328] the one proposed in The Hague was conditional. Recourse to force was still allowed for the collection of private pecuniary claims under the above-stated conditions. Therefore, the *Porter Doctrine* aimed at limiting the states' *ius ad bellum,* but it did not attempt to go as far as Calvo's or Drago's propositions or as the treaty concluded at the *Second Pan-American Conference.*

In the discussions in The Hague, the Latin American states did not fail to stress the importance of the implementation of a provision for the limitation of the practice of collecting private debts by force. For example, Francisco L. de la Barra, a Mexican delegate, declared that "[…] the fact that a State may not interfere in the affairs of another State, unless it be in exceptional circumstances determined by international law, is a natural consequence of the prin-

327 James Brown Scott (ed.), *The Proceedings of the Hague Conferences: The Conference of 1907*, vol. 2 (n 144 in Chapter 6) 227.

328 'Treaty of Arbitration for Pecuniary Claims', accessible in James Brown Scott (ed.), *The International Conferences of American States 1889–1928* (n 1 in Chapter 4) 104.

ciple of the sovereignty and independence of the States."[329] But they remained one of the few Latin American countries to support the U.S.-American initiative.[330] Most of the other Latin American delegates criticized the U.S.-American proposal as insufficient and aimed for introducing amendments in order to give it a more absolute character. The Argentinian delegation argued – in person of Luis Drago – for a non-conditional prohibition of force with regards to the collection of pecuniary claims and the delegations of Venezuela, the Dominican Republic,[331] Chile,[332] Colombia, and several other Latin American states issued similar requests as well.[333] They concurred in their demand for a prohibition of the use of force in this regard and for the introduction of an unrestricted arbitration obligation for this type of conflict. Drago reasoned the position of his government by declaring that "[...] in accepting this part of the proposition of the United States which appeals to force in order to carry out arbitration decisions that have been disregarded, we would be taking a great step backwards."[334] Instead, the Latin American nations strove for a treaty similar to the one on the collection of pecuniary claims from Mexico City, or even for the full implementation of the *Drago Doctrine*.

Elihu Root criticized the position of the Latin American countries because he thought that they did not show the slightest bit of willingness to compromise and depart from their absolute demands.[335] By upholding this attitude, he was convinced that they risked the entire project and ran the danger of leaving the conference empty-handed. It was only in later discussions on this topic that the Latin American states, in fact, seem to have realized this point and to have adapted their position, at least slightly. Antônio Augusto Cançado Trindade (*'The Presence and Participation of Latin America at the Second Hague Peace Conference of 1907'* from 2008), explicitly referred to this process of rethinking the positions among the Latin American delegations. He took the Argentinian delegation as an example and argued that Luis Drago and his

329 James Brown Scott (ed.), *The Proceedings of the Hague Conferences: The Conference of 1907*, vol. 2 (n 144 in Chapter 6) 240.

330 For example, the delegation of Panama did so too by referring to the U.S.-American proposal as "[...] the one which approaches nearest to the ideal." Compare: ibid 244.

331 Ibid 908, 910–912 (Annexes 51, 57).

332 Ibid 908 (Annex 52).

333 According to an internal report of the Colombian delegation, identical arguments were invoked by the representatives of Chile, Argentina, Peru, Bolivia, Guatemala, El Salvador, Mexico, etc. Compare: Jorge Holguín (ed.) *La Delegación Colombiana, Segunda Conferencia internacional de la Haya* (Imprenta Nacional 1908) 29.

334 James Brown Scott (ed.), *The Proceedings of the Hague Conferences: The Conference of 1907*, vol. 2 (n 144 in Chapter 6) 250.

335 Lars Schoultz, *Beneath the United States* (n 19 in Chapter 4) 195.

colleagues had initially regarded the original U.S.-American proposal as to stand in a clear contradiction to their own position.[336] It was only because of further adjustments of the U.S.-American proposal and – presumably – because of the insight that a strict refusal of the U.S.-American proposal would not lead to any results at all, that the Argentinian delegation decided to vote in favor of this initiative. However, Luis Drago and his colleagues decided to invoke certain reservations at the same time. Hence, they declared the following when it came to the final voting on the adoption of the *Convention concerning the Limitation of the Employment of Force for the Recovery of Public Contract Debts* in the plenary meeting of the First Commission on October 16, 1907:

> 1. "With regard to debts arising from ordinary contracts between the *ressortissani* of a nation and a foreign Government, recourse shall not be had to arbitration except in the specific case of denial of justice by the courts of the country which made the contract, the remedies before which courts must first have been exhausted.
> 2. Public loans, secured by bond issues and constituting the national debt, shall in no case give rise to military aggression or the material occupation of the soil of American nations."[337]

Many other Latin American states made the same – or very similar[338] – reservations; for example, the Dominican Republic, Paraguay, Nicaragua, Guatemala, Ecuador, and Uruguay. In the end, the convention was adopted with 39 votes in its favor and 5 abstentions.[339] But even though the numbers seem to constitute evidence for a general acceptance of this doctrine in The Hague, this impression is highly deceptive. It might appear as if there had been a broad, almost unanimous, consensus on the limitation of the use of force for the collection of private contract debts in the proposed way. But, due to the numerous Latin American reservations, the convention did not consti-

336 Antônio Augusto Cançado Trindade, 'The Presence and Participation of Latin America at the Second Hague Peace Conference of 1907' (n 318 in Chapter 6) 57–58.

337 James Brown Scott (ed.), *The Proceedings of the Hague Conferences: The Conference of 1907*, vol. 1 (n 129 in Chapter 6) 330–331.

338 For example, the delegation of Peru declared the following (whereby she seems to have aimed for preserving the applicability of the *Calvo Clauses*): "That the principles established in this proposition cannot be applied to claims or controversies arising out of contracts made by the Government of a country with foreign subjects, when in these contracts it is expressly stipulated that these claims or controversies should be submitted to the judges of the tribunals of the country." Compare: ibid 331.

339 Ibid 332.

tute a uniform system. Instead, the Western countries concluded the actual text of the convention without any (far-going) reservations. Therefore, they secured themselves the right in the context of private pecuniary claims to intervene militarily in the debtor states if the governments of the debtor states had refused the request for arbitration, or if they had not complied with an arbitral award. However, at the same time, the Latin American countries aimed for upholding the practice of the *Calvo Clauses* (according to which creditors had to refer to national courts before taking recourse to arbitration), for realizing the *Drago Doctrine*, and for implementing a complete prohibition of the use of force for the collection of debts.

By including corresponding reservations, a very heterogeneous set up was created. Although *ius ad bellum* was – in theory – successfully limited by the conclusion of the *Convention concerning the Limitation of the Employment of Force for the Recovery of Public Contract Debts*, it did not result into a common framework for dealing with this type of conflict in practice in a coherent manner. Since several Latin American countries demanded that national remedies first had to be exhausted before arbitration could be requested, this arrangement bore a lot of potential for further conflicts and for making the *Porter Doctrine* obsolete in state practice. This was the case because if any Western creditor state had requested an arbitration of a dispute of a private pecuniary nature, and if the Latin American countries responded by referring to their reservations, there would have been a situation in which the Latin American state would have practically rejected the arbitration. Thus, the Western states would have been entitled – at least according to their interpretation of the convention – to pursue the claims of their nationals by force. This dilemma substantially reduced the applicability of the convention in state practice and basically led it *ad absurdum*.

Nevertheless, the convention can still be considered as a first step towards the limitation of *ius ad bellum* by law. The Western powers agreed – for the first time – to a reduction of their right to wage war. Furthermore, they accepted a multi-lateral and universal obligation agreement, which ordered them to take recourse to arbitration instead of using force for the settlement of conflicts; which was an achievement that they had failed to make in the context of the conclusion of a general obligatory arbitration treaty. Therefore, the *Convention concerning the Limitation of the Employment of Force for the Recovery of Public Contract Debts* provided for a true novelty in the history of international law,[340] despite the Latin American reservations and the resulting

340 As mentioned above, multi-lateral obligations to arbitrate certain types of conflicts had already existed before; for example, in the context of the *Universal Postal Union* (com-

incoherent understanding of the *Porter Doctrine* thereof in different world regions.

2.6 *The Results of the Second Hague Peace Conference*

In some respects, the *Second Hague Peace Conference* was nothing but a complete success and definitely a highly remarkable event in history. It was the first global conference in which 44 states participated, which accounted for almost all recognized countries at this point. It was also the first time that Latin American countries participated in such an event in greater numbers. Furthermore, the invitation of the Latin American nations also marked a milestone in their development towards their full recognition as sovereign equals and independent countries.

Regarding other topics, however, the conference achieved mixed results. The German Empire once more successfully prevented any progress with regards to obligatory arbitration and, thereby, frustrated most of the other participants. Germany had already done so at the *First Hague Peace Conference*. However, the wave of conclusions of bi-lateral obligatory arbitration treaties between 1903 and 1905 had left most states with the impression that obligatory arbitration had finally become a universally accepted principle, especially since Germany had participated in this development too. One of the primary expectations for the *Second Hague Peace Conference* had, therefore, been that the event would result in the conclusion of a universal multilateral (special) obligatory arbitration treaty. Hence, the German opposition was a great shock for the other delegations. It left them bewildered, startled, and disappointed. Furthermore, the German rejection could not simply be outvoted because of the country's status as a great power, and it turned out to be impossible to change the mind of the German government in this regard. Although the majority of states declared their support and dedication to obligatory arbitration at the *Second Hague Peace Conference*, no progress could be achieved in relation to this topic.

As for the *International Prize Court* and the *Court of Arbitral Justice*, the advocates of these two court projects struggled with similar problems as the ones for an obligatory arbitration treaty. Surprisingly, however, Germany did not play the role of their major opponent. Instead, the German delegates were

---

pare pages 95–97 of the present book). But these obligations only concerned limited topics of (usually) secondary importance. The chance for them to escalate into actual wars was very low. On the other hand, the forceful collection of private contract debts by the home countries of the creditors had been an actual problem in the 19th and early 20th century, which had caused numerous armed conflicts and interventions (mostly in Latin America).

even among their most enthusiastic supporters (a fact which stood in complete contrast to the German policy at the first conference).[341] What is exceptional with regards to these initiatives is certainly the fact that they both aimed for the creation of permanent international courts of law. During the discussions on these projects, similar problems occurred concerning the proposed methods for appointing judges. In the case of the IPC, the Latin American countries criticized but – in the end – accepted a solution that was based on national quotas. However, regarding the CAJ they were not willing to do the same (again). They upheld an uncompromising approach because they were convinced that the proposed method for appointing judges for the CAJ contravened the principle of full equality of states. Since the Latin American states felt that they had been put at a systematic disadvantage, they declared to reject this project if this system was upheld. During most of the negotiations on the CAJ, the Western countries did not show any interest in compromising on this point. They only began to change their attitude and attempted to find a common solution (also suitable to the Latin American states) when the positions had already hardened and when the differences were no longer bridgeable. Hence, this change of mind came too late to prevent the project from failing. In the end, the participating states did not conclude more than a '*vœu*' at the *Second Hague Peace Conference* in which they expressed their general favor for the future realization of the CAJ (once a generally acceptable solution was found for the nomination of judges). On the other hand, however, they agreed to establish the IPC. The court was to be brought into existence soon after the end of the conference. According to Article 10 of the *Convention relative to the Creation of an International Prize Court*, its judges (and the deputy judges) were to be appointed "[…] within six months after the ratification of the present Convention".[342]

Finally, the efforts made regarding the conclusion of a multi-lateral treaty for the limitation of the use of force for the collection of private pecuniary claims also only led to mixed results. On the one hand, the participating states concluded a multi-lateral treaty, which banned the use of force in the context of such cases. But, on the other hand, it did so only under the condition that the debtor states did not refuse requests to arbitrate such disputes and that they did not ignore arbitral awards. Otherwise, the home countries of the private creditors were still entitled to employ claims by force. Furthermore, it should be noted that the Latin American states made numerous reserva-

341 Compare pages 166–170 of the present book.

342 James Brown Scott (ed.), *The Proceedings of the Hague Conferences: The Conference of 1907*, vol. 1 (n 129 in Chapter 6) 662.

tions, which aimed for granting themselves further going rights, for constituting a full prohibition of the use of force in this type of conflicts, and for setting up the requirement to exhaust national remedies before turning to international arbitration was to be allowed. Therefore, no uniform framework was established through the conclusion of the *Convention concerning the Limitation of the Employment of Force for the Recovery of Public Contract Debts*. Instead, different interpretations and understandings of the legal situation prevailed in the context of these questions in the North Atlantic world and in Latin America. This led the convention (at least to a certain extent) *ad absurdum*. However, its conclusion can still be considered a success for the peace movement and for the cause of *peace through law* because it constituted the first actual limitation of the *ius ad bellum* (through a universal multilateral treaty).

Taking all of these points into consideration, it could appear – at least at first glance – that the *Second Hague Peace Conference* was rather a failure than a success; and that the peace movement must have been furious to condemn the states for not having achieved further going results. In fact, hardly any of the expected outcomes had been achieved and only little progress was made with regards to the topic of *peace through law*. However, another *'vœu'* also concluded at The Hague turned the press coverage and the views of the conference observers (and of its participants) in its favor again (to a certain extent at least). According to this *'vœu,'* the conference recommended "[...] to the Powers the assembly of a Third Peace Conference, which might be held within a period corresponding to that which has elapsed since the preceding Conference."[343] The *'vœu'* was proposed by the delegates of the United States and all participating states immediately expressed their support for a *Third Hague Peace Conference* in a series of very favorable statements, adopting the proposition unanimously.[344] Consequently, a third conference was to be envisaged for 1915 and, according to James Brown Scott (*'Should there be a Third Hague Peace Conference?'* from 1925), "[...] the governments were to take charge of the conference and its preparation, instead of Russia, in the future; a form of organization and procedure for the conference was to be devised as for a permanent institution, and a committee of the Powers, meeting some two years in advance of the conference, was to determine its program."[345] In the follow-

343 Ibid 226.

344 Ibid 172.

345 James Brown Scott, 'Should there be a Third Hague Peace Conference?' (1925) 87, no. 1 Advocate of Peace through Justice 31. Scott argued for the detachment of the Hague Conferences from the mood and the willingness of a single monarch. Instead, he wanted

ing, Scott argued that because of this 'institutionalization' of the preparatory work and because the decision for a follow-up conference was already taken in 1907,

> [...] it is evident that that a third would have been called, and that the system of conferences would have become an international institution, freed from the domination of any one Power, with an organization and procedure of its own, with individual conferences meeting at regular intervals, with programs prepared in advance by an international body appointed by and having the confidence of nations.[346]

As mentioned above, the hope to turn *The Hague Conferences* into a series of periodic conferences, and to establish them as a permanent institution, had already been expressed by members of the U.S.-American peace movement before the opening of the *Second Hague Peace Conference.*[347] Furthermore, in his instructions to the U.S.-American delegates, Secretary of State Elihu Root had expressed the hope for institutionalization as well.[348] It had even been among Root's foremost goals to adapt a resolution at the *Second Hague Peace Conference* "[...] providing for the holding of further conferences within fixed periods and arranging the machinery by which such conferences may be called and the terms of the programme may be arranged, without awaiting any new and specific initiative on the part of the Powers or any one of them."[349]

Several other authors seem to have held similar (or even more extensive) views too. The most progressive authors regarded *The Hague Conferences* as

---

to establish a structured mode for the calling and initiation of these meetings. By doing so, Scott seems to have aimed for institutionalizing the Hague Conferences.

346 Ibid. It should, however, be noted that this only represents Scott's opinion from 1925. In an article from 1908, he had held the following, decisively different view: "The conference, however, did not attempt to perpetuate itself by declaring that conferences should be held in the future at regular and recurring intervals, but limited itself to a recommendation for a third conference to meet at a specific date." Compare also: James Brown Scott, 'Recommendation for a Third Peace Conference at The Hague' (1908) 2 The American Journal of International Law 818.

347 Compare pages 220–221, 250, 265–266 of the present book.

348 James Brown Scott, 'Recommendation for a Third Peace Conference at The Hague' (n 346 in Chapter 6) 818.

349 James Brown Scott, *The Hague Peace Conferences of 1899 and 1907*, vol. 2 (n 118 in Chapter 6) 184. Compare also: Calvin DeArmond Davis, *The United States and the Second Hague Peace Conference* (n 28 in Chapter 1) 286. According to the Davis, the periodization/institutionalization of the Hague Conferences became even more important to the U.S.-American delegation than the court project.

already having constituted an established federation of states[350] or went, at least, as far as to claim that the determination to hold a third conference had to be understood as a periodization and, therefore, as an institutionalization of *The Hague Conferences*. For example, Walther Schücking (*The International Union of the Hague Conferences'* from 1918) argued that either "[...] a loose federation [... or ...] a mere judicial union"[351] had already been created under the roof of *The Hague Conferences*. According to him, the aim of this federation was the further development and protection of international law, and *The Hague Conferences* were its principal organ (and its legislative body).[352] Others regarded the scheduling of a third conference only as a step in this direction,[353] although even the delegates of the conference often seem to have assumed that *The Hague Conferences* were just about to become permanent institutions, if not even a formal world organization.[354] According to Arthur

350 Compare, e.g., also: Thomas Joseph Lawrence, *International Problems and Hague Conferences* (J.M. Dent & Company 1908) 42. According to him, at the Second Hague Peace Conference "[n]early the whole of civilized humanity was represented, and something like a parliament of mankind came together for the first time. [...] Unless the views of the leading rulers and nations of the world undergo a sudden and complete change, not only will a third Hague Conference be held after the laps of a few years, but a series of such Conferences may be expected with reasonable confidence. [...] In all probability we have obtained at length a legislative or quasi-legislative organ of the great Society of Nations. From it are developing judicial organs in the shape of Courts of Arbitration and an International Prize Court." Also: William I. Hull, *The two Hague Conferences and their Contributions to International Law* (n 39 in Chapter 5) 497–498. According to him, the features of the two Hague Conferences "[...] may justify the appellation of the *federation* of the world. The legislative, judicial, and executive organs of this federation are still rudimentary, of course, but they have come to life, thanks to the Peace Conferences, and give promise of larger growth." See also: Warren F. Kuehl, *Seeking World Order* (n 16 in Chapter 3) 104–105. Kuehl concluded the following concerning authors such as Raymond Bridgman and Benjamin Trueblood. According to him, they found that the decision on regular congresses "[...] revealed that evolutionary process which would culminate in 'a legislative world-assembly'. The four-month sessions had laid the foundation for a 'future deliberative and federative union'. In a burst of enthusiasm, Trueblood predicted that such a body, even with limited powers, could solve 'all the problems of international interest' then current."

351 Walther Schücking, *The International Union of the Hague Conferences* (n 233 in Chapter 6) 182.

352 Walther Schücking, *Die Organisation der Welt* (n 181 in Chapter 6) 80.

353 Compare: Lassa Oppenheim, *The Future of International Law* (n 130 in Chapter 2) 7. According to him, the '*vœu'* for a third conference "[...] gives the first impetus towards making the Hague Conferences a permanent institution and so ensuring their periodic assembly without the need of initiative on part of some power or another."

354 Calvin DeArmond Davis, *The United States and the Second Hague Peace Conference* (n 28 in Chapter 1) 277–278.

Eyffinger (*'A highly critical Moment: Role and Record of the 1907 Hague Peace Conference'* from 2007), thereby, "[...] a first if perhaps only semi-conscious effort was made to establish a Hague System of World Organization."[355] Consequently, numerous scholars of international law looked rather favorably upon *The Hague Conferences*. The failure of the *Second Hague Peace Conference* to produce any progressive changes of the international legal order, with regards to arbitration or adjudication (except of the IPC), did not let these authors condemn the conference. They were (most probably) disappointed but they chose to look ahead and to deal with the chances of achieving further going results at the next occasion rather than to mourn over the failure of the last one.

The overwhelming majority of European peace activists, on the other hand, was highly disappointed by the outcomes of the *Second Hague Peace Conference* and criticized the governments for them.[356] If the peace activists saw any positive point in the *Second Hague Peace Conference*, then it was only the fact that the conference seemed to have contributed to the international understanding and cooperation in an atmosphere of equals and that the *Second Hague Peace Conference* could be regarded as – according to Léon Bourgeios, a member of the French delegation – "the germ of a 'society of nations'".[357] At least some of them shared, therefore, the notion of the above-cited scholars, which considered *The Hague Conferences* as an already institutionalized and established series of periodic conferences (or even as the embodiment of an international federation). However, most of the members of the European peace movement continued to be highly unsatisfied with the results of the conference and expressed their disappointment at the upcoming meetings of the *Universal Peace Congress* (in Munich in 1907) and of the *Inter-Parliamentary Union* (in Berlin in the same year).[358] In comparison to that, the mood on the other side of the Atlantic does not seem to have been as negative as in Europe. U.S.-American scholars of international law and peace activists did not give up on their expectations and hopes towards a *Third Hague Peace Conference* and started to prepare themselves on a series of occasions for achieving better and further going results at a third meeting in The Hague; for example, at the *Lake Mohonk Conferences* in 1913 and 1914.[359]

355 Arthur Eyffinger, 'A highly critical Moment: Role and Record of the 1907 Hague Peace Conference' (2007) 54 The Netherlands International Law Review 224.

356 Sandi E. Cooper, *Patriotic Pacifism* (n 156 in Chapter 3) 109–110.

357 The quote stems from: ibid 110.

358 Ibid 109–110.

359 Compare in this regard: *Report of the 19th Annual Lake Mohonk conference on International Arbitration, May 14th, 15th and 16th, 1913* (Lake Mohonk Arbitration Conference

The delegates at the *Second Hague Peace Conference* did not share the negative reception of the European peace activists regarding the event and its outcomes either.[360] According to Calvin DeArmond Davis (*'The United States and the Second Hague Peace Conference'* from 1975), most delegates found it

> [...] far more satisfactory than they had expected during the dull, rambling debates of its first weeks. True, it had amassed a long record of failures. It had swept aside the armaments question; it had failed to complete agreements necessary to create the Court of Arbitral Justice: it had failed to do anything effective in regard to obligatory arbitration; whether or not it had framed the International Prize Court convention in such a way that it would be ratified was uncertain. But the delegates pointed to the resolution for a third conference and to the recommendations that the conference take up these matters. More important were the thirteen conventions and the declaration awaiting signature. Surely, some of the latter agreements would prove useful additions to international law.[361]

Even Choate and Scott did not consider the conference to be a complete failure;[362] although they could neither achieve the conclusion of a universal treaty of obligatory arbitration nor the establishment of the CAJ at The Hague. For

---

1913). Also: *Report of the 20th Annual Lake Mohonk Conference on International Arbitration, May 27th, 28th, and 29th, 1914* (Lake Mohonk Arbitration Conference 1914).

360 Warren F. Kuehl, *Seeking World Order* (n 16 in Chapter 3) 104.

361 Calvin DeArmond Davis, *The United States and the Second Hague Peace* (n 28 in Chapter 1) 290.

362 James Brown Scott, 'The Work of the Second Hague Peace Conference' (1908) 2 The American Journal of International Law 1. There, Scott concluded the work of the conference as follows: "The conference of 1907, no more than its immediate predecessor, satisfied the leaders of humanitarian thought. War was not abolished, nor was peace legislated into existence. Universal disarmament was as unacceptable in 1907 as in 1899, and some few nations were still unwilling to bind themselves to refer all international disputes not involving independence, vital interests, or national honor to a court of arbitration. Deeply interested in the success of these projects, the great public felt that their failure necessarily involved the failure of the conference, notwithstanding that many wise and humanitarian measures failing short of the goal were incorporated into the law of nations. But we should not in our disappointment, and perhaps bitterness of soul, overlook positive and beneficent progress, and if we could not take the advanced position outlined by the friends of peace, we should nevertheless rejoice that many a mile-stone has been passed. We must not forget that an international conference is different from a parliament; that independent and sovereign nations are not bound by majorities, and that positive results are obtained by compromising upon desirable but perhaps less advanced projects. The aim of a conference is to lay down a law for all, not

Scott the court project had been a matter of personal importance and he had put a lot of effort into its realization. However, Scott acknowledged that it had already been a great success that (almost) all nations had come to The Hague in order to discuss the establishment of peace and the replacement of war by law. In addition to that, Scott and Root were quite optimistic regarding the future, especially with regards to a third conference. According to Ralph D. Nurnberger (*James Brown Scott: Peace Through Justice'* from 1975),

> [t]he Secretary of State believed that the main accomplishment of the 1899 meeting was to set the stage for the discussions in 1907. The world, he hoped, had finally entered an orderly process, so that through a series of conferences a firm framework for peace could be brought into existence. Each conference would start where its predecessors had concluded, so that even items that were not ratified at one meeting could be picked up and developed in the future. Only through this slow and gradual process would a lasting, firm world peace be possible.[363]

Especially the fact that the general idea for an international court of law had received such widespread support, gave them further hope for its future realization.[364] Consequently, Scott concluded after the *Second Hague Peace Conference* that "[i]t is of little importance whether the court is constituted now or later, for the recognition of the idea makes the ultimate realization a certainty."[365] But despite their cautious statements, neither Scott nor Root was willing to wait for long to see their court project realized. Soon after the end of the *Second Hague Peace Conference*, they took actions for its implementation. Therefore, the results of the conference do not seem to have discouraged them; instead, Scott and Root henceforth pursued their goals even more enthusiastically and with full of determination.

From today's perspective, it can therefore be concluded that the conference failed in achieving far going, presentable results. None of the prestigious pro-

---

for the many, much less for the few; to establish a law which will be international because it is accepted and enforced by all nations."

363 Ralph D. Nurnberger, *James Brown Scott: Peace Through Justice* (n 1 in Chapter 5) 156–157.

364 John Hepp, 'James Brown Scott and the Rise of Public International Law' (2008) 7 The Journal of the Gilded Age and Progressive Era 167. See also: Ralph D. Nurnberger, *James Brown Scott: Peace Through Justice* (n 1 in Chapter 5) 93. According to him, Scott optimistically concluded – despite the failure of creating the CAJ at The Hague – that the "[...] Permanent Court will come, because it is necessary."

365 Cited in: Ralph D. Nurnberger, *James Brown Scott: Peace Through Justice* (n 1 in Chapter 5) 158.

jects of the peace movement (the conclusion of a general obligatory arbitration treaty and the creation of a permanent and general international court of law) had been realized, wherefore the reception of the peace movement was accordingly modest. However, despite the disappointment among peace activists, it must also be taken into consideration that the *Second Hague Peace Conference* was only the second meeting of this kind ever in history; a multi-lateral conference that dealt with a multitude of different topics, which all affected the core and the essence of the international legal order. Regarding the fact that it was even the first truly global meeting (of almost all recognized states), the *Second Hague Peace* constituted an entire novum. Against this background, it cannot surprise that it was not possible in the end to realize all the (ambitious) projects. Some of the initiatives presented at The Hague even took the participating states completely by surprise, such as the proposal for the *Court of Arbitral Justice*. However, all these projects were discussed in an atmosphere of goodwill and, in most cases at least, with a lot of openness to adopt them and to compromise. The *Second Hague Peace Conference* was therefore – despite the failure to realize most of these projects – a true forum for the exchange of ideas and for the discussion of the future shape of the international legal order among all states. It provided a basis for international negotiations and understanding, and it was regarded by international scholars, delegates, and even some of the peace activists as only the beginning of an institutionalized series of similar events, which were meant to contribute decisively to the realization of further going results in the fields of obligatory arbitration and adjudication, to the juridification of international relations, and to the replacement of war by law in the future.

3 The Period between 1907 and 1914

Many members of the peace movement – and also several legal scholars, delegates, politicians, and observers of the *Second Hague Peace Conference* – were still disappointed that the project for a permanent international court of law had failed to be realized at the *Second Hague Peace Conference*. Such an institution would have constituted a novelty at the international level and would have been a great step forward for the cause of *peace through law*. However, almost all participating states had declared their general favor at the conference for the creation of such an institution; even though the idea for an international court of law had mainly been prominent in the United States before the opening of this event (while it had hardly attracted any public attention in Europe). European peace activists had concentrated on other means of conflict settlement, primarily obligatory arbitration. Consequently, the proposal for the creation of the CAJ must have taken most delegates of the European powers by surprise. Nevertheless, they had shown a very positive attitude towards it in The Hague. Never before in history had the states been as close to creating a permanent international court of law than they were at the *Second Hague Peace Conference*; and despite the failure to create the CAJ in the end, they had at least been able to find a compromise concerning the establishment of the IPC, also a permanent international court of law.

The powers had demonstrated a compromising and benevolent mood at the conference and seem to have been open for changes and the further development of the international legal order. They had been working together, at least to a certain extent, in a friendly atmosphere and had seriously discussed a number of highly advanced and progressive topics. However, this situation changed soon after the end of the conference. The two European power blocks – the *Triple Alliance* and the *Triple Entente* – confronted each other in a series of conflicts and *realpolitik* remained to be a decisive factor in international politics. The achievement of national goals was often regarded as more important than the desire for peace and the balancing of power. Imperialism, the German attempt at becoming a world power, and the armament races are some of the reasons that brought the two power blocks on a course for confrontation.[366] Crises such as the *Young Turk Revolution* (1908), the annexation of Bosnia and Herzegovina by Austria-Hungary (also 1908), the *Second Morocco Crisis* (1911), or the *Italo-Turkish War* (1911–12), marked the period between the closure of the *Second Hague Peace Conference* and the outbreak of *World War I*.[367] Moreover, according to Jörg Fisch (*'Europa zwischen Wachstum und Gleichheit 1850–1914'* from 2002), war "[...] remained a legitimate political instrument, not least because only few people foresaw its highly destructive nature."[368]

3.1 *The* Washington Conference (*1907*)

The first attempt to continue the work of the *Second Hague Peace Conference* was not made in Europe or among the North Atlantic states. It took place in the Pan-American context at the so-called *Washington Conference*. The meeting was held between November 14 and December 20, 1907, in the U.S.-American capital only a few months after the end of the *Second Hague Peace*

366 Michael Epkenhans, *Der Erste Weltkrieg* (n 156 in Chapter 5) 11 et seq.

367 Calvin DeArmond Davis, *The United States and the Second Hague Peace Conference* (n 28 in Chapter 1) 303.

368 Ibid.

Conference. On the initiative of the United States and Mexico, the five countries from Central America (Guatemala, Nicaragua, El Salvador, Costa Rica, and Honduras) were invited to this meeting in order to establish peace on the isthmus.

Root and Scott were eager to use this opportunity to prove the workability and functionality of the concept for a permanent court of law at the (regional) international level. Therefore, the two U.S.-American statesmen did their best to convince the other governments represented at this meeting of joining their efforts for the creation of an institution shaped in accordance with the proposed CAJ. Juan Pablo Scarfi (*'The Hidden History of International Law in the Americas'* from 2017) remarked the following on the developments regarding the striving for the creation of a permanent international court of law, which followed the events of the *Second Hague Peace Conference*:

> At The Hague there was a tension between the 'doctrinal legalism' of Barbosa and 'pragmatic institution building' of Scott, but the legacy of Scott's approach and the US proposal prevailed and proved to be more influential and lasting in the following years within the international law community.[369]

Peace had always been a fragile commodity in Central America throughout the entire 19th century. After the disintegration of the Federal Republic of Central America (1823–1841),[370] the region was dominated by repressive dictatorships, constant social unrests, and border conflicts.[371] Furthermore, European powers (especially Great Britain) initially pursued imperialist ambitions on the isthmus – and were then replaced by the United States as the hegemonic power in the 1860s/70s.[372] But the United States did not only reach for control over the region because of strategic and geopolitical reasons. Central America also began to play an important role for the U.S.-American economy. Companies such as the United Fruit Company as well as a number of coffee and banana producers established businesses in Central America in the last decade of the 19th century.[373] As a result, each of the wars between Central American states (as well as social unrests) that continued to occur regularly bore a substantial threat for the U.S.-American investments and financial

369 Juan Pablo Scarfi, *The Hidden History of International Law in the Americas* (n 8 in Chapter 6) 29.

370 Lynn V. Foster, *A Brief History of Central America* (n 5 in Chapter 4) 134–136.

371 Ibid 186.

372 Compare pages 139–142 of the present book.

373 Juan Pablo Scarfi, *El Imperio de la Ley* (n 144 in Chapter 4) 73.

interests. Therefore, the United States showed a quickly growing interest in securing peace and stability in Central America to protect their citizens' investments.

In the beginning, the U.S.-American attempts to establish peace on the isthmus were little fruitful. Nicaragua and Guatemala were competing for the dominant position among the Central American states since 1898. This conflict spread soon and involved all the other nations from the region as well. Honduras, e.g., being located right between the Nicaragua and Guatemala, was especially affected. Due to that conflict, the country experienced years of extreme political instability and was subject to numerous *coups d'état* and revolutions.[374] The situation finally escalated in 1906 when Nicaragua (with the help of Costa Rica and El Salvador) invaded Guatemala. To protect U.S.-American investments and interests in the region, the United States interfered (with the help of Mexico) in this conflict.[375] The two major regional powers managed to bring the conflicting parties together in San José in 1906 where the Central American republics negotiated a general treaty of peace.[376] Several other treaties were concluded at the occasion as well which assigned the U.S.-American and Mexican Presidents the role of umpires in the case of conflict settlements.[377] But neither the peace agreement nor any other treaty concerning the peaceful (and obligatory) settlement of mutual conflicts between the Central American states could put an end to this dispute.[378] They all turned out to be incapable of preserving peace in the region; which became plainly apparent again in February 1907 when Nicaragua started to launch another attack against Honduras.[379] The United States and Mexico intervened again, wherefore they called the states together for the *Washington Conference*. The two regional powers participated in the event in order to negotiate terms and conditions for peace between the opponents and for making sure that a compromise could be found. James Brown Scott (*'Elihu Root'* from 1963) mentioned in this regard that

---

374 Lynn V. Foster, *A Brief History of Central America* (n 5 in Chapter 4) 190.

375 Juan Pablo Scarfi, *El Imperio de la Ley* (n 144 in Chapter 4) 74.

376 Regarding this meeting, the 'Treaty of the Marblehead' (1906), and other Central American attempts to establish peace (also with the help of multi-lateral obligatory arbitration treaties and the formation of a Central American Court of Arbitration), please see: James Brown Scott, 'The Central American Peace Conference of 1907' (1908) 2 The American Journal of International Law 125–126.

377 James Brown Scott, 'Elihu Root' (n 12 in Chapter 6) 262.

378 Ibid 263.

379 Philip Marshall Brown, 'American Intervention in Central America' (1914) 4 The Journal of Race Development 410.

> [...] although Mexico and the United States should not be contracting parties to any agreements to be reached in the proposed conference, a representative from each of the two countries should attend the sessions and lend, as it were, the moral sanction of Mexico and the United States to the understandings which should be reached.[380]

At the inaugural session of the *Washington Conference*, Secretary of State Elihu Root urged the delegates of the Central American states to establish lasting and durable peace between them.[381] But the Central American delegates struggled in the beginning of the meeting to find a solution. Some of them preferred the establishment of a federation, while others strove for an economic integration or favored other approaches, which were less radical than the establishment of another federation in Central America.[382] Due to this deadlock, the U.S.-Americans took the initiative and William I. Buchanan, a member of their delegation, proposed the creation of the *Central American Court of Justice* (hereinafter CACJ), which was supposed to be modeled in accordance with the plans for the CAJ.[383] According to James Brown Scott, it was Root who had instructed Buchanan to introduce this plan at the *Washington Conference* and to seek

> [...] to have a Central American court of justice established, whereby the disputes between the republics could be submitted to judicial settlement by a court of their own creation, and determined by the principles of international law, before the controversies had become embittered to such an extent that war might be the consequence.[384]

---

380 James Brown Scott, 'Elihu Root' (n 12 in Chapter 6) 263. The quote encourages the assumption that the United States and Mexico were to serve as the guarantee powers of peace in Central America (and of the other agreements concluded at the Washington Conference).

381 William I. Buchanan, *The Central American Peace Conference held at Washington D.C. 1907* (United States Government Printing Office 1908) 5.

382 Benjamin Allen Coates, *Legalist Empire* (n 311 in Chapter 5) 119. Also: William I. Buchanan, *The Central American Peace Conference held at Washington D.C. 1907* (n 381 in Chapter 6) 6–7. According to Buchanan, the initiative for the formation of a Central American union came from Honduras and was supported by Nicaragua and El Salvador. Guatemala and Costa Rica, on the other hand, objected to the project.

383 Benjamin Allen Coates, *Legalist Empire* (n 311 in Chapter 5) 119.

384 James Brown Scott, 'Elihu Root' (n 12 in Chapter 6) 266.

The proposal was supported by Mexico[385] and the Central American states soon agreed to it as well. James Brown Scott (*'The Central American Peace Conference of 1907'* from 1908) pointed out in this regard that "[t]he conference recognized that peace is the great need of the Central American republics, and this peace should be based not upon force but upon the administration of justice."[386] Therefore, the participating states joined the United States in their approach and in their striving for the establishment of a permanent court of international justice – and, as claimed by Scarfi, they thereby turned away from Barbosa's doctrinal legalism.

The *Convention for the Establishment of a Central American Court of Justice*[387] was signed on December 20, 1907, and it was ratified in 1908. It formed the basis for the creation of the CACJ, which was officially brought into existence on May 25, 1908. The court was the first permanent genuine judicial tribunal at the international level (the creation of the IPC was delayed because of political reasons) and – according to Coates – it was also "the realization of a legalist dream".[388] According to Article VI of the convention, the court was composed of five judges, "[...] one being appointed by each Republic and selected from among the jurists who possess the qualification which the laws of each country prescribe for the exercise of high judicial office."[389] Furthermore, Article I provided that the Central American states bound themselves to "[...] submit all controversies or questions which may arise among them, of whatever nature and no matter what their origin may be, in case the respective Departments of Foreign Affairs should not have been able to reach an understanding."[390] According to Article II, the CACJ was even supposed to

> [...] also take cognizance of the questions which individuals of one Central American country may raise against any of the other contracting Governments, because of the violation of treaties or conventions, and other causes of an international character; no matter whether their own Government supports said claim or not.[391]

385 Benjamin Allen Coates, *Legalist Empire* (n 311 in Chapter 5) 119.

386 James Brown Scott, 'The Central American Peace Conference of 1907' (n 376 in Chapter 6) 134.

387 William I. Buchanan, *The Central American Peace Conference held at Washington D.C. 1907* (n 381 in Chapter 6) 43 et seq.

388 Benjamin Allen Coates, *Legalist Empire* (n 311 in Chapter 5) 119.

389 Article VI of the Convention for the Establishment of a Central American Court of Justice, published in: William I. Buchanan, *The Central American Peace Conference held at Washington D.C. 1907* (n 381 in Chapter 6) 45–46.

390 Ibid 44.

391 Ibid.

Therefore, the contracting states created a truly judicial and permanent court at the regional (international) level, which was composed of judges appointed for pre-determined tenures of five years (Article VIII). The salaries of the judges were to be paid by the treasury of the court to which all the Central American states agreed to contribute (Article VII). These provisions aimed at guaranteeing the highest level of independence and impartiality of the judges by enabling them to exercise their offices without being (financially) dependent on their home countries. Furthermore, the CACJ was designed to have a general obligatory jurisdiction over all controversies, which arose between the Central American nations, and which could not be settled by diplomacy. Even individuals could file cases before the court against other Central American states (but not against their home countries). Therefore, the jurisdiction of the CACJ was extremely broad. It went even beyond the scope and design of the projected CAJ (the so-far most advanced initiative for the creation of a general international court, which had ever been seriously discussed among states). Finally, the convention for the CACJ provided for the complete abolishment of war in the mutual relations between the Central American countries. All of their conflicts had to be settled on the basis of law and through a genuine judicial tribunal.

Luis Anderson, Minister of Foreign Affairs of Costa Rica, commented on the creation of the CACJ (*'The Peace Conference of Central America'* from 1908) by declaring that the court

> [...] shall be, it is hoped, a strong and durable defense for international peace and fraternity in Central America [...]. The establishment of the Central American Court of Justice will be the practical realization of the ingenious plans formulated and recommended by the American delegates at the Second Peace Conference at The Hague, plans which, it will be remembered, were received with enthusiastic applause, though unfortunately they had no immediate success. The Court of Justice will be, in some degree, the child of that bright idea, the happy performance of that which was a happy thought.[392]

Furthermore, he also expressed the hope that the establishment of the CACJ would result in a signal effect and that it would serve as an example for other nations to take similar actions so that, "[...] little by little, the idea will take root in the hearts of the nations, and that the ultimate result will be the grand

---

392 Luis Anderson, 'The Peace Conference of Central America' (1908) 2 The American Journal of International Law 145–146.

success of a great and valuable institution dedicated to the work of combating international discord and misery, and of promoting international peace and prosperity."[393] At the last session of the conference the Mexican ambassador added in this regard that "[a]s far as the world is concerned it is the organization of an international court, which brings hopes for universal peace. Its success must be interesting to all the nations of the globe."[394] With these words, Luis Anderson and the Mexican ambassador expressed similar hopes as Elihu Root and James Brown Scott who had aimed for using the *Washington Conference* to establish a permanent and truly judicial court of law on a limited regional international level (in Central America) to prove to the rest of the world (and especially to the other great powers) the workability and functioning of their plan for the establishment of the CAJ.[395] With the creation of the CACJ, they succeeded in this regard and took the first step in this direction.

3.2 *Follow-Up Events*

In the subsequent years, a number of follow-up events took place involving the United States and several European countries. At these occasions, the United States did not tire to strive for the realization of their plan for the establishment of a truly permanent and international court of law. Alongside a far-reaching proposal to realize this idea, which was made at the *London Naval Conference* in 1908/09, Root also tried, for example, to revive the earlier initiative of John Hay for the conclusion of a series of bi-lateral obligatory arbitration treaties.[396] As mentioned above in Chapter V, Hay had concluded eleven treaties of this kind between November 1904 and February 1905 (the so-called *Hay Arbitration Conventions*).[397] But none of them had been ratified due to domestic struggles in the United States between the Senate and the President. Root was convinced that such agreements would constitute an

393 Ibid 146.

394 William I. Buchanan, *The Central American Peace Conference held at Washington D.C. 1907* (n 381 in Chapter 6) 89.

395 James Brown Scott, 'The Central American Peace Conference of 1907' (n 376 in Chapter 6) 143. Also: Juan Pablo Scarfi, *El Imperio de la Ley* (n 144 in Chapter 4) 77–79. James Brown Scott, 'Elihu Root' (n 12 in Chapter 6) 267. In this publication, Scott claimed that the "[…] court was not destined to be a paper court". But although the CACJ settled ten cases before its extinction in 1918, it should also be acknowledged that the court was not able to effectively preserve peace in the region. Revolutions and wars still took place in the Central American context during its existence. Compare: Manley O. Hudson, 'The Central American Court of Justice' (n 216 in Chapter 5) 768 et seq. Also: Lynn V. Foster, *A Brief History of Central America* (n 5 in Chapter 4) 197–198.

396 Francis Anthony Boyle, *Foundations of World Order* (n 28 in Chapter 1) 32–33.

397 Compare pages 219–220 of the present book.

immense advance in comparison to a non-regulated state. After the failure to conclude a multi-lateral obligatory arbitration treaty in The Hague, he, therefore, (according to James Brown Scott, *'Elihu Root'* from 1963) "[...] set to work to conclude a series of treaties of this kind, frankly accepting the requirement of the Senate that the special agreement should also be advised and consented to by that body as a formal treaty."[398] Hence, Root concluded twenty-five bi-lateral obligatory arbitration treaties with most of the great powers and other influential nations, with the exception of Germany, between 1908 and 1909 (the so-called *Root Arbitration Conventions*).[399] All these treaties provided that

> [...] differences which may arise of a legal nature, or relating to the interpretation of treaties existing between the two Contracting Parties, and which it may not have been possible to settle by diplomacy, shall be referred to the Permanent Court of Arbitration [...], provided, nevertheless, that they do not affect the vital interests, the independence, or the honor of the two Contracting States, and do not concern the interests of third Parties.[400]

Therefore, the United States did not focus entirely on purely judicial settlements of international conflicts at that time. Their representatives were also aware that arbitration remained a key instrument in this regard. They did not abandon arbitration or refuse to conclude further bi-lateral obligatory arbitration treaties. Instead, as it has already become apparent in the context of the *Second Hague Peace Conference*, the United States endorsed the approval of a multi-lateral treaty of obligatory arbitration too. Since this project had failed in The Hague, the United States returned to concentrate on bi-lateral agreements and expanded the net of this kind of treaties to bind as many states as possible.

By doing so, the U.S.-American government proved that it did not place all its hopes on a single solution. However, the creation of a permanent international court of law remained its first choice, as it became apparent (once more) in the context of the *London Naval Conference* in 1908/09. The confer-

398 James Brown Scott, 'Elihu Root' (n 12 in Chapter 6) 225.

399 Ibid.

400 Compare: Article 1 of the Convention signed at Washington on February 10, 1908, between the United States and France, published in: Charles I. Bevans (ed.), *Treaties and other International Agreements of the United States of America 1776–1949, Vol. 7: Denmark – France* (United States Government Printing Office 1971), 870. Also: James Brown Scott, 'Elihu Root' (n 12 in Chapter 6) 225.

ence was called on the initiative of the British government, which sent a convening note to Germany, Spain, France, Italy, Russia, Japan, Austria-Hungary, and the United States on February 27, 1908.[401] The decision to abstain from inviting smaller states to this event complied to a great extent with the prevailing mood among the great powers at that time after they had had to face claims for sovereign equality by smaller states (especially the Latin American ones) at the *Second Hague Peace Conference*.[402] The British government then declared in the circular that it would not ratify the convention for the establishment of the IPC at the current point of time.[403] Instead, they proposed to come together for another conference to settle the difficulties, which arose from the vagueness of Article 7 of the convention. This article provided that if the court could not base its decision on an established international treaty, it should refer to general principles of law and equity.[404] According to Calvin DeArmond Davis (*'The United States and the Second Hague Peace Conference'* from 1975), the British government had concerns against this provision because "British naval leaders feared that in a war with Germany or another continental power, the prize court would free ships seized by His Majesty's navy. The admiralty insisted on clarification of international law before ratification."[405] Furthermore, the British government feared – according to Isabel V. Hull (*'A Scrap of Paper'* from 2014) – that "[…] the new court might reject many customary British practices at sea because most of its judges would be

401 'British Circular' (February 27, 1908), in: James Brown Scott (ed.), *The Declaration of London February 26, 1909* (Oxford University Press 1919) 13. In the end, the Netherlands was also invited; compare: Calvin DeArmond Davis, *The United States and the Second Hague Peace Conference* (n 28 in Chapter 1) 304–305.

402 Compare: Gerry Simpson, *Great Powers and Outlaw States: Unequal Sovereigns in the International Legal Order* (n 51 in Chapter 2) 150. Also: Ellery C. Stowell, 'The International Naval Conference and the Declaration of London' (1909) 3 The American Political Science Review 492.

403 'British Circular' (n 401 in Chapter 6) 15 (No. 7). See also: Charles H. Stockton and Charles S. Sperry, 'The London Naval Conference' (1909) 3 The Proceedings of the American Society of International Law at Its Annual Meeting (1907–1917) 62. According to them, a number of other states (Germany, Brazil, China, Spain, Italy, Japan, Portugal, Russia, and Turkey) had not ratified the convention in the beginning of 1908 either.

404 Calvin DeArmond Davis, *The United States and the Second Hague Peace Conference* (n 28 in Chapter 1) 304. Also: Isabel V. Hull, *A Scrap of Paper: Breaking and Making International Law during the Great War* (Cornell University Press 2014) 142.

405 Calvin DeArmond Davis, *The United States and the Second Hague Peace Conference* (n 28 in Chapter 1) 304.

from neutral or Continental countries."[406] Therefore, the British invited the other great powers to London to determine the law of the sea in greater detail.

At the *London Naval Conference*, the powers discussed the enactment of a corpus of elaborated laws of naval warfare. By the end of the conference, they even unanimously adopted a declaration, the so-called *Declaration Concerning the Laws of Naval War*[407] (the *London Declaration*), which was never ratified in the end.[408]

Nevertheless, the *London Naval Conference* is highly interesting – but for another reason: The United States attempted to realize the draft convention for the CAJ within the framework of the IPC at this very occasion. Root and Scott wanted to extend the competences of the IPC through an additional protocol. It would have allowed the IPC to "[…] sit as a court of arbitral justice for powers willing to accept such a procedure."[409] The representatives of the United States had placed a lot of hope in the IPC after the closure of the *Second Hague Peace Conference*. They wanted the court to serve as an example for the functionality of a permanent and international court of law. They expected a positive experience with the work of the IPC to convince other states of the need to create an actual world court, shaped in accordance with the draft convention for the CAJ. According to Elihu Root's speech delivered at the *Sixth Annual Meeting of the American Society of International Law* in 1912, he had been convinced after the conference in The Hague that the IPC "[…] became the advance guard of the proposed judicial system, the experiment upon which the success of the whole plainly depends."[410] President Roosevelt expressed a similar thought in his message to Congress of December 3, 1907, in which he declared the following:

> Not only will the International Prize Court be the means of protecting the interest of neutral, but it is in itself a step toward the creation of the most general court for the hearing of international controversies, to which reference has just been made. The organization and action of

406 Isabel V. Hull, *A Scrap of Paper* (n 404 in Chapter 6) 142. Also: Charles H. Stockton, 'The International Naval Conference of London, 1908–1909' (1909) 3 The American Journal of International Law 597.

407 Published in: The American Journal of International Law, Vol. 3, No. 3, Supplement: Official Documents (1909) 186 et seq.

408 Compare: 'Editorial Comment: Status of the Declaration of London' (1915) 9 The American Journal of International Law 199.

409 Calvin DeArmond Davis, *The United States and the Second Hague Peace Conference* (n 28 in Chapter 1) 307.

410 Elihu Root, 'The Real Significance of the Declaration of London' in James Brown Scott (ed.), *The Declaration of London February 26, 1909* (n 401 in Chapter 6) 10.

> such a Prize Court can not fail to accustom the different countries to the submission of international questions to the decision of an international tribunal, and we may confidently expect the results of such submission to bring about a general agreement upon the enlargement of the practice.[411]

These words support the assumption that the United States had been willing to follow and support such a gradual development towards a world court. But, taking into consideration the initiative at the *London Naval Conference*, their representatives seem to have abandoned their patient attitude once more and already proposed an extension of the jurisdiction of the IPC in London on February 6, 1909. The U.S.-American plan provided for the conclusion of an additional agreement between two or more signatory states. According to it,

> […] any signatory of the convention for the establishment of the prize court may provide further in the act of ratification thereof that the international court of prize shall be competent to accept jurisdiction of and decide any case arising between the signatories of this proposed article submitted to it for arbitration, and the international prize court shall thereupon accept jurisdiction and adopt for its consideration and decision of the case the project of convention for the establishment of a court of arbitral justice adopted by the second Hague conference, the establishment of which was recommended by the powers through diplomatic channels.[412]

Hence, the United States wanted to extend the jurisdiction of the IPC through an additional protocol. According to it, the draft code for the CAJ was to be applied by the IPC in cases between contenting states.[413] This agreement would have turned the IPC into a world court shaped in accordance with the proposed CAJ, at least for those states that decided to adhere to the additional protocol. However, the delegates of the other states declared at the *London Naval Conference* that they were not authorized to negotiate such far-reaching agreements and that the U.S.-American proposal exceeded the scope

---

411 Published in: ibid 10–11.

412 Quoted in: Philander C. Knox, 'Identic Circular Note of the Secretary of State of the United States Proposing Alternative Procedure for the International Prize Court and the Investment of the International Prize Court with the Functions of a Court of Arbitral Justice' (1910) 4 The American Journal of International Law – Supplement: Official Documents 109.

413 Francis Anthony Boyle, *Foundations of World Order* (n 28 in Chapter 1) 45.

of the conference.[414] But at the same time, they encouraged the United States, according to the new U.S.-American Secretary of State Philander C. Know (1853–1921),[415] to "[...] prosecute through diplomatic channels a matter of such magnitude."[416]

Root's direct successors in the office of the Secretary of State – Robert Bacon (as interim holder of the office) and Philander C. Know (introduced to the office on March 6, 1909) – as well as new U.S.-American president William H. Taft (1857–1930) were just as keen as Root and Scott to create a general court of international law and supported Root's approach for turning the IPC into such an institution, even after Root had resigned from his office.[417] Taft even publicly declared on March 22, 1910, that there were no questions – not even those concerning national honor or the interest of civilized nations – which could not be determined by judicial decision.[418] Because of this approach, and because of what happened at the *London Naval Conference*, the U.S.-American representatives followed the advice and encouragement of the other powers and issued a so-called *Identic Circular Note* on March 5, 1909, directly following the end of the conference. It contained the same proposal (in a very similar wording) as the above-quoted plan from the *London Naval Conference*.[419] The United States probably proposed this solution because it would have impeded the re-occurrence of discussions on the mode for the appointment of judges for the thereby created world court (and the disputes concerning the compliance of this mode with the principle of full sovereign equality). This was the case because there already existed a settled method for the nomination of judges for the IPC. Extending the jurisdiction of this institution (the IPC) through an additional protocol would not have changed anything with regards to the nomination procedure. Consequently, introducing the CAJ in this way, namely within the framework of the IPC, would have allowed the

---

414 Ibid 46. See also: Charles H. Stockton, 'The International Naval Conference of London 1908–1909' (n 406 in Chapter 6) 616–617.

415 Calvin DeArmond Davis, *The United States and the Second Hague Peace Conference* (n 28 in Chapter 1) 313.

416 Philander C. Knox, 'Identic Circular Note' (n 412 in Chapter 6) 110. Also: James Brown Scott, *The Status of the International Court of Justice* (American Society for Judicial Settlement 1916) 42.

417 Calvin DeArmond Davis, *The United States and the Second Hague Peace Conference* (n 28 in Chapter 1) 313.

418 Nicholas Murray Butler, 'Are we Our Brothers' Keeper? Opening Address as Chairman of the Lake Mohonk Conference on International Arbitration, May 18, 1910' in Charles F. Howlett (ed.), *Nicholas Murray Butler's International Mind: An Argument for the Judicial Settlement of International Disputes* (Information Age Publishing Inc. 2013) 19.

419 Philander C. Knox, 'Identic Circular Note' (n 412 in Chapter 6) 111.

adhering states to stick to the established system. No further negotiations would have been necessary. The court could have just worked in accordance with the settled provisions and the system, which the great powers had preferred from the beginning for the nomination of judges and the composition of the tribunal.

Furthermore, attempting to conclude the additional protocol only among the participating states from the *London Naval Conference* would have meant that the members of the additional protocol were all members of the North Atlantic world (except Japan), and this group of states was exclusively comprised of great powers. Since the vast majority of them had already supported the proposal for the CAJ in The Hague, and since none of the Latin American countries (almost all of them voted against the CAJ in The Hague) were invited to adhere to the additional protocol (yet), the major opponents against the projected CAJ were simply not involved. Therefore, the court would have been a primarily North Atlantic organization and further ratification by other states was an option for the future in order to turn the court into an actual world court. Consequently, this additional protocol was supposed to be open only for this limited group of addressed states to – according to James Brown Scott ('*The Status of the International Court of Justice*' from 1916) –

> [...] try the experiment on a smaller scale, for we must admit that an international court is an experiment, before attempting it upon a large scale, in the hope that experience will demonstrate the usefulness of the court and the appropriate method of constituting it for all members of the society of nations [...]. Such a tribunal would be temporary in the sense that it might be replaced by the larger court, should an agreement be reached upon its constitution, and the writer ventures the suggestion that the attempt should be made in the very near future, so that before the meeting of the Third Conference it should be found in existence.[420]

The reactions to this note were mixed. In general, the addressed states seem to have supported the initiative.[421] However, they appear to have preferred the establishment of the court in the form of a separate institution (instead of creating it within the framework of the IPC).[422] Due to these differences –

420 James Brown Scott, *The Status of the International Court of Justice* (n 416 in Chapter 6) 48–49.

421 Calvin DeArmond Davis, *The United States and the Second Hague Peace Conference* (n 28 in Chapter 1) 313.

422 James Brown Scott, *The Status of the International Court of Justice* (n 416 in Chapter 6) 45.

and maybe also because the states lacked the necessary public pressure from the *Second Hague Peace Conference* and no longer felt the need to achieve representable results in order to turn this conference into a great success in the eyes of the global public – the initiative amounted to nothing. However, Scott was inspired by their responses to pick up the idea for a separate international court of law afresh and dealt with it in his writings. For example, he proposed (in '*The Status of the International Court of Justice*' from 1916) to establish a separate international court of law – at first – only between the eight largest powers (Germany, the United States, Austria-Hungary, France, Great Britain, Italy, Japan, and Russia). But other nations were to be entitled to bring cases before the tribunal as well.[423] He seems to have hoped for creating a shining example on this way for other states in order to convince them of joining a (potential) later initiative for a universal court of law (or: to join this court). Therefore, Scott supported the idea for a separate international court of law and argued that

> [...] the larger powers are convinced of the utility of such a court [...]. It is believed that the institution and successful operation of the court would not merely justify the powers in establishing it, but would convince non-contracting powers of its utility, which perhaps hesitate to pledge themselves to judicial settlement. Theory is one thing; practice is another, and practical demonstration is, with nations as with individuals, more conclusive than theoretical exposition.[424]

Although Root and Scott were no longer in charge in the U.S.-American Department of State, their government continued to put a lot of effort into convincing other nations of the establishment of a world court over the following years.[425] Furthermore, the State Department nominated James Brown Scott for representing the United States at the so-called *Four-Power Conference(s)* in Paris in March and July 1910 with representatives from Germany (Johannes Kriege), Great Britain (Eyre Crowe), and France (Louis Renault). The three European powers had proposed such a meeting in their replies to the (aforementioned)

423 Ibid 50. According to Scott, the great powers were supposed to hold permanent seats in the court. Only if non-contracting states had brought cases to the court, these states would have been entitled to nominate a judge of their own choice for the trial this specific case. This was supposed to guarantee equal representation in the procedures of the court for all parties.

424 Ibid 51–52.

425 Francis Anthony Boyle, *Foundations of World Order* (n 28 in Chapter 1) 46. Also: James Brown Scott, *The Status of the International Court of Justice* (n 416 in Chapter 6) 313.

Identic Circular Note[426] and the United States gladly accepted. On the conference, the participating states dealt with the idea to create the CAJ as initially discussed at The Hague (including the rotational system for the nomination of judges); instead of extending the jurisdiction of the IPC as proposed in the aforementioned additional protocol (introduced by the United States at the *London Naval Conference*).[427]

At the end of the Paris conference, on September 19, 1910, the representatives of the four powers signed a convention for the establishment of a court of arbitral justice, which was supposed to be open for ratification by all interested states. While the eight greatest powers were intended to enjoy permanent representation in the court, the smaller states were – according to Scott ('*Memorandum of James Brown Scott*' from 1916) – to be given "[...] a larger or smaller representation, conditioned upon their commercial interests."[428] Therefore, a method for the nomination of judges was chosen, which resembled the one that had already been (fiercely) discussed at the *Second Hague Peace Conference*. Furthermore, Scott stated also that

> [...] the method of appointing the judges of the Prize Court was adopted by the commission, and that the four powers agreed to take steps, after the constitution of the Prize Court, for the establishment of the Court of Arbitral Justice, provided eighteen powers, including therein the four powers specified, should agree to the establishment of the Court of Arbitral Justice.[429]

It seems reasonable to assume that the representatives of the four powers would have thought at this point that they had just taken the final step towards the establishment of a permanent international court of law; at least for a limited number of states. From the correspondence before the meetings and from the statements at these occasions, the conclusion can be drawn that all four of them were committed to the idea of the establishment of such a

426 'Memorandum of James Brown Scott, accompanying his Letter of January 12, 1914, to the Netherland Minister of Foreign Affairs, Proposing the Establishment of a Court of Arbitral Justice by and for Germany, the United States, Austria-Hungary, France, Great Britain, Italy, Japan, the Netherlands and Russia' in James Brown Scott, *An International Court of Justice* (Oxford University Press 1916) 74.

427 Francis Anthony Boyle, *Foundations of World Order* (n 28 in Chapter 1) 46. Calvin DeArmond Davis, *The United States and the Second Hague Peace Conference* (n 28 in Chapter 1) 313–314.

428 'Memorandum of James Brown Scott' (n 426 in Chapter 6) 74.

429 Ibid.

court.[430] At the *Sixteenth Annual Meeting of the Lake Mohonk Conference* in May 1910 – while the *Four-Power-Conferences* were still in progress – an official message from Secretary of State Philander C. Knox was read. According to it, he was optimistically looking ahead in this regard, and he was convinced that

> […] a truly permanent court of arbitral justice, composed of judges acting under a sense of judicial responsibility, representing the various judicial systems of the world and capable of insuring the continuity of arbitral jurisprudence, will be established in the immediate future and that the Third Peace Conference will find it in successful operation at The Hague.[431]

However, one (minor) issue turned out to be fatal for the project, resulting in its failure. This was the fact that the states held the belief that the establishment of the CAJ depended on the prior institution of the IPC.[432] According to them, the CAJ could only be created after the IPC had finally come into existence. They assumed the existence of an inherent connection between these two projects – although it must seem, at least from a today's perspective, that there was no need for assuming this connection and that both institutions could have existed independently from each other. But because this connection was held to exist, because the realization of the IPC depended on the ratifications of its constituting convention and of the *Declaration of London*, and because Great Britain refused to ratify both documents, the CAJ was never established.

In the end, neither the IPC nor the CAJ came into existence; despite a series of further efforts taken by the U.S.-American government, peace activists, and international scholars – all of which failed. James Brown Scott was again amongst the strongest advocates of these attempts. Moreover, he was backed by Philander C. Knox. In 1912, Knox sent Scott on a trip to Europe in order to

430 H.B.F. Macfarland, 'The Hopefulness of the Knox Proposition' in *Report of the Sixteenth Annual Meeting of the Lake Mohonk Conference on International Arbitration, May 18th, 19th, and 20th 1910* (Lake Mohonk Arbitration Conference 1910) 76.

431 'Official Message from Philander C. Knox regarding the International Court of Arbitral Justice' in *Report of the Sixteenth Annual Meeting of the Lake Mohonk Conference on International Arbitration, May 18th, 19th, and 20th 1910* (n 430 in Chapter 6) 9.

432 Calvin DeArmond Davis, *The United States and the Second Hague Peace Conference* (n 28 in Chapter 1) 314. Also: David S. Patterson, *Towards a Warless World* (n 147 in Chapter 3) 163. Or: Francis Anthony Boyle, *Foundations of World Order* (n 28 in Chapter 1) 47. According to Boyle, however, the document did not state this condition.

initiate another series of negotiations on the topic.[433] Additionally, Scott also made another attempt in 1914 to bring together representatives of the mentioned eight greatest powers in order to realize the plan for the CAJ by requesting help from the Dutch ministry of foreign affairs.[434] The U.S.-American government even took a final attempt in this regard only few months before the outbreak of *World War I*. According to the *Draft of a Memorandum approved by Secretary of State Knox*,

> [...] the Department of State proposed that the question of the Arbitral Court and its establishment in the immediate future be taken up and considered by the powers which negotiated the draft convention of March, 1910, in the hope that an agreement may be reached without further delay upon this important question, which, in the opinion of the Secretary of State, vitally concerns the maintenance of international peace.[435]

This position was also shared by members of the U.S.-American peace movement and international lawyers.[436] These groups, however, were even more focused on and paid particular attention to the projected *Third Hague Peace Conference* (scheduled for 1915) in the period between 1910 and 1914. In this regard, they discussed potential developments, which they wanted to achieve in the context of this event and the political agenda which the U.S.-American delegation should pursue in The Hague.[437]

U.S.-American international lawyers looked upon the third meeting in The Hague with a lot of optimism, especially regarding the creation of the CAJ.[438] For example, James L. Tryon (*'A Permanent Court of International Justice'* from 1913) argued in favor of changing the structure of the PCA at the *Third Hague Peace Conference* by creating two chambers within its framework. One of them should remain voluntary and would be supposed to settle semi-political disputes (as the PCA used to do it so far); the other chamber was intended to have

433 Francis Anthony Boyle, *Foundations of World Order* (n 28 in Chapter 1) 47.

434 Ibid. Compare also: 'Letter of James Brown Scott to the Netherland Minister of Foreign Affairs, dated January 12, 1914, concerning the Establishment of a Court of Arbitral Justice' in James Brown Scott, *An International Court of Justice* (n 426 in Chapter 6) 1–5.

435 'Draft of a Memorandum approved by Secretary of State Knox, proposing the Establishment of the Court of Arbitral Justice recommended by the Second Hague Peace Conference of 1907' in James Brown Scott, *An International Court of Justice* (n 426 in Chapter 6) 17.

436 Ralph D. Nurnberger, *James Brown Scott: Peace Through Justice* (n 1 in Chapter 5) 230.

437 Compare: William Cullen Dennis, 'The Necessity for an International Code of Arbitral Procedure' (1913) 7 The American Journal of International Law 285.

438 Francis Anthony Boyle, *Foundations of World Order* (n 28 in Chapter 1) 84.

an "[...] obligatory jurisdiction and be strictly judicial in its procedures."[439] Furthermore, Arthur K. Kuhn (*'The existing and proposed International Courts as Subjects for the Deliberations of the Third Hague Peace Conference'* from 1913) proposed the establishment of a court at the Third Hague Peace Conference which "[...] is to be a new organ with new functions, permanent as a court, not merely as a panel, continuous in its judicature, administering law divested of mere compromise and hence, within its sphere, a *new* force making the peace of the world."[440] A similar view was also held by Edward A. Harriman (*'The Work of the Hague Conferences – Past and Future'* from 1914). According to him, "[t]here are many things which a third Hague Conference should consider, – details of the rules of international law affecting nations in war and peace, – but to my mind the greatest object [...] should be the provision for the actual establishment of a real International Court of Justice."[441] Harriman's contribution also demonstrated that (at least some) U.S.-American international lawyers and peace activists finally differentiated very clearly between 'arbitration' and 'adjudication.' This becomes apparent, for example, in the following statement of his:

> [...] the fundamental ideas of arbitration and judicial justice are radically different, and there is no such thing known to jurisprudence as arbitral justice. From a legal standpoint, the administration of justice consists, first, in the determination of the facts in the case; second, in the ascertainment of the rules of law applicable to those facts, and, third, in a judgment applying the law to the facts and fixing the respective obligations of the parties to the proceeding.[442]

Hence, the U.S.-American peace activists and international lawyers held great hopes regarding the *Third Hague Peace Conference*. In order to achieve them, they also made use of their grown political influence. Above all, Elihu Root and James Brown Scott (as well as Nicholas Murray Butler) used their close

439 James L. Tryon, 'A Permanent Court of International Justice: A Suggestion for the Consideration of the Programme Committee of the Third Hague Conference' (1913) 22 The Yale Law Journal 203–204.

440 Arthur K. Kuhn, 'The Existing and Proposed International Courts as Subjects for the Deliberations of the Third Hague Peace Conference' in *Report of the Nineteenth Annual Lake Mohonk Conference on International Arbitration, May 14th, 15th, and 16th 1913* (Lake Mohonk Arbitration Conference 1913) 100.

441 Edward A. Harriman, 'The Work of the Hague Conferences – Past and Future' in *Report of the Twentieth Annual Lake Mohonk Conference on International Arbitration, May 27th, 28th, and 29th 1914* (Lake Mohonk Arbitration Conference 1914) 93.

442 Ibid.

relations to governmental officials, political decision-makers, and the White House to convince the U.S.-American government of taking preparatory steps for the third conference and for realizing the idea of an international court of law at this occasion.[443] According to Ralph D. Nurnberger (*'James Brown Scott: Peace Through Law'* (from 1975), Scott and Root were quite successful in this regard. They managed to convince President Taft of creating a *National Advisory Committee* on June 10, 1912, which was assigned with the preparatory work for the agenda of the United States at this conference.[444] Other nations had also just taken similar steps – such as Denmark, France, the Netherlands, Norway, and Sweden.[445] The United States did not wish to stand behind in this regard. Secretary of State William Jennings Bryan (1860–1925) even sent a circular note to the American diplomatic missions (which was to be forwarded to the respective foreign governments in the host countries). In this letter, Bryan proposed the creation of an *International Preparatory Committee* in order to set the agenda for the *Third Hague Peace Conference*.[446] On July 6, 1914, the Dutch and Russian governments finally took over the initiative and invited all nations represented at the *Second Hague Peace Conference* to participate in the work of such a preparatory committee.[447] However, the Dutch-Russian invitation was submitted eight days after the assassination of the Austrian Archduke Francis Ferdinand. Hence, the events leading to *World War I* were already gathering momentum. It should also be taken into consideration that – according to Warren F. Kuehl (*'Seeking World Order'* from 1969) – the chances that the *Third Hague Peace Conference* took place in 1915 had generally been very low, regardless of the war. It had seemed as if the meeting could not be held before 1916 or 1917.[448] In this regard, Kuehl stated that "[t]he armament race and the aura of suspicion permeating the diplomacy of the time would have undermined the venture. The mood and attitude of nations by 1914 was far different from what it had been in 1899 or even 1907."[449]

While the situation between the great power blocks was very tense and, to a certain extent, gridlocked, it was not entirely hopeless. The powers were

---

443 Warren F. Kuehl, *Seeking World Order* (n 16 in Chapter 3) 158.

444 Ralph D. Nurnberger, *James Brown Scott: Peace Through Justice* (n 1 in Chapter 5) 229–230.

445 Ibid 232.

446 Ibid 233.

447 Ibid 233–234. According to Nurnberger, the Preparatory Committee "[…] would consist of one representative from each nation and would meet at The Hague on June 1, 1915." Also: Warren F. Kuehl, *Seeking World Order* (n 16 in Chapter 3) 158.

448 Warren F. Kuehl, *Seeking World Order* (n 16 in Chapter 3) 159. See also the following article: 'Things International' (June 22, 1914) 78 The Independent 533.

449 Warren F. Kuehl, *Seeking World Order* (n 16 in Chapter 3) 159.

still communicating with one another. Furthermore, Great Britain, Germany, France, and the United States had just met in Paris in 1910 to draft a convention for the establishment of the CAJ. All four states seem to have aimed for realizing the project and to have worked together for the achievement of this goal. It had only failed in the end because of Great Britain's decision not to ratify the *London Declaration* as well as the convention for the establishment of the IPC. Consequently, it does not seem as if the initiative for a *Third Hague Peace Conference* was doomed to failure before the outbreak of the war. The situation, and the relationship between the European great power blocks, was not catastrophic and hostile enough to prevent the conference from taking place at all. Instead, it seems as if the event did stand a chance to achieve presentable results. This understanding of the situation in 1913/14 is further supported by the fact that (at least) a number of smaller states as well as France, Russia, and the United States decided to take preparatory steps for setting an agenda for the meeting. In the end, however, *World War I* prevented the conference from being realized and froze any attempt for potential further developments and advancements in the field of international law for the next years, at least in the sense of developing a more peace-oriented and rule of law-based international legal order. Initiatives for the establishment of an international court of law, the creation of a league of nations, and the preservation of *peace through law* only surfaced again in 1918/19.[450]

3.3 *Arbitration and Commissions of Inquiry*

As shown on the previous pages, the creation of an international court of law stood in the focus of attention of many peace activists and international lawyers, especially those from the United States. However, despite the popularity of adjudication, arbitration and commissions of inquiry did not disappear from international law, political discussions, or the agenda of the peace movement between 1907 and 1914.

As mentioned above, Elihu Root had already concluded a series of bi-lateral obligatory arbitration treaties between 1908 and 1909 and had thereby revived John Hay's initiative for this type of agreement in the United States.[451] The new Secretary of State William Jennings Bryan not only strove for additional

---

450 Compare in this regard: David J. Hill, 'International Law and International Policy' (1919) 209 no. 760 The North American Review 315–329; Manley O. Hudson, *A Treatise on the Permanent Court of International Justice* (n 116 in Chapter 2) 85–96; Francis Anthony Boyle, *Foundations of World Order* (n 28 in Chapter 1) 47–48.

451 Compare pages 330–331 of the present book.

agreements of that kind,[452] but he also took the initiative in 1913 for the conclusion of a new type of bi-lateral peace treaty. In the context of these agreements, he pursued a decisively different approach. Instead of concluding purely obligatory arbitration treaties, he aimed for advancing the cause of general peace by introducing a new kind of clause. According to the U.S.-American scholar George A. Finch (*'The Bryan Peace Treaties'* from 1916) "[a]ll of these treaties are based upon the same principle, namely, that disputes which the high contracting parties are unable to adjust by diplomacy or arbitration shall be referred to a commission for investigation and report and that hostilities may not be resorted to in the meantime."[453] Bryan concluded such treaties with at least nineteen countries by October 1916;[454] and all of which contained a provision that limited the *ius ad bellum* of the adhering parties in the described manner. The contracting states either had to settle their disputes by diplomacy, arbitration, or with the help of a commission of inquiry. Therefore, none of the parties were allowed to wage war while any of these procedures were still in progress and while these options had not yet been exhausted; which constituted a wide-reaching prohibition of armed struggles. The inherent delay of the use of force until the end of all these procedures granted time for the parties to re-consider their situations. It allowed them to cool down and take a well-considered decision instead of a hasty and maybe premature one. Thereby, they had the chance to re-evaluate whether they really wanted to take recourse to force. It also created the moral obligation for them to take into consideration arbitral decisions and the results of the investigations of the commissions. If any of the parties ignored them, these nations could lose all support and backing from the international community and could be condemned as warmongers that referred to force out of selfish and unlawful reasons. Therefore, Bryan seems to have expected his peace treaties to have a substantial effect on the preservation of peace and to prevent conflicts from escalating into open wars.

Apart from the *Bryan Treaties*, interesting findings can also be made regarding the practical use of arbitration. According to A.M. Stuyt (*'Survey of International Arbitrations 1794–1989'* from 1990), 29 cases were settled by arbitration between the end of the *Second Hague Peace Conference* (October 18, 1907)

452 Calvin DeArmond Davis, *The United States and the Second Hague Peace Conference* (n 28 in Chapter 1) 335.

453 Georg A. Finch, 'The Bryan Peace Treaties' (1916) 10 The American Journal of International Law 882.

454 Ibid. According to him, these states were: Bolivia, Chile, China, Costa Rica, Denmark, Ecuador, France, Great Britain, Guatemala, Honduras, Italy, Norway, Paraguay, Peru, Portugal, Russia, Spain, Sweden, and Uruguay.

and the Austrian declaration of war against Serbia (July 28, 1914).[455] These numbers account for a frequency of 4.14 arbitrations per year during that period. In comparison, this figure was at 1.45 arbitrations per year for the period between 1871 and 1899 and at 7.13 arbitrations per year between the end of the *First* and the beginning of the *Second Hague Peace Conference* (1899–1907).[456] Before this background, it seems as if the deterioration of the relations between the great powers also had an impact on their willingness to settle conflicts by arbitration. As it can be deduced from these above-given numbers, the frequency of arbitrations per year was almost reduced by half in the period after the *Second Hague Peace Conference*.

That being said, one remarkable development should still be noted regarding the use of arbitration between 1907 and 1914. According to Calvin DeArmond Davis, "[…] the Permanent Court of Arbitration was functioning with a vigor which seemed to refute the criticism it received at the *Second Hague Peace Conference*. Between 1909 and 1914 the court made awards in ten cases involving thirteen governments. Most of these decisions were about minor matters but a few touched important issues."[457] One of those cases settled by the PCA and dealing with key interests of the involved parties was a dispute between Germany and France. It concerned Morocco and bore the potential of leading to another crisis between the two countries – and due to their alliances also beyond their bi-lateral relationship.[458] The decision of the court (issued on September 25, 1908) prevented an escalation and offered a peaceful alternative which Germany and France willingly accepted. The most important case settled by the PCA was, however, the so-called *North Atlantic Coast Fisheries Case* between the United States and Great Britain.[459] In an editorial comment on this particular case from the American Journal of International Law, the following was stated:

> But the great importance of the arbitration can hardly be said to lied in the award: the example of two great and powerful nations submitting to

---

455 A.M. Stuyt, *Survey of International Arbitrations 1794–1989* (n 125 in Chapter 3) 292–325.

456 Ibid 292–325, 233–291. With regards to these figures, Francis Anthony Boyle refers to the period between 1899–1914 as "the Golden Age of Modern International Arbitration"; compare: Francis Anthony Boyle, *Foundations of World Order* (n 28 in Chapter 1) 34–35.

457 Calvin DeArmond Davis, *The United States and the Second Hague Peace Conference* (n 28 in Chapter 1) 314.

458 A.M. Stuyt, *Survey of International Arbitrations 1794–1989* (n 125 in Chapter 3) 289.

459 Ibid 309. See also: Luis M. Drago, 'United States versus Great Britain in the Matter of the North Atlantic Coast Fisheries' (1910) 4 The American Journal of International Law 948–988.

> judicial determination an acute controversy involving a question of sovereignty and its exercise is likely to influence other nations to resort to this peaceable method of settling intricate disputes dangerous to their peace, and the award is calculated to create confidence in the method. [...] Every war, it is said, carries with it the seeds of future wars; it may be said with greater confidence that each arbitration leads inevitably to arbitration and accustoms the world to the peaceful settlement of international disputes.[460]

Therefore, the popularity of the PCA and the willingness of the states to refer cases – even important ones – to this institution grew between the *Second Hague Peace Conference* and the outbreak of *World War I*. Despite the decreasing number of arbitrations in general, the PCA became a considerably more accepted institution. Although peace activists and international lawyers strove for the establishment of a purely judicial court at the international level and although they had several reservations concerning the structure of the PCA, they still propagated its use and further involvement in the settlement of international disputes. The PCA was the best and most capable institution for the peaceful settlement of international conflicts that was available at that time; therefore, most peace activists and international lawyers did not want it to be abolished or to fall into oblivion. Instead, they aimed for creating a judicial court, which was supposed to exist side by side with the PCA. Accordingly, it seems completely logical that peace activists and international lawyers still attached so much hope to the work of the PCA and to its potential role as a savior of peace.

The belief in the functioning of the existing system for conflict settlement was still strong, even after the assassination at Sarajevo in June 1914. During the subsequent month, in the course of which the situation between the European great powers escalated into *World War I*, most people in the United States and Europe seem to have shared the expectation that the issue was to be settled peacefully.[461] On July 31, 1914, – 3 days after the Austrian declaration of war against Serbia – Philip Stanhope, president of the *Inter-Parliamentary Union*, still claimed that "[t]he prevailing nervousness is natural, but I hope

460 'Editorial Comment: North Atlantic Fisheries' (1910) 4 The American Journal of International Law 903–904.

461 Sandi E. Cooper, *Patriotic Pacifism* (n 156 in Chapter 3) 186. Also: David S. Patterson, *Towards a Warless World* (n 147 in Chapter 3) 229 et seq.

and believe, exaggerated. Neither France nor Germany desire War, I do not think that Court circles in Russia desire it either."[462]

British, French, and Russian diplomats were, indeed, trying to mediate between the parties and to prevent the situation from escalating.[463] Efforts were made to reach an agreement, to have the case settled by the PCA, or to revive the *Concert of Europe*; and Serbia even yielded to the majority of the Austrian demands.[464] However, neither the offer to arbitrate the dispute nor diplomacy succeeded in the end in the attempt to settle the crisis. Austria (backed by the German Empire) rejected the Serbian offer to take the case to The Hague, and they did the same regarding the British proposal to negotiate terms for its settlement on a conference of ambassadors as well.[465] Soon thereafter, Austria-Hungary declared war against Serbia (on July 28, 1914).[466] Thereby, a development was set in motion, which resulted in the clash of the two great power alliances in Europe and which thrusted the world into a devastating war costing the lives of millions of people.

4 Conclusions

In his article *'A highly critical Moment: Role and Record of the 1907 Hague Peace Conference'* (from 2007) Arthur Eyffinger came up with the following, very interesting conclusion regarding the developments between 1906 and 1914:

> Often ignored and ridiculed, the Second Hague Peace Conference was a unique exchange of views at a moment of paramount interest for the history of Europe. Its debate impeccably touched upon the sore of early 20th century international society. Its failure to reach agreement on all too many vital issues had dramatic consequences: 1907 proved the last stop of the nations on their head-long race for Verdun. At The Hague, the die was cast. Prussian arrogance and bigotry blew up what little credibility was left from under the system of Concert and Balance.[467]

462 Quoted in: Sandi E. Cooper, *Patriotic Pacifism* (n 156 in Chapter 3) 186.

463 Ibid.

464 Calvin DeArmond Davis, *The United States and the Second Hague Peace Conference* (n 28 in Chapter 1) 339.

465 Ibid 340.

466 Compare: Oona A. Hathaway and Scott J. Shapiro, *The Internationalists* (n 11 in Chapter 1) 101 et seq.

467 Arthur Eyffinger, 'A highly critical Moment' (n 355 in Chapter 6) 228.

He draws a very dark picture – probably too dark – when it comes to the proceedings and results of the *Second Hague Peace Conference*. As shown above, the agenda of the conference was very progressive and touched upon a number of topics, which had never before been discussed by representatives from almost all existing states on an event of global dimensions. It was the first world conference in history and some points of its agenda were of crucial importance for the principle of *peace through law*, such as the conclusion of an obligatory arbitration treaty, the establishment of the IPC and of the CAJ, and the discussions about the *Porter Doctrine*. The chance of reaching an agreement regarding all three of these points had been rather small from the beginning. Furthermore, there are good reasons to regard the *Second Hague Peace Conference* not only as an isolated event but as an element of a series of developments reaching from the end of the 19th century until the middle of the 20th century (and beyond). Before *World War I*, the *First Pan American Conference* (1889/1890), the *First Hague Peace Conference* (1899), the *Second* and *Third Pan-American Conferences* (1901/1902 and 1906), the *Second Hague Peace Conference* (1907), and the subsequent events between 1907 and 1914 were the most important elements of this development. After *World War I*, the process towards the realization of the principle of *peace through law*, the creation of institutions for the judicial settlement of international conflicts, the implementation of the rule of law in international relations, and the limitation of the *ius ad bellum* were even taken up again and further pursued; for example, through the *Treaty of Versailles* (1919), the creation of the *League of Nations* (1920), the constitution of the *Permanent Court of International Justice* (1922), the conclusion of the *Briand-Kellogg Pact* (1928), and the *Saavedra Lamas Treaty* (1933). At every one of these occasions, the realization of similar goals was striven for – especially regarding the creation of a world court, the preservation of peace, and the limitation/abolition of war.

Consequently, the *Second Hague Peace Conference* should rather be understood as an important, but still early, step in this course of events. Deep-going changes of the international order require a lot of time to be implemented and (usually) only take place in form of gradual developments. The above-cited statements issued by international lawyers and state officials show that most of them were well aware of this fact, wherefore they regarded the *Second Hague Peace Conference* only as the starting point for further developments in favor of the cause of peace. By the end of the conference, and despite its shortcomings, they continued to look to the future optimistically. They hoped for the realization of their goals on future occasions. Nevertheless, it cannot be denied either that the *Second Hague Peace Conference* did not result in very presentable, prominent, and highly progressive achievements in the fields of obligatory arbitration or adjudication, despite the decision to establish the IPC and the conclusion of the *Porter Doctrine*. Both major projects regarding the preservation of peace – the creation of a general international court of law and the conclusion of a multi-lateral obligatory arbitration treaty – had failed; even though these two topics were controversially discussed and that the vast majority of the participating states had supported them. Therefore, the general mood in The Hague seems to have been benevolent and supportive of these progressive ideas, which had aimed at the realization of the principle of *peace through law*. The main reasons for the failure of these projects laid in the fact that minor groups of states objected to them and that the conference failed to come to suitable compromises acceptable for everybody.

Above all other countries, the United States took a leading role with regards to the attempt to establish a general international court of law in the period between 1906 and 1914. After having already striven for a tribunal of a very advanced nature at the *First Hague Peace Conference*, they took the lead once more at the follow-up meeting in 1907 and introduced the draft code for the CAJ to its discussions. Despite the failure of the *Second Hague Peace Conference* to come to terms for the realization of this project, the United States continued to promote this project on several occasions between 1907 and 1914, most notably at the *London Naval Conference* (1908/09) and at the *Four-Power-Meeting* in Paris (1910). None of these attempts resulted in the actual realization of the CAJ; however, it can be concluded from the reactions to these proposals, that the idea to create a general international court of law had already found numerous supporters among the states before the outbreak of *World War I*. Consequently, the (intellectual) foundations for the developments in the aftermath of this war – especially the creation of the *Permanent Court of International Justice* – were laid between 1906 and 1914.

This conclusion is further supported by the achievements made at the *Washington Conference* (1907). At this occasion, the United States (and Mexico) managed to convince the Central American countries to establish the *Central American Court of Justice*, the first permanent international court of law in history. The creation of the CACJ was a huge success for peace activists, international lawyers, and especially for the U.S.-American government, in particular Elihu Root and James Brown Scott. They regarded the foundation of this regional international court of law as a necessary and very promising step in the gradual development of an international judiciary. After this success, they hoped to achieve similar results at the global level. The *Third Hague Peace Conference* played a major role in this regard because it was deemed to be the perfect opportunity to approach this topic again before the entire world community and to convince the participating states of taking the necessary steps for the creation of a global court of law. Therefore, lots of hope and expectations were attached to the event. However, the outbreak of *World War I* prevented the conference from ever taking place. Even though no such court was created at the global level before *World War I* – despite numerous U.S.-American attempts in this direction – the mentioned developments show that the *Second Hague Peace Conference* set a movement in motion, which resulted in the creation of the *Permanent Court of International Justice* and, in the long-run, the *International Court of Justice* (in 1945). Therefore, the *Second Hague Peace Conference* cannot only be considered as an isolated event, but it should be seen as the starting point of the development leading to the creation of an international judiciary.

Moreover, the thinking of progressive international lawyers and peace activists in the period between 1906 and 1914 was dominated by the idea of institutionalizing adjudication in form of a permanent international court of law. During these years, this concept developed from a utopian idea – only prominent in legal scholarship and in the publications of the peace movement – into a well-received and warmly welcomed scheme among governments. Additionally, it can also be found that arbitration remained an option for the peaceful settlement of international conflicts as well. It was regularly invoked for the settlement of state-to-state disputes, numerous bi-lateral obligatory arbitration treaties were concluded, and the PCA was called on no less than ten times between 1907 and 1914 (in some cases even to settle important issues). Many international lawyers and peace activists no longer believed arbitration to be the most suitable means for pacific conflict settlement. Adjudication was considered to be far more promising in this regard. However, arbitration was well-established and widely accepted within the community of states. Moreover, unlike adjudication, it was actually practiced by states. The idea to preserve peace through the establishment of a permanent international court of law may have enjoyed considerably more prominence. However, arbitration was the only available and established means in state practice for (*quasi-*)judicial settlements of conflicts before the outbreak of *World War I*. It was the instrument on which states relied on a quickly increasing basis since 1899 and it was invoked to settle (mostly) minor conflicts between them. In a gradually growing number of cases, it was also used to address more important issues. Therefore, arbitration did not simply fade into the background when adjudication became more prominent. Instead, it continued to play an essential role during these years, especially when it came to state practice. Adjudication only became more dominant and was institutionalized on the global level in the form of a permanent international court of law after the end of *World War I*.

CHAPTER 7

Conclusions

> The feeling that the present war is a disastrous failure of civilization, and that at its close all should be done that human wisdom and foresight can devise, to prevent the recurrence of such a catastrophe, is, we believe, general, if not universal, among all the nations concerned.[1]
>
> JAMES BRYCE, *'Proposals for the Avoidance of War'* (*1915*)

1 Summarizing the Subsequent Developments

David S. Patterson (*'Toward a Warless World'* from 1976) described the peace movement in the years before *World War I* as highly heterogenic. According to him, "[w]ith so many individuals involved in the cause, it is not surprising that there were numerous approaches to peace."[2] One group – comprised of lawyer-statesmen and activists such as Elihu Root, James Brown Scott, and William J. Bryan – believed that judicial procedures such as arbitral courts and the codification of international law were the most suitable means for securing peace.[3] Several other approaches were heavily discussed among peace activists at that time as well; and especially, James Bryce, a former British ambassador to the United States, played a key role in this regard. He and a group of like-minded thinkers supported the idea to create an international union – and, thus, revived similarly shaped projects from the 19th century – which was competent and powerful enough to prevent peace and to enforce its decisions through collective measures against the will of law-breaking and warmongering nations. For realizing this goal, Bryce and his colleagues prepared the so-called *Proposals for the Avoidance of War* in 1915. According to Martin

1 James Bryce, *Proposals for the Avoidance of War with a Preparatory Note by Viscount Bryce* (1915) 7; the treatise was not intended for publication but can be found here: <https://archive.org/details/proposalsforavoi00brycuoft/page/n1/mode/2up> accessed August 26, 2021.

2 David S. Patterson, *Towards a Warless World* (n 147 in Chapter 3) 181.

3 Ruth Henig, *The League of Nations* (n 27 in Chapter 1) 11–12.

 | DOI:10.1163/9789004754126_008

D. Dubin (*'Toward the Concept of Collective Security'* from 1970), it was "[…] the single most influential scheme for a league of nations produced during the First World War."[4] Dubin continued his remarks by claiming that the document was even "[…] the source of key concepts and language embodied in 1919 in the Covenant of the League of Nations and subsequently in the Statute of the Permanent Court of International Justice and of its successor, the International Court of Justice."[5]

The question of whether Dubin's claim is fully correct shall remain unanswered here. It is at least likely that Bryce's *Proposals* contributed to the development, which finally led to the creation of the *League of Nations* in 1920. The two courts, the PCIJ and the ICJ, on the other hand, seem to have had their roots in the *Hague Conferences* and the other developments descried above. However, it is only important to note at this point that the idea to create an international union of states became highly prominent among peace activists once more, at the latest after the outbreak of *World War I*. In this regard, Bryce himself stated the following:

> The project of a world-State, or even of a European Federation, we do not here advocate. It is perhaps a possibility of the distant future, and it well deserves the discussion it has provoked. But we do not believe it to be practicable at any near date. Our aim is a more modest one. We desire to give definite shape to that idea of an association or union of Sovereign States which is advocated by many leading men both in Europe and in America, and which, we believe, could be realized immediately at the conclusion of the war.[6]

Bryce clearly distinguished between a federation (or a world state) and an association. By the latter, he meant (in comparison to an actual federation) a loose alliance of states, whose members kept their sovereignty and independence. However, he did not shy away from demanding that its member states bound themselves to refer all disputes (if diplomacy had failed to settle them) to an international judicial court or to a council for investigation and report.[7] Consequently, no wars and hostilities were to be allowed between the member states of this association until the court (or council) had taken a decision

4 Martin D. Dubin, 'Toward the Concept of Collective Security: The Bryce Group's "Proposal for the Avoidance of War," 1914–1917' (1970) 24 International Organization 288.

5 Ibid.

6 James Bryce, *Proposals for the Avoidance of War with a Preparatory Note by Viscount Bryce* (n 1 in Chapter 7) 7.

7 Ibid 8.

on the conflict. Thereby, Bryce, and his supporters intended to eliminate anarchy from international relations, which they held to be one of the major reasons for the outbreak of *World War I* (besides militarism).[8] Even the British Prime Minister Herbert H. Asquith (1852–1928) affiliated with ideas that were very similar to the concepts proposed by Bryce. In a speech held in Dublin on September 25, 1914, Asquith declared the following:

> The idea of public right, what does it mean when translated into concrete terms?
>
> [...] it means, finally, or it ought to mean, perhaps by a slow and gradual process, the substitution for force, for the clash of competing ambitions, for groupings and alliances and a precarious equipoise, the substitution for all these things of a real European partnership, based on the recognition of equal right and established and enforced by a common will. A year ago that would have sounded like a Utopian idea. It is probably one that may not or will not be realized either to-day or to-morrow. If and when this war is decided in favour of the Allies, it will at once come within the range, and before long within the grasp, of European statesmanship.[9]

U.S. President Woodrow Wilson (1856–1924) contributed to this development as well. In 1918, he presented his famous *Fourteen Points* before the U.S.-American Congress, which provided (in its point XIV) for the creation of a "[...] general association of nations [...] for affording mutual guarantees of political independence and territorial integrity to great and small states alike."[10] This was not the first time Wilson thought about the establishment of such an institution. He had already dealt with the idea before. According to Warren F. Kuehl ('*Seeking World Order*' from 1969), Wilson had

> [...] joined the American Peace Society in 1908, delivered addresses at pacifist meetings, and must have been introduced to the Ladd-Trueblood concept of a congress of nations and a world court. He knew of the evolutionary tends at The Hague and recognized the importance of arbitration when he endorsed the Taft treaties in 1911.[11]

8 Martin D. Dubin, 'Toward the Concept of Collective Security' (n 4 in Chapter 7) 289.

9 Herbert H. Asquith, 'Speech at Dublin, September 25, 1914' in James Bryce, *Proposals for the Avoidance of War with a Preparatory Note by Viscount Bryce* (n 1 in Chapter 7) 14.

10 President Woodrow Wilson's 'Fourteen Points' (Jan. 8, 1918), <http://avalon.law.yale.edu/20th_century/wilson14.asp> accessed August 21, 2018.

11 Warren F. Kuehl, *Seeking World Order* (n 16 in Chapter 3) 224.

Furthermore, Wilson mentioned in 1914 to his brother-in-law that "[…] there must be an association of the nations, all bound together for the protection of the integrity of each, so that any one nation breaking from this bond will bring upon herself war; that is to say punishment, automatically."[12] Moreover, Wilson's friend and advisor Colonel Edward M. House presented a draft for an institutionalized cooperation in the inter-American context for the preservation of peace in the region and to make an example for Europe.[13] British and French committees worked on the idea of creating international associations too, and seem to have inspired Wilson in this regard.[14]

Apart from political leaders, peace activists embraced and propagated concepts for the creation of world unions soon after the outbreak of the war as well. The experiences and horrors of *World War I* had convinced people of the need for international structures and mechanisms for maintaining peace. After the end of hostilities in 1918, they considered it to be the perfect occasion to introduce concepts for world organizations once more.[15] For example, the *League to Enforce Peace* was created in the United States in 1915 and soon developed into an influential peace society.[16] U.S.-American peace activists had been shocked by the outbreak of *World War I*. They had to realize that all previous efforts that they had made had been fruitless in establishing a system capable of preserving peace. But according to Warren F. Kuehl, "[…] virtually all thought and action in regard to world co-operation immediately before 1914 had been channeled along the lines of arbitral, legal, and judicial agreements. The war had proven how ineffective such machinery could be in time of crisis."[17] As shown in the previous chapters, this conclusion surely was not unfounded. Most attempts made between the late 19th century and 1914 to create an international system for the preservation of peace and for the peaceful settlement of state-to-state disputes had aimed for the establishment of (autonomous) arbitral and judicial institutions and for the conclusion of obligatory arbitration treaties. However, both approaches (the arbitral as well as the judicial one) had proven to be incapable of preventing the outbreak of *World War I*. Moreover, cases of primary importance had only occasionally been settled by arbitration (or by the

12 The quote stems from: ibid 224; no original source indicated. See also: Ruth Henig, *The League of Nations* (n 27 in Chapter 1) 13.

13 Ruth Henig, *The League of Nations* (n 27 in Chapter 1) 13.

14 Christian J. Tams, 'League of Nations', *Max Planck Encyclopedia of Public International Law* (online).

15 Manley O. Hudson, *The Permanent Court of International Justice 1920–1942* (The Macmillan company 1943) 85.

16 Warren F. Kuehl, *Seeking World Order* (n 16 in Chapter 3) 200.

17 Ibid 172–173.

PCA) before 1914, and even the projected and highly progressive CAJ was intended to be of a purely voluntary nature. Consequently, this court would not have been equipped with the necessary competences to prevent the war from breaking out either. Finally, in several cases, bi-lateral obligatory arbitration agreements turned out to be rather ineffective in practice. *World War I* had shattered the conviction that states would honor bi-lateral treaty obligations that demanded arbitral or judicial settlements in cases of crucial disputes.[18] The system that international lawyers, peace activists, and progressive members of the governments had striven for so far, turned out in 1914 to be incapable of effectively preventing wars. This was due to its voluntary nature, its reliance on bi-lateral agreements, and the fact that it lacked an institutional background that was competent and powerful enough to enforce its decisions.

After the outbreak of *World War I*, numerous peace activists drew conclusions from these new insights and from the failure of the existing system to prevent the war. They intensified the promotion of the creation of an international court of law that was equipped with obligatory competences. This had already been a long-term goal of the peace movement but many of its members seem to have considered it to be too utopian (during the pre-war period) to actually be realized. As shown in the context of the *Second Hague Peace Conference*, this assessment of the prevailing situation on the international level and of the states' view on such an idea appears to be well founded. The members of the U.S.-American delegation had even explicitly abstained in The Hague from proposing the award of obligatory competences to a potential international court of law because they had not believed that such a project could be realized at this point in time. The negotiations on the conclusion of a multi-lateral obligatory arbitration must also have confirmed this view. The German government (and some of its supporters) had rejected all initiatives in this regard. However, the prevailing notion on this topic changed decisively during *World War I*, at least among peace activists (and especially among the members of the *League to Enforce Peace*). They openly demanded the introduction of an obligatory judicial system on the international level to deprive states of the chance to avoid pacific settlements of their disputes and of the option to go to war directly. Therefore, the number of supporters for the creation of a world association and for the establishment of an international court of law equipped with obligatory competences in the framework of the latter association rose substantially after 1914. But although supporters of this approach acquired an influential position in the U.S.-American peace movement, their approach did not reflect the entire range of views

18 Both quotes stem from: ibid 173.

on the preservation of peace on the international level at that time.[19] There were several other tendencies and ideas pursued by peace groups and individuals; and the concept of an autonomous international court of law – which had developed into a highly prominent idea among peace activists and international lawyers between 1906 and 1914 – did not disappear either.[20] In this regard, James Brown Scott mentioned in 1915 that "[w]e have societies galore advocating a parliament of man, and an equally large number of organizations and people advocating a supreme court of the world, all of them making innumerable suggestions and proposals at different times."[21]

After the end of *World War I*, the *League of Nations* was established (in 1920). It had a truly judicial court, the *Permanent Court of International Justice*, and complied to a great extent with Woodrow Wilsons' (above described) concept for an alliance of states. For example, authors such as Charles G. Fenwick had already stressed in 1917 that it would not be enough to only create an international court of law. According to him, it was also necessary to introduce instruments for the enforcement of decisions that were issued by such a court. Otherwise, the court would run the risk of becoming useless in practice.[22] In his contribution *'International Organization – Judicial'* (from 1917), Fenwick consequently declared the following in this regard:

> We cannot refuge in abstract mediation and speculate upon the ideal judicial organization of an ideal international community. It will not do to propose a court, however nicely its jurisdiction and membership be adjusted in theory [...].

---

19 Ibid 200.

20 Between 1906 and 1914 the striving of Elihu Root, James Brown Scott, and many other peace activists and international lawyers for the pacification of international relations had rested to a great extent on the idea to create an autonomous international court of law. This approach had widely replaced the idea of creating a world union in whose framework an international court (of law) settled all arising conflicts between the member states of the association (compare pages 248 et seq. of the present book). Only the horrors of World War I and the realization that autonomous (and voluntary) judicial/arbitral courts alone were not powerful enough to prevent major wars from breaking out, peace activists and international lawyers again turned to promote the creation of world associations to provide the necessary institutional background for preserving peace.

21 'James Brown Scott to J.G. Schmidlapp' (February 2, 1915). See also: Sally Marks, *The Illusion of Peace: International Relations in Europe, 1918–1933* (Palgrave Macmillan Ltd. 2003) 7.

22 Charles G. Fenwick, 'International Organization – Judicial' (1917) 11 Proceedings of the American Society of International Law at Its Annual Meeting 65.

> [...] As in the case of national courts, [....] there can be no authoritative decision except on the knowledge that behind the award of the court stands the organized force of the community pledged to support it. The jurisdiction of the international court will, therefore, be largely dependent upon the existence of an international legislature, and its authority will be greater or less according to the character of the international executive which supports its decrees.[23]

Other authors joined Fenwick's approach and openly declared that they did not consider an autonomous judicial system as being capable of preserving peace. Instead, they demanded that judicial decisions and international law be backed by enough power to enforce them. To achieve this goal, they wanted to create an international union, whose members mutually guaranteed each other collective security in order to put an end to war.[24] U.S. President Wilson shared this approach as well and favored collective security over adjudication.[25] Moreover, he strove for putting an end to war itself due to its destructive nature and danger to all states (neutrals and conflict parties alike).[26]

In 1920, Wilson's goal became a reality: The *League of Nations* was established as an association of nations bound together through a system of collective security. This approach was supposed to guarantee the territorial integrity and sovereignty of states[27] and, in particular, the maintenance of peace. Collective security was explicitly introduced through Article 11 of the *Covenant of the League of Nations*. The norm provided that "[a]ny war or threat of war, whether immediately affecting any of the Members of the League or not, is hereby declared a matter of concern to the whole League, and the League shall take any action that may be deemed wise and effectual to safeguard the peace of nations."[28] Additionally, Article 12 determined that in the event of the emergence of a dispute between them, the members of the *League* had to "[...] submit the matter either to arbitration or judicial settlement or to enquiry by the Council, and they agree in no case to resort to force until three months

23 Ibid.

24 Paolo Amorosa, *The American Project and the Politics of History: James Brown Scott and the Origins of International Law* (Doctoral dissertation at University of Helsinki 2018) 129–130; <https://helda.helsinki.fi/bitstream/handle/10138/233591/TheAmeri.pdf?sequence=1&isAllowed=y> accessed August 26, 2021.

25 Ibid.

26 Charles G. Fenwick, 'International Law: The Old and the New' (1966) 60 The American Journal of International Law 476–477.

27 Compare: Article 10, Covenant of the League of Nations; available online: <http://avalon.law.yale.edu/20th_century/leagcov.asp> accessed August 19, 2018.

28 Ibid Article 11.

after the award by the arbitrators or the judicial decision, or the report of the Council."[29] The competent body for judicial settlements was determined to be the PCIJ, an institution that was to be established in accordance with Article 14 of the *Covenant* in the following years.[30] Compliance with these obligations was supposed to be guaranteed through Article 16. The norm provided that if any member of the *League* disregarded its covenants under Articles 12, 13, or 15, this state "[…] shall ipso facto be deemed to have committed an act of war against all other Members of the League."[31] In such cases, the other states were entitled to take appropriate measures – in the form of collective actions – against the law-breaking state to penalize its behavior and to "protect the covenants of the League."[32] Therefore, Article 16 established guarantees for the functioning of the convention and attempted to secure the compliance of its members with its obligations.

The *Covenant* provided, thereby, for a limitation of the *ius ad bellum* but not for a full prohibition of war under international law. This step was only accomplished in 1928 with the conclusion of the *Briand-Kellogg Pact* (and the *Saavedra Lamas Treaty* in 1933) that condemned "[…] recourse to war for the solution of international controversies, and renounce it, as an instrument of national policy with one another."[33] Nevertheless, the *Covenant* already determined that war was no longer allowed to be waged without prior attempts to settle the underlying conflicts peacefully by arbitration, before the PCIJ, or by the *Council of the League of Nations*. Furthermore, a period of restraint (or "cooling off period")[34] was imposed on the conflicting parties (in Article 12). They were only entitled to wage war after a period of three months had passed since a decision had been issued by any of the named institutions. Thereby, the states were given the chance to re-consider whether they really wanted to go to war or not. They could take another attempt at settling the dispute diplomatically as they had enough time to cool down their tempers and had the chance to search for alternatives to emotion-driven reactions.

Moreover, the introduction of the *Covenant* set a development in motion that would finally result in the ban of war in the *Briand-Kellogg Pact* from 1928, the *Saavedra Lamas Treaty* from 1933, and the *Charter of the United Nations*

29 Ibid Article 12.

30 Ibid Article 14.

31 Ibid Article 16.

32 Ibid Article 16 (paragraph 2).

33 'Briand-Kellogg Pact', Article 1; <http://avalon.law.yale.edu/20th_century/kbpact.asp> accessed August 22, 2018. See also: Randall Lesaffer, 'Briand-Kellogg Pact (1928)', *Max Planck Encyclopaedia of Public International Law* (*online*).

34 Christian J. Tams, 'League of Nations' (n 14 in Chapter 7).

from 1945. Unlike during the years prior 1914, the *interbellum* system was no longer based on (mostly voluntary) international (arbitral) courts and bilateral obligatory arbitration treaties. Instead, it was driven by the recent experiences and the horrors of *World War I*. A system of collective security was created among most states (but not joint, for example, by the United States).[35] This step was supposed to close conceptual gaps and shortcomings of the former international system. The member states of the *League of Nations* were not only obliged to guarantee the sovereignty and territorial integrity of all its members and, therefore, to step in for each other in the event of aggressions. But they also had to subject all of their mutual conflicts to pacific settlement before they were legally entitled to wage war. It meant that a multi-lateral treaty was finally concluded, which obliged its signatory states to take recourse to peaceful methods of conflict settlement.

A closer look at the PCIJ reveals that – according to James Brown Scott (*'A Permanent Court of International Justice'* from 1920) – it was "[...] a permanent Court of Justice, not of Arbitration."[36] It was established in 1922 by the member states of the *League*, but it was not an organ of this institution. Instead, the PCIJ was established as an autonomous body for the judicial settlement of conflicts, open to members as well as non-members of the *League*.[37] Manley O. Hudson (*'The Permanent Court of International Justice'* from 1943) postulated the following concerning possible influences around 1920 on the drafting process of the *Statute* of the court:

> The work of the 1920 Committee of Jurists was greatly influenced by the deliberations of the Peace Conferences at The Hague in 1899 and 1907, and by the 'Five-Power-Plan' drawn up at a Conference of representatives of formerly neutral States held at The Hague in February 1920, many of the Committee's proposals with reference to the procedure of the Court were borrowed from provisions of the 'Five-Power-Plan', which had in turn adapted them from the Hague Conventions for Pacific Settlement. The project *annexed* to the Final Act of the Hague Conference of 1907, relating to the creation of a Court of Arbitral Justice, furnished ideas for the organization of the Court, also. Indeed, a careful review of the history of the

35 Charles G. Fenwick, 'International Law: The Old and the New' (n 26 in Chapter 7) 477. Also: John Milton Cooper, Jr., *Breaking the Heart of the World: Woodrow Wilson and the Fight for the League of Nations* (Cambridge University Press 2001).

36 James Brown Scott, 'A Permanent Court of International Justice' (1920) 14 The American Journal of International Law 582.

37 Shabtai Rosenne, 'Permanent Court of International Justice (PCIJ)', *Max Planck Encyclopaedia of Public International Law (online)*.

> drafting of the Statute leaves the impression that it contains but few new ideas, and that many of its provisions are based either upon previous experience or upon draft previously elaborated.[38]

Hence, Hudson concluded that the PCA and the CAJ acted as examples, inspirations, and sources for the PCIJ.[39] This assumption seems to be well founded, especially when looking at the composition of the *Committee of Jurists* – the body responsible for drafting the PCIJ statue. The committee was established by the *Council of the League of Nations* in February 1920, and it was composed of ten well-known and reputable jurists.[40] Several of them had already taken part in the *Second Hague Peace Conference,*[41] such as Francis Hangerup (Norway) and Arturo Ricci-Busatti (Italy). Elihu Root was appointed to the committee as well, and he was once again accompanied by James Brown Scott.[42] Furthermore, some of the other participants were progressive peace activists or international lawyers, for example, Albert de Lapradelle (France) and Edouard Descamps (Belgium).[43] Therefore, the majority of the committee was very familiar with earlier concepts and projects for the creation of international courts (of law) and some of them – especially Root and Scott – had even been among the primary advocates and pioneers of the creation of an international judiciary prior to 1914. The fact that they strove for a continuation of their earlier attempts and continued to follow the conceptual lines of these projects appears only logical. Moreover, proof of this assumption can also be found in the proto-

---

38 Manley O. Hudson, *The Permanent Court of International Justice 1920–1942* (n 16 in Chapter 7) 143–144.

39 Compare: ibid 81. There, Hudson stated the following: "Though the Court of Arbitral Justice planned in 1907 was never established, the promulgation of the project by the Second Peace Conference had a profound effect on world opinion in the succeeding years, and it later assisted in establishing a conviction, already quite general in 1914, that a new judicial institution was needed. Moreover, it supplied a set of definite ideas which could be used in fresh efforts in the future, and it was naturally taken as a point of departure when the Statue of the Permanent Court of International Justice was drafted in 1920." See also: Noelle Higgins, *Regulating the Use of Force in Wars of National Liberation – The Need for a New Regime* (Nijhoff 2010) 30.

40 Shabtai Rosenne, 'Permanent Court of International Justice (PCIJ)' (n 37 in Chapter 7).

41 Ibid.

42 Ole Spiermann, 'Historical Introduction' in Andreas Zimmermann, Christian Tomuschat, Karin Oellers-Frahm, and Christian J. Tams (eds.), *The Statute of the International Court of Justice* (Oxford University Press 2012) 52–53.

43 Regarding the composition of the Committee of Jurists, see: Manley O. Hudson, *The Permanent Court of International Justice 1920–1942* (n 16 in Chapter 7) 115–116. Also: James Brown Scott, 'A Permanent Court of International Justice' (n 36 in Chapter 7) 582.

cols of the work of the committee (in form of numerous references to the CAJ and the PCA).[44] Hudson affirmed this finding by declaring the following:

> Though the Court of Arbitral Justice planned in 1907 was never established, the promulgation of the *project* by the Second Peace Conference had a profound effect on world opinion in the succeeding years, and it later assisted in establishing a conviction, already quite general in 1914, that a new judicial institution was needed. Moreover, it supplied a set of definite ideas which could be used in fresh efforts in the future, and the 1907 *project* naturally served as a point of departure when the Statue of the Permanent Court of International Justice was drafted in 1920. Credit is therefore due to the men who struggled so valiantly to establish the Court of Arbitral Justice, for without their effort, the world might have been unprepared to take the step forward which was achieved in 1920.[45]

With these words, Hudson clearly connected the work of advocates of an international judiciary before 1914 with the developments following the end of *World War I*. He praised their work as having established the conceptual and ideological foundation for the creation of the PCIJ; and, due to the above-listed reasons, there is plenty of reason to follow his arguments.

Before the PCIJ was finally established in 1922, one more problem had to be overcome. This problem was one that had already caused the failure of the CAJ at the *Second Hague Peace Conference*: The method for the selection of judges for the new institution. But unlike in 1907, the states managed to find a solution. It was possible for them to compromise in this regard because the *League of Nations* had two important political organs, the *Council* and the *Assembly*. While the five great powers (the United States, Great Britain, France, Italy, and Japan) dominated the *Council*, the smaller states were in the clear majority in the *Assembly*.[46] On the proposal of Elihu Root, judges were to "[…] be selected by the concurrent action of the Council and the Assembly."[47] According to Root, this plan had the advantage of "[…] removing any possibility of unfair-

---

44 'Documents presented to the Committee Relating to Existing Plans for the Establishment of a Permanent Court of Justice' (presented 1920 in London); <https://www.icj-cij.org/public/files/permanent-court-of-international-justice/serie_D/D_documents_to_comm_existing_plans.pdf> accessed June 15, 2017.

45 Manley O. Hudson, *The Permanent Court of International Justice 1920–1942* (n 16 in Chapter 7) 83–84.

46 Compare: Article 4 Covenant of the League of Nations. See also: Christian J. Tams, 'League of Nations' (n 14 in Chapter 7).

47 James Brown Scott, 'A Permanent Court of International Justice' (n 36 in Chapter 7) 583.

ness by giving the small nations the veto on everything which took place in the Council, and by giving the large nations a veto on all the decisions taken by the Assembly."[48] Thanks to this solution, the so-called *Root-Phillimore Plan*, a truly judicial and general international court was finally established in 1922.

It was possible to accomplish these steps – the creation of a truly judicial and permanent international court equipped with obligatory competences, the establishment of a world association, and a far-reaching limitation of the *ius ad bellum* through legal means – because of the following reasons. First of all, the failure of the pre-1914 system of preventing the outbreak of *World War I* played a decisive role in this regard. It showed that a functional and effective system required a powerful world association, as well as an obligatory judicial court, to settle conflicts peacefully. These experiences and insights drove the states to finally agree on uniting within the framework of a world organization. Secondly, they subjected themselves to a general commitment to peaceful settlements of conflicts and imposed the obligation on conflicting states to observe a *cooling period* before using forces after such a decision had been issued. Thirdly, the formation of the *League of Nations* also provided the necessary structure for solving the problem of how to find the best, i.e., a universally acceptable, method of selecting judges for the court. Finally, this structure also strengthened the obligation to take recourse to peaceful methods of conflict settlement. The *League of Nations* was powerful enough to enforce these decisions; as it determined non-compliance as a breach of the covenant and, therefore, as a case which triggered collective measures against the covenant-breaking state.

This arrangement paved the way for the establishment of a stronger and more powerful system at the international level, although – as history taught us – it was still not sufficient to prevent *World War II* from breaking out. Nonetheless, the *interbellum* system represented an enormous step forward compared to the time before *World War I*. The international community now had an actual world organization that was intended to strengthen cohesion between states and provide an institutionalized solution to international disputes. The interwar system was based in several points on efforts and attempts made before 1914 in order to create an international court of law, on the experiences with the PCA, and on other previous conceptual, legal theoretical, and ideological works. These impressions, the conceptual groundwork, and experiences during 1899 and 1914 were merged after the end of *World War I* with the newly arisen insight that it also took a strong and power-

48 Cited in: Manley O. Hudson, *The Permanent Court of International Justice 1920–1942* (n 16 in Chapter 7) 151.

ful world organization, and a system of collective security, to enforce judicial decisions and to preserve peace. Therefore, the PCIJ (and to a certain extent, also the *League of Nations*) was based on these earlier endeavors. The pre-1914 ideas and concepts for an international court of law were finally realized, following the end of *World War I*, in form of the PCIJ, an institution equipped with so-far unknown and unique competences and a very wide-reaching obligatory jurisdiction. This step not only constituted the realization of Root's and Scott's dreams but also of those of countless other peace activists, international lawyers, and progressive politicians from before 1914. It is a tragedy that it needed *World War I* and millions of deaths to finally realize them.

2 Conclusion

The findings of the present book confirm the assumption, according to which the basis was laid between the late 19th century and 1914 for the developments after the end of *World War I*, which initially led to the limitation of *ius ad bellum* and finally to its replacement by *ius contra bellum*. In the pre-war period, concepts were discussed among peace activists, international lawyers, but also – and, especially, on the above-listed major international conferences – among representatives of (almost) all existing states that aimed for decisive restrictions of *ius ad bellum* and the introduction of *peace through law*. Some of these concepts were even realized already in form of international courts, obligations to use peaceful means of conflict settlement, and limitations of the right to wage war.

Regarding arbitration, its acceptance by the community of states, its development into an integral instrument in international relations and international law, and the effects of all these arbitration-related developments on the understanding of *ius ad bellum* between the late 19th century and 1914, it can be concluded that an enormous and substantial change took place during this period. During the first half of the 19th century, arbitration did not yet play a major role in international relations. It was not yet (neither in its isolated, but especially not in its obligatory form) commonly used or widespread in state practice. However, the U.S.-American and the British peace movements already propagated the implementation of arbitration at the international level, organized several conferences on this topic (*inter alia* in continental Europe), and managed to significantly increase the attention which was paid to their agenda and their ideas. During the second half of the 19th century, more and more states began to show a considerably grown readiness to take recourse to isolated arbitration for the settlement of their mutual conflicts.

During the 1880s and 1890s, the use of this instrument even reached a first major peak. It was more often and more regularly invoked at that time for the settlement of state-to-state conflicts than ever before. Furthermore, the overwhelming majority of states participated in the trend to refer conflicts (of mostly secondary importance) to arbitral decisions. In 1899, at the eve of the *First Hague Peace Conference*, isolated arbitration was, therefore, an already widely accepted and frequently used instrument in international relations and under international law. The *First Hague Peace Conference* then marked a milestone in the further development of arbitration into a widely accepted and frequently invoked instrument among states.

According to David D. Caron (*'War and International Adjudication'* from 2000), it is indispensable for the understanding of the importance of the *First Hague Peace Conference* to "[...] appreciate the spirit of the nineteenth century and the contemporary concern about the growing horrors of war, the concomitant drive for peace, and the belief that international arbitration, if improved through the establishment of a permanent court, offered the promise of ending war."[49] At least in the beginning of the conference, it appeared as if (some of) these hopes could actually have been fulfilled at this event. The conclusion of a multi-lateral treaty of obligatory arbitration seemed to be within the realms of possibility, although it was not realized in the end. However, the participating states managed to agree on the establishment of the PCA, the first (voluntary) body for the settlement of state-to-state conflicts. This step constituted a novum in the history of international law and a major achievement. But, at the same time, it was also just a minimum consensus. The achievement of considerably further-going results might have been possible if (in particular) the German delegation had not held such a relentlessly negative stance in this regard. Jost Dülffer (*'Regeln gegen den Krieg?'* from 1981) stated the following concerning the (untapped) potential of the *First Hague Peace Conference*:

> It can be concluded that all European great powers except for the German Empire were willing to conclude measures at the Hague which went beyond considering arbitration only as a voluntary instrument for conflict settlement. Three European powers (Russia, England, and Italy) and the United States presented their own plans, whereas Austria-Hungary and France showed willingness to adapt their [initially negative] approaches in order to achieve presentable results at this conference.

49 David D. Caron, 'War and International Adjudication' (n 14 in Chapter 5) 5–6.

> A combination of the most far-reaching proposals would have resulted into obligatory arbitration of non-political cases (Russia). Within the framework of this system, those cases would have been decided by a permanent tribunal which was widely autonomous in its rulings (USA). Such far-reaching regulations would have constituted a deep impact on the prevailing international order. Combining them with later arising concepts for the award of competences to the arbitral tribunal in order to initiate procedures on its own decision, could have formed the core of a new global order in which international relations were continuously more and more subjected to law and legal decisions.[50]

Therefore, the *First Hague Peace Conference* could have already resulted in distinctively different and substantially more far-reaching results. The PCA could have been equipped with a greater jurisdiction and with more extensive competences, which would have resulted in a considerably greater step ahead regarding the attempt to transform the international order into a system in which the use of force was replaced by arbitration (or even by adjudication). The establishment of the PCA in 1900 was, nevertheless, a huge step forward for the further development of international law, for the institutionalization of methods of peaceful conflict settlement, and for the goal of the peace movement to create a system based on the principle of *peace through law*. Those who had represented the United States at the *First Hague Peace Conference* expressed the hope that the PCA would serve as a starting point for further going and more extensive projects,[51] for example, in the form of an extension of the competences of the court at a later occasion. In the following years, the PCA proved its functionality (against all criticism) by settling 14 cases between 1902 and 1914. Some of them were even of crucial importance for the relationships between the conflicting parties. Consequently, the creation of the PCA was more than only an interim stage within the development towards an international judiciary.

Furthermore, the failure to come to an agreement concerning the conclusion of a multi-lateral obligatory arbitration treaty at the *First Hague Peace Conference* did not bring about an end to attempts to introduce such commitments to international law. In fact, very soon thereafter, obligatory arbitration developed into a common phenomenon and into an often-invoked instru-

---

50 Analogously translated by the author of the present book from: Jost Dülffer, *Regeln gegen den Krieg?* (n 20 in Chapter 1) 88.

51 Compare pages 184–186 of the present book.

ment in international relations. Before the turn of the century, obligatory arbitration had been particularly common in inter-Spanish American relations and, at least to a certain extent, in European/American relations; in comparison, it was rarely used in inter-European relations and by the great powers during this period. The reasons for this achievement can be traced back to two important developments. First, there were two multi-lateral obligatory arbitration treaties concluded at the *Second Pan-American Conference* in Mexico City (1901/02), which had a pioneering character, since they were the first agreements extending the competences of the PCA (by determining that parts of their mutual conflicts fell within the jurisdiction of the PCA).[52] Second, Article 19 of the *Hague Convention* determined that that all adhering states had the right to subject (parts of) their mutual relations through bi- or multi-lateral obligatory arbitration agreements to the jurisdiction of the PCA. France and Great Britain made use of this provision by entering a bi-lateral agreement in 1903. In accordance with the encouragement of Article 19, it subordinated certain areas of their mutual relationship to obligatory arbitration by the PCA. This step not only extended the competences of the court but also set in motion a wave of concluding similar treaties between 1903 and 1905.[53] Thereby, obligatory arbitration developed into a widely accepted and integrated tool in international relations and international law – which raised hopes for further achievements among peace activists, international lawyers, and progressive members of the governments. Given the very favorable attitude that the overwhelming majority of states had shown during this wave of conclusions of bilateral obligatory arbitration agreements, expectations were high concerning the conclusion of a multi-lateral obligatory arbitration treaty at the *Second Hague Peace Conference*. However, to great surprise, all attempts that were made in The Hague in this regard (in 1907) failed. The project was rejected (again) by a minority of nations around the German Empire. Walter Schücking (*'Die Organisation der Welt'* from 1909) commented on this situation as follows:

> The population of the 32 countries (including their colonies) voting in favor of the principle of obligatory arbitration accounts for around 1200 million people, whereas the population of the 9 opposing states only equates 220 million (for the most part from the Balkans). The popu-

52 Regarding the proceedings and results of the Second Pan-American Conference, compare pages 190–207 of the present book.

53 Compare pages 207 et seq. of the present book.

> lation of those states abstaining from voting finally accounted for around 95 million.[54]

By giving these numbers, Schücking showed that the majority of states supported the conclusion of a multi-lateral obligatory arbitration agreement at the *Second Hague Peace Conference*. The Latin American states had already been strong supporters of such agreements before (given their long history of conclusions of bi-lateral agreements, the attempts to create Spanish American unions, and the developments at the *Second Pan-American Conference*). The United States wanted to secure a far-reaching treaty as well, and even most European countries voted in favor of such a commitment. Therefore, it can be concluded that – although the attempt failed to reach an obligatory arbitration agreement at the *Second Hague Peace Conference* due to a rejection by a minority of nations – the prevailing mood among most of the participating states concerning this instrument had substantially changed between the 19th and the beginning of the 20th centuries. Whereas most European countries had still hesitated to subject themselves to obligatory arbitration by the end of the 19th century, the majority of all states welcomed those commitments at the *Second Hague Peace Conference*.

That the overwhelming majority of states bound themselves by bi-lateral obligatory arbitration commitments between the late 19th century and the outbreak of *World War I* and that many of them were even ready to enter into a universal agreement of that type in 1907 leads to another important conclusion. By subjecting conflicts (affecting certain or even all aspects of their mutual relations) to compulsory arbitral settlement, these states also showed their willingness to limit the *ius ad bellum*. At least in theory, bi-lateral obligatory arbitration treaties entailed limitations concerning the use of force in certain situations by imposing the obligation on states to take recourse to arbitration, instead of waging war. This constituted a legally binding restriction regarding the enforcement of the states' right to use force against the other treaty parties. Given the fact that numerous countries had signed and ratified such agreements in their bi-lateral relations between the late 19th century and 1914, there must have existed a comparably close, but still not universal, net of agreements that limited the treaty parties' *ius ad bellum* in their respective bi-lateral relations. Thus, a quickly growing number, or even a majority (given the overwhelming support shown at the *Second Hague Peace Conference*), of states showed a lot of willingness to limit their right to wage war between 1899 and

54 Walther Schücking, *Die Organisation der Welt* (n 181 in Chapter 6) 73. Originally the text is in German, the (analogous) translation was produced by the author of the present book.

1914 through (special) obligatory arbitration in the form of legally binding commitments. Moreover, it constituted a first step in the development towards a system in which war was banned and states were legally obliged to take recourse to peaceful instruments instead. Therefore, the basis was laid in these years for further developments, such as the introduction of Article 2.4 UN Charter or the conclusion of the *'Briand-Kellogg Pact'* in 1928.

Apart from arbitration, important developments also took place before *World War I* in the field of adjudication. The idea to create an international court of law stemmed from William Ladd, the leader of the U.S.-American peace movement in the 1830s. In the subsequent decades, however, adjudication did not enjoy outstanding attention in the considerations and writings of the peace movement or legal scholarship because of its comparably utopian character. This arrangement prevailed until the beginning of the 20th century when international lawyers and peace activists began to deal with concepts for the creation of autonomous international courts of law and pushing aside the idea to create them as parts of world unions. Leading political figures and international lawyers such as Elihu Root and James Brown Scott took up this approach and used their enormous influence to establish the striving for the realization of an (autonomous) international judiciary as a dominant aspect in the agenda of the U.S.- American government as well as in the one of the peace movement. The *Second Hague Peace Conference* was the first occasion at which ideas for the institutionalization of international adjudication were discussed by the wider community of states. The initiative for this development stemmed from the United States, whose delegates presented the plan for an autonomous and truly permanent international tribunal. They had already proposed the creation of such an institution (albeit of an arbitral nature) at the previous conference. However, this time, the initiative for the so-called *Court of Arbitral Justice* aimed explicitly for the foundation of a purely judicial (but still voluntary) court. Despite its voluntary nature, it stands to reason that the United States hoped that the creation of the CAJ would also be another step forward in the aspired development towards the establishment of a compulsory international legal system that was based on the principles of the rule of law and *peace through law*. Consequently, the U.S.-American representatives seem to have regarded the voluntary CAJ as a starting point for this development and hoped to gradually extend the competences and jurisdiction of the court over the subsequent years.

When the U.S.-American plan for the creation of the (voluntary) CAJ was first presented at the *Second Hague Peace Conference*, it was (surprisingly) well received by the majority of participating states. But despite the initial overwhelming support for this project, the participating states failed to come to an agreement concerning its actual realization. Instead, they only concluded a *vœu* at The Hague, which encouraged the signatory states to create the CAJ once a solution was found regarding the major obstacle for its realization – the procedure for the appointment of the court's bench of judges in a way that was suitable to all participating countries, and which did not collide with the principle of sovereign equality. Consequently, there existed a wide open window of opportunity at the *Second Hague Peace Conference* in 1907 to create an actual international court of law. Although the project failed, the general approach of the international community towards adjudication and the creation of an international court of law was, consequently, very positive.

Another attempt made at the *Second Hague Peace Conference* to introduce adjudicative measures to international law – namely in the field of international prize law – was more successful. The participating states were able to overcome the obstacles that had prevented the establishment of the CAJ, since the Latin American countries proved their willingness to compromise for the sake of the creation of this institution. Therefore, the *Second Hague Peace Conference* could adopt the plan for the creation of the *International Prize Court*. At first, this decision was regarded as a major success for the conference. The body would have been the first truly judicial international court of law in history. However, it soon turned out that the actual establishment of the court was severely hampered due to the British decision to abstain from ratifying the underlying agreement. To settle this situation, and in order to finally create the court, nine major powers (seven European countries plus the United States and Japan) met for the *London Naval Conference* in 1908/09. The United States attempted to use the meeting to discuss the extension of the competences of the IPC by presenting a plan for the realization of the draft convention for the *Court of Arbitral Justice* in the framework of the prize court. They wanted the IPC to serve as a general international court of law, shaped in accordance with the model of the proposed CAJ – but it should do so only for signatory states of an additional protocol. Although the other powers did not consider the meeting in London to be the right occasion to discuss this issue, they gave generally favorable feedback. Consequently, the United States further pursued this idea in the aftermath of the meeting. They even convinced France, Great Britain, and Germany to send delegates to Paris in 1910 to discuss this topic with U.S.-American representatives at the so-called *Four-Power Conference*. In the course of the negotiations in Paris, the participating states came to an agreement and concluded a convention for the establishment of a (autonomous) court of arbitral justice. This agreement was supposed to enter into force once that eighteen states had ratified it. U.S. Secretary of State Philander C. Knox was so elated by the result of the conference and the prospect of finally seeing the CAJ becoming a reality that he declared at the *Sixteenth Annual Meeting of the Lake Mohonk Conference* that

> [...] a truly permanent court of arbitral justice, composed of judges acting under a sense of judicial responsibility, representing the various judicial systems of the world and capable of insuring the continuity of arbitral jurisprudence, will be established in the immediate future and that the Third Peace Conference will find it in successful operation at The Hague.[55]

Despite their joint effort for an international judiciary at these occasions, despite the decision taken at the *Second Hague Peace Conference* to create the IPC, and despite the overwhelming support for the general idea for a permanent international court of law (which the majority of the participating states had expressed at the same conference), no universal, purely judicial international court was established on the global level before 1922. In the aftermath of the *Second Hague Peace Conference*, the concept was continuously brought up again (usually by the United States) and international adjudication, therefore, continued to be a prominently discussed topic. Therefore, it can be concluded that there existed a highly favorable and receptive mood among the states between 1907 and 1914 regarding international adjudication and the creation of a permanent and autonomous international court of law. Furthermore, it appears highly likely that the creation of an international court of arbitral justice would have resulted – despite its voluntary character – into another important step towards the limitation of the *ius ad bellum* and the submission of international relations to (the rule of) law. By taking this step, it would have been possible to get significantly closer to the realization of the dream of many peace activists and international lawyers to replace war by law and to achieve the ideal of *peace through law* in the international legal order. However, it must also be borne in mind that a voluntary international court of law would not have effectively limited the *ius ad bellum*. It would have only constituted another, important, development towards the fulfillment of this long-cherished dream (and, of course, the moral obligations of states to bring their disputes before the international court).

Most attempts to establish international courts of law failed before 1914. However, there was one case in which the efforts taken in favor of inter-

55 'Official Message from Philander C. Knox regarding the International Court of Arbitral Justice' in *Report of the Sixteenth Annual Meeting of the Lake Mohonk Conference on International Arbitration, May 18th, 19th and 20th 1910* (n 430 in Chapter 6) 9.

national adjudication resulted in actual success: The constitution of the *Central American Court of Justice*. The CACJ was created by the five Central American states Nicaragua, Costa Rica, Honduras, El Salvador, and Guatemala at the *Washington Conference* in late 1907 and was the first (regional) international court of law in history. The meeting in Washington was organized by Mexico and the United States, and these two states played – according to Michla Pomerance (*'The United States and the World Court as a 'Supreme Court of the Nations''* from 1996) – "[...] a pivotal role in the establishment of the Court which, apart from intrinsic virtues, was seen as an experiment which could stimulate emulation and generalization."[56] Despite the intended role of the tribunal as a prototype and a shining example for the workability of the concept of an international court of law, the CACJ is also important because of its extensive competences. It was equipped with general and unlimited obligatory jurisdiction over all kinds of international conflicts between the adhering states. Even nationals of the five nations were entitled to bring cases before the court.[57] Thereby, the court became the realization of – what Benjamin Allen Coates (*'Legalist Empire'* from 2016) called – "[...] a legalist dream."[58] Instead of settling disputes by force, all emerging conflicts had to be decided through judicial means before the CACJ. Consequently, the *ius ad bellum* was highly limited (if not to say, completely replaced by an *ius contra bellum*) in the Central American mutual relations and the regional international system was – at least, in theory – entirely juridified.

All the above-described achievements from the period between the late 19th century and 1914 paved the way for further developments and set the tone for the creation of more complex and powerful institutions for (obligatory) conflict settlement in the aftermath of *World War I*. The accomplishments prior to 1914 should be understood as intermediate steps on the way to the establishment of the PCIJ in 1922, the conclusion of the *Briand-Kellogg Treaty* in 1928, the formation of the ICJ as well as the introduction of Article 2.4 *UN Charter* both in 1945. The developments (prior to 1914) also demonstrate that the (majority of the) community of states was already attempting to limit the *ius ad bellum* during the period between the late 19th century and 1914. By subjecting themselves to obligatory arbitration in numerous bi-lateral treaties, they promised to abstain from the use of force for the settlement of (certain types of) their mutual conflicts. The instruments and institutions for pacific

56 Michla Pomerance, *The United States and the World Court as a 'Supreme Court of the Nations'* (n 47 in Chapter 3) 60.

57 Compare pages 328–329 of the present book.

58 Benjamin Allen Coates, *Legalist Empire* (n 311 in Chapter 5) 119.

conflict settlement that were introduced during the period under consideration were, of course, still limited and some states (such as the German Empire) were rather hesitant to follow these developments in their entirety. Furthermore, the concluded obligatory arbitration commitments proved incapable in the end to prevent the outbreak of *World War I*. However, the atmosphere and the general mood between the late 19th century and 1914 was on many occasions – and especially at the major international meetings – very peace-oriented and benevolent to the further development of international law. Despite imperialist considerations, continuous struggles between the European great powers and the on-going armament races, states came together on these occasions to discuss methods for the preservation of peace. Furthermore, ideas for the further development of the existing instruments of conflict settlement, for the introduction of new ones, and for the creation of international institutions for the same purpose – overall for the replacement of the use of force by law and judicial procedures – were prominently discussed on multiple events at that time. These topics were no longer purely utopian concepts only dealt with and propagated by peace activists or in legal scholarship. Between the end of the 19th century and 1914, they reached the international sphere and attracted the interest and support of numerous governments. Therefore, several achievements were already made to limit the *ius ad bellum*, to juridify international relations, and to replace, or at least to restrict, the use of force by law during these years.

Moreover, first achievements were already made with regards to adjudication as well. The CACJ was established at that time as the first international court of law in history and the concept of adjudication found its way from the discussions among peace activists and international lawyers onto the foreign political agenda of the overwhelming majority of the members of the community of states. The reception of attempts to realize adjudication in the form of the creation of international courts of law was, as mentioned before, overwhelmingly positive. Although the establishment of the CACJ remained the only real success in this regard before 1914, and although all the other attempts failed in the end, the sole fact that international adjudication became a prominently discussed and well-received topic on numerous international conferences was already a great achievement. It clearly demonstrates the changed mood of many states with regards to this topic. Between the end of the 19th century and the outbreak of *World War I*, states demonstrated considerably more willingness than ever before to seriously consider the introduction of new forms of conflict settlement to international law, to attribute a remarkably more important role to international law, and to take the first steps towards the realization of a rule-of-law-based international order in which war was replaced by judicial procedures. This change in the mindset and the welcoming attitude towards juridified international relations were substantial and groundbreaking processes, which set the tone and paved the way for the developments taking place after 1914.

In this regard, notice should also be taken of the fact that the concept of creating international tribunals – regardless of whether of an arbitral or an adjudicative nature – had traditionally been closely linked throughout the 19th century, with the idea to introduce world unions; an idea considered to be too utopian and radical by the majority of legal scholars, peace activists, and in particular, the governments. Taking into consideration the constant imperialist struggles, fierce rivalries, and competition over global influence among the great powers at that time, it does seem reasonable to assume that chances of convincing the whole community of states of changing the international order so substantially were relatively marginal. Consequently, it meant that chances for the creation of international courts were equally small, at least so long as this concept continued to be linked with the claim for the formation of world unions. This situation only changed when the first proposals for autonomous international courts came up in the 1890s and when the idea to introduce tribunals outside of the framework of world unions became increasingly more prominent over the following years. When Czar Nicholas II proposed the *First Hague Peace Conference* in 1898 and when the idea to institutionalize arbitration (in the form of an autonomous body) found its way onto the agenda of this conference, this approach was immediately successful and resulted into the formation of the PCA. Moreover, when adjudication and the formation of establishing an international court of law became prominent topics in 1905/06, advocates of these ideas – such as Root, Scott, and many other progressive scholars – followed the same path as well. All of them promoted the formation of autonomous institutions, instead of returning to demand world unions. Due to the states' manifold and repeatedly shown support for international courts of law since 1907, this approach developed into a very prominent topic and states became familiar with it.

Thereby, the foundations were laid for further going developments. When peace activists, international lawyers, and governments called for the introduction of a global court of law after 1914 (and especially after 1918), this demand no longer constituted a novum. It was already a wide-spread and accepted concept in international legal scholarship as well as in state-to-state discussions. Furthermore, in the light of the failure of the (voluntary) pre-war system to prevent *World War I* from breaking out and to provide effective instruments for forcing conflicting parties to settle major disputes peacefully, a window of opportunity opened after the end of the war for reconnecting the demand for an international court of law with the idea for a world union. As described above, after 1914, many peace activists and international lawyers began to claim that only a world union could provide the necessary mechanisms through collective security to enforce arbitral/judicial decisions, to enforce treaty obligations, to put its own acts into effect, and to bring conflicting powers to the negotiation table when they faced conflicts with one another, which bore the potential of resulting in a war. Only world unions were considered to have enough power to deter conflicting parties from taking recourse to force. By demanding states to settle disputes peacefully and by threatening them (in the case of non-compliance with this demand) with the power of the joined forces of all the other union members, peace was supposed to be better preservable.

It appears highly unlikely that the developments after 1918 could have taken place in the way they did, if discussions among peace activists and international lawyers had not shifted since the 1890s from considering international courts only as organs of potential world unions to proposing them in the form of autonomous and independent institutions. Without this intellectual shift in the peace movement and international legal scholarship, states would probably not have discussed the creation of autonomous international courts in the pre-1914-period because they would have rejected the prospect of an introduction of international unions (with which the idea for international tribunals still would have been linked). In this case, states would not have become familiar with autonomous international courts at that time. Consequently, only because the described developments took place, the window of opportunity for the introduction of such courts opened (again) after the outbreak of *World War I* and quickly a growing number of states realized that it took far more extensive, compulsory, and powerful mechanisms for the preservation of peace. By linking the concept of international courts again with the demand for collective security, world unions became an actual option, and this idea was even realized in the end in form of the *League of Nations*. Hence, the developments between the late 19th century and 1914 paved the way and laid the foundation for the formation of the *League of Nations* in 1920, for the creation of the *Permanent Court of International Justice* in 1922, and for all the subsequent developments in this regard.

Taking all these findings, conclusions, and insights into consideration, it becomes apparent that during the early 20th century, international law was still in a stage of development. Nevertheless, peaceful methods for conflict settlement already played a significant role. In comparison to the 19th century, states recognized isolated arbitration after the *First Hague Peace Conference* as a common and fully integrated tool in their set of foreign political instruments. They already created the first arbitral institution (PCA) and even an entirely judicial institution for peaceful conflict settlement (CACJ). Moreover, they entered into obligatory arbitration treaties on a regular basis. Finally, they discussed the establishment of a series of other institutions for peaceful conflict settlement. In conclusion, states showed a lot of willingness to introduce limitations to the *ius ad bellum*, to (further) juridify international relations, and to subject themselves to a compulsory rule-of-law-based system between 1899 and 1914.

In the course of the developments during this period, the community of states installed an international system that allowed them to handle conflicts peacefully. By concluding a quickly growing net of bi-lateral obligatory arbitration treaties, they imposed restrictions on themselves regarding their right to use force in their respective bi-lateral relations. Moreover, adjudication was already a widely discussed and highly prominent concept under international law as well. Although only one purely judicial court was established in the form of the CACJ before the outbreak of *World War I*, and although this tribunal only existed in a regionally very limited context, many other ideas and proposals for the creation of international courts of law were enthusiastically discussed within the community of states; and they were received remarkably positively by most of the states. The failure to establish an actual global court of law at the *Second Hague Peace Conference* and thereafter, only resulted from (minor) conceptual discords. Therefore, the fact that the concept for the creation of such a tribunal was not realized before 1922 did not derive from a rejection of this idea as a whole. Its general reception by the states was even overwhelmingly good. All the points listed above indicate that the international order already reached an advanced stage in the period under consideration, concerning the striving for replacing the use of force in international relations through arbitral and adjudicative procedures.

Moreover, the system established between the *First Hague Peace Conference* and the eve of *World War I* was already decisively different and substantially advanced in comparison to the 19th century. In fact, the vast majority of states showed a very benevolent and welcoming attitude towards new ideas concerning the preservation of peace and the limitation of the use of force under international law. This was especially the case regarding the institutionalization of measures for peaceful conflict settlement and the conclusion of obligatory arbitration commitments, which were groundbreaking and very well-received achievements. By taking all these measures and by changing the international system in the ways mentioned, the community of states showed its willingness to take first steps towards the submission of the international order to the rule of law, to the juridification of international relations, and to the limitation of the *ius ad bellum*. Although actual and direct restrictions of this right (the *ius ad bellum*) were – apart from bi-lateral obligatory arbitration agreements – not yet that common and were only established in thematically very limited fields, it can still be concluded that the achievements from the period between the late 19th century and 1914 went beyond taking mere first steps and toward laying the conceptual foundations for developments that took place after the end of *World War I*.

Finally, since the institutionalization of adjudication in the form of voluntary international courts of law was openly declared by several actors as only an intermediate step on the way towards the realization of an international system that was fully juridified and under which all state-to-state conflicts were obligatorily subjected to settlement by an international judicial tribunal, the conclusion can be drawn that there already existed a substantially changed mood prior to *World War I* concerning the use of force under international law. Instead of considering the *ius ad bellum* as widely unrestricted (as it used to be the case during the 19th century), lots of states demonstrated their willingness, at multiple occasions during that period, to introduce limitations of this right to international law – in the form of bi- or multi-lateral obligatory arbitration agreements, compulsory bodies for conflicts settlement, or prohibitions of the use of force. Although many of these initiatives failed due to the complicated political situation and ongoing rivalries between the great powers, the majority of states still showed a keen interest in limiting the right to wage war, in submitting international relations to a considerably greater extent to international law, and in creating international institutions that were competent to settle state-to-state conflicts on the basis of arbitration or even of law. Moreover, it is not only international law scholars and peace activists who adopted this new approach, but also the (the majority of the) community of states. For the first time in history, states showed their willingness to establish a system in which law played a significantly greater role than pure power and the use of force. In 1945 – and after having experienced a second devastating World War that (again) cost the lives of dozens of millions of people – the concepts and ideas that had been developed during in the pre-*World War I* period and the first attempts that had been made at that time in order to realize a rule-of-law-based international order finally concluded in the adoption of the *UN Charter*, the introduction of Article 2.4, the creation of the *International Court of Justice* (as the continuation of the PCIJ), and, therefore, in the replacement of the *ius ad bellum* with an *ius contra bellum*.

Bibliography

Books

Abbenhuis M et al. (eds.), *War, Peace and International Order? The Legacies of the Hague Conferences of 1899 and 1907* (Routledge 2017).

Abbenhuis M et al. (eds.), *The Hague Conferences and International Politics, 1898–1915* (Bloomsbury Academic 2018).

Adams JT, *The History of New England*, vol. 3 (Little, Brown 1927).

Alcorta A, *Cours de Droit International Public*, vol. 1 (Lajouane 1887).

Amorosa P, *The American Project and the Politics of History: James Brown Scott and the Origins of International Law* (Doctoral dissertation at University of Helsinki 2018); <https://helda.helsinki.fi/bitstream/handle/10138/233591/TheAmeri.pdf?sequence=1&isAllowed=y> accessed August 26, 2021.

Althammer B, *Das Bismarckreich 1871–1890* (Ferdinand Schöningh 2009).

Alvarez A, *Le Droit International Américan* (Institut américain du droit international 1910).

Arend AC and Beck RJ, *International Law and the Use of Force: Beyond the UN Charter Paradigm* (Routledge 1993).

Ash C, *Kruger, Kommandos and Kak: Debunking the Myths of the Boer War* (30 Degree South Publ. 2014).

Atkins GP, *Encyclopedia of the Inter-American System* (Greenwood Press 1997).

Balch T, *International Courts of Arbitration* (Allen, Lane, and Scott 1912; first published 1874).

Bailey TA, *A Diplomatic History of the American People* (Prentice-Hall 1974, 9th ed.).

Barrows SJ, *Tour of the Interparliamentary Union Tendered by the Government of the United States* (United States Government Printing Office 1904).

Baty T, *International Law* (John Murray 1909).

Beales ACF, *The History of Peace: A Short Account of the Organised Movements for International Peace* (Bell 1931).

Becker Lorca A, *Mestizo International Law: A Global Intellectual History 1842–1933* (Cambridge University Press 2014).

Bender S, *Der Burenkrieg und die deutschsprachige Presse* (Brill 2009).

Benzinger Brothers, *The 'Summa Theologica' of St. Thomas Aquinas, Part II* (Benziger Bros. 1917).

Best A, Hahimäki JM, Maiolo JA, and Schulze KE, *International History of the Twentieth Century and Beyond* (Routledge 2004).

von Beyme K, *Politische Theorien im Zeitalter der Ideologien 1789–1945* (VS Verlag für Sozialwissenschaften 2002).

Bloch IS, *Is War Now Impossible? Being an Abridgment of 'The War of the Future in its Technical, Economic and Political Relations'* (Richards 1898/99).

Bluntschli JC, *Das moderne Völkerrecht der civilisirten Staaten: Als Rechtsbuch dargestellt* (C.H. Beck 1868).

Bluntschli JC, *Gesammelte kleine Schriften*, vol. 2 (C.H. Beck 1881).

Börnsen N, *Nationales Recht in Investitionsschiedsverfahren* (Mohr Siebeck 2016).

Bourgeois L, *Solidarité* (A. Colin et cie 1896).

Bourne K, *Britain and the Balance of Power in North America 1815–1908* (University of California Press 1967).

Bowring J (ed.), *The Works of Jeremy Bentham, vol. 2: Judicial Procedure, Anarchical Fallacies, works on Taxation* (William Tait 1843).

Boyle FA, *Foundations of World Order: The Legalist Approach to International Relations 1898–1922* (Duke University Press 1999).

Boyle FA, *World Politics and International Law* (Duke University Press 1985).

Brewer SA, *Why America Fights: Patriotism and War Propaganda from the Philippines to Iraq* (Oxford University Press 2009).

Bridge FR and Bullen R, *The Great Power and the European States System 1814–1914* (Pearson Longman 2005).

Brown GS, *Latin American Rebels and the United States: 1806–1822* (McFarland et Company 2015).

Brown M, *Informal Empire in Latin America: Culture, Commerce and Capital* (Blackwell 2008).

Brownlie I, *International Law and the Use of Force by States* (Oxford University Press 1963).

Brownlie I, *The Rule of Law in International Affairs* (Nijhoff 1998).

Bryce J, *Proposals for the Avoidance of War with a Preparatory Note by Viscount Bryce* (1915); <https://archive.org/details/proposalsforavoi00brycuoft/page/n1/mode/2up> accessed August 26, 2021.

Buchanan WI, *The Central American Peace Conference held at Washington D.C. 1907* (United States Government Printing Office 1908).

Buckman RT, *Latin America* (Stryker-Post Publications 2015).

Cable J, *Gunboat Diplomacy 1919–1979: Political Applications of Limited Naval Force* (Macmillan 1981).

Cady DL, *From Warism to Pacifism: A Moral Continuum* (Temple University Press, U.S. 2010).

Calvert P, *The International Politics of Latin America* (Manchester University Press 1994).

Calvo C, *Derecho Internacional Teórico y Práctico de Europa y América*, vol. 1 (D'Amyot 1868).

Calvo C, *Le Droit International Théorique et Practique 2* (Guillaumin 1880).

Campbell RG, Neutral Rights and Obligations in the Anglo-Boer War (The Johns Hopkins Press 1908).

Carlisle RP and Golson JG, *Manifest Destiny and the Expansion of America* (ABC Clio 2007).

Carr W and Hearder H, *The Wars of German Unification 1864–1871* (Routledge 1999).

Chitty J, *The Law of Nations or Principles of the Law of Nature Applied to the Conduct and Affairs of Nations and Sovereigns from the French Monsieur de Vattel* (T.&J.W. Johnson 1852).

von Clausewitz C, *On War* (trans. and edited by Michael Howard and Peter Paret, University Press Group 1993).

Clayton LA, *Peru and the United States: The Condor and the Eagle* (University of Georgia Press 1999).

Coates BA, *Legalist Empire: International Law and American Foreign Relations in the Early Twentieth Century* (Oxford University Press 2016).

de la Codre JM, *L'Opinion Publique et l'Extinction de la Guerre* (Dentu) 1867.

Coerver DM and Hall LB, *Tangled Destinies: Latin America and The United States* (The University of New Mexico Press 1999).

Collier S, *Chile: The Making of a Public 1830–1865* (Cambridge University Press 2003).

Connell-Smith G, *The Inter-American System* (Oxford University Press 1966).

Conway C (ed.), *The U.S.-Mexican War: A Binational Reader* (Hackett Publishing Company 2010).

Cooper JM, Jr., *Breaking the Heart of the World: Woodrow Wilson and the Fight for the League of Nations* (Cambridge University Press 2001).

Cooper L (ed.), *The Rhetoric of Aristotle* (D. Appleton and Co. 1932).

Cooper SE, *Patriotic Pacifism: Waging War on War in Europe 1815–1914* (Oxford University Press 1991).

Connell-Smith G, *The Inter-American System* (Oxford University Press 1966).

Cortright D, *Peace: A History of Movements and Ideas* (Cambridge University Press 2008).

Cory HM, *Compulsory Arbitration of International Disputes* (Columbia University Press 1932).

Craig GA, *Geschichte Europas 1815–1980: Vom Wiener Kongreß bis zur Gegenwart* (C.H. Beck 1983).

Crowe MB, *The Changing of the Profile of the Natural Law* (Springer 1977).

Crucé E, *Le nouveau Cynée ou discours d'Estat représentant les occasions et moyens d'establir une paix géneralle et la liberté de commerce par tout le monde* (J. Villery 1623).

Cullum W (ed.), *The Second International Peace Conference, held at The Hague from June 15 to October 18, 1907* (United States Government Printing Office 1908).

Curti ME, *Peace or War: The American Struggle 1636–1936* (Garland Pub. 1972).

Darby WE, *International Arbitration; International Tribunals: A Collection of the various Schemes which have been produced; and of Instances in the Nineteenth Century* (J.M. Dent 1904).

Davis CD, *The United States and the Second Hague Peace Conference: American Diplomacy and International Organization 1899–1914* (Duke University Press 1975).

Davis GB, *The Elements of International Law* (Harper & Brothers 1915).

Dennson S, *Joaquim Nabuco: Monarchism, Panamericanism and Nation-Building in the Brazilian Belle Epoque* (P. Lang 2006).

Depkat V, *Geschichte Nordamerikas* (UTB GmbH 2008).

Descamps E, *Die Organisation des internationalen Schiedsgerichts* (A. Schupp 1897).

Dhokalia RP, *The Codification of Public International Law* (Manchester University Press 1970).

Díaz-Bonilla E and del Campo MV, *A long and winding Road: The Creation of the Inter-American Development Bank* (lulu.com 2010).

Donahue JF, *Food and Drink in Antiquity: Readings from the Graeco-Roman World* (Bloomsbury Academic 2015).

Dülffer J, *Regeln gegen den Krieg? Die Haager Friedenskonferenzen von 1899 und 1907 in der internationalen Politik* (Ullstein 1981).

Ebel F and Thielmann G, *Rechtsgeschichte: Von der Römischen Antike bis zur Neuzeit* (C.F. Muller 2003).

Epkenhans M, *Der Erste Weltkrieg* (Ferdin and Schöningh 2015).

Erasmus D, *Querela Pacis* (originally published in 1517).

Eyffinger A, *The 1899 Hague Peace Conference: The Parliament of Man, the Federation of the World* (Kluwer Academic Publishers 1999).

Eyffinger A, *Dreaming the Ideal, Living the Attainable – T.M.C. Asser [1838–1913]: Founder of The Hague Tradition* (TMC Asser Press 2011).

Eyffinger A and Witteveen A, *The International Court of Justice 1946–1996* (Kluwer Law International 1996).

Fagg JE, *Latin America: A General History* (Macmillan 1963).

Field DD, *Outline of an International Code*, vol. 1 (Baker 1872).

Finnemore M, *The Purpose of Intervention: Changing Beliefs about the Use of Force* (Cornell University Press 2003).

Fisch J, *Europa zwischen Wachstum und Gleichheit 1850–1914* (UTB 2002).

Fischer F, *Krieg der Illusionen* (Droste 1969).

La Fontaine H, *Pasicrisie Internationale: Histoire documentaire des arbitrages internationaux* (Impr. Stämpfli & cie 1902).

Foster JW, *Arbitration and the Hague Court* (Houghton, Mifflin and Company 1904).

Foster LV, *A Brief History of Central America* (Facts on File Inc. 2007).

Fried AH, *Handbuch der Friedensbewegung* (Outlook Verlag 2011).

Fried AH, *Handbuch der Friedensbewegung*, vol. 1 (Friedens-Warte 1911).

Fried AH, *Handbuch der Friedensbewegung*, vol. 2 (Friedens-Warte 1913).

Fried AH, Handbuch der Friedensbewegung (Oesterreichische Friedensgesellschaft 1905).

Fried AH, *Pan-Amerika: Entwicklung, Bedeutung und Umfang der pan-amerikanischen Bewegung* (Maritima 1910).

García-Salmones Rovira M, *The Project of Positivism in International Law* (Oxford University Press 2013).

Gargarella R, *The Legal Foundations of Inequality: Constitutionalism in the Americas, 1776–1860* (Cambridge University Press 2010).

Gbosoe GT, *Modernization of Japan* (iUniverse 2006).

Göhler H, *Freies Kriegsführungsrecht und Kriegsschuld* (Noske 1931).

Goertz G, Diehl PF, and Balas A, *The Puzzle of Peace: The Evolution of Peace in the International System* (Oxford University Press 2016).

Goldberg A, *Honor, Politics and the Law in Imperial Germany: 1871–1914* (Cambridge University Press 2010).

Graham R, *Britain and the Onset of Modernization in Brazil 1850–1914* (Cambridge University Press 1972).

Gratianus (de Clusio), *Decretum magistri Gratiani* (1140), re-published, e.g., by Aemilius Friedberg in 1879.

Grewe W, *Die Epochen der Völkerrechtsgeschichte* (Nomos 1984).

Grewe W, *The Epochs of International Law* (De Gruyter 2000).

Grewe W, (as editor) *Fontes Historiae Iuris Gentium*, vol. 1 (De Gruyter 1995).

Griswold del Castillo R, *The Treaty of Guadalupe Hidalgo: A Legacy of Conflict* (University of Oklahoma Press 1990).

Hugo Grotius, *De Iure Belli Ad Pacis* (1631); <https://archive.org/details/bub_gb_VIRnoA4gKxwC> accessed August 10, 2018.

Gruen ES, *The Hellenistic World and the Coming of Rome*, vol 1 & 2 (University of California Press 1984).

Hall WE, *International Law* (Clarendon Press 1880).

Hall WE, *A Treatise on International Law* (Clarendon Press 1909).

Halleck HW, *International Law; Or, Rules Regulating the Intercourse of States in Peace and War* (D. Van Nostrand 1861).

Hannigan RE, *The New World Power: American Foreign Policy, 1898–1917* (University of Pennsylvania Press 2002).

Hathaway OA and Shapiro SJ, *The Internationalists: And their Plan to Outlaw War* (Simon & Schuster 2018).

Healy D, *James G. Blaine and Latin America* (Missouri University of Missouri Press 2001).

Heilborn P, *Handbuch des Völkerrechts*, vol. 1 (W. Kohlhammer 1912).

Henig R, *The League of Nations* (Haus Publishing 2010).

Hietala TR, *Manifest Design: American Exceptionalism and Empire* (Cornell University Pres 1985).

Higgins N, *Regulating the Use of Force in Wars of National Liberation: The Need for a New Regime* (Nijhoff 2010).

Hinshaw J and Stearns PN, *Industrialization in the Modern World: From the Industrial Revolution to the Internet*, vol. 1 (ABC Clio 2013).

von Hippel W and Stier B, *Europa zwischen Reform und Revolution 1800–1850* (UTB 2012).

Hixson WL, *The Myth of American Diplomacy: National Identity and U.S. Foreign Policy* (Yale University Press 2008).

Hobe S, *Einführung in das Völkerrecht* (10th edn, UTB 2014).

Hollander N, *Elusive Dove: The Search for Peace during World War I* (McFarland & Company, Inc., Publishers 2013).

Holls FW, *The Peace Conference at The Hague and its Bearings on International Law and Policy* (Macmillan 1900).

Honsell H and Mayer T-Maly, *Rechtswissenschaft: Eine Einführung in das Recht und seine Grundlagen* (Springer 2015).

Hudson MO, *A Treatise on the Permanent Court of International Justice* (The Macmillan company 1934).

Hudson MO, *International Tribunals: Past and Future* (Rumford Press 1944).

Hudson MO, *The Permanent Court of International Justice 1920–1942* (The Macmillan company 1943).

Hull IV, *A Scrap of Paper: Breaking and Making International Law during the Great War* (Cornell University Press 2014).

Hull WI, *The two Hague Conferences and their Contributions to International Law* (Ginn & Company 1908).

Hüppauf B, *Was ist Krieg? Zur Grundlegung einer Kulturgeschichte des Kriegs* (Transcript 2013).

Imberg KE, *Die Stellung der Vereinigten Staaten zur internationalen Schiedsgerichtsfrage* (F. Vahlen 1914).

Inman SG, *Inter-American Conferences 1826–1954: History and Problems* (Washington University Press 1965).

Inter-American Institute of International Legal Studies, T*he Inter-American System: Its Development and Strengthening* (Oceana Publications 1966).

Jahn E, Politische Streitfragen, Band 4: Weltpolitische Herausforderungen (Springer VS 2015)

Janis MW, *The American Tradition of International Law: Great Expectations 1789–1914* (Oxford University Press 2004).

Janis MW, *America and the Law of Nations 1776–1939* (Oxford University Press 2010).

Jenkins D, *The Final Frontier: America, Science, and Terror* (Verso 2002).

Jenkins R, *Gladstone* (England Papermac 1995).

Jones R and Sherman SS, *The League of Nations from Idea to Reality: Its Place in History and in the World of To-Day* (Pitman 1927).

Justenhoven HG, *Internationale Schiedsgerichtsbarkeit: Ethische Normen und Rechtswirklichkeit* (Kohlhammer 2006).

Kamarowsky L, *Le Tribunal International* (A. Durand et Pedone-Lauriel 1887).

Kant I, *Zum Ewigen Frieden* (Friedrich Nicolovius 1795).

Karnes TL, *The Failure of Union: Central America 1824–1975* (Tempe Arizona State University 1976).

Kennedy P, *Aufstieg und Fall der großen Mächte* (Fischer 1991).

Kirgis FL, *The American Society of International Law's First Century: 1906–2006* (Nijhoff 2006).

Kissinger H, *Diplomacy* (Simon & Schuster 1994).

Klüber JL, *Europäisches Völkerrecht*, vol. 1 (Cotta 1821).

von dem Knesebeck P, *Soldaten, Guerilleros, Terroristen: Die Lehre des gerechten Krieges im Zeitalter asymmetrischer Konflikte* (Springer 2014).

Koskenniemi M, *The Gentle Civilizer of Nations: The Rise and Fall of International Law 1870–1960* (Cambridge University Press 2002).

Krieger H (ed.), *East Timor and the International Community: Basic Documents* (Cambridge University Press 1997).

Kuehl WF, *Seeking World Order: The United States and International Organization to 1920* (Vanderbilt University Press 1969).

Ladd W, *An Essay on a Congress of Nations* (Whipple and Damrell 1840).

Ladd W, *Prize Essays on a Congress of Nations* (Whipple and Damrell 1840).

Laity P, *The British Peace Movement 1870–1914* (Clarendon 2001).

Lammasch H, *Die Lehre von der Schiedsgerichtsbarkeit in ihrem ganzen Umfange* (W. Kohlhammer 1913).

Langley LD, *The Banana Wars: United States Intervention in the Caribbean, 1898–1934* (SR Books 2002).

Langley LD, *America and the Americas: The United States in the Western Hemisphere* (University of Georgia Press 2010).

de Lapradelle AG, *Recueil des arbitrages internationaux*, vol. 1 1798–1855 (A.W. Sijthoff's Publishing Co. 1905).

Lauterpacht H, *The Function of Law in the International Community* (Oxford University Press 1933).

Lauterpacht H, *The Function of Law in the International Community* (Oxford University Press 2000).

de la Laveleye E, *Des Causes Actuelles de Guerre in Europe et de l'Arbitrage* (C. Muquardt 1873).

Lawrence TJ, *International Problems and Hague Conferences* (J.M. Dent & Company 1908).

Lennox C (ed.), *Maximilien de Béthune, duc de Sully, The memoirs of the Duke of Sully, prime-minister to Henry the Great* (Printed by W. Bulmer and co. 1817).

Lens S, *The Forging of the American Empire: From the Revolution to Vietnam: A History of U.S. Imperialism* (Pluto Press 2003).

Lesaffer R, *European Legal History: A Cultural and Political Perspective* (Cambridge University Press 2012).

Liedtke R, *Die industrielle Revolution* (Böhlau Verlag 2012).

van der Linden WH, *The International Peace Movement 1815–1874* (Tilleul Publications 1987).

Lingens KH, *Internationale Schiedsgerichtsbarkeit und Jus publicum europaeum 1648–1794* (Duncker & Humblot 1988).

Lock T, *Das Verhältnis zwischen dem EuGH und internationalen Gerichten* (Mohr Sibeck 2010).

Longo B, *Spurious Coin: A History of Science, Management, and Technical Writing* (State University of New York Press 2000).

Lowe J, *The Great Powers, Imperialism, and the German Problem, 1865–1925* (Routledge 1994).

Lynch J, *The Spanish American Revolutions 1808–1826* (Weidenfeld and Nicolson 1973).

Maclachlan CM and Beezley WH, *Mexico's Crucial Century, 1810–1910* (University of Nebraska Press 2010).

Marks S, *The Illusion of Peace: International Relations in Europe, 1918–1933* (Palgrave Macmillan Ltd. 2003).

von Martens GF, *Précis du droit des gens moderne de l'Europe fondé sur les traités et les usages: Pour servir d'introduction à un cours politique et diplomatique* (3rd ed., J.C. Dieterich 1821).

von Martens GF, *Précis du droit des gens moderne de l'Europe fondé sur les traités et les usages: Pour servir d'introduction à un cours politique et diplomatique* (3rd ed., J.C. Dieterich 1821).

Marx C, *Geschichte Afrikas: Von 1800 bis zur Gegenwart* (UTB 2004).

McPherson A, *A Short History of U.S. Interventions in Latin America and the Caribbean* (John Wiley & Sons, Inc. 2016).

McWhinney E, *The International Court of Justice and the Western Tradition of International Law* (Martinus Nijhoff Publishers 1987).

Mecham JL, *The United States and Inter-American Security 1889–1960* (University of Texas Press 1961).

Meiser JW, *Power and Restraint: The Rise of the United States, 1898–1941* (Georgetown University Press 2015).

Ter Meulen J, *Der Gedanke der Internationalen Organisation in seiner Entwicklung*, vol. 2.1 (M. Nijhoff 1929).

Ter Meulen J, *Der Gedanke der Internationalen Organisation in seiner Entwicklung*, vol. 2.2 (M. Nijhoff 1940).

Milej T, *Entwicklung des Völkerrechts: Der Beitrag internationaler Gerichte und Sachverständigengremien* (De Gruyter 2014).
Miles CA, *Provisional Measures before International Courts and Tribunals* (Cambridge University Press 2017).
Miles JB, *Le Tribunal International* (Debons et Ce 1874).
Miles K, *The Origins of International Investment Law: Empire, Environment and the Safeguarding of Capital* (Cambridge University Press 2013).
Mill JS, *Auguste Comte and Positivism* (Trübner 1866).
Miller W, *Cicero de Officiis: With an English Translation by Walter Miller* (Heinemann 1928).
Mills B, *U.S.-Mexican War* (Chelsea House 2003).
Moch G, *Histoire Sommaire de l'Arbitrage permanent* (Institut international de la paix 1905).
Montt S, *State Liability in Investment Treaty Arbitration: Global Constitutional and Administrative Law in the BIT Generation* (Hart 2009).
Moore JB, *History and Digest of the International Arbitrations to which the United States has been a Party*, vol. 1 (Gov. Print. Off. 1898).
Morgenthau HJ, *Politics among Nations* (Knopf 1949).
Moriarty JT, *Manifest Destiny: A Primary Source History of America's Terrestrial Expansion in the 19th Century* (Rosen Publications Group 2005).
Neff S, *War and the Law of Nations: A General History* (Cambridge University Press 2005).
Neff S, *Justice Among Nations* (Harvard University Press 2014).
Nippold O, Die Fortbildung des Verfahrens in völkerrechtlichen Streitigkeiten (Duncker & Humblot 1907).
Nish I, *The Origins of the Russo-Japanese War* (Routledge 2014).
Nonn C, *Das 19. und 20. Jahrhundert* (UTB 2014).
von Nostiz H, *Bismarcks unbotmäßiger Botschafter Fürst Münster von Derneburg, 1820–1902* (Vandenhoeck & Ruprecht 1968).
Nurnberger R, *James Brown Scott: Peace through Justice* (Georgetown University 1975).
Nussbaum A, *Geschichte des Völkerrechts* (C.H. Beck 1960).
Nußberger A, *Das Völkerrecht: Geschichte, Institutionen, Perspektiven* (C.H. Beck 2009).
Nys E (ed.), *De Indis et De Iure Relections: Being Parts of Relections Theologicae XII* (Oceana Publications Inc. 1917).
O'Brien TF, *The Century of U.S. Capitalism in Latin America* (University of New Mexico Press 1999).
Okimoto K, *The Distinction and Relationship between Jus ad Bellum and Jus in Bello* (Hart Publishing 2011).
Oppenheim L, *International Law: A Treatise*, vol. 2 (Longmans 1906).
Oppenheim L, *The Future of International Law* (Clarendon Press 1921).

Osterhammel J, *Die Verwandlung der Welt. Eine Geschichte des 19. Jahrhunderts* (C.H. Beck 2009).

Paddeu F, *Justification and Excuse in International Law: Concept and Theory of General Defenses* (Cambridge University Press 2018).

Parry J, *The Politics of Patriotism: English Liberalism, National Identity and Europe, 1830–1886* (Cambridge University Press 2006).

Patterson DS, *Towards a Warless World: The Travail of the American Peace Movement 1887–1914* (Indiana University Press 1976).

Payk MM, *Frieden Durch Recht? Der Aufstieg des modernen Völkerrechts und der Friedensschluss nach dem ersten Weltkrieg* (De Gruyter Oldenbourg 2018).

Pendle G, *A History of Latin America* (Penguin Books 1963).

Penn W, *Essay Towards the Present and Future Peace of Europe* (printed and sold by Randal Taylor 1693).

Peterson S, *Crisis Bargaining and the State: The Domestic Politics of International Conflict* (University of Michigan Press 1996).

Phillipson C, *Termination of War and Treaties of Peace* (The Lawbook Exchange 2008).

Pohl H, *Deutsche Prisengerichtsbarkeit. Ihre Reform durch das Haager Abkommen* (J.C.B. Mohr 1911).

Pomerance M, *The United States and the World Court as a 'Supreme Court of the Nations': Dreams, Illusions and Disillusion* (Springer Netherland 1996).

Preuss O, *Bridging the Island: Brazilian's Views of Spanish America and Themselves, 1865–1912* (M. Vervuert 2011).

Proudhon PJ, *La Guerre et la Paix* (3rd ed., A. Lacroix, Verboeckhoven & Co 1861).

Pustagarov VV and Butler WE, *Our Martens: F.F. Martens, International Lawyer and Architect of Peace* (Simmonds & Hill 2000).

Quesada G, *Arbitration in Latin America* (Wyt 1907).

Ralston JH, *International Arbitration from Athens to Locarno* (Stanford University Press 1929).

Ralston JH, *International Arbitration from Athens to Locarno* (Clark 2004).

von Rauchhaupt FW, *Völkerrechtliche Eigentümlichkeiten Amerikas, insbesondere Hispano-Amerikas* (H. Sack 1924).

Rey MF, *La Unión Centro-Americana: Estudio Relativo á las Instituciones creadas en Washington por la Conferencia de Paz Centro-Americana de 1907* (Oficina Internacional Centro-Americana 1911).

Rech W, *Enemies of Mankind: Vattel's Theory of Collective Security* (Brill 2013).

Reinalda B, *Routledge History of International Organizations: From 1815 to the Present Day* (Routledge 2009).

Reinold T, *Sovereignty and the Responsibility to Protect: The Power of Norms and the Norms of the Powerful* (Routledge 2013).

Reinsch PS, *Public International Unions: Their Work and Organization* (Boston Ginn 1911).

Renehan E, *The Monroe Doctrine: The Cornerstone of American Foreign Policy* (Chelsea House 2007).

Rossi CR, *Broken Chain of Being: James Brown Scott and the Origins of Modern International Law* (Kluwer Law International 1998).

Ross A, A Textbook of International Law: General Part (The Lawbook Exchange 2006).

Rousseau JJ, *A Lasting Peace through the Federation of Europe and the State of War* (Constable 1917, originally published in French in 1761).

de Sá Vienna M, *De la Non-Existence d'un Droit International Américain* (L. Figueredo 1912).

de Saint-Pierre CI, *Projet pour rendre la paix perpétuelle en Europe* (Chez A. Schouten 1713).

Salacuse JW, *The Law of Investment Treaties* (Oxford University Press 2015).

Scarfi JP, *El Imperio de la Ley: James Brown Scott y la Construcción de un Orden jurídico interamericano* (Fondo de Cultura Económica de Argentina 2014).

Scarfi JP, *The Hidden History of International Law in the Americas: Empire and Legal Networks* (Oxford University Press 2017).

Schoultz L, *Beneath the United States: A History of U.S. Policy toward Latin America* (Harvard University Press 1998).

Walther Schücking, *Die Organisation der Welt* (A. Kröner 1909).

Walther Schücking, *The International Union of The Hague Conferences* (H. Milford 1918).

Scott JB (ed.), *An Essay on a Congress of Nations by William Ladd* (Oxford University Press 1915); re-print from the original: Ladd W, *An Essay on a Congress of Nations* (Whipple and Damrell 1840).

Scott JB (ed.), *The Status of the International Court of Justice* (American Society for Judicial Settlement 1916).

Scott SV, *International Law, US Power: The United States' Quest for Legal Security* (Cambridge University Press 2012).

Seebohm F, *On International Reform* (Longmans, Green and Co. 1871).

Seijas RF, *El derecho internacional Hispano-Americano* (El Monitor 1884).

Sexton J, *The Monroe Doctrine: Empire and Nation in the Nineteenth-Century America* (Hill & Wang 2011).

Shaw CM, *Cooperation, Conflict, and Consensus in the Organization of American States* (Palgrave Macmillan 2004).

Shire LC, *The Threshold of Manifest Destiny: Gender and National Expansion in Florida* (University of Pennsylvania Press 2016).

Simpson G, *Great Powers and Outlaw States: Unequal Sovereigns in the International Legal Order* (Cambridge University Press 2004).

Skousen M (ed.), *The Autobiography of Benjamin Franklin*, vol. 2 (Regnery History 2007).

Smith J, *The United States and Latin America: A History of American Diplomacy, 1776–2000* (Routledge 2005).

Smith J,*Unequal Giants: Diplomatic Relations between the United States and Brazil, 1889–1930* (University of Pittsburgh 1991)Stadtmüller G, *Rechtsidee und Machtpolitik in der amerikanischen Geschichte* (Isar 1957).

Steller V, *Diplomatie von Angesicht zu Angesicht: Diplomatische Handlungsformen in den deutsch-französischen Beziehungen 1870–1919* (Schöningh 2011).

Stinger M, *The Legacy of Positivism* (Palgrave Macmillan 2005).

Stone O and Kuznick P, *The Untold History of the United States* (Ebury Press 2012).

de Strada J, *L'Europe sauvée, et la Fédération* (A. Le Chevalier 1868).

Stuyt AM, *Survey of International Arbitrations 1794–1970* (A. W. Sijthoff. Dobbs Ferry, N.Y. Oceana 1972).

Stuyt AM, *Survey of International Arbitrations 1794–1989* (M. Nijhoff 1990).

Trendelenburg FA, *Lücken im Völkerrecht: Betrachtungen und Vorschläge aus dem Jahre 1870* (Hirzel 1870).

Tripp D, Der *Einfluß des naturwissenschaftlichen, philosophischen und historischen Positivismus auf die deutsche Rechtslehre im 19. Jahrhundert* (Duncker & Humblot 1983).

Turner B, *Latin America* (Rowman & Littlefield 2017).

Ullmann E, *Völkerrecht* (J. C. B. Mohr 1908).

de Vattel E, *The Law of Nations or Principles of the Law of Nations* (printed and sold by Samuel Campbell 1858; first published in French in 1758).

de Vattel E, *The Law of Nations or Principles of the Law of Nature* (T.&J. W. Johnson 1853; originally published in 1758).

Vavasour Noel J, *History of the Second Pan-American Congress* (Guggenheimer, Weil & Co. 1902).

Verzijl JHW, *International Law in Historical Perspective, Part VIII: Inter-State Disputes and their Settlement* (A. W. Sijthoff 1976).

Verzijl JHW, *International Law in Historical Perspective, Part III: State Territory* (A.W. Sijthoff 1970).

Vogler G, *Europas Aufbruch in die Neuzeit 1500–1650* (Ulmer 2003).

de Vries HP, *The Law of the Americas: An Introduction to the Legal Systems of the American Republics* (Oceana Publications 1965).

Weatherall T, *Ius Cogens – International Law and Social Contract* (Cambridge University Press 2015).

Weeks GB, *U.S. and Latin American Relations* (Wiley-Blackwell 2015).

Wehberg H, *The Problem of an International Court of Justice* (Clarendon Press 1918).
Westlake J, *International Law – Part 1: Peace* (Cambridge University Press 1910).
Wheaton H, *Elements of International Law: With a Sketch of the History of the Science* (Carey, Lea & Blanchard 1836).
Whitaker AP, *The Western Hemisphere: its Rise and Decline* (Cornell University Press 1954).
White AD, *Autobiography of Andrew Dickson White*, Vol II (Century 1905).
Wiarda HJ, *American Foreign Policy Toward Latin America in the 80s and 90s: Issues and Controversies from Reagan to Bush* (New York University Press 1992).
Williams ME, *Understanding U.S.-Latin American Relations: Theory and History* (Routledge 2012).
Williams WA, *The Tragedy of American Diplomacy* (W.W. Norton, cop. 2009).
Williamson DG, *Bismarck and Germany: 1862–1890* (Longman 2011).
Wright TC, *Latin America since Independence: Two Centuries of Continuity and Change* (Rowman & Littlefield Publ. 2017).
Wright Q, *The Role of International Law in the Elimination of War* (Manchester University Press 1961).
Zifcak S (ed.), *Globalisation and the Rule of Law* (Routledge 2005).
Zöllner R, *Geschichte Japans: Von 1800 bis zur Gegenwart* (Ferdinand Schöningh 2013).

Book Chapters

Alonso CJ, 'The Criollista Novel' in Roberto González Echevarría and Enrique Pupo-Walker (eds.), *The Cambridge History of Latin American Literature, vol. 2: The Twentieth Century* (Cambridge University Press 1996).
Birle P, 'Zwischenstaatliche Konflikte in Südamerika Vom 19. Jahrhundert bis heute. Ursachen, Lösungsansätze, Perspektiven' in Lothar Mark and Erich G. Fritz (eds.): *Lateinamerika im Aufbruch. Eine kritische Analyse* (Athena 2009).
Blanchard P, 'Pan Americanism and Slavery in the Era of Latin American Independence' in David Sheinin (ed.), *Beyond the Ideal: Pan Americanism in Inter-American Affairs*, published 2000 in Westport/London.
Blokker N, 'The Security Council and the Use of Force on Recent Practice' in Niels Blokker and Nico Schrijver (eds.), *The Security Council and the Use of Force: Theory and Reality – A Need for Change?* (Brill 2005).
Bouchez LJ, 'The Netherlands and the Law of International Rivers' in H.F. van Panhuys, W.P. Heere, J.W. Josephus Jitta, Ko Swan Sik, and A.M. Stuyt (eds.), *International Law in the Netherlands*, vol. 1 (Sitjhoff & Noordhoff 1978).

Brock L, 'Frieden Durch Recht: Anmerkungen Zum Thema in Historischem Kontext' in Peter Becker, Reiner Braun & Dieter Deiseroth (eds.), *Frieden durch Recht?* (Berliner Wissenschafts-Verlag 2010).

Butler NM, 'Are We Our Brothers' Keeper? Opening Address as Chairman of the Lake Mohonk Conference on International Arbitration, May 18, 1910' in Charles F. Howlett (ed.), *Nicholas Murray Butler's International Mind: An Argument for the Judicial Settlement of International Disputes* (Information Age Publishing Inc. 2013).

Cançado Trindade AA, 'Reflections on a Century of International Justice and Prospects for the Future' in Giorgia Gaja and Jenny Grote Stoutenburg (eds.), Enhancing the Rule of Law through the International Court of Justice (Brill–Nijhoff 2012).

Cançado Trindade AA, 'The Presence and Participation of Latin America at the Second Hague Peace Conference of 1907' in Yves Daudet, *Actualité de la Conférence de La Haye de 1907, deuxième Conférence de la paix: colloque, La Haye, 6–7 septembre 2007* (Nijhoff 2008).

Cassese A, 'States: Rise and Decline of the Primary Subjects of the International Community' in Bardo Fassbender and Anne Peters (eds.), *The Oxford Handbook of the History of International Law* (Oxford University Press 2012).

Cede F, 'The Settlement of International Disputes by Legal Means: Arbitration and Judicial Settlement' in Jacob Bercovitch (ed.), *The SAGE Handbook of Conflict Resolution* (SAGE Publications 2009).

Cooper SE, 'The Origins and Development of European Peace Movements: from Vienna to Frankfurt' in Gernot Heiss and Heinrich Lutz (eds.), *Friedensbewegungen: Bedingungen und Wirkungen* (Oldenbourg Wissenschaftsverlag 1984).

Craven M, 'Colonialism and Domination' in Bardo Fassbender and Anne Peters (eds.), *The Oxford Handbook of the History of International Law* (Oxford University Press 2012).

Doerr PW, 'Anglo-Japanese Alliance' in Spencer C. Tucker (ed.), *World War I: The Definite Encyclopedia and Document Collection*, vol. 1 (ABC Clio 2014).

Elihu Root, 'the Real Significance of the Declaration of London' in James Brown Scott (ed.), *The Declaration of London February 26, 1909* (Oxford University Press 1919).

Esquirol JL, 'Latin America' in Bardo Fassbender and Anne Peters (eds.), *The Oxford Handbook of the History of International Law* (Oxford University Press 2012).

Haggenmacher P, 'People in Portrait: Hugo Grotius' in Bardo Fassbender and Anne Peters (eds.), *The Oxford Handbook of the History of International Law* (Oxford University Press 2012).

Haruto T, 'Approaching Total War: Ivan Bloch's Disturbing Vision' in John Steinberg, et al. (eds.), *The Russo-Japanese War in Global Perspective: World War Zero*, vol. 2 (Brill 2007).

Humphreys RA, 'Chapter XXV: The States of Latin America' in John Patrick Tuer Bury (ed.), *The New Cambridge Modern History, vol. 10: The Zenith of European Power 1830–70* (Cambridge University Press 1960).

Janis MW, 'North America: American Exceptionalism in International Law' in Bardo Fassbender and Anne Peters (eds.), *The Oxford Handbook of the History of International Law* (Oxford University Press 2012).

Johnson C, 'Understanding the American Empire: Colonialism, Latin Americanism, and Professional Social Science, 1898–1820' in Alfred W. McCoy and Francisco A. Scarano (eds.), *Colonial Crucible: Empire in the Making of the modern American State* (University of Wisconsin Press 2009).

Keiger J, 'How the Entente Cordiale Began' in Richard Mayne, Douglas Johnson, and Robert Tombs (eds.), *Cross Channel Currents: 100 Years of the Entente Cordiale* (Routledge 2004).

Koskenniemi M, 'The Ideology of International Adjudication and the 1907 Hague Conference' in Yves Daudet (ed.), *Topicality of the 1907 Hague Conference, the Second Peace Conference* (Brill 2008).

Kowner R, 'Preface' in Rotem Kowner (ed.), *The Impact of the Russo-Japanese War* (Routledge 2007).

Lesaffer R, 'Too Much History: from War as Sanction to the Sanctioning of War' in Marc Weler (ed.), *The Oxford Handbook of the Use of Force in International Law* (Oxford University Press 2015).

Lesaffer R, 'Peace through Law: the Hague Peace Conferences and the Rise of the *Ius Contra Bellum*' in Maartje Abbenhuis et al. (eds.), *War, Peace and International Order? The Legacies of the Hague Conferences of 1899 and 1907* (Routledge 2017).

Lev A, 'the Transformation of International Law in the Nineteenth Century' in Alexander Orakhelashvili (ed.), *Research Handbook on the Theory and History of International Law* (Edward Elgar Pub 2011).

Lingens KH, 'Der Jay-Vertrag (1794) Als Geburtsstunde der Modernen Internationalen Schiedsgerichtsbarkeit? Zur Entstehung Eines Undifferenzierten Geschichtsbildes' in Miloš Vec & Serge Dauchy (eds.), *Les Conflits entre Peiples* (Nomos 2011).

Luf L, 'der "Gerechte Krieg" – Rechtsphilosophische Überlegungen Zur Renaissance Eines Überwunden Geglaubten Konzepts', in Daniela Demko, Kurt Seelmann, and Gerd Brudermüller (eds.), *Kriegs-Recht* (Königshausen u. Neumann 2013).

Lynch C, 'Peace Movements, Civil Societies, and the Development of International Law' in Bardo Fassbender and Anne Peters (eds.), *The Oxford Handbook of the History of International Law* (Oxford University Press 2012).

Mendelsohn E, 'Knowledge and Power in the Sciences' in Roderick W. Home (ed.), *Science under Scrutiny: The Place of History and Philosophy of Science* (Reidel 1983).

Mourra MH, 'The Conflicts and Controversies in Latin American Treaty-Based Disputes' in Mary Hellen Mourra (ed.), *Latin American Investment Treaty Arbitration: The Controversies and Conflicts* (Kluwer Law International 2008).

Muntarbhorn V, 'The 1899 Hague Peace Conference and the Development of the Laws of War: Asia's Contribution to the Quest for Humanitarianism?' in Timothy L.H.

McCormack, Michael Tilbury, and Gillian D. Triggs (eds.), *A Century of War and Peace: Asia-Pacific Perspectives on the Centenary of the 1899 Hague Peace Conference* (Kluwer Law International 2001).

Murase S, 'The Presence of Asia at the 1907 Hague Conference' in Yves Daudet (ed.), *Topicality of the 1907 Hague Conference, the Second Peace Conference* (Brill 2008).

Obregón L, 'Latin American International Law' in James D. Armstrong (ed.), *Routledge Handbook of International Law* (Routledge 2009).

Obregón L, 'The Civilized and the Uncivilized' in Bardo Fassbender and Anne Peters (eds.), *The Oxford Handbook of the History of International Law* (Oxford University Press 2012).

O'Connell ME, 'Historical Development and Legal Basis' in Dieter Fleck (ed.), *The Handbook of International Humanitarian Law* (3rd ed., Oxford University Press 2013).

O'Connell ME, 'The Prohibition of the Use of Force' in Nigel D. White and Christian Henderson (eds.), Research Handbook on the International Conflict and Security Law (Edward Elgar Pub 2013).

O'Connell ME, 'Arbitration and Avoidance of War: the Nineteenth-Century American Vision' in Cesare P.R. Romano (ed.), *The Sword and the Scales: The United States and International Courts and Tribunals* (Cambridge Univ. Press 2009).

O'Connell ME and Vanderzee L, 'The History of International Adjudication' in Cesare P.R. Romano, Karen J. Alter & Yuval Shany (eds.), *The Oxford Handbook of International Adjudication* (Oxford University Press 2014).

Odello M and Seatzu F, 'Introduction' in Marco Odello and Francesco Seatzu (eds.), *Latin American and Caribbean International Law* (T.M.C. Asser Press 2015).

Oldfield J, 'Remembering the Maine: the United States, 1898 and Sectional Reconciliation' in Angel Smith and Emma Dávila-Cox (eds.), *The Crisis of 1898: Colonial Redistribution and Nationalist Mobilization* (Palgrave Macmillan 1999).

Prados de la Escosura L, 'The Economic Consequences of Independence in Latin America' in Victor Bulmer-Thomas, John Coatsworth, and Roberto Cortes-Conde (eds.), *The Cambridge Economic History of Latin America* (Cambridge University Press 2005).

Rivarola Puntigliano A, 'Geopolitics and Integration: A South American Perspective' in Andrés Rivarola Puntigliano and José Briceño-Ruiz (eds.), *Resilience of Regionalism in Latin America and the Caribbean: Development and Autonomy* (Palgrave Macmillan 2013).

Roelofsen CG, 'International Arbitration and Courts' in Bardo Fassbender and Anne Peters (eds.), *The Oxford Handbook of the History of International Law* (Oxford University Press 2012).

Romano CPR, 'Trial and Error in International Judicialization' in Cesare P. R. Romano, Karen J. Alter, and Yuval Shany (eds.), *The Oxford Handbook of International Adjudication* (Oxford University Press 2014).

Sassòli M, 'Ius ad Bellum and Ius in Bello – The Separation between the Legality of the Use of Force and Humanitarian Rules to Be Respected in Warfare: Crucial or Outdated?' in Michael Schmitt and Jelena Pejic (eds.), *International Law and Armed Conflict: Exploring the Faultiness: Essays in Honour of Yoram Dinstein* (Martinus Nijhoff Publishers 2007).

Schulz M, 'Paradoxes of a Great Power Peace: the Case of the Concert of Europe', in Thomas Hippler and Miloš Vec (eds.), *Paradoxes of Peace in Nineteenth Century Europe* (Oxford University Press 2015).

Seibert-Fohr A, 'International Judicial Ethics' in Cesare PR Romano, Karen J Alter & Yuval Shany (eds.), *The Oxford Handbook of International Adjudication* (Oxford University Press 2014).

Sheinin D, 'Rethinking Pan Americanism: An Introduction' in David Sheinin (ed.), *Beyond the Ideal: Pan Americanism in Inter-American Affairs* (Greenwood Press 2000).

de Sillac J, 'Les Conférences Périodiques de La Paix' in Gustave Spiller, *Mémoires sur le Contact des Races: Communiques au Premier Congres Universel des Races tenu a l'Universite de Londres du 26 au 29 juillet 1911* (P.S. King 1911).

Smith J, 'The First Conference of American States (1889–1890) and the Early Pan American Policy of the United States' in David Sheinin (ed.), *Beyond the Ideal: Pan Americanism in Inter-American Affairs* (Greenwood Press 2000).

Strachan H, 'Military Modernization 1789–1918' in CW Blanning (ed.), *The Oxford History of Modern Europe* (Oxford University Press 2000).

Vec M, 'From the Congress of Vienna to the Paris Peace Treaties of 1919' in Bardo Fassbender and Anne Peters (eds.), *The Oxford Handbook of the History of International Law* (Oxford University Press 2012).

Viñuales JE and Langer MJ, 'Foreign Investment in Latin America: between Love and Hatred' in Claude Auroi and Aline Helg (eds.), *Latin America 1810–2010: Dreams and Legacies* (Imperial College Press 2012).

Visser D, 'a Brief Perspective on Military Preparedness in History' in Thean Potgieter and Ian Liebenberg (eds.), *Reflections on War: Preparedness and Consequences* (SUN Press 2012).

Webster A, 'Reconsidering Disarmament at the Hague Peace Conference of 1899, and after', in Maartje Abbenhuis et al. (eds.), *War, Peace and International Order? The Legacies of the Hague Conferences of 1899 and 1907* (Routledge 2017).

Webster A, 'Internationalism' in Gordon Martel (ed.), A Companion to International History 1900–2001 (Blackwell 2007).

Wessel RA, 'Towards a United Europe? A Legal Perspective on European Institutionalization and Integration' in Jaap de Wilde and Hakan Wilberg (eds.), *Organized Anarchy in Europe: The Role of States and Intergovernmental Organizations* (Tauris Academic Studies 1996).

Whyte J, '"Always on Top?" The "Responsibility to Protect" and the Persistence of Colonialism' in Jyotsna G. Singh and David D. Kim (eds.), *The Postcolonial World* (Routledge 2017).

Articles and Encyclopedia/Commentary Entries

Abrams I, 'The Emergence of the International Law Societies' (1957) 19 The Review of Politics.

Adriansen I and Christensen JO, *The Second Schleswig War 1864* (Museum Sønderjylland 2013); <http://www.museum-sonderjylland.dk/siderne/Det-sker/documents/1864-Engelsk.pdf> accessed January 8, 2015.

Alcorta A, 'La ciencia del derecho internacional. A propósito de la obra de Calvo' (1883) 7 Nueva Revista.

Alvarez A, 'Latin America and International Law' (1907) 3 The American Journal of International Law (1907).

Anderson L, 'The Peace Conference of Central America' (1908) 2 The American Journal of International Law.

Anon., 'The German Empire '(April 1871) CXXXIII Edinburg Review.

Baker B, 'The Hague Conferences (1899 and 1907)' in Max Planck Encyclopedia of Public International Law (online), accessed online: November 16, 2017.

Bates RH, Coatsworth JH, and Williamson JG, 'Lost Decades: Postindependence Performance in Latin America and Africa' (2007) 67 The Journal of Economic History.

Becker Lorca A, 'International Law in Latin America or Latin American International Law? Rise, Fall, and Retrieval of a Tradition of Legal Thinking and Political Imagination' (2006) 47 Harvard International Law Journal.

Bernhardt R, 'Preferential Claims against Venezuela Arbitration' in Rudolf Bernhardt, Rudolf L Bindschedler, and Rudolf Dolzer (eds.), *Encyclopedia of Public International Law, vol. 2: Decisions of International Court and Tribunals and International Arbitrations* (North-Holland Publ. Co. 1981).

Bingham T, 'The Alabama Claims Arbitration' (2005) 54 The International and Comparative Law Quarterly.

Brower CH II, 'Arbitration', *Max Planck Encyclopedia of International Law* (online; accessed online: April 28, 2016).

Brown HB, 'The Proposed International Prize Court' (1908) 2 The American Journal of International Law.

Brown PM, 'American Intervention in Central America' (1914) 4 The Journal of Race Development.

Buchanan WI, 'Latin America and the Mexican Conference' (1903) 22 The Annals of the American Academy of Political and Social Science.

Caron DD, 'War and International Adjudication: Reflections on the 1899 Peace Conference' (2000) 94 The American Journal of International Law.

Castro-Ruiz C, 'The Monroe Doctrine and the Government of Chile' (1917) 11 The American Political Science Review.

Chester A, 'A Permanent Court' in *Report of the 5th Annual Meeting of the Lake Mohonk Conference on International Arbitration 1899* (Lake Mohonk Conference on International Arbitration 1899).

Clarke RF, 'A Permanent Tribunal of International Arbitration: Its Necessity and Value' (1907) 1 The American Journal of International Law.

Collier S, 'Nationality, Nationalism, and Supranationalism in the Writings of Simón Bolívar' (1983) 63 The Hispanic American Historical Review.

Corrales J and Feinberg RE, 'Regimes of Cooperation in the Western Hemisphere: Power. Interests, and Intellectual Traditions' (1999) 43 International Studies Quarterly (1999).

Davis CD, 'Elihu Root' in Edward S. Mihalkanin (ed.), *American Statesmen: Secretaries of State from John Jay to Colin Powell* (Greenwood Press 2004).

Dawson FG, 'Contributions of Lesser Developed Nations to International Law: The Latin American Experience' (1981) 13 Case Western Reverse Journal of International Law.

Dennis WC, 'The Necessity for an International Code of Arbitral Procedure' (1913) 7 The American Journal of International Law.

Drago LM, 'United States versus Great Britain in the Matter of the North Atlantic Coast Fisheries' (1910) 4 The American Journal of International Law.

Dubin MD, 'Toward the Concept of Collective Security: The Bryce Group's "Proposal for the Avoidance of War," 1914–1917' (1970) 24 International Organization.

'Editorial Comment: The Second Peace Conference of The Hague' (1907) 1 The American Journal of International Law.

'Editorial Comment: Treaties of Arbitration since the First Hague Conference' (1908) 2 The American Journal of International Law.

'Editorial Comment: North Atlantic Fisheries' (1910) 4 The American Journal of International Law.

'Editorial Comment: Status of the Declaration of London' (1915) 9 The American Journal of International Law.

von Elbe J, 'The Evolution of the Concept of the Just War in International Law' (1939) 33 The American Journal of International Law.

Esthus RA, 'Nicholas II and the Russo-Japanese War' (1981) 40 The Russian Review.

Everett G, 'International Arbitration in the Americas' (1939/40) 17 New York University Law Quarterly Review.

Eyffinger A, 'A highly critical Moment: Role and Record of the 1907 Hague Peace Conference' (2007) 54 The Netherlands International Law Review.

Fawcett L, 'Between West and non-West: Latin American Contributions to International Thought' (2012) 34 The International History Review.

Fenwick CG, 'International Organization: Judicial' (1917) 11 Proceedings of the American Society of International Law at Its Annual Meeting.

Fenwick CG, 'International Law: The Old and the New' (1966) 60 The American Journal of International Law.

Finch GA, 'The Bryan Peace Treaties' (1916) 10 The American Journal of International Law.

La Fontaine H, *Histoire Sommaire et Chronologique des Arbitrages Internationaux (1794–1900)* (Revue de Droit International et de Législation Comparée 1902).

Ford TK, 'The Genesis of the First Hague Peace Conference' (1936) 51 Political Science Quarterly.

Franklin JH, 'The Southern Expansionists of 1846' (1959) 25 The Journal of Southern History.

Gent SE, 'The Politics of International Arbitration and Adjudication' (2013) 2 Penn State Journal of Law & International Affairs.

Gilderhus MT, 'The Monroe Doctrine: Meaning and Implications' (2006) 36 Presidential Studies Quarterly.

Goddard SE, 'When Right Makes Might: How Prussia Overturned the European Balance of Power' (2008/09) 33 International Security.

Godwin RK, 'Russia and the Portsmouth Peace Conference' (1950) 9 The American Slavic and East European Review.

Dr. Goldschmidt, 'Ein Reglement für internationale Schiedsgerichte' (1875) 2 Zeitschrift für das Privat- und Öffentliche Recht der Gegenwart.

Greenwood C, 'The Relationship between ius ad bellum and ius in bello' (1983) 9 Review of International Studies.

Grigera Naón HA, 'Arbitration and Latin America: Progress and Setbacks' (2005) 21 Arbitration International.

Harrer GA, 'Cicero on Peace and War' (1918) 13 The Classical Journal.

Harriman EA, 'The Work of the Hague Conferences: Past and Future' in *Report of the Twentieth Annual Lake Mohonk Conference on International Arbitration, May 27th, 28th and 29th 1914* (Lake Mohonk Arbitration Conference 1914).

Henderson JB, 'The Hague Tribunal Does Not Go Far Enough' in William J. Rose (ed.), *Report of the Tenth Annual Meeting of the Lake Mohonk Conference on International Arbitration 1904* (Lake Mohonk arbitration conference 1904).

Hepp J, 'James Brown Scott and the Rise of Public International Law' (2008) 7 The Journal of the Gilded Age and Progressive Era.

Hershey AS, 'History of International Law Since the Peace of Westphalia' (1912) 6 The American Journal of International Law.

Hershey AS, 'The Coming Peace Conference at The Hague' (1906) LXI The Independent.

Hershey AS, 'An International Prize Court' (1907) 19 The Green Bag.

Hill DJ, 'The Second Peace Conference at the Hague' (1907) 1 The American Journal of International Law.

Hill DJ, 'International Law and International Policy' (1919) 209 no. 760 The North American Review.

Hobe S and Fuhrmann J, 'Vom *ius in bello* zum *ius contra bellum*: Der Beitrag der Zweiten Haager Friedenskonferenz zur Entwicklung des modernen Völkerrechts' (2007) 82 Die Friedens-Warte.

Howland D, 'Sovereignty and the Laws of War: International Consequences of Japan's 1905 Victory over Russia' (2011) 29 Law and History Review.

Hudson MO, 'The Central American Court of Justice' (1932) 26 The American Journal of International Law.

Hye CC, 'Legal Problems Capable of Settlement by Arbitration' in Charles Edward Beales, *Proceedings of the Second National Peace Congress* (Peterson Linotype Co. 1909).

Jones FL, 'The Concert of America. The New World's League of Nations' in (1925) 11 Transactions of the Grotius Society.

Jones H, 'Anglophobia and the Aroostook War' (1975) 48 The New England Quarterly.

Juillard P, 'Calvo Doctrine/Calvo Clause', *Max Planck Encyclopedia of Public International Law* (online), accessed online: March 14, 2017.

Kamarowsky L, 'De l'idée d'un tribunal international' (1883) 15 Revue de Droit International et de Législation Comparée.

Keene E, 'The Treaty-Making Revolution of the Nineteenth Century' (2012) 34 The International Historical Review.

Kohen MG, 'La Contribución de América Latina al Desarrollo progresivo del Derecho Internacional en Materia territorial' (2001) 17 Anuario Español de Derecho Internacional.

Kotzur M, 'Ex Aequo et Bono', *Max Planck Encyclopedia of International Law* (online; accessed August 16, 2018).

Kuhn AK, 'The Existing and Proposed International Courts as Subjects for the Deliberations of the Third Hague Peace Conference' in *Report of the Nineteenth Annual Lake Mohonk Conference on International Arbitration, May 14th, 15th and 16th 1913* (Lake Mohonk Arbitration Conference 1913).

de Lapradelle AG and Stowell EC, 'Latin America at the Hague Conference' (1908) 17 The Yale Law Journal.

Lesaffer R, 'Aggression before Versailles' (2018) 29 The EuropeanJournal of International Law.

Lesaffer R, 'The Grotian Tradition Revisited: Change and Continuity in the History of International Law' (2002) 73 The British Yearbook of International Law.

Lesaffer R, 'The Temple of Peace: The Hague Conferences, Andrew Carnegie and the Building of the Peace Palace 1898–1913' in *Mededelingen van de Koninklijke Nederlandse Vereniging voor Internationaal Recht, Preadviezen.* vol. 140 (2013).

Lesaffer R, 'Briand-Kellogg Pact (1928)', *Max Planck Encyclopedia of Public International Law (online)*.

Levie HS, 'Final Settlement of the Pious Fund Case' (1969) 63 The American Journal of International Law.

Levi L, 'Draft Project of a Council and High Court of International Arbitration', reprinted in: William Evans Darby, *International Arbitration; International Tribunals.*

Lihr T, 'Elihu Root and International Legalism: Legalist Remarks on Collective Security and American Realism' (2014) 1 Helsinki Law Review.

Mace G, 'Regional Integration in Latin America: A Long and Winding Road' (1988) 43 International Journal.

Macfarland HBF, 'The Hopefulness of the Knox Proposition' in *Report of the Sixteenth Annual Meeting of the Lake Mohonk Conference on International Arbitration,* May *18th, 19th and 20th 1910* (Lake Mohonk Arbitration Conference 1910).

Macnamara HTJ, 'The Second Paper' in Peace Society Office, *The Proceedings of the First General Peace Convention* (Ward and Co 1843).

Mallet JA, 'War and Peace in Plato's Political Thought' (2017) 1 The Philosophical Journal of Conflict and Violence.

Mandel R, 'The Effectiveness of Gunboat Diplomacy' (1986) 30 International Studies Quarterly.

de Martens F, 'The Portsmouth Peace Conference' (1905) 181 The North American Review.

von Martitz F, 'Das internationale System zur Unterdrückung des Afrikanischen Sklavenhandels in seinem heutigen Bestande' (1886) 1 Archiv des öffentlichen Rechts.

Mauser G, 'Der Vergessene Kontinent: Lateinamerika zwischen Diktatur und Demokratie' (1959) 7 Vierteljahreshefte für Zeitgeschichte.

McDonald WE, 'The Pious Fund of the Californias' (1934) 19 The Catholic Historical Review.

Miller LH, 'The Contemporary Significance of the Doctrine of Just War' (1964) 16 World Politics.

Mitchener KJ and Weidenmier M, 'Empire, Public Goods, and the Roosevelt Corollary' (2005) 65 The Journal of Economic History.

Möller F, 'Vom revolutionären Idealismus zur Realpolitik. Generationswechsel nach 1848?' (2003) 36 Historische Zeitschrift. Beihefte, New Series.

Moore JB, 'Historical Notes on International Arbitration', *The American Conference on International Arbitration held in Washington D.C. April 22 and 23 1896* (Baker & Taylor 1896).

Morrill DL, 'Nicholas II and the Call for the First Hague Conference' (1974) 46 The Journal of Modern History.

Motyl AJ, 'Latin American Nationalism' in Alexander J. Motyl (ed.), *Encyclopedia of Nationalism, vol. 2: Leaders, Movements, and Concepts* (Academic Press 2001).

Mueller J, 'Changing Attitudes towards War: The Impact of the First World War' (1991) 21 British Journal of Political Science.

Münch F, 'Das Institut de Droit international' (1990) 28 Archiv des Völkerrechts.

Murphy JD, 'Insular Cases' in Spencer C. Tucker (ed.), *The Encyclopedia of the Spanish-American and Philippines-American Wars* (ABC Clio 2009).

Nicholls D, 'Richard Cobden and the International Peace Congress Movement, 1848–1853' (1991) 30 Journal of British Studies.

Nuermberger GA, 'The Continental Treaties of 1856: An American Union "Exclusive of the United States"' (1940) 20 The Hispanic American Historical Review.

Obregón L, 'Regionalism Constructed: A Short History of "Latin American International Law"' (2015) 5 European Society of International Law: Conference Paper Series.

Obregón L, 'Between Civilisation and Barbarism: Creole Interventions in International Law' (2006) 27 Third World Quarterly.

Oellers-Frahm K, 'International Courts and Tribunals, Judges and Arbitrators', *Max Planck Encyclopedia of Public International Law* (accessed online: August 17, 2018).

Offner JL, 'McKinley and the Spanish-American War' (2004) 34 Presidential Studies Quarterly.

Oppenheim L, 'The Science of International Law: Its Task and Method' (1908) 2 The American Journal of International Law.

Orakhelashvili A, 'The Idea of European International Law' (2006) 17 The European Journal of International Law.

Orr WJ, Jr., 'British Diplomacy and the German Problem, 1848–1850' (1978) 10 Albion: A Quarterly Journal Concerned with British Studies.

O'Sullivan J, 'Annexation' (1845) 17 United States Magazine and Democratic Review.

Parsons EB, 'Roosevelt's Containment of the Russo-Japanese War' (1969) 38 Pacific Historical Review.

Patterson DS, 'The United States and the Origins of the World Court' (1976) 91 Political Science Quarterly.

Peceny M, 'A Constructivist Interpretation of the Liberal Peace: The Ambiguous Case of the Spanish-American War' (1997) 34 Journal of Peace Research.

Pellet A, 'Article 38' in Andreas Zimmermann, Christian Tomuschat, Karin Oellers-Frahm, and Christian J. Tams (eds.), *The Statute of the International Court of Justice: A Commentary* (Oxford University Press 2012).

Pellet A, 'Judicial Settlement of International Disputes', *Max Planck Encyclopedia of Public International Law* (accessed online: August 18, 2018).

Penfield WL, 'The Anglo-German Intervention in Venezuela' (1903) 177 The North American Review.

Penfield WL, 'International Arbitration' (1907) 1 The American Journal of International Law.

Ralston JH, 'Some Suggestions as to the Permanent Court of Arbitration' (1907) 1 The American Journal of International Law.

Reinsch PS, 'The Concept of Legality in International Arbitration' (1911) 5 The American Journal of International Law.

Renger N and Kennedy-Pipe C, 'The State of War' (2008) 84 International Affairs.

Ritter M, 'Deutschland und der Ausbruch des Weltkrieges' (1919) 121 Historische Zeitschrift.

Rolin-Jaequemyns G, 'De la nécessité d'organiser une institution scientifique permanente pour favoriser l'étude et le progrès du droit international' (1873)1 Revue de Droit Internationale et de Législation Comparée.

Romano CPR, 'The Shift from the Consensual to the Compulsory Paradigm in International Adjudication: Elements for a Theory of Consent' (2006/07) 39 New York University Journal of International Law and Politics.

Ronzitti N, 'International Prize Court (IPC)' in *Max Planck Encyclopedia of Public International Law* (online), accessed: January 16, 2018.

Root E, 'The Real Monroe Doctrine' (1914) 199 The North American Review.

Root E, 'The Need of Popular Understanding of International Law' (1907) 1 The American Journal of International Law.

del Rosario Rodríguez Díaz M, 'La misión diplomática de Elihu Root en América Latina y el Caribe, 1906' (2004) 9 Revista Mexicana del Caribe.

Rosenne S, 'Permanent Court of International Justice (PCIJ)', *Max Planck Encyclopaedia of Public International Law (online)*.

Scarfi JP, 'In the Name of the Americas: The Pan-American Redefinition of the Monroe Doctrine and the Emerging Language of American International Law in the Western Hemisphere, 1893–1933' (2016) 40 Diplomatic History.

Scarfi JP, 'Excepcionalismo Estadounidense y Hegemonia Legal Hemisferica: La Corte Suprema de Estados Unidos como Modelo Imperial de Justicia Internacional para Contramerica y America Latina, y su Inlufjo en el Sistema Interamericano (1906–1938)' (2016) 4 Revista Latinoamericana de Derecho Internacional.

Schimmelpenninck van der Oye D, 'Rewriting the Russo-Japanese War: A Centenary Retroperspective' (2008) 67 The Russian Review.

Schlochauer HJ, 'Arbitration' in Rudolf Bernhardt, *The Encyclopedia of Public International Law*, vol. 1 (Elsevier 1992).

Schimmelpenninck van der Oye D, 'Die Entwicklung der internationalen Schiedsgerichtsbarkeit' (1962/63) 10 Archiv des Völkerrechts.

Schroeder PW, 'The 19th-Century International System: Changes in the Structure' (1986) 39 World Politics.

Schroeder PW, 'The Nineteenth Century System: Balance of Power or Political Equilibrium?' (1989) 15 Review of International Studies.

Schulz CA, 'Civilisation, Barbarism and the Making of Latin America's Place in the 19th Century International Society' (2014) 42 Millennium Journal of International Studies.

Scott JB, 'The Evolution of a Permanent International Judiciary' (1912) 6 The American Journal of International Law.

Scott JB, 'The Proposed Court of Arbitral Justice' (1908) 2 The American Journal of International Law.

Scott JB, 'Elihu Root: An Appreciation' (1939) 31 Proceedings of the American Society of International Law at its Annual Meeting.

Scott JB, 'Elihu Root' in Samuel Flagg Bemis (ed.), *The American Secretaries of State and their Diplomacy*, vol. IX (Cooper Square Publishers 1963).

Scott JB, 'Recommendation for a Third Peace Conference at The Hague' (1908) 2 The American Journal of International Law.

Scott JB, 'The Work of the Second Hague Peace Conference' (1908) 2 The American Journal of International Law.

Scott JB, 'The Central American Peace Conference of 1907' (1908) 2 The American Journal of International Law.

Scott JB, 'A Permanent Court of International Justice' (1920) 14 The American Journal of International Law.

Scott JB, 'Should there be a Third Hague Peace Conference?' (1925) 87, no. 1 Advocate of Peace through Justice.

Slade WF, 'The Federation of Central America' (1917) 8 The Journal of Race Development.

Smith RC, 'the Need and Advantages of an International Court of Justice' in James Brown Scott (ed.) *Proceedings of the Third National Conference of the American Society for Judicial Settlement of International Disputes, December 20–21, 1912* (Williams & Wilkins Company 1913).

Sokoloff KL and Engerman SL, 'History Lessons: Institutions, Factors Endowments, and Paths of Development in the New World' (2000) 14 The Journal of Economic Perspectives.

Spiermann O, 'Historical Introduction' in Andreas Zimmermann, Christian Tomuschat, Karin Oellers-Frahm, and Christian J. Tams (eds.), *The Statute of the International Court of Justice* (Oxford University Press 2012).

Steinberg JW, 'Was the Russo-Japanese War World War Zero?' (2008) 67 The Russian Review (2008).

von Stengel K, *Die Haager Friedenskonferenz und das Völkerrecht* (J.C.B. Mohr 1900).

Stockton CH, 'The Declaration of Paris' (1920) 14 The American Journal of International Law.

Stockton CH, 'The International Naval Conference of London, 1908–1909' (1909) 3 The American Journal of International Law.

Stowell EC, 'The International Naval Conference and the Declaration of London' (1909) 3 The American Political Science Review.

Summers LM, 'The Calvo Clause' (1933) 19 Virginia Law Review.

Tams CJ, *World Peace Through International Adjudication?* (2016) 3; available online <https://papers.ssrn.com/sol3/papers.cfm?abstract_id=2733307> uploaded: February 15, 2016.

Tams CJ, 'League of Nations', in: Max Planck Encyclopedia of Public International Law (accessed online September 10, 2018).

Temperley H, 'The Treaty of Paris of 1856 and Its Execution' (1932) 4 The Journal of Modern History.

Thayer WW, 'International Arbitration of Justiciable Disputes' (1913) 26 Harvard Law Review.

Thorson WB, 'American Public Opinion and the Portsmouth Peace Conference' (1948) 53 The American Historical Review.

Tomuschat C, 'International Courts and Tribunals', *Max Planck Encyclopedia of Public International Law* (accessed online: August 17, 2018).

James L. Tryon, 'Proposals for an International Court' (1914) 23 The Yale Law Journal.

James L. Tryon, 'A Permanent Court of International Justice: A Suggestion for the Consideration of the Programme Committee of the Third Hague Conference' (1913) 22 The Yale Law Journal.

Tyrrell A, 'Making the Millennium: The Mid-Nineteenth Century Peace Movement' (1978) 21 The Historical Journal.

Verdebout A, 'The Contemporary Discourse on the Use of Force in the Nineteenth Century: A Diachronic and Critical Analysis' (2014) 1 Journal on the Use of Force and International Law.

Waldman T, 'Politics and War: Clausewitz's Paradoxical Equation' (2010) 40 Parameters.

Wehberg H, 'Restrictive Clauses in International Arbitration Treaties' (1913) 7 The American Journal of International Law.

Weidmaier MC, 'Contracting for State Intervention: The Origins of Sovereign Debt Arbitration' (2010) 73, n 4 Law and Contemporary Problems.

Whitaker AP, 'The Origin of the Western Hemisphere Idea' (1954) 98 Proceedings of the American Philosophical Society.

Wickham FR, 'Pan-Americanism: A Dream or a Reality?' (1935) 18 Hispania.

Wilgus AC, 'James G. Blaine and the Pan American Movement' (1922) 5 The Hispanic American Historical Review (1922).

Wilson RR, 'Reservation Clauses in Agreements for Obligatory Arbitration' (1929) 23 The American Journal of International Law.

Winkel L, 'Francisco de Vitoria on Just War on Both Sides and on the Legal Position of Burgundy' (2007) 57 The Legal History Review.

Wolfrum R, 'International Law', *The Max Planck Encyclopedia of Public International Law* (Oxford University Press 2012).

Zasloff J, 'Law and the Shaping of American Foreign Policy: From the Gilded Age to the New Era' (2003) 78 NYU Law Review.

Ziegler KH, 'Zur Entwicklung von Kriegsrecht und Kriegsverhütung im Völkerrecht des 19. und frühen 20. Jahrhunderts' (2005) 42 Archiv des Völkerrechts.

Documents, Official Declarations and Cases

'Additional Articles to the Treaty of Commerce of 15 September 1846 between Chile and France', signed at Santiago, 30 June 1852 (available: Oxford Historical Treaties; OUP reference: 108 CTS 213).

'Address by President John F. Kennedy to the UN General Assembly', September 25, 1961.

Address of Congratulation and Commendation of the New York State Bar Association to His Imperial Majesty, Nicholas II, Emperor of all Russians, on the Occasion of the Peace Congress at The Hague and Recommending the Creation of an International Court (New York State Bar Association 1899).

'Address of President James Brown Scott' in American Society for Judicial Settlement of International Disputes, *Proceedings of the International Conference under the Auspices of the American Society for Judicial Settlement of International Disputes, December 15–17, 1910 in Washington, D.C.* (Waverly Press 1911).

'Address of the Hon. Elihu Root, Secretary of State of the United States, When Calling the Conference to Order on November 14, 1907' in *Papers relating to the Foreign Affairs of the United States with the Annual Message of the President transmitted to Congress December 3, 1907*, vol 2 (United States Government Printing Office 1910).

Adolf Baron Marschall Von Bieberstein, *Die Gruppierung der Staaten auf der Haager Konferenz* (accessible at: Politisches Archiv des Auswärtigen Amts, R 172).

Adolf Baron Marschall von Bieberstein, *Die Verhandlung der zweiten Haager Friedenskonferenz 1907: Allgemein* (accessible at: Politisches Archiv des Auswärtigen Amtes, R 176).

'Amendment to the Russian Draft regarding Mediation and Arbitration Submitted by His Excellency Count Nigra', in: James Brown Scott (ed.), *The Proceedings of The Hague Peace Conferences: The Conference of 1899* (Oxford University Press 1920).

American Peace Society, *Official report of the Fifth Universal Peace Congress held at Chicago, United States of America, August 14 to 20, 1893, under the auspices of the World's congress auxiliary of the World's Columbian exposition* (American Peace Society 1893).

'Annual Message of the President to Congress, December 5, 1905' in: *Papers relating to the Foreign Relations of the United States, with the annual message of the president transmitted to Congress December 5, 1905* (United States Government Printing Office 1906).

'Articles of Confederation and Perpetual Union'; <https://www.govinfo.gov/content/pkg/SMAN-107/pdf/SMAN-107-pg935.pdf> accessed December 13, 2016.

Asquith HH, 'Speech at Dublin, September 25, 1914' in James Bryce, *Proposals for the Avoidance of War with a Preparatory Note by Viscount Bryce* (1915); <https://archive.org/details/proposalsforavoi00brycuoft/page/n1/mode/2up> accessed August 26, 2021.

'Award of the Permanent Court of Arbitration in the matter of the Japanese House Tax Case, rendered May 22, 1905'; <https://pca-cpa.org/en/cases/69/> accessed August 11, 2017.

'Award of the Permanent Court of Arbitration in the matter of the Pious Fund of the Californias, rendered on October 14, 1902'; <http://www.pca-cpa.org/The%20Pious%20Funde37e.pdf?fil_id=1820> accessed December 11, 2015.

'Award of the Permanent Court of Arbitration in the matter of the Venezuela Preferential Case, rendered February 22, 1904'; <http://legal.un.org/riaa/cases/vol_IX/99-110.pdf> accessed August 23, 2017.

Blaine JG, 'Note of the Secretary of State of the United States Inviting the Republics of America to a Pan-American Congress' (1910) 4 The American Journal of International Law, Supplement: Official Documents.

'Briand-Kellogg Pact'; <http://avalon.law.yale.edu/20th_century/kbpact.asp> accessed August 22, 2018.

'British Circular' (February 27, 1908), in: James Brown Scott (ed.), *The Declaration of London February 26, 1909* (Oxford University Press 1919).

'Case Concerning the Payment of Various Serbian Loans Issues in France', published in: Publications of the Permanent Court of International Justice, Series A., No 20 (1929).

Channing WE, in a Letter to John O'Sullivan (From May 7, 1841), in William Ellery Channing, *Memoir with extracts from his correspondence and manuscripts* (Routledge 1870).

'Circular Invitation Addressed by Simón Bolívar to the Governments of Colombia, Mexico, Central America, the United Provinces of Buenos Aires, Chile and Brazil', available in: James Brown Scott (ed.), *The International Conferences of American States 1889–1928* (Carnegie Endowment for International Peace 1931).

'Constitución de la República Dominicana (1880)', Art. 97; <http://www.consultoria.gov.do/constituciones%201844-2008/Constitucion%201880.pdf> accessed June 5, 2016.

'Consular and Establishment and Extradition Conventions between Italy and Romania', signed at Bucharest, August 5 and 17, 1880; <http://www.prassi.cnr.it/prassi/content.html?id=1249> accessed February 28, 2019.

'Continental Treaty of Alliance and Reciprocal Assistance', signed at the Congress of Santiago in 1856; <http://www.oas.org/sap/peacefund/VirtualLibrary/ContinentalCongressofSantiago/TratadoContinental1856.pdf> accessed January 30, 2017.

'Convention between Buenos Aires and France', signed at Buenos Aires', October 29, 1840; available: Oxford Historical Treaties; OUP reference: 91 CTS 111.

'Convention between the Netherlands and Portugal Relative to Commerce, Navigation, Boundaries and Mutual Rights of Pre-Emption in the Timor and Solor Archipelago', signed at Lisbon, June 10, 1893; available in: Krieger H (ed.), *East Timor and the International Community: Basic Documents* (Cambridge University Press 1997).

'Convention for the Peaceful Settlement of International Disputes (1899)'; <http://avalon.law.yale.edu/19th_century/hague01.asp> accessed June 1, 2017.

'Convention Signed at Washington on February 10, 1908, between the United States and France', published in: Charles I. Bevans (ed.), *Treaties and other International Agreements of the United States of America 1776–1949, Vol. 7: Denmark–France* (United States Government Printing Office 1971).

'Covenant of the League of Nations'; <http://avalon.law.yale.edu/20th_century/leagcov.asp> accessed August 31, 2018.

'Declaration Concerning the Laws of Naval War', in: The American Journal of International Law, Vol. 3, No. 3, Supplement: Official Documents (1909).

'Documents presented to the Committee Relating to Existing Plans for the Establishment of a Permanent Court of Justice' (presented 1920 in London); <https://www.icj-cij.org/public/files/permanent-court-of-international-justice/serie_D/D_documents_to_comm_existing_plans.pdf> accessed June 15, 2017.

'Draft of a General Arbitration Treaty' in *Union Interparlementaire pour l'Arbitrage International – XIII. Conférence Tenue à Bruxelles du 28 au 31 août 1905* (E. Guyot 1905).

'Draft of a Memorandum Approved by Secretary of State Knox, Proposing the Establishment of the Court of Arbitral Justice Recommended by the Second Hague Peace Conference of 1907' in James Brown Scott, *An International Court of Justice* (Oxford University Press 1916).

'Elihu Root's Address at the Proceedings of the Special Session Held in Honor of the Honorable Elihu Root, Secretary of State of the United States of America, and

Honorary Vice-President of the Conference (July 31, 1906)' in *Report of the Delegates of the United States to the Third International Conference of the American States held at Rio de Janeiro, July 21, to August 26, 1906* (United States Government Printing Office 1907).

'Elihu Root's Reply to Luis Drago's Speech at the Banquet at the Opera House in Buenos Aires, August 17, 1906' in Robert Bacon and James Brown Scott (eds.), *Latin America and the United States: Addresses by Elihu Root* (Harvard University Press 1917).

Ely RE (ed.), *Proceedings of the National Arbitration and Peace Congress, New York, April 14th to 17th, 1907* (National Arbitration and Peace Congress 1907).

'Emile Arnaud's report of the work of *'Commission B'* of the 15th Meeting of the Universal Peace Congress (1906)' in *Bulletin Officiel du 15. Congrès Universel de la Paix tenu à Milan du 15 au 22 septembre 1906* (Impr. Büchler & Co. 1906).

'Frederick Theodore Frelinghuysen to Osborn, 9 Aug. 1882' in *Papers Relating to the Foreign Relations of the United States, Year: 1882* (United States Government Printing Office 1883).

'General Report of the Commission' in James, Brown Scott (ed.), *The Hague Peace Conferences 1899 and 1907, vol. II: Documents* (Oxford University Press 1909).

'General Treaty of Peace between Great Britain, Austria, France, Prussia, Russia, Sardinia, and Turkey', signed at Paris, 30th March 1856 (available: Augustus Oakes & R.B. Mowat (eds.), *The Great European Treaties of the Nineteenth Century* (Clarendon Press 1930) 176 et seq.).

'Historic Activation of the Crime of Aggression', <http://www.coalitionfortheicc.org/explore/icc-crimes/crime-aggression> accessed October 29, 2018.

'Historical Resumé', in: James Brown Scott (ed.), *Instructions to the American Delegates to The Hague Peace Conferences and their Official Reports* (Oxford University Press 1916).

Holguín J (ed.) *La Delegación Colombiana, Segunda Conferencia internacional de la Haya* (Imprenta Nacional 1908).

Hugo V, 'Inaugural Address', in: Henry Richard and Elihu Burritt (eds.), *Report of the Proceedings of the Second General Peace Congress held in Paris on the 22nd, 23rd and 24th of August 1849*.

'Instructions to the American Delegates to the Hague Conference of 1899', in James Brown Scott (ed.), *Instructions to the American Delegates to The Hague Peace Conferences and their Official Reports* (Oxford University Press 1916).

'Instructions to the American Delegates to the Hague Conference of 1907', in James Brown Scott (ed.), *Instructions to the American Delegates to The Hague Peace Conferences and their Official Reports* (Oxford University Press 1916).

'Instructions to the International (Peace) Conference at the Hague, by U.S. Secretary of State John Hay, Annex A' in James Brown Scott (ed.), *The Hague Peace Conferences of 1899 and 1907*, vol. 2 (The John Hopkins Press 1909).

'Instructions to the United States Delegates' in John Vavasour Noel, *History of the Second Pan-American Congress* (Guggenheimer, Weil & Co. 1902).

International Law Association, *Report of the Twenty-Second Conference held at Christiania, September 1st–4th 1905* (West, Newman & Co. 1906).

'Jamaica Letter'; <http://www.oas.org/sap/peacefund/VirtualLibrary/CongressofPanama/JamaicaLetter.pdf> accessed February 8, 2017.

'Kellogg-Briand Pact'; <http://avalon.law.yale.edu/20th_century/kbpact.asp> accessed March 3, 2016.

Knox PC, 'Identic Circular Note of the Secretary of State of the United States Proposing Alternative Procedure for the International Prize Court and the Investment of the International Prize Court with the Functions of a Court of Arbitral Justice' (1910) 4 The American Journal of International Law – Supplement: Official Documents.

'Letter of James Brown Scott to the Netherland Minister of Foreign Affairs, Dated January 12, 1914, Concerning the Establishment of a Court of Arbitral Justice' in James Brown Scott, *An International Court of Justice* (Oxford University Press 1916).

'Memorandum from the Russian Embassy Handed to the President of the United States, September 13, 1905, Proposing a Second Peace Conference at the Hague' in James Brown Scott (ed.), *The Hague Conventions and Declarations of 1899 and 1907* (Oxford University Press 1915).

'Memorandum of James Brown Scott, Accompanying His Letter of January 12, 1914, to the Netherland Minister of Foreign Affairs, Proposing the Establishment of a Court of Arbitral Justice by and for Germany, the United States, Austria-Hungary, France, Great Britain, Italy, Japan, the Netherlands and Russia' in James Brown Scott, *An International Court of Justice* (Oxford University Press 1916).

Message from the President of the United States, transmitting a Communication from the Secretary of State, submitting the Report, with accompanying Papers, of the Delegates of the United States to the Second International Conference of American States, held at City of Mexico from October 22, 1901, to January 22, 1902 (United States Government Printing Office 1902).

'Message from Us Secretary of State Richard Olney to Us Ambassador to the United Kingdom Thomas F. Bayard' in Jeffrey F. Taffet and Dustin Walcher, *The United States and Latin America: A History with Documents* (Routledge 2017).

'Official Message from Philander C. Knox regarding the International Court of Arbitral Justice' in *Report of the Sixteenth Annual Meeting of the Lake Mohonk Conference on International Arbitration, May 18th, 19th and 20th 1910* (Lake Mohonk Arbitration Conference 1910).

Papers relating to the Foreign Relations of the United States, with the annual message of the president transmitted to Congress December 2, 1902 (United States Government Printing Office 1902).

'Plan for an International Tribunal', in: James Brown Scott (ed.), *Instructions to the American Delegates to The Hague Peace Conferences and their Official Reports* (Oxford University Press 1916).

'Plan for Arbitration', Adopted at the First International Conference of American States in Washington (October 2, 1889–April 19, 1890) in James Brown Scott (ed.), *The International Conferences of American States 1889–1928* (Carnegie Endowment for International Peace 1931).

'Preliminary Address of the Committee of Arrangements of the World's Congress Auxiliary on a Congress of Arbitration and Peace' (1893) 55 American Advocate of Peace.

President Woodrow Wilson's 'Fourteen Points' (Jan. 8, 1918); <http://avalon.law.yale.edu/20th_century/wilson14.asp> accessed August 21, 2018.

'Prospectus: The Aim and Scope of the American Society of International Law' (1907) 1 The American Journal of International Law.

'Report of Messrs. White, Low and Holls to the American Delegation to the First Hague Conference, regarding the Work of the Third Commission of the Conference', in: James Brown Scott (ed.), *Instructions to the American Delegates to The Hague Peace Conferences and their Official Reports* (Oxford University Press 1916).

'Report of the Committee on Custom Regulations' in James Brown Scott (ed.), *the International Conferences of American States 1889–1928* (Carnegie Endowment for International Peace 1931).

Adams MD, *Report of the First Annual Meeting of the Lake Mohonk Conference on International Arbitration in 1895* (The Lake Mohonk Arbitration Conference 1895).

Report of the 19th Annual Lake Mohonk conference on International Arbitration, May 14th, 15th and 16th, 1913 (Lake Mohonk Arbitration Conference 1913).

Report of the 20th Annual Lake Mohonk Conference on International Arbitration, May 27th, 28th and 29th, 1914 (Lake Mohonk Arbitration Conference 1914).

'Report to the Secretary of State of the Delegates to the First Hague Conference', in: James Brown Scott (ed.), *Instructions to the American Delegates to The Hague Peace Conferences and their Official Reports* (Oxford University Press 1916).

'Report to the Secretary of State of the Delegates of the United States to the Second Hague Conference', in: James Brown Scott (ed.), *Instructions to the American Delegates to The Hague Peace Conferences and their Official Reports* (Oxford University Press 1916).

Richard H and Burritt E (eds.), *Report of the Proceedings of the Second General Peace Congress held in Paris on the 22nd, 23rd and 24th of August 1849* (Gilpin 1849).

'Russian Circular Note Proposing the Program of the First Conference from 30 December 1898', published, e.g., in James Brown Scott (ed.), *Instructions to the American Delegates to The Hague Peace Conferences and their Official Reports* (Oxford University Press 1916).

'Saavedra Lamas Pact' (1934) 28 American Journal of International Law – Supplement: Official Documents (Jul. 1934).

Scott JB, *The Hague Peace Conferences of 1899 and 1907*, vol. 1 (The John Hopkins Press 1909).

Scott JB, *American Addresses at the Second Hague Peace Conference* (World Peace Foundation 1916).

Scott JB, *Instructions to the American Delegates to The Hague Peace Conferences and their Official Reports* (Oxford University Press 1916).

Scott JB, *The Hague Peace Conferences of 1899 and 1907*, vol. 2 (The John Hopkins Press 1909).

Scott JB, *The Proceedings of The Hague Peace Conferences: The Conference of 1899* (Oxford University Press 1920).

Scott JB, The International Conferences of American States 1889–1928 (Carnegie Endowment for International Peace 1931).

Scott JB, *The Proceedings of the Hague Conferences: The Conference of 1907*, vol. 1 (Oxford University Press 1920).

Scott JB, *The Proceedings of the Hague Conferences: The Conference of 1907*, vol. 2 (Oxford University Press 1921).

'James Brown Scott to J.G. Schmidlapp' (February 2, 1915).

'State of the Union Address delivered by U.S. President Theodore Roosevelt before the United States Congress on December 6, 1904'; <http://www.presidency.ucsb.edu/ws/index.php?pid=29545> accessed June 28, 2017.

'State of the Union Address Delivered by U.S. President Theodore Roosevelt before the U.S. Congress on December 5, 1905' in Theodore Roosevelt, *Presidential Addresses and State Papers* (P.F. Collier & Son 1905).

'State of the Union Address of President William McKinley to the Senate and the House of Representatives on December 5, 1899'; <http://www.thisnation.com/library/sotu/1899wm.html> accessed June 14, 2017.

Stockton CH and Sperry CS, 'the London Naval Conference' (1909) 3 The Proceedings of the American Society of International Law at Its Annual Meeting (1907–1917).

'Jonkheer van Tets van Goudriaan's (Dutch Minister of Foreign Affairs) Address on the Opening Meeting of the Second Hague Peace Conference', in: James Brown Scott (ed.), *The Proceedings of the Hague Conferences: The Conference of 1907*, vol. 1 (Oxford University Press 1920).

'The American Society for the Judicial Settlement of International Disputes' (1910) 4 The American Journal of International Law.

'The London Naval Conference' (1909) 3 The American Journal of International Law – Supplement: Official Documents.

'The Papers of James Brown Scott', box 1 (1891–1967).

The Second American Conference on International Arbitration held in Washington, D.C., January 12, 1904(Gibson Bros. 1904).

'the Secretary of State of the United States to the American Diplomatic Representatives Accredited to the Governments Signatory to the Acts of the First Hague Conference (October 21, 1904)' in James Brown Scott (ed.), *The Hague Conventions and Declarations of 1899 and 1907* (Oxford University Press 1915).

'the Secretary of State of the United States to the American Diplomatic Representatives Accredited to the Governments Signatory to the Acts of the First Hague Conference (December 16, 1904)' in: James Brown Scott (ed.), *The Hague Conventions and Declarations of 1899 and 1907* (Oxford University Press 1915).

'The Treaty of Portsmouth and the Russo-Japanese War, 1904–1905'; <https://history.state.gov/milestones/1899-1913/portsmouth-treaty> accessed February 9, 2016.

'The World at Six Billion' 4; by the Population Division, Department of Economic and Social Affairs at United Nations Secretariat (ESA/P/WP.154) from 12 October 1999.

'Translation of the Protocol of Adherence to the Conventions of the Hague' in *Message from the President of the United States, transmitting a Communication from the Secretary of State, submitting the Report, with accompanying Papers, of the Delegates of the United States to the Second International Conference of American States, held at City of Mexico from October 22, 1901, to January 22, 1902* (United States Government Printing Office 1902).

'Tratado de Confederación entre las Republicas del Perú, Bolivia, Chile, Ecuador y Nueva Granada', signed at Lima, February 8, 1848; <http://www.oas.org/sap/peacefund/VirtualLibrary/CongressofLima1847/Treaty/TratadoConfederacionPeruBoliviaChileEcuadorNuevaGranada.pdf> accessed October 12, 2016.

'Treaty Concerning the Formation of a General Postal Union', signed on October 9, 1874; <http://avalon.law.yale.edu/19th_century/usmu010.asp> accessed August 3, 2016.

'Treaty of Arbitration for Pecuniary Claims' in James Brown Scott (ed.), *The International Conferences of American States 1889–1928* (*Carnegie Endowment for International Peace 1931*).

'Treaty of Friendship, Commerce and Navigation between Belgium and Peru', signed at London, 16 May 1850; available: Oxford Historical Treaties, OUP reference: 104 CTS 103.

'Treaty of Peace and Friendship between Peru and Spain' from 1853; <https://archive.org/stream/colecciondelost06peru#page/116/mode/2up> accessed January 7, 2015.

'Treaty of Perpetual Union, League, and Confederation'; <http://www.oas.org/sap/peacefund/VirtualLibrary/CongressofPanama/Treaties/TreatyPerpetualUnion.pdf> accessed September 26, 2016.

'Treaty on the Preservation of Peace' from 1864; <http://www.oas.org/sap/peacefund/VirtualLibrary/SecondCongressofLima/TratadoSobreConservacionPazEntreEstadosdeAmericaContratantes.pdf> accessed January 30, 2017.
'UN Charter'; <http://www.un.org/en/sections/un-charter/chapter-i/index.html> accessed October 22, 2018.

Newspaper/Non-scientific Articles

'A Programme for The Hague' (October 7, 1905) The Outlook.
'A Stated International Congress' (1903) LXV No. 2 Advocate for Peace.
Burrit E, 'Congress and Supreme Court of Nations' (May 1848) Bond of Brotherhood.
Call AD, 'The War Has Not Destroyed X: The Will to End War' (1920) 82 Advocate of Peace through Justice.
The Advocate of Peace, Vol. 69, No. 3 (March 1907).
Herald of Peace from July 1, 1886 (82).
Herald of Peace from September 1, 1886 (pages 107 et seq.).
Herald of Peace from September 1, 1887 (page 263).
'Things International' (June 22, 1914) 78 The Independent.
Withnall A, 'World Peace? These Are the Only 11 Countries in the World that Are Actually Free from Conflict' (The Independent, August 14, 2014); <https://www.independent.co.uk/news/world/politics/world-peace-these-are-only-11-countries-world-are-actually-free-conflict-9669623.html> accessed October 22, 2018.

Index

www.ingramcontent.com/pod-product-compliance
Lightning Source LLC
Chambersburg PA
CBHW071332230926
51849CB00002B/379